Stay on a farm

JARROLD
PUBLISHING

1/98
Published by Jarrold Publishing, Whitefriars,
Norwich NR3 1TR
in association with the Farm Holiday Bureau (UK) Ltd,
the English Tourist Board and the National Tourist Boards
of Scotland, Wales and Northern Ireland
© Farm Holiday Bureau (UK) Ltd 1998
National Agricultural Centre, Stoneleigh Park,
Warwickshire CV8 2LZ

All our rights reserved. No part of this publication may
be reproduced, stored in a retrieval system, or
transmitted, in any form or by any means, electronic,
mechanical, photocopying, recording or otherwise,
without the prior permission in writing of the publishers.

ISBN 0 7117 1070 8

The information contained in this Guide has been
published in good faith on the basis of the details
submitted by the proprietors of the premises listed.
These proprietors are current members of the Farm
Holiday Bureau (UK) Ltd and have paid for their entries
in this Guide. Whilst every effort has been made to
ensure accuracy in this publication, neither the publisher,
the Farm Holiday Bureau (UK) Ltd, the National Tourist
Boards nor their agents can guarantee the accuracy of
the information in this Guide and accept no responsibility
for any error or misrepresentation. All liability for loss,
disappointment, negligence or other damage caused by
reliance on the information contained in this Guide, or in
the event of bankruptcy, or liquidation, or cessation of
trade of any company, individual or firm mentioned is
hereby excluded.

The Farm Holiday Bureau (UK) Ltd gratefully
acknowledges the continuing assistance and advice
offered by the National Tourist Boards, the Farming and
Rural Conservation Agency (FRCA) of the Ministry of
Agriculture, the Scottish Agricultural Organisations
Society Ltd, and all those who seek to maintain a balance
in the rural community.

Produced for the Tourist Boards by The Pen and Ink
Book Company Limited, Huntingdon, Cambridgeshire.

*Front cover photograph supplied by Jarrold Publishing,
Norwich.
Back cover, bottom left, by Mike Williams Photography.*

Printed and bound in Great Britain.

Contents

Welcome to the Farm Holiday Bureau	4
Stay on a farm	5
Walk on the wild side – Simon King	7
How to use this guide	8
Where to go	8
How the farm entries are listed	8
Making your booking	8
Compliments and complaints	9
Where to go maps	10
Accommodation symbols and awards	13
Explanation of facilities symbols	16
UK map section	17

Farm listings

Scotland	
Scottish Highlands & Islands	33
Scottish Lowlands	47
England	
England's North Country	**68**
England's Heartland	**128**
South & South East England	**205**
England's West Country	**236**
Wales	
North Wales	**307**
Mid Wales	**322**
South & West Wales	**333**
Northern Ireland	**345**
Farm Holiday Bureau Group contacts	360
European contacts	365
Further information	366
Index to farms	367

3

Welcome to the Farm Holiday Bureau

The Farm Holiday Bureau (FHB) is a network of over 1,000 farming families throughout the United Kingdom who provide value for money, good food and a warm welcome in quality bed and breakfast and self-catering accommodation.

All members belong to one of 92 local FHB Groups which, together with the National Tourist Boards, inspect all FHB properties to ensure high standards for guests.

We hope you enjoy your stay on a farm, and would like to ask you to help us provide an even better guide. Please send us your views and ideas.

Thank you for choosing to stay on a farm. We all hope you enjoy the opportunity to discover our countryside.

Farm Holiday Bureau (UK) Ltd
National Agricultural Centre
Stoneleigh Park
Warwickshire
CV8 2LZ

☎ 01203 696909
Fax: 01203 696630
E-mail: admin@fhbaccom.demon.co.uk
http://www.webscape.co.uk/farmaccom/

Stay on a farm –

for the best welcome to the British countryside

Here is your guide to more than a thousand farms, offering the best accommodation at unbeatable value. They are spread throughout the UK, in England, Scotland, Wales, Northern Ireland and the Isle of Man. Staying on a farm here doesn't mean *working* (as it does in some countries!), or roughing it. All our accommodation is graded under the national grading schemes, and a large proportion comes into the high-quality bracket.

Farming families have grown up on the land and moulded it. Their intimate knowledge of the landscape, the country way of life and all the attractions it has to offer, is unsurpassed. They can tell you all there is to know about the best (and often the quietest) places to go. This, combined with their warm welcome and friendly help during your stay, will give you a real chance to discover the countryside.

Many farms can cater for activity holidays, and symbols indicate those that can offer waymarked walks on their land, riding and fishing. There are many more activities besides – from bread-making to participating in some of the jobs on the farm. All you have to do is ask! Children in particular will love the variety that only a stay on a farm can bring.

Most farms now cater for business people. A warm welcome at the end of a long day means so much to the weary traveller. Some farms can also cater for small meetings. What better way to concentrate on major decisions and long-term policy than to be in a farmhouse – where peace, quiet, security and anonymity can be guaranteed?

Television's wildlife expert *Simon King* invites you to

Walk on the wild side

BBC Natural History
Unit Picture Library

The British countryside is, by and large, man made. Over the millennia we have altered the wild face of the land to suit our needs, clearing forests, draining wetlands, shifting the course of rivers and building defences against the sea.

You might think then that we live in an impoverished desert whose natural glory has been completely stifled and crushed, but this is not so. For hundreds of years there has been a harmony between the people who work the land for our benefit and the wild things which share their space.

By staying on one of the working farms in this guide, you will begin to see just how deep that sense of understanding and co-operation runs. Many of the farms offer a green oasis, a balance between economic efficiency and environmental sensitivity. It is no coincidence that British farmland is host to hundreds of thousands of wintering wildfowl, or that it shelters one of the strongest populations of badgers in Europe. Barn owls, deer, hares and many more depend absolutely on the conscientious management of the land around them.

Many of the farms you can visit offer not only a traditionally warm, friendly welcome, but also a window onto the wild world that we all cherish. It may no longer be a wilderness, but British farmland offers some of the finest natural diversity to be found anywhere in the world.

All the benefits of a retreat in a rural area – the peace, the tranquillity, the gentle pace of life – can be found within these pages. So too can the opportunity to dip into our very own wild inheritance. Enjoy your stay.   **Simon King**

How to use this guide

Where to go

Stay on a farm lists all the members of the Farm Holiday Bureau (FHB), within Scotland, England, Wales and Northern Ireland. Browse the comprehensive UK map section (pages 17–32) for ideas of places to visit, then turn to the Where to go maps on pages 10–12 to find the key to the appropriate region or county/area.

How the farm entries are listed

This year, to make the guide easier to use, the farms are arranged under **counties or tourism areas** within their appropriate regional sections.

There are ten regional sections, each introduced with a key map showing which counties/tourism areas are included and a list of appropriate page numbers for easy reference. Each county/area section opens with a description of the area covered and an outline map showing the location of each farm.

Within each county/area section, farms are listed alphabetically under type of accommodation: Bed & Breakfast, Self-Catering, Camping & Caravanning, and/or Bunkhouses/Camping Barns. Each illustrated farm entry clearly sets out the information about the farm, its accommodation and facilities, making it easy to choose somewhere to stay.

FHB Group contacts

All the farms listed here belong to one of 92 FHB Groups. The local FHB Group contacts listed on pages 360–363 will be pleased to help you find a vacancy in your chosen area.

Index to farms

The comprehensive index on pages 367–396 lists all the farms in this guide under the appropriate country and county/area. As well as giving the page number for each farm, it indicates those farms that:

- offer access to disabled visitors (see page 15 for explanation of symbol)
- offer camping/caravanning facilities
- are working farms (and also those that welcome safe participation by guests)
- offer stabling/grazing for guests' horses
- offer en suite facilities
- welcome business people (with meeting room capacity where provided)
- accept *Stay on a farm* gift tokens (see page 6).

Making your booking

All you have to do is telephone or write to the farm of your choice. Remember to provide the following information when making your booking:

- First of all, please mention this guide.
- State your planned arrival and departure dates.
- State the exact number in your party or family, including children.
- State the accommodation needed and any particular requirements, eg twin beds, family room, private bath, ground floor, cot.

❶ **Honeybrook Farm,** Ramsbury, Nr Swindon, Wiltshire SN12 3RT

❷ Mrs Jill Whitehead
❸ ☎/Fax 01552 224553
❹ BB From £22–£25
❺ Sleeps 6
❻ ♿ ...
❼ ❦❦ Highly Commended

Example only

❽ Honeybrook Farm is a Grade II listed building in an idyllic rural setting just one mile from the pretty village of Ramsbury. Small, family-run farm with dairy cows and sheep. All bedrooms en suite with colour TV and hospitality tray. We offer a warm, friendly welcome and delicious breakfasts using local produce, served in our conservatory. Open Mar-Dec.

Key

❶ Farm name and address
❷ Contact name
❸ Telephone and fax number
❹ Prices
❺ Number of bed spaces
❻ Facilities symbols (see pages 15–16)
❼ Accommodation symbol/award given by National Tourist Board (see pages 13–14)
❽ Description (provided by owner)

- Specify the terms required, eg B&B, evening meal. Evening meal times vary and high tea may be available for children. Farms offering evening meals do not necessarily do so all year round, so do check.
- State special requirements, eg special diets, facilities for disabled people, arrangements for children, dogs, horses.
- Check prices and what they include and also any reductions that may be offered.
- When booking self-catering accommodation, it is advisable to find out whether linen or gas, electricity and telephone charges are included.
- Check the required method and date of payment.
- Check whether a deposit is payable and, if so, what charges will apply if the booking is cancelled (see 'Cancellations' right). Please note a deposit will normally be required with written confirmation of booking, and this will be deducted from the final bill.
- Check whether B&B access is restricted through the day. Many farms are happy for guests to stay in the house all day, but on some farms this is not practical and guests are asked to be out of the farmhouse between 10.30am and 4.30pm. Remember, it is essential that children are carefully supervised at all times on and around the farm.
- Check the best time to arrive and what time you must leave by.
- Ask for directions to the farm. (When you are near your destination, look out for the FHB member sign at the end of the drive. Your host will be happy to direct you by telephone if you get lost.)
- Give your name, address and telephone number.

NB We recommend that, time permitting, all telephone bookings are confirmed in writing, specifying exactly what you have booked and the price you expect to pay.

If the accommodation you want is not available, the owner will be happy to refer you to similar FHB accommodation, as will the local FHB Group contact (see pages 360–363).

Many FHB members also offer a 'book a bed ahead' service to their guests. If you are touring, just tell your host where you wish to visit next and he or she can make the booking for you.

Cancellations

Once a booking has been agreed, on the telephone or by letter, a legally binding contract has been made with the host. If you cancel a reservation, fail to take up the accommodation or leave prematurely (regardless of the reasons), the host may be entitled to compensation if it cannot be relet for all or a good part of the booked period. If a deposit has been paid it is likely to be forfeited and an additional payment may be demanded.

Insurance

Travel and holiday insurance protection policies can be taken out to safeguard visitors in the event of cancellation or curtailment. Insurance of personal property can also be sought. Hosts cannot accept liability for any loss or damage to visitors' property, however caused. Do make sure that your valuables are covered by your household insurance before you take them away.

For overseas visitors

- **Host and Guest Service** – FHB-appointed central reservations service for overseas visitors
- Easy and convenient way to book your farm holiday accommodation
- Itineraries arranged if you require more than one location

Host and Guest Service
103 Dawes Road
London SW6 7DU
Tel: 0171 385 9922
Fax: 0171 386 7575
E-mail: farm@host-guest.co.uk
Internet: http://www.host-guest.co.uk

Or you can, of course, book direct with the farm of your choice (see opposite).

Compliments and complaints

Many visitors write to the Farm Holiday Bureau saying how much they have enjoyed their stay. If you feel that something or someone deserves acknowledgement, or if you have a suggestion about how to improve the guide, please write to the Farm Holiday Bureau (UK) Ltd, National Agricultural Centre, Stoneleigh Park, Warwickshire CV8 2LZ, or ring 01203 696909.

If you are dissatisfied, please make your complaint to the host there and then. This gives an opportunity for rectifying action to be taken at once. It is usually difficult to deal with a complaint if it is reported at a later date. If the host fails to resolve the problem, please write to the FHB. We shall be happy to help.

Where to go

These country outline maps show how the United Kingdom is divided into ten regional sections in this guide. Each region is picked out in a different colour and divided into county sections (for England and Northern Ireland) and tourism areas (for Scotland and Wales).

All the farm entries are listed in the guide under their appropriate county or area. The coloured regional panels alongside these country maps give the page number for each regional section, and list those counties/areas that contain farm entries, together with appropriate page numbers.

For more detail, see the comprehensive UK map section on pages 17–32.

Scotland

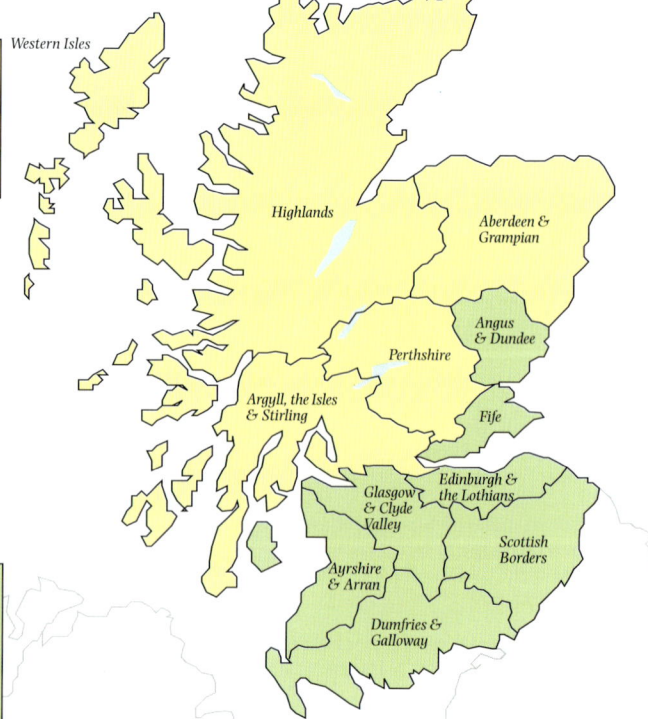

SCOTTISH HIGHLANDS & ISLANDS 33
Highlands 34
Aberdeen & Grampian 38
Perthshire 40
Argyll, the Isles & Stirling 43

SCOTTISH LOWLANDS 47
Angus & Dundee 48
Fife 50
Glasgow & Clyde Valley 52
Edinburgh & the Lothians 55
Ayrshire & Arran 58
Scottish Borders 61
Dumfries & Galloway 65

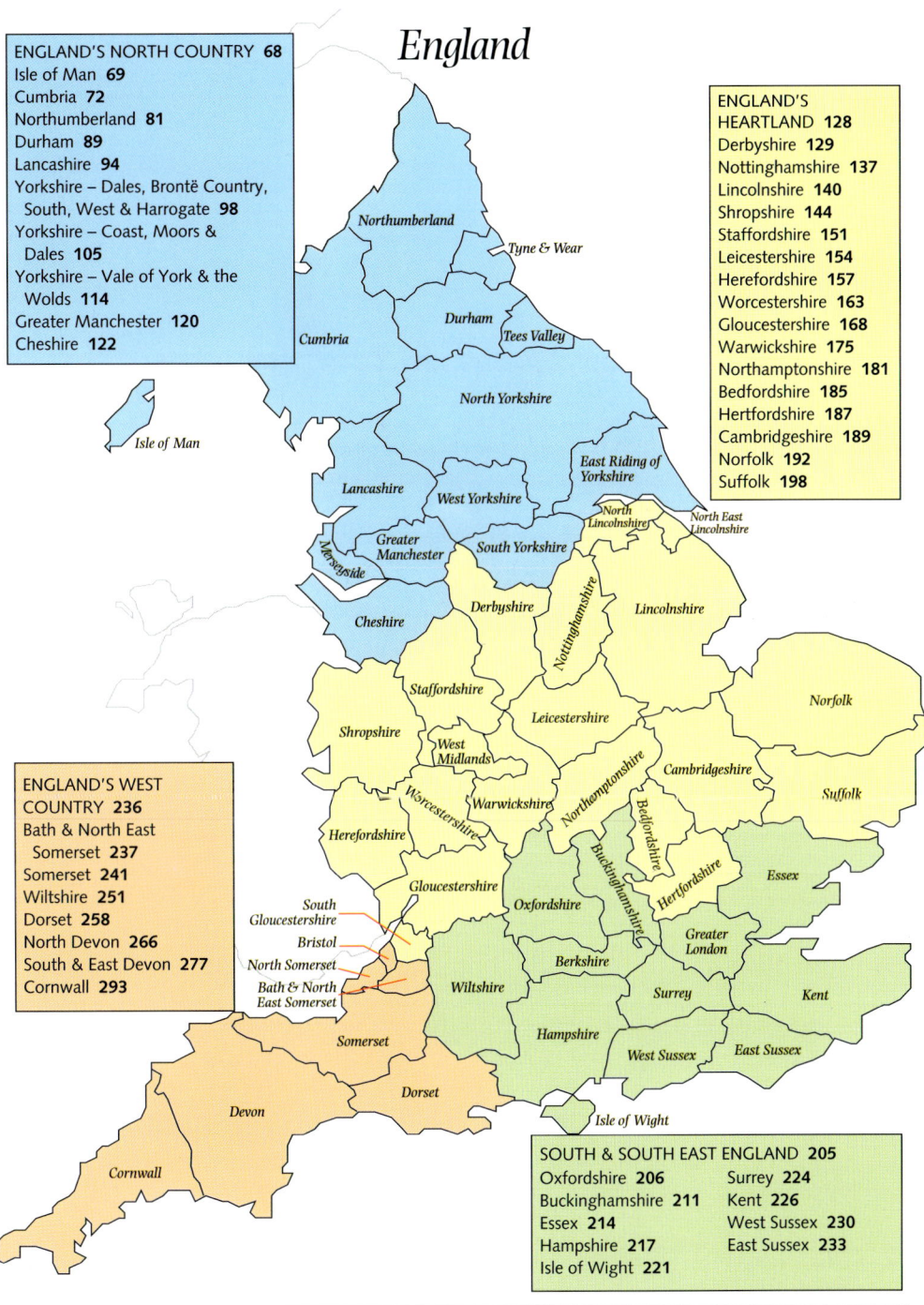

England

ENGLAND'S NORTH COUNTRY 68
Isle of Man 69
Cumbria 72
Northumberland 81
Durham 89
Lancashire 94
Yorkshire – Dales, Brontë Country, South, West & Harrogate 98
Yorkshire – Coast, Moors & Dales 105
Yorkshire – Vale of York & the Wolds 114
Greater Manchester 120
Cheshire 122

ENGLAND'S HEARTLAND 128
Derbyshire 129
Nottinghamshire 137
Lincolnshire 140
Shropshire 144
Staffordshire 151
Leicestershire 154
Herefordshire 157
Worcestershire 163
Gloucestershire 168
Warwickshire 175
Northamptonshire 181
Bedfordshire 185
Hertfordshire 187
Cambridgeshire 189
Norfolk 192
Suffolk 198

ENGLAND'S WEST COUNTRY 236
Bath & North East Somerset 237
Somerset 241
Wiltshire 251
Dorset 258
North Devon 266
South & East Devon 277
Cornwall 293

SOUTH & SOUTH EAST ENGLAND 205
Oxfordshire 206
Buckinghamshire 211
Essex 214
Hampshire 217
Isle of Wight 221
Surrey 224
Kent 226
West Sussex 230
East Sussex 233

Where to go (continued)

Wales

NORTH WALES 307
The Isle of Anglesey **308**
Snowdonia – Mountains & Coast **311**
North Wales Coast & Borderlands **319**

MID WALES 322
Ceredigion, Cardigan Bay **323**
Mid Wales, Lakes & Mountains **327**

SOUTH & WEST WALES 333
Pembrokeshire **334**
Carmarthenshire & the Gower **340**
Wye Valley & Vale of Usk **342**

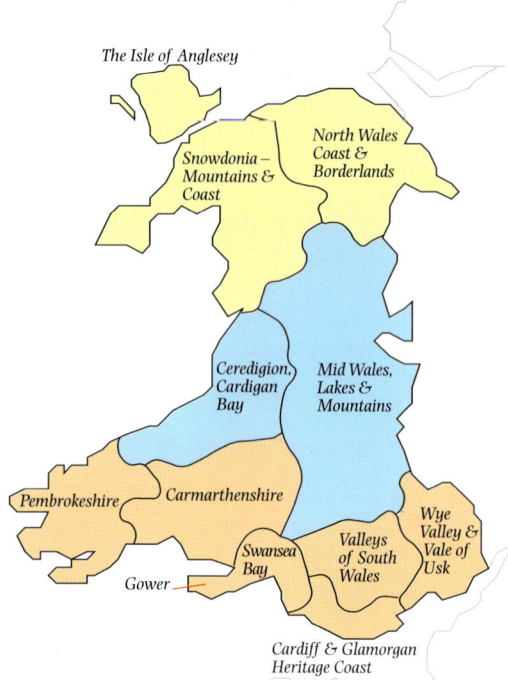

Northern Ireland

NORTHERN IRELAND 345
County Londonderry **346**
County Antrim **349**
County Tyrone **352**
County Armagh **354**
County Down **356**

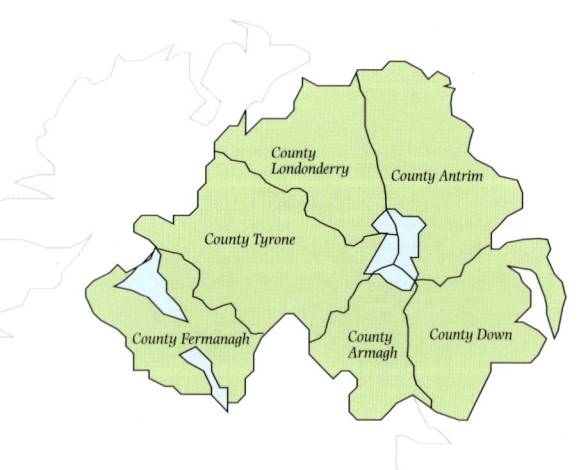

Accommodation symbols and awards

Farm Holiday Bureau members are inspected by their appropriate Group to ensure that a high standard of cleanliness, courtesy and service is maintained. All members must also be inspected by their National Tourist Board and agree to meet its Minimum Standards and observe its Code of Conduct. Any farm that was awaiting Tourist Board inspection at the time of going to press will show the word 'Applied' in place of a symbol or award.

Classification/grading schemes

Each National Tourist Board operates its own classification/grading schemes for serviced accommodation and self-catering properties. This year, the Scottish and Wales Tourist Boards are launching new schemes. New schemes will be in place for England and Northern Ireland from the end of 1999.

Scotland

Serviced and self-catering accommodation
The Scottish Tourist Board has introduced a new Star Scheme for both serviced and self-catering accommodation where the Star award is determined by quality, not by the size of the accommodation or the range of facilities.

For self-catering accommodation, the quality standard of the fabric, furnishings, decor, equipment and ambience of the property result in the Star awards. For serviced accommodation, the award also takes account of the welcome and service, the food and the hospitality. Awards range from **1–5 Stars**:

★	Fair and acceptable
★★	Good
★★★	Very good
★★★★	Excellent
★★★★★	Exceptional, world-class

In ★★★★ and ★★★★★ self-catering properties you will be guaranteed a wider range of equipment.

England

Serviced accommodation
The English Tourist Board currently classifies serviced accommodation, according to the range of facilities provided, within six bands from '**Listed**' and then from **1–5 Crowns**. The more Crowns, the more extensive the range of facilities.

♛
♛ ♛
♛ ♛ ♛
♛ ♛ ♛ ♛
♛ ♛ ♛ ♛ ♛

Accommodation is also assessed for a separate quality grading of '**Approved**', '**Commended**', '**Highly Commended**' or '**De Luxe**' and this grading appears alongside the classification symbol.

Self-catering
Self-catering accommodation is currently classified by the English Tourist Board, according to the range of facilities provided, in a range from **1–5 Keys**.

⚷
⚷ ⚷
⚷ ⚷ ⚷
⚷ ⚷ ⚷ ⚷
⚷ ⚷ ⚷ ⚷ ⚷

Holiday homes are also quality graded '**Approved**', '**Commended**', '**Highly Commended**' or '**De Luxe**' alongside the classification symbol.

Accommodation symbols and awards (continued)

Wales

Serviced accommodation
The Wales Tourist Board has introduced a new Star Quality Grading Scheme, from **1–5 Stars**, for serviced accommodation, with the emphasis on quality. High awards reflect the standard of welcome, ambience and furnishings, comfort, service and guest care. The awards are:

★	Fair to good
★★	Good
★★★	Very good
★★★★	Excellent
★★★★★	Exceptional

As this is a new scheme, some properties have not yet received their new award. In such cases their entry will show a **'provisional'** award, provided the accommodation was quality graded under the old scheme.

Self-catering
As in previous years, quality standards of holiday homes are graded on a scale of **1–5 Dragons**.

🐉
🐉 🐉
🐉 🐉 🐉
🐉 🐉 🐉 🐉
🐉 🐉 🐉 🐉 🐉

Northern Ireland

All visitor accommodation is inspected annually by the Northern Ireland Tourist Board under a statutory system, and all the farms listed offer a high standard.

Holiday caravan, camping and chalet parks

The National Tourist Boards operate a common quality grading scheme, the **British Graded Holiday Parks Scheme**. The scheme grades parks according to the relative quality of what is offered, in a range of **1–5 'ticks'**. The more 'ticks', the higher the quality.

Wheelchair accessibility symbols

All the places that display one of the symbols shown here have been checked by a Tourist Board Inspector against standard criteria that reflect the practical needs of wheelchair users. There are three categories of accessibility:

Category 1:
Accessible to all wheelchair users including those travelling independently

Category 2:
Accessible to a wheelchair user travelling with a helper

Category 3:
Accessible to a wheelchair user able to walk short distances and up three steps

Please check at the time of booking if you have special needs.

Inspected accessible schemes have been developed throughout the UK by the National Tourist Boards and Tourism for All Consortium in conjunction with the Holiday Care Service. They are designed to provide disabled travellers with reliable information on standards and facilities. Additional help and guidance on finding suitable holiday accommodation for those with special needs can be obtained from the Holiday Care Service on 01293 774535.

Welcome Host

The National Tourist Boards operate a Welcome Host scheme and training programme which places the emphasis on warm hospitality and first-class service. Recipients of the Welcome Host certificate or badge are part of a fine tradition – a tradition of friendliness.

Look at the entries to find those farms participating in the Welcome Host scheme.

 Scotland

 England

 Wales

 Northern Ireland

Wales Farmhouse Award

The Farmhouse Award is given to those proprietors who have successfully completed a Wales Tourist Board-approved course in farm-based tourism, as well as the Welcome Host course. Their accommodation is of high quality and you can expect a high level of customer care. This award applies to serviced accommodation only.

Explanation of facilities symbols

Symbol	Explanation	French	German
♿	Wheelchair accessibility category (see page 15)	Symbole d'accessibilité aux fauteuils roulants	Zeichen der Zugänglichkeit für Rollstuhlfahrer
⚘(3)	Children welcome (minimum age)	Enfants bienvenus (âge minimum)	Kinder willkommen (Mindestalter)
🐕	Dogs by arrangement	Chiens autorisés sous réserve d'accord préalable	Hunde nach Vereinbarung
🚭	No smoking	Non fumeurs de préférence	Nichtraucher bevorzugt
💳	Credit cards accepted	Cartes de crédit acceptées	Kreditkarten werden akzeptiert
💼	Business people welcome	Facilités pour hommes et femmes d'affaires	Geschäftsreisende willkommen
🚶	Waymarked walks on farm	Itinéraires fléchés sur la propriété de la ferme	Wanderwege gezeichnet
🗣	Foreign language(s) spoken	Langue(s) étrangère(s) parlée(s)	Hier werden Fremdsprachen gesprochen
🐎	Riding on farm	Randonnée à poney ou équitation à la ferme	Reiten auf Ponys oder Pferden
🎣	Fishing on farm	Pêche à la ferme	Angeln
🏠	Country house, not a working farm	Manoir (non pas ferme en exploitation)	Landhaus, kein aktiver Bauernhof
⛺	Camping facilities	Camping	Camping – Einrichtungen
🚐	Caravanning facilities	Caravaning	Caravan – Einrichtungen
🏅	Welcome Host certificate holder (see page 15)	Détenteur du certificat 'Welcome Host'	Absolventen der 'Welcome Host'
	Prices	**Prix**	**Preise**
BB	Price per person per night for bed and breakfast	Prix par personne par nuit pour chambre + petit déjeuner	Preis pro Person pro Nacht für Bett und Frühstück
EM	Price per person for evening meal	Prix par personne pour repas du soir	Preis pro Person für Abendessen
SC	Price per unit per week self-catering	Prix par location par semaine	Preis pro Einheit pro Woche bei Selbstversorgung
Tents	Price per tent pitch per night	Prix par emplacement de tente par nuit	Preis pro Zeltaufstellung pro Nacht
Caravans	Price per caravan pitch per night	Prix par emplacement de caravane par nuit	Preis pro Caravanaufstellung pro Nacht
Bunkhouses/ Camping Barns	Price per person per night	Gîtes d'étape/Refuges – Prix par personne par nuit	Übernachtungs-/ Camping-Hütte – Preis pro Person pro Nacht
	All prices include VAT and service charge if any.	TVA et service compris dans le prix	Alle Preise inklusive MWSt und Bedienungsgeld, wenn überhaupt

MAP 2

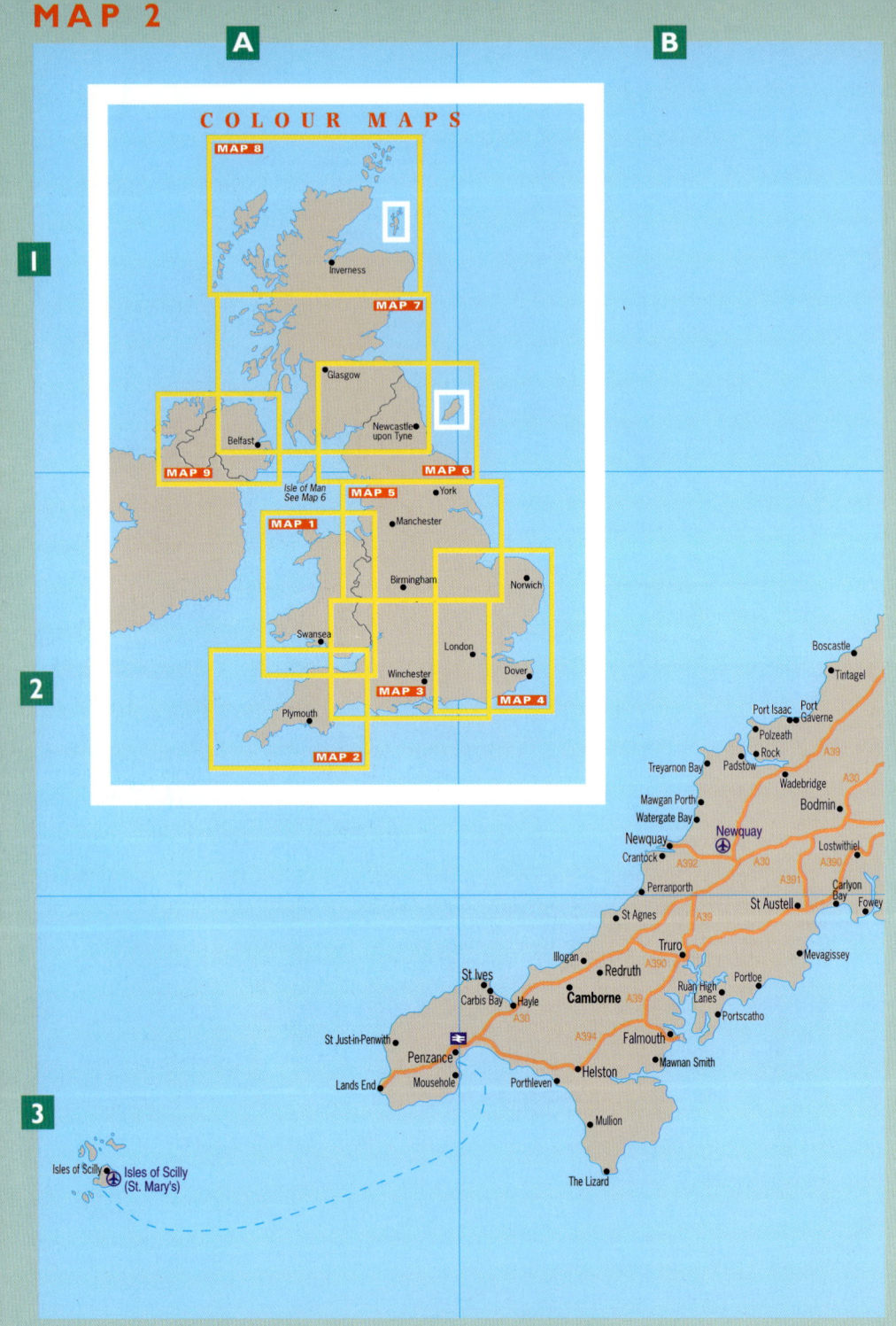

MAP 3

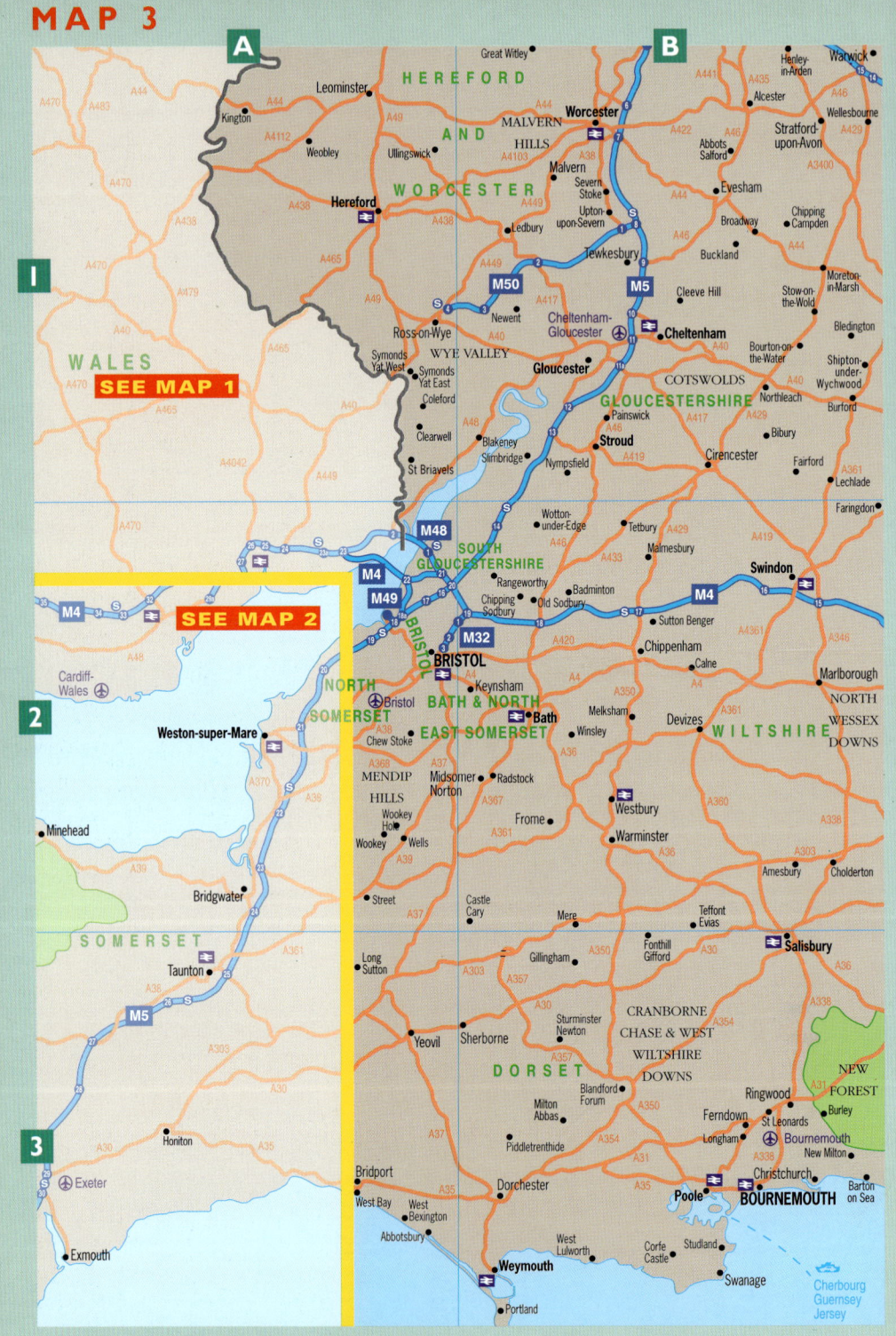

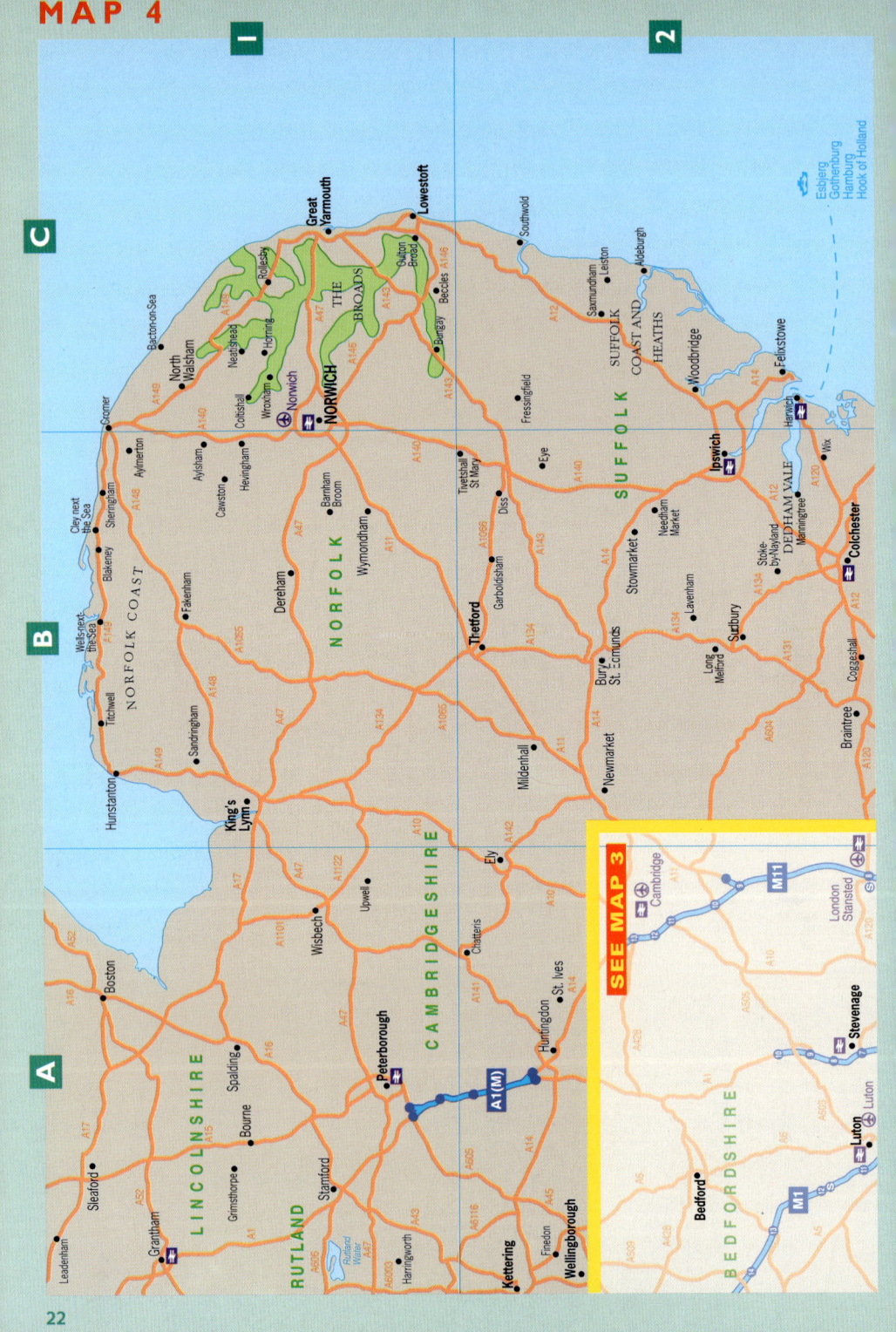

MAP 6

MAP 6

Scottish Highlands & Islands

Farm entries in this regional section are listed under those areas shown in green on the key map. Look at the index below to find on which page the entries start. You will see that we have listed the areas geographically so that you can turn more easily to find farms in neighbouring areas.

At the start of each area section is a detailed map with numbered symbols indicating the location of each farm. Different symbols denote different types of accommodation; see the key below each area map. Farm entries are listed alphabetically under type of accommodation. Some farms offer more than one type of accommodation and therefore have more than one entry.

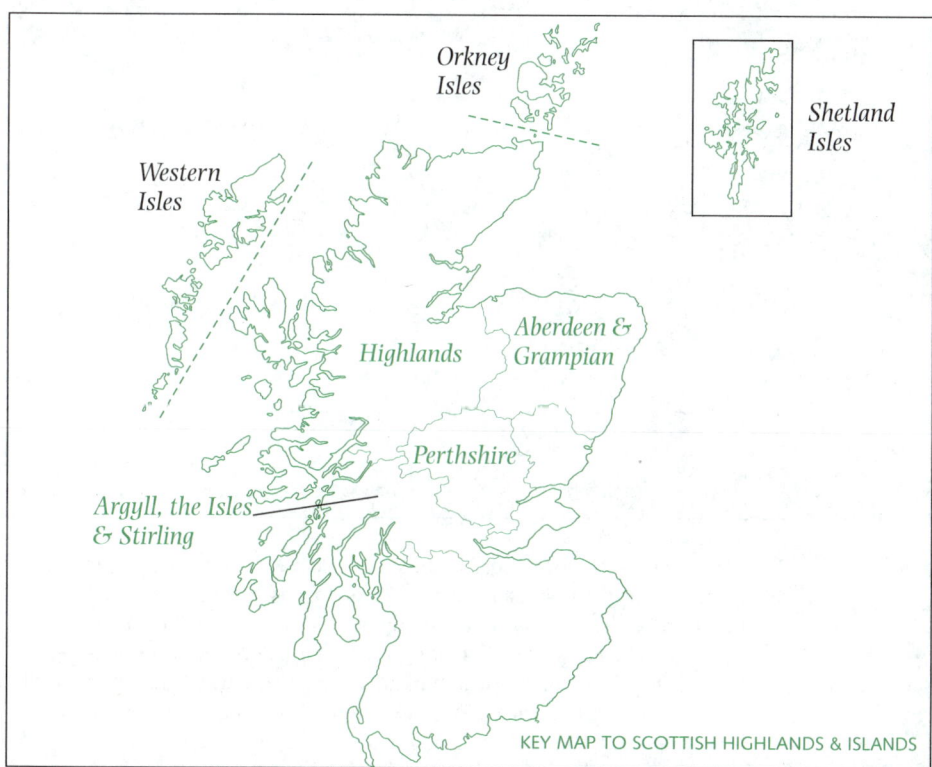

KEY MAP TO SCOTTISH HIGHLANDS & ISLANDS

Highlands *page 34*
John O'Groats, Moray Firth, Glen Affric, Loch Ness, Cairngorms & Ben Nevis

Aberdeen & Grampian *page 38*
Moray Firth, Spey & Don Valleys, Royal Deeside, Lochnagar & the Mounth

Perthshire *page 40*
Rannoch, Faskally & Ben Lawers

Argyll, the Isles & Stirling *page 43*
Mull, Jura, Loch Lomond, the Trossachs & the Argyll & Queen Elizabeth Forest Parks

Highlands

John O'Groats, Moray Firth, Glen Affric, Loch Ness, Cairngorms & Ben Nevis

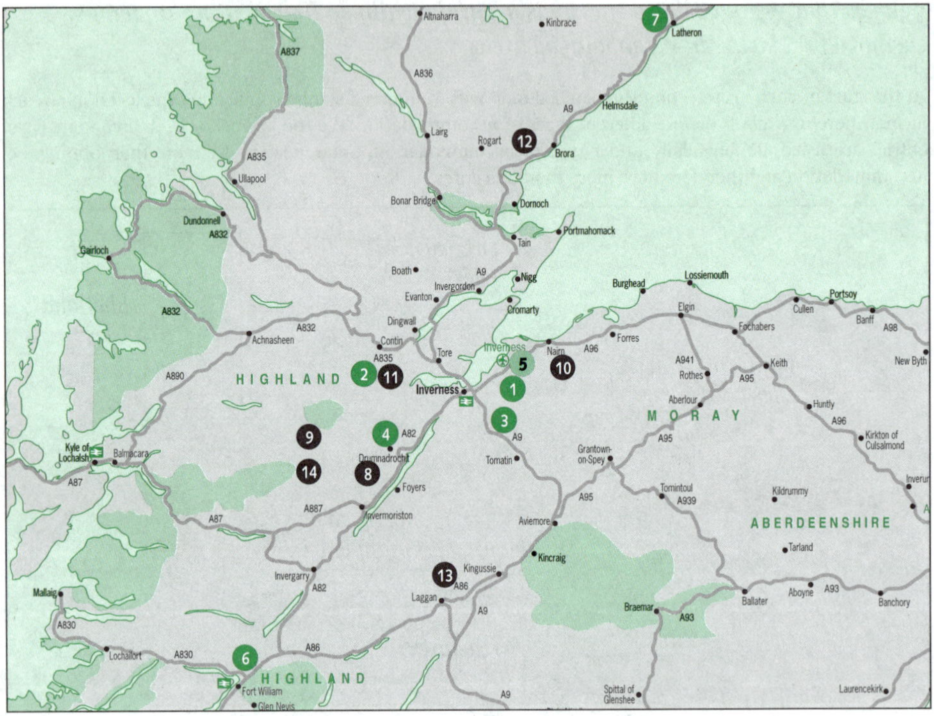

Key

- 1 Bed & Breakfast
- 1 Self-Catering
- 1 B&B and SC
- 1 Camping Barns
- Camping & Caravanning

'Ceud mìle faìlte' – a hundred thousand welcomes – to the Highlands and Islands, nearly 15,000 square miles of unsurpassed scenic beauty in mountains, glens, lochs, lonely sandy beaches and rugged, unspoilt coastline. There is something for everyone here. Enthusiasts of boating, fishing, golf, walking, birdwatching and geology are well catered for. In the land where deer and eagle roam free, wildlife lovers can also observe seals, osprey and otters in their natural habitat. Old castles, battlefield monuments and folk museums testify to a past rich in history, culture and folklore. The traditional Highland welcome is famed throughout the world. Come and try it.

If you would like help in finding suitable farm accommodation, turn to the full listing of farm groups on pages 360 to 363 to find appropriate contact details for this area.

Highlands   Scotland

Bed and Breakfast
(and evening meal)

Balaggan Farm, Culloden Moor, By Inverness, Inverness-shire IV1 2EL

Mrs Phyllis Alexander
☎/Fax 01463 790213
BB From £16
EM From £10
Sleeps 5
★★★
BED & BREAKFAST

A warm welcome awaits you on our small stock rearing farm set in peaceful surroundings. Good home cooking and baking is served. Log fires burn in lounge and dining room. 1 family and 1 twin bedroom, with electric blankets and tea/coffee-making facilities. No smoking in bedrooms. Ideal for touring Highlands with Culloden battlefield and Cawdor Castle. Many places of interest close by. Open April–Nov.

Cherry Trees, Kiltarlity, Beauly, Inverness-shire IV4 7JQ

Mrs J Matheson
☎ 01463 741368
BB From £15–£19
Sleeps 4
Applied

A warm welcome awaits you on our small stock rearing farm. Choice of breakfasts. Tea and coffee served in the lounge on request. Log fires in lounge and breakfast room. Central heating and electric blankets. Near Loch Ness, fishing and golf. Easy access to the North and West. Open Mar–Nov.

Daviot Mains Farm, Daviot, Nr Inverness, Inverness-shire IV1 2ER

Margaret & Alex Hutcheson
☎ 01463 772215
Fax 01463 772099
BB From £19–£25
FM From £13
Sleeps 6
★★★★
BED & BREAKFAST

Comfortable early 19th century listed farmhouse in quiet situation near Inverness. Relax in the warm atmosphere of this friendly home where delicious meals are thoughtfully prepared for you (residents' licence). Log fires in sitting and dining rooms. En suite/private facilities. The perfect base for exploring the Scottish Highlands. Selected by "Taste of Scotland", recommended by Elizabeth Gundrey's S.O.T.B.T. and Fodor. Closed Christmas.

Drumbuie Farm, Drumbuie, Loch Ness, Drumnadrochit, Inverness-shire IV3 6XP

Mrs Caroline Urquhart
☎ 01456 450634
Fax 01456 450595
BB From £17–£22
Sleeps 6
★★★★
BED & BREAKFAST

Custom-built farmhouse with en suite accomodation overlooking Loch Ness and sorrounding hills. Farm is mostly cattle including several Highland (hairy) cows and calves. Drumnadrochit is the perfect base when visiting the Highlands. Skye, Ullapool and the North all within easy reach. You are assured of a Scottish welcome at Drumbuie. Open all year.

Easter Dalziel Farm, Dalcross, Inverness, Inverness-shire IV1 2JL

Bob & Margaret Pottie
☎/Fax 01667 462213
BB From £17–£20
EM From £12
Sleeps 6
★★★★
BED & BREAKFAST

Relax in the traditional style of our lovely early Victorian home. Comfortable guest rooms and delicious home cooking. This stock/arable farm provides the ideal Highland touring base. Many recommendations including *The Good Guide to Britain* and *The Best Bed and Breakfast* guide. Open all year except Christmas & New Year.

Scotland — Highlands

6 Strone Farm, By Banavie, Fort William PH33 7PB

Eileen Cameron
☎ 01397 712773
BB From £18–£25
EM From £10
Sleeps 6
⌂(5) ♦
★★★
BED & BREAKFAST

A friendly welcome awaits you in our beautiful farmhouse which sits in a rural setting with magnificent panoramic views of Ben Nevis and Caledonian Canal. All double bedrooms tastefully decorated with en suite facilities and hostess tray. Large lounge with woodburning stove. Fresh food well presented. Open Feb–Sept.

7 Upper Latheron Farm, Latheron, Caithness KW5 6DT

Mrs Camilla Sinclair
☎ 01593 741224
BB From £16–£17
Sleeps 6
⌂ ⚲ ⚔ ♦ ⚘ W
★★★★
BED & BREAKFAST

Relax in the romantic Highlands amidst tranquil surroundings and enjoy magnificent coastal scenery from your bedroom windows. Beautifully renovated farmhouse offers high standard of food, comfort and cleanliness. For the energetic there is a wide range of outdoor activities. Enjoy a day trip to Orkney and John O'Groats. Perfect centre for exploring the far North and discovering its exceptional attractions. AA Recommended QQQ. Open May–Sept.

Self-Catering

8 Achmony Holidays, Drumnadrochit, by Loch Ness IV3 6UX

Mrs Elizabeth Mackintosh
☎ 01456 450357
Fax 01456 450830
SC From £190–£510
Sleeps 6
⌂ ⚲ ♦ ⚔ ⚘ W
★★★★
SELF CATERING

Enjoy your holiday in an idyllic location above Loch Ness. Each 3 bedroomed chalet bungalow is situated to afford maximum privacy in over 40 acres of silver birch-studded hillside. Central for touring (car essential), Drumnadrochit has several hotels, restaurants, shops, exhibition centres, pony trekking, fishing and boat trips on Loch Ness. Open Mar–Nov.

9 Culligran Cottages, Glen Strathfarrar, Struy, Nr Beauly, Inverness-shire IV4 7JX

Frank & Juliet Spencer-Nairn
☎/Fax 01463 761285
SC From £99–£399
Sleeps 5/7
⌂ ⚔ ⚘ ♦ W
★★ – ★★★
SELF CATERING

A regular? You soon could be. So don't delay – send for a brochure! This is your opportunity to stay on a deer farm within the beautiful Strathfarrar Nature Reserve. Watch the wild deer from your window and feed the farm deer during a conducted tour. Choice of chalet or cottage. Bikes for hire. Salmon and trout fishing. Hotel and inn nearby. Open late Mar–mid Nov.

5 Easter Dalziel Farm, Dalcross, Inverness, Inverness-shire IV1 2JL

Bob & Margaret Pottie
☎/Fax 01667 462213
SC From £120–£410
Sleeps 4/6
⌂ ⚔ ⊞ ♦ ⚘ W
★★★ – ★★★★
SELF CATERING

Enjoy a relaxing holiday in our cosy, traditional stonebuilt cottages. Between Inverness and Nairn on our stock/arable farm. A truly central location from which to explore the Highlands. The local area offers a wide range of activities to suit the sports-minded, tourer or walker alike. Look out for dolphins, badgers and buzzards, visit Cawdor, Culloden, Fort George and Loch Ness. Short breaks or long stays welcome all year. Brochure. Open all year.

Highlands   Scotland

Laikenbuie Holidays, Grantown Road, Nairn, Moray Firth IV12 5QN   ⑩

Thérèse Muskus
☎ 01667 454630
SC From £100–£456
Sleeps 6
★★★★
SELF CATERING

Watch roe deer and osprey among the abundant wildlife on tranquil organic croft (cows, sheep, hens) with beautiful outlook over trout loch amid natural birch woods. Large warm chalet (quality unbeaten) or residential caravan provide luxury accommodation. Excellent holiday centre, safe for children, low rainfall, plentiful sunshine, sandy beaches and dolphins. Near Loch Ness, Cairngorms, Cawdor Castle. Colour brochure. No smoking inside.

Mains of Aigas, By Beauly, Inverness-shire IV4 7AD   ⑪

Mrs Jessie Masheter
☎ 01463 782942
Fax 01463 782423
SC From £160–£400
Sleep 4/6
Guide dogs only
★★★ – ★★★★
SELF CATERING

Absorb the peace and quiet of this beautiful, unspoilt area. Enjoy special guest rates on our own challenging 9-hole golf course, tour the Highland beauty spots, study the abundant wildlife or simply "stay at home", relax and unwind. Comfortable attractive courtyard house and self-contained apartments. Open Mar–Nov.
E-mail: aigas@cali.co.uk

Milton Bank, c/o St Callan's Old Manse, Rogart, Sutherland, IV28 3XE   ⑫

Robert & Caroline Mills
☎ 01408 641363
Fax 01408 641313
SC From £90–£300
EM From £10
Sleeps 4
★★★
SELF CATERING

Lovely views in every direction. Farm kitchen has dishwasher, microwave, electric cooker and utility room with washer/dryer. Study with desk and books, double aspect sitting room with hi-fi/CD. Two twin bedrooms can be made up as doubles. Large bathroom with double ended tub. Shower room and WC. Payphone. Open all year.
E-mail: catadata@aol.com

Strone Cottage, c/o Lochbuie Croft, Newtonmore, Inverness-shire PH20 1BA   ⑬

Mary Mackenzie
☎/Fax 01540 673504
SC From £180–£430
Sleeps 6
★★★
SELF CATERING

You'll be very welcome at our croft on the outskirts of our lovely Highland village. Cosy renovated cottage has open fire, double glazing and CH. Downstairs en suite bedroom, upstairs 2 bedrooms and bathroom with small drying area. Electricity & coal incl. Enjoy peace and scenery, visit local attractions or take part in varied activities. Central for touring. Edinburgh 2 hours, Loch Ness 1 hour, Aviemore 15 mins. Brochure/special offers. Open all year.
E mail: mmackenzie@sprite.co.uk

Tomich Holidays, Guisachan Farm, Tomich, by Beauly, Inverness-shire IV4 7LY   ⑭

Mr & Mrs D J Fraser
☎ 01456 415332
Fax 01456 415499
SC From £150–£475
Sleeps 4–6
★★★ – ★★★★
SELF CATERING

Our magnificent farm steading houses three luxury cottages and a heated indoor swimming pool. Other accommodation is in spacious chalets set in woodland and a Victorian dairy. All have central heating, hot water and electricity included in the price. Tomich, in the depths of the Highlands near Glen Affric, is an ideal base for walking, touring or just relaxing. Open all year.

Our farms offer a range of facilities that are illustrated by symbols in each entry. Turn to page 16 for an explanation of the symbols.

Aberdeen & Grampian

Moray Firth, Spey & Don Valleys, Royal Deeside, Lochnagar & the Mounth

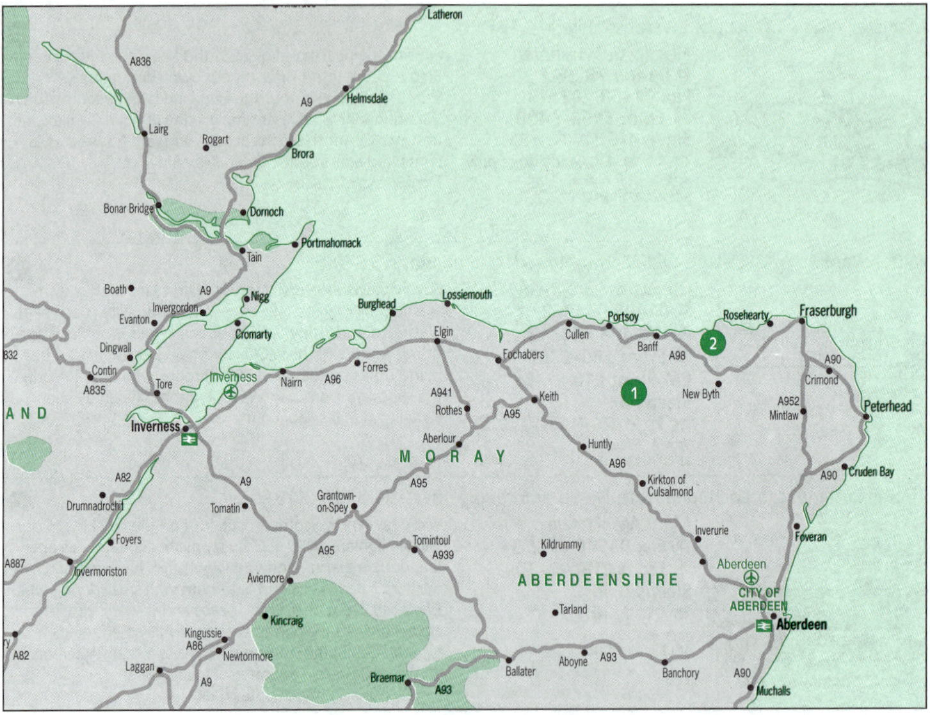

Key
- 1 Bed & Breakfast
- 1 Self-Catering
- 1 B&B and SC
- 1 Camping Barns
- ▲ Camping & Caravanning

The eagle soaring in the sky over a vastness of magnificent scenery sets the stage for this beautiful part of Scotland. On your travels take in the heather-clad mountains, home of the red deer; the unspoilt north-east where farming and fishing go hand in hand; the long winding rivers of the Spey and Dee; sophisticated Aberdeen, the 'Granite City', and picturesque fishing villages and harbours. Agricultural shows and Highland Games are held throughout the summer. Explore Royal Deeside and follow a Castle, Whisky, Coastal or Victorian Heritage 'Trail', or try one of the many championship golf courses. Come and enjoy a holiday to remember.

If you would like help in finding suitable farm accommodation, turn to the full listing of farm groups on pages 360 to 363 to find appropriate contact details for this area.

Aberdeen & Grampian   Scotland

Bed and Breakfast
(and evening meal)

Bandora, Yonder Bognie, Forgue, By Huntly, Aberdeenshire AB54 6BR

Paula Ross
☎ 01466 730375
BB From £15–£18
EM From £8
Sleeps 4
★★
BED & BREAKFAST

Comfortable accommodation near Huntly on castle and whisky trails. Central heating throughout, residents' lounge with colour TV. En suite bedrooms have electric blankets, colour TV, tea/coffee-making facilities and hairdryers. Food hygiene certificate held. French and Italian spoken. Warm welcome assured. Open all year.

The Palace Farm, Gamrie, Banff, Aberdeenshire AB45 3HS

Mrs Pat Duncan
☎ 01261 851261
BB From £19–£20
Sleeps 6
★★★
BED & BREAKFAST

Enjoy a warm Scottish welcome on our mixed arable farm. Late 18th century farmhouse set in wooded garden amidst rolling farm landscapes. Beautiful, quaint fishing villages of Gardenstown and Pennan only 5 minutes away, waiting to be explored. Fresh farm produce and seafood from along the Moray Firth shores. Certificate of Excellence and Scotland's Best. Open Mar–Nov.

Our Internet address is
http://www.webscape.co.uk/farmaccom/

CONFIRM BOOKINGS

Disappointments can arise from misunderstandings over the telephone. Please write to confirm your booking.

Perthshire

Rannoch, Faskally & Ben Lawers

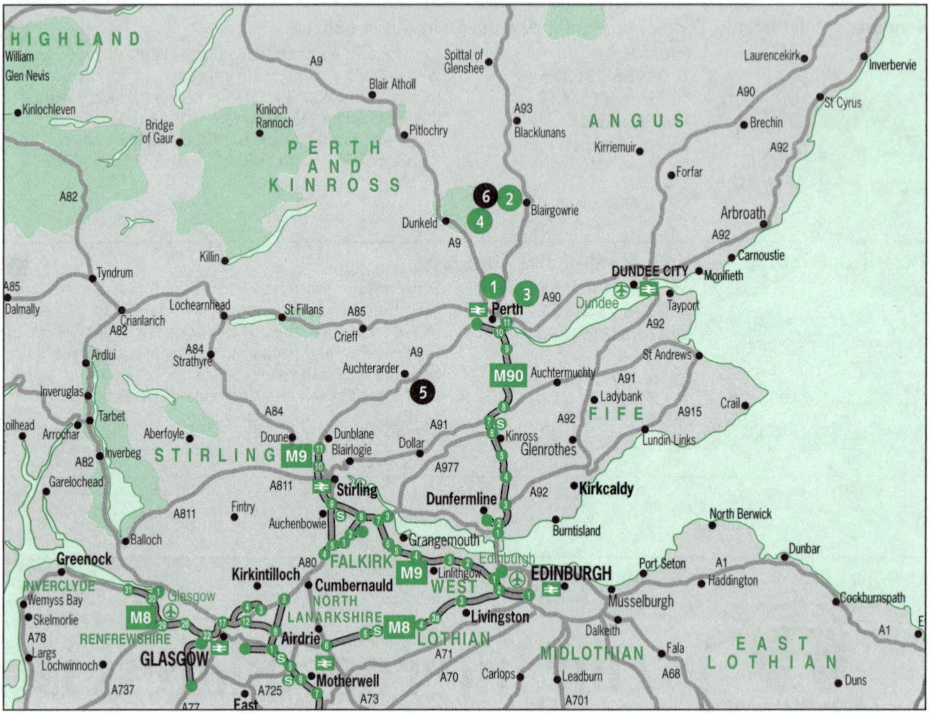

Key

1 Bed & Breakfast
1 Self-Catering
1 B&B and SC
1 Camping Barns
1 Camping & Caravanning

Perthshire lies at the very centre of Scotland so it is the ideal base for your holiday. Here you'll find the grandeur of mountains and glens, the glimmer of lochs and the River Tay, an angler's paradise. See Perthshire at work producing top-quality glass, pottery, hand-knitted woollens, leather goods, hornware and the 'water of life' in its four malt whisky distilleries. There's something for everyone – historic castles, houses and gardens, the world's highest beech hedge, Europe's oldest living tree, Perth's ultra-modern leisure pool, 25 golf courses, theatres and numerous highland nights and ceilidhs.

If you would like help in finding suitable farm accommodation, turn to the full listing of farm groups on pages 360 to 363 to find appropriate contact details for this area.

Perthshire   Scotland

Bed and Breakfast
(and evening meal)

'Avonlea' at Pitmurthly, Redgorton, Nr. Luncarty, Perth PH1 3HX

Mrs Christine Smith
☎ 01738 828363
Fax 01738 828053
[BB] From £18–£22
Sleeps 5
★★★★
BED & BREAKFAST

Quiet, comfortable farmhouse in ideal touring location set amidst lovely countryside yet only 5 minutes from historic Perth with its unique shops and excellent restaurants. Log fires and full CH. Working farm with plenty to watch. Golf, fishing, riding and swimming can be arranged. Warm welcome assured. Open all year except Dec & Jan.

Bankhead, Clunie, Blairgowrie, Perthshire PH10 6SG

Mrs H Wightman
☎/Fax 01250 884281
[BB] From £18–£20
EM From £8
Sleeps 5
★★
BED & BREAKFAST

A friendly and peaceful atmosphere awaits you on our family-run farm. Traditional farmhouse cooking using our own free range eggs and raspberries. Log fire, CH. Two ground floor bedrooms with electric blankets, tea/coffee facilities. Ideally situated for touring Perthshire and beyond. Enjoy birdwatching at Loch of Lowes, walking on hills above Dunkeld, fishing on local lochs. Glenshee ski slopes 40 mins. Open Jan–Nov.

Blackcraigs Farm, Scone, Perthshire PH2 7PJ

Irene Millar
☎/Fax 01821 640254
[BB] From £16–£20
Sleeps 6
★★★
BED & BREAKFAST

18th century farmhouse set in a well maintained garden where a warm welcome awaits you. Relax and enjoy the quiet, peaceful surroundings. Comfortable bedrooms all with colour TV and tea/coffee-making facilities. Elegant residents' lounge with an open fire. The Fair City of Perth has lots of charm and many amenities and is only 4 miles away. Golf and fishing nearby. Ideally situated for a quiet holiday. Open all year.

Letter Farm, Loch of the Lowes, By Dunkeld, Perthshire PH8 0HH

Jo Andrew
☎/Fax 01350 724254
[BB] From £20–£27
Sleeps 6
★★★★
BED & BREAKFAST

Enjoy our recently renovated farmhouse, kingsize beds in en suite rooms, log fire in guest lounge and good home baking. Our family-run stock farm nestles next to the Loch of Lowes Wildlife Reserve, home to ospreys, otters and others. It exudes peace and tranquillity – come see for yourselves, you'll be warmly welcomed. Open May–Nov.

Please mention **Stay on a Farm** when booking

Scotland — Perthshire

Self-Catering

5 Milton of Duchally Cottage, Millhill Farm, Auchterarder PH3 1PQ

Jennifer Davidson
☎ 01764 662227
Fax 01764 664033
SC From £230–£390
Sleeps 4 + cot
★★★
SELF CATERING

Very comfortable, well equipped, two bedroomed detached cottage. Tumble drier, auto washing machine, microwave, coffee maker, colour TV, video, living room with open fire. Cot, high chair, play pen, stairgates available. Fenced garden with furniture. Ideal for golfing and touring central Scotland. Three miles from shops. If you like peace and quiet this is the cottage for you. Open Apr–Oct.

6 Wester Riechip, Laighwood, Butterstone, Dunkeld, Perthshire PH8 0HB

W & Wl Bruges
☎ 01350 724241/724208
SC From £380–£568
Sleeps 8
★★★★
SELF CATERING

Wester Riechip has been constructed from the west wing of a 19th century shooting lodge to create a luxurious detached holiday house with superb modern facilities. Comfortably accommodates 8. Spectacular views over surrounding hills and lochs. An ideal base for touring, golfing and birdwatching. Shooting and fishing available on our family-run hill farm. Open all year.

NO ANSWER?
Farmers are mostly out and about during the day.
Try to telephone before 9.30am or after 4pm.

FINDING YOUR ACCOMMODATION

The local FHB Group contacts listed on pages 360 to 363 can always help you find a vacancy in your chosen area.

Please mention **Stay on a Farm** when booking

Argyll, the Isles & Stirling

Mull, Jura, Loch Lomond, the Trossachs & the Argyll
& Queen Elizabeth Forest Parks

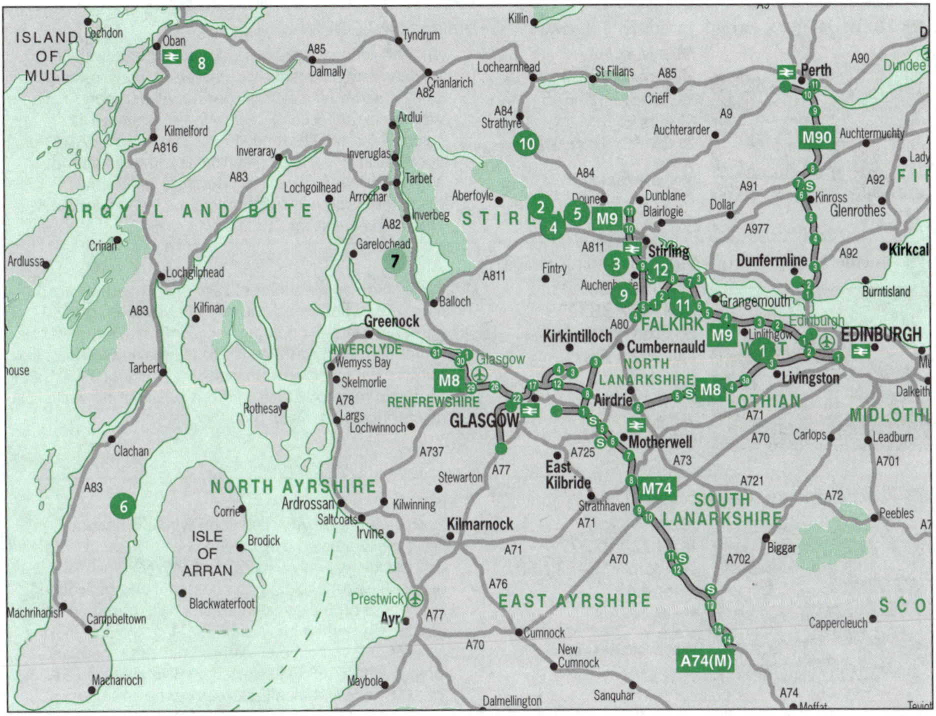

Key

- 🟢 1 Bed & Breakfast
- ⚫ 1 Self-Catering
- 🟢 1 B&B and SC
- 🟥 1 Camping Barns
- 🔺 Camping & Caravanning

Here, at the very crossroads of Scotland, the Highlands meet the Lowlands against a scenic backdrop of mountains, lochs and glens. There's so much to do. Walk in the Campsie Fells, Ochil Hills or Arrochar Alps. Explore the stately homes, lovely gardens, historic sites, castles, nature trails, sandy beaches and the beautiful islands a short distance away. Visit Glasgow, Edinburgh, Perth and Linlithgow. Journey from Loch Awe to Carradale, cruise shimmering Loch Lomond, explore the Trossachs and the hills walked by Rob Roy. Don't miss Royal Stirling, near the battle site where William Wallace led his army to glorious victory. Discover the magnificent diversity of Scotland's scenery, history and culture, with the bonus of good food and comfortable farm accommodation.

If you would like help in finding suitable farm accommodation, turn to the full listing of farm groups on pages 360 to 363 to find appropriate contact details for this area.

Scotland
Argyll, the Isles & Stirling

Bed and Breakfast
(and evening meal)

---

① Belsyde Farm, Lanark Road, Linlithgow, West Lothian EH49 6QE

Mrs Nan Hay
☎/Fax 01506 842098
BB From £16–£25
Sleeps 6
★★★
BED & BREAKFAST

An 18th century farmhouse located in large, secluded gardens with panoramic views over the Forth estuary. Golfing and fishing available locally. All bedrooms have washbasin (hot & cold), tea/coffee-making facilities, colour TV, central heating, 1 bedroom en suite. AA listed. Located close to M8, M9 and M90 and to Edinburgh airport. Follow A706 south-west from Linlithgow (1½ miles); first entrance on left after crossing Union Canal. Open all year except Christmas.

---

② Inchie Farm, Port of Menteith, Stirling FK8 3JZ

Mrs Norma Erskine
☎ 01877 385233
BB From £15–£16
EM From £10
Sleeps 5
★★★
BED & BREAKFAST

Family farm on the shores of Lake of Menteith where ospreys nest between April and Sept. Featured in 'Wish You Were Here' TV programme. Comfortable twin/family rooms both with washbasins and tea-making facilities, also guests' own bathroom and lounge with colour TV. Central heating throughout. Ideal for trout fishing or hill walking in nearby Trossachs. Open Mar–Oct.

---

③ Lochend Farm, Carronbridge, Denny, Stirlingshire FK6 5JJ

Jean Morton
☎ 01324 822778
BB From £18–£22.50
Sleeps 4
★★★★
BED & BREAKFAST

Peace, panoramic view and good wholesome food. Delightfully situated overlooking Loch Coulter in unspoiled countryside, yet only 5 miles from M9/M80 (jct 9). A perfect base for exploring this beautiful part of Scotland. Farmhouse centrally heated, traditionally furnished. 2 double bedrooms with washbasin, TV, radio, tea-making facilities; also guests' own bathroom, dining room and lounge with colour TV. Selected by *'Which' Good Bed & Breakfast Guide.* Open Easter–Oct or by arrangement.

---

④ Lochend Farm, Port of Menteith, Stirling FK8 3JZ

Mrs Rhona Millar
☎ 01877 385235
Fax 01786 480550
BB From £18–£20
EM From £10
Sleeps 4
★★★
BED & BREAKFAST

Enjoy a peaceful stay at Lochend, a mixed arable stock farm next to Scotland's only Lake in the heart of the Trossachs. Farmhouse dates back to 1726 being the former dower house of the estate. Spacious accommodation with en suite bedrooms. A warm friendly atmosphere and good home cooking await. Open April–Oct.

---

⑤ Lower Tarr Farm, Ruskie, Port of Menteith, Stirling FK8 3LG

Mrs Effie Bain
☎/Fax 01786 850202
BB From £18–£20
EM From £10
Sleeps 6 + cot
★★★
BED & BREAKFAST

On our mixed farm guests can dine in our conservatory and enjoy the peaceful situation, panoramic views and pretty garden, with Ruskie burn flowing past. Good home cooking and baking are served, ensuring an enjoyable stay. Cattle, sheep and hens plus interesting wildlife can be seen. Central for touring the Trossachs, Loch Lomond, Stirling and Edinburgh. En suite room. Open Feb–Nov.

Argyll, the Isles & Stirling   Scotland

Mains Farm, Carradale, Campbeltown, Argyll PA28 6QG   ⑥

Mrs Dorothy MacCormick
☎ 01583 431216
BB From £16.50
EM from £7
Sleeps 6
★★
BED & BREAKFAST

Comfortable accommodation in traditional farmhouse five minutes' walk from mile-long safe beach, forest walks. Golf and river fishing. Scenic views of Isle of Arran over the Kilbrannon Sound and picturesque fishing harbour. Good home cooking and warm hospitality with coal fires and heating in rooms. Not suitable for disabled visitors. Open Apr–Oct.

Shantron Farm, Luss, Alexandria, Dumbartonshire G83 8RH   ⑦

Anne M Lennox
☎/Fax 01389 850231
Mobile 0468 378400
BB From £20–£25
Sleeps 11
★★★
BED & BREAKFAST

Enjoy a relaxing break in a spacious bungalow with outstanding views of Loch Lomond. The farm is Morag's croft in 'High Road' and other scenes. Four miles south of Luss. Ideal for touring, hillwalking, fishing, watersports and golf on the new Loch Lomond Golf Course. En suite available. Open Mar–Nov.
E mail: rjlennox@shantron.u-net.com

Thistle-Doo, Kilchrenan, by Taynuilt, Oban, Argyll PA35 1HF   ⑧

K Lambie
☎ 01866 833339
BB From £17–£21
EM from £10
Sleeps 6
★★★
BED & BREAKFAST

Awe-inspiring view of Loch Awe from our friendly family-run establishment. Ideal for all outdoor activities. Very peaceful and relaxing. 20 miles east of Oban, taking the B845 off the A85 at Taynuilt to the shore of Loch Awe. Open all year.

The Topps Farm, Fintry Road, Denny, Stirlingshire FK6 5JF   ⑨

Mrs Jennifer Steel
☎ 01324 822471
Fax 01324 823099
BB From £19–£32
EM From £16
Sleeps 14
★★★
GUEST HOUSE

A modern farmhouse guesthouse in a beautiful hillside location with stunning, panoramic views. Family, double or twin-bedded rooms available, all en suite with tea/coffee, shortbread, TV, radio, telephone. Food a speciality ("Taste of Scotland" listed). Restaurant open to non-residents. A la carte menu only. Easy access to all major tourist attractions. Your enjoyment is our aim and pleasure! Open all year.

Trean Farm, Leny Feus, Callander, Perthshire FK17 8AS   ⑩

Janette Donald
☎/Fax 01877 331160
BB From £18–£21
Sleeps 6
★★★
BED & BREAKFAST

A working farm situated in open parkland beside Callander with a 15 minute walk to shops. Outstanding views of Ben Ledi. An ideal base for touring and hill walking. 2 en suite rooms with TV and 1 with washbasin. Tea/coffee facilities. Residents' lounge. Open May–Oct.

Wester Carmuirs Farm, Larbert, By Falkirk, Stirlingshire FK5 3NW   ⑪

Mrs Sheila Taylor
☎ 01324 812459
BB From £19
Sleeps 6
★★
BED & BREAKFAST

Relax and enjoy friendly hospitality and good food in our comfortable home on mixed farm on A803 near Falkirk (M9/A80). Comfortable twin/double/family rooms all with washbasins and tea/coffee. Guests' own bathroom, shower room, dining room and TV room with log fire. Ideal centre to visit local attractions, eg. Mariner Centre with swimming pool; also Trossachs, Loch Lomond, Stirling, Glasgow and Edinburgh. Open Jan–Oct.

Scotland — *Argyll, the Isles & Stirling*

(12) West Plean, Denny Road, Stirling FK7 8HA

Mrs Moira Johnston
☎ 01786 812208
Fax 01786 480550
BB From £20–£24
Sleeps 6
🐴🐎🐾🐕🐖🐐 W
★★★
BED & BREAKFAST

Enjoy warm Scottish farming hospitality in a historic setting, with sweeping lawns, walled garden, extensive woodland walks, surrounded by our mixed farm. We offer quality food, spacious comfort, bedrooms en suite, hot drink facilities and attentive hosts. Riding and fishing can be arranged locally. Located on the A872 Denny road, 2 minutes from M9/M80 (jct9). Open Feb–Nov.
E-mail: west.plean@virgin.net

Self-Catering

(7) Shemore Farm Cottage, Shantron Farm, Luss, Alexandria, Dumbartonshire G83 8RH

Mrs Anne M Lennox
☎/Fax 01389 850231
Mobile 0468 378400
SC From £150–£350
Sleeps 6
🐕🐟🐾🐖 W
★★
SELF CATERING

Regulars often return to this traditional stone cottage attractively situated on a hill sheep farm, 300 ft above Loch Lomond, over which the cottage has magnificent views. The farm has often been filmed for 'High Road' TV series. Four miles south of picturesque village of Luss. Edinburgh, Oban, Fort William, Ayr – 1½ hours. Ideal for hillwalking, fishing, watersports. Children love to feed lambs. Short breaks available. Open all year.
E mail: rjlennox@shantron.u-net.com

Our farms offer a range of facilities that are illustrated by symbols in each entry.
Turn to page 16 for an explanation of the symbols.

USE THE INDEX

The comprehensive Index shows which farms offer access to disabled visitors; caravanning/camping facilities; the chance to participate on a working farm; stabling/grazing for visiting horses; en suite rooms; a welcome to business people; acceptance of *Stay on a Farm* gift tokens.

Scottish Lowlands

Farm entries in this regional section are listed under those areas shown in green on the key map. Look at the index below to find on which page the entries start. You will see that we have listed the areas geographically so that you can turn more easily to find farms in neighbouring areas.

At the start of each area section is a detailed map with numbered symbols indicating the location of each farm. Different symbols denote different types of accommodation; see the key below each area map. Farm entries are listed alphabetically under type of accommodation. Some farms offer more than one type of accommodation and therefore have more than one entry.

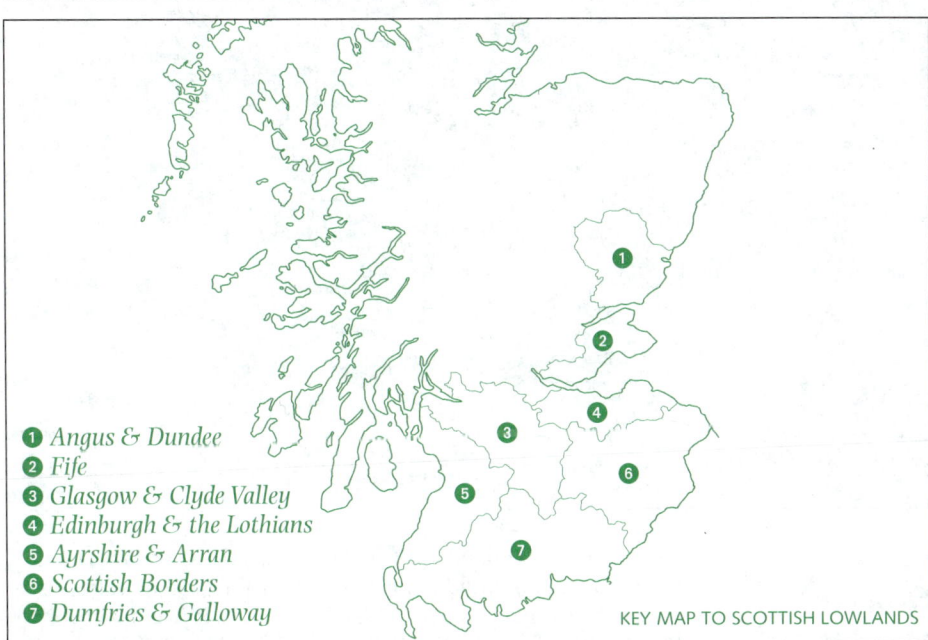

❶ Angus & Dundee
❷ Fife
❸ Glasgow & Clyde Valley
❹ Edinburgh & the Lothians
❺ Ayrshire & Arran
❻ Scottish Borders
❼ Dumfries & Galloway

KEY MAP TO SCOTTISH LOWLANDS

Angus & Dundee *page 48*
Angus Glens, Strathmore & Sidlaw Hills

Fife *page 50*
Fife Ness & Firth of Forth

Glasgow & Clyde Valley *page 52*
Inverclyde, Renfrewshire, City of Glasgow, North and South Lanarkshire.

Edinburgh & the Lothians *page 55*
Firth of Forth & Pentland, Moorfoot & Lammermuir Hills

Ayrshire & Arran *page 58*
North Arran, Goat Fell & Ayrshire coast

Scottish Borders *page 61*
Upper Tweeddale, Eildon Hills, the Merse, Teviotdale, Eskdale, Southern Upland Way & the Borders Forest Park

Dumfries & Galloway *page 65*
Moffat & Annandale Valley, Galloway Forest Park, Solway Coastline

Angus & Dundee

Angus Glens, Strathmore & Sidlaw Hills

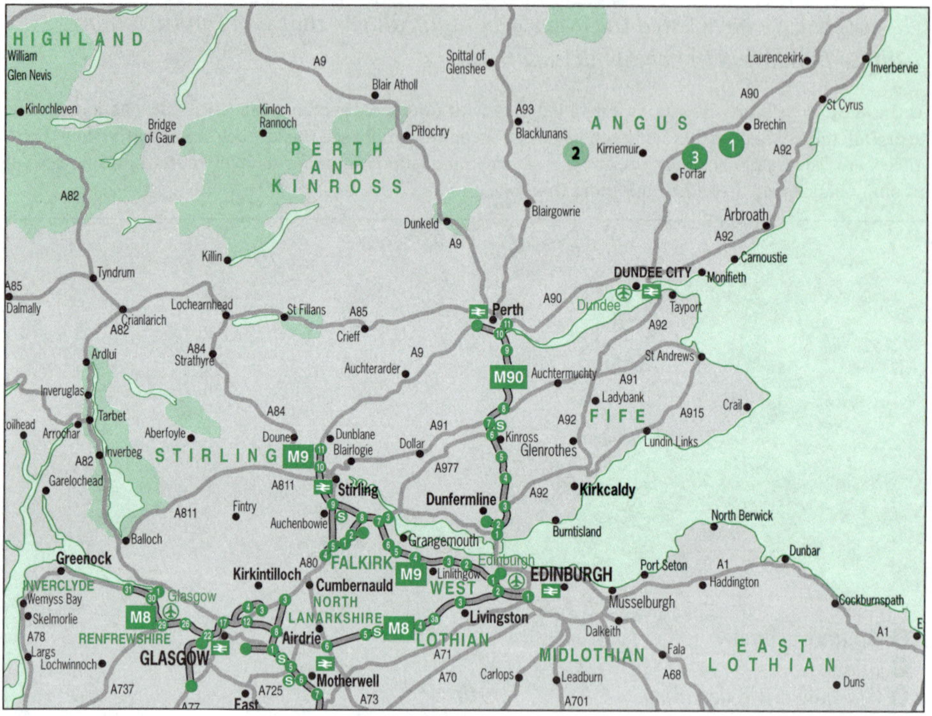

Key

1 Bed & Breakfast
1 Self-Catering
1 B&B and SC
1 Camping Barns
1 Camping & Caravanning

Whatever you seek in Scotland you'll find in Angus where the Braes of Angus meet the valley of Strathmore, from glens with gushing waterfalls to numerous sandy beaches and bays. Visit Glamis Castle, former home of Queen Elizabeth the Queen Mother, or Kirriemuir, birthplace of J.M. Barrie, author of *Peter Pan*. Opportunities abound to fish and golf and the Heritage Trail is a must for the visitor. Arbroath Abbey, Brechin Cathedral, Restenneth Priory and various Pictish standing stones and hill forts testify to a fascinating past. Dundee is famed for its 3km railway bridge spanning the River Tay. This area is an ideal touring base for your Scottish holiday.

If you would like help in finding suitable farm accommodation, turn to the full listing of farm groups on pages 360 to 363 to find appropriate contact details for this area.

Angus & Dundee   Scotland

Bed and Breakfast
(and evening meal)

Blibberhill Farm, By Brechin, Angus, Tayside DD9 6TH

Mrs Wendy Stewart
☎/Fax 01307 830323
BB From £16
EM From £9
Sleeps 6
★★★
BED & BREAKFAST

Peacefully situated between the Angus glens and coast, Glamis and Edzell Castles nearby. Under 1 hour's drive from Royal Deeside and St Andrews and Perth. Central to many golf courses, fishing and hillwalking. Tastefully decorated and furnished en suite rooms. Open fires and electric blankets keep you cosy in winter. All home cooking. Beautiful large garden. Excellent children's facilities. Evening meal optional. Open all year excluding Christmas.

Purgavie Farm, Lintrathen, Kirriemuir DD8 5HZ

Mrs Moira Clark
☎/Fax 01575 560213
BB From £19–£21
EM From £11
Sleeps 6
★★★★
BED & BREAKFAST

A warm welcome in homely accommodation on our farm set in peaceful countryside with excellent views. All rooms have private or en suite bathroom, TV and tea-making facilities. Good home cooking providing traditional Scottish fayre. Fishing on Lintrathen loch, pony trekking and hillwalking in Glen Isla. Glamis Castle 10 miles. Located 7 miles from Kirriemuir, follow the B951 to Glen Isla; farm signposted at roadside. Open all year.

Wemyss Farm, Montrose Road, Forfar, Angus DD8 2TB

Mrs Deanna Lindsay
☎/Fax 01307 462887
BB From £15.50
EM From £10
Sleeps 6
★★
BED & BREAKFAST

190-acre mixed farm situated on the B9113 with a wide variety of animals. Ideal for touring Angus Glens, St Andrews, Royal Deeside, Aberdeen, Edinburgh, east coast resorts. Glamis Castle nearby. Shooting, fishing, golf, swimming, all in the area. Bedrooms overlooking beautiful countryside. Children made welcome, reduced rates. Evening dinner optional, packed lunches. Quiet and peaceful, yet within easy reach of all amenities. Food hygiene certificate held. Open all year.

Self-Catering

Purgavie Farm, Lintrathen, Kirriemuir DD8 5HZ

Mrs Moira Clark
☎/Fax 01575 560213
SC From £200–£400
EM From £12
Sleeps 4/6
★★ – ★★★★
SELF CATERING

Escape the stress and relax in our Swedish log house or bungalow and enjoy the panoramic views of the lovely countryside. Explore the hills and see the wildlife or fish in Lintrathen loch. Properties furnished to a high standard with dishwasher, shower, fridge freezer, washer dryer, payphone and microwave. Open fire in bungalow. Located 7 miles from Kirriemuir, follow B951 signposted at roadside. Open all year.

Fife

Fife Ness & Firth of Forth

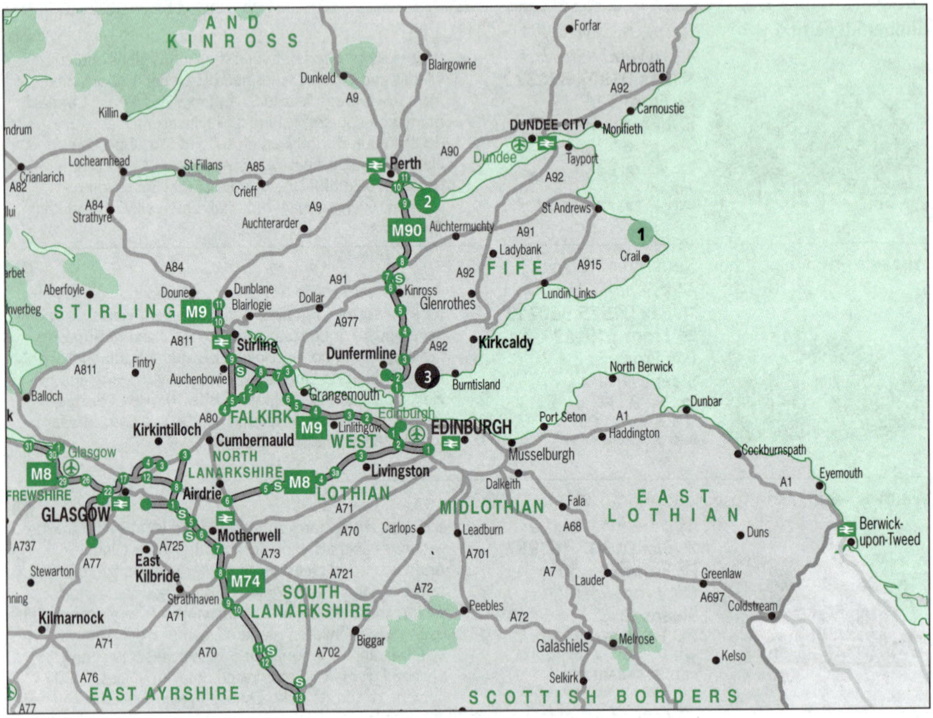

Key

- 1 Bed & Breakfast
- 1 Self-Catering
- 1 B&B and SC
- 1 Camping Barns
- 1 Camping & Caravanning

Fife is blessed with a sunny climate and miles of clean sandy beaches and quaint fishing villages. Visit the Fisheries Museum at Anstruther and the Sea Life Centre at St Andrews where you can watch the seals being fed. There are country parks and many fascinating museums such as the Ceres Folk Museum and the Secret Bunker. Dunfermline Abbey, Falkland with its Royal Palace and Kellie Castle near Pittenweem are rich in history. Wildlife lovers will enjoy the Scottish Deer Centre near Cupar and Fife Animal Park, while famous St Andrews is a mecca for golfers. Fife makes an ideal touring base for visiting Dundee, Edinburgh and Perth. Come and enjoy our warm hospitality.

If you would like help in finding suitable farm accommodation, turn to the full listing of farm groups on pages 360 to 363 to find appropriate contact details for this area

Fife   *Scotland*

Bed and Breakfast
(and evening meal)

Cambo House, Kingsbarns, St Andrews, Fife KY16 8QD

Mr & Mrs Peter Erskine
☎ 01333 450054/450313
Fax 01333 450987
BB From £40–£55
EM From £25
Sleeps 4
★★★★
BED & BREAKFAST

Come and lose yourself in a glorious four-poster bed in our magnificent Victorian family home hardly touched by time, set in parkland and woods that meander down to an unspoilt coastline with a fine sweeping beach. Only 10 minutes from St. Andrews. Open all year except Christmas and New Year.
E-mail: 100130,1660@compuserve.com

Easter Clunie Farmhouse, Easter Clunie, Newburgh, Fife KY14 6EJ

Mrs Kathleen Baird
☎ 01337 840218
Fax 01337 842226
BB From £16–£20
Sleeps 6
★★
BED & BREAKFAST

David and Kathleen Baird warmly welcome you to their 18th century centrally heated home on a working farm. Comfortable bedrooms with en suite or private facilities. Home baking and tea on arrival. Relax in walled garden, enjoy panoramic views of the River Tay. Surrounding countryside provides a wealth of scenic walks. Ideal touring base for Fife and Perthshire. Situated on A913. Open Mar–Nov. E-mail: cluniefarm.@aol.com

Self-Catering

Cambo House, Kingsbarns, St Andrews, Fife KY16 8QD

Mr & Mrs Peter Erskine
☎ 01333 450054/450313
Fax 01333 450987
SC From £190–£750
Sleeps 2/8
★★
SELF CATERING

Come and lose yourself on an enchanting wooded coastal estate hardly touched by time. Only 10 minutes from St Andrews, the home of golf. Cottages and apartments in a magnificent country house. Ideal for families and groups of up to 32. Open all year.
E-mail: 100130,1660@compuserve.com

Parkend Cottage, Parkend Farm, Crossgates, Cowdenbeath KY4 8EX

June Weatherup
☎/Fax 01383 860277
SC From £225–£375
Sleeps 6
★★★★★
SELF CATERING

Luxury traditionally refurbished 3-bedroom cottage enjoying beautiful and peaceful location on working dairy farm, 2 miles from Aberdour, with panoramic views to Firth of Forth and famous bridges. A true family 'home from home' with a warm welcome assured. Fully equipped to highest standard. Ideal base for touring Fife, Perthshire, Stirling and Edinburgh. Open all year.

Glasgow & Clyde Valley

Inverclyde, Renfrewshire, City of Glasgow, North & South Lanarkshire.

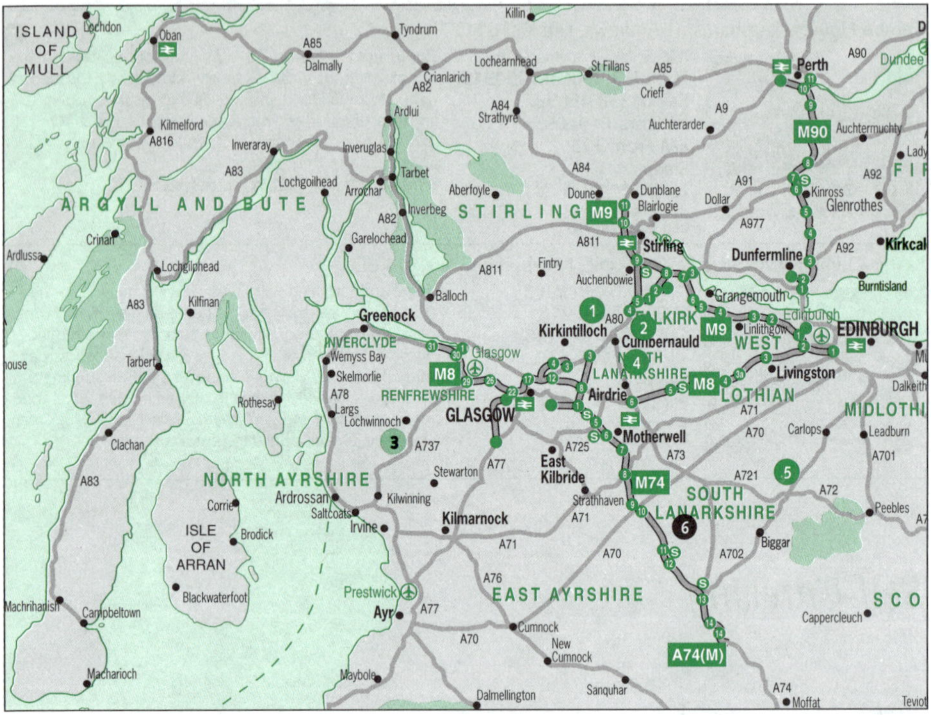

Key

- 1 Bed & Breakfast
- 1 Self-Catering
- 1 B&B and SC
- 1 Camping Barns
- 1 Camping & Caravanning

Welcome to the many different worlds of Greater Glasgow and Clyde Valley, where city life blends with country life. Glasgow, Scotland's largest city and cultural capital, city of architecture and design, has many fascinating buildings and museums including the famous Burrell Collection and the Art Nouveau designs of Charles Rennie Mackintosh. Glasgow is paradise for shoppers. From Biggar to Gourock enjoy the famous River Clyde: the area is steeped in history. Both city and town are complemented by the spectacular scenery and the hidden picturesque villages, such as New Lanark World Heritage Village. Numerous lush golf courses, country parks, canals, castles and museums – experience it all and don't forget, whenever you arrive, both far and wide, a traditional warm Scottish welcome awaits you.

If you would like help in finding suitable farm accommodation, turn to the full listing of farm groups on pages 360 to 363 to find appropriate contact details for this area.

Glasgow & Clyde Valley   Scotland

Bed and Breakfast
(and evening meal)

Allanfauld Farm, Kilsyth, Glasgow G65 9DF ①

Libby MacGregor
☎/Fax 01236 822155
BB From £16
Sleeps 4
★★
BED & BREAKFAST

A working family farm situated close to the town of Kilsyth at the foot of the Kilsyth Hills, a great base to explore central Scotland. Located near A803 with easy access to M8 and M9. Golf, fishing, hill walking and a swimming pool are all within half a mile. Glasgow, Stirling 20 minutes. 1 twin/family room, 1 single room, both with TV and tea/coffee facilities. Open all year.

Bandominie Farm, Walton Road, Castlecary, Bonnybridge FK4 2HP ②

Jean Forrester
☎ 01324 840284
BB From £16–£17
Sleeps 5
★★
BED & BREAKFAST

A working farm located 2 miles from the A80 at Castlecary (B816). Easy access from Glasgow and Edinburgh. Lovely view with a homely atmosphere. Central heating, TV lounge. Ample parking. Open all year except Christmas & New Year.

East Lochhead, Largs Road, Lochwinnoch PA12 4DX ③

Janet Anderson
☎/Fax 01505 842610
BB From £30–£32
Sleeps 2–6
★★★★
BED & BREAKFAST

East Lochhead is a 100 year old farmhouse standing in 2 acres of beautiful landscaped gardens. Both bedrooms, one of which is on the ground floor, have magnificent views over Barr Loch and the Renfrewshire hills. The Irvine/Paisley cycle track passes close to the house. Janet would be delighted to cook you an evening meal by prior arrangement. AA Premier Selected QQQQQ. Open all year. E mail: winnoch@aol.com.uk

---

Easter Glentore Farm, Slamannan Road, Greengairs, Airdrie, Lanarkshire ML6 7TJ ④

Elsie Hunter
☎/Fax 01236 830243
Mobile 0370 746950
BB From £22
Sleeps 6
★★★★
BED & BREAKFAST

Enjoy a warm, homely atmosphere with Scottish hosts in our 18th century ground floor farmhouse. Panoramic views. Quality accommodation, en suite or private bathroom, radio/alarms, tea/coffee facilities with home baking, lounge with TV. Evening tea tray. Excellent touring base, Glasgow and Stirling 15 miles, Edinburgh 28 miles. Near central Scotland's canals. Selected by 'Which' Good Bed and Breakfast Guide. Open all year except Christmas.

Walston Mansion Farmhouse, Walston, Carnwath, Lanark ML11 8NF ⑤

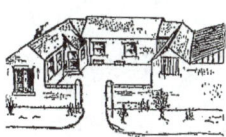

Mrs Margaret Kirby
☎/Fax 01899 810338
BB £15–£17
EM From £8
Sleeps 6
★★
BED & BREAKFAST

A very pleasant family home situated 5 miles from Biggar. A friendly and relaxed atmosphere; children most welcome. Good home cooking with home-produced meat, eggs and organic vegetables. Two en suite rooms, guests' lounge with log fire, TV/video and children's games. An ideal base for touring Strathclyde, Lothian and the Borders; Lanark, Edinburgh and Glasgow only a short drive away. Open all year.

Scotland — *Glasgow & Clyde Valley*

Self-Catering

⑥ Carmichael Country Cottages, Estate Office, Westmains, Carmichael, Biggar, Lanarkshire ML12 6PG

Richard Carmichael of Carmichael
☎ 01899 308336
Fax 01899 308481
[SC] From £180–£450
EM From £7.50
Sleeps 2/7
★★ – ★★★★
SELF CATERING

Fifteen 200-year-old stone cottages nestle among the woods and fields of our 700-year-old family estate. Enjoy our private tennis court and fishing loch. We guarantee comfort, warmth and a friendly welcome in an accessible, unique rural and historic time capsule. We farm deer, cattle and sheep and sell meats and tartan – Carmichael, of course. Breakfast and evening meal available. Visitor centre. Open all year. E mail: chiefcarm@aol.com.

③ East Lochhead, Largs Road, Lochwinnoch PA12 4DX

Janet Anderson
☎/Fax 01505 842610
[SC] From £160–£500
EM From £16
Sleeps 2–5
★★★★
SELF CATERING

Three cosy comfortable cottages newly converted from our old byres. Furnished and equipped to a high standard. Beautiful views over Barr Loch and the Renfrewshire hills. Linen is included and home cooking is available. The Paisley/Irvine cycle track passes close to the house. Convenient base for touring Glasgow, Ayrshire, Trossachs and Loch Lomond. Open all year.
E mail: winnoch@aol.com.uk

STAY ON A FARM GIFT TOKENS

FARM HOLIDAY BUREAU

If you have enjoyed your Stay on a Farm, why not treat your friends and relatives to *Stay on a Farm* gift tokens? Available from the Bureau office (tel: 01203 696909), they can be redeemed against accommodation and are accepted by the majority of farms (see Index). Please check when booking to avoid disappointment.

FOLLOW THE COUNTRY CODE

Leave nothing but footprints,
Take nothing but photographs,
Kill nothing but time!

Edinburgh & the Lothians

Firth of Forth & Pentland, Moorfoot & Lammermuir Hills

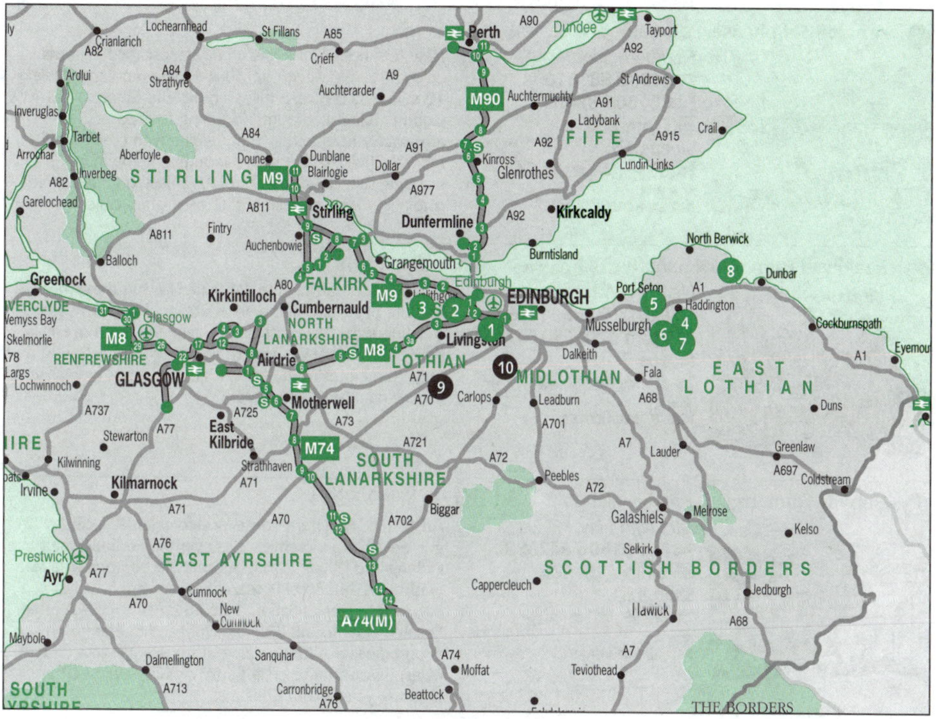

Key

- **1** Bed & Breakfast
- **1** Self-Catering
- **1** B&B and SC
- **1** Camping Barns
- **1** Camping & Caravanning

Edinburgh generates excitement. Visual drama, arresting skylines, historic buildings, elegant architecture, a guardian castle... this is Edinburgh, endlessly appealing. On its doorstep lie 40 miles of beautiful sandy beaches, rocky shores and a rolling landscape chequered with castles. Romance, history, splendour... Marvel at Linlithgow Palace, birthplace of Mary Queen of Scots. Admire the elegant grandeur of Adam's Hopetoun House, the tantalising carvings of gothic Rosslyn Chapel or spectacular Bass Rock seabird colony. Cruise canals or escape under the dramatic Forth Bridges to lovely Inchcolm Island or awe-inspiring Deep Sea World. Sample Scotland's golden water of life at Glenkinchie distillery... or attempt par on a world-renowned golf-link. And for youngsters? A tree-top adventure, a butterfly walk in Dalkeith? Linger in the Lothians: it's no lottery... everyone wins.

If you would like help in finding suitable farm accommodation, turn to the full listing of farm groups on pages 360 to 363 to find appropriate contact details for this area.

Scotland   Edinburgh & the Lothians

Bed and Breakfast
(and evening meal)

---

① Ashcroft Farmhouse, East Calder, Nr Edinburgh EH53 0ET

Elizabeth Scott
☎ 01506 881810
Fax 01506 884327
[BB] From £26
Sleeps 16
★★★★
GUEST HOUSE

New farmhouse set in beautifully landscaped gardens enjoying lovely views over surrounding farmland. Only 10 miles city centre, 5 miles airport, city by-pass, M8/M9. Good parking. Bedrooms, including four-poster, attractively furnished in antique pine with co-ordinating fabrics. Choice of breakfasts including home made sausage, salmon, kippers, etc. AA Selected QQQQ. No smoking. Open all year. E-mail: ashcrofta@aol.com

---

② Bankhead Farm, Dechmont, Broxburn, West Lothian EH52 6NB

Heather Warnock
☎/Fax 01506 811209
[BB] From £20–£30
Sleeps 5
★★★
BED & BREAKFAST

This livestock farm in the Bathgate Hills has three modern en suite bedrooms and private kitchen. Panoramic views of Edinburgh, West Lothian and over the Forth to Fife belie the fact that we are close to three historic towns, and only 20 minutes from Scotland's capital city. Open all year. E-mail: bankheadbb@aol.com

---

③ Belsyde Farm, Lanark Road, Linlithgow, West Lothian EH49 6QE

Mrs Nan Hay
☎/Fax 01506 842098
[BB] From £16–£25
Sleeps 6
★★★
BED & BREAKFAST

An 18th century farmhouse located in large, secluded gardens with panoramic views over the Forth estuary. Golfing and fishing available locally. All bedrooms have washbasin (hot & cold), tea/coffee-making facilities, colour TV, central heating, 1 bedroom en suite. AA listed. Located close to M8, M9 and M90 and to Edinburgh airport. Follow A706 south-west from Linlithgow (1½ miles); first entrance on left after crossing Union Canal. Open all year except Christmas.

---

④ Carfrae Farmhouse, Carfrae, Nr Garvald, Haddington, East Lothian EH41 4LP

Mrs Dorothy Gibson
☎ 01620 830242
Fax 01620 830320
[BB] From £18.50–£27
Sleeps 6
★★★★
BED & BREAKFAST

Set on 800-acre mixed farm, beautifully furnished farmhouse overlooking walled garden with uninterrupted views of the Lammermuir Hills. Close to many golf courses, own fishing loch. Edinburgh 35 minutes. Open Apr–Oct.

---

⑤ Coates Farm, Longniddry, East Lothian EH32 0PL

Zoë Peace
☎/Fax 01620 822131
[BB] From £23
Sleeps 4
★★★★
BED & BREAKFAST

Spacious Georgian farmhouse tastefully decorated and furnished throughout. Ideally situated for exploring countryside, coastline or visiting Edinburgh. Train station nearby. Comfortable bedrooms with private facilities. Separate lounge and dining room for guests. Large, well tended, interesting garden. Excellent local pubs and restaurants. Coates is 1¾ miles from the A1. Open May–Sept.

Edinburgh & the Lothians   Scotland

Eaglescairnie Mains, Gifford, Haddington, East Lothian EH41 4HN ⑥

Mrs Barbara Williams
☎/Fax 01620 810491
BB From £18–£25
Sleeps 6
★★★
BED & BREAKFAST

Join us at Eaglescairnie Mains, a beautifully furnished Georgian house on our 350-acre arable/sheep farm which recently won a National Conservation Award. Near A1, ideal for the coast, golf courses, the Borders or Edinburgh. Double, twin and single rooms – some en suite, full CH, basins, tea/coffee trays. Conservatory, tennis court and games room. Open all year (closed Christmas and New Year). E-mail: williams.eagles@btinternet.uk

Rowan Park, Longnewton Farm, Gifford, East Lothian EH41 4JW ⑦

Mrs Margaret Whiteford
☎ 01620 810327
BB From £18
Sleeps 6
★★★★
BED & BREAKFAST

Our family farm of 450 acres consists of cattle, cereals and ponies. Situated at the foot of the Lammermuir Hills, with magnificent views to the Forth. Only 30 minutes from Edinburgh and near to the Border Country with its stately homes. Golf, fishing, tennis, swimming and pony trekking nearby. Furnished to a high standard, CH, guests' lounge, dining room and ground floor bedrooms, also welcome tray. A warm welcome awaits you. Open Mar–Nov.

Whitekirk Mains, Whitekirk, North Berwick, East Lothian EH42 1XS ⑧

Mrs J Tuer
☎ 01620 870245/870300
Fax 01620 870330
BB From £22–£25
Sleeps 6
★★★★
BED & BREAKFAST

Spacious Georgian farmhouse on a 600-acre mixed farm at the edge of a historic village. Large en suite rooms with tea/coffee facilities and colour TV. Oak panelled dining/drawing rooms, log fires, superb views. Country and beach walks. 20 miles Edinburgh/Lammermuir Hills. Adjoining our new Whitekirk Golf Course and club house, restaurant/bar. Open Mar–Oct.

Self-Catering

Crosswoodhill Farm, By West Calder, West Lothian EH55 8LP ⑨

Mrs Geraldine Hamilton
☎ 01501 785205
Fax 01501 785308
SC From £230–£500
Sleeps 5/6
★★ – ★★★★
SELF CATERING

Imagine the best of both worlds…historic Edinburgh just ½ hour by car…rural tranquillity on our hill livestock farm with 1700 acres to roam. Perfectly placed for exploring the Borders, Fife, Glasgow, Rob Roy and Braveheart Country. Choose between a gem of a cottage on the Pentland Hills, the wing of our handsome 18th century farmhouse or imaginatively designed Steading Cottage. All thoughtfully equipped. Cosy peat fires, relaxing atmosphere. CH. Own phones. Car essential. Brochure. Open all year.

Eastside Farm, Penicuik, Midlothian EH26 9LN ⑩

Susan Cowan
☎/Fax 01968 677842
SC From £200–£450
Sleeps 4
★★ – ★★★★
SELF CATERING

Relax in this beautifully converted 18th century farm-steading located on a working family sheep farm in the scenic Pentland Hills Regional Park. Historic Edinburgh is only an eight mile drive away while New Lanark and the Border towns are a few miles further. Horseriding, fishing and golf nearby. Open all year.

Ayrshire & Arran

North Arran, Goat Fell & Ayrshire coast

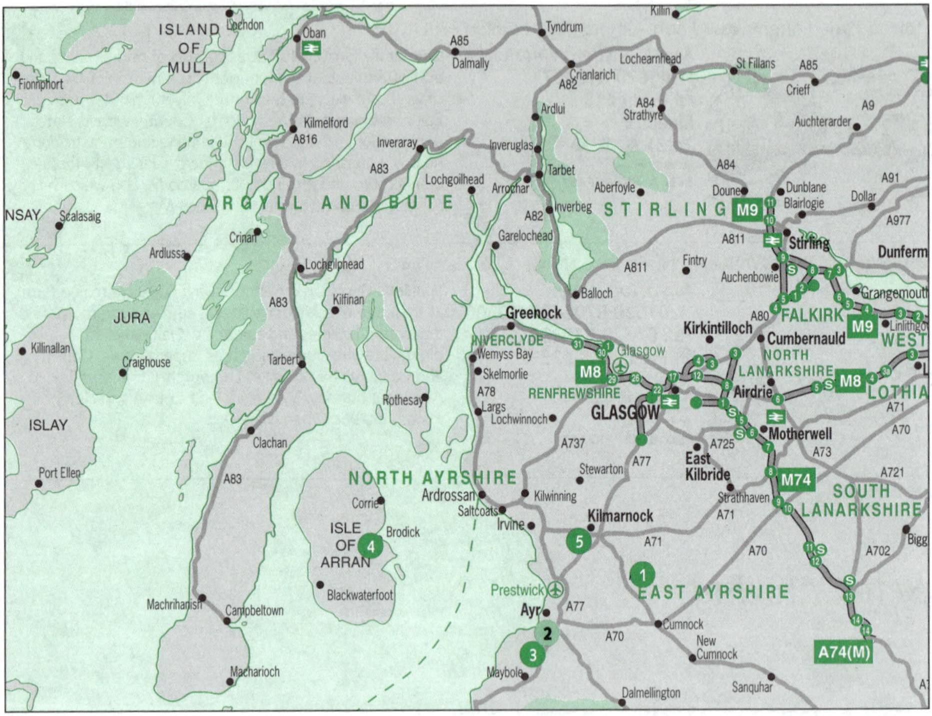

Key
- 1 Bed & Breakfast
- 1 Self-Catering
- 1 B&B and SC
- 1 Camping Barns
- Camping & Caravanning

Wherever you travel in Ayrshire, you experience a sense of other ages, and the area's many museums and visitor centres bring them to life. The coast is lined with ancient castles such as Turnberry and the vast Culzean Castle with its lovely country park and gardens. No stay in Ayrshire is complete without a visit to Burns' Cottage, birthplace of Scotland's national poet, and the Burns experience in Alloway. From Ardrossan take the ferry to the mystical island of Arran, Scotland in miniature with rugged mountains in the north sloping to green pasture in the south. Brodick Castle is a must, as is Goat Fell, Arran's tallest mountain, for its superb views over south-west Scotland and Ireland.

If you would like help in finding suitable farm accommodation, turn to the full listing of farm groups on pages 360 to 363 to find appropriate contact details for this area

Bed and Breakfast
(and evening meal)

Auchencloigh Farm, Galston, Ayrshire KA4 8NP

Mrs Jessie Bone
☎/Fax 01563 820567
From £18.50
Sleeps 4
★★★
BED & BREAKFAST

Auchencloigh is a 250-acre beef and sheep farm in central Ayrshire situated on B7037. The tranquil setting of this 18th century spacious farmhouse, set in mature gardens, offers guests old and new a warm and relaxing atmosphere after a day spent visiting the many attractions in Ayrshire. Please send for brochure. AA recommended QQQ. Open Easter–Nov.
E-mail: jessie.bone@btinternet.com

Dunduff Farm, Dunure, Ayr KA7 4LH

Agnes Gemmell
☎ 01292 500225
Fax 01292 500222
From £20–£25
Sleeps 6
★★★★
BED & BREAKFAST

Dunduff Farm is a 650-acre beef and sheep farm overlooking the Firth of Clyde to the Holy Isle and Arran. Culzean Castle, Burns Cottage, Turnberry and many more are nearby. All rooms have en suite facilities or private bathroom and sea view. So come and enjoy the ambience of the Ayrshire coastline where a cheerful, warmhearted welcome awaits you. AA Selected QQQQ. Open Feb–Nov.

Fisherton Farm, Dunure, Ayr KA7 4LF

Mrs Lesley Wilcox
☎/Fax 01292 500223
From £17.50–£20
Sleeps 4–6
★★
BED & BREAKFAST

Delightful traditional Scottish farmhouse in coastal location on working farm. Convenient for Turnberry, Prestwick Airport, Troon and many golf courses, also agate picking, fishing, walking, touring Burns Country and Culzean Castle. Ground floor en suite bedrooms with tea/coffee-making facilities and colour TV. TV lounge. Open all year except Christmas.

Glen Cloy Farmhouse, Brodick, Isle of Arran KA27 8DA

Mark and Vicki Padfield
☎ 01770 302351
From £21–£26
EM From £15
Sleeps 9
★★★
GUEST HOUSE

Glen Cloy farmhouse is a century-old farmhouse set in a quiet glen just outside Brodick. The house is surrounded by a mixed farm and offers warm, cosy rooms and excellent cooking using homegrown produce. A log fire burns cheerily in the drawing room. Taste of Scotland selected member. Close to golf, pony trekking, castle and mountains. Open Mar–mid Nov.
E-mail: mvpglencloy@compuserve.com

Muirhouse Farm, Gatehead, Kilmarnock KA2 0BT

Mrs Martha S Love
☎ 01563 523975
From £17
Sleeps 6
★★
BED & BREAKFAST

A warm welcome is assured on our family-run dairy farm. In our traditional stone-built farmhouse all rooms have private or en suite bathrooms, TV and tea-making facilities. Near to Troon, we are ideally situated for golfers. Easy access to Glasgow also Arran ferry. Choice of excellent eating places nearby. Open all year.

Scotland Ayrshire & Arran

Self-Catering

② Bothy Cottage, Dunduff Farm, Dunure, Ayr KA7 4LH

Agnes Gemmell
☎ 01292 500225
Fax 01292 500222
SC From £190–£225
Sleeps 6
★★★
SELF CATERING

Bothy Cottage is situated five miles south of Ayr at the coastal village of Dunure on a working farm. Overlooking Firth of Clyde to Arran. It has two double rooms, one is en suite, lounge and kitchen. Ideal for Culzean Castle and Parks, Burns Cottage, Galloway Forest, Farm Parks and many more. Capture this country coastal farm atmosphere at its best. Open Feb–Nov.

USE THE INDEX

The comprehensive Index shows which farms offer access to disabled visitors; caravanning/camping facilities; the chance to participate on a working farm; stabling/grazing for visiting horses; en suite rooms; a welcome to business people; acceptance of *Stay on a Farm* gift tokens.

THE 1000+ BUREAU MEMBERS OFFER A UNIQUE LINK TO CUSTOMERS ACROSS THE UK

All Bureau members belong to a local Group. Each member can refer you to an equally high quality member within the Group... or across the UK: England, Northern Ireland, Scotland, Wales.

FOLLOW THE COUNTRY CODE

Leave nothing but footprints,
Take nothing but photographs,
Kill nothing but time!

Scottish Borders

Upper Tweeddale, Eildon Hills, the Merse, Teviotdale, Eskdale, Southern Upland Way & the Borders Forest Park

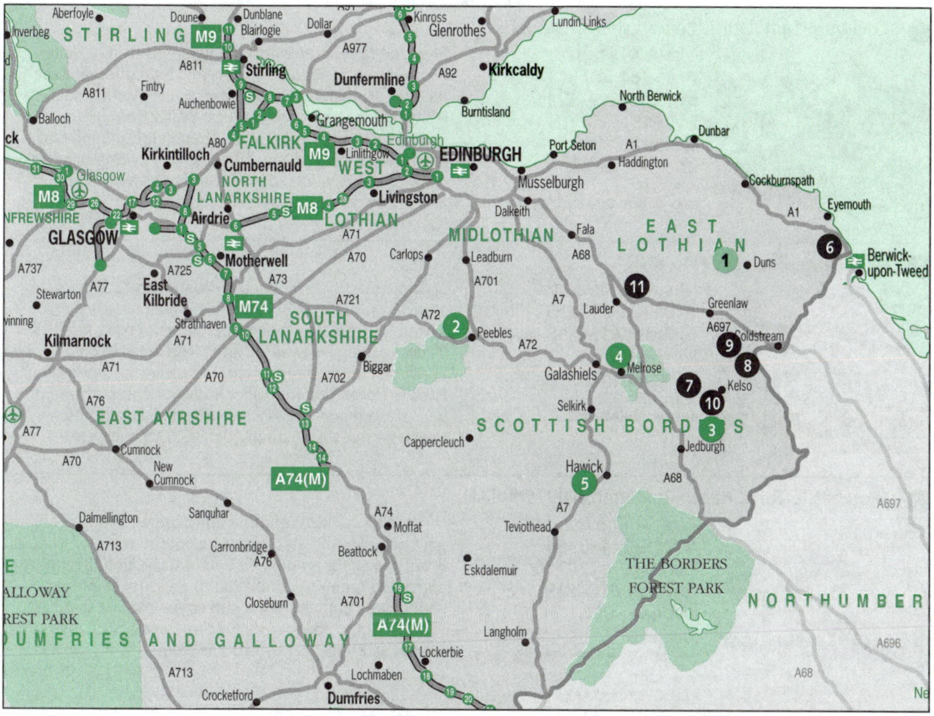

Key

- 1 Bed & Breakfast
- 1 Self-Catering
- 1 B&B and SC
- 1 Camping Barns
- ▲ Camping & Caravanning

In this tranquil landscape that once bore witness to raids and battles, you'll travel quiet roads through rolling farmlands to discover bustling towns and tiny hamlets. There are historic houses and gardens of all periods, from Scott's Abbotsford to Mellerstain, the finest complete Adam house in Scotland, while the ruined abbeys of Kelso, Jedburgh, Melrose and Dryburgh stand testament to more troubled times. Everyone has their favourite view in this lovely area – the sun-dappled River Tweed, the majestic Eildon Hills, the broad sweep of the Merse. Come and discover yours in the beautiful Scottish Borders.

If you would like help in finding suitable farm accommodation, turn to the full listing of farm groups on pages 360 to 363 to find appropriate contact details for this area.

Scotland — Scottish Borders

Bed and Breakfast
(and evening meal)

① Cockburn Mill, Duns, Berwickshire TD11 3TL

Mrs A M Prentice
☎ 01361 882811
BB From £19–£21
EM £13
Sleeps 4
★★
BED & BREAKFAST

Riverside farmhouse offering 2 luxurious twin en suite bedrooms with electric blankets and tea/coffee-making facilities. Within sight and sound of River Whiteadder. Home baking and farm produce. Water from hillside spring. Trout fishing included. Abundant plant and bird life. Ideal for hill-walking, birdwatching, cycling or just relaxing. Hens, ducks, donkeys and pet lambs. Brochure and colour photo available. Open Mar–Nov.

② Lyne Farm, Peebles EH45 8NR

Mrs Arran Waddell
☎ 01721 740255
BB From £16–£19
Sleeps 6
★★
BED & BREAKFAST

Spacious Georgian farmhouse situated on 1300 acre arable/stock farm with outstanding panoramic views. Tastefully decorated rooms, tea/coffee-making facilities. Walled garden. Hillwalking and picnic areas to enjoy. Excellent pubs and restaurants in picturesque town of Peebles. Ideal base for castles, historic houses, museums and outdoor pursuits. A warm welcome awaits you. Peebles 4 miles, Edinburgh 20 miles. Open all year.

③ Morebattle Tofts, Kelso, Roxburghshire TD5 8AD

Mrs Debbie Playfair
☎ 01573 440364
Fax 01573 420750
BB From £18–£19
EM from £11
Sleeps 6
★★
BED & BREAKFAST

Large, elegant 18th century farmhouse set in 3 acres of garden beside the River Kale. Area of Outstanding Natural Beauty, ideal for touring, walking, fishing, golf. Beautifully appointed rooms, 2 double rooms en suite, twin room with private bathroom. Tea and coffee-making facilities. Tennis court, croquet lawn. Brochure available. Open Mar–Nov. E-mail: debbytofts@aol.com

④ Over Langshaw Farm, Langshaw, Galashiels, Selkirkshire TD1 2PE

Sheila Bergius
☎ 01896 860244
BB From £18–£22
Sleeps 6
★★
BED & BREAKFAST

Our beautifully situated rambling farmhouse extends a warm welcome and provides delicious food from the kitchen. Near Galashiels and Melrose, Edinburgh 34 miles. The specially large family bedroom has a dressing room and private bathroom. Very attractive double room with en suite shower room. Cot available. Our farm has dairy and beef cows, Scottish Mule and Blackface Ewes. Southern Upland Way nearby. Open all year.

⑤ Wiltonburn Farm, Hawick, Roxburghshire TD9 7LL

Mrs Sheila Shell
☎ 01450 372414
Mobile 0374 192551
BB From £18
EM From £10
Sleeps 6
★★
BED & BREAKFAST

You will be warmly welcomed and cared for as you unwind on our friendly, working mixed farm. Enjoy our rolling green hills and idyllic valley, 2 miles from Hawick, the centre of Scottish textiles. Your base for walking, riding, fishing, golf, castles and stately homes. Log fires, cosy rooms and our showroom containing designer cashmere knitwear, paintings, jewellery and small gifts will make your stay more pleasurable. Closed Christmas.

Scottish Borders   Scotland

Self-Catering

Broadmeadows Holiday Cottages, Hutton, Nr Berwick-upon-Tweed TD15 1TN ❻

Mrs CM McCrone
☎ 01289 386229
Fax 01289 386667
SC From £200–£420
Sleeps 2–6
★★★★
SELF CATERING

Delightful cottages on a 400-acre estate which is a stock breeding farm with Highland cattle, Shetland ponies, llamas and rare breeds of sheep. Refurbished to a very high standard of comfort with log fires. Ideal base for touring, coast 6 miles and Holy Island approx 15 miles. A warm welcome is assured at Broadmeadows. Open all year.

The Cottage, Cockburn Mill, Duns, Berwickshire TD11 3TL ❶

Ann Prentice
☎ 01361 882811
SC From £130–£275
Sleeps 4/5 + cot
★★
SELF CATERING

Stone-built cottage within sight and sound of River Whiteadder. Children welcome. Barbecue, colour TV. Overnight storage heating included. Trout fishing included. Water from hillside spring. Abundant plant and bird life. Chicks, donkeys, ducklings and pet lambs. Coast, beaches, Edinburgh, Border keeps and abbeys within easy reach on quiet roads. Pets by arrangement only. Brochure and colour photo available. Open all year.

Craggs Cottage, Cliftonhill Farm, Ednam, Kelso, Roxburghshire TD5 7QE ❼

Archie & Maggie Stewart
☎ 01573 225028
Fax 01573 226416
SC From £180–£370
Sleeps 5
★★★
SELF CATERING

A terraced sandstone cottage, lovingly restored, maintaining its character and charm. One double room – large and luxurious, 1 twin bedroom and 1 small single bedroom. Large comfortable kitchen with oil-fired red Rayburn cooker. CH. Sitting room with log fire and colour TV and video. Enclosed colourful garden, garden furniture. Delightful restaurant 3 miles. Coast 18 miles, Edinburgh 35 miles. Short breaks and special winter break offer. Open all year.
E-mail: archie@sol.co.uk

Kerchesters Cottages, Kerchesters, Kelso, Roxburghshire TD5 8HR ❽

Mrs M Clark
☎ 01573 224321
Fax 01573 226609
SC From £110–£320
Sleeps 5/7
★★
SELF CATERING

Cockerlaw and Todrig cottages are warm, welcoming terraced cottages on a working farm. Relax in front of an open fire in well equipped surroundings. Shower, colour TV. Three miles east of Kelso. Well placed for touring Borders and Northumbria. Edinburgh 1 hour, beach 30 minutes. Golf, swimming, good walking locally. Linen included. Brochure on request. Open all year.

Rowan Tree Cottage, Karingal, Lochton, Coldstream, Berwickshire TD12 4NH ❾

Mrs Rosalind Aitchison
☎ 01890 830205
Fax 01890 830210
SC From £200–£350
Sleeps 2–6
★★★
SELF CATERING

A warm welcome awaits you at Rowan Tree, a south-facing terraced cottage with views over beautiful Borders countryside. Three charming bedrooms, bathroom/power shower, delightful lounge, wood burning stove, CH, fully equipped kitchen/utility area, downstairs cloakroom. Garden patio. Trout fish on River Tweed, walk, cycle, birdwatch or just relax, enjoy our space. Edinburgh 1 hour. Open all year. E-mail: lochton@btinternet.com.uk

Scotland — Scottish Borders

⑩ Roxburgh Newtown Farm, Kelso, Roxburghshire TD5 8NN

Mrs Pauline Twemlow
☎/Fax 01573 450250
[SC] From £120–£300
Sleeps 2–6
★★★
SELF CATERING

In a picturesque rural location 5 miles west of Kelso, Swallow and Jimmy's Cottages have been modernised and offer spacious, comfortably furnished accommodation. Jimmy's sleeps 6 and Swallow 2/4. Colour TV, microwave, dishwasher, central heating, electricity and linen included. Large play area. Ample parking. Open all year.
E-mail: pauline.twemlow@which.net

⑪ Thirlestane Farm Cottages, Thirlestane, Lauder, Berwickshire TD2 6SF

Mrs Caroline Barr
☎ 01578 722216
[SC] From £180–£300
Sleeps 6
★★★
SELF CATERING

Renovated to retain their original charm and character, these cottages each provide 3 bedrooms (to sleep 6), large sitting room with open fire and panoramic view, pine kitchen/dining area. Rent includes bedlinen and fuel. Ideal for touring, walking, fishing, riding, easy access to all border towns, only 28 miles from Edinburgh. Pets by arrangement. Open all year.

NO ANSWER?
Farmers are mostly out and about during the day.
Try to telephone before 9.30am or after 4pm.

CONFIRM BOOKINGS
Disappointments can arise from misunderstandings over the telephone. Please write to confirm your booking.

FARM HOLIDAY BUREAU

Our Internet address is
http://www.webscape.co.uk/farmaccom/

Dumfries & Galloway

Moffat & Annandale Valley, Galloway Forest Park, Solway Coastline

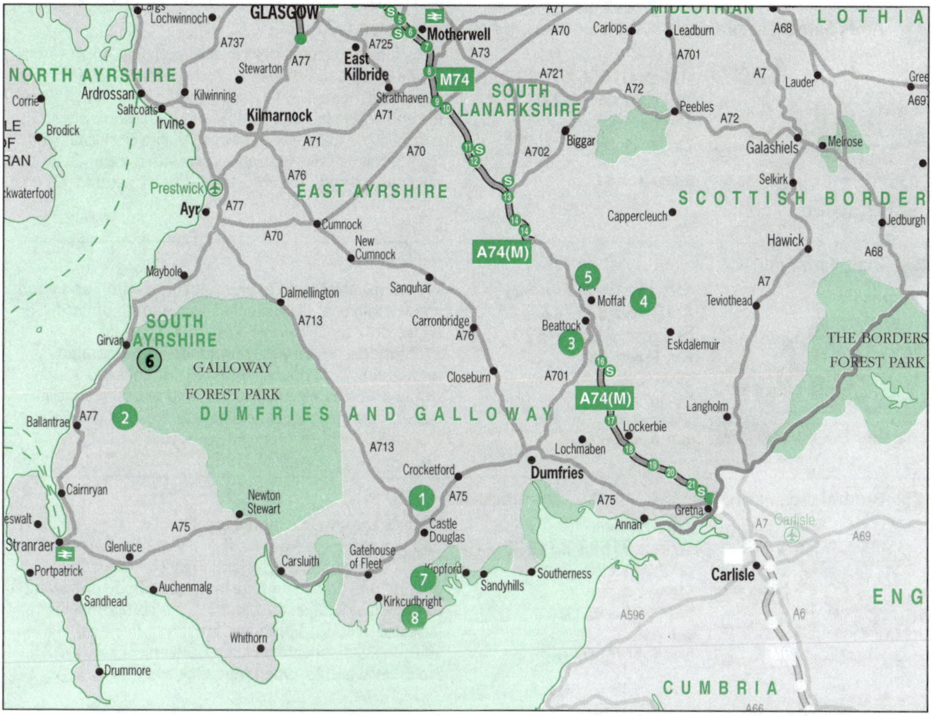

Key

- 1 Bed & Breakfast
- 1 Self-Catering
- 1 B&B and SC
- 1 Camping Barns
- ▲ Camping & Caravanning

From the miles of beautiful coastline to the rugged Moffat Hills with the spectacular 'Grey Mare's Tail' and the striking 'Devil's Beef Tub', here is a variety of scenery unmatched in Britain. You will find quiet lanes winding through lush green countryside, busy small towns with a variety of interesting shops, numerous challenging golf courses and excellent fishing and walking. Visit the excellent Robert Burns Centre in Dumfries and the archaeological dig at Whithorn where St Ninian founded the first Christian church. This is a peaceful, undiscovered yet easily accessible part of Scotland and, with its mild climate, what more could you ask?

If you would like help in finding suitable farm accommodation, turn to the full listing of farm groups on pages 360 to 363 to find appropriate contact details for this area.

Scotland — Dumfries & Galloway

Bed and Breakfast
(and evening meal)

---

① Airds Farm, Crossmichael, Castle Douglas, Kirkcudbrightshire DG7 3BG

Tricia Keith
☎/Fax 01556 670418
BB From £15–£22
Sleeps 10
★★★
GUEST HOUSE

Airds farmhouse overlooks lovely Loch Ken, 4 miles from Castle Douglas on the A713. All bedrooms tastefully decorated, heated, with wash handbasins, colour TV and tea and coffee facilities. Family and twin rooms are en suite. Private lounge with colour TV. Fire certificate held. Non-Smoking only. Pleasant walks within grounds. A warm welcome and comfortable stay are assured. Open all year.

---

② Blair Farm, Barrhill, Girvan, Ayrshire KA26 0RD

Mrs Elizabeth Hughes
☎ 01465 821247
BB From £16.50–£20
EM From £9
Sleeps 6
★★★★
BED & BREAKFAST

We warmly invite you to enjoy peace, comfort and good home cooking at Blair, situated 1 mile south of Barrhill on A714, close to Galloway Forest Park. Spacious accommodation, tastefully furnished and decorated throughout. One double en suite, 1 double and 1 twin with washbasin, electric blankets and tea/coffee facilities. Visitors' lounge, central heating, log fires, TV etc. Fishing available. Brochure. Open Easter–Oct.

---

③ Broomlands Farm, Beattock, Moffat, Dumfriesshire DG10 9PQ

Kate Miller
☎/Fax 01683 221900
BB From £20
Sleeps 4
★★★★
BED & BREAKFAST

A lovely comfortable farmhouse situated in the Annandale Valley only 2 miles from Moffat, a wonderful area to tour, walk, play golf, etc. High standard accommodation offering one double en suite on ground floor, one twin en suite on first floor, with colour TV, tea/coffee-making facilities. Delicious farmhouse breakfast. Personal attention. Safe private parking. Convenient for A/M74. Brochure available. Open Mar–Oct.

---

④ Coxhill Farm, Old Carlisle Road, Moffat, Dumfriesshire DG10 9QN

Mrs Sandra Long
☎ 01683 220471
BB From £17
Sleeps 6
★★★★
BED & BREAKFAST

A very attractive farmhouse in 70 acres of unspoilt countryside with outstanding views, beautiful rose gardens and ample parking. 2 double, 1twin bedrooms, all with washbasins, tea/coffee-making facilities and central heating. Situated 1 mile south of the charming town of Moffat, and 1½ miles from Southern Upland Way. Excellent base for golf, tennis, fishing and touring SW Scotland. Open Mar–Oct.

---

⑤ Ericstane, Moffat, Dumfriesshire DG10 9LT

Robert Jackson
☎ 01683 220127
BB From £18–£23
Sleeps 4
★★★
BED & BREAKFAST

Ericstane offers peace and quiet in attractive surroundings on a working hill farm 4 miles from Moffat. Period farmhouse with twin and double-bedded rooms with en suite facilities, TV, tea/coffee-making facilities. Central heating. In *Staying Off the Beaten Track* and *The Which Good Bed and Breakfast Guide*. Open all year.

Dumfries & Galloway *Scotland*

Glengennet Farm, Barr, Girvan, Ayrshire KA26 9TY

Vera Dunlop
☎/Fax 01465 861220
BB From £19–£21
Sleeps 4
★★★★
BED & BREAKFAST

Original Victorian shooting lodge with lovely views over the Stinchar valley and neighbouring Galloway Forest Park. One double and one twin, both en-suite with tea trays. Guests' lounge/dining room with colour TV. Two miles from Barr village where good meals are available. Good base for forest walking/ cycling, golf, Ayrshire coast, Burns country, Culzean Castle and Glentrool National Park. Open Apr–Oct.

6

Mains of Collin, Auchencairn, Castle Douglas, Kirkcudbrightshire DG7 1QN

Fiona Wallace
☎ 01556 640211
BB From £16–£18
Sleeps 2+cot
★★★
BED & BREAKFAST

An old stone-built farmhouse, nestling in the valley and surrounded by the green rolling hills of Galloway. Quietness, solitude and tranquillity, good food, caring, attentive hosts, and charming, comfortable accommodation. Colour TV and hospitality tray. Excellent base for touring. Pub meals available in Auchencairn (2 miles). Brochure and weekly terms on request.

7

Rascarrel Cottage, Rascarrel Farm, Auchencairn, Castle Douglas, Kirkcudbrightshire DG7 1RJ

Ellice Hendry
☎ 01556 640214
BB From £19–£21
Sleeps 4
★★★★
BED & BREAKFAST

You will find peace, comfort and wonderful views at our attractive, well-appointed cottage. Situated on an 18th century smuggling route overlooking our 400 acre farm and the Solway Firth, it is 500 yards from the sea and 2 miles from village where good meals are available.
1 double en suite on ground floor, 1 twin en suite on first floor. Tea trays, CH, bright spacious lounge with colour TV, sunroom/dining room. Open Mar–Oct.

8

Self-Catering

Upper Barr Farm, Glengennet, Barr, Girvan, Ayrshire KA26 9TY

Vera Dunlop
☎/Fax 01465 861220
SC From £150–£470
Sleeps 6/8 + cot
★★ – ★★★★
SELF CATERING

Choose between detached period black and white farmhouse, recently modernised to provide centrally heated accommodation for 8 in 4 bedrooms (one en suite) or farmhouse wing sleeps 6 (one ground floor bedroom and bathroom). On working hill farm in peaceful Stinchar Valley, lovely views to Galloway Forest Park. Short breaks offseason, brochure. Open all year.

6

 Please mention *Stay on a Farm* when booking

England's North Country

Farm entries in this regional section are listed under those counties shown in green on the key map. Look at the index below to find on which page the entries start. You will see that we have listed the counties geographically so that you can turn more easily to find farms in neighbouring areas.

At the start of each county section is a detailed map with numbered symbols indicating the location of each farm. Different symbols denote different types of accommodation; see the key below each county map. Farm entries are listed alphabetically under type of accommodation. Some farms offer more than one type of accommodation and therefore have more than one entry.

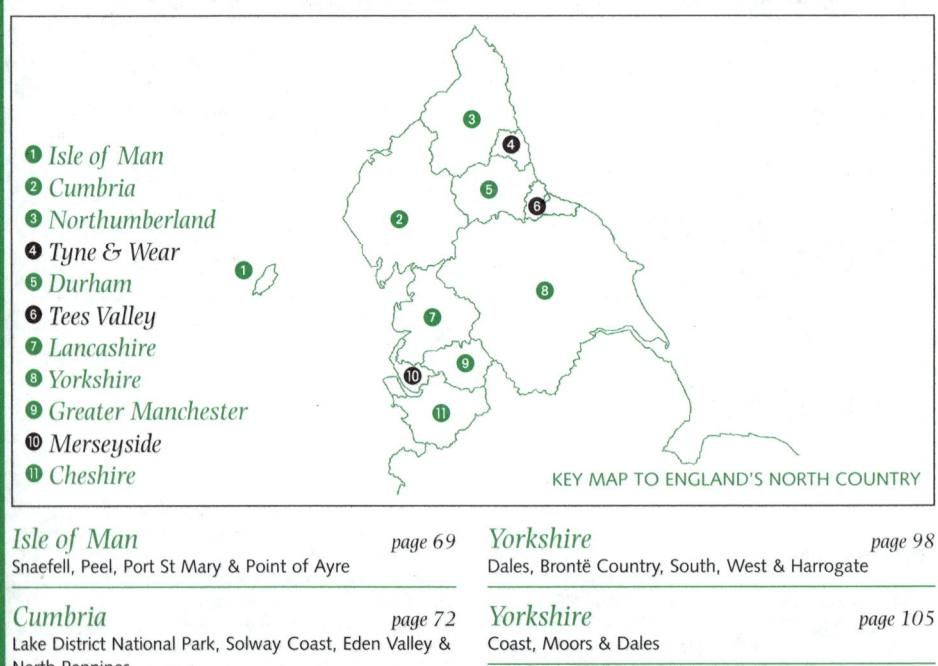

❶ Isle of Man
❷ Cumbria
❸ Northumberland
❹ Tyne & Wear
❺ Durham
❻ Tees Valley
❼ Lancashire
❽ Yorkshire
❾ Greater Manchester
❿ Merseyside
⓫ Cheshire

KEY MAP TO ENGLAND'S NORTH COUNTRY

Isle of Man	*page 69*	**Yorkshire**	*page 98*
Snaefell, Peel, Port St Mary & Point of Ayre		Dales, Brontë Country, South, West & Harrogate	
Cumbria	*page 72*	**Yorkshire**	*page 105*
Lake District National Park, Solway Coast, Eden Valley & North Pennines		Coast, Moors & Dales	
		Yorkshire	*page 114*
		Vale of York & the Wolds	
Northumberland	*page 81*		
Cheviot Hills, Northumberland National Park, Northumberland Coast, Kielder Forest & Hadrian's Wall		**Greater Manchester**	*page 120*
		South Pennines & Colne Valley	
Durham	*page 89*		
North Pennines, Weardale, Teesdale & High Force		**Cheshire**	*page 122*
		Delamere Forest, Cheshire Plain, Shropshire Union Canal, Alderley Edge & Peak District National Park	
Lancashire	*page 94*		
Arnside & Silverdale, Morecambe Bay, Vale of Lune, Pennine Way, Forest of Bowland & Ribble Valley			

Isle of Man

Snaefell, Peel, Port St Mary & Point of Ayre

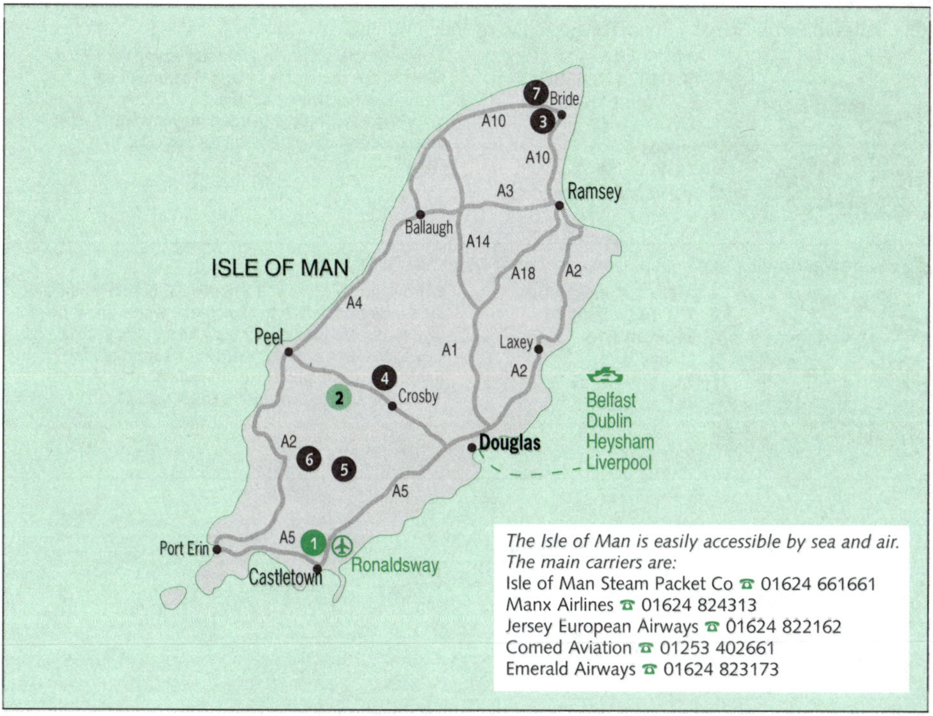

The Isle of Man is easily accessible by sea and air. The main carriers are:
Isle of Man Steam Packet Co ☎ 01624 661661
Manx Airlines ☎ 01624 824313
Jersey European Airways ☎ 01624 822162
Comed Aviation ☎ 01253 402661
Emerald Airways ☎ 01624 823173

Key
- 1 Bed & Breakfast
- 1 Self-Catering
- 1 B&B and SC
- 1 Camping Barns
- ▲ Camping & Caravanning

The Isle of Man's 100 miles of coastline varies from rocky cliffs to sandy beaches and shingle ridges. The contrast of inland scenery is equally varied, from wooded glens through patchwork fields to open moorland and mountain. The island has retained a rich transport system from Victorian times, with steam trains to seaside villages, an electric tram up the highest mountain, and horse-drawn trams along Douglas sea front. Laxey has the largest working waterwheel in Europe and the castles of Peel and Castletown must be seen. We have our own language, currency and culture but are only 35 minutes from Liverpool Airport or a short sail from Heysham or Liverpool. Do come.

If you would like help in finding suitable farm accommodation, turn to the full listing of farm groups on pages 360 to 363 to find appropriate contact details for this area.

North Country   *Isle of Man*

Bed and Breakfast
(and evening meal)

---

① Ballavell Farm, Grenaby Road, Ballasalla, Isle of Man IM9 3DP

Mrs H E Duggan
☎ 01624 824306
BB From £16.50
EM From £7
Sleeps 6
♿ 👣 ✂ ♨ ⛺
♣ Highly Commended

Family-run dairy farm in a tranquil setting with lovely views of the south of the island. The traditional Manx farmhouse has been refurbished and is fully equipped for a luxurious stay. There is a large sunny garden to relax in. An ideal base for walkers and car tourers alike. Open May–Oct.

---

② Kerrowgarrow Farm, Greeba, Douglas, Isle of Man IM4 3LQ

Mrs Jean Jackson
☎ 01624 801871
BB From £16
Sleeps 5
♿ 👣 ✂ ⛳ ♨ ⛺
♣ Commended

Kerrowgarrow offers you a homely atmosphere and an ideal base from which to explore the whole island by foot, bike or car. TV, tea-making facilities and CH in all rooms. Cows, chickens and Manx cat. Walks arranged for naturalists. Good pub food and restaurant in St Johns 1 mile. Air or sea travel arranged for you. Open Mar–Nov.

Self-Catering

---

③ Ballachrink Bungalow, Ballachrink Farm, Bride, Isle of Man IM7 4AP

Mrs Val Teare
☎/Fax 01624 880364
SC From £175–£280
Sleeps 4
♿ 👣 ♨
🏠🏠🏠🏠 Commended

Situated in the north of the island, enjoying magnificent views of the Manx countryside, our bungalow offers you a comfortable base from which to explore the island. Well equipped with towels and linen provided. Just the place to get away from it all and relax. Open all year.

---

④ Cronk-Dhoo Farm Cottages, Cronk-Dhoo Farm, Greeba IM4 2DX

Ms Lin Kermode
☎ 01624 851327
SC From £150–£450
Sleeps 4
♿ 👣 ✂ ⛳ ⛺
🏠🏠🏠🏠🏠 Commended – Highly Commended

Lovely farmhouse and converted barn with southerly aspect over the central valley. Refurbished to a high standard, fully equipped with colour TV, satellite, microwave, CH. Towels and linen provided. Private garden, barbecue area, plenty of parking. 100 meters main bus route, near craft centre, pubs and restaurants. Ideal base for keen conservationists. Open all year.

Isle of Man   *North Country*

Kionslieu Farm Cottages, Higher Foxdale, Isle of Man IM4 3HB

Mrs Fiona Barker
☎/Fax 01624 801349
SC From £210–£550
Sleeps 2–6
♠ ♞ ⊨ ⚒
₰₰₰₰ Highly Commended

Beautiful farm cottages on a traditional sunny courtyard. Fully equipped and furnished to highest standards. Centrally situated in peaceful Foxdale countryside, 10 min walk village shop and inn and 10/15 min drive Douglas, Castletown and Peel. Friendly animals, play area, laundry, payphone and delightful rural views make Kionslieu your ideal holiday home. Open all year.

Little Cresta, Lower Gleneedale, St Johns, Douglas, Isle of Man IM4 3BF

Mrs G C Osborne
☎ 01624 801237
SC From £150–£250
Sleeps 2+cot
☆ ♞ ☂
₰₰₰ Commended

This delightful, renovated cottage stands adjacent to owners' smallholding and enjoys superb views across surrounding countryside. Featuring a slate fireplace in the lounge, a fitted kitchen and shower, the cottage retains much original character with exposed beams. Excellent area for walking and a good general base from which to explore the whole island. Short drive to beautiful beach at Peel. Open Mar–Oct.

Smeale Cottage, Andreas, Isle of Man IM7 3EB

Beth and Steve Martin
☎ 01624 880888
Fax 01624 880955
SC From £200–£320
Sleeps 5 + cot
☆ ⚒
₰₰₰ Highly Commended

Treat yourselves to a memorable Manx holiday in our comfortable, well appointed, semi-detached farm cottage surrounded by the family-run sheep farm. Enjoy the wonderful views and spacious, private garden. Children very welcome. Fully equipped with CH, washing machine, linen, etc. Ample parking. Perfect base for exploring our beautiful island. All-inclusive price. Brochure available. Open all year.

Soalt Veg, Kerrowgarrow Farm, Greeba, Douglas, Isle of Man IM4 3LQ

Mrs Jean Jackson
☎ 01624 801871
SC From £250–£425
Sleeps 6
☆ ♞ ♘ ♠ ⚒ ☂
₰₰₰₰ Highly Commended

Traditional Manx stone barn carefully converted to provide comfortable centrally heated accommodation, whilst retaining all the character of country living. Ideally situated for exploring the whole island. Enclosed garden, children's games, TV, washing machine, tumble dryer, microwave. Air or sea travel arranged for you. Open all year.

THE 1000+ BUREAU MEMBERS OFFER A UNIQUE LINK TO CUSTOMERS ACROSS THE UK

FARM HOLIDAY BUREAU

All Bureau members belong to a local Group. Each member can refer you to an equally high quality member within the Group... or across the UK: England, Northern Ireland, Scotland, Wales.

Cumbria

Lake District National Park, Solway Coast, Eden Valley
& North Pennines

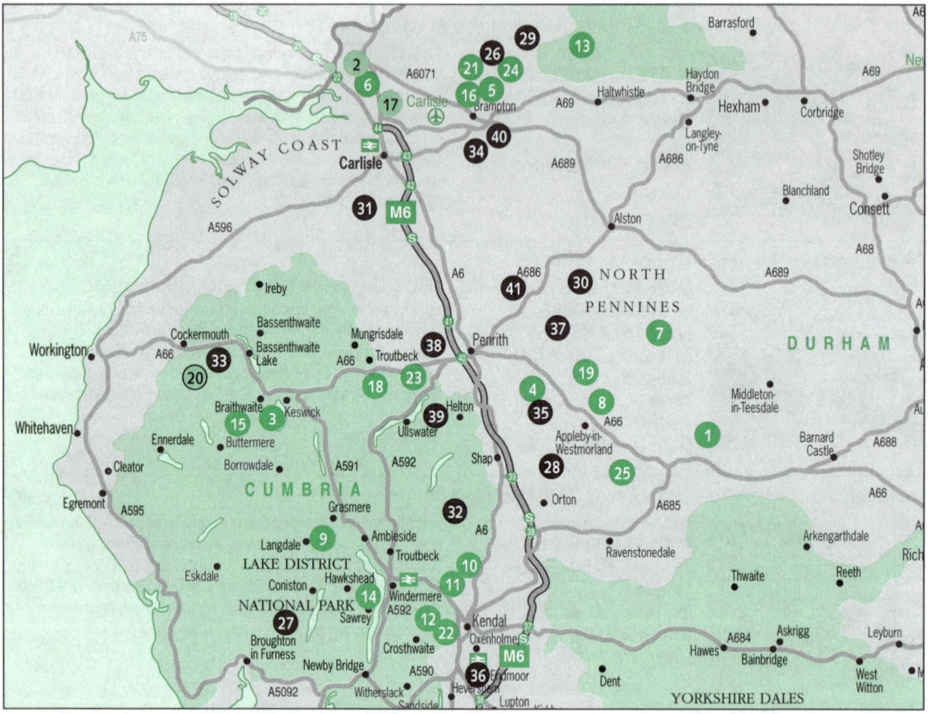

Key

- 1 Bed & Breakfast
- 1 Self-Catering
- 1 B&B and SC
- 1 Camping Barns
- 1 Camping & Caravanning

Find complete peace in Cumbria. To the north lie the Solway Coast and historic Carlisle, while charming market towns such as Alston and Appleby nestle among the hills of the North Pennines. Follow the River Eden to Penrith, gateway to the Lakes. The Carlisle-Settle railway runs right through the lush Eden Valley or try the miniature steam railway at Ravenglass. The Lake District, inspiration of Wordsworth and Beatrix Potter, is one of the best-loved parts of England with its mountains, woods and lakes. Visit the centres of Windermere, Keswick and Kendal and venture out to Wasdale, Buttermere and Longsleddale, great for fell walking. See local shows, crafts, Cumberland and Westmorland wrestling, fell running and hound trailing. It's all here in Cumbria.

If you would like help in finding suitable farm accommodation, turn to the full listing of farm groups on pages 360 to 363 to find appropriate contact details for this area.

Cumbria   *North Country*

Bed and Breakfast
(and evening meal)

Augill House Farm, Brough-under-Stainmore, Kirkby Stephen, Cumbria CA17 4DX   ①

Jeanette Atkinson
☎ 017683 41305
[BB] From £20–£22
EM From £12
Sleeps 4
ප(12) ⌇ ✕ ♿ ⓢ
☻ ☻ *Highly Commended*

Enjoy good food and hospitality at this much recommended farmhouse in the Upper Eden Valley. En suite bedrooms with colour TV and hospitality tray. Ideal for visiting the Lakes, Dales and North Pennines. Breakfast and dinner served in our lovely conservatory overlooking the garden. RAC Highly Acclaimed. AA QQQQ Selected. Open Apr–Nov.

Bessiestown Farm Country Guest House, Catlowdy, Longtown, Carlisle, Cumbria CA6 5QP   ②

Margaret Sisson
☎ 01228 577019/577219
Fax 01228 577219
[BB] From £21.50–£24.50
EM From £11
Sleeps 8
ප ⌇ 🚭 ♿ ✕ ⓢ
☻ ☻ *Highly Commended*

An award-winning farm guesthouse overlooking Scottish Borders. Friendly, relaxing atmosphere assured. Warm, pretty en suite bedrooms with colour TV, radio and tea/coffee. Delicious home cooking using traditional recipes. Residential drinks licence. Indoor heated swimming pool (May–Sept). AA QQQQQ Premier Selected. Stop off Scotland and Northern Ireland. M6 J44, A7 to Longtown, then follow signs to Catlowdy. Open all year.

Birkrigg Farm, Newlands, Keswick, Cumbria CA12 5TS   ③

M M Beaty
☎ 017687 78278
[BB] From £16–£18
Sleeps 12
ප ⌇ ✕ ♿
Listed Approved

Birkrigg is a dairy and sheep farm very pleasantly situated with excellent outlook in the peaceful Newlands Valley, 5 miles from Keswick. Surrounded by mountains, this is an ideal place to walk and climb. Central for touring. Clean, comfortable accommodation. The breakfasts are good too! Meals available at inns nearby. Packed lunches provided. Open Mar–Dec.

Bridge End Farm, Kirkby Thore, Penrith, Cumbria CA10 1UZ   ④

Mrs Yvonne Dent
☎ 01768 361362
[BB] From £19–£21
EM From £10
Sleeps 6
ප(12) ⌇ 🐾 ♿
☻ ☻ *Highly Commended*

Relax in 18th century farmhouse on a dairy farm in the Eden Valley near Appleby. Lovely, spacious, antique-furnished en suite rooms featuring patchwork quilts. Delicious homemade breakfast and dinner served in dining room. All food is freshly prepared and you will never forget Yvonne's sticky toffee pudding. Finish with a a stroll along the River Eden. Open all year except Christmas.

Cracrop Farm, Kirkcambeck, Brampton, Cumbria CA8 2BW   ⑤

Marjorie Stobart
☎ 016977 48245
Fax 016977 48333
[BB] From £25
EM From £17
Sleeps 6
ප(12) 🅿 ⌇ 🐾 ✕ ♿
☻ ☻ *Highly Commended*

Looking for somewhere special? Then try our superbly appointed large (1847) farmhouse. Set in peaceful countryside with super views, excellent for birdwatching and walking. Spacious en suite bedrooms, hostess tray, colour TV, fresh flowers. Relax in spa bath or sauna. Games room. Near Roman Wall, Borders, 1 mile from B6318. Excellent pubs nearby. AA selected QQQQ. Every effort has been made to ensure a memorable stay.

North Country   *Cumbria*

⑥ Craigburn Farm, Catlowdy, Longtown, Carlisle, Cumbria CA6 5QP

Jane & Jack Lawson
☎ 01228 577214
Fax 01228 577014
BB From £21–£22
EM From £12
Sleeps 12

Carlisle's Border Country, one of the most peaceful places in England. We offer a warm welcome and hospitality you will certainly want to come back to. One of the best for food (City and Guilds Distinction held) – desserts our speciality. Stopover to and from Scotland and Northern Ireland. 'We look forward to meeting you'. Open all year.

♛ ♛ *Commended*

---

⑦ Crossgill Farm, Garrigill, Alston, Cumbria CA9 3HE

Helen Dent
☎ 01434 382079
BB From £16–£20
EM £11
Sleeps 4

A large, family-run hill farm where visitors are welcome to wander. A warm welcome awaits you at our warm, tastefully furnished home, formerly a shooting lodge. One double and one family en suite. Tea trays, central heating, electric blankets. All good home cooking including our own bread. Closed Christmas & April for lambing.

♛ *Highly Commended*

---

⑧ Dufton Hall Farm, Appleby in Westmorland, Cumbria CA16 6DD

Mrs EM Howe
☎/Fax 01768 351573
BB From £18–£20
EM £10
Sleeps 6

Spacious Grade II listed farmhouse in the centre of the beautiful Pennine village of Dufton. 3½ miles from Appleby in Westmorland. En suite rooms with TV, tea/coffee facilities. Guests' lounge. No smoking or pets please. Off road parking. Village pub 200 yards. Superb walking area. Open Mar–Nov.

♛ *Approved*

---

⑨ Fell Foot Farm, Little Langdale, Ambleside, Cumbria LA22 9PE

Mrs S Harryman
☎ 015394 37294
BB From £17
EM From £10.50
Sleeps 6

Nestling at the foot of the famous Wrynose Pass, this 17th century farmhouse was once a coaching Inn. Owned by the National Trust, it contains fine oak beams and panelling. The house offers warm, comfortable accommodation with beautiful views and excellent home cooking. Three rooms, 1 en suite, tea/coffee-making facilities. Open Easter–Nov.

Listed Commended

---

⑩ Garnett House Farm, Burneside, Kendal, Cumbria LA9 5SF

Mrs Sylvia Beaty
☎ 01539 724542
BB From £16–£20.50
EM From £9
Sleeps 10

AA/RAC acclaimed 15th century farmhouse, just ½ mile from A591 Windermere Road, village inn, shops and public transport. Bedrooms have colour TV, washbasins and tea-making facilities, en suites available. Oak panelled lounge, dining room with choice of breakfast and 5 course dinners. Lovely views of our countryside and close to Windermere. Golf and fishing 1 mile. Good parking. Nov–Mar 3 night breaks £48, en suite £55. Closed Christmas.

♛ ♛ *Commended*

---

⑪ Gateside Farm, Windermere Road, Kendal, Cumbria LA9 5SE

Mrs June Ellis
☎/Fax 01539 722036
BB From £17.50–£21
EM £8.50
Sleeps 10

Traditional Lakeland working farm, 2 miles north of Kendal on A591. Easily accessible from M6 (jct36). Ideal for touring Lakes and Yorkshire Dales. 16th century farmhouse, all bedrooms have colour TV, tea/coffee facilities, most en suite. Short or weekly stays welcome. Good home cooked breakfasts and evening meals. Lovely walks from the farm with maps provided. Golf and fishing 2 miles. AAQQQ. Open all year.

♛ ♛ *Commended*

Cumbria **North Country**

High Gregg Hall, Underbarrow, Kendal, Cumbria LA8 8BL

Mrs Ciceley Simpson
☎ 015395 68318
BB From £15–£16
Sleeps 4
➤ ♘ ♠ ❦ ❈
☺ Commended

100-acre dairy/sheep farm in the Lake District National Park within easy reach of M6 jct36. Guests' sitting room, colour TV, tea-making facilities. Bath/shower room. 1 double, 1 twin with washbasins, shaver points. Pub within walking distance. Golf, swimming, horse riding 2–4 miles, Kendal 4 miles, Windermere 6 miles. Open Apr–Nov.

Howard House Farm, Gilsland, Carlisle, Cumbria CA6 7AN

Elizabeth Woodmass
☎ 016977 47285
BB From £18.50–£21
EM From £9.50
Sleeps 6
➤(5) ❦ ♠ ⓢ
☺☺ Highly Commended

A warm welcome and comfortable accommodation await you on beef/sheep farm. Situated on an elevated site enjoying magnificent views over 2 counties in the heart of Roman wall country. Guests lounge, colour TV, tea/coffee-making facilities. Dinner by arrangement or bar meals nearby. Discount on 3 night stay. Open all year, except Christmas.

Howe Farm, Hawkshead, Nr Ambleside, Cumbria LA22 0QB

Lisa Woodhouse
☎ 015394 36345
BB From £16–£17
Sleeps 6
➤ ⚒ ♠ ❈
Listed Commended

Dating back to 1698, Howe Farm is a traditional stone-built Lakeland farmhouse overlooking Esthwaite Lake. Tastefully decorated with many original features including oak panelling, staircase and log fires. A warm welcome awaits and an excellent breakfast greets you in the morning. Open all year except Christmas and New Year.

Keskadale Farm, Newlands, Keswick, Cumbria CA12 5TS

Mrs M Harryman
☎ 017687 78544
BB From £16.50–£18.50
Sleeps 6
➤ ⚒ ⚘ ❈ ♠ ⓢ
☺ Commended

Traditional Lakeland hill farm in the magnificent setting of the Newlands Valley. Ideal for walking or touring the lakes and mountains. All rooms have tea/coffee, washbasin, CH. On chilly evenings relax by a real open fire in the lounge and enjoy TV or a Lakeland book. Packed lunches available. A warm welcome awaits one and all. Open Mar–Dec.

Low Rigg Farm, Walton, Brampton, Cumbria CA8 2DX

Ann Thompson
☎ 01697 73233
BB From £15–£20
EM From £10
Sleeps 6
➤ ♞ ♠ ⓢ
Listed Commended

The Thompson family would like to welcome you to Low Rigg, a family-run dairy farm in beautiful Hadrian's Wall country. Ideal area for touring, walking, cycling, etc. The farmhouse is comfortably furnished with spacious guest rooms with king size or twin beds. Freshly baked bread and rolls, free range eggs and homemade preserves are served for breakfast. Evening meal by arrangement. Reductions for children and weekly bookings. Closed Christmas and New Year.

New Pallyards, Hethersgill, Carlisle, Cumbria CA6 6HZ

Mrs Georgina Elwen
☎/Fax 01228 577308
BB From £19–£22
EM From £13
Sleeps 6
➤ ♞ ⚘ ⓔ ♘ ❦ ❈ ♠ ⚒ ⓢ
☺☺☺ Highly Commended

Friendly hospitality, warmth and comfort await you in this modernised 18th century farmhouse. Situated in the peaceful countryside, surrounded by nature yet easily accessible from M6, A7, M74. All bedrooms en suite, tea/coffee facilities, disabled people welcome. A wide range of leisure and recreational activities are within a few minutes' drive from the farm. National Gold Award winner. Discount promotions. Open all year.

North Country Cumbria

18 Park House Farm, Dalemain, Penrith, Cumbria CA11 0HB

Mrs Mary Milburn
☎ 017684 86212
BB From £18–£20
Sleeps 6
Commended

Peace and tranquillity in our valley – you can relax and enjoy stunning views of Lakeland fells. 3 miles from Lake Ullswater or M6 (J40) on A592 entering via Dalemain Mansion (historic house) ignoring the 'no cars' sign. Cumbrian hospitality assured, home baking and generous breakfast. Evening meals available locally. 2 family en suite bedrooms, electric blanket, heater, tea/coffee facilities. Bathroom and shower room. TV lounge with open fire. Open Apr–Oct.

19 Slakes Farm, Milburn, Appleby in Westmorland, Cumbria CA16 6DP

Mrs C Braithwaite
☎ 017683 61385
BB From £18
EM from £10
Sleeps 6
Listed Commended

Slakes Farm was built in 1734 and is situated between the villages of Milburn and Knock 6 miles from Appleby. The farm is approx 40 acres rearing cattle and sheep. It makes an ideal base for walking and touring, returning to good farmhouse cooking using fresh local produce. Open Easter–Nov.

20 Stanger Farm, Cockermouth, Cumbria CA13 9TS

Mrs Carolyn Heslop
☎ 01900 824222
BB From £16.50–£18
Sleeps 4
Commended

With breathtaking fell views, yet only 2 miles from the lovely market town of Cockermouth, Stanger Farm lies peacefully beside the River Cocker in the beautiful Lorton Valley. Comfortable lounge and dining room with log fires, spacious bedrooms with tea-making facilities, a traditional farmhouse breakfast and good old-fashioned hospitality all await you. Open all year except Christmas and New Year.

21 Town Head Farm, Walton, Brampton, Cumbria CA8 2DJ

Mrs Una Armstrong
☎ 016977 2730
BB From £14–£15
EM From £9
Sleeps 4
Listed Commended

Relax in the friendly atmosphere of our beef/sheep farm. Our cosy farmhouse overlooks the village green with play area and small nature trail. Scenic views of Pennines and Lakeland Hills. Ideal base for walking/touring. Near Hadrian's Wall, Lakes, Scottish Borders and Northumbria. 10 miles M6 jct43. Bar meals at local pub (400 yds). Special breaks. Open all year except Christmas and New Year.

22 Tranthwaite Hall, Underbarrow, Nr Kendal, Cumbria LA8 8HG

Mrs D Swindlehurst
☎ 015395 68285
BB From £20–£21
Sleeps 4
Highly Commended

Magnificent old farmhouse dating back to 11th century. Beautiful oak beams, doors and rare antique fire range. Tastefully modernised with full CH, pretty en suite bedrooms with tea/coffee, radio and hairdrier. Colour TV lounge, separate dining room. This dairy/sheep farm is set in a small, picturesque village between Kendal and Windermere. Walking, golf, pony trekking. Many good pubs and inns nearby. SAE for brochure. Open all year except Christmas.

23 Tymparon Hall, Newbiggin, Stainton, Penrith, Cumbria CA11 0HS

Mrs Margaret Taylor
☎ 017684 83236
BB From £20–£24
EM From £12
Sleeps 8
Commended

A spacious farmhouse and colourful summer garden situated on a 150 acre sheep farm in a peaceful rural area. Good home cooking. Tea/coffee-making facilities, electric blankets in bedrooms. Open fire in lounge. Lake Ullswater 10 minutes away. Reduction for under 12s; no charge for cot. 4 miles from M6 (jct.40). Open Feb–Nov.

Cumbria *North Country*

Walton High Rigg, Walton, Brampton, Cumbria CA8 2AZ

Margaret Mounsey
☎ 016977 2117
BB From £15–£16.50
EM From £9
Sleeps 4
❦ Commended

Working dairy/sheep farm with attractive 18th century listed farmhouse near Walton and Roman Wall. Friendly welcome, excellent home cooking, panoramic views of the Lakes and Pennines. Convenient also for Northumbria and Scottish Borders. Patio, children's play area. Follow the farm trail to the waterfall, help feed the animals or relax in the garden. Good parking. Golf courses and riding nearby. Closed Christmas and New Year.

 24

Wickerslack Farm, Crosby Ravensworth, Penrith, Cumbria CA10 3LN

Mrs Christine Jackson
☎ 01931 715236
BB From £15–£20
Sleeps 6
❦ ❦ Commended

A warm welcome awaits you on our family-run working farm in the beautiful Eden Valley. Spacious, beautifully decorated farmhouse with superb views. Two double rooms (one en suite) and one twin, all with refreshments. Traditional English breakfast. Guest's lounge with log fire, accessible all day. Light suppers available. Open Mar–Oct.

25

Self-Catering

Arch View and Riggfoot Cottages, Midtodhills Farm, Roadhead, Carlisle, Cumbria CA6 6PF

Jean James
☎/Fax 016977 48213
SC From £130
Sleeps 2/8
♛ ♛ ♛ ♛ ♛ Up to Highly Commended

Arch View and Riggfoot Cottages are on a 320-acre working farm close to Cumbria/Scotland/Northumbria/borders. Ideal for touring Hadrian's Wall, Gretna Green, Kielder, Carlisle and Lakes. The barn conversion has 5 bedrooms, 2 bathrooms, kitchen/diner, lounge. The 2-bedroomed cottages have four-poster beds, dishwasher, washer, microwave, payphone, video, garden, barbecue. Good walking, trekking, fishing. Open all year.

 26

Bessiestown Farm, Catlowdy, Longtown, Carlisle, Cumbria CA6 5QP

Margaret Sisson
☎ 01228 577019/577219
Fax 01228 577219
SC From £75–£340
EM From £11
Sleeps 4–5
♛ ♛ ♛ Commended

Three tastefully converted two bedroomed courtyard cottages enjoying extensive views over Border country. Well furnished, spacious, warm and welcoming. Swim in the pool, meander through the meadows, picnic by the stream, dine in the main house – simply unwind. Indoor heated swimming pool (mid May–mid Sept). Special winter breaks. Phone for colour brochure. Open all year.

2

Birchbank Cottage, Birchbank, Blawith, Ulverston, Cumbria LA12 8EW

Mrs Linda Nicholson
☎ 01229 885277
SC From £125–£265
Sleeps 4+ cot
♛ ♛ ♛ ♛ Commended

Relax and unwind in this comfortable beamed cottage on a Lakeland sheep farm only 5 miles from Coniston Water. Enjoy marvellous views of the Duddon estuary and Coniston Old Man while walking on the fells around the farm. One double, 1 twin, linen and electricity included. Short breaks in low season. Open all year.

27

North Country Cumbria

17 Burn and Meadow View, New Pallyards, Hethersgill, Carlisle, Cumbria CA6 6HZ

Georgina Elwen
☎/Fax 01228 577308
From £80–£395
Sleeps 5/8

Up to Highly Commended

Set amidst beautiful countryside close to the Scottish Borders, our fully centrally heated cottages offer a high standard of accommodation with all modern-day facilities. A wide range of leisure and recreational activities are within a few minutes' drive from the farm. Our on-site games and dining room will make your stay more enjoyable. Discount promotions. Open all year.

28 Chestnuts, Meaburn Hill Farm, Maulds Meaburn, Penrith, Cumbria CA10 3HN

Ruth Tuer
☎/Fax 01931 715205
From £300–£350
Sleeps 6

Highly Commended

Lovely cottage converted from traditional Cumbrian long barn, with unsurpassed views of tranquil Lyvennet Valley and village green. Enjoy a peaceful break in this bright, cheerful cottage, mainly on one floor, with excellent standards of facilities, furnishing and decoration. Full oil CH. Small conservatory and garden area, patio, barbecue, parking. Linen and heating included. Short breaks. Open all year.

29 Collin Bank, Bewcastle, Carlisle, Cumbria CA6 6PU

Mrs J Moscrop
☎/Fax 01697 748408
From £230–£390
Sleeps 6

Approved

High on the fells of Bewcastle is Collin Bank Farm with wonderful views of the surrounding countryside. The area is ideal for walking (Hadrian's Wall is not far away), riding and birdwatching. Our chalet is well equipped and comfortable. You can enjoy a swim in our indoor heated pool. Open all year.

30 Ghyll Burn Cottage, Hartside Nursery Garden, Nr Alston, Cumbria CA9 3BL

Mrs Susan Huntley
☎ 01434 381372/381428
Fax 01434 381372
From £160–£355
Sleeps 4/6 + cot

Commended

Recently renovated farm buildings dating back to 1630 offer spacious and comfortable accommodation for 4/6 people. Kitchen/diner, large lounge with oak beams and wood burning stove on first floor. Attractive twin and double bedrooms, bathroom, are downstairs. Full gas central heating. The cottage is set in a secluded valley with small nursery garden. Ideal for bird wildlife and gardening enthusiasts. Open all year.

31 Green View Lodges & Well Cottage, Green View, Welton, Nr Dalston, Carlisle, Cumbria CA5 7ES

Anne Ivinson
☎ 016974 76230
Fax 016974 76523
From £150–£507
Sleeps 2/7

Highly Commended

Superb Scandinavian lodges in peaceful garden setting. 17th century oak-beamed cottages oozing character, one with open fire. Also for non-smokers only, a tastefully converted Wesleyan chapel (regret no pets). Own gardens. In tiny, picturesque hamlet with unspoilt views to Caldbeck Fells 3 miles. Every home comfort provided for a relaxing country holiday. CH, telephones. ½ hr's drive from Keswick, Lake Ullswater, Gretna Green. Hotel leisure facilities. Open all year.

32 High Swinklebank Farm, Longsleddale, Nr Kendal, Cumbria LA8 9BD

Mrs Olive Simpson
☎ 01539 823682
From £100–£200
Sleeps 4

Commended

High Swinklebank is near the head of the beautiful Longsleddale Valley with lovely views and walking. A recent conversion which is well appointed includes fitted carpets throughout. Comprising lounge with electric fire, bed settee, TV, lovely kitchen, shower room, 2 bedrooms – double and bunk. Children welcome. Linen provided. Weekends available. Cleanliness and personal attention assured. Open all year.

Cumbria   *North Country*

Jenkin Cottage, Embleton, Cockermouth, Cumbria CA13 9TN

Mrs Margaret Teasdale
☎ 017687 76387
SC From £230–£350
Sleeps 6
Commended

Jenkin Cottage has a spectacular outlook over open countryside extending to the Solway Firth and Scottish Lowlands. We are a working family hill farm in a beautiful quiet part of the Lake District. The cottage is fully equipped with all fuel, bed linen, towels provided. Open fire. Ideal base for fell walking or touring the Lakes by car. Sorry no pets. Open all year.

Long Byres, Talkin Head Farm, Talkin, Brampton, Cumbria CA8 1LT

Mrs Harriet Sykes
☎ 016977 3435
Fax 016977 2228
SC From £98–£272
Sleeps 2–5
Commended

Seven specially designed, fully equipped, warm holiday cottages on North Pennine hill farm. Freshly home-cooked meal service. Enjoy walking (access direct to fells); cycling (green and quiet roads); bird watching (RSPB reserve next door); touring centre for Scottish Borders, Hadrian's Wall, Lake District. Golf, boating, fishing and good pubs close by. Open all year. Email: harriet@talkinhead.demon.co.uk

Lyvennet Cottages, Keld Farm, Kings Meaburn, Penrith, Cumbria CA10 3BS

Mrs DM Addison
☎ 01931 714226
Fax 01931 714598
SC From £160–£400
Sleeps 3–6
Up to Highly Commended

Four different cottages in and around a small farming village in beautiful, unspoilt Lyvennet Valley. Ideal touring centre for the Lakes or Dales. Attractively furnished with either electric storage heaters, oil CH or log and coal fires in winter inclusive. Also free fly fishing. Children and pets welcome. Open all year.

Preston Patrick Hall Cottage, Preston Patrick Hall, Crooklands, Milnthorpe, Cumbria LA7 7NY

Mrs Jennifer Armitage
☎/Fax 015395 67200
SC From £110–£310
Sleeps 2/6
Commended

Green fields with sheep and cows will be your first sight as you open your bedroom curtains. Our cottage is a self-contained, fully equipped wing of a magnificent medieval manor house. You may spend your time walking the quiet lanes, swimming in our pool or perhaps take advantage of the easy access to the Lakes, Dales and Morecambe Bay. Brochure available. Open all year.

Skirwith Hall Cottage, Skirwith Hall, Skirwith, Penrith, Cumbria CA10 1RH

Mrs Laura Wilson
☎/Fax 01768 88241
SC From £160–£350
Sleeps 8+cot
Commended

Georgian farmhouse wing overlooking large landscaped garden and stream on 400-acre mixed dairy farm. Exposed beams and open fire in lounge, CH, electric and Rayburn cookers. Two double rooms and one with twin beds and bunks. Cot and high chair. Ideal for Lakes, North Pennines or Borders, or simply relaxing in peaceful idyllic rural surroundings. Well behaved children and dogs welcome. Brochure. Short breaks in low season. Open all year.

Smithy Cottage, c/o Skirwith Hall, Skirwith, Penrith, Cumbria CA10 1RH

Mrs Laura Wilson
☎/Fax 01768 88241
SC From £125–£260
Sleeps 4+cot
Commended

Originally the home of the village blacksmith. Situated on the outskirts of an unspoilt village in the shadow of Crossfell. Tastefully and comfortably furnished with 1 twin and 1 double room. Nightstore heaters and open fires in sitting and dining rooms. Colour TV, telephone, cot, high chair. Private garden by stream. Good pubs, Carlisle–Settle railway, golf, riding, fishing nearby. Ideal for walking or touring Lakes, Pennine Dales or Borders. Open all year.

 **North Country** *Cumbria*

20 Stanger Farm, Cockermouth, Cumbria CA13 9TS

Mrs Carolyn Heslop
☎ 01900 824222
SC From £180–£350
Sleeps 4+cot
Commended

Set amidst magnificent fell views this is an ideal base for exploring the whole of the Lake District. The Stable is a recently converted 17th century barn adjoining the farmhouse. The open plan lounge with log fire and dining and fully equipped kitchen areas are "upstairs" to benefit from view across the River Cocker and open fields. Fishing, central heating, logs, bed linen all included. Open all year.

38 Stonefold, Newbiggin, Stainton, Penrith, Cumbria CA11 0HP

Mrs Gill Harrington
☎ 01768 866383
SC From £120–£320
Sleeps 2–4
Applied

A warm welcome awaits you at Stonefold. Our three cottages are set in a beautiful panoramic position overlooking the Eden Valley, with the majestic Pennine Hills in the background. Stonefold makes a superb base to explore the northern Lake District and the unspoilt Eden Valley. Ullswater 4 miles. Open all year.

39 Swarthbeck Farm, Howtown-on-Ullswater, Penrith, Cumbria, CA10 2ND

Mr & Mrs WH Parkin
☎ 01768 486432
SC From £195–£450
Sleeps 6–12
Up to Commended

Individual 18th century properties overlooking Ullswater, with own lake frontage, boat launching and direct access to fell. Boats and bikes for hire. Bring your own horses – miles of open bridleways. Ideal for active group/family holidays, also for peace and quiet (couples and small parties equally welcome). Open all year.

40 Tarnside Cottages, Tarnside, Farlam, Brampton, Cumbria CA8 1LA

Vicky Reed
☎ 01697 746675
SC From £190–£340
Sleeps 1/4 + cot
Highly Commended

Two excellently equipped cottages, each with lounge, dining/kitchen, bathroom and twin bedroom downstairs and spiral staircase to double bedroom. Electricity and heating included, initial supply of logs. Located near Eden Valley, Lake District, Hadrians Wall and the Borders. Tarnside is an excellent base for exploring the area. Open all year. E-mail: creed10110@aol.com.uk

41 West View Cottages, West View Farm, Winskill, Penrith, Cumbria CA10 1PD

Alan and Susan Grave
☎/Fax 01768 881356
SC From £180–£370
Sleeps 2–5
Commended

A roomy cottage and 2 barn conversions on a mixed working farm. All units have central heating, TV, modern kitchen, washing facilities, and linen provided. Ideally situated for touring and within easy reach of the lakes, North Pennines and Scotland. Local facilities include children's play area, open air swimming pool, walking. Sleeps 2/4/5. Short breaks available in low season. Brochure sent on request. Open all year.

LET THE TELEPHONE RING!
Some farmhouses are big places. Let the telephone ring long enough to give the owner time to answer it.

Northumberland

Cheviot Hills, Northumberland National Park,
Northumberland Coast, Kielder Forest & Hadrian's Wall

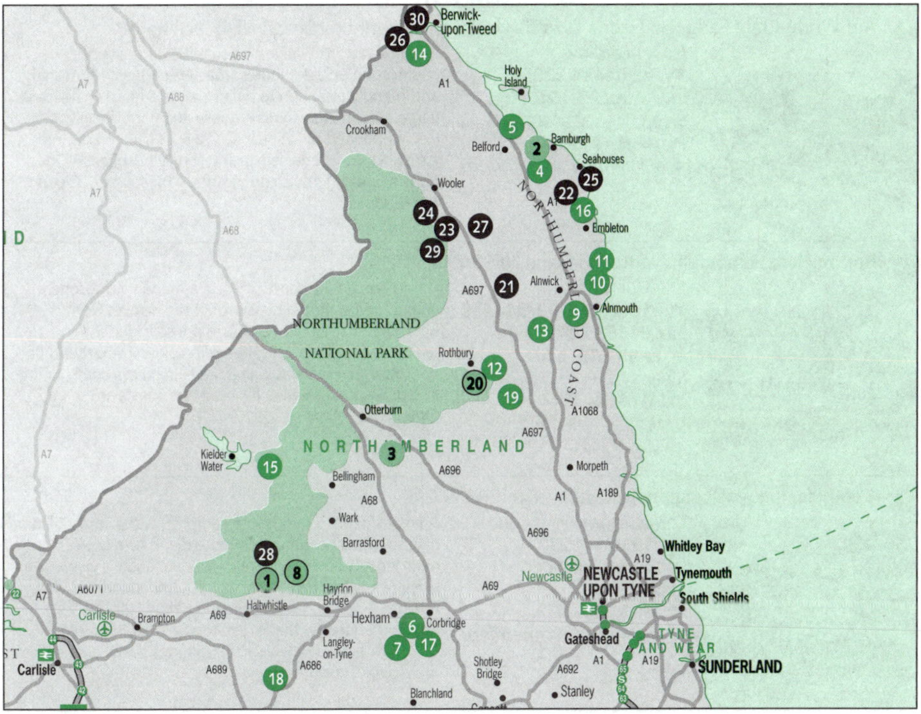

Key

- 1 Bed & Breakfast
- 1 Self-Catering
- 1 B&B and SC
- 1 Camping Barns
- 1 Camping & Caravanning

This is an exciting county for the heritage enthusiast with Hadrian's Wall and many other Roman sites, the Border abbeys, the heritage coastline with castles such as Lindisfarne, Bamburgh and Dunstanburgh and, inland, Hexham Abbey and the historic homes of Alnwick Castle, Wallington Hall and Cragside. The Northumberland National Park is a haven of peace and solitude while Kielder Water offers many water activities, birdwatching and magnificent forest surroundings. We have quiet roads, charming country inns, bustling market towns, such as Berwick-upon-Tweed and Alnwick, and friendly people. When are you coming?

If you would like help in finding suitable farm accommodation, turn to the full listing of farm groups on pages 360 to 363 to find appropriate contact details for this area.

North Country   Northumberland

Bed and Breakfast
(and evening meal)

---

① Ald White Craig Farm, Nr. Hadrian's Wall, Haltwhistle, Northumberland NE49 9NW

Isobel Laidlow
☎/Fax 01434 320565
[BB] From £22–£26
Sleeps 4
♨ ⊞ ⬚ ♣ ⊚
♛ ♛ Highly Commended

Peaceful, award-winning en suite B&B in scenic countryside only 2 minutes from A69. Quality furnishings and friendly attention to detail ensure a relaxing holiday. Large garden with summerhouse and panoramic views. Recommended by 'Which' Good B&B Guide. No gimmicks, just genuine North Country hospitality! Good pubs nearby. Plenty to do yet space for solitude. Open Apr–Oct.

---

② Burton Hall, Bamburgh, Northumberland NE69 7AR

Eve Humphreys
☎ 01668 214213/214458
Fax 01668 214538
[BB] From £19–£30
Sleeps 17
ಕ(4) 🐾 ♣ ⊚
Listed *Commended*

A traditional farmhouse offering a friendly atmosphere with a high standard of service only 1½ miles from Bamburgh Castle. All bedrooms are spacious with tea/coffee facilities, en suites with colour TV. Ground floor bedrooms available as well as an elegant residents' lounge and dining room where delicious breakfasts are served. Open Easter–Nov.

---

③ Cornhills, Kirkwhelpington, Northumberland NE19 2RE

Lorna Thornton
☎ 01830 540232
[BB] From £20–£25
Sleeps 6
ಕ ♨ ♣ ♣
♛ ♛ Highly Commended

A large Victorian farmhouse complete with mosaic tiled hall, spacious beautifully decorated and furnished bedrooms (two en suite), all with outstanding views. Our stock farm is in the centre of Northumberland, ideal for visiting Cragside, Wallington and Belsay Hall. Recommended by the *Which* report *The Good Bed & Breakfast* guide. Newcastle 30 minutes away, 1 mile from the A696. Closed April.

---

④ Elford Farmhouse, Elford, Seahouses, Northumberland NE68 7UT

Mrs M Robinson
☎/Fax 01665 720244
[BB] From £17.50–£20
Sleeps 6
ಕ(12) ⌚ ♣ ♣ ⚛
Listed *Highly Commended*

An old stone farmhouse of great character on an arable farm near the villages of Bamburgh and Seahouses, 1½ miles from the sea. Nearby are beautiful beaches, castles, golf, riding and boat trips to the Farnes and Holy Island. Good local restaurants. Comfortable bedrooms with central heating, colour TV, hair dryers and tea/coffee facilities. Elegant dining room. Some use of outdoor heated swimming pool and lawn tennis court in summer. Open Mar–Oct.

---

⑤ Fenham-le-Moor Farmhouse, Belford, Northumberland NE70 7PN

Mrs K Burn
☎/Fax 01668 213247
[BB] From £18–£22
Sleeps 3
ಕ(12) ♨ ♣ ♣ ⊚
♛ ♛ Highly Commended

A comfortable stone-built farmhouse in a peaceful situation with magnificent views overlooking farmland and the bay of Lindisfarne Nature Reserve. An area of outstanding natural beauty and excellent centre for birdwatching, golf, good beaches and visiting many castles. One twin room en suite, one single. Open Easter–Oct.

Northumberland / North Country

Flothers Farm, Slaley, Hexham, Northumberland NE47 0BJ

Susan Dart
☎ 01434 673240/673587
Mobile 0585 038432
BB From £17.50–£25
Sleeps 5
🐕 🐎 🛄 ⓟ
☕☕ Commended

We are a typical Northumbrian dairy farm, set in beautiful countryside. Accommodation in self-contained area. Easy reach of Ikea, Metro Centre, and Beamish Museum. Full central heating, all rooms en suite, tea/coffee and colour TV. Country pubs within walking distance. Excellent breakfasts provided and packed lunches, if required. Open all year except Christmas.

Gairshield Farm, Whitley Chapel, Hexham, Northumberland NE47 0HS

Mrs Hilary Kristensen
☎ 01434 673562
BB From £20–£25
Sleeps 3
🐕(6) 🍴 🎎 🛄
Listed Highly Commended

A comfortable 17th century farmhouse on a quiet hill farm (1,000 ft above sea level), with superb views over open countryside. 20 mins south of Hexham. Ideal for exploring this beautiful historic region. Perfect walking and horse-riding area; horses very welcome. Relaxed, friendly atmosphere. Tastefully decorated with large attractive family bedroom. Guests' dining room/lounge with TV and tea/coffee-making facilities. Open Apr–Oct.

Gibbs Hill Farm, Bardon Mill, Hexham, Northumberland NE47 7AP

Mrs Valerie Gibson
☎/Fax 01434 344030
BB From £17.50–£20
Sleeps 6
🐕(12) 🍴 🛄 🐎 🎎
☕☕ Commended

Spacious farmhouse accommodation of highest standard on traditional 700-acre hill farm/nature reserve in National Park. Beautifully fuirnished rooms, 1 twin, 1 double (both en suite) with tea/coffee and colour TV and spectacular views. Excellent breakfasts in huge farmhouse kitchen, guests' lounge. Private fishing on own small lake, walking, riding, birdwatching from bird hide overlooking Greenlee Lough. Five minutes to Roman Wall and main Roman sites. Open Apr–Oct.

Hawkhill Farmhouse, Hawkhill, Lesbury, Alnwick, Northumberland NE66 3PG

Mrs Margery Vickers
☎/Fax 01665 830380
BB From £22.50–£30
Sleeps 6
🐕(12) 🛄
☕☕ Highly Commended

Large traditional farmhouse set in extensive, secluded grounds with magnificent views of the Aln valley and surrounding countryside. Midway Alnwick/Alnmouth, ideal for good beaches, castles and places of interest. One double and 2 twin rooms, all en suite with TV, tea/coffee. Very spacious guests' sitting room and dining room. Full CH and private parking. Open Easter–Oct.

Hipsburn Farm, Lesbury, Alnmouth, Northumberland NE66 3PY

Hilda Tulip
☎ 01665 830206
BB From £20–£30
Sleeps 6
🐕(12) 🍴
☕ Highly Commended

A spacious farmhouse situated ½ mile from Alnmouth, overlooking the Aln estuary. Rooms comfortably furnished, one double en suite, one twin or double en suite and one double with private bathroom. TV, tea/coffee-making facilities in all bedrooms. All rooms are centrally heated, dining room – lounge. Ideal area for golfers, walkers and birdwatchers. Private parking. Open Easter–Oct.

Howick Scar Farm, Craster, Alnwick, Northumberland NE66 3SU

Mrs Celia Curry
☎ 01665 576665
BB From £16
Sleeps 4
🐕(5) 🎎 🛄
☕☕ Commended

Comfortable farmhouse accommodation on mixed farm situated on the coast between the villages of Craster and Howick. Ideal base for walking or exploring the coast, moors and historic castles. Guests have their own television lounge/dining room, double bedrooms with washbasins and full central heating. Open May–Nov.

North Country   Northumberland

---

(12) The Lee Farm, nr Rothbury, Longframlington, Morpeth, Northumberland NE65 8JQ

Mrs Susan Aynsley
☎ 01665 570257
[BB] From £17.50–£20
Sleeps 5
♞ ☙ ⚘
♥♥ Highly Commended

Large traditional farmhouse on 1,200 acre farm. Comfortable bedrooms with tea/coffee-making facilities and washbasins, one en suite. Guests' lounge with log fire and dining room. Central heating throughout. Excellent central location for walking or exploring Northumberland's many attractions. Fishing, riding and golf available nearby. Open Mar–Nov.

---

(13) Lumbylaw Farm, Edlingham, Alnwick, Northumberland NE66 2BW

Mrs Sally Lee
☎/Fax 01665 574277
[BB] From £21
Sleeps 6
⚘ ♞ ☙ ⚘
♥ Highly Commended

Friendly hospitality in a comfortable stone farmhouse on a beef and sheep farm. 6 miles between Alnwick and Rothbury. Outstanding views of the 13th century Edlingham Castle and Victorian disused railway viaduct in farm grounds. Two twin bedrooms, one double (all with washbasin; one with en suite shower). Guest's bathroom, CH throughout. Excellent local eating places available. Open May–Oct.

---

(14) Middle Ord Manor House, Middle Ord Farm, Berwick-on-Tweed TD15 2XQ

Joan Gray
☎ 01289 306323
Mobile 01410 295004
Fax 01289 308423
[BB] From £26
Sleeps 6
⚘ ♣ ☙ ⚘ ◉
♥♥ De Luxe

Feeling stressed, want to unwind, or are you just wanting to indulge yourself? Either way, why not visit our elegant home and experience the warmth and quality of gracious living in a secluded, tranquil setting. Relax in our spacious en suite rooms (four poster if desired). Holder of Pride of Northumbria Best B&B and England for Excellence Awards. Sorry no children or pets. Open Easter–Oct.

---

(15) Ridge End Farm, Falstone, Hexham, Northumberland NE48 1DE

Mrs Karen Hodgson
☎ 01434 240395
[BB] From £18–£25
Sleeps 5
♞ ☙ ⚘ ♣ ⚘
♥♥ Commended

Working hill farm within Northumberland National Park, next to Kielder Water and Forest Park. This 16th century Bastle house, former home of Border Reivers, has 5ft thick walls. Roaring log fire in winter. Surrounded by magnificent scenery, close to Hadrian's Wall, Scottish Borders, watersports, mountain bike trails and wildlife. Walker's paradise. Pub nearby. Open all year.

---

(16) Rock Farmhouse, Rock Village, Alnwick, Northumberland NE66 3SB

Douglas Turnbull
☎ 01665 579235
Fax 01665 579215
[BB] From £21–£25
Sleeps 6
♞ ♣ ⚘ ▣ ♠ ♣ ☙ ⚘
♥♥ Commended

Listed 16th century farmhouse with mature walled garden and tennis court, three miles from the coastal path at Dunstanburgh Castle. Award-winning beaches at Newton Bay and the Cheviot hills are nearby. Ten miles of woodland and nature trails. Home cooking with free range eggs and home made bread. Open all year except Christmas & New Year.
E-mail: 100701.2640@compuserve.com.uk

---

(17) Rye Hill Farm, Slaley, Nr Hexham, Northumberland NE47 0AH

Elizabeth Courage
☎ 01434 673259
Fax 01434 673608
[BB] From £20–£24
EM From £12
Sleeps 15
♞ ♣ ▣ ♠ ⚘ ♣ ◉
♥♥♥ Highly Commended

We are a small family-run livestock farm set in beautiful countryside with 360-degree panoramic views. We have recently converted some of the old byres into superb modern guest accommodation. We aim for high standards with a homely atmosphere. Good, fresh, homemade cooking. All rooms are en suite and have large bath towels. Well mannered children and pets welcome. Open all year. Email:enquiries@consult-courage.co.uk

Northumberland   *North Country*

Struthers Farm, Catton, Allendale, Hexham, Northumberland NE47 9LP

Mrs Ruby Keenleyside
☎ 01434 683580
[BB] From £17.50–£20
EM From £9.50
Sleeps 5
Applied

A small working livestock farm situated in a designated area of natural beauty. Quiet country walks, ample safe parking. Children and pets by arrangement. We offer spacious double/twin en suite rooms, Guests' lounge/dining/TV room. Fresh home cooking. Come and enjoy our countryside. Open all year.

Thistleyhaugh Farm, Longhorsley, Morpeth, Northumberland NE65 8RG

Enid Nelless
☎/Fax 01665 570629
[BB] From £18–£21
EM From £12
Sleeps 6
Highly Commended

Thistleyhaugh Farm is a spacious farmhouse situated on the banks of the River Coquet. Furnished to a high standard, all rooms are en suite, one with a private bathroom. Evening meals include wine and are followed by coffee in the lounge, with large open fires, exclusive to guests. We are a working farm with a wide variety of animals.

Tosson Tower Farm, Great Tosson, Rothbury, Morpeth, Northumberland NE65 7NW

Mrs Ann Foggin
☎/Fax 01669 620228
[BB] From £18.50–£20
Sleeps 6
Highly Commended

Breathtaking views over Coquet Valley and Cheviots combined with traditional farmhouse comforts in this former coaching inn nestling in peaceful hamlet. Border history starts on doorstep with ruined 15th century Tosson Pele Tower. Surrounding hills and forests provide invigorating challenges for serious walkers or a peaceful return to nature for ramblers. Private fishing. Cosy en suite bedrooms, hairdryers, electric blankets, beverages at anytime. CH, real log fires. Closed Christmas & New Year.

Self-Catering

Ald White Craig Farm Cottages, Nr. Hadrian's Wall, Haltwhistle, Northumberland NE49 9NW

Isobel Laidlow
☎/Fax 01434 320565
[SC] From £120–£420
Sleeps 2/5 + cot
Highly Commended

Warm and comfortable, these farm cottages offer you award-winning accommodation. Nearby are country inns, restaurants and varied attractions including Hadrian's Wall with its stunning scenery and peaceful moorland. On the edge of Northumberland National Park overlooking North Pennine Fells. Open all year.

Broome Hill Farm, Alnwick, Northumberland NE66 2BA

Mrs Margaret McGregor
☎/Fax 01665 574460
[SC] From £250–£490
Sleeps 4/6+cot
Highly Commended

Our two cottages have recently been completely renovated to a very high standard with landscaped gardens and secure private heated storage for personal leisure equipment. They are ideally situated for the coast and hills. Open log fires, CH and solid pine furniture. All fuel, electricity and linen inclusive. Sorry no pets or smoking. Open all year.

North Country — Northumberland

② Doxford Newhouses, Doxford Farm, Chathill, Northumberland NE67 5DY

Sarah Shell
☎ 01665 579348
Fax 01665 579331
[SC] From £225–£495
Sleeps 4
🐎 🐕 ⌂ 🍴 ☆
♛♛♛♛ Highly Commended

A delightful 17th century stone cottage with well maintained garden ideally situated midway between the Cheviot foothills and the heritage coastline. Tastefully modernised, the open beams have been retained and a woodburning stove installed in the huge stone fireplace. The cottage is very comfortable and well furnished, heated and equipped to a high standard. All fuel power and bed linen provided. Pets are welcome. Open all year.

② East Burton Farm Holiday Cottages, East Burton, Bamburgh, Northumberland NE69 7AR

Eve Humphreys
☎ 01668 214213/214458
Fax 01668 214538
[SC] From £250–£500
Sleeps 4–6
🐎 🍴 ⊙
♛♛♛♛ Up to Highly Commended

Six comfortable cottages on a working farm 1½ miles from Bamburgh, all well equipped and furnished. Heat, light, sheets and towels included in rent. Ideal base for birdwatching, golf, sightseeing or relaxing. Open all year.

㉓ The Farmhouse, Northfield Farm, Glanton, Alnwick, Northumberland NE66 4AG

Jackie Stothard
☎ 01665 578203
[SC] From £180–£350
Sleeps 4–6
🐎 ⌂ ☆
Applied

Traditional 18th century farmhouse, with many original features, on our 15-acre smallholding with a variety of livestock. We are in a peaceful yet central location with panoramic views. 2 miles from National Park. Ideal centre for exploring the delights of Northumberland. Comfortable, well equipped accommodation with all mod cons. Open all year.

㉔ Firwood Bungalow & Humphreys House, Earle Hill Head Farm, Wooler, Northumberland NE71 6RH

Mrs Sylvia Armstrong
☎/Fax 01668 281243
[SC] From £200–£650
Sleeps 6/10
🐎 🍴 ⌂ 🐕 ☆
♛♛♛ – ♛♛♛♛ Highly Commended

Firwood and Humphreys, a choice of two beautiful homes offering a unique and private situation. Standing in 1.5 acres of well maintained gardens within the National Park at the foot of the Cheviots. Ideal for walking and wildlife throughout the year. Every comfort, open fires, central heating. Aga in Firwood. Pride of Northumbria award 1997. Open all year.

㉕ Gardeners & Dunes Cottages, Annstead Farm, Beadnell, Chathill, Northumberland NE67 5BT

Mrs Susan Mellor
☎ 01665 720387
Fax 01665 721494
[SC] From £160–£450
Sleeps 4/6
🐎 🍴
Applied

Recently renovated stone cottages situated on working farm ½ mile from Beadnell village in one of the most beautiful coastal areas in Northumberland. Equipped to high standard – heating, lighting and linen included. Ideal for walking, fishing, golfing and birdwatching or as a base to explore the surrounding area – 500yards from beautiful sandy beach. Open all year.

⑧ Gibbs Hill Farm Cottages, Bardon Mill, Hexham, Northumberland NE47 7AP

Mrs Valerie Gibson
☎/Fax 01434 344030
[SC] From £100–£400
Sleep 2–5 + cot
🐎 🍴 ⌂ 🐕 ☆
♛♛♛♛ Up to De Luxe

Superb stone cottages on 700-acre traditional hill farm nature reserve in National Park. Central heating, log fires. Outstanding views, walking, riding, trout fishing in own small lake. Birdwatching from bird hide. 5 minutes to Roman Wall and main Roman forts. Centrally placed for north east coast, Tynedale and Lakes. Brochure available. Short breaks. Open all year.

Northumberland   North Country

The Herdsman Cottage, Cornhills, Kirkwhelpington, Northumberland NE19 2RE

Lorna Thornton
☎ 01830 540232
[SC] From £180–£330
Sleeps 5
Commended

A beamed 19th century farm cottage, provides comfortable accommodation for 5 people (double, twin, single). The fully fitted kitchen is equipped with fridge, microwave, washing machine, night storage heaters, open fire. All fuel included in price. Bed linen provided. Enjoy the peace on our stock farm, in the centre of Northumberland. Open all year.

Honeysuckle Cottage, West Longridge Farm, Berwick upon Tweed, Northumberland TD15 2JX

Mr Robert S Whitten
☎ 01289 331112
Fax 01289 304591
[SC] From £150–£365
Sleeps 6+cot
Highly Commended

This charming stone-built cottage has been modernised, decorated and furnished to high standards, and provides very attractive accommodation in this beautiful area just 4 miles west of the historic market town of Berwick upon Tweed. The cottage enjoys uninterrupted picturesque views of the Cheviot Hills. Bed linen provided. Open fire. Sorry no pets. Open all year.

Keepers Cottages, Tosson Tower Farm, Great Tosson, Rothbury, Northumberland NE65 7NW

Mrs Ann Foggin
☎/Fax 01669 620228
[SC] From £170–£460
Sleeps 4–6
Up to Highly Commended

Four delightful cottages situated in the Coquet Valley enjoying panoramic views of the Cheviot Hills. Cosy, comfortable, centrally heated, well equipped and all with enclosed gardens. Set in National Park with many forest and moorland walks clearly marked. Private fishing. 2 miles from Rothbury and the NT property of Cragside. Very central for touring all Northumberland. Bedlinen provided. Log fires during winter. Open all year.

Lumbylaw and Garden Cottages, Lumbylaw Farm, Edlingham, Alnwick, Northumberland NE66 2BW

Mrs Sally Lee
☎/Fax 01665 574277
[SC] From £148–£440
Sleeps 2/6 + cot
Highly Commended

The two cottages are situated in a beautiful valley with extensive hill views, rich in wildlife with a 13th century castle ruin and a Victorian viaduct providing easy walking along the disused railway line. Centrally heated, prettily decorated, furnished and equipped to a high standard. Own garden. All fuel, power, bedlinen, towels included in rent. Sorry no pets or smokers. Open all year.

Nos. 1, 2 and 3 Cottages, Titlington Hall Farm, Alnwick, Northumberland NE66 2EB

Mrs Vera Purvis
☎/Fax 01665 578253
[SC] From £175–£305
Sleep 2–10
Commended

Two lovely country cottages available for holiday lets all year round. They are situated in a beautiful area with many interesting places close by. Facilities include central heating, TV, fridge, washing machine, microwave, tumble dryer and all linen. Children and pets welcome. Can sleep families of up to 10. Open all year.

Rowan Cottage, High Edges Green, Cawburn, Haltwhistle, Northumberland NE49 9PP

Mrs Margaret Swallow
☎ 01434 320352
[SC] From £125–£275
Sleep 2
Highly Commended

Beautiful converted barn retaining many original features, 4 miles from the scenic town of Haltwhistle. Lovely views of Hadrian's Wall. Private garden with patio and barbecue. Oil fired CH and open fire. En suite bedroom. Well-equipped kitchen with washing machine, dishwasher, fridge, microwave and electric cooker. Short breaks. A warm welcome guaranteed. Open all year.

 *North Country*   Northumberland

㉙ Shepherd's Cottage, Ingram Farm, Powburn, Alnwick, Northumberland NE66 4LT

Sarah Wilson
☎/Fax 01665 578243
[SC] From £235–£400
Sleeps 7
🪑 🛏 ♨ ☂ 🐕
🔑🔑🔑🔑 *Commended*

On a working family farm in the beautiful Breamish Valley, the cottage has superb scenery on the doorstep. Explore the unspoilt Cheviot Hills or the coast and castles. Most mod cons are provided and there are no extras – fuel, linen and towels all included. Central heating from open fire. Night storage heating. Open all year except Christmas and New Year.

㉚ West Ord Holiday Cottages, West Ord Farm, Berwick-upon-Tweed, Northumberland TD15 2XQ

Mrs Carol Lang
☎ 01289 386631
Fax 01289 386800
[SC] From £110–£390
Sleeps 2–6
🪑 🛏 🐕
🔑🔑🔑 – 🔑🔑🔑🔑
Highly Commended

Six charming cottages within 10 mins' drive of Berwick town centre, offering accommodation for 2–6 people. Ranging from cosy riverside cottages to a tasteful and spacious garden cottage. All are thoughtfully equipped and furnished. We can offer tennis and fishing on the farm and beautiful walks. Colour brochure. Short breaks also available. Open all year.

LET THE TELEPHONE RING!
Some farmhouses are big places. Let the telephone ring
long enough to give the owner time to answer it.

STAY ON A FARM GIFT TOKENS

If you have enjoyed your Stay on a Farm, why not treat your friends and relatives to *Stay on a Farm* gift tokens? Available from the Bureau office (tel: 01203 696909), they can be redeemed against accommodation and are accepted by the majority of farms (see Index). Please check when booking to avoid disappointment.

FOLLOW THE COUNTRY CODE

Leave nothing but footprints,
Take nothing but photographs,
Kill nothing but time!

Durham

North Pennines, Weardale, Teesdale & High Force

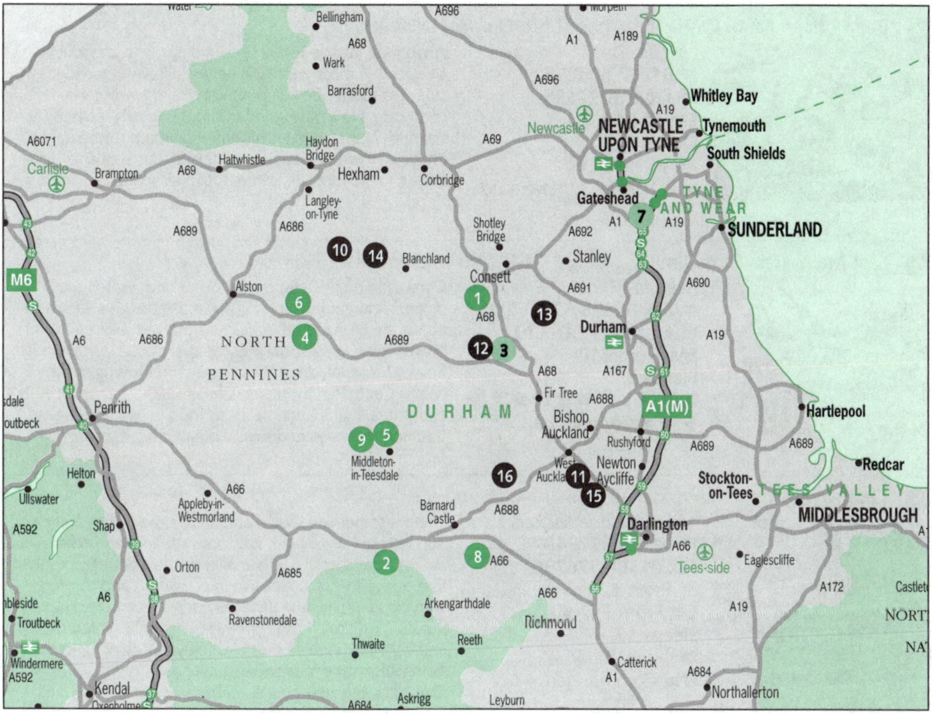

Key

- 1 Bed & Breakfast
- 1 Self-Catering
- 1 B&B and SC
- 1 Camping Barns
- 1 Camping & Caravanning

There's plenty to do and see in County Durham: the historic city of Durham itself with its cathedral and castle; the Open Air Museum at Beamish where you can experience life at the turn of the century; the reconstructed Killhope lead mine high up in Weardale; the largest waterfall in England at High Force in Teesdale; impressive castles and fortified farmhouses; the Bowes Museum's collections of 18th century furniture, paintings and ceramics, and the breathtaking scenery of the high, wild fells and wooded valleys of 'England's last wilderness'. Add to that the proximity of vibrant Tyneside and Teesside and you have all you need for a wonderful holiday.

If you would like help in finding suitable farm accommodation, turn to the full listing of farm groups on pages 360 to 363 to find appropriate contact details for this area.

North Country *Durham*

Bed and Breakfast
(and evening meal)

---

① Bee Cottage Farm, Castleside, Consett, Co Durham DH8 9HW

Liz Lawson
☎ 01207 508224
BB From £22–£35
EM £14.50
Sleeps 34
♥♥ *Highly Commended*

A working farm in lovely surroundings with unspoilt views, situated 1½ miles west A68 between Tow Law and Castleside. Tea room open daily. Quiet country walks. Fire certificate. No smoking in farmhouse. Ideally located for Beamish Museum, Metro Centre, Durham Cathedral or a break on a journey between England and Scotland. You will be made most welcome. Open all year.

---

② East Mellwaters Farm, Bowes, Barnard Castle, Co Durham DL12 9RH

Patricia Milner
☎/Fax 01833 628269
BB From £17.50–£20
EM From £10
Sleeps 9
♥♥ *Commended*

Come and meet Dolly, our highland cow, watch the dippers and golden plovers or glimpse badgers. Learn about the Bronze Age on our waymarked walks. Fish for brown trout, we'll show you the best pools. Visit Beamish, Bowes Museum, ancient castles, market towns or the Metro Centre for shopping (Christmas?). Then relax with a cup of tea, log fire and delicious food in best farmhouse tradition. Holidays and special break rates. Open mid Jan–mid Dec.

---

③ Greenwell Farm, Nr Wolsingham, Tow Law, Bishop Auckland, Co Durham DL13 4PH

Mike & Linda Vickers
☎ 01388 527248
Fax 01388 526735
BB From £20
EM From £12.50
Sleeps 12
♥♥ *Commended*

There is something special about Greenwell Farm and its 300 year-old stone barn, now converted into accommodation. That speciality is homeliness, the unique atmosphere that our visitors come for. We offer warmth and comfort with blend of pine and dark oak antique furniture. High quality food using home produced, naturally reared meat and vegetables where possible. Enjoy our working mixed farm with nature trails and beautiful countryside. Closed Christmas and New Year. E-mail:greenwel1@aol.com.uk

---

④ Lands Farm, Westgate-in-Weardale, Co Durham DL13 1SN

Mrs Barbara Reed
☎ 01388 517210
BB From £20–£25
Sleeps 5
♥♥ *Highly Commended*

A friendly welcome awaits you on our 280-acre beef and sheep farm peacefully situated in beautiful Weardale. All bedrooms have luxury en suite facilities, TV and tea/coffee. Conveniently located for Durham City, Beamish Museum, Hadrian's Wall, High Force and walking in the North Pennines. Open Mar–Nov.

---

⑤ Lonton South Farm, Middleton-in-Teesdale, Barnard Castle, Co. Durham DL12 0PL

Mrs Irene Watson
☎ 01833 640409
BB From £16–£17
Sleeps 5
Listed *Commended*

A working dairy and sheep farm with beautiful views and quiet situation, one mile south of Middleton-in-Teesdale on B6277. Ideal for walking. Good local pubs for meals. One double, one twin, one single room, all with washbasins, tea/coffee-making facilities and CH. Private bathroom, TV lounge. Open Mar–Oct.

Durham — North Country

Low Cornriggs Farm, Cowshill-in-Weardale, Bishop Auckland, Co Durham DL13 1AQ ❻

Mrs Janet Ellis
☎/Fax 01388 537600
[BB] From £19.50–£26
EM From £9.80
Sleeps 6
🛏(4) 🐕 ⊞ ♿ ♙ 💼 ⓜ
👑👑 *Commended*

Luxury 200-year-old farmhouse with wonderful views over High Pennines. Antiques, en suite rooms, electric blankets, tea trays. Log fires, stone floors, beams, pine doors, full CH. Take breakfast in large conservatory, enjoy wonderful home-cooked food in licensed dining room. TV lounge. We are an Approved British Riding School offering lessons, treks, riding holidays. Good walking, Green Tourism Award Winner. Open all year.

Low Urpeth Farm, Ouston, Chester Le Street, Co Durham DH2 1BD ❼

Hilary Johnson
☎ 0191 410 2901
Fax 0191 410 0081
[BB] From £20–£25
Sleeps 6
🛏(12) ⚘ 💼 ♙ ⓜ
Listed Highly Commended

Traditional stone farmhouse with spacious and tastefully furnished rooms with TV/beverage facilities, easy chairs one double with washbasin, 2 twin en suite. Within easy reach of Beamish Museum, Durham and castles and coast of Northumberland. Directions – leave A1(M) at Chester Le Street, follow A693, at 2nd roundabout fork right to Ouston, continue 1½ miles down hill, over roundabout, turn left at 'Trees Please' sign. Closed Christmas and New Year.

Wilson House, Barningham, Richmond, North Yorkshire DL11 7EB ❽

Mrs Helen Lowes
☎ 01833 621218
[BB] From £16–£20
EM From £10
Sleeps 6
🛏 ✗ ⚘ ♙ 💼
👑👑 *Highly Commended*

Relax and unwind in a traditional country retreat. Set amidst magnificent scenery, Wilson House offers a high standard of accommodation, a relaxing atmosphere and friendly welcome. (FHG Diploma 1997.) Tour the Dales by car or take one of the many beautiful walks then return to the open fire and smell of home cooking. Varied menus using fresh local/home produce and tailored to your tastes. Open all year except Christmas.

Wythes Hill Farm, Lunedale, Middleton-in-Teesdale, Co Durham DL12 0NX ❾

Mrs June Dent
☎ 01833 640349
[BB] From £17–£18
EM From £9
Sleeps 5
🛏 ♙
👑 *Commended*

Wythes Hill is a working stock-rearing farm with panoramic views from all rooms. Situated on the Pennine Way route with many picturesque walks in Teesdale. Visit the Bowes Museum, Raby Castle and High Force Waterfall. Good plain cooking. One family room with H&C, one twin en suite. All rooms with tea/coffee-making facilities. Lounge with coal fire. Open Mar–Nov.

Self-Catering

Bail Hill, Allenshields, Blanchland, Consett, Co Durham DH8 9PP ❿

Jennifer Graham
☎ 01434 675274
[SC] From £130–£230
Sleeps 5
🛏 ⊞ ♙ 💼 ✿
🐾🐾🐾 *Commended*

Centrally heated, 2-bedroomed farmhouse with breathtaking views to Derwent Reservoir near Blanchland. Enjoy the peaceful surroundings of a typical hill farm or use as a central location for Tynedale, Durham and N E Coast. Blanchland is one of the most picturesque of Northumbrian historic villages with Abbey, pub and post office. Open fire and well-equipped kitchen. Enclosed garden and parking outside the house. Open all year.

North Country — Durham

11. Brackenbury Leases Farm, c/o Brackenbury House, Bildershaw, West Auckland, Co Durham DL14 9PL

Mrs RP Pickering
☎ 01388 832484
SC From £140–£250
Sleeps 7
Commended

This modernised farmhouse offers bright, cheerful rooms with attractive rural views. CH, double glazing, open fire, well equipped kitchen with dining area and garden make this ideal for family holidays. Central for touring Teesdale, Weardale and Northumbria. The old towns of Barnard Castle, Richmond and Durham are within easy driving distance. Open all year. Email:brackenbury@clara.net

12. Bradley Burn Holiday Cottages, Wolsingham, Weardale, Co Durham DL13 3JH

Mrs Judith Stephenson
☎/Fax 01388 527285
SC From £130–£330
Sleeps 2–6
Up to Highly Commended

Explore our fields and woods, observe modern farming, watch for owls and herons. Stay in one of four comfortable, well equipped cottages adjoining the farmhouse at Bradley Burn, at the gateway to Weardale and the North Pennines. Excellent sightseeing and walking base, or just unwind. Granary Cottage is ideal for families, Stable and Harvest Cottages perfect for couples. Our brochure has full details. Short breaks available. Open all year. Email:selfcatering@bradleyburn.demon.co.uk

13. Browney Cottage, c/o Hall Hill Farm, Lanchester, Durham DH7 0TA

Mrs Pat Gibson
☎/Fax 01388 730300
SC From £150–£260
Sleeps 4
Up to Commended

Browney Cottages are one mile from our family-run open farm. During your stay visitors can bottle feed the lambs, see fluffy chicks and lots more. Both cottages have 1 double and 1 twin. Kitchen with fridge/freezer, microwave, washer and tumble dryer. Bedlinen included. Ample parking. Open all year except Christmas.

14. Buckshott Farm Cottage, Blanchland, Consett, Co Durham DH8 9PL

Lorraine Bainbridge
☎ 01434 675227
SC From £130–£245
Sleeps 6
Commended

Attractive 2-bedroom cottage which adjoins the farmhouse and overlooks the beautiful Derwent Valley. Central heating, fitted kitchen, private garden, ample parking. Blanchlands historic village has a shop, post office, pub and a 12th century abbey. Hexham, Durham, Beamish Open Air Museum, Gateshead Metro Centre and the Northumberland coast are all within an easy day's outing. Open Apr–Oct.

3. Greenwell Hill Stables & Byre, c/o Greenwell Farm, Nr Wolsingham, Tow Law, Co Durham DL13 4PH

Linda & Mike Vickers
☎ 01388 527248
Fax 01388 526735
SC From £165–£385
Sleeps 2/6
Highly Commended

Enjoy a relaxing stay in one of two quality cottages. This is a traditional farm in peaceful countryside. Marvellous views, pleasant walks and our own nature trail with conservation area. The larger cottage has a four poster bed, dishwasher and en suite bedrooms. Both are well equipped with gas central heating, double glazing, natural beams, pine furniture, fitted carpets, comfy chintzy suites and woodburing stoves. Evening meals available. Open all year. E-mail: greenwel1@aol.com.uk

15. High House Farm Cottages, High House Farm, Houghton Le Side, Darlington DL2 2UU

Harry & Peggy Wood
☎/Fax 01388 834879
SC From £140–£340
Sleeps 2–6
Highly Commended

Gateway to Northumbria with panoramic views across Teesdale to North Yorks Moors. Near A1(M), A68 scenic route and Dere Street Roman Road. Home of 'Fairisle' Shetland sheep and 'Aymara' alpacas. Smithy, Granary and Coach House conversions, sensitively combining four-poster, beams and log burning stove with night storage heaters, power showers, TVs and other modern amenities. Open all year.

Durham   *North Country*

Katie's Cottage, c/o Low Urpeth Farm, Ouston, Chester Le Street, Co.Durham DH2 1BD   ❼

Hilary Johnson
☎ 0191 410 2901
Fax 0191 410 0081
SC From £210–£285
Sleeps 4

Highly Commended

Katie's Cottage is tastefully furnished, most comfortable and very cosy. The ground floor accommodation offers two en suite bedrooms and a delightful living area with timber beams. All linen, towels, electricity and CH are included. Excellent base for Durham, Beamish Museum, Northumberland and Hadrian's Wall. Open all year.

Stonecroft, Low Lands Farm, Low Lands, Cockfield, Bishop Auckland DL13 5AW   ⓰

Mr K & Mrs A Tallentire
☎/Fax 01388 718251
SC From £150–£250
Sleeps 4 + cot

Highly Commended

Charming old farmworker's cottage recently renovated and decorated to retain its traditional style and character. On the borders of wonderfully unspoilt Teesdale, Weardale and Durham Dales. Set in an area full of historic towns and sights. Ideally suited for walkers, families and professionals wanting a quiet restful break. Open all year.

Our farms offer a range of facilities that are illustrated by symbols in each entry.
Turn to page 16 for an explanation of the symbols.

CONFIRM BOOKINGS

Disappointments can arise from misunderstandings over the telephone.
Please write to confirm your booking.

FARM HOLIDAY BUREAU

Our Internet address is
http://www.webscape.co.uk/farmaccom/

Lancashire

Arnside & Silverdale, Morecambe Bay, Vale of Lune, Pennine Way, Forest of Bowland & Ribble Valley

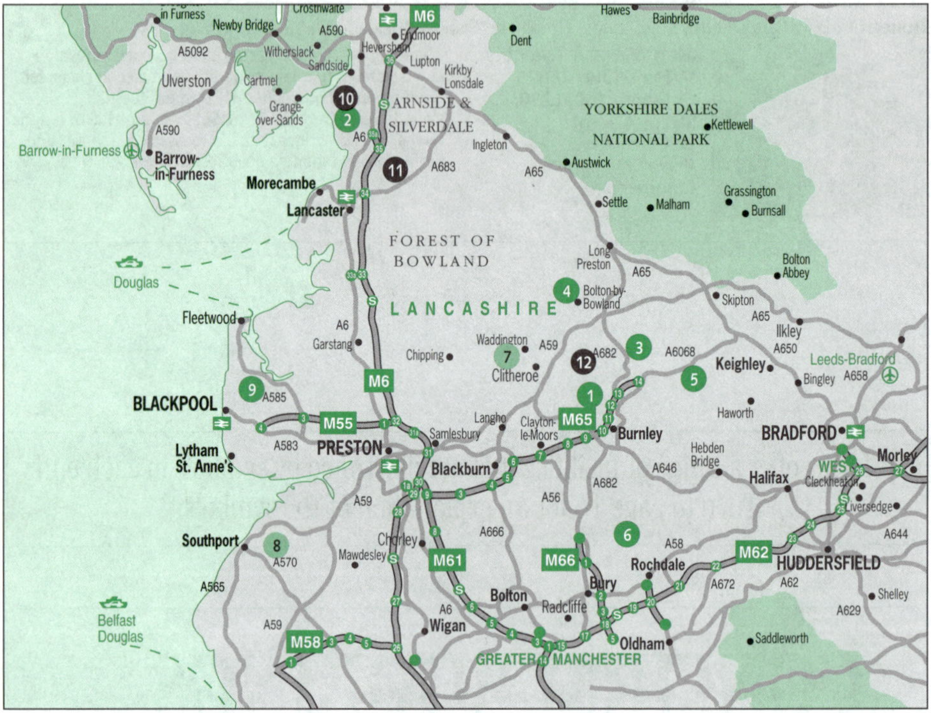

Key
1 Bed & Breakfast
1 Self-Catering
1 B&B and SC
1 Camping Barns
1 Camping & Caravanning

Lancashire is a truly beautiful county, areas of which still await discovery by many visitors – a treat lies in store for them. The bracing, northern coastline encompasses the resorts of Morecambe, Arnside and Silverdale, lively Blackpool with its famous illuminations and elegant Southport. The scenic countryside of Forest of Bowland, Ribble Valley and Pendle are rich in wildlife and offer excellent walking. While market towns like Clitheroe with its castle and such unspoilt villages as Barley, Downham (where 'Whistle Down the Wind' was filmed) and Wycoller offer havens away from the hustle and bustle. The area is also known for its 'Hetty Wainthrop' connections; and for bargain hunters, we have some of the best mill shops in the country.

If you would like help in finding suitable farm accommodation, turn to the full listing of farm groups on pages 360 to 363 to find appropriate contact details for this area.

Lancashire North Country

Bed and Breakfast
(and evening meal)

Blakey Hall Farm, Red Lane, Colne, Lancashire BB8 9TD

Mrs R Boothman
☎ 01282 863121
BB From £18–£22
EM From £7.50
Sleeps 6
Listed Commended

Delightful old Grade II listed working dairy farm. Oliver Cromwell is reputed to have stayed here. Ideally situated to provide the holidaymaker with a good base to visit the Yorkshire Dales/Brontë Country and Lake District. Full English breakfast. Comfortable accommodation, guests' own TV lounge. 3 bedrooms, 1 en suite, tea/coffee facilities. Open all year.

Galley Hall Farm, Shore Road, Carnforth, Lancashire LA5 9HZ

Vera Casson
☎ 01524 732544
BB From £16–£18
EM From £10
Sleeps 5
Listed Commended

Galley Hall is situated on the coast within easy reach of the Lake District, the Dales and historic Lancaster. We offer a warm and friendly welcome to all at our working farm and 17th century farmhouse with views of Lakeland hills and Morecombe Bay. Share the comforts of our large lounge with TV and log fires. Bedrooms have washbasins, tea-making facilities and TV on request. 5 minutes from M6 J35. Open Jan–Nov.

Higher Wanless Farm, Red Lane, Colne, Lancashire BB8 7JP

Carole Mitson
☎ 01282 865301
BB From £19–£24
EM From £11
Sleeps 4
Highly Commended

Ideally situated for visiting 'Pendle Witch' country, Haworth or Yorkshire Dales – the farm nestles peacefully alongside the Leeds/Liverpool Canal. Shire horses and sheep are reared on the farm, where the warmest of welcomes awaits you. Spacious and luxurious bedrooms (1 en suite) offer every comfort for our guests. Several country inns nearby offering wide range of meal facilities. AA selected establishment. Open mid Jan–mid Dec.

Middle Flass Lodge, Settle Road, Bolton-by-Bowland, Nr Clitheroe, Lancashire BB7 4NY

Joan M Simpson
☎ 01200 447259
Fax 01200 447300
BB From £20–£27.50
EM From £14
Sleeps 11
Commended

Our tastefully converted barn/cow byre, based on the family farm, has idyllic views of the surrounding countryside. An ideal touring base, being situated on Lancashire and Yorkshire border. Full en suite facilities, tea/coffee, CH, TV, etc. Comfortable lounge with stove. Cosy dining room with chef prepared cuisine. Licensed. Open all year.

Parson Lee Farm, Wycoller, Colne, Lancashire BB8 8SU

Patricia Hodgson
☎ 01282 864747
BB From £15–£17
EM £7
Sleeps 6
Commended

There's a warm welcome at our 110-acre sheep farm on the edge of beautiful Wycoller Country Park. The 250-year old farmhouse, with exposed beams and mullion windows, is peacefully located and perfect for walking, being on the Brontë and Pendle Ways. Easy access to Lancashire or Yorkshire. Pendle Way walking breaks with transport. En suite bedrooms, furnished in country style, have tea/coffee-making facilities. Open all year except Christmas & New Year.
E-mail: pathodgson@hotmail.com

North Country   Lancashire

6 Pasture Bottom Farm, Bacup, Lancashire OL13 9UZ

Ann Isherwood
☎/Fax 01706 873790
[BB] From £15
EM From £7
Sleeps 4
♿ 🐕 ♨
♿ Approved

We offer farmhouse accommodation in a quite rural area on a true working beef farm in a relaxed away-from-it-all atmosphere. Magnificent country views. Centrally located for Pennines and Yorkshire moors, Lancashire hill country and within easy reach of Manchester by M66, making it ideal for business people. Closed Christmas and New Year.

7 Rakefoot Farm, Chaigley, Nr Clitheroe, Lancashire BB7 3LY

Mrs Pat Gifford
☎ 01995 61332
0589 279063
[BB] From £13.50–£18.50
EM £10
Sleeps 6
♿ 🐕 ♨ ♟ ▪ ✿ ◉
Applied

A warm welcome awaits on peaceful 100-acre family farm in beautiful Forest of Bowland in 17th century farmhouse and traditional stone barn conversion. Refreshments on arrival, superb home cooking (EM by arrangement). Excellent accommodation, panoramic views. Laundry, log fires, CH, games room, babysitting. 3 miles Chipping village, 8 miles M6 J31A. Open all year.

8 Sandy Brook Farm, Wyke Cop Road, Scarisbrick, Southport, Lancashire PR8 5LR

Mrs W E Core
☎ 01704 880337
[BB] From £17
Sleeps 15
♿ 🐎 ▪ ✿
♿ ♿ Commended

This small, comfortable arable farm is situated in the rural area of Scarisbrick, midway between the seaside town of Southport and the ancient town of Ormskirk. A570 ½ mile. The converted farm buildings are attractively furnished, and all bedrooms have en suite facilities, colour TV and tea/coffee facilities. Silver winners NWTB Place to Stay, 'Commended' award Holiday Care Service. Open all year except Christmas.

9 Todderstaffe Hall Farm, off Fairfield Road, Singleton, Poulton-le-Fylde, Lancashire FY6 8LF

Mrs Maureen Smith
☎/Fax 01253 882537
[BB] From £18–£25
Sleeps 4
♿ 🐕 ✂ 🍴 ✿ ▪
♿ ♿ Highly Commended

A warm welcome awaits you at Todderstaffe as well as a pot of tea! We are just 4 miles from the attractions of Blackpool in a peaceful corner of the Fylde. Oak beams and open fires maintain the charm of the old farmhouse but comfort and good food are a priority. One en suite twin/family room with colour TV, and tea making facilities. Children welcome. Open Jan–Nov.

Self-Catering

10 Brackenthwaite Cottages, Brackenthwaite Farm, Yealand Redmayne, Carnforth LA5 9TE

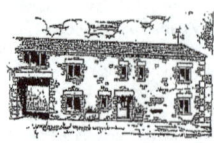

Susan Clarke
☎/Fax 015395 63276
[SC] From £95–£330
Sleeps 4/6
♿ 🐕 ♨ ▪
🗝🗝 – 🗝🗝🗝
Commended

Relax comfortably in one of our three cottages. Walk our nature trail or through nearby nature reserves in AONB. Children can play on the adventure playground and feed the animals. Keepers Cottage has all rooms on a single level, the Old Stables have beams and exposed limestone. Laundry room available. Short lets Nov–Easter. Open all year.

Lancashire   North Country

Garden Cottage, High Snab, Gressingham, Lancaster LA2 8LS

Mrs Margaret Burrow
☎ 015242 21347
SC From £200–£280
Sleeps 4 + cot
Commended

Garden cottage, with its own private drive and garden, adjoins our farmhouse on a working dairy and sheep farm in a quiet location. Ideal for touring lakes, dales and coast. Award winner. Conservatory and utility room with washer and drier. Well equipped kitchen/oak beamed lounge. Two bedrooms, 1 double, 1 twin, snooker table, bathroom with shower. CH from farmhouse, cot/high chair available. Electric and linen included. 5 miles M6 J35. Brochure. Open Mar–Nov.

11

Higher Gills Farm, Rimington, Clitheroe, Lancashire BB7 4DA

Freda M Pilkington
☎ 01200 445370
SC From £180–£280
Sleeps 6
Commended

A traditional stable converted into two holiday apartments with spectacular views of the Ribble Valley, situated on a family working hill farm. Footpaths leading to open moorland. 4 miles from Gisburn. 'Granary' on first floor has exposed beams. 'Lower Laithe' on ground floor has Grade 2 wheelchair access. Both have large patio and safe grassed area. Open all year.

12

Rakefoot Barn, Rakefoot Farm, Chaigley, Nr Clitheroe, Lancashire BB7 3LY

Mrs Pat Gifford
☎ 01995 61332
0589 279063
SC From £75–£395
Sleeps 2–8
Up to Highly Commended

A warm welcome awaits on peaceful 100-acre family farm in Forest of Bowland. Traditional stone barn conversion, original features, superbly furnished. Fully fitted kitchens, CH, woodburners, en suite bedrooms (some ground floor). Meals service, laundry, games room, play areas, patios, gardens, panoramic views. Babysitting. 3 miles Chipping village, 3 miles M6 J31A. 3 properties can be internally interlinked to sleep 16. Open all year.

7

Sandy Brook Farm, Wyke Cop Road, Scarisbrick, Southport PR8 5LR

Mr W H Core
☎ 01704 880337
SC From £100–£260
Sleeps 2/6
Commended

Our newly converted 18th century barn, which stands in peaceful countryside, offers five superbly equipped and traditionally furnished holiday apartments. We are 3½ miles from the seaside town of Southport and close to many other places of interest. The apartments sleep 2/6 and 'The Dairy' is especially equipped for disabled guests. Open all year.

8

Our Internet address is
http://www.webscape.co.uk/farmaccom/

FARM HOLIDAY BUREAU

Yorkshire

Dales, Brontë Country, South, West & Harrogate

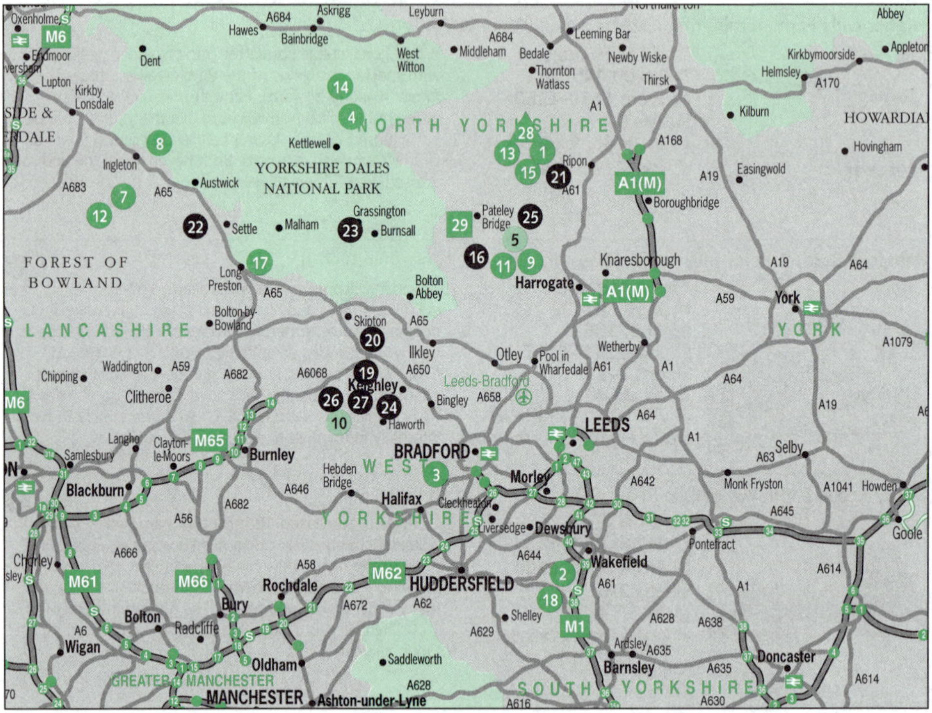

Key

- 1 Bed & Breakfast
- 1 Self-Catering
- 1 B&B and SC
- 1 Bunkhouses Camping Barns
- 1 Camping & Caravanning

Mention the Yorkshire Dales and you evoke lush, green valleys, dry stone walls and fields dotted with stone barns, clear tumbling streams, quaint villages and warm, friendly people. 'Brontë Country' conjures up images of windswept moors, heather, romance, deep valleys, woollen mills and industrial heritage. For history and heritage visit Haworth and the Brontë Parsonage, Bolton Abbey, Skipton Castle and the Bradford Industrial Museum. Elegant Harrogate is famed for its wide open spaces and gardens, while *Last of the Summer Wine* Country' can be found around Holmfirth. Shop til you drop in mill shops and open-air markets or take a ride on one of our steam railways. It's all here!

If you would like help in finding suitable farm accommodation, turn to the full listing of farm groups on pages 360 to 363 to find appropriate contact details for this area

Yorkshire  North Country

Bed and Breakfast
(and evening meal)

Bay Tree Farm, Aldfield, Nr Fountains Abbey, Ripon, North Yorkshire HG4 3BE

Valerie Leeming
☎/Fax 01765 620394
BB From £22.50–£25
EM From £12
Sleeps 12

Highly Commended

As featured in *Which* B&B, this 17th century converted stone hay barn combines character with comfort in quiet hamlet. Beautiful Fountains Abbey, ½ mile. York, Harrogate and Dales all in easy reach. Lovely circular walks from our door returning to open fires and super cooking (HE trained). All rooms en suite, CH, beverages, TV. Kettle always on the boil. Ideal for 'get togethers' or just a peaceful few days. Colour brochure. Open all year.

Birch Laithes Farm, Bretton Lane, Bretton, Wakefield, West Yorkshire WF4 4LF

Pat Hoyland
☎ 01924 252129
BB From £17–£19
Sleeps 6

Commended

A mixed working farm with 18th century house. Comfortable bedrooms, tea/coffee-making facilities, TV, separate dining room and TV lounge, central heating. Ideally situated for Yorkshire towns and countryside, Yorkshire Sculpture Park nearby. 1½ mile J38/39 M1. Open all year.

Brow Top Farm, Baldwin Lane, Clayton, Bradford, West Yorkshire BD14 6PS

Margaret Priestley
☎/Fax 01274 882178
BB From £17.50–£20
Sleeps 4

Highly Commended

Visitors are most welcome to our family dairy and beef farm. The farmhouse has recently been modernised to a very high standard with central heating throughout. 1 double, 1 twin and 1 family room all with private bathroom, colour TV, fridge and tea/coffee-making facilities. Conveniently situated for visiting the Dales and Brontë Country. Plenty of good eating places in the area. Open all year (closed Christmas).

Bushey Lodge Farm, Starbotton, Skipton, North Yorkshire BD23 5HY

Rosie Lister
☎/Fax 01756 760424
BB From £20–£22.50
Sleeps 4

Highly Commended

Traditional Dales farmhouse in quiet position in Upper Wharfedale village, with extensive views along the valley, much of which is owned and protected by the National Trust. Superb walking and sightseeing area. Local inns provide excellent evening meals. Each bedroom has en suite bathroom, TV and tea/coffee-making facilities, hairdryer. Open all year except Christmas.

Clough House Farm, Summerbridge, Harrogate, North Yorkshire HG3 4JR

Mrs Brenda Walmsley
☎ 01423 780823
BB From £22.50–£45
EM From £10
Sleeps 14

Commended

17th century farmhouse/attached farm building converted into 8 delightful en suite bedrooms (three ground floor) tastefully decorated with CH and tea/coffee-making facilities. Peaceful position with far-reaching views. Private guests' sitting and dining room. Private horse riding lessons or hack around beautiful countryside. Featured in the *Which? Good Bed and Breakfast Guide* and recommended by the *Good Bed and Breakfast Guide.* Open all year.

North Country   Yorkshire

6 Far Laithe Farm, Laycock, Keighley, West Yorkshire BD22 0PU

Sylvia Lee
☎ 01535 661993
BB From £19.50–£21.50
EM From £12
Sleeps 4
⌕(12) ⊞ ♨
♛♛ Highly Commended

Traditional Yorkshire farm close to Haworth, Skipton and the Dales, set in the heart of open countryside. Tea-making facilities and colour TV in all bedrooms. Luxury en suite facilities. Enjoy dinner in our licensed oak-furnished dining room. We pride ourselves on the quality of our food and hospitality and look forward to welcoming you to our home. Open all year.

---

7 Fowgill Park Farm, High Bentham, Nr Lancaster, North Yorkshire LA2 7AH

Shirley Metcalfe
☎ 01524 261630
BB From £16–£18
EM From £10
Sleeps 4
⌕ 🐎 ✂ ♨ ◉
♛♛ Commended

Fowgill is a stock rearing farm, ideal for those who wish to stay where it is quiet. Guests enjoy panoramic views of the Dales and Fells. A good centre for visiting the Lakes, Dales, coast, waterfalls and caves. Beamed bedrooms have washbasins, shaver points and tea/coffee-making facilities; two bedrooms en suite. Comfortable beamed lounge with television. Separate dining room. Bedtime drink included. Open Easter–Oct.

---

8 Gatehouse Farm, Far Westhouse, Ingleton, North Yorkshire LA6 3NR

Nancy Lund
☎ 015242 41458/41307
BB From £17–£20
EM From £9
Sleeps 6
⌕ 🐎 ✂ ♨ 🚬 ◉
♛♛ Commended

Bryan and Nancy welcome you to our dairy and sheep farm built in 1740, rooms with old oak beams in elevated position enjoying panoramic views over open countryside in the YORKSHIRE DALES NATIONAL PARK. Guests' dining room, and lounge with colour TV. Bedroom with private facilities and tea trays. Welcome drink on arrival. 15 miles J34 M6, also J36 1½ miles west of Ingleton just off A65. Open all year (closed Christmas and New Year).

---

9 Graystone View Farm, Graystone Plain Lane, Hampsthwaite, Harrogate, North Yorkshire HG3 2LY

Gloria Metcalfe
☎ 01423 770324
Fax 01423 772536
BB From £20–£25
Sleeps 6
⌕ 🐎 ♨ ⚘ ◉
♛♛ Commended

18th century farmhouse in tranquil setting with comfortable rooms to come back to after a lovely day seeing the wonderful sights that Yorkshire has to offer. Bedrooms have tea/coffee-making facilities. We are a family run farm set in 100 acres and located ¼ mile from the A59 west of Harrogate. Open all year except Christmas and New Year.

---

10 Hole Farm, Dimples Lane, Haworth, Keighley, West Yorkshire BD22 8QT

Janet Milner
☎/Fax 01535 644755
BB From £20–£22
Sleeps 4
⌕(12) ✂ ⚘ ♨ ◉
♛♛ Highly Commended

17th century farmhouse, on 8 acre small holding 5 minutes walk from Brontë Parsonage and 2 minutes from the moors. One twin and one double en suite rooms, central heating, colour TV; tea.coffee-making facilities. Full English breakfast. Have your breakfast watching the peacocks on the lawn. Open all year except Christmas.

---

11 Knabbs Ash, Skipton Road, Kettlesing, Felliscliffe, Nr Harrogate, North Yorkshire HG3 2LT

Sheila Smith
☎ 01423 771040
Fax 01423 771515
BB From £22.50
Sleeps 6
⌕(10) ✂ 🚬 ♨ ◉
♛♛ Highly Commended

White Rose Award-winning B&B. Recommended by *Which? Good Bed and Breakfast Guide*. Smallholding 6 miles west of Harrogate off the A59 in a tranquil position with delightful views over the countryside. En suite rooms enhanced by quality furnishings, colour TV, hair dryer, tea/coffee-making facilities, CH. Private guest sitting and dining room with separate tables. Ideal area for walking and touring. Good local inns. Open all year except Christmas.

Yorkshire North Country

Lane House Farm, High Bentham, Lancaster, North Yorkshire LA2 7DJ

Betty Clapham
☎ 015242 61479
BB From £16.50–£18
Sleeps 6
⌂ ⚞ ✂ ♨ ♠ ⊕
♛ ♛ Commended

Enjoy a relaxing break at our 17th century beamed farmhouse, within ½ mile of the Forest of Bowland, with beautiful views of the Yorkshire Dales. 1 mile from the market town of High Bentham, ½ hour from M6. Ideal for caves, waterfalls, touring the Lakes. Bedrooms have washbasins and tea-making trays. En suite facilities. Guests' lounge with colour TV. Separate dining room. Open Mar–Nov.

North Pasture Farm, Brimham Rocks, Summerbridge, Harrogate, North Yorkshire HG3 4DW

Eileen Payne
☎ 01423 711470
BB From £22–£24
EM From £13.50
Sleeps 4
✂ ⚞ ♨ ♠ ⊕
♛ ♛ ♛ Highly Commended

North Pasture Farm, a 14th century listed farmhouse, beamed and mullioned and oozing with character, awaits discerning guests. Warm and cosy with central heating throughout, together with en suite bedrooms and separate dining room and separate TV lounge. Peaceful and quiet, sheltered by Brimham Rocks. Within easy reach of Harrogate, Ripon, Skipton, York and Fountains Abbey. Open Mar–Nov.

Redmire Farm, Buckden, Nr Skipton, North Yorkshire BD23 5JD

Mrs Julia Horner
☎ 01756 760253
Fax 01756 760360
BB From £20–£22.50
EM £12.50
Sleeps 6
✂ ♠ ♛ ♨ ⊕
♛ ♛ Highly Commended

Family-run, traditional working hill farm set in heart of Yorkshire Dales. 1,600 acres of stunning woodland, moorland and farmed parkland bound by 2½ mile stretch of the River Wharfe. Former shooting lodge, now sympathetically restored and very comfortably refurbished, with 2 double and 1 twin rooms, all en suite with CH, colour TV and beverages. House accessible all day, cosy lounge. A welcoming family providing a wholesome table of mainly home-reared and locally produced food. Open all year except Christmas.

St George's Court, Old Home Farm, High Grantley, Ripon, North Yorkshire HG4 3EU

Mrs Sandra Gordon
☎ 01765 620618
BB From £21–£22.50
Sleeps 12
⌂(2) ⚞ ♿ ♠ ♛ ♨ ⊕
♛ ♛ Commended

Beautifully situated accommodation in renovated farm buildings. Comfortable ground floor en suite rooms with colour TV and tea/coffee facilities, all with views of open countryside. Breakfast in our beautiful listed farmhouse and enjoy the view from our conservatory dining room. Peace and tranquillity are our passwords. Open all year.

Scaife Hall Farm, Blubberhouses, Otley, West Yorkshire LS21 2PL

Christine Ryder
☎/Fax 01943 880354
BB From £21
Sleeps 6
⌂ ✂ ♨ ♠ ⊕
♛ ♛ Highly Commended

Scaife Hall is a working farm set in a tranquil, rural location. Recommended by *Which? Good Bed and Breakfast Guide*, our 19th century farmhouse offers two double and one twin bedded rooms, each tastefully decorated. All en suite with beverage tray, clock radio, hairdryer, CH. Private guests' lounge with colour TV, dining room for hearty breakfasts. Local inns provide excellent meals. Open all year except Christmas and New Year.

Wenningber Farm, Hellifield, Nr Skipton, North Yorkshire BD23 4JR

Mrs Barbara Phillip
☎ 01729 850856
BB From £19–£21
Sleeps 4
⌂ ⚞ ✂ ♨ ♠ ♛ ⊕
♛ Highly Commended

Wenningber Farm is a charming 16th century farmhouse just 4 miles from Malham in the heart of the Yorkshire Dales. Furnished to a very high standard with oak beams and inglenook fireplace. Full central heating, H&C in both rooms, tea and coffee-making facilities. Warm welcome assured. Open all year except Christmas.

North Country   *Yorkshire*

(18) White Cross Farm, Ash Lane, Emley, Nr Huddersfield, West Yorkshire HD8 9QU

Marie Gill
☎ 01924 848339
BB From £17–£19
Sleeps 5
Listed *Approved*

Mixed working farm with listed farmhouse. Some buildings date from 12th century when monks from Byland Abbey lived here and dug for iron ore and kept sheep. Set in rolling Pennine countryside. Tea/coffee-making facilities, TV, central heating in all bedrooms. Close to Yorkshire Mining Museum, Yorkshire Sculpture Park and Holmfirth (Last of Summer Wine country). 3 miles from M1 (jct. 38/39). Open all year.

Self-Catering

(19) Bottoms Farm Cottages, Bottoms Farm, Laycock, nr Keighley, West Yorkshire BD22 0QD

Mrs J Parr
☎/Fax 01535 607720
SC From £140–£270
Sleep 2/4

Highly Commended

Bottoms Farm is a rural 35-acre sheep farm situated on the south side of a beautiful valley with spectacular views. Howarth 4 miles, Skipton 7 miles. These luxury cottages have been recently converted to the highest standard from 200 years mistal/barn. Fully equipped. Heating and linen included. Sorry no pets. Open all year.

(20) Cawder Hall Cottages, c/o Cawder Hall, Cawder Lane, Skipton, North Yorkshire BD23 2QQ

Anne Pearson
☎ 01756 791579
Fax 01756 797036
SC From £130–£360
Sleeps 2/6

Up to Highly Commended

Enjoy the peace and quiet of our warm, welcoming cottages which, while being surrounded by fields of animals are only 1 mile from Skipton with its thriving street market, medieval castle and church. Each cottage is well equipped (colour TV, video, microwave) and is suitable for disabled guests. There is a lawned garden, barbecue, phone, laundry room and children's play area. Linen, gas and electricity included as are cots and high chairs. Open all year.

(5) Clough House Farm, Summerbridge, Harrogate, North Yorkshire HG3 4JR

Mrs Brenda Walmsley
☎ 01423 780823
SC From £120–£280
EM from £12.50
5 cottages + flat

Commended

Clough House Farm offers five delightful small stone cottages and one 2-bedroom flat. Tastefully decorated, fully equipped, heating and linen included. Breakfast and evening meals also available. Village of Summerbridge 5-minute walk. Brimham Rocks and Fountains Abbey close by. Featured in the *Which? Good Bed and Breakfast Guide* and recommended by the *Good Bed and Breakfast Guide*. Open all year.

(21) Dukes Place, Fountains Abbey Road, Bishop Thornton, Harrogate, North Yorkshire HG3 3JY

Jaki Moorhouse
☎ 01765 620229
Fax 01765 620454
SC From £145–£350
Sleeps 2–6

Up to Highly Commended

Situated in the heart of Nidderdale yet close to Harrogate, Dukes Place is a well-maintained property comprising the owners' 18th century farmhouse and cottage-style apartments developed from the original farm buildings. Working stables from which riding can be arranged. Pets welcome. Open all year.

Yorkshire *North Country*

Heather & Bilberry Cottages, Hole Farm, Dimples Lane, Haworth, Keighley, West Yorkshire BD22 8QT

Mrs Janet Milner
☎/Fax 01535 644755
SC From £225–£550
Sleeps 4/8 + cot
Highly Commended

The old barn has been carefully converted to make two cottages with most bedrooms en suite. We are a small working farm, the sort that appears in children's Ladybird books. Gloria the sow, Gilbert the turkey, foals and calves. Ideal for children. A short walk to the village to see the Brontë Museum or a walk on the moors 2 minutes from our door. Sorry no pets. Open all year.

Layhead Farm Cottages, Field House, Rathmell, Settle, North Yorkshire BD24 0LD

Rosemary Hyslop
☎ 01729 840234
Fax 01729 840775
SC From £190–£340
Sleeps 7
Applied

Layhead Farm Cottages are located on a working farm on the edge of the Dales village of Rathmell, quiet and peaceful yet only 4 miles from the market town of Settle. The conversion of an old stone barn has resulted in two cottages, modern and comfortable yet full of charm and character. Open all year.

Maypole Cottage, Blackburn House Farm, Thorpe, Skipton, North Yorkshire BD23 6BJ

Liz Gamble
☎ 01756 720609
SC From £190–£330
Sleeps 4
Highly Commended

An 18th century stable converted to a particularly high standard in the tiny hamlet of Thorpe near Burnsall. This well equipped cottage has full central heating, exposed beams and stonework open fire. Colour TV, microwave, washer/dryer. Bathroom with shower. Linen provided. Large walled garden, ample parking. Open all year.

Meadow & Field Cottages, The Coach House, Spring Head, Tim Lane, Haworth, West Yorks BD22 7RX

David and Hilary Freeman
☎ 01535 644140
SC From £120–£270
Sleeps 4
Highly Commended

A warm Yorkshire welcome is assured at our two cosy cottages, converted from a 200-year-old barn, ½ mile from the Brontë sisters' Haworth and within easy reach of the Yorkshire Dales. We pride ourselves on our high standard of cleanliness and comfort. Each cottage has full CH, with colour TV, cooker, fridge, microwave, washer, dryer. Gas, electricity, linen and towels, cot, highchair inclusive. Pets by arrangement. Open all year.

Old Spring Wood Lodges, Helme Pasture, Hartwith Bank, Summerbridge, Harrogate, N Yorks HG3 4DR

Rosemary Helme
☎ 01423 780279
Fax 01423 780994
SC From £165–£510
Sleeps 2–8
Up to Highly Commended

Exclusive Scandinavian lodges in woodland setting overlooking the Nidd Valley. Also converted Dales farmhouse – mind your head on the beams! Excellently equipped, with CH. Colour TV, payphone, laundry, easy parking. Extensive woodland tracks, magnificent views. Ideal centre for Harrogate, York, Dales, coast and Herriot Country. Warm personal welcome. Pets also welcome! Open all year.

Well Head Cottage, Hanging Gate Lane, Oxenhope, Keighley, West Yorkshire BD22 9RJ

Mrs Nicola Binns
☎ 01535 647966
SC From £200–£400
Sleeps 4
Highly Commended

Delightful, well equipped stone-built cottage, full of character and old oak beams. Recently renovated and refurbished to a high standard. Enjoy the magnificent view and peaceful, rural setting while only a short walk from the centre of Haworth. Non-smokers preferred. Open all year.

North Country   *Yorkshire*

㉗ Westfield Farm Cottages, c/o Westfield Farm, Tim Lane, Haworth, West Yorkshire BD22 7SA

Clare Pickles
☎ 01535 644568
Fax 01535 646686
SC From £150–£420
Sleeps 2/6

Highly Commended

Delightful cottages with stunning views overlooking Brontë Parsonage and moorland. Hundreds of acres of grazed farmland. Sheep, hens, haymaking. Peace and tranquillity. Farm trail, safe river. Farmhouse sleeps 6, cottages sleep 2–6. Cottage for 2 disabled guests. Colour TV, automatic washer, microwave in each. Dogs by arrangement. Children's outdoor play area and indoor barn. Open all year. E-mail: c.p.pickles@bradford.ac.uk

Camping and Caravanning

㉘ Woodhouse Farm Caravan Park, Winksley, Nr Ripon, North Yorkshire HG4 3PG

Alison Hitchen
☎ 01765 658309
Fax 01765 658882
SC From £160–£200

✓✓✓✓

Woodhouse Farm and Country Park is set amidst 56 acres of natural woodland and meadows with its own 2½ acre coarse fishing lake, children's play area and games room. Close by are Fountains Abbey and Brimham rocks with Ripon, Britain's smallest city and famous for its cathedral, just 6 miles away. Open Easter–Oct.

Bunkhouse/Camping Barn

㉙ West End Outdoor Centre, Whitmoor Farm, West End, Summerbridge, Harrogate, North Yorkshire HG3 4BA

Margaret Verity
☎/Fax 01943 880207
SC Sole use of centre £800 per week
From £5 pppn
Sleeps 30

Inspected

Set amidst stunning scenery overlooking Thruscross reservoir in a Designated Area of Outstanding Natural Beauty adjoining the Dales National Park. The Centre offers excellent facilities for 30 people in 9 bedrooms. No meters, AGA cooker, private parking. 12 miles Harrogate and Skipton, 30 miles York. Ideal venue for the larger family. Open all year.

Yorkshire
Coast, Moors & Dales

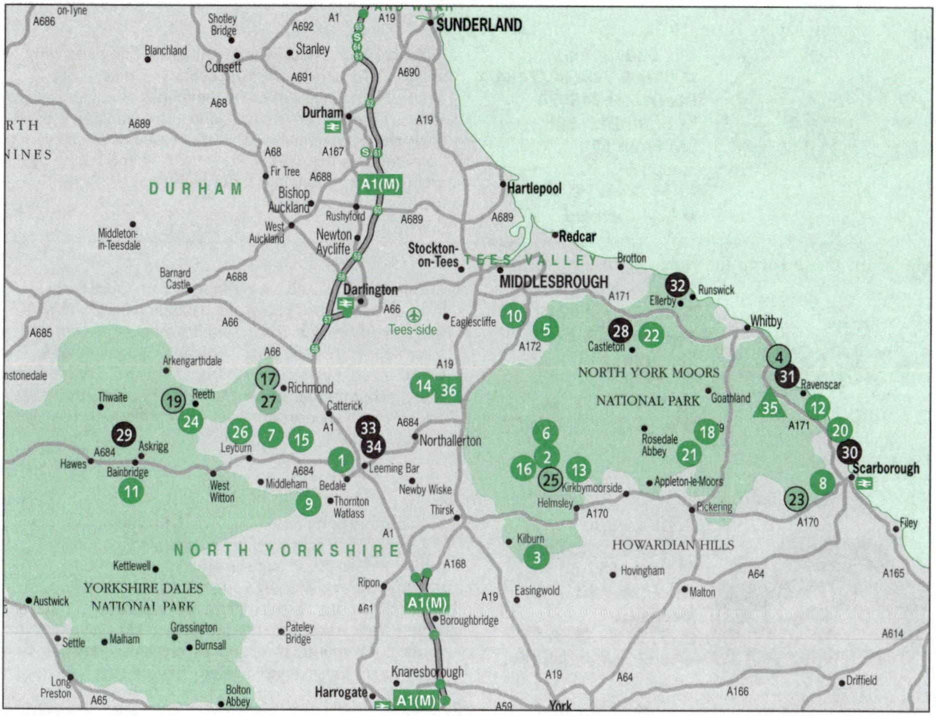

Key

- **1** Bed & Breakfast
- **1** Self-Catering
- **1** B&B and SC
- **1** Bunkhouses Camping Barns
- **1** Camping & Caravanning

Take a trip around North Yorkshire and sample for yourself the delights of this area as portrayed in James Herriot's *All Creatures Great and Small*, based in Thirsk, and TV's *Heartbeat* which is centred on Goathland. Coast and countryside are both near at hand. Quaint Robin Hood's Bay contrasts with the lively seaside resorts of Whitby and Scarborough. Inland, enjoy the spendour of Swaledale and Wensleydale with their tumbling waterfalls and historic castles, and sample the local fayre, including cheeses and beer. Explore the many romantic ruined abbeys, take a nostalgic trip on the North Yorkshire Moors Steam Railway or pay respects to Captain Cook in Great Ayton, his former home. Or maybe just take a picnic onto the moors and breathe in the beauty of the area.

If you would like help in finding suitable farm accommodation, turn to the full listing of farm groups on pages 360 to 363 to find appropriate contact details for this area.

North Country Yorkshire

Bed and Breakfast
(and evening meal)

① **Ainderby Myers Farm,** Nr Hackforth, Bedale, North Yorkshire DL8 1PF

Mrs Valerie Anderson
☎ 01609 748668/748424
Fax 01609 748424
BB From £16–£18
EM From £10
Sleeps 6
ぢ ⅍ ♞ ■ ⅋ ⦿
♛ Commended

Historical manor house set amidst moors and dales with origins going back to the 10th century. Terrific atmosphere. Once farmed by the monks of Jervaulx Abbey. Sheep, crops, pastures and a stream. Walk the fields and discover the wildlife. Visit castles and abbeys. Excellent base for walkers. Pony trekking and fishing by arrangement. Traditional Yorkshire breakfasts. Picnic facilities. Open all year.

② **Barn Close Farm,** Rievaulx, Helmsley, North Yorkshire YO62 5LH

Joan Milburn
☎ 01439 798321
BB From £20–£22
EM From £12
Sleeps 5
ぢ ⅍ ♞ ⅋ ♞ ■
♛♛♛ Commended

Comfortable, relaxed atmosphere at Barn Close Farm set in an idyllic wooded valley of outstanding beauty close to Rievaulx Abbey and Old Byland. Farmhouse cooking recommended by the Daily Telegraph. Speciality home baked bread. Riding, walking from farmyard. Central for touring countryside, 1 hour from York or coast. 1 en suite, 1 family with private bathroom, tea/coffee-making facilities. Open all year.

③ **Carr House Farm,** Shallowdale, Ampleforth, York, North Yorkshire YO6 4ED

Anna Lupton
☎ 01347 868526
BB From £17.50
EM From £10
Sleeps 6
ぢ(7) ⅍ ♞ ⅋ ■ ⦿
♛ ♛ Commended

16th century farmhouse filled with memorabilia. Part of 400-acre family farm for 5 generations. Internationally recommended, 'fresh air fiend's dream! Good food, walking, warm welcome'. Romantic four-poster bedroom en suite. Relaxing, peaceful, informal – 'heartbeat country'. ½ hour York. Make your holiday memorable – own spring water, north country sheep, ponds, orchards, green fields, wild flowers. Open all year (closed Christmas and New Year).

④ **Croft Farm,** Church Lane, Fylingthorpe, Whitby, North Yorkshire YO22 4PW

Pauline Featherstone
☎/Fax 01947 880231
BB From £20
Sleeps 6
ぢ(5) ⅍ ■ ⅋ ⦿
Listed *Highly Commended*

18th century farmhouse in lawned garden on small working farm overlooking Robin Hood's Bay. Tastefully furnished in the 'olde worlde' charm with open beams, staircase and fireplaces. Rooms with washbasins (1 en suite) all with tea-making facilities and panoramic views of the sea, moors and country-side. Guests' lounge, bathroom. Ideal base for coastal resorts, walking and touring the beauty spots of North Yorkshire. Our speciality is a good hearty breakfast. Open Easter–mid-Oct.

⑤ **Dromonby Hall Farm,** Busby Lane, Kirkby-in-Cleveland, Stokesley, Middlesbrough TS9 7AP

Mrs Patricia Weighell
☎/Fax 01642 712312
BB From £17.50–£19
Sleeps 6
ぢ(2) ♜ ⅍ ♟ ■ ⅋ ⦿
♛ Commended

Modern farmhouse on 170-acre working farm with superb views of Cleveland Hills. Ideal for walking or touring by car. Easy access from A19 and B1257, 8 miles south of Middlesbrough. ½ hr drive from coast and from Teesside. A warm welcome and good food. Horse riding available locally. Enjoy the peace and beautiful surroundings. Open all year.

Yorkshire — North Country

Easterside Farm, Hawnby, Helmsley, North Yorkshire YO62 5QT ⑥

Mrs Sarah Wood
☎ 01439 798277
From £20–£22
EM From £12
Sleeps 12

Commended

A large 18th century Grade II listed farmhouse, nestling on Easterside Hill and enjoying panoramic views. Ideal base for walking, touring, the coast and the city of York. Enjoy good food and a warm welcome in comfortable surroundings. All rooms have en suite facilities. Open all year (closed Christmas).

Elmfield Country House, Arrathorne, Bedale, North Yorkshire DL8 1NE ⑦

Edith & Jim Lillie
☎ 01677 450558
Fax 01677 450557
From £22–£31
EM From £12
Sleeps 20

Highly Commended

Situated between Richmond and Bedale. Superb views of surrounding countryside, relaxed friendly atmosphere in luxurious country house. 9 spacious bedrooms (all en suite) including a four-poster bed, twin and family rooms. 2 bedrooms equipped for disabled. All with colour TV (satellite channel), radio, phone, tea/coffee-making facilities, CH. Lounge and bar (residential licence), dining room, games room, large conservatory and solarium. Excellent home cooking. Open all year.

The Grainary, Keasbeck Hill Farm, Harwood Dale, Scarborough, North Yorkshire YO13 0DT ⑧

John & Lynda Simpson
☎/Fax 01723 870026
From £19–£23
EM From £8.50
Sleeps 35

Commended

Midway between Scarborough and Whitby, set in 200 acres of National Park countryside, we are a mixed farm with lots of friendly animals. Close to Heartbeat Country, coast and moors, six specially created conservation areas and wildlife trails. All rooms en suite. Relax in our licensed country tea rooms. Out of season special breaks available. Open all year.

Haregill Lodge, Ellingstring, Masham, Ripon, North Yorkshire HG4 4PW ⑨

Mrs Rachel Greensit
☎/Fax 01677 460272
From £18–£19
EM From £9
Sleeps 6

Commended

Wanting a peaceful break? Then come and join us in our 18th century farmhouse set on a mixed farm. Secluded garden with play area overlooking Hambleton Hills, Vale of York. Ideal for Dales, moors and Herriot Country. Two rooms en suite and one with private facility, TV/radio, tea/coffee. Log fire, CH, satellite TV lounge, games room. Excellent home cooking with supper tray. Fishing and trekking nearby. A warm welcome awaits you.

Harker Hill Farm, Harker Hill, Seamer, Stokesley, Nr Middlesbrough, North Yorkshire TS9 5NF ⑩

Pam & John Fanthorpe
☎/Fax 01642 710431
From £17–£18
EM From £8
Sleeps 6

Listed Commended

Harker Hill is a two hundred year old farm offering warmth and comfort. The cosy accommodation includes full central heating, log fires, lounge and television. Home cooked food is served at times to suit you so businessmen visiting Teesside can enjoy early cooked breakfasts and late evening meals. Open all year except Christmas.

High Force Farm, Bainbridge, Leyburn, North Yorkshire DL8 3DL ⑪

Margaret Iveson
☎ 01969 650379
From £16–£18.50
Sleeps 6

Commended

Working hill farm used in James Herriot TV programme. Ideal centre for exploring the Dales offering guests a warm welcome in a relaxed atmosphere. A non-smoking establishment. Open Jan–Nov.

North Country　　　Yorkshire

12 Island Farm, Staintondale, Scarborough, North Yorkshire YO13 0EB

Mary Clarke
☎ 01723 870249
BB From £18–£20
Sleeps 6
♥ ♥ Commended

Relax in our spacious and comfortable farmhouse and garden. All bedrooms have en suite facilities. Being close to coast and in open countryside, it is ideal for walking or visiting many places of interest. Visitors appreciate our large games room with toys, full size snooker table and tennis court. Brochure on request. Open Easter–Nov.

13 Laskill Farm Country House, Hawnby, Nr Helmsley, North Yorkshire YO62 5NB

Sue Smith
☎/Fax 01439 798268
BB From £20.50–£25
EM From £12
Sleeps 8
♥ ♥ Commended

Amidst beautiful North Yorkshire Moors, in heart of James Herriot and Heartbeat Country. Attractive farmhouse with own lake/large walled garden. Own natural spring water. High standard of food and comfort. Rooms have en suite, colour TV, beverage tray. Ideal for nearby places of interest and scenic beauty, or simply enjoy tranquil surroundings. Recommended in the *Sunday Times* and the BBC *Holiday Programme*. Open all year except Christmas Day.

14 Lovesome Hill Farm, Lovesome Hill, Northallerton, North Yorkshire DL6 2PB

Mrs Mary Pearson
☎ 01609 772311
BB From £19.50
EM From £12
Sleeps 9
♥ ♥ Commended

Come and experience life on our working farm just north of Northallerton. Relax in our individually furnished en suite rooms (two on the ground floor). CLA commendation for conversion. For that little extra Gate Cottage offers a romantic feel, with half-tester bed, corner bath and own patio. A warm welcome of tea and homemade biscuits and meals awaits you. You'll 'love' it. Brochure available. Open Mar–Nov.

15 Mill Close Farm, Patrick Brompton, Bedale, North Yorkshire DL8 1JY

Mrs Patricia Knox
☎ 01677 450257
Fax 01677 450585
BB From £19–£22
Sleeps 4
♥ ♥ Highly Commended

17th century working farm surrounded by beautiful rolling countryside at foothills of Yorkshire Dales. 2 miles from A1. Charming bedrooms. Guests' private bathrooms (one en suite), dining and sitting room with log fires. Highland cattle, sheep, calves, pony, wild flowers and woodland. A relaxing, peaceful atmosphere. Romantic walled garden with pond and summerhouse. Sumptuous breakfasts in our conservatory dining room. Colour brochure. Open Mar–Nov.

16 Mount Grace Farm, Cold Kirby, Thirsk, North Yorkshire YO7 2HL

Joyce Ashbridge
☎/Fax 01845 597389
BB From £21–£24
Sleeps 6
♥ ♥ Highly Commended

A warm welcome awaits you on working farm surrounded by beautiful open countryside with magnificent views. Ideal location for touring, or exploring the many walks in the area. Luxury en suite bedrooms with tea/coffee facilities. Spacious guests' lounge with colour TV. Garden. Enjoy delicious, generous farmhouse breakfasts cooked on our Aga. Weekly rates. Open all year except Christmas.

17 Mount Pleasant Farm, Whashton, Richmond, North Yorkshire DL11 7JP

Alison Pittaway
☎/Fax 01748 822784
BB From £20–£25
EM From £10
Sleeps 12
♥ ♥ Commended

A very warm welcome to our comfortable farmhouse set in beautiful, peaceful countryside with lovely views. Three miles from Richmond and ideally situated for exploring the North Yorkshire Dales. Renovated farm buildings offer cosy cottage-style en suite rooms, each with own front door, colour TV and beverage tray. All home cooking using fresh local produce. Table licence and friendly atmosphere. This really is a pleasant place to stay for your special holiday or short break. Open all year except Christmas.

Yorkshire *North Country*

Newgate Foot Farm, Saltersgate, Pickering, North Yorkshire YO18 7NR

Mrs Alison Johnson
☎/Fax 01751 460215
BB From £18–£23
EM From £12
Sleeps 5
⌂(5) ⌘ ⚤ ⚹ ▪ ⚘
☘ ☘ *Highly Commended*

Just 1 mile off the A169, but in a world of its own in the middle of the moors with no neighbours in sight! Enjoy walking on the moors, through the forest, or trout fishing in our own lake. See the ewes and lambs and thoroughbred mares and foals. Whitby 14 miles, York 35 miles, "Aidensfield" 6 miles. One en suite bedroom, 1 twin/3 bedded, 1 single. Open all year except Christmas.

Oxnop Hall, Low Oxnop, Gunnerside, Richmond, North Yorkshire DL11 6JJ

Annie Porter
☎/Fax 01748 886253
BB From £23–£24
EM From £14
Sleeps 11
⌂(5) ⚹ ⚤ ▪ ⊚
☘ ☘ ☘ *Commended*

Stay with us on our working hill farm with beef cattle and Swaledale sheep. Oxnop Hall is of historical interest and has recently been extended with all en suite rooms. Ideal walking and touring. We are in the Yorkshire Dales National Park, Herriot Country, an Environmentally Sensitive Area which is renowned for its stone walls, barns and flora. Good farmhouse food. Tea/coffee-making facilities. Open all year except Christmas.

Plane Tree Cottage Farm, Staintondale, Scarborough, North Yorkshire YO13 0EY

Mrs Marjorie Edmondson
☎ 01723 870796
BB From £18
EM From £10
Sleeps 4
⚤ ▪ ⚹ ⊚
Listed Approved

Plane Tree Cottage is situated on the coast, about halfway between Scarborough and Whitby. We have beautiful open views of the sea and lovely countryside. This is a small working farm with sheep, pigs, free range hens, and a very friendly cat called Danny. This small cottage is homely and cosy, and offers meals to a very high standard. Home grown produce as available. Often recommended.

Seavy Slack, Stape, Pickering, North Yorkshire YO18 8HZ

Anne Barrett
☎ 01751 473171
BB From £15–£17
EM From £12
Sleeps 6
⌂(5) ⚞ ▪ ⚹ ⊚
Listed Approved

Relax and enjoy good food and a very warm welcome on our 160-acre stock and arable farm situated on the edge of the North Yorkshire Moors. Pickering 7 miles, Whitby, Scarborough and York within easy reach. One double, one family room both with tea-making facilities. Guests' lounge/dining room with colour TV. Open all year except Christmas and New Year.

Stonebeck Gate Farm, Little Fryup, Danby, Whitby, North Yorkshire YO21 2NS

Jill Kelly
☎/Fax 01287 660363
BB From £15–£20
EM From £10
Sleeps 6
⌂ ⚹ ⚞ ▪ ⚹
Applied

Jill and Andrew Kelly welcome you to Little Fryup in the heart of the North Yorkshire Moors National Park. We offer you a comfortable base for your holiday, with guests' own bathroom, dining room and lounge (with satellite TV). Bedrooms are spacious with fine views. Evening meal by prior arrangement. Open all year.

Studley House, 67, Main Street, Ebberston, Scarborough, North Yorkshire YO13 9NR

Ernie & Jane Hodgson
☎/Fax 01723 859285
BB From £18–£20
Sleeps 6
⌂ ⊞ ⚃ ▪ ⚹ ⊚
☘ ☘ *Commended*

Studley House is situated in a pretty village with much charm and character. Enjoy an excellent Yorkshire breakfast then take a leisurely stroll by the stream. All bedrooms are en suite with hospitality trays, colour TV, own keys. CH throughout. We are central for moors, coast, pretty villages and historic York. A friendly welcome awaits. Open all year except Christmas.

North Country — Yorkshire

㉔ Summer Lodge, Low Row, Richmond, North Yorkshire DL11 6NP

Carol Porter
☎ 01748 886504
BB From £19
Sleeps 5
⛚ Commended

Set in the Yorkshire Dales National Park and the heart of Herriot Country. Working hill farm pleasantly situated in its own little valley near Low Row in Swaledale, renowned for buildings, flora, fauna and wildlife in an environmentally sensitive area. Ideal walking area. Two bedrooms, both with washbasin, CH, tea/ coffee and colour TV. Large south-facing garden. A warm welcome is assured. Open Mar–Nov.

㉕ Valley View Farm, Old Byland, Helmsley, York, North Yorkshire YO62 5LG

Sally Robinson
☎/Fax 01439 798221
BB From £25–£29
EM From £13
Sleeps 10
⛚ Highly Commended

Enjoy the delights of traditional Yorkshire hospitality, hearty country breakfasts and delicious farmhouse fayre. Relax in the beautiful countryside of the North York Moors National Park or see the many places of interest and visit historic towns. Rooms are tastefully furnished and en suite. Guests' lounge with open fire. Licensed. Way marked walks from the farmyard. Open all year.

㉖ Walburn Hall, Downholme, Richmond, North Yorkshire DL11 6AF

Diana Greenwood
☎/Fax 01748 822152
BB From £22–£24
Sleeps 5
⛚ Highly Commended

Walburn Hall is one of the few remaining working farms with a fortified farmhouse, an enclosed cobbled courtyard and terraced garden. For guests' comfort there is a separate lounge and dining room with beamed ceilings, stone fireplaces and log fires (when required). Centrally heated. Double/twin rooms (en suite) with tea/coffee-making facilities. Ideally situated between Richmond and Leyburn for exploring the Dales. Open Mar–Nov.

㉗ Whashton Springs Farm, Richmond, North Yorkshire DL11 7JS

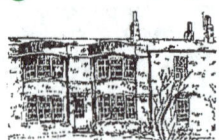

Fairlie Turnbull
☎ 01748 822884
Fax 01748 826285
BB From £20–£23
Sleeps 18
⛚ Highly Commended

400-acre beef/sheep, family working farm in heart of Herriot Country. Delightful Georgian farmhouse, featured on 'Wish You Were Here', 1988 AA 'Farmhouse of the North' Award, unusual bay windows, overlooking lawns sloping to a sparkling stream. Real Yorkshire breakfast. Home cooking using local produce. All 8 bedrooms have en suite baths/showers, TV, phone. One 4-poster bedroom. Historic Richmond 3 miles away. Open all year except Christmas & Jan.

Self-Catering

㉘ Blackmires Farm, Danby Head, Danby, Whitby, North Yorkshire YO21 2NN

Gillian & Lewis Rhys
☎ 01287 660352
SC From £200–£350
Sleeps 6
⛚ Commended

Stone cottage for six. Two bedrooms and bathroom on ground floor, twin bedroom upstairs. Garden, swing and sandpit. Quiet situation adjacent to moors in an area of outstanding natural beauty. Our small working farm is in Danby Dale, 3 miles from Danby, Castleton and the North York Moors National Park Information Centre. Open all year.

Yorkshire — North Country

Clematis, Well & Shepherds Cottage, c/o Mile House Farm, Hawes, Wensleydale, North Yorkshire DL8 3PT

Anne Fawcett
☎ 01969 667481
SC From £165–£500
Sleeps 4/8
Highly Commended

Three lovely old Dales stone cottages of character with open fires, exposed beams and Laura Ashley prints. All cottages are peacefully situated with spectacular views over Wensleydale. Fully renovated to a high standard, these cottages provide charming, spacious accommodation with lovely, old fashioned walled gardens. Free trout fishing on farm. Private parking. Open all year.

The Coach House, Whashton Springs Farm, Richmond, North Yorkshire DL11 7JS

Fairlie Turnbull
☎ 01748 822884
Fax 01748 826285
SC From £165–£270
Sleeps 4–5
Highly Commended

The Coach House offers luxury accommodation on our 400-acre working family farm near Richmond, gateway to the Dales. This warm spacious house sleeps 4–5 in double and twin bedrooms. Beamed lounge and well equipped kitchen with washer, freezer, microwave, etc. Heating and bed linen included in tariff. Good local hospitality. Open all year.

Croft Farm Cottage, Croft Farm, Church Lane, Fylingthorpe, Whitby, North Yorkshire YO22 4PW

Pauline Featherstone
☎/Fax 01947 880231
SC From £150–£285
Sleeps 4
Commended

Forget the pressures of everyday living! Come and relax in the cottage attached to our 18th century farmhouse on a working farm, offering spectacular views, home comforts, peace and tranquillity. Overlooking Robin Hood's Bay, within easy reach of coastal resorts, Moors Railway and termination of well-known walks. 2 bedrooms, 1 double and 1 with built-in bunk beds. Fully equipped including linen. Colour TV and sun lounge. Open all year.

Dufton's House, Low Oxnop, Gunnerside, Richmond, North Yorkshire DL11 6JJ

Annie Porter
☎/Fax 01748 886253
SC From £300–£500
Sleeps 7
Commended

Come and relax in peace and comfort in our cottage on family-run farm in Upper Swaledale renowned for its walls, barns and wild flowers. 1 twin and 1 double room with washbasin, 1 family en suite. Cot available. Sitting room with open fire and colour TV, modern kitchen, CH. Bedlinen, towels, electricity and fuel included. Regret no pets, no smoking. Open all year.

The Farm Cottage, Town Farm, Cloughton, Scarborough, North Yorkshire YO13 0AE

Mr & Mrs Joe Green
☎ 01723 870278
Fax 01723 870968
SC From £150–£375
Sleeps 5/6
Applied

Delightful cottage situated on working farm in centre of village. Completely refurbished to provide comfortable accommodation to a high standard. Set between the east coast resorts of Scarborough and Whitby, on the edge of the North York Moors National Park, the cottage provides an ideal base for walking and touring. Open all year.

Farsyde Farm Cottages, Farsyde House Farm, Robin Hood's Bay, Whitby, North Yorkshire YO22 4UG

Angela Green
☎ 01947 880249
Fax 01947 880877
SC From £130–£495
Sleeps 20
Up to *Highly Commended*

Yorkshire stone cottages on private stud farm with land reaching the sea. Spectacular coastal, country and heather moors scenery, near Robin Hood's Bay. Close to beautiful Esk Valley and Heartbeat Country, and an hours' drive from York. Riding and private use of chalet swimming pool. Spacious parking. Open all year.

North Country   Yorkshire

17 Mount Pleasant Farm, Whashton, Richmond, North Yorkshire DL11 7JP

Alison Pittaway
☎/Fax 01748 822784
SC From £180–£280
Sleeps 4
Commended

Enjoy a break in one of our two newly converted cottages, set in lovely peaceful countryside with superb views. Three miles from Richmond and ideally situated for touring the North Yorkshire Dales. Each cottage comprises 1 double and 1 twin bedroom, lounge with dining area, fully equipped kitchen, shower room, colour TV, CH. Electricity, linen and heating included. Good local hospitality. Open all year.

32 Rhuss Cottage, Hinderwell, c/o Broom House Farm, Ugthorpe, Whitby, North Yorkshire YO21 2BJ

Mrs Louise Robson
☎/Fax 01947 840454
SC From £180–£350
Sleeps 4/5+cot
Applied

17th century beamed cottage situated in lovely village between Staithes and Runswick Bay (Whitby 6 miles). Clean, comfortable, owner maintained, with luxury oak-fitted kitchen. Linen, storage heating, real fire. Garden and private patio. Scenic walks in area of outstanding beauty. Close to good beaches. Also a chance to visit our farm and watch the cows being milked, etc. Open all year.

33 Stanhow Farm Bungalow, c/o Stanhow Farm, Great Langton, Northallerton, North Yorks DL7 0TJ

Lady Mary Furness
☎ 01609 748614
SC From £180–£350
Sleeps 6
Commended

Peacefully situated on a 230-acre working family farm, a cosy spacious detached bungalow with private garden and parking. Lovely views of Swaledale and Herriot Country. Heating, CTV, video, open fire. Fully equipped kitchen, washer/dryer, fridge/freezer, microwave, etc. One double, 2 twin bedrooms (bed linen included). Good local hospitality. A warm welcome assured. Brochure available. Open all year.

23 Studley House, 67, Main Street, Ebberston, Scarborough, North Yorkshire YO13 9NR

Ernie & Jane Hodgson
☎/Fax 01723 859285
SC From £165–£280
Sleeps 4
Commended

Come and relax in this cosy country hideaway in the pretty village of Ebberston. The cottage is very well equipped and offers every comfort. Accommodation is all on one level, suitable for partially disabled. Central for Yorkshire moors, coast, forests and historic York. Sorry no pets. Colour brochure. Open all year.

25 Valley View Farm, Old Byland, Helmsley, York, North Yorkshire YO62 5LG

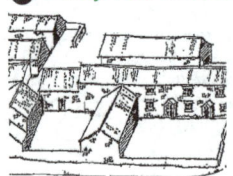

Sally Robinson
☎/Fax 01439 798221
SC From £200–£460
Sleeps 2–6
Highly Commended

A beef, sheep and pig farm set on the edge of small village. Newly converted barn furnished with traditional farm theme. The cottages have TV, video, dishwasher, washer/dryer, open fires, CH. All bedrooms are en suite, beds double or twin. Delicious farmhouse meals available (see B&B listing). Phone for colour brochure. Open all year.

34 Wren Cottage, c/o Street House Farm, Little Holtby, Northallerton, North Yorkshire DL7 9LN

Mrs Jennifer Pybus
☎ 01609 748622
SC From £145–£260
Sleeps 4
Commended

This cosy cottage in Kirkby Fleetham overlooks the village green, with pub serving food and shop/PO nearby. Ideal centre for exploring Yorkshire Dales and North Yorkshire Moors and within easy reach of York and Durham. The cottage with its traditional oak beams and open fire in the lounge has a fully equipped kitchen with electric cooker and microwave. Also night storage heaters and telephone. Electricity included. Open all year.

Yorkshire   North Country

Camping and Caravanning

Pond Farm, Fylingdales, Whitby, North Yorkshire YO22 4QJ

Grace Cromack
☎ 01947 880441
SC From £120–£200
Sleeps 6
Tourist Board Inspected

We offer one 6-berth caravan, situated on 400-acre mixed stock farm edging the North Yorkshire Moors and near to Robin Hood's Bay. It is situated in a walled garden with open views and has all mains services including shower, toilet. TV, fridge, double and bunk-bedded rooms. Ideal for visiting historic towns, coastal resorts. Forest and moorland walks, pony trekking and clay pigeon shooting nearby. Short breaks out of season. Open Apr–Nov.

Bunkhouse/Camping Barn

Lovesome Hill Barn, Lovesome Hill, Northallerton, North Yorkshire DL6 2PB

Mrs Mary Pearson
☎ 01609 772311
SC From £3.50
Sleeps 15
YHA Inspected

A former cornstore, this building is in the farmyard at Lovesome Hill Farm. Facilities include electricity/shower (metered), toilets, heating, cooking/eating area and sleeping area. Many nearby walks to explore the Yorkshire Dales and North York Moors National Parks. Only 200 yards from the Coast to Coast walk. Brochure available. Open all year except Christmas and New Year.

FARM HOLIDAY BUREAU

USE THE INDEX

The comprehensive Index shows which farms offer access to disabled visitors; caravanning/camping facilities; the chance to participate on a working farm; stabling/grazing for visiting horses; en suite rooms; a welcome to business people; acceptance of *Stay on a Farm* gift tokens.

Yorkshire
Vale of York & the Wolds

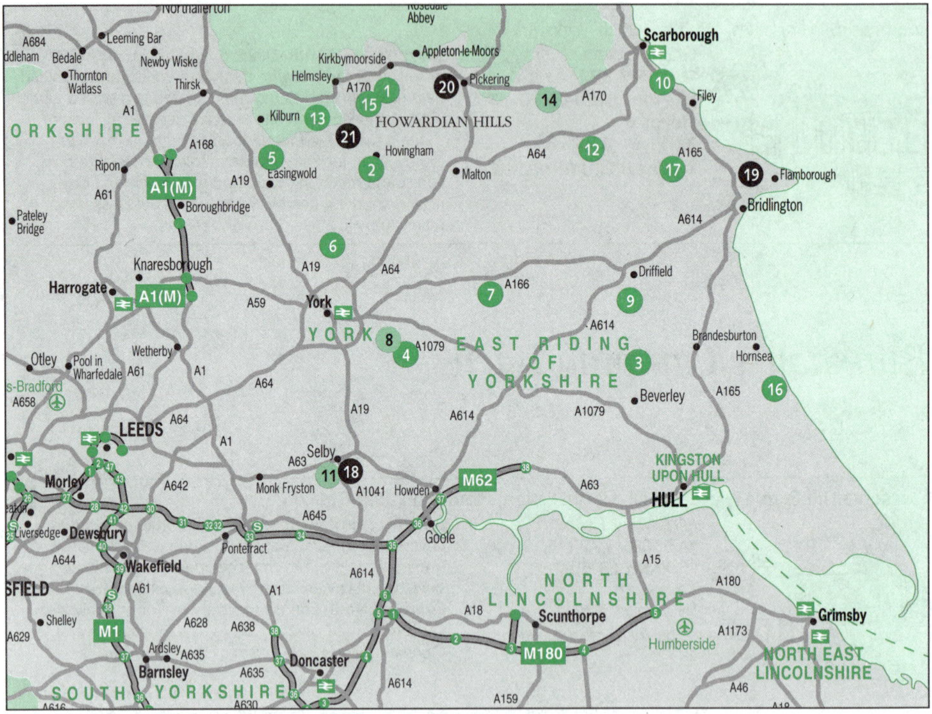

Key
- 1 Bed & Breakfast
- 1 Self-Catering
- 1 B&B and SC
- 1 Camping Barns
- 1 Camping & Caravanning

When you come to stay with us on our farms you are within easy reach of the ancient city of York with its beautiful Minster, city walls and fascinating Railway Museum and Jorvik Centre. Whilst in the area see Castle Howard where *Brideshead Revisited* was filmed and the abbeys of Rievaulx, Byland and Selby. Eden Camp at Malton is well worth a visit and the children will love Flamingoland. The historic market town of Pickering offers you access to the North York Moors National Park and steam railway. The market town of Driffield is the capital of the Wolds and reputed burial place of King Alfred. Beverley is a delight with its cobbled streets, 'bars' or town gates and Minster. You can walk for miles on the Cleveland Way between Helmsley and Filey.

If you would like help in finding suitable farm accommodation, turn to the full listing of farm groups on pages 360 to 363 to find appropriate contact details for this area.

Yorkshire North Country

Bed and Breakfast
(and evening meal)

Beech Tree House Farm, South Holme, Slingsby, York YO62 4BA

Mrs Carol Farnell
☎ 01653 628257
[BB] £17
EM £8
Sleeps 10
Listed *Commended*

Large Victorian farmhouse on 260-acre arable farm with sheep, pigs, poultry. In peaceful valley ¼ mile inland, close to Castle Howard, central for York, moors, dales, coast and Flamingoland. 1 family, 2 doubles, 1 twin room, 3 guest bathrooms. Lounge with log fire, TV. Snooker/games room. Large garden with safe play area, toys and cycles available. Children welcome at reduced rates. Babysitting. Open all year except Christmas.

Church Farm, Scackleton, York, North Yorkshire YO6 4NB

Mrs Cynthia Firby
☎/Fax 01653 628403
[BB] From £17–£20
Sleeps 6
Listed *Highly Commended*

A spacious, comfortable stone farmhouse on our sheep and arable farm in a quiet hamlet in the Howardian Hills designated Area of Outstanding Natural Beauty. 1 double en suite, 1 family en suite. Tea/coffee-making facilities in all bedrooms. Central heating, good home cooking, wonderful views. Ideal base for walking or visiting York, the moors and coast. Open Feb–Nov inclusive.

Clematis House, 1 Eastgate, Lund, Nr Driffield, East Yorkshire YO25 9TQ

Mrs Gill Lamb
☎/Fax 01377 217204
[BB] From £19.50–£21
EM From £10
Sleeps 4
Commended

Family-run 389-acre arable and livestock farm in pretty rural village. Farmhouse with character, spacious yet cosy. En suite rooms with TV and tea/coffee-making facilities. Lounge with log fire. Secluded south-facing walled garden and off road parking. Ideal for visiting York, Hull, Beverley, the coast and North Yorkshire Moors. Open all year except Christmas.

Cuckoo Nest Farm, Wilberfoss, York YO4 5NL

Joan Liversidge
☎ 01759 380365
[BB] From £18–£22
Sleeps 6
Commended

Situated 7 miles east of York off A1079 Hull road, 200-year-old traditional red-brick farmhouse on cattle/dairy/arable farm. Oak-beamed rooms, pleasant sitting room and separate dining room. One en suite bedroom; one double and one twin, both H&C. Good country pubs nearby. Easy drive to coast, dales and moors. A warm welcome awaits you here. Open all year except Christmas.

Dimple Wells, Thormanby, Easingwold, North Yorkshire YO61 4NL

Lorna & Neville Huxtable
☎/Fax 01845 501068
[BB] From £24–£26
Sleeps 5
Highly Commended

Our country house is easily found, set within extensive grounds, with the backdrop of the Hambleton Hills and White Horse of Kilburn. En suite rooms have colour TV and tea/coffee tray. Aga–cooked breakfasts. York, Thirsk and Easingwold are nearby. A relaxing home from home. Open all year except Christmas and New Year.

115

North Country — Yorkshire

⑥ Goose Farm, Eastmoor, Sutton-on-the-Forest, York YO61 1ET

Susan Rowson
☎/Fax 01347 810577
BB From £20–£22
Sleeps 6
⌖ ⌖ ⌖ ⌖
⌖ ⌖ Commended

150-year old brick farmhouse situated 5 miles from York Minster in open countryside just off the B1363 and within easy access of Herriot Country and the Yorkshire coast. Large rooms, all en suite with TV and tea/coffee-making facilities. Central heating throughout and as warm as the welcome to yourselves. Open all year.

⑦ High Belthorpe, Bishop Wilton, York, YO42 1SB

Meg Abu Hamdan
☎ 01759 368238
Mobile 0973 938528
BB From £17.65
Sleeps 6
⌖ ⌖ ⌖ ⌖ ⌖ ⌖
⌖ Commended

Set on an ancient moated site in the Yorkshire Wolds, this large Victorian farmhouse has spacious bedrooms with uninterrupted panoramic views. The centre of a working livery yard, the house has own private fishing lake and access to fabulous country walks. Croquet, small snooker table available. York 12 miles, coast 20 miles. Open all year except Christmas.

⑧ High Catton Grange, High Catton, near Stamford Bridge, York YO41 1EP

Sheila Foster
☎/Fax 01759 371374
BB From £16.50–£22.50
Sleeps 6
⌖ ⌖ ⌖ ⌖ ⌖
⌖ ⌖ Commended

Only 8 miles east of York, High Catton Grange is a 300-acre mixed farm with comfortable 18th century farmhouse. Friendly, relaxed atmosphere and attractive bedrooms, 2 with washbasin, 1 en suite, guest bathroom, central heating, tea/coffee-making facilities. Within 2 miles, local country inns providing excellent meals. Ample private parking. Open all year except Christmas and New Year.

⑨ Kelleythorpe Farm, Kelleythorpe, Great Driffield, East Riding of Yorkshire YO25 9DW

Mrs Tiffy Hopper
☎ 01377 252297
BB From £17
EM From £10
Sleeps 6
⌖ ⌖ ⌖ ⌖ ⌖
Listed Commended

Imagine peacocks strutting, ducks swimming and trout rising. Enjoy tea on the sun terrace overlooking a crystal clear shallow river, the friendly atmosphere of our lovely Georgian farmhouse with its mellow antique furniture, pretty chintz and new bathrooms, 1 en suite, is sure to captivate you. Delicious country cooking. Children very welcome. Ideally placed for touring. Open all year (closed Christmas & New Year).

⑩ Killerby Cottage Farm, Killerby Lane, Cayton, Scarborough, North Yorkshire YO11 3TP

Valerie Green
☎ 01723 581426
Fax 01723 585465
BB From £18–£25
Sleeps 6
⌖ ⌖
⌖ ⌖ Commended

Simon and Val Green welcome you to Killerby Cottage Farm in the pleasant countryside between Scarborough and Filey. The farmhouse has many charming features and our double and twin bedded rooms all have en suite facilities. Guests' lounge with log fires, sun room, lovely garden, good food – all for you to enjoy. Open all year.
E-mail: val@green–glass.demon.co.uk

⑪ Lund Farm, Gateforth, Selby, North Yorkshire YO8 9LE

Chris & Helen Middleton
☎ 01757 228775
Fax 01757 228004
BB From £20–£28
EM From £7
Sleeps 6
⌖ ⌖ ⌖ ⌖ ⌖ ⌖
⌖ Highly Commended

Convenient for York and the Dales, our peaceful 18th century farmhouse has en suite rooms, pine beams and log fires. Children most welcome; 200-acre farm with lambs, eggs to collect, Shetland pony, bicycles, baby listening and nursery teas. Evening meals on request. Lambing breaks Dec–Mar. Business visitors welcome too; phone and fax available. Open all year.

Yorkshire   North Country

Manor Farm, East Heslerton, Malton, North Yorkshire YO17 8RN ⑫

David & Elizabeth Lumley
☎/Fax 01944 728268
BB From £17.50
Sleeps 6

Commended

Comfortable, relaxing atmosphere in our Victorian farmhouse set in large gardens with rose garden and orchard. Very spacious centrally heated bedrooms are en suite with tea, coffee and biscuits. Our 400-acre mixed farm with farm walks and private fishing is centrally located for coast, moors, forestry and York. Open Mar–Oct. E-mail: d.c.lum@farmline.com

Oldstead Grange, Oldstead, Coxwold, York YO61 4BJ ⑬

Anne Banks
☎/Fax 01347 868634
BB From £21
Sleeps 6

Highly Commended

Lying amongst its beautiful fields, woods and valleys near Byland Abbey, Oldstead Grange is perfectly situated within the NYM National Park for visiting Thirsk, Helmsley and York. Our 17th century farmhouse has a hidden priest hole, but now guests enjoy newly appointed luxury en suite rooms with the highest standard of comfort and facilities – large comfortable beds, TV, CH, log fires, hearty breakfasts, good local inns and eating places. Open all year. E-mail: tom.banks@farmline.com

Rains Farm, Allerston, Pickering, North Yorkshire YO18 7PQ ⑭

Jean or Lorraine Allanson
☎/Fax 01723 859333
BB From £20–£25
EM From £14
Sleeps 9

Commended

Very peacefully set in Ryedale's beautiful open countryside. Relax and unwind in our recently refurbished farmhouse. Quality en suite accommodation and delicious farmhouse fayre. Five pretty en suite rooms (one ground floor), all with CH TV, hospitality tray, hairdriers. Centrally situated for moors, Dales, coast, attractions. Private parking. Totally non-smoking. Closed Christmas and New Year.

Sunley Court, Nunnington, York, North Yorkshire YO62 5XQ

Mrs Joan Brown
☎ 01439 748233
BB From £15–£17.50
EM £10
Sleeps 6

Commended

Sunley Court is a comfortable modern farmhouse with open views in a quiet secluded area. The farm is arable with sheep and horses. All bedrooms have tea/coffee-making facilities, washbasins, electric blankets, 2 have shower/toilet en suite, 2 single bedrooms. Good home cooking. Central for York, moors and coast. Open all year except Christmas.

West Carlton, Carlton Lane, Aldbrough, Hull HU11 4RB ⑯

Caroline Maltas
☎ 01964 527724
Mobile 0467 830868
BB From £18–£20
Sleeps 6

Applied

Lovely south-facing Georgian farmhouse on 330-acre mixed farm. Ideally situated in a very quiet rural location yet convenient for Beverley, Hull, York. 4 miles from a sandy beach, 6 miles from Hornsea. Beautiful en suite rooms coordinated with Laura Ashley fabrics. Children's playroom, guests' own lounge and dining room. Large garden. Ring for a brochure – you won't be disappointed. Open all year.

The Wold Cottage, Wold Newton, Driffield YO25 3HL ⑰

Mrs Katrina Gray
☎/Fax 01262 470696
BB From £20
EM From £12
Sleeps 6

Highly Commended

"Just what you always hope to find." Georgian farmhouse set in own grounds overlooking new and mature woodlands and continuous wold land. Come and relax and forget the pressures of everyday life. Stroll around our field margins and observe the wildlife and history. Spacious four-poster room with spa bath. All rooms en suite. Lambing breaks Jan–Mar. Open all year.

North Country   Yorkshire

Self-Catering

⑧ The Cottage, High Catton Grange, High Catton, near Stamford Bridge, York YO41 1EP

Sheila Foster
☎/Fax 01759 371374
SC From £150–£290
Sleeps 4–6
♣♣♣♣ Commended

This former gig shed and stable has been converted to a high standard yet retains many original features. Comfortable and tastefully furnished with colour TV, electric cooker, automatic washer/dryer, fridge, microwave, storage heaters,etc. Patio doors onto large private patio and garden furniture. Glorious views across green meadows. Working farm in peaceful, rural setting, ideally situated for York or touring. Linen/fuel included. Open all year.

⑱ Dove Cottage, Primrose Hill Farm, c/o Staynor Hall, Selby, North Yorkshire YO8 8EE

Jenny Webster
☎ 01757 708931
Fax 01757 704386
SC From £160–£320
Sleep 5+cot
♣♣♣ Highly Commended

A warm welcome awaits at our beautifully renovated 19th century cottage with all modern amenities. Relax in comfort and peace whilst experiencing life on a working family farm. Enjoy our animals, country walks, bird watching and abundant wildlife. Golf, fishing and horse riding nearby. Well placed for York, Dales and Moors. Children welcome. Open all year.

⑲ Field House, Jewison Lane, Sewerby, Bridlington, East Yorkshire YO16 6YG

Angela & John Foster
☎ 01262 674932
Fax 01262 608688
SC From £250–£375
Sleeps 6 + cot
♣♣♣♣ Highly Commended

Our highly rated farmhouse with walled garden, tennis court and croquet lawn is an excellent base from which to explore a spectacular coastline or, within an hour's drive, some of Yorkshire's finest features. Sample life on a large dairy/arable farm. Children especially welcome. Open all year.

⑪ Lund Farm Cottage, Lund Farm, Gateforth, Selby, North Yorkshire YO8 9LE

Chris & Helen Middleton
☎ 01757 228775
Fax 01757 228004
SC From £250–£350
EM From £7
Sleeps 6
♣♣♣ Highly Commended

Convenient for York and the Dales, our 18th century farmyard cottage has beams, fireside range, safe patio and lawn, with barbecue, and friendly owners next door. Children most welcome. 200-acre farm with lambs, eggs to collect, Shetland pony, and bicycles. Evening meals available. Lambing breaks Dec–Mar. Prices fully inclusive. Open all year.

⑳ Manor Cottage, Sinnington Manor, Sinnington, York YO6 6SN

Mrs J M Wilson
☎/Fax 01751 433296
SC From £150–£350
Sleeps 4/5
Applied

Relax in our newly restored cottage adjoining Grade II listed house. Built of plum-red brick, retaining original features such as exposed beams and Victorian 'copper' and water pump. Spacious, comfortable rooms – two en suite bedrooms, one with four-poster. CH throughout. Beautiful views over lawns, duck pond, woods and hedged fields. Farm walks, calves and foals – a peaceful rural haven. Prices fully inclusive. Children, dogs and horses welcome. Open all year.

Yorkshire **North Country**

Rains Farm, Allerston, Pickering, North Yorkshire YO18 7PQ ⑭

Jean or Lorraine Allanson
☎/Fax 01723 859333
SC From £150–£395
Sleeps 2/6

♘ ♦ ✝ ⌂ ■ ⊛
♙♙♙ – ♙♙♙♙ Highly Commended

Five warm and comfortable newly converted barns. Very peaceful, magnificent views. Relax, unwind and ease away the pressures of life in this idyllic rural retreat. Gaze on the ponies grazing in the paddocks. Furnished, decorated and equipped for luxury living. We are centrally situated for many attractions. Safe parking. Colour brochure. Open all year.

Sunset Cottages, Grimston Manor Farm, Gilling East, York YO61 4HR ㉑

Heather Kelsey
☎ 01347 888654
Fax 01347 888347
SC From £150–£375
Sleeps 3–6
♘ ♦ ⚶
♙♙♙ Commended

In an envied location in the middle of the Howardian Hills AONB, 17 miles north of York. Six stone-built barn and granary conversions on 175-acre sheep and arable farm. Warm and comfortable, tremendous character, thoughtfully planned. Enjoy excellent walks and our fine garden. Colour brochure. Open all year.

STAY ON A FARM GIFT TOKENS

If you have enjoyed your Stay on a Farm, why not treat your friends and relatives to *Stay on a Farm* gift tokens? Available from the Bureau office (tel: 01203 696909), they can be redeemed against accommodation and are accepted by the majority of farms (see Index). Please check when booking to avoid disappointment.

THE 1000+ BUREAU MEMBERS OFFER A UNIQUE LINK TO CUSTOMERS ACROSS THE UK

All Bureau members belong to a local Group. Each member can refer you to an equally high quality member within the Group... or across the UK: England, Northern Ireland, Scotland, Wales.

FOLLOW THE COUNTRY CODE

Leave nothing but footprints,
Take nothing but photographs,
Kill nothing but time!

Greater Manchester

South Pennines & Colne Valley

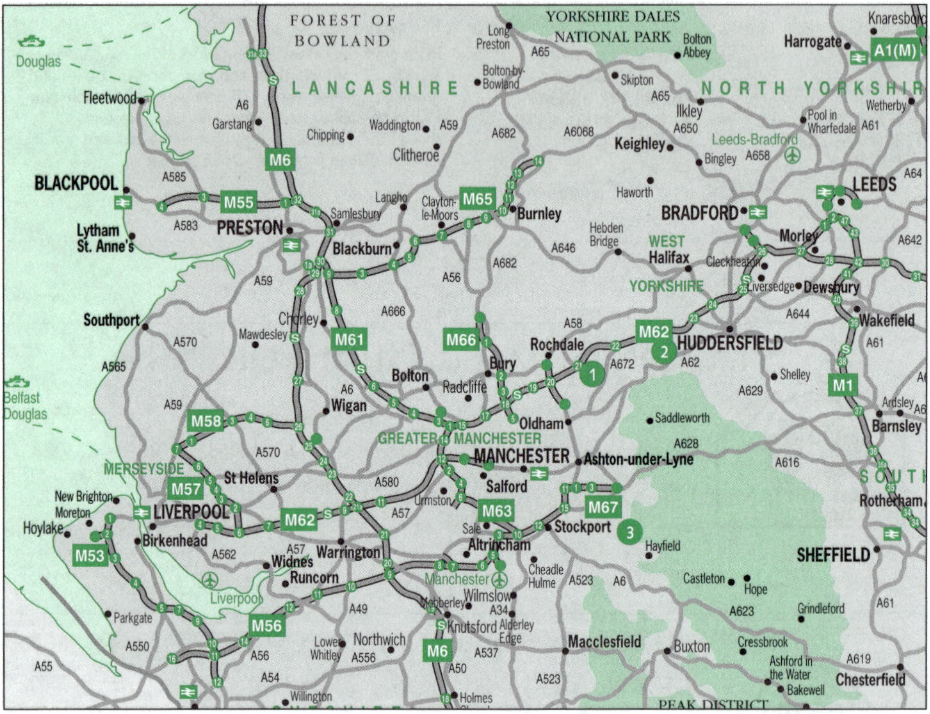

Key
- **1** Bed & Breakfast
- **1** Self-Catering
- **1** B&B and SC
- **1** Camping Barns
- **1** Camping & Caravanning

A warm and friendly welcome awaits visitors to the dramatic South Pennines, an area still remarkably untouched by tourism. Walkers on the Pennine Way will find attractive valley towns like Delph, Uppermill, Marsden and Hebden Bridge and there are equally interesting routes over Blackstone Edge with the Roman Road, the Rossendale Way, the Calderdale Way and the Colne Valley Circular. Our textile heritage is magnificently illustrated in Golcar's Colne Valley Museum, the Helmshore Museum at Haslingden, and the Saddleworth Museum at Uppermill, and craft centres and mill shops abound. For shopping, restaurants and nightlife you can't beat cosmopolitan Manchester.

If you would like help in finding suitable farm accommodation, turn to the full listing of farm groups on pages 360 to 363 to find appropriate contact details for this area.

Greater Manchester   North Country

Bed and Breakfast
(and evening meal)

Boothstead Farm, Rochdale Road, Denshaw, Oldham, Greater Manchester OL3 5UE ①

Mrs Norma Hall
☎ 01457 878622
BB From £17–£20
Sleeps 4
Listed *Commended*

An 18th century hill farm catering for people in the area on business or taking a relaxing break. Ideally situated within 3½ miles of M62 Junctions 21 and 22 (A640). Cosy lounge with open fire, TV, tea/coffee-making facilities, wash basins in rooms. Good base for touring neighbouring counties and beauty spots. Close to Saddleworth leisure amenities, ie. golf, swimming, walking, sailing. Open 2 Jan–22 Dec.

Globe Farm, Huddersfield Road, Standedge, Delph, Nr Oldham, Greater Manchester OL3 5LU ②

Jean Mayall
☎/Fax 01457 873040
BB From £20–£23
EM From £8.25
Sleeps 23
Commended

Overlooking the picturesque valleys of Saddleworth but within easy reach of M62 junction 22, Manchester Airport, Yorkshire Dales and Peak District. Only ¼ mile from Pennine Way. All rooms en suite. Evening meal can be provided if required. Colour TV, CH, drying room, tea/coffee-making facilities. Good home cooking and real northern hospitality. Open all year (closed Christmas & New Year).

Needhams Farm, Uplands Road, Werneth Low, Gee Cross, near Hyde, Cheshire SK14 3AQ ③

Mrs Charlotte Walsh
☎ 0161 368 4610
Fax 0161 367 9106
BB From £19–£20
EM From £7
Sleeps 14
Commended

Farmhouse accommodation dating back to the 16th century, offering 5 en suite rooms. Evening meals available each evening. Residential licence. Surrounded by lovely views. Ideal for Manchester Airport and city centre. Courtesy service from airport and Piccadilly station for a small charge. Six bedrooms in all. Open all year.

LET THE TELEPHONE RING!
Some farmhouses are big places. Let the telephone ring long enough to give the owner time to answer it.

USE THE INDEX

The comprehensive Index shows which farms offer access to disabled visitors; caravanning/camping facilities; the chance to participate on a working farm; stabling/grazing for visiting horses; en suite rooms; a welcome to business people; acceptance of *Stay on a Farm* gift tokens.

Cheshire

Delamere Forest, Cheshire Plain, Shropshire Union Canal, Alderley Edge & Peak District National Park

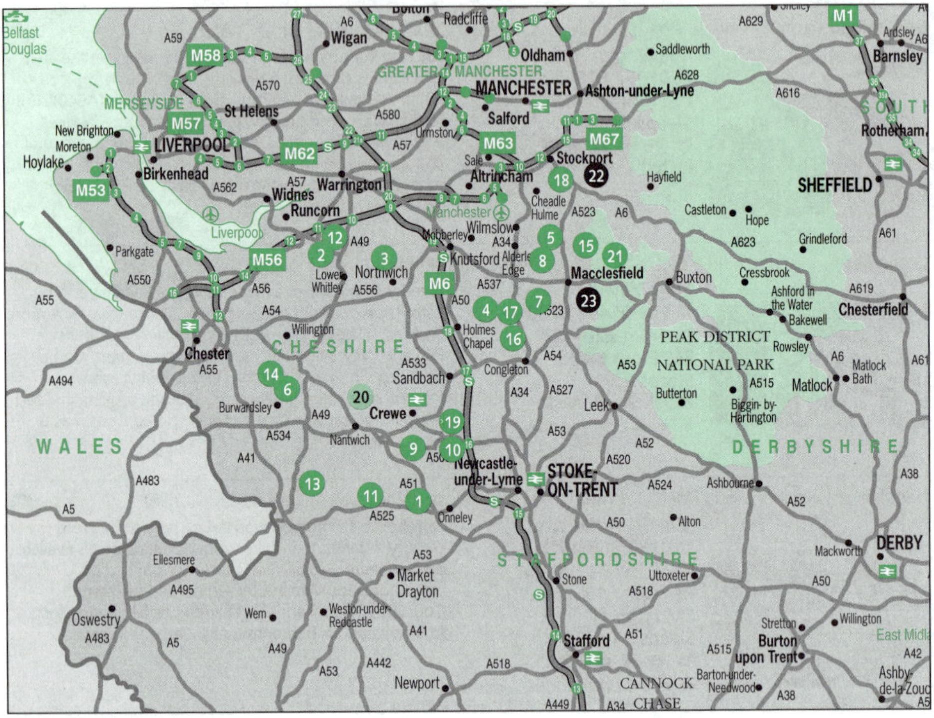

Key

- 1 Bed & Breakfast
- 1 Self-Catering
- 1 B&B and SC
- 1 Camping Barns
- 1 Camping & Caravanning

Cheshire is one of England's undiscovered counties. Renowned for lovely black-and-white architecture and its superb cheese, it is a county of contrasts. From the majesty of the Peak District across the Cheshire Plain to the Dee estuary, from North Wales to Manchester, from the Shropshire Hills to Liverpool, Cheshire has something for everyone. The county has a rich history, with Roman remains, a splendid cathedral and the unique 'Rows' in Chester, Elizabethan towns like Nantwich, fine castles and country mansions, and excellent museums about the Industrial Revolution. There are beautiful gardens, canals, wonderful walking, cycling and fishing. Come and discover us.

If you would like help in finding suitable farm accommodation, turn to the full listing of farm groups on pages 360 to 363 to find appropriate contact details for this area.

Cheshire   North Country

Bed and Breakfast
(and evening meal)

Adderley Green Farm, Heighley Castle Lane, Betley, Nr Crewe, Cheshire CW3 9BA

Mrs Sheila Berrisford
☎ 01270 820203
Fax 01270 820542
BB From £16–£20
Sleeps 6
🐴 🐕 🛅 🌳 ♿ ⊚
♛♛ *Highly Commended*

Relax in our lovely Georgian farmhouse on a 250-acre dairy farm set in large garden along a pretty country lane near an old ruined castle. Full CH. Colour TV, radio, washbasin and tea tray in all bedrooms. En suites available, draped and 4-poster beds. Beautifully decorated in the Laura Ashley style, separate tables in dining room. Ideally situated for Stapeley Water Gardens, Alton Towers and Chester. Near Keele University and Potteries, 10 mins M6 J16. Open all year except Christmas and New Year.

Ash House Farm, Chapel Lane, Acton Bridge, Northwich, Cheshire CW8 3QS

Mrs Sue Schofield
☎ 01606 852717
BB From £18–£22
Sleeps 6
🐴 🐕 🛅 🌳 ♿
Listed Commended

A warm welcome awaits you at Ash House Farm, a mixed working farm in the heart of Cheshire in peaceful, scenic surroundings. Relax in our lovely Georgian farmhouse which is full of traditional architectural features. Guests' TV lounge and dining room with log fire. Tea/coffee facilities in bedrooms. Very rural, excellent for country walks yet only short distance from M56 J10. Secure parking. Open all year.

Beechwood House, 206 Wallerscote Road, Weaverham, Northwich, Cheshire CW8 3LZ

Janet Kuypers
☎ 01606 852123
BB From £16.50
Sleeps 4
✘ ♿
♛ *Commended*

Peaceful, comfortable 1830s farmhouse and small stock farm 1 mile from Weaverham in easy reach of M56, M6. Guests' dining room/lounge with TV and hot drinks. 1 twin en suite, 2 single bedrooms with H&C; all with tea/coffee trays, radios and individual control radiators. Diets catered for. No smoking please. Recommended by 'Which'. Open all year except Christmas.

Bridge Farm, Bridge Lane, Blackden, Holmes Chapel, Cheshire CW4 8BX

Mrs A Massey
☎ 01477 571202
BB From £17–£20
Sleeps 6
🐴 🐕 🛅 🌳 ⊚
♛ *Commended*

Here at Bridge Farm, only 500 yards from Jodrell Bank Telescope with its famous Visitors' Centre, we offer a warm welcome and comfortable accommodation in our 300 year old family farmhouse. Well appointed rooms and visitors' lounge overlooking 12 acres of wildflower meadows. En suite available. Situated 3 miles from M6 J18, close to Knutsford, central to Macclesfield, Chester and the Potteries. Open all year.

Carr House Farm, Mill Lane, Adlington, Macclesfield, Cheshire SK10 4LG

Mrs Isobel Worthington
☎ 01625 828337
BB From £16–£18
Sleeps 5
🐴 🐕 🛅 🌳
Listed Commended

We extend a warm welcome to our cattle and sheep rearing farm, and offer you comfortable accommodation in our 200 year-old farmhouse in a garden setting. Tea and coffee facilities in bedrooms. Visitors' own lounge and dining room. Adlington Hall one mile, Manchester Airport approx six miles. Situated four miles north of Macclesfield just off the A523. Open Feb–Nov.

North Country   Cheshire

6 **Ford Farm,** Newton Lane, Tattenhall, Chester, Cheshire CH3 9NE

Audrey Charmley
☎ 01829 770307
BB £15
Sleeps 6
Listed *Commended*

A friendly welcome to our dairy farm set in beautiful countryside with views of Beeston and Peckforton Castles. Close to ice cream farm and Cheshire workshops and many tourist attractions. Chester 7 miles, Oulton Park 8 miles. Guests' own lounge and dining room with TV. Two double rooms and one twin, tea/coffee-making facilities and TV in all rooms. Bathroom with shower. Open all year.

7 **Golden Cross Farm,** Siddington, Nr Macclesfield, Cheshire SK11 9JP

Hazel Rush
☎ 01260 224358
BB From £16–£20
Sleeps 6
Commended

Small organic farm, 100 yards from the A34 on the B5392 in picturesque surroundings. Central for Macclesfield, Congleton, Holmes Chapel and Alderley Edge. Places of local interest include Capesthorne Hall, Gawsworth Hall, Tatton Hall, Styal Mill and Nether Alderley Mill. 2 double rooms, 2 single rooms, all with washbasins and tea/coffee-making facilities. Central heating, guests' lounge, colour TV. Open all year (closed Christmas & New Year).

8 **Goose Green Farm,** Oak Road, Mottram St Andrew, Nr Macclesfield, Cheshire SK10 4RA

Dyllis Hatch
☎ 01625 828814
BB From £20–£24
Sleeps 6
Commended

Welcome to our farm set in beautiful countryside with panoramic views. Near the A538 between Wilmslow and Prestbury, in easy reach of M6, M56 and Manchester Airport. Own fishing, stabling available. Log fire, separate dining room. Pay phone. Double en suite, twin and single rooms, all with washbasin, TV, CH and tea/coffee-making facilities. Open all year (closed Christmas).

9 **Henhull Hall,** Welshmans Lane, Nantwich, Cheshire CW5 6AD

Joyce Percival
☎/Fax 01270 624158
BB From £20–£25
Sleeps 4
Highly Commended

Welcome to our spacious farmhouse,
View the garden, duckpond, cows,
Walk to Nantwich, drive to Chester,
Along the canalside you may wander.
Beds and bathrooms are luxurious
Wait no longer, come and join us.

10 **Lea Farm,** Wrinehill Road, Wybunbury, Nantwich, Cheshire CW5 7NS

Allen & Jean Callwood
☎/Fax 01270 841429
BB From £15
EM From £16–£18
Sleeps 6
Commended

A charming farmhouse set in landscaped gardens where peacocks roam a pedigree dairy farm. Spacious, attractive bedrooms with washbasins, TV and tea/coffee-making facilities, two en suite. Luxurious lounge with open log fire, with dining room overlooking garden. Snooker, pool table, fishing available. Near to Stapeley Water Gardens and Bridgemere Garden World. M6 J16, Chester and Alton Towers. Open all year (closed Christmas & New Year).

11 **Little Heath Farm,** Audlem, Nantwich, Crewe, Cheshire CW3 0HE

Hilary Bennion
☎/Fax 01270 811324
BB From £17–£24
EM From £8.50
Sleeps 6
Commended

17th century farmhouse on a working dairy farm on the A529, 6 miles from Nantwich in lovely canalside village with shops, pubs, church and village trails. Large, warm bedrooms with all facilities. Beamed lounge and dining room traditionally furnished. Ideal for Chester, Shrewsbury (Ironbridge) and Potteries. We are close to Bridgemere Garden World and Stapeley Water Gardens. We look forward to meeting you! Closed Christmas.

Cheshire

North Country

Manor Farm, Cliff Road, Acton Bridge, Northwich, Cheshire CW8 3QP

Mrs T H Campbell
☎/Fax 01606 853181
BB From £20–£27
Sleeps 5

♥ Highly Commended

Set in secluded location down private drive with fields and walks beside the River Weaver. Convenient for M6, M56 (J10), Chester, Northwich and Merseyside. We give a warm welcome to our quiet country house. Comfortable bedrooms, each with private/en suite facilities. Tea/coffee, hairdrier, trouser press, drying, own TV lounge and peaceful garden. English breakfast served in elegant oak-furnished dining room. Safe car park. Open all year.

Millmoor Farm, Nomansheath, Malpas, Cheshire SY14 8ED

Mrs Sally-Ann Chesters
☎ 01948 820304
BB From £16–£20
EM From £10
Sleeps 4

Listed Commended

Set amongst the beautiful valleys on the South Cheshire/Shropshire border, Millmoor Farm is a wonderful setting to escape the hurly burly of modern life. The 17th century farmhouse has recently been refurbished and boasts an exquisite en suite four-poster double bedroom. Within easy reach of Chester, North Wales and Shropshire's many attractions. Great pub meals within walking distance. Open all year.

Newton Hall, Tattenhall, Chester, Cheshire CH3 9AY

Mrs Anne Arden
☎ 01829 770153
Fax 01829 770655
BB From £20–£25
Sleeps 5

♥ Highly Commended

A warm welcome to our part 16th century oak-beamed farmhouse. Set in large well kept grounds, with fine views of historic Beeston and Peckforton Castles and close to the Sandstone Trail. Six miles south of Chester off A41 and ideal for Welsh Hills. Rooms are en suite or have adjacent bathroom. TV in bedrooms. Guests' own sitting room. Full central heating.

Oldhams Hollow Farm, Manchester Road, Tytherington, Macclesfield, Cheshire SK10 2JW

Brenda Buxton
☎/Fax 01625 424128
BB From £17.50–£18.50
EM From £9.50
Sleeps 6

Listed Commended

Welcome to Oldhams Hollow – a 16th century listed farmhouse one mile north of Macclesfield, close to the peaks and plains of Cheshire. Snug, warm and restful with oak beams, large lounge, open fire, spacious dining room, central heating. Comfortable bedrooms with colour TV, washbasins, tea/coffee-making facilities, electric blankets.

Sandhole Farm, Hulme Walfield, Congleton, Cheshire CW12 2JH

Veronica Worth
☎ 01260 224419
Fax 01260 224766
BB From £24–£39
Sleeps 36

♥ Highly Commended

The comfortable traditional farmhouse and delightful converted stable block are situated 2 miles north of Congleton on A34, 15 mins from M6 and 30 mins from Manchester airport. Most of our rooms have modern en suite facilities and all have the usual extras, including hairdryer, remote control teletext TV plus trouser press and direct dial telephone. Large comfortable lounge, separate newly built conservatory/dining room. Cheshire Tourism Award Winner. Now approved for Civil Marriages. Open all year.

Sandpit Farm, Messuage Lane, Marton, Macclesfield, Cheshire SK11 9HS

Mrs I H Kennerley
☎ 01260 224254
BB From £17.50–£20
Sleeps 6

♥ Commended

A friendly welcome to our 300 year old farmhouse surrounded by 100 acres of grassland. Traditional farmhouse with oak timber features and heated throughout. Separate dining room and TV lounge. H&C in T/S, en suite facilities in double and twin, all with tea/coffee and TV. Excellent touring centre for Peak District, Potteries, Chester. Manchester Airport 14 miles, NT properties, stately homes and Jodrell Bank Science Centre nearby. Open all year.

125

North Country — Cheshire

18 Shire Cottage Farmhouse, Benches Lane, Chisworth, Marple Bridge, Stockport, Cheshire SK6 5RY

Monica Sidebottom
☎ 01457 866536
BB From £19–£24
Sleeps 6
♿ 🐴 ⚞ ⚘ 🛄
☕ ☕ *Commended*

Real home from home accommodation in peaceful location. Magnificent views overlooking Etheroe Country Park. Convenient for Manchester Airport, city centre, Peak District, stately homes and numerous places of interest. Ground floor bedrooms and bathroom. All rooms have vanity units/shaver points/tea-making facilities/TV. Family room has own shower and toilet. Bathroom has shower and bidet. Early breakfast for businessmen and travellers. Open all year.

19 Snape Farm, Snape Lane, Weston, Nr Crewe, Cheshire CW2 5NB

Mrs Jean Williamson
☎/Fax 01270 820208
BB From £16–£20
EM From £9
Sleeps 6
♿ 🐴 ⚞ 🛄 ⓢ
☕ ☕ *Commended*

Enjoy a warm welcome to our centrally heated farmhouse on a 150-acre beef/arable farm set in rolling countryside. 3 miles from Crewe. A good centre for visiting Nantwich, Chester or the Potteries. Guests' lounge and snooker room. 1 twin (en suite), 1 twin, 1 double room, each with colour TV and tea/coffee-making facilities. 4 miles from M6 (J 16). Open all year except Christmas.

20 Stoke Grange Farm, Chester Road, Nantwich, Cheshire CW5 6BT

Georgina West
☎/Fax 01270 625525
BB From £20–£25
Sleeps 6
♿ ⚞ ⚘ 🛄 ⚘ ⓢ
☕ ☕ *Highly Commended*

In a picturesque setting, an attractive canalside farmhouse, with large car park and beautiful garden. Spacious en suite bedrooms with colour TV and hot drink facilities. Comfortable guest lounge with TV, dining room with log fire. Honeymoon suite with four-poster bed. Warm welcome and excellent breakfast. Vegetarians catered for. Past Cheshire Tourism Development Award winner. Short walk to pub and village. Open all year.

21 Yew Tree Farm, North Rode, Congleton, Cheshire CW12 2PF

Mrs Sheila Kidd
☎ 01260 223569
BB From £19
EM From £10
Sleeps 6
♿ 🐴 ⚞ ⚘ ⚘ 🛄 ⓢ
Listed *Commended*

Discover an oasis of freedom, relaxation, wooded walks and beautiful views. Meet a whole variety of pets and farm animals on this friendly working farm. Your comfort is our priority. Good food is a speciality. Generous, scrummy breakfasts and traditional evening meals. A true taste of the countryside – just for you! Open all yaer.

Self-Catering

22 Lake View, Ernocroft Farm, Marple Bridge, Stockport, Cheshire SK6 5RY

Monica Sidebottom
☎ 01457 866536
SC From £275–£330
Sleeps 6 + cot
♿ ⚘ 🛄
🐎 🐎 🐎 *Commended*

A new, self-catering farm bungalow, 2 miles Marple Bridge, 4 miles Glossop. Overlooking Etherow Country Park. Ideal base for exploring Peak District, Marple locks and waterways, country parks and stately homes. Peaceful location. Accommodates 6 with all mod cons. TV. Cot available. Open all year.

Cheshire   **North Country**

The Old Byre, Pye Ash Farm, Leek Road, Bosley, Macclesfield, Cheshire CW12 3QD

Dorothy Gilman
☎ 01260 273650
Fax 01260 297115
[SC] From £200–£400
Sleeps 8 + cot
↟ ☙ ▪ ◉
🗝🗝 *Commended*

The Old Byre is especially designed so two families may holiday together. Cows, sheep, hens, ducks, etc make this a country paradise. Roomy enough to dine together, or good pub food is ½ mile walk away. The Peak District, Staffordshire Moorlands, Alton Towers, National Trust properties all easily reached.

Stoke Grange Mews, Stoke Grange Farm, Chester Road, Nantwich, Cheshire CW5 6BT

Georgina West
☎/Fax 01270 625525
[SC] From £200–£375
Sleeps 2–6 + cot
☙ ☙ ▪ ◉
🗝🗝🗝 *Highly Commended*

Holiday home created from a fine old barn near the owner's canalside farmhouse and dairy farm in lush heritage rich countryside 15 miles south Chester. Each has exposed beams, quality furniture, and offers fully equipped accommodation. Linen and towels provided. Small rear patio, large shared garden with canal access. Children's play area and farm pets corner. Barbeque area. Past Cheshire Tourism Development Award winner. Open all year.

NO ANSWER?
Farmers are mostly out and about during the day.
Try to telephone before 9.30am or after 4pm.

CONFIRM BOOKINGS
Disappointments can arise from misunderstandings over the telephone.
Please write to confirm your booking.

Our Internet address is
http://www.webscape.co.uk/farmaccom/

England's Heartland

Farm entries in this regional section are listed under those counties shown in green on the key map. Look at the index below to find on which page the entries start. You will see that we have listed the counties geographically so that you can turn more easily to find farms in neighbouring areas.

At the start of each county section is a detailed map with numbered symbols indicating the location of each farm. Different symbols denote different types of accommodation; see the key below each county map. Farm entries are listed alphabetically under type of accommodation. Some farms offer more than one type of accommodation and therefore have more than one entry.

1. Derbyshire
2. Nottinghamshire
3. Lincolnshire
4. Shropshire
5. Staffordshire
6. Leicestershire
7. Herefordshire
8. Worcestershire
9. Gloucestershire
10. West Midlands
11. Warwickshire
12. Northamptonshire
13. Bedfordshire
14. Hertfordshire
15. Cambridgeshire
16. Norfolk
17. Suffolk

KEY MAP TO ENGLAND'S HEARTLAND

Derbyshire *page 129*
Derwent Valley, Peak District National Park, Dovedale, Manifold Valley & Heights of Abraham

Nottinghamshire *page 137*
Sherwood Forest & the Dukeries

Lincolnshire *page 140*
Lincolnshire Wolds & Tennyson Country

Shropshire *page 144*
Shropshire Union Canal, the Wrekin, Ironbridge Gorge, Shropshire Hills, the Long Mynd, Wenlock Edge, Clun Forest & the Marches

Staffordshire *page 151*
Peak District National Park, Cannock Chase, Trent Valley & the Potteries

Leicestershire *page 154*
Vale of Belvoir, Rutland Water & Grand Union Canal

Herefordshire *page 157*
Wye Valley & Golden Valley

Worcestershire *page 163*
Wyre Forest, Severn Valley, Malvern Hills & Vale of Evesham

Gloucestershire *page 168*
Forest of Dean, Cotswolds & Slad Valley

Warwickshire *page 175*
Shakespeare Country & Fosse Way

Northamptonshire *page 181*
Rockingham Forest, Nene Valley & Grand Union Canal

Bedfordshire *page 185*
Ivel & Ouse Valleys

Hertfordshire *page 187*
The Chilterns

Cambridgeshire *page 189*
The Fens & Grafham Water

Norfolk *page 192*
The Broads, Norfolk Coast, the Wash, Wensum Valley & Thetford Forest

Suffolk *page 198*
Constable Country, Waveney Valley, Suffolk Coast & Heaths

Derbyshire

Derwent Valley, Peak District National Park, Dovedale, Manifold Valley & Heights of Abraham

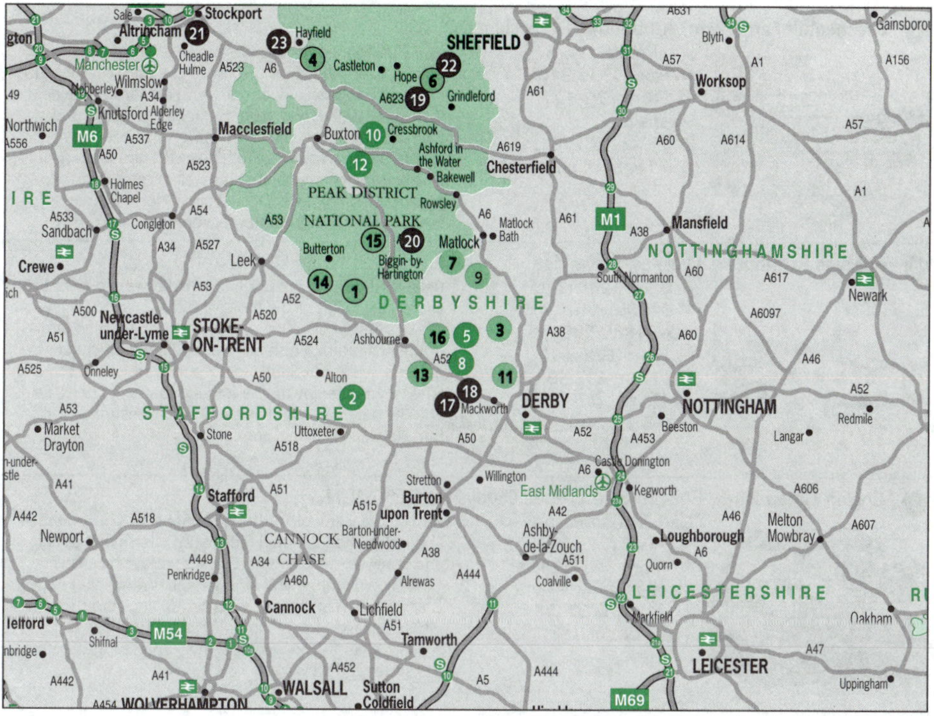

Key

- 1 Bed & Breakfast
- 1 Self-Catering
- 1 B&B and SC
- 1 Camping Barns
- 1 Camping & Caravanning

This is the home of the Peak District, Britain's first National Park. From the mellow lowlands of the south to the rugged peaks of the north, from picturesque villages to busy market towns like Ashbourne and Bakewell, from historic houses such as Chatsworth, Haddon and Hardwick to the excitement of Alton Towers and the American Adventure, a warm welcome awaits you in every corner of Derbyshire. At Matlock cable cars glide majestically across an awe-inspiring gorge, while Castleton is known for its show caves and Blue John stone. Dovedale and the Manifold Valley are justly famous for their scenery. This is ideal walking, cycling, pony trekking and fishing country, perfect for your stay on a farm.

If you would like help in finding suitable farm accommodation, turn to the full listing of farm groups on pages 360 to 363 to find appropriate contact details for this area.

Heartland — Derbyshire

Bed and Breakfast
(and evening meal)

---

① Beechenhill Farm, Ilam, Ashbourne, Derbyshire DE6 2BD

Sue Prince
☎/Fax 01335 310274
BB From £20–£27
Sleeps 5
🐎 ✂ ♿ ⓘ
♛♛ Highly Commended

Wake up to wonderful views over a country garden, grazing cows and sheep, Florence the goat, walkable hills and explorable valleys, at our warm old farmhouse near Dovedale. We've two delightful rooms; 1 family and 1 double, both en suite, own lounge, all beautifully decorated by artist Sue! Fruit, yoghurts and famous Beechenhill porridge feature as well as carefully cooked farmhouse breakfasts. Open March–Nov.
E-mail: beechenhill@btinternet.com.uk

---

② Beeches Farmhouse, Waldley, Doveridge, Nr Ashbourne, Derbyshire DE6 5LR

Barbara Tunnicliffe
☎ 01889 590288
Fax 01889 590559
BB From £28–£42
EM From £13.50
🐎 ⓘ ♿ ⓘ
♛♛♛ Highly Commended

Relax and unwind in our rural retreat after exploring the Derbyshire Dales or the thrills of Alton Towers. Dine in our AA Rosette award-winning 18th century licensed farm-house restaurant. Fresh English food and homemade desserts. Meet our Shetland pony, pigs, dogs, rabbits and kittens, whilst enjoying the freedom of the gardens, fields and the beautiful countryside. Closed Christmas.
E-mail: beechesfa@aol.com.uk

---

③ Chevin Green Farm, Chevin Road, Belper, Derbyshire DE56 2UN

Carl & Joan Postles
☎/Fax 01773 822328
BB From £15–£21
Sleeps 14
🐎 ✂ 🚗 🧳 🎋 ⓘ
♛♛ Commended

Relax in peaceful picturesque countryside. Our extended and refurbished beamed farmhouse offers twin, double and family en suite rooms. Enjoy generous breakfasts. Guests own lounge and dining room. Within easy reach of Dales, Peak District, stately homes (6) and Alton Towers. Pleasant walks, riding and golf nearby. Reductions for children sharing and weekly terms. Open all year except Christmas and New Year.

---

④ Cote Bank Farm, Buxworth, Whaley Bridge, High Peak, Derbyshire SK23 7NP

Pamela Broadhurst
☎/Fax 01663 750566
BB From £20–£25
Sleeps 5
🐎(6) ✗ ✂ 🧳 🎋 ⓘ
♛♛ Highly Commended

Good old fashioned hospitality, a kettle always on the boil and a breakfast worth waking for! Treat yourself to a relaxing stay on our peaceful sheep farm with stunning views across the hills and excellent walks. A home from home for business travellers (1 mile Chinley, 3 miles A6) and a welcoming base for holidaymakers. Guest lounge with log fire; 1 double, 1 family, both en suite, with TV, radio, tea/coffee. Open Mar–Dec.
E-mail: cotebank@btinternet.com.uk

---

⑤ Dannah Farm Country Guest House, Bowmans Lane, Shottle, Belper, Derbyshire DE56 2DR

Joan & Martin Slack
☎ 01773 550273/550630
Fax 01773 550590
BB From £35–£55
EM From £16.95
Sleeps 18
🐎(8) ⓘ 🎋 🧳 ⓘ
♛♛♛ Highly Commended

Winners Bed & Breakfast of the Year '94, also top national award for farm catering. Hopefully we have it all, from pot-bellied pigs to award-winning food and, above all, the warmest of welcomes! Relax in our lovely Georgian farmhouse on our mixed working farm. All rooms en suite. Colour TVs, fully licensed. AA QQQQQ Premier Selected, RAC Highly Acclaimed. Johansens recommended. Open all year except Christmas. E-mail: dannah.demon.co.uk

Derbyshire — Heartland

Lane End Farm, Abney, Hathersage, Hope Valley, via Sheffield, Derbyshire S32 1AH

Mrs Jill Salisbury
☎/Fax 01433 650371
BB From £18–£28
Sleeps 6
Listed *Highly Commended*

Award-winning farmhouse on sheep farm above the Hope Valley. Wake up to unrivalled views from delightful bedrooms. Start the day with a large traditional English breakfast, then take to footpaths or explore the farm nature trail. Whether for pleasure or business, the farmhouse offers superb accommodation. Antiques and country fabrics. 3 bedrooms (1 en suite) all with tea/coffee facilities. CH. TV lounge. Own horse welcome. Open all year except Christmas. E-mail: laneendfarm@btinternet.com.uk

Lydgate Farm, Aldwark, Grange Mill, Matlock, Derbyshire DE4 4HW

Joy Lomas
☎/Fax 01629 540250
BB From £18–£22
Sleeps 6
Commended

A warm welcome and good food await you in our 17th century house on a 300-acre dairy and sheep farm. Lydgate is ideally situated for visiting Chatsworth, Haddon Hall and all Derbyshire has to offer. Central heating and hot drink facilities in all rooms, one family en suite, one twin en suite, one double. Guests' own dining room and sitting room. Open Jan–Nov.
E-mail: joy.lomas@btinternet.com.uk

Mercaston Hall, Mercaston, Brailsford, Ashbourne, Derbyshire DE6 3BL

Angus & Vicki Haddon
☎ 01335 360263
Fax 01335 361399
BB From £20–£22.50
Sleeps 6
Commended

Timber-framed, historic, listed building in a quiet countryside location. Situated off the A52 halfway between Derby and Ashbourne. An ideal centre for visits to the Peak District, many tourist attractions and the commercial towns and cities of the Midlands. Kedleston Hall (NT) 1 mile. Hard tennis court. Open all year except Christmas.

Middlehills Farm, Grange Mill, Matlock, Derbyshire DE4 4HY

Mrs Linda Lomas
☎/Fax 01629 650368
BB From £20
Sleeps 9
Commended

Escape the rat race – taste the fresh air, absorb the peace, feast your eyes on the beautiful scenery and magnificent views that surround our small working farm 5 miles west of Matlock on the A5012. Large walled garden, two en suite family rooms, one en suite twin, all with tea/coffee facilities. Comfortable lounge with TV and pool table.
E-mail: l.lomas@btinternet.com.uk

The Old Bake & Brewhouse, Blackwell Hall, Blackwell in the Peak, Taddington, nr Buxton, Derbys SK17 9TQ

Mrs Christine Gregory
☎ 01298 85271
BB From £18–£21
Sleeps 4
Commended

Early 18th century much loved farmhouse with its old oak, chintz and the scent of beeswax and honeysuckle, set in a peaceful, mature garden. Our home is in the Peak National Park and the farm has archaeological and conservation sites. From our door join the lovely River Wye as it meanders through spectacular Chee Dale and Monsal Dale. Delicious, hearty Derbyshire breakfasts with home made preserves. Open all year.
E-mail: christine.gregory@btinternet.com.uk

Park View Farm, Weston Underwood, Ashbourne, Derbyshire DE6 4PA

Mrs Linda Adams
☎/Fax 01335 360352
BB From £22.50–£28
Sleeps 6
Highly Commended

Enjoy country house hospitality in our elegant farmhouse set in large gardens with lovely views overlooking the National Trust's magnificent Kedleston Park, hence the farm's name. Double en suite rooms with antique four-poster beds, twin with handbasin and bathroom. Drinks facilities. Guests' sitting room and delightful dining room. Superb English breakfasts. Country pubs and restaurants close by. AA QQQQQ Premier Selected. Closed Christmas.

Heartland   Derbyshire

12 Shallow Grange, Chelmorton, nr Buxton, Derbyshire SK17 9SG

Christine Holland
☎ 01298 23578
Fax 01298 78242
BB From £22–£30
Sleeps 6
⚘ (5) ⚘ ⚘ ⚘ ⚘ ⚘
⚘⚘ *Highly Commended*

Spectacular views, wide open spaces and a piece of rural England all await you at Shallow Grange. Luxury accommodation includes all rooms en suite, colour TVs, etc. This working dairy farm has numerous unspoilt walks whilst Chatsworth, Buxton and Bakewell are all within a short drive. We also have 20-pitch caravan site. *Which?* recommended. Open all year.

13 Shirley Hall, Shirley, Ashbourne, Derbyshire DE6 3AS

Mrs Sylvia Foster
☎/Fax 01335 360346
BB From £18–£25
Sleeps 6
⚘ (10) ⚘ ⚘ ⚘ ⚘
⚘⚘ *Highly Commended*

Enjoy the tranquillity of our lovely old, part moated, timbered farmhouse, surrounded by large lawned garden and rolling dairy/arable farm just 4 miles from Ashbourne. Our English breakfasts are renowned. Village pub within walking distance for excellent evening meals. Free coarse fishing. Woodland walks. 2 double bedrooms en suite. 1 twin with handbasin and guest's bathroom. All with CH, TV and drinks facilities. Guests' sitting room. Open all year.

14 Throwley Hall Farm, Ilam, Ashbourne, Derbyshire DE6 2BB

Mrs MA Richardson
☎ 01538 308202
Fax 01538 308243
BB From £20–£25
Sleeps 9
⚘ ⚘ ⚘ ⚘ ⚘
⚘⚘ *Commended*

Large Georgian farmhouse on working hill farm with beef and sheep. Nestling in beautiful countryside in the Manifold Valley, close to Dovedale. Superb walking country, Alton Towers a short drive. All rooms have tea/coffee facilities, TV and washbasin, some en suite. Full English breakfast. Open all year.

15 Wolfscote Grange Farm, Hartington, Nr Buxton, Derbyshire SK17 0AX

Jane Gibbs
☎ 01298 84342
BB From £19–£24
Sleeps 6
⚘ ⚘ ⚘ ⚘ ⚘
Applied

Find an ideal 'country hideaway' on our secluded hill farm with beautiful views over the Dove Valley. Along a stone-walled road from picturesque Hartington village. Feel at home in our ancient 15th century farmhouse with all its character, original oak beams, mullion windows, spiral staircase. Spacious guests' lounge, 2 pretty bedrooms, 1 family, 1 double en suite, tea/coffee facilities. Breakfast, then explore the many footpaths leading to hidden Dales below. Open Mar–Nov.

16 Yeldersley Old Hall Farm, Yeldersley Lane, Bradley, Ashbourne, Derbyshire DE6 1PH

Mrs Janet Hinds
☎/Fax 01335 344504
BB From £19–£25
Sleeps 6
⚘ ⚘ ⚘ ⚘
⚘⚘ *Commended*

Yeldersley Old Hall Farm is a family-run dairy farm of 112 acres. The Grade II listed farmhouse is situated in pleasant and quiet rural surroundings just 3 miles from the market town of Ashbourne and within easy reach of Dovedale, Alton Towers, Matlock and many stately homes. Farmhouse breakfast provided. Lounge with log fire. All rooms en suite. Non-smokers only please. Open Mar–Nov.

Our farms offer a range of facilities that are illustrated by symbols in each entry. Turn to page 16 for an explanation of the symbols.

Derbyshire Heartland

Self-Catering

Archway Cottage, Lane End Farm, Abney, Hathersage, Hope Valley, via Sheffield, Derbys S32 1AH

Jill Salisbury
☎/Fax 01433 650371
SC From £180–£275
Sleeps 2/4
Commended

Beams, pine furniture, lovely decor make our well-equipped cottage a must for the discerning visitor to the Peak District. Tucked away on our working hill farm in a small hamlet. Superb views, many fabulous walks. Ideally situated for all Derbyshire attractions. 1 double bedroom, sofa bed in lounge. Linen, electricity included. No pets. Own horse welcome. Open all year.
E-mail: laneendfarm@btinternet.com.uk

Beechenhill Cottage & The Cottage by the Pond, Beechenhill Farm, Ilam, Ashbourne, Derbys, DE6 2BD

Mrs Sue Prince
☎/Fax 01335 310274
SC From £100–£430
Sleeps 2–6
Highly Commended

Beechenhill Cottage, tiny and warm in pretty walled garden, a secluded holiday just for two.
The Cottage by the Pond, award-winning cottage, for all including wheelchair users. Sleeps six in three bedrooms, two bathrooms. Both cottages have real fires and beautiful decoration by artist Sue! Meet Florence the goat, Scrabble, Boggle and Meg! Open all year.
E-mail: beechenhill@btinternet.com.uk

Briar, Bluebell & Primrose Cottages, c/o Yeldersley Old Hall Farm, Yeldersley Lane, Bradley, Ashbourne, Derbyshire DE6 1PH

Mrs Janet Hinds
☎/Fax 01335 344504
SC From £150–£310
Sleep 5/6
Commended

Situated on a working family dairy farm in rural surroundings, our Grade II listed barn has been converted into 3 self-catering cottages. Two accommodate 5 people (maximum), one 6 people. Each has three bedrooms with bathroom containing bath and shower, fitted kitchen, colour TV. Ample parking area. Ideal spot for touring Derbyshire. Ashbourne 3 miles. Short breaks. Open all year.

Chapelgate Cottage, c/o Lydgate Farm, Aldwark, Grange Mill, Matlock, Derbyshire DE4 4HW

Joy Lomas
☎/Fax 01629 540250
SC From £200–£280
Sleeps 5 + cot
Highly Commended

Beautiful oak beamed, stone mullioned cottage with lovely views and garden, set in the peaceful hamlet of Aldwark. Well appointed open plan kitchen/living area with log fire and colour TV. Two bedrooms and bathroom/shower room. The cottage is centrally heated, double glazed and fully carpeted throughout. Towels, fresh linen and electricity are included. Chapelgate Cottage will give you a wonderful holiday in the heart of the Peak District. Open all year. E-mail: joy.lomas@btinternet.com.uk

Chevin Green Farm, Chevin Road, Belper, Derbyshire DE56 2UN

Carl & Joan Postles
☎/Fax 01773 822328
SC From £100–£315
Sleeps 4/6
Commended

Enjoy a holiday in one of our four attractive cottages of character overlooking picturesque countryside. The cottages with original beams are fully equipped to a high standard. Lounge, fully fitted kitchen, bathroom, 2 or 3 bedrooms, one is specially adapted for the disabled. Ideally situated for all places of interest, Alton Towers, Dales, Peak District and 6 stately homes. Open all year except Christmas and New Year.

Heartland — Derbyshire

17 The Chop House, Windle Hill Farm, Sutton-on-the-Hill, Ashbourne, Derbyshire DE6 5JH

K E & J Lennard
☎/Fax 01283 732377
[SC] From £140–£350
Sleeps 6

Commended

The Chop House was originally built in 1858 as the farm corn shed. It has been carefully converted to offer cosy, well-equipped family accommodation on our small working farm. Centrally heated, fully insulated, ideal for winter or summer lets. 3 twin bedrooms, kitchen/dining room, separate living room. Sheltered garden. Set amidst tranquil countryside south of Ashbourne. Open all year.

---

4 Cote Bank Farm Cottages, Buxworth, Whaley Bridge, High Peak, Derbyshire SK23 7NP

Pamela Broadhurst
☎/Fax 01663 750566
[SC] From £190–£460
Sleeps 2/6 + cot

Highly Commended

Two warm, welcoming cottages on peaceful sheep farm with magnificent views and excellent walks. Chinley 1 mile, Buxton 7 miles. Children can feed the hens with farmer Nic and see happy animals reared naturally. Each cottage has 3 bedrooms (double, twin, bunks), lounge with logfire, TV and video, dining room, modern kitchen, full CH. 'Amongst the best farm cottages we know' – *Good Holiday Cottage Guide 1998*. Short breaks Nov–March. Open all year.
E-mail: cotebank@btinternet.com.uk

---

15 Cruck & Wolfscote Cottages, Wolfscote Grange Farm, Hartington, Nr Buxton, Derbyshire SK17 0AX

Jane Gibbs
☎/Fax 01298 84342
[SC] From £140–£430
Sleeps 4–6 + cot

Highly Commended

Enjoy spectacular scenery from our superb cottages. Cruck Cottage 'peaceful and away from it all with no neighbours only cows and sheep!', nestling above the beautiful Dove Valley. Wolfscote Cottage in a unique position with panoramic views across open meadows, hills and dales, on a secluded working sheep farm. Cosy welcoming cottages prettily stencilled, original features. 'Enjoy the views, relax in peaceful surroundings or explore the Derbyshire Dales on the cottage doorstep.' Open all year.

---

18 Culland Mount Farm, Brailsford, Ashbourne, Derbyshire DE6 3BW

Carolyn Phillips
☎/Fax 01335 360313
[SC] From £150–£320
Sleeps 4/6

Commended

Come and enjoy a relaxing holiday in our magnificent Victorian farmhouse with splendid views of rolling countryside. Whilst retaining many original features (marble fire grate), the house is divided making a luxurious holiday home – equally attractive to holiday makers and business people. Signposted walks all around and we welcome visitors to walk around the farm to see the cows and calves.

---

13 Hall Farm Bungalow, New House Farm & The Saddlery, c/o Shirley Hall, Shirley, Ashbourne, Derbyshire DE6 3AS

Mrs Sylvia Foster
☎/Fax 01335 360346
[SC] From £130–£360
Sleeps 4/8

Commended

Relax in one of our superb properties at separate locations in unspoilt countryside 4 miles from Ashbourne. Bungalow near Shirley village has 3 bedrooms, large garden, lovely views. Peacefully situated 18th century farmhouse at Mercaston near Brailsford has 4 bedrooms. The Saddlery is a listed self-contained 1st floor barn conversion (family bedroom) on our farm. All very comfortable and well appointed. Private coarse fishing. Open all year.

---

19 The Hayloft, Stanley House Farm, Great Hucklow, Buxton, Derbyshire SK17 8RL

Margot Darley
☎ 01298 871044
[SC] From £140–£295
Sleeps 4

Commended

Enjoy a relaxing holiday in peaceful surroundings in our stone barn conversion which offers excellent accommodation for four people. Spacious beamed sitting room with log fire and colour TV. Quality fitted kitchen/dining room, modern bathroom/WC. The Hayloft offers an ideal centre for exploring the Peak District. All linen, towels and fuel included in price. Open all year except Christmas and New Year.
E-mail: stan'house@btinternet.com.uk

Derbyshire   Heartland

Honeysuckle & Brook Cottages, c/o Park View Farm, Weston Underwood, Ashbourne, Derbys DE6 4PA **11**

Mrs Linda Adams
☎/Fax 01335 360352
SC From £130–£395
Sleeps 4/6 + cot
Commended

Honeysuckle is a truly delightful country cottage set in its own secluded garden with wonderful views over the Derbyshire countryside. Full of character and charm, furnished to a very high standard, with beamed sitting room, antique furnishings and pretty four poster bed. Accommodation for 6 persons in 3 bedrooms. Brook is a welcoming village cottage with 2 bedrooms (double and twin). Short breaks. Open all year.

Honeysuckle, Jasmine & Clematis Cottages, Middlehills Farm, Grange Mill, Matlock, Derbys DE4 4HY **9**

Linda Lomas
☎/Fax 01629 650368
SC From £140–£450
Sleeps 4/8
Commended

Take a break from the treadmill of life. Relax on the patio beneath the sweetly scented honeysuckle and jasmine. Enjoy the peace and tranquillity at our recently converted cottages. Full of character – beams, parquet floors, rustic rose arches, yet equipped with all modern conveniences – double glazing, CH, living flame fire. Clematis Cottage, available for 1998, one level especially designed for the less able. Open all year. E-mail: l.lomas@btinternet.com.uk

The Old House, Cote Bank Farm, Buxworth, Whaley Bridge, High Peak, Derbyshire SK23 7NP **4**

Pamela Broadhurst
☎/Fax 01663 750566
SC From £170–£270
Sleeps 2
Applied

A honeymoon hideaway in romantic self-contained Tudor wing of farmhouse. Cleverly modernised but with original 16th century beams, mullions and oodles of character! Kitchen/diner, bathroom, large bedroom with king size bed, lounge with inglenook fireplace and log burner. Logs, coal, CH, electricity, fresh linen and towels included. Glorious views, wonderful walks, perfect peace. Chinley 1 mile. Open all year. E-mail: cotebank@btinternet.com.uk

Old House Farm Cottage, Old House Farm, Newhaven, Hartington, Buxton, Derbyshire SK17 0DY **20**

Sue Flower
☎/Fax 01629 636268
SC From £180–£330
Sleeps 6 + cot
Commended

Explore 'Peak Practice' Country from our warm well appointed cottage. Stay on a real working dairy/sheep farm where a high standard is maintained. Lambing time a must in April. We run a busy family farm, still having time to answer your questions and delighted to let you watch our farm activities. Off road cycling trails lead from our farm. Short breaks Nov–Mar. Brochure. Open all year. E-mail: s.flowerfarmaccom@btinternet.com

Plattwood Farm Cottage, Lyme Park Disley, Cheshire SK12 2NT **21**

Jill Emmott
☎/Fax 01625 872738
SC From £250–£450
Sleeps 6
Highly Commended

Beautiful location within the National Trust's Lyme Park (of Pride and Prejudice fame). Excellent walks, superb views over rolling countryside, an ideal base to explore the Peak District. Cosy and welcoming, the cottage is tastefully furnished. The master bedroom has a four-poster bed and en suite facilities. Landscaped garden and colourful courtyard. Open all year.
E-mail: plattwood farm@btinternet.com

Shatton Hall Farm Cottages, Bamford, Hope Valley, nr Sheffield, Derbyshire S33 0BG **22**

Angela Kellie
☎ 01433 620635
Fax 01433 620689
SC From £175–£350
Sleeps 4/6 + cot
Up to Highly Commended

Our comfortable, well equipped cottages are stone barn conversions around the Elizabethan farmstead in a peaceful setting. Streamside and woodland walks. Fishing, riding, cycle hire nearby. Each cottage has terrace/garden. Ample car parking. Open plan living room, open fires, CH, colour TV, well equipped kitchen. 2 double bedrooms, linen included. Put-u-up and cot available. Laundry facilities. Hard tennis court. Open all year.
E-mail: a.j.kellie@virgin.net.uk

Heartland   Derbyshire

㉓ Shaw Farm, Shaw Marsh, New Mills, High Peak, Derbyshire SK22 4QE

Mrs Nicky Burgess
☎ 0161 427 1841
SC From £185–£325
Sleeps 8
Commended

Views and cows, walks to suit, a picnic in the wood. Come to us we have it all, a real farm delight. Three bedroomed cottage, price reduced if family room not required. Full CH, south-facing garden with patio, children's play area. Pub with grub 5 mins' walk. Short breaks. Open all year.

⑭ Throwley Moor Farm & Throwley Cottage, Ilam, Ashbourne, Derbyshire DE6 2BB

Mrs MA Richardson
☎ 01538 308202
Fax 01538 308243
SC From £180–£600
Sleeps 7–12
Commended

Attractive self-catering farmhouse and cottage conveniently situated near to the beautiful Manifold Valley and Dovedale. Superb scenery and walking country, Alton Towers is a short drive away. Both well equipped with fridge, freezer, microwave, dishwasher, washing machine, TV and video. Open all year.

LET THE TELEPHONE RING!
Some farmhouses are big places. Let the telephone ring long enough to give the owner time to answer it.

STAY ON A FARM GIFT TOKENS

If you have enjoyed your Stay on a Farm, why not treat your friends and relatives to *Stay on a Farm* gift tokens? Available from the Bureau office (tel: 01203 696909), they can be redeemed against accommodation and are accepted by the majority of farms (see Index). Please check when booking to avoid disappointment.

Our Internet address is
http://www.webscape.co.uk/farmaccom/

Nottinghamshire

Sherwood Forest & the Dukeries

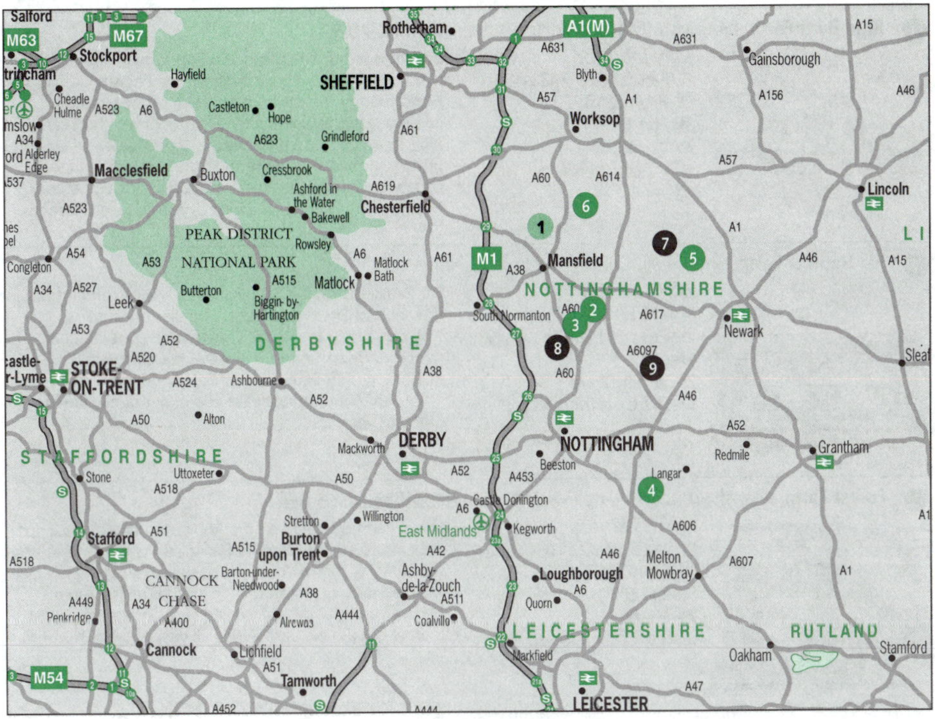

Key

 Bed & Breakfast
 Self-Catering
 B&B and SC
 Camping Barns
 Camping & Caravanning

Think of Nottinghamshire and you think of Sherwood Forest; think of Sherwood Forest and you think of Robin Hood. He can still be found here, at the Sherwood Forest Visitor Centre near Edwinstowe and also in Nottingham, in a statue outside the castle. At the foot of Castle Rock is the Brewhouse Yard Museum illustrating the city's social history while nearby the Canal Museum and the Musem of Costume and Textile show other aspects of Nottingham's heritage. Worksop and Retford are pleasant market towns and the open-air markets at Newark and Mansfield are popular with visitors. Southwell, though hardly more than a village, has an impressive Minster which is well worth a visit.

If you would like help in finding suitable farm accommodation, turn to the full listing of farm groups on pages 360 to 363 to find appropriate contact details for this area.

Heartland — Nottinghamshire

Bed and Breakfast
(and evening meal)

① Blue Barn Farm, Langwith, Mansfield, Nottinghamshire NG20 9JD

June Ibbotson
☎/Fax 01623 742248
BB From £18–£22
Sleeps 6
Commended

Welcome to our family-run 450-acre farm in peaceful surroundings on the edge of Sherwood Forest in Robin Hood country, 5 miles from M1 (J30) off A616. Many interesting places catering for all tastes only a short car journey away. Suitable for the business traveller, a place to unwind. 1 double, 1 twin en suite, 1 family, all with tea/coffee-making facilities and washbasins. Cot available. Dining room, lounge, TV. Open all year (closed Christmas Day & New Year).

② Far Baulker Farm, Southwell, Oxton, Nottinghamshire NG25 0RQ

Janette Esam
☎ 01623 882375
BB From £16–£25
Sleeps 6
Listed Commended

Far Baulker Farm is a 300-acre arable/livestock farm set in the heart of Sherwood Forest 10 miles north of Nottingham on the A614. One double en suite, one double with washbasin, one twin, tea/coffee-making facilities and TV in all rooms. Visitors lounge with TV/video. A welcome awaits you in our family home. Open all year.

③ Forest Farm, Mansfield Road, Papplewick, Nottinghamshire NG15 8FL

Mrs E J Stubbs
☎ 0115 9632310
BB From £16–£20
Sleeps 5
Listed Commended

Forest Farm is located on the A60 standing well back up the farm road away from traffic noise. Pleasant views from south-facing rooms, 1 double en suite, 1 single, 1 twin, all with tea-making facilities. TV in lounge/dining room. Midway between Mansfield and Nottingham, and ideal touring or business base. Open all year except Christmas.

④ Jerico Farm, Fosse Way, Nr Cotgrave, Nottinghamshire NG12 3HG

Mrs Sally Herrick
☎/Fax 01949 81733
BB From £19–£28
Sleeps 6
Commended

A working farm with attractive accommodation surrounded by our own farmland with lovely views. Good firm beds, tea/coffee/chocolate trays and TVs in all bedrooms, (one en suite). Guests' sitting room. Good pubs nearby. Excellent location for visiting Nottingham, its universities, sports venues and tourist sites. Located down a farm drive off A46, 1 mile north of A46/A606 jct, south of Cotgrave village. Open all year (closed Christmas).

⑤ Manor Farm, Moorhouse Road, Laxton, Newark, Nottinghamshire NG22 0NU

Mrs Pat Haigh
☎ 01777 870417
BB From £16–£17
EM From £8.50
Sleeps 6
Listed Commended

Manor Farm is a family-run dairy and arable farm of 137 acres, in the historic medieval village of Laxton, situated 10 miles north of Newark, and on the verge of the popular tourist area of Sherwood Forest in Nottinghamshire. 2 family rooms, 1 double room, tea/coffee-making facilities available. Visitors' lounge and dining room. Access to rooms at all times. Open all year (closed Christmas & New Year).

Nottinghamshire   Heartland

Norton Grange Farm, Norton, Cuckney, Mansfield, Nottinghamshire NG20 9LP ⑥

        Fernie Palmer
        ☎ 01623 842666
        BB *From £17–£18*
        Sleeps 4
        Commended

Norton Grange is a Grade II listed farmhouse set in the heart of the Welbeck Estate, part of the world-famous Sherwood Forest. Ideally situated for overnight stops or touring the very beautiful countryside and the many attractions, in Nottinghamshire and Derbyshire. One double room and one twin room, both with washbasin and tea/coffee-making facilities. Open all year except Christmas & New Year.

Self-Catering

Blue Barn Cottage, c/o Blue Barn Farm, Langwith, Mansfield, Nottinghamshire NG20 9JD ①

        June Ibbotson
        ☎/Fax 01623 742248
        SC *From £375–£425*
        Sleeps 8 + cot
        Commended

Do come and relax in peace and comfort on our family-run farm in Robin Hood country. Visit quiet villages, stately homes rich in history, ramble through country parks or hunt bargains in thriving market towns. Blue Barn is off the A616 near Cuckney. 4 bedrooms, bathroom, breakfast kitchen, dining room, lounge, TV, washing machine and dryer. CH and linen included. Open all year.

Foliat Cottages, c/o Jordan Castle Farm, Wellow, Newark, Nottinghamshire NG22 0EL ⑦

        Mrs Janet Carr
        ☎/Fax 01623 861088
        SC *From £200–£325*
        Sleeps 6 + cot
        Commended

Close to the heart of Sherwood Forest, our Edwardian cottages have beautiful pastoral views across our working family farm. Peaceful and cosy, with central heating, colour TV, microwave and washer/dryer. Each has 1 double and 2 twin bedrooms, bathroom and shower room. Cot and highchair available. Enclosed south-facing gardens with patios. Linen provided. Brochure available. Open all year. E-mail: janet.carr@farmline.com.uk

The Granary, Top House Farm, Lamins Lane, Mansfield Road, Arnold, Nottingham, Notts NG5 8PH ⑧

        Mrs Ann Lamin
        ☎ 0115 9268330
        SC *From £250–£295*
        Sleeps 3/4
        Commended

Charming granary flat with beams, open fireplace, CH. Lounge has colour TV, patio doors onto garden. Kitchen has electric and microwave ovens, use of automatic washer and dryer. Within easy reach of Nottingham, Newstead Abbey, Southwell Minster, the Dukeries, Sherwood Forest, Derbyshire and the National Watersports Centre. Open all year.

The Mews, Eastwood Farm, Hagg Lane, Epperstone, Nottingham NG14 6AX ⑨

        Susan Santos
        ☎ 0115 9663018
        SC *From £140–£190*
        Sleeps 4 +cot
        Approved

Our peaceful, homely self-contained flat, with lovely views, is within easy reach of Nottingham, Southwell, Newark and Mansfield. At first floor level, adjacent to the farmhouse, it comprises 1 double, 1 twin bedroom, bathroom, living/dining room (colour TV), and well equipped kitchen. CH included in rental. Garage parking. Golf courses, Trent river and pond fishing nearby. Ideal leisure, touring or business base. Open all year.

Lincolnshire

Lincolnshire Wolds & Tennyson Country

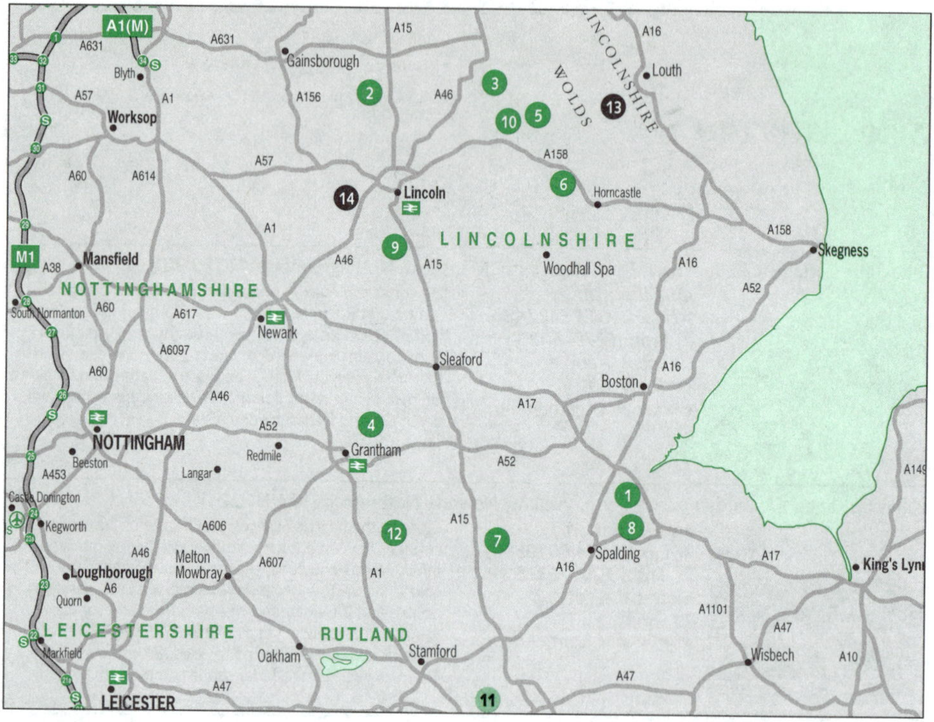

Key

- 1 Bed & Breakfast
- 1 Self-Catering
- 1 B&B and SC
- 1 Camping Barns
- 1 Camping & Caravanning

A frequent comment of first-time visitors to Lincolnshire is: "I never realised there was so much to see and do". Don't miss Lincoln with its magnificent cathedral, castle and Museum of Lincolnshire Life; Belton House near Grantham; Stamford, a near-perfect stone town or its brick-built equivalent, Louth; and Elizabethan houses such as Doddington Hall and Burghley House. Explore the hidden lanes of Tennyson Country in the south of the lovely Lincolnshire Wolds. Visit unspoilt market towns, walk part of the Viking Way, see Boston and its Stump, the memorial marking the spot where the Pilgrim Fathers tried to leave England... Sorry, no more space – you'll just have to come and see for yourself!

If you would like help in finding suitable farm accommodation, turn to the full listing of farm groups on pages 360 to 363 to find appropriate contact details for this area.

Lincolnshire   Heartland

Bed and Breakfast
(and evening meal)

Cackle Hill House, Cackle Hill Lane, Holbeach, Lincolnshire PE12 8BS

Maureen Biggadike
☎ 01406 426721
Fax 01406 424659
[BB] From £20–£24
Sleeps 6
🐴(10) 🐓 ⚡ 💼
🌿🌿 *Highly Commended*

We welcome you to our farm situated in rural position just off the A17. Comfortable accommodation (en suites and private facilities) and traditional farmhouse fare. Farm walks, large patio and gardens. Close to the shores of the Wash with its marshes, trails and mature reserves, Spalding, Boston, Norfolk and Cambridgeshire. Open all year.

Church Farm, Fillingham, Gainsborough, Lincolnshire DN21 5BS

Christine Ramsay
☎ 01427 668279
Fax 01427 668025
[BB] From £17–£20
EM From £8
Sleeps 6
🐴(5) ⚡ 💼 ◎
Listed *Highly Commended*

Church Farm is an 18th century stone farmhouse set in a peaceful garden that has sweeping and well cut lawns – they are surrounded by flower-filled troughs and the only sound is of birdsong. All bedrooms have wonderful countryside views. Hemswell Antique Centre and Lincolnshire Showground close by. Open all year except Christmas and New Year.

East Farm House, Middle Rasen Road, Buslingthorpe, Market Rasen, Lincolnshire LN3 5AQ

Mrs Gill Grant
☎ 01673 842383
[BB] From £20
EM From £12
Sleeps 4
🐴 🐓 ⚡ 🎯 💼 🐾
🌿🌿 *Highly Commended*

Peace and relaxation await you in beamed 18th century listed farmhouse on 410 acre conservation award-winning farm with farm trail overlooking unspoilt countryside. Situated 4 miles SW of Market Rasen, ideal for rambling, touring beautiful Lincolnshire Wolds, coast, historic Lincoln and market towns. Wholesome farmhouse food, spacious bedrooms, TV and tea/coffee makers. 1 double en suite, 1 twin with private facilities. Guests' lounge. Business people welcome. Open all year.

Gelston Grange Farm, Nr Marston, Grantham, Lincolnshire NG32 2AQ

Janet Sharman
☎/Fax 01400 250281
[BB] From £17.50–£25
Sleeps 6
🐴(5) ⚡ 💼
🌿🌿 *Commended*

We are known for our welcome and homely atmosphere. Comfortable beds, 1 four poster en suite room, 1 double, 1 twin, all with HC, tea/coffee trays, TV, CH and tastefully decorated. Full English breakfast. Large garden. Lots of places to visit – Belton House, Lincoln, Newark, Boston and the coast, Robin Hood country. Northward on A1 take first right turn for Marston (after Grantham roundabout). Open all year except Christmas and New Year.

The Grange, Torrington Lane, East Barkwith, Market Rasen, Lincolnshire LN8 5RY

Mrs Sarah Stamp
☎ 01673 858670
[BB] From £22–£28
Sleeps 4
🐴 ⚡ 🚗 ☕ 🎯 💼 ◎
🌿🌿 *Highly Commended*

The Stamp family gives you a warm welcome to Grange Farm, a beautiful, spacious Georgian farmhouse peacefully situated with views of Lincoln Cathedral to the west and the Wolds to the east. Two double en suite rooms with TV and tea/coffee trays. Guests' sitting room, log fires. Lawn tennis. Unwind on the award winning farm trail, stopping for a break at the secluded trout lake. Open all year except Christmas and New Year.

Heartland — Lincolnshire

6 Greenfield Farm, Minting, near Horncastle, Lincolnshire LN9 5RX

Mrs Judy Bankes Price
☎/Fax 01507 578457
BB From £20
Sleeps 6
☼(10) ⅍ ♠ ▪ ◉
♛ ♛ Highly Commended

Judy and Hugh welcome you to their comfortable farmhouse set in a quiet location yet central for all the major Lincolnshire attractions. Play tennis, relax by the large garden pond or enjoy the forest walks that border the farm. Modern en suite shower rooms, heated towel rails, radios, tea/coffee facilities, CH. Ample parking. Excellent pub with traditional country cooking 1 mile. AA Selected QQQQ. Open mid Jan–mid Dec.

7 Greenoaks, Pinfold Lane, Pointon, Sleaford, Lincolnshire NG34 0NB

Mrs Ann Firth
☎ 01529 240193
Fax 01529 240612
BB From £20–£25
Sleeps 5
☼(10) ⅍ ▪ ◉
♛ ♛ Highly Commended

Ann and Anthony welcome you to their Georgian farmhouse set in mature grounds in a peaceful village. Centrally situated for stately homes – Belvoir Castle, Burghley House, Belton House. Spacious sitting room with French windows to garden and separate dining room. Ann enjoys cooking and offers evening meals by prior arrangement. All rooms centrally heated. Closed Christmas and New Year.
E-mail: ranthony.firth@btinternet.com.uk

8 Guy Wells Farm, Eastgate, Whaplode, Spalding, Lincolnshire PE12 6TZ

Anne Thompson
☎/Fax 01406 422239
BB From £19–£23
EM From £10
Sleeps 6
☼(5) ♠ ⅍ ▪
♛ ♛ Highly Commended

Anne and Richard welcome you to their listed Queen Anne farmhouse set in a peaceful country garden, close to the famous fenland churches, the Wash, Sandringham, the coast, Boston, Stamford and Peterborough. Guy Wells is their home offering a few guests (non-smokers) spacious en suite accommodation with full CH, flowers, log fires and TV. Closed Christmas and New Year.

9 The Manor House, Manor Farm, Sleaford Road, Bracebridge Heath, Lincoln, Lincolnshire LN4 2HW

Mrs Jill Scoley
☎ 01522 520825
Fax 01522 542418
BB From £21–£26
Sleeps 6
☼(10) ⅍ ▪ ◉
♛ ♛ Highly Commended

Welcome to Lincolnshire. Stay in a lovely Georgian farmhouse situated in large walled garden. 3 miles south of Lincoln. Comfortable bedrooms two en suite, one with private facilities, all with radio, tea/coffee facilities. Large lounge with log fire for cooler evenings. Open all year (closed Christmas and New Year).

10 The Manor House, West Barkwith, Market Rasen, Lincoln LN8 5LF

Mrs J A Hobbins
☎/Fax 01673 858253
BB £25
EM From £10.50
Sleeps 4
☼(12) ⅍
♛ ♛ Highly Commended

The Manor Farm is a 400-acre arable farm. The house stands in extensive landscaped grounds overlooking lawns, ornamental pond, rock garden and lake. Screened from the road by mature trees providing an attractive setting and seclusion. All rooms enjoy an uninterrupted view of the lake. An ideal base for touring the Wolds and historic Lincoln. Closed Christmas and New Year.

11 Midstone Farmhouse, Southorpe, Stamford, Lincolnshire PE9 3BX

Mr & Mrs C Harrison-Smith
☎/Fax 01780 740136
BB From £20–£30
EM From £10
Sleeps 8
☼ ♠ ▪ ◉
Listed Commended

Midstone House is an 18th century farmhouse where a warm welcome awaits you. Many original features remain although we provide all the best modern standards of comfort and amenity. A private lounge is available for guests to use. We have a small herd of Dexter cattle, ponies, ducks and a potbellied pig named 'George'. Brochure on request. Open all year except Christmas.

Lincolnshire   Heartland

Sycamore Farm, Bassingthorpe, Grantham, Lincs NG33 4ED

Mrs Sue Robinson
☎ 01476 585274
BB From £20
EM From £10
Sleeps 6
🛏(12) ⚲ 🛄 ⓘ
♨♨ Highly Commended

Set in peaceful unspoilt countryside Sycamore Farm offers the perfect place to relax and unwind. Spacious, pretty bedrooms with en suite bathrooms (1 private) and lovely views, comfortable guests' lounge with guide books, board games and log fire on chilly evenings. Ideally placed for A1 (4 miles), Stamford, Lincoln, historic Belton and Burghley. Open Mar–Nov.

Self-Catering

Bridle Cottage, Midstone Farmhouse, Southorpe, Stamford, Lincolnshire PE9 3BX

Mrs A Harrison-Smith
☎/Fax 01780 740136
SC From £200–£250
Sleeps 2/4 + cot
🛏 🐎 ⚲ 🛄 ⓘ
🏠🏠🏠 Highly Commended

A former coachhouse and stables tastefully converted into a comfortable cottage providing ground floor accommodation close to the farmhouse. Our farm has a small herd of Dexter cattle and a pot-bellied pig named 'George'. Open all year.

Mill Lodge, Benniworth House Farm, Donington on Bain, Louth, Lincs LN11 9RD

Mrs Pamela M Cade
☎/Fax 01507 343265
SC From £250–£350
Sleeps 4
🛏(10) ⚲ 🎄 🛄
🏠🏠🏠 Commended

Ezra and Pamela Cade welcome you to a delightful cottage on a traditional farm/Nature reserve in the beautiful Bain valley. Spacious grounds with conservatory, patio, lawn, flowering shrubs and lock up garage. Lovely walks with well maintained footpaths. Many species, some rare. Children welcome. Open all year.

Red House Farm Cottage, Red House Farm, Spalford Lane, North Scarle, Lincoln LN6 9HB

Mrs Helen Jones
☎ 01522 778224
SC From £160–£260
Sleeps 4/6
🛏 🛄 ⓘ
🏠🏠 Commended

Our brick and pantile cottage is ideally situated between Lincoln and Newark. The cottage offers spacious and comfortable accommodation with all modern amenities. Coarse fishing is available f.o.c. on our private lake. Colour brochure available. Open all year.

NO ANSWER?
Farmers are mostly out and about during the day.
Try to telephone before 9.30am or after 4pm.

Shropshire

Shropshire Union Canal, the Wrekin, Ironbridge Gorge, Shropshire Hills, the Long Mynd, Wenlock Edge, Clun Forest & the Marches

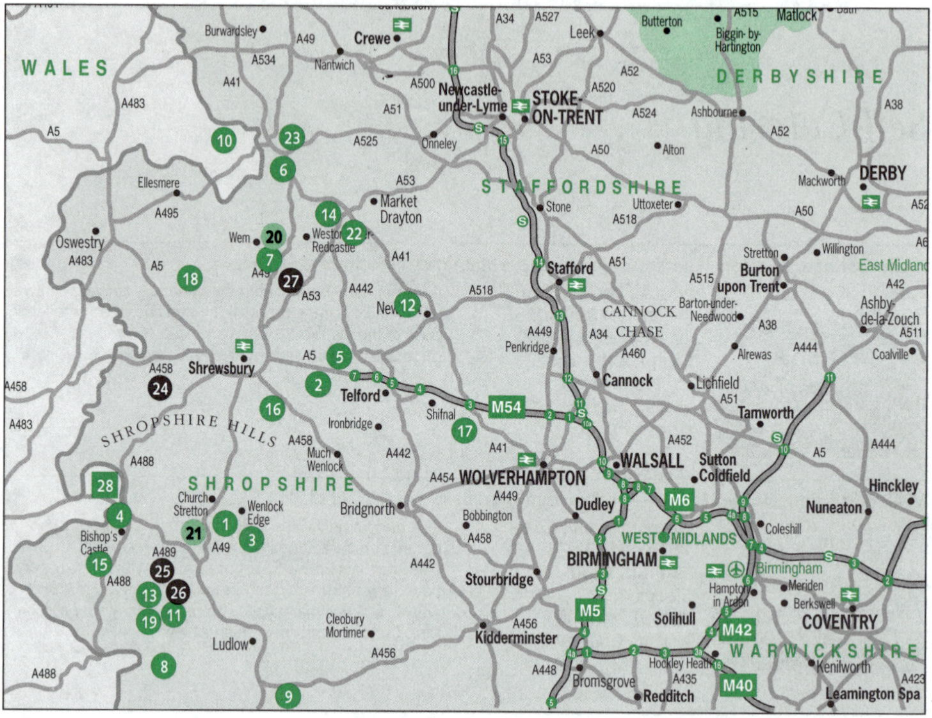

Key

- 1 Bed & Breakfast
- 1 Self-Catering
- 1 B&B and SC
- 1 Bunkhouses Camping Barns
- 1 Camping & Caravanning

Shropshire, with its wealth of historic houses, castles and abbeys, is England's largest landbound county. Medieval Shrewsbury, the county town, and up-to-date Telford are the principal centres with attractive market towns such as Craven Arms, Church Stretton and historic Ludlow scattered around. The World Heritage Site of Ironbridge, birthplace of the Industrial Revolution, is a must with its six fascinating museums. Being so large, the county caters for every need, with its own lake district at Ellesmere, hill country in South Shropshire, the Llangollen and Shropshire Union Canals, Severn Valley Steam Railway and miles of truly glorious countryside.

If you would like help in finding suitable farm accommodation, turn to the full listing of farm groups on pages 360 to 363 to find appropriate contact details for this area.

Shropshire   Heartland

Bed and Breakfast
(and evening meal)

Acton Scott Farm, Church Stretton, Shropshire SY6 6QN ①

Mary Jones
☎ 01694 781260
[BB] From £18–£22
Sleeps 6
Commended

Situated in beautiful countryside, adjacent to an historic working farm, the 17th century farmhouse of character has comfortable and spacious rooms, all with washbasin and en suite facilities or private bathroom. The spectacular hills and valley of Church Stretton are nearby and we are central for visiting Shrewsbury, Ludlow and Ironbridge. We look forward to welcoming you. Open mid Feb – mid Nov.

Avenue Farm, Uppington, Telford, Shropshire TF6 5HW ②

Mrs Mig Jones
☎ 01952 740253
Fax 01952 740401
[BB] From £18–£20
Sleeps 4
(5)
Commended

Charming 18th century farmhouse situated in the quiet, unspoilt village of Uppington. Set in extensive gardens with magnificent views of the Wrekin. Conveniently situated near Shrewsbury, Ironbridge and Telford, 2 miles from M54 J7. Guests' private sitting room with TV. Open all year.

Brereton House, Woolston Farm, Church Stretton, Shropshire SY6 6QD ③

Joanna Brereton
☎/Fax 01694 781201
[BB] From £19
EM From £9
Sleeps 6
Commended

Relax, unwind and enjoy the fine views of rolling countryside from the extensive garden on our working farm. Our Victorian farmhouse offers very spacious, comfortable, en suite rooms with beverage trays. Good hearty food is served. Close to Long Mynd and Ironbridge. Open Feb–Nov.

Broughton Farm, nr Bishop's Castle, Montgomery, Powys SY15 6SZ ④

Mrs Kate Bason
☎ 01588 638393
[BB] From £16–£20
Sleeps 6
Commended

A 140-acre cattle and sheep farm located near the Welsh border. The house is oak-framed and dates back to the 15th century. Traditional country house furnishings. Central heating. Comfortable bedrooms (one en suite) have washbasins and tea/coffee trays. Stroll around the farm and meet the animals or relax in the garden and enjoy the views. Open all year.

Church Farm, Wrockwardine, Wellington, Telford, Shropshire TF6 5DG ⑤

Mrs Jo Savage
☎/Fax 01952 244917
[BB] From £20–£25
EM From £16
Sleeps 8
(10)
Highly Commended

Down a lime tree avenue, in a peaceful village betwixt Shrewsbury and Telford, lies our superbly situated Georgian farmhouse. Mature gardens with medieval stonework, old roses and many unusual plants. Attractive bedrooms with TVs, tea/coffee/chocolate, some en suite with ground floor available. Enormous inglenook fireplace in spacious guests' lounge. Delicious breakfasts helped by free range hens! Minutes from Ironbridge, Shrewsbury and Telford. 1 mile M54 (J7) and A5. Open all year.

Heartland   Shropshire

⑥ Dearnford Hall, Whitchurch, Shropshire SY13 3JJ

Charles & Jane Bebbington
☎ 01948 662319
Fax 01948 666670
BB From £35–£40
Sleeps 4
⛄🐕♿🍴♨️Ⓢ
☘️☘️ Highly Commended

Splendid country house, home to the Bebbington family who have farmed here for 36 years. The atmosphere is relaxed and friendly. Cosy sofas, log fires, sounds of music and memorable breakfasts. Beautiful en suite bedrooms and guests' drawing room overlook sweeping lawns and walled garden. A paradise for garden lovers, antiques browsers, golfers and lovers of country pursuits. Excellent fly-fishing on our own trout pool. Superb eating places nearby to round off your day. Closed Christmas.

⑦ Grove Farm, Preston Brockhurst, Shrewsbury, Shropshire SY4 5QA

Mrs Janet Jones
☎/Fax 01939 220223
BB From £19–£21
Sleeps 6
⛄🍴Ⓢ
☘️ Highly Commended

Step into Shropshire and enjoy quality accommodation and fine home cooking using local produce. Our 322-acre farm is set in a small village 7 miles north of Shrewsbury on the A49. The 17th century house is traditionally furnished and offers warmth and comfort after the day's activities. Ideally situated for Ironbridge World Heritage Site, Shrewsbury, Chester, Potteries and Wales. Brochures available. Open mid Jan–mid Dec.

⑧ The Hall, Bucknell, Shropshire SY7 0AA

Mrs Christine Price
☎/Fax 01547 530249
BB From £18–£20
EM £10
Sleeps 6
⛄(7)⛄♨️
☘️☘️ Commended

The Hall is a working farm with spacious Georgian farmhouse and peaceful garden to relax in, after a day walking or exploring the Welsh Borderland with its historic towns and castles, also the black and white villages of North Herefordshire. Guest lounge, 1 twin en suite, 2 double with washbasins, shaving points. Colour TV and tea-making facilities. Open Feb–Nov.

⑨ Haynall Villa, Little Hereford, Nr Ludlow, Shropshire SY8 4BG

Mrs Rachel Edwards
☎/Fax 01584 711589
BB From £17–£24
EM From £13
Sleeps 6
⛄(6)🐕⛄🍴♨️
☘️☘️ Approved

Farmhouse B&B as featured in the *Daily Telegraph*, nestling in Teme Valley 6m from historic Ludlow, 2m from A49. Spacious bedrooms (1 en suite) offer comfort, views to 3 counties, vanity units, tea/coffee-making facilities. Guests' bathroom. Delicious farmhouse fayre (vegetarian and special diets). Relax in lounge with TV or attractive garden. Open all year except Christmas and New Year.

⑩ Horseman's Green Farm, Horseman's Green, Nr Whitchurch, Shropshire SY13 3EA

Mrs Gillian Huxley
☎ 01948 830480
Fax 01948 780552
BB From £20–£25
Sleeps 2
⛄🍴♨️🌿
★★ FARM

A very special Grade I listed 14th century hall house, on a working farm, with many original timbers including a rare aisle truss. Very comfortable accommodation with all private facilities and galleried sitting room. Convenient for Chester, Shrewsbury and Llangollen, the hills and coasts of North Wales within easy reach. Excellent unspoilt walking. Local and home made produce. Open Mar–Nov.

⑪ Hurst Mill Farm, Clun, Craven Arms, Shropshire SY7 0JA

Joyce Williams
☎ 01588 640224
BB From £18–£20
EM From £8
Sleeps 6
⛄🍴🐎🐕♨️🌿Ⓢ
☘️☘️ Commended

Winner of 'Shropshire Farm Breakfast Challenge'. A warm welcome to this working farm where the 'kettle's always on'. Well appointed bedrooms, double en suite. Riverside farmhouse and spacious gardens. Nestling in the delightful Clun Valley, between historic Clun and Clunton. Woodland and hills on either side. Two quiet riding ponies, kingfishers and herons. Pets welcome. Log fires. Also 2 luxury cottages. AA QQQ recommended. Closed Christmas.

Shropshire   Heartland

Lane End Farm, Chetwynd, Newport, Shropshire TF10 8BN   ⑫

Mrs Janice Park
☎ 01952 550337
[BB] From £18–£25
EM from £11
Sleeps 4
Commended

Relax and feel at home in our friendly, interesting farmhouse set amidst lovely countryside. Large bedrooms with en suite facilities. Good woodland walks nearby. Located on A41 two miles North of Newport; ideal for visiting Ironbridge, Weston Park, Cosford, Potteries, Chester, etc. Working sheep farm – see the lambs in spring! Open all year.

Llanhedric, Clun, Craven Arms, Shropshire SY7 8NG   ⑬

Mrs Mary Jones
☎/Fax 01588 640203
[BB] From £17–£20
EM From £10
Sleeps 6
Commended

Relax in traditional style in characteristic farmhouse set in the splendours of the Clun Valley. Awake to the smell of good home cooking. Enjoy the life of a modern working farm, feel the fresh breeze as you explore the beautiful countryside, then unwind in the guests' lounge by a warm inglenook fire. Comfortable bedrooms overlooking attractive gardens, double en suite, tea/coffee facilities, CH. Open Apr–Nov.

Mickley House, Faulsgreen, Tern Hill, Market Drayton, Shropshire TF9 3QW   ⑭

Mrs Pauline Williamson
☎/Fax 01630 638505
[BB] From £20–£26
Sleeps 6
Highly Commended

Discover peace, quiet and comfort in our home with its oak doors, beams, leaded windows and landscaped gardens. Stroll through rose-scented pergolas to pools with trickling waterfall. Restful drawing room beckons after sightseeing and meal at local restaurants/pubs. Individually styled en suite bedrooms, master bedroom with Louis XIV king-size bed. Ground floor available. All facilities. 2 miles off A41. Business visitors welcome. Closed Christmas.

New House Farm, Clun, Shropshire SY7 8NJ   ⑮

Miriam Ellison
☎ 01588 638314
[BB] From £22.50–£25
Sleeps 4
Highly Commended

Peaceful isolated 18th century farmhouse high in Clun Hills. Near Welsh border – with Iron Age hill fort. Walks from doorstep, Offa's Dyke and Shropshire Way. Large bedrooms furnished to a high standard with scenic views. Tea/coffee facilities, colour TV. Books to browse in a large garden. Open Easter–Oct.

North Farm, Eaton Mascot, Shrewsbury, Shropshire SY5 6HF   ⑯

Mrs Vanessa Bromley
☎ 01743 761031
[BB] From £18–£20
Sleeps 4
Listed Commended

Traditional farmhouse situated on a 270-acre mixed arable farm within a private estate in unspoilt countryside. Easy access to Shrewsbury and M54. Two double bedrooms (one with traditional brass bed), both with hospitality tray and colour TV. Separate bathroom and WC. Guests' sitting/dining room with log burner. CH throughout. Guests are always welcome to explore the garden and surrounding countryside, and enjoy this very special part of Shropshire. Ample car parking. Closed Christmas.

Parkside Farm, Holyhead Road, Albrighton, Nr Wolverhampton WV7 3DA   ⑰

Margaret Shanks
☎ 01902 372310
Fax 01902 375013
[BB] From £20–£23
Sleeps 6
Commended

Looking for warm and friendly welcome? Want to relax, or just need a convenient location for work or pleasure? Well look no further! Kick start your day with a farmhouse breakfast, while enjoying the view of the beautiful garden. All rooms have TV and tea/coffee facilities. Plenty of attractions to visit. Near A464 and just 2 mins' walk to a real ale pub/restaurant. Open all year.

Heartland Shropshire

---

18 Petton Hall Farm, Petton, Burlton, Shrewsbury, Shropshire SY4 5TH

Mrs Mary Kennerley
☎/Fax 01939 270601
BB From £18–£22
Sleeps 4/6
☒ ♞ ⚲ ☂ ♨
♛ ♛ Commended

Petton Hall Farm is situated between historic Shrewsbury and the beautiful meres of Ellesmere, a haven for birdwatching. Our two en suite bedrooms offer comfort with character. Come and enjoy traditional home cooking from the Aga and relax in front of a real open fire on those colder evenings. Ironbridge, Hawkstone, the Potteries and more so near! Open all year except Christmas.

---

19 Pool House Farm, Clunbury, Craven Arms, Shropshire SY7 0HG

Janice Barrett
☎/Fax 01588 660414
BB From £17–£19
EM From £9
Sleeps 3
☒ ⚲ ♨
Listed Commended

Traditional farmhouse tucked under Clunbury Hill. Friendly pet farm animals, chickens in the yard, ducks on the pond. Charming garden to be enjoyed. Country-style bedrooms, shared guests' bathroom, CH. Guests' lounge with log stove. Hearty breakfasts. Wonderful walking/riding country. Quality stabling for guests' horses. Open all year except Christmas and New Year.

---

20 Soulton Hall, near Wem, Shropshire SY4 5RS

Ann Ashton
☎ 01939 232786
Fax 01939 234097
BB From £27.50–£34.50
Sleeps 12
☒ ♞ ☏ ☂ ♨ ⚲ ✲ ◉
♛ ♛ ♛ ♛ Commended

Sample English country life in an Elizabethan manor house offering very relaxing holiday. Bird watching, fishing, riding. Good food, home produce where possible, super meals. Walled garden. Licensed bar. Direct dial telephones. We welcome you. Open all year.
E-mail: j.a.ashton@farmline.co.uk

---

21 Strefford Hall Farm, Strefford, Craven Arms, Shropshire SY7 8DE

Mrs Caroline Morgan
☎/Fax 01588 672383
BB From £20–£21
EM £11
Sleeps 6
⚲ ☒ ♞ ☂ ♨ ◉
♛ ♛ Commended

Set in an Area of Outstanding Natural Beauty in the quiet hamlet of Strefford, against the wooded backdrop of the Wenlock Edge and with uninterrupted views of the Long Mynd and Church Stretton hills. Spacious accommodation in 2 doubles, 1 twin (all en suite) with tea/coffee and colour TV. Full English breakfast, special diets catered for. Evening meals by arrangement. Non smoking household. Closed Christmas and New Year.

---

22 Willow House, Shrewsbury Road, Tern Hill, Market Drayton, Shropshire TF9 3PX

Mrs Moira Roberts
☎ 01630 638326
BB From £16–£18
Sleeps 4
☒ ♞ ⚲ ♨ ◉
Listed Commended

A warm and friendly welcome awaits you at our modern farmhouse with 1 double, 1 twin room and guests' own bathroom/shower. Both rooms have hot drink facilities. Guests have a separate lounge with colour TV. A good base for touring Shropshire, Cheshire, Staffordshire and local attractions of Ironbridge, Hodnet gardens, Hawkstone Follies and the Potteries. Open all year.

---

23 Wood Farm, Old Woodhouses, Whitchurch, Shropshire SY13 4EJ

Mrs Val Mayer
☎ 01948 871224
BB From £17–£20
Sleeps 6
☒ ⚲ ♨ ☏ ◉
Listed Commended

Down in the meadow,
Where the green grass grows,
There's a farm that nobody knows.
Pine, patchwork, pot-pourri,
Biscuits and cakes for afternoon tea,
Visit us soon and you will see!!

Central to Chester, Shrewsbury, Ironbridge and the Potteries.

Shropshire   Heartland

Self-Catering

Garden Cottage, Whitton Hall, Westbury, Shrewsbury, Shropshire SY5 9RD

Mrs CW Halliday
☎ 01743 884270
Fax 01743 884158
SC From £200–£250
Sleeps 4
Commended

This spacious 18th century cottage, on the Welsh border, has its own small walled garden and lies by the pool and close to the farm and the Jersey herd. In good walking country. Linen and CH included.

The Granary, Rowton Grange, Aston on Clun, Craven Arms, Shropshire SY7 0PA

Frank and Linda Morgan
☎/Fax 01588 660227
SC From £160–£220
Sleeps 2/4
Commended

Situated in the beautiful Clun Valley, the Granary has been recently converted and furnished to a high standard. Rowton Grange is a family-run, 300-acre farm with arable, beef, cattle, sheep and horses. The surrounding area is excellent for walking and we are within easy reach of Ludlow, Shrewsbury and Ironbridge. Open Mar–Nov.

Hesterworth, Hopesay, Craven Arms, Shropshire SY7 8EX

Roger and Sheila Davies
☎ 01588 660487
SC From £91–£335
Sleeps 2–8
Up to Commended

A selection of comfortable country cottages and apartments surrounded by 12 acres of beautiful gardens and grounds. Large dining room ideal for families and groups. Meal service and short breaks available. Ideal for walking or visiting Shropshire's many attractions. Ludlow 10 miles. Open all year.

Keepers Cottage, Soulton Hall, Near Wem, Shropshire SY4 5RS

Ann Ashton
☎ 01939 232786
Fax 01939 234097
SC From £190–£460
Sleeps 6
Commended

Keepers Cottage nestles on south side of 50-acres of Oak woodland offering really relaxing holidays. Woodland and riverside walks, CH, TV, log fires in season. Evening meals available at Soulton Hall from £17.50, by arrangement. Shrewsbury, Chester, Ironbridge, North Wales, Potteries – all within easy reach. Open all year.
E-mail: j.a.ashton@farmline.co.uk

The Sett, Village Farm, Stanton-upon-Hine Heath, Shrewsbury, Shropshire SY4 4LR

Brenda & Jim Grundey
☎/Fax 01939 250391
SC From £160–£240
Sleeps 6
Applied

The Sett is a special place, share our secret. Escape for a well earned rest. Be warm and comfortable, hide yourselves away. We won't tell! Open all year.

Heartland *Shropshire*

21 Strefford Hall Farm, Strefford, Craven Arms, Shropshire SY7 8DE

Mrs Caroline Morgan
☎/Fax 01588 672383
SC From £170–£230
Sleeps 2 + cot
Commended

Set in the lovely South Shropshire countryside, surrounded by fields and close to Wenlock Edge. The coachhouse provides two luxury self-catering units, Swallows Nest on the ground floor is ideal for frail or disabled guests, Wrens Nest is on the first floor. Each has double en suite bedroom, fitted kitchen, large sitting/dining room, fitted carpets and patio area with seating. Open all year.

Bunkhouse/Camping Barn

28 Broughton Bunkhouse, nr Bishop's Castle, Montgomery, Powys SY15 6SZ

Mrs Kate Bason
☎ 01588 638393
SC From £8
Sleeps 12
Applied

Comfortable accommodation in converted 17th century oak-framed stable. Separate sleeping areas for men and women. Self-catering, all cooking equipment provided, or breakfasts available. Centrally heated, showers, drying facilities. Bed and breakfast in adjoining farmhouse. Transport provided to and from Shropshire Way (1mile) and Offa's Dyke (4 miles).

USE THE INDEX

The comprehensive Index shows which farms offer access to disabled visitors; caravanning/camping facilities; the chance to participate on a working farm; stabling/grazing for visiting horses; en suite rooms; a welcome to business people; acceptance of *Stay on a Farm* gift tokens.

Our Internet address is
http://www.webscape.co.uk/farmaccom/

Staffordshire

Peak District National Park, Cannock Chase, Trent Valley & the Potteries

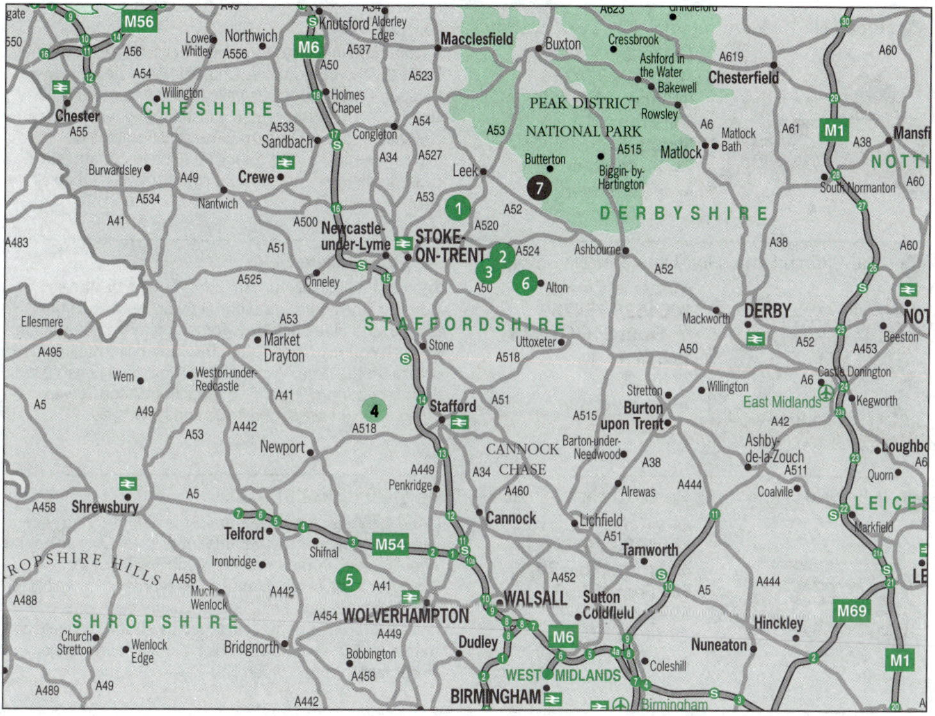

Key
- **1** Bed & Breakfast
- **1** Self-Catering
- **1** B&B and SC
- **1** Camping Barns
- **▲** Camping & Caravanning

The varied landscape of Staffordshire ranges from that of the Peak District National Park, through the moorlands in the north to the fertile valleys of the Trent and its tributaries in the south. In the heart of the county is the extensive Cannock Chase, an Area of Outstanding Natural Beauty. The county has two excellent leisure parks: Alton Towers, famous for its exciting rides, and Drayton Manor Park. Many visitors seek out the potteries and visitor centres which offer the chance to see crafts being made and find a bargain at the factory shops. Heritage lovers should visit Stafford, Tamworth, Burton on Trent, Tutbury and the cathedral city of Lichfield, birthplace of Dr Samuel Johnson.

If you would like help in finding suitable farm accommodation, turn to the full listing of farm groups on pages 360 to 363 to find appropriate contact details for this area.

 Heartland   *Staffordshire*

Bed and Breakfast
(and evening meal)

---

① Brook House Farm, Cheddleton, Leek, Staffordshire ST13 7DF

Elizabeth Winterton
☎ 01538 360296
BB From £17–£19
EM From £10
Sleeps 10
Commended

A dairy farm in a picturesque and peaceful valley. Central for Peak District, Potteries, Churnet Valley steam railway, Cauldon Canal, Coombes Valley RSPB Reserve and Alton Towers. 3 spacious rooms in a tastefully converted cowshed and 2 in the farmhouse, all en suite with tea/coffee-makers and colour TV. Dine in our attractive conservatory with magnificent country views. Open all year.

---

② The Church Farm, Holt Lane, Kingsley, Stoke on Trent, Staffordshire ST10 2BA

Mrs Jane Clowes
☎ 01538 754759
BB From £16.50–£18
Sleeps 4
Commended

Relax in traditionally furnished rooms with oak beams. Country pine bedrooms with Victorian brass and iron double, and pine bunk beds forming family suite. Wander through country lanes, footpaths, lush meadows, orchard, or laze on the lawn. Watch the milking, feed hens, collect eggs for your breakfast. Five miles from Alton Towers. Open all year except Christmas and New Year.

---

③ Ley Fields Farm, Leek Road, Cheadle, Stoke-on-Trent, Staffordshire ST10 2EF

Mrs Kathryn Clowes
☎ 01538 752875
BB From £18–£20
EM From £9.50
Sleeps 6
Commended

Listed Georgian farmhouse amidst beautiful countryside with local walks offering abundant wildlife. Convenient for Alton Towers, Pottery museums and Peak District. Spacious, traditionally furnished accommodation includes guests' lounge and dining room. Luxury bedrooms with hot drink facilities, family suite, family en suite, double en suite. CH. Excellent home cooking and a warm welcome to our family home. Open Feb–Dec.

---

④ Oulton House Farm, Norbury, Stafford, Staffordshire ST20 0PG

Mrs Judy Palmer
☎/Fax 01785 284264
BB From £20–£25
Sleeps 6
Highly Commended

A 300-acre dairy farm situated on the Shropshire/Staffordshire border. Our large Victorian farmhouse offers warm, comfortable and well appointed en suite bedrooms, all with tea trays and TV. From your peaceful, rural base discover our many local attractions from the heritage of Ironbridge Gorge, the splendours of Shugborough to the bargains of the Potteries factory shops. Many local pubs and restaurants. Peace and quiet guaranteed. Open all year except Christmas.

---

⑤ Parkside Farm, Holyhead Road, Albrighton, Nr Wolverhampton WV7 3DA

Margaret Shanks
☎ 01902 372310
Fax 01902 375013
BB From £20–£23
Sleeps 6
Commended

Looking for warm and friendly welcome? Want to relax, or just need a convenient location for work or pleasure? Well look no further! Kick start your day with a farmhouse breakfast, while enjoying the view of the beautiful garden. All rooms have TV and tea/coffee facilities. Plenty of attractions to visit. Near A464 and just 2 mins' walk to a real ale pub/restaurant. Open all year.

Staffordshire — Heartland

Ribden Farm, Nr Oakamoor, Stoke-on-Trent, Staffordshire ST10 3BW ❻

Christine Shaw
☎/Fax 01538 702830
BB From £20–£24
Sleeps 20
Highly Commended

Ribden Farm is an 18th Century farmhouse c1748 which is situated 1,000 ft high in the Weaver Hills yet is only 5 minutes from Alton Towers. Plenty of underused footpaths. Local inns. All rooms en suite with colour TV, coffee/tea-making facilities, some with four-poster beds. Separate TV lounge and dining room. Secure off road parking. RAC Highly Acclaimed. AA QQQQ selected. Open all year except Christmas.

Self-Catering

Rosewood Holiday Flats, Lower Berkhamsytch Farm, Bottom House, Nr Leek, Staffordshire ST13 7QP ❼

Edith & Alwyn Mycock
☎/Fax 01538 308213
SC From £120–£215
Sleeps 7
Commended

Two delightful self-contained flats on stock rearing farm each with own private entrance and within walking distance of 2 pubs serving meals. Lounge/diner with colour TV and double bed-settee. Well equipped kitchen, 1 double bedroom, 1 twin, shower room with toilet and washbasin. Ideal for Alton Towers, Potteries, Peak District and moorland beauty spots. Electricity, heating, linen included. Laundry room. Short breaks early and late season. Open all year.

Swallows Nest, Oulton House Farm, Norbury, Stafford, Staffordshire ST20 0PG ❹

Mrs Judy Palmer
☎/Fax 01785 284264
SC From £130–£270
Sleeps 4 + cot
Highly Commended

Swallows Nest has been designed with the comfort of our guests in mind. We think it is special. It is self-contained, fully equipped and all inclusive. An ideal base for a relaxing holiday: patchwork quilts, pine, pot pourri, peace and quiet   perfect. See why the swallows return! Larger cottages available soon. Open all year.

FOLLOW THE COUNTRY CODE

Leave nothing but footprints,
Take nothing but photographs,
Kill nothing but time!

Leicestershire

Vale of Belvoir, Rutland Water & Grand Union Canal

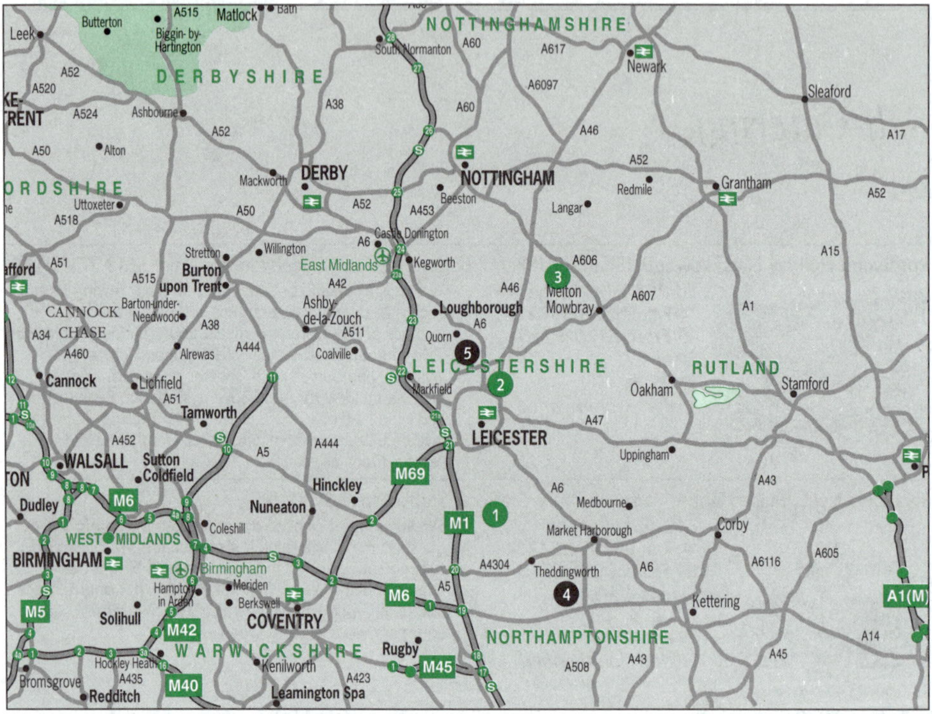

Key

- 1 Bed & Breakfast
- 1 Self-Catering
- 1 B&B and SC
- 1 Camping Barns
- ▲ Camping & Caravanning

Leicestershire is a land of tranquil beauty spread with reminders of a turbulent history. To find the true Leicestershire just travel over high horizons and narrow farm tracks, explore vast Rutland Water and the lazy green banks of the Grand Union Canal, take a nostalgic trip on one of our many steam railways, walk in historic Bradgate Park or 'do battle' in Bosworth Field. Explore the county's curious annual events such as Bottle Kicking and the Hare Pie Scramble between Hallaton and Medbourne, or visit our castles and museums, timber-framed cottages and grand mansions, theatres and theme parks. Find all this and more in this green and undulating county.

If you would like help in finding suitable farm accommodation, turn to the full listing of farm groups on pages 360 to 363 to find appropriate contact details for this area.

Leicestershire   Heartland

Bed and Breakfast
(and evening meal)

Knaptoft House Farm, Bruntingthorpe Road, Nr Shearsby, Lutterworth, Leicestershire LE17 6PR

Mrs AT Hutchinson
☎/Fax 01162 478388
BB From £19–£29
Sleeps 6
🐕(5) ⌂ ⇆ 🌲 ♨ 🍴
🌷🌷 *Highly Commended*

Easy access from the motorways and Leicester (A50/5119), yet very quietly situated overlooking undulating farm land. Our accommodation is warm and welcoming, all rooms with bespoke beds, TV, hospitality tray, en suite or adjacent facilities Furnishings are carefully chosen and co-ordinated. Interesting china, pictures, family history memorabilia/books. Secluded car parking. Excellent local pubs. Brochure. Closed Christmas and New Year.
E-mail: knight@bruntingthorpe.softnet.co.uk

Three Ways Farm, Melton Road, Queniborough, Leicester LE7 3FN

Mrs Janet S Clarke
☎ 0116 260 0472
BB From £17–£20
Sleeps 5
🐕 🐎 🐴 ⇆ ♨
Listed Commended

It's hard to believe you're only 6 miles north of Leicester in lovely Queniborough with its ancient church, thatched cottages and two good pubs. You'll be welcomed at the Clarke's bungalow in peaceful fields. All bedrooms have colour TV, tea/coffee facilities. West of Melton Road, ¼ m A607 Queniborough roundabout, connects with Leicester A46 bypass. Nottingham and Birmingham NEC 40 mins. Open all year except Christmas.

White Lodge Farm, Nottingham Road, Ab Kettleby, Melton Mowbray, Leicestershire LE14 3JB

Margaret Spencer
☎ 01664 822286
BB From £18–£20
Sleeps 6
🐕(9) ✂ ■ ♨
Listed Commended

A warm welcome and comfortable accommodation await you on our working farm at the edge of the Vale of Belvoir, 3 miles north of Melton Mowbray, home of the pork pie and Stilton cheese. Ground floor, self-contained rooms overlook the garden, all en-suite with CH, colour TV, tea coffee-making facilities and electric blankets. Open all year.

Self-Catering

Brook Meadow Holiday Chalets, Welford Road, Sibbertoft, Market Harborough, Leicestershire LE16 9UJ

Mary and Jasper Hart
☎/Fax 01858 880886
SC From £130–£400
Sleep 3/6
🐕 🐴 🏕 ⌂ ⇆ ■ 🌲
♣ ♣ ♣ *Approved*

Stay in one of our holiday chalets in the peaceful lakeside setting at the heart of our farm. Imagine sipping a glass of wine from a complimentary bottle, relaxing in a rocking chair, whilst the sun sets over the fishing lake. Two chalets sleep 3 and one sleeps 4/6 in luxurious comfort; all are fully equipped including bed linen. Pets welcome. Colour brochure available. Open all year.

Heartland — Leicestershire

(5) Stonehurst, Bond Lane, Mountsorrel, Leicestershire LE12 7AR

Marilyn Duffin
☎ 01509 413216
[SC] From £175–£350
Sleeps 8
🐕 🐎 🎿 ♿ ☕ ✲
Applied

This comfortable, modern, well-equipped family house with five bedrooms, a private garden and barbecue is attached to Stonehurst Family Farm and Museum, to which free admission is given during stay. Teashop and restaurant on farm. All amenities in the village. The farm is 12 minutes from M1 J21A. Open all year.

USE THE INDEX

The comprehensive Index shows which farms offer access to disabled visitors; caravanning/camping facilities; the chance to participate on a working farm; stabling/grazing for visiting horses; en suite rooms; a welcome to business people; acceptance of *Stay on a Farm* gift tokens.

STAY ON A FARM GIFT TOKENS

If you have enjoyed your Stay on a Farm, why not treat your friends and relatives to *Stay on a Farm* gift tokens? Available from the Bureau office (tel: 01203 696909), they can be redeemed against accommodation and are accepted by the majority of farms (see Index). Please check when booking to avoid disappointment.

THE 1000+ BUREAU MEMBERS OFFER A UNIQUE LINK TO CUSTOMERS ACROSS THE UK

All Bureau members belong to a local Group. Each member can refer you to an equally high quality member within the Group... or across the UK: England, Northern Ireland, Scotland, Wales.

Herefordshire
Wye Valley & Golden Valley

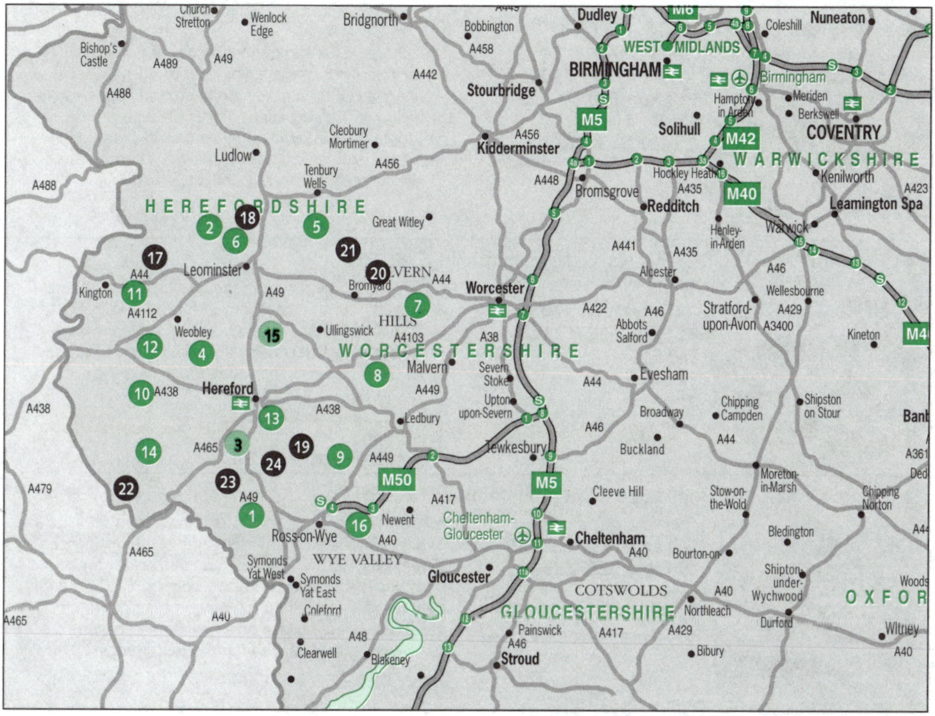

Key

- 🟢 1 Bed & Breakfast
- 🟢 1 Self-Catering
- 🟢 1 B&B and SC
- 🟢 1 Camping Barns
- 🟢 1 Camping & Caravanning

Herefordshire is a land of red earth, green meadows, quiet woods, streams and pretty black and white villages. In the south are the spectacular gorges of the River Wye and the lovely woodland trails of the Forest of Dean; westward lies the tranquil Golden Valley leading into Offa's Dyke. To the east, Elgar Country rises to the Malvern Hills with one of the finest ridge walks in England. The county's historic sites span every period of British history, from Iron Age hill forts, Roman remains, Norman castles and medieval manor houses to stately homes and their gardens and heritage museums. Street markets abound and Hay-on-Wye is famous for its second-hand bookshops. Come and browse.

If you would like help in finding suitable farm accommodation, turn to the full listing of farm groups on pages 360 to 363 to find appropriate contact details for this area.

Heartland   Herefordshire

Bed and Breakfast
(and evening meal)

① Amberley, Aberhall Farm, St Owen's Cross, Hereford HR2 8LL

Freda Davies
☎/Fax 01989 730256
BB From £18.50–£22
Sleeps 4
☼(10) ⚹ ⛟ ⊙
♣♣ Highly Commended

Savour the peace and tranquillity of our home with panoramic views of the rolling countryside. 132-acre working family farm offering one ground floor en suite twin/double and, upstairs, one double with private bathroom. Guests' own lounge and dining room. Tea/trays, excellent cuisine, 'home from home'. Large garden with patio. Open Mar–Nov.

② The Barn Farm, Leinthall Starkes, Ludlow, Shropshire SY8 2HP

Sylvia Price
☎/Fax 01568 770388
BB From £18–£21
EM £15
Sleeps 6
☼ ⚹ ⛟
♣♣ Approved

A warm welcome, comfort and a relaxed atmosphere await you. Our traditional mixed farm is 5 miles west of Ludlow. Cosy bedrooms, 2 double en suite, tea trays. Meals served in our conservatory dining room. Special diets. Guests' own sitting room. Open Mar–Nov.

③ Grafton Villa Farm, Grafton, Hereford, Herefordshire HR2 8ED

Jennie Layton
☎/Fax 01432 268689
BB From £20–£25
Sleeps 6
☼ ⚹ ⚐ ⛟ ⚒ ⚘ ⊙
♣♣ Highly Commended

A farmhouse of great character and warmth set in an acre of beautiful lawns and gardens amidst the picturesque Wye Valley. Beautiful fabrics and antiques throughout, charming, peaceful en suite bedrooms with TV and drinks tray. Guests' private bathroom or en suite. We offer our guests a relaxing holiday on a 'real farm', enjoying a sumptuous breakfast with farmhouse portions. Open Feb–Nov.

④ Hill Top Farm, Wormsley, Nr Weobley, Hereford, Herefordshire HR4 8LZ

Mr & Mrs P Jennings
☎/Fax 01981 590246
BB From £17–£19.50
Sleeps 5
☼ ⚹ ⚐ ⛟ ⚒ ⛟
♣♣ Commended

A working farm offering real peace and relaxation. Glorious views in all directions. The character farmhouse is fully modernised with rooms en suite or with private bathroom. Tea/coffee facilities. An abundance of flora and fauna and many walks and sports facilities locally, including golf. Our friendly welcome and personal attention will make your stay a delight. Open all year except Christmas.

⑤ The Hills Farm, Leysters, Leominster, Herefordshire HR6 0HP

Jane & Peter Conolly
☎/Fax 01568 750205
BB From £24–£27
EM £17
Sleeps 10
⚐ ⚹ ⊞ ⛟
♣♣♣ Highly Commended

We have five charming, well equipped bedrooms – three are in delightfully converted barns, so you have your own front door! Scrumptious food including vegetarian is served, all home cooked. We try to offer everything for a comfortable, relaxing break, be it one night or many more. No smoking. Brochure. Open Mar–end Oct.

Herefordshire　　　　　　　　　　　　　　　Heartland

Home Farm, Bircher, Nr Leominster, Herefordshire HR6 0AX　　6

Doreen Cadwallader
☎ 01568 780525
BB From £20–£22
Sleeps 6
Commended

We welcome you to a traditional livestock farm offering you excellent service and accommodation. Set in a peaceful, secluded area on the Welsh Border, it's 4 miles north of Leominster, 7 miles south of Ludlow, and close to Croft Castle, Berrington Hall and other attractions. All rooms have tea/coffee-making facilities. TV and washbasins. Light evening meals by request. Open all year.

Linton Brook Farm, Bringsty, Bromyard, Herefordshire WR6 5TR　　7

Sheila & Roger Steeds
☎/Fax 01885 488875
BB From £18.50–£22.50
Sleeps 6
Applied

A warm welcome awaits you at our fascinating 17th century home. This former hop farm has large en suite rooms and a comfortable sitting room with oak beams, log fires and flag and oak plank floors. Home-smoked foods provide a delicious breakfast bonus. Our rolling hills offer glorious walks; views over 8 or more counties and quite exceptional wildlife. Open Apr–early Nov.

Moor Court Farm, Stretton Grandison, Nr Ledbury, Herefordshire HR8 2TP　　8

Elizabeth Godsall
☎ 01531 670408
BB From £17.50
EM From £12.50
Sleeps 6
Highly Commended

Relax and enjoy our beautiful 15th century timber-framed farmhouse with adjoining oast houses in a peaceful location. It's a traditional working Herefordshire hop and livestock farm, in scenic countryside central to the major market towns. Easy access to the Malverns, Wye Valley and Welsh borders. Spacious bedrooms, en suite or private bathroom, tea/coffee-making facilities. Oak beamed lounge and dining room. Open all year.

New House Farm, Much Marcle, Ledbury, Herefordshire HR8 2PH　　9

Mrs Anne Jordan
☎ 01531 660604/660674
BB From £15
EM From £10
Sleeps 4
Approved

A friendly welcome awaits you at our delightful farmhouse enjoying panoramic views over Herefordshire, Worcestershire and Gloucestershire. Relax by a log fire on chilly evenings, or enjoy a swim in our outdoor pool during summer. Horses welcome by arrangement. Open all year.

Old Court Farm, Bredwardine, Herefordshire HR3 6BT　　10

Sue Whittall
☎ 01981 500375
Mobile 0421 424575
BB From £20–£25
EM From £16
Sleeps 6
Commended

Old Court (featured on BBC Food programme) is a 14th century mediaeval manor situated on the banks of the River Wye. Ideal for the Wye Valley Walk. It has been carefully restored to preserve a wealth of beams and a 15ft fireplace. Central heating. Gardens enjoy beautiful views to the river. There are 2 four-poster bedrooms, 2 en suite and four-poster family room with private bathroom, all with teamakers. Evening meals. Phone for opening times.

Penrhos Farm, Lyonshall, Kington, Herefordshire HR5 3LH　　11

Sally Williams
☎ 01544 231467
BB From £18–£25
EM From £10
Sleeps 6
Commended

Spacious farmhouse, recently decorated and offering a hearty breakfast, garden and parking. One mile from Kington. Double en suite, twin and single with private bathroom. TV, tea/coffee facilities. Open Mar–Nov.

Heartland — Herefordshire

12 Red Ley Farmhouse, Red Ley, Letton, Herefordshire HR3 6DT

Mary King
☎/Fax 01981 500438
BB From £20–£25
EM From £12
Sleeps 6
♦(5) ✗ ♣ ♠ ●
♥♥♥ Highly Commended

Experience the friendly beamed atmosphere of Red Ley and its picturesque gardens, situated in the upper Wye Valley midway between Hay on Wye and Hereford. Safe parking, en suite rooms and delicious food. Open all year except Christmas.

13 Sink Green Farm, Rotherwas, Hereford HR2 6LE

David Jones
☎ 01432 870223
BB From £19–£25
Sleeps 6
♦ ♞ ✗ ♣ ♠
♥♥ Commended

Sink Green awaits you with a warm, friendly welcome to its 16th century farmhouse overlooking the River Wye and picturesque Herefordshire countryside yet only 3 miles from the cathedral city of Hereford. Comfortable bedrooms, one with four-poster bed, all en suite, tea/coffee-making facilities and colour TV. Large oak-beamed lounge and traditional farmhouse fare. Children welcome, pets by arrangement. AA listed. Open all year.

14 Upper Gilvach Farm, St Margarets, Vowchurch, Hereford HR2 0QY

Mrs Ruth Watkins
☎/Fax 01981 510618
BB From £20–£28
EM From £12
Sleeps 6
♦ ♞ ✗ ⊞ ♠ ♘ ♣ ♠
♥♥ Commended

Family-run farm between Golden Valley and Black Mountains. This 300-year-old farmhouse offers three spacious, attractively furnished bedrooms, all en suite with colour TV and hospitality trays. Peace and comfort in a relaxing atmosphere. Delicious evening meals and hearty farmhouse breakfasts using local wines and produce. Licensed, dinner optional. AA QQQQ Selected. Open all year.

15 The Vauld House Farm, Marden, Herefordshire HR1 3HA

Mrs Judith Wells
☎ 01568 797347
Fax 01568 797366
BB From £18–£20
EM From £13.50
Sleeps 5
♦ ♞ ✗ ⊞ ♠ ♣
♥♥♥ Highly Commended

Situated 6 miles north of Hereford in beautiful countryside, this 17th century farmhouse offers traditionally furnished, comfortable en suite accommodation with guests' own lounge and dining room. Open log fires. All home cooking to a very high standard using fresh local produce. Guests may enjoy relaxing in the wooded and lawned gardens with carp ponds. Open all year except Christmas and New Year.

16 Warren Farm, Warren Lane, Lea, Ross on Wye, Herefordshire HR9 7LT

Mrs Christine Whitehouse
☎/Fax 01989 750272
BB From £22–£26
Sleeps 6
✗ ♞ ♠ ♣
♥♥ Highly Commended

A warm welcome awaits you in our beautifully restored 16th century Grade II listed farmhouse with a multitude of exposed beams and three inglenooks. Set in peaceful countryside on a mixed working farm. 1 double en suite, 1 twin en suite, 1 double with private bathroom. All have TV, tea/coffee facilities. Two 18-hole golf courses within 3 miles and ideally situated for touring the Royal Forest of Dean, Wye Valley and the Vale of Leadon. Open Mar–Oct.

NO ANSWER?
Farmers are mostly out and about during the day.
Try to telephone before 9.30am or after 4pm.

Herefordshire　　　　　　　　　　　　　　　　Heartland

Self-Catering

Anvil Cottage, Grafton Villa, Grafton, Hereford, Herefordshire HR2 8ED ③

Jennie Layton
☎/Fax 01432 268689
SC From £180–£350
Sleeps 5
Highly Commended

Beams, natural wood and beautiful fabrics make our recently converted wainhouse into a very well equipped cottage for the discerning visitor. Comfortable, spacious twin and double bedded rooms, each en suite. Lovely open plan lounge leading to a sheltered patio. Suitable for disabled and wheelchair guests. Linen, electricity and CH included. Open all year.

Brick House Farm, Byton, Presteigne, Powys LD8 2HY ⑰

Mr & Mrs David Johnstone
☎ 01544 267306
Fax 01544 260601
SC From £175–£325
Sleeps 5 + cot

Situated in beautiful Welsh Border countryside, in peaceful Lugg Valley. Good walking, lovely scenery. Old-fashioned smallholding/nature reserve where participation in animal care is encouraged. Children especially welcome; everything we do is safe, educational and fun. Dairy, sheep, pigs and poultry. The cottage is comfortable, spacious and really well equipped.
E-mail: dmfj@johnstone.kc3ltd.co.uk

Brooklyn, c/o Marlbrook Hall, Elton, Ludlow, Shropshire SY8 2HR ⑱

Mrs Valerie Morgan
☎ 01568 770230
SC From £165–£295
Sleeps 6
Commended

Situated on the Herefordshire/Shropshire border, ideal for exploring the market town of Ludlow, Mortimer Forest and Welsh Borders. Spacious accommodation consists of three bedroomed house with garden and garage. Fitted carpets and tastefully decorated. Colour TV, microwave oven, washing machine, tumble dryer, linen and towels included in price. Open all year.

Carey Dene and Rock House, Carey, c/o Folly Farm, Holme Lacy, Hereford HR2 6LS ⑲

Mrs Rita Price
☎/Fax 01432 870259
SC From £170–£390
Sleeps 4/8 + cot
Commended

Two oak-beamed cottages on traditional farm overlooking River Wye. Beautiful area between Hereford and Ross on Wye, for a peaceful holiday or short break. Access to the river, two minutes' walk to pub serving meals. Washing machine, microwave, colour TV, central heating. Electricity and linen included in charge. Open all year.

Grafton Cottage, Grafton Farm, Bockleton, Tenbury Wells, Worcestershire WR15 8PT ⑳

Mrs S Thomas
☎ 01568 750602
SC From £130–£280
Sleeps 8 + cot
Approved

Large semi-detached red brick cottage, well equipped and full of character, set in unspoilt countryside. Explore the 300-acre working stock farm and its wildlife. Ideal for touring with black and white village trail and Welsh border country close by. Riding lessons and trekking available on the farm. Open Mar–Nov.

Heartland *Herefordshire*

㉑ Mill House Flat, Woonton Court Farm, Leysters, Leominster, Herefordshire HR6 0HL

Mrs Elizabeth Thomas
☎/Fax 01568 750232
[SC] From £160–£250
Sleeps 3/4 + cot
Commended

Half-timbered brick and stone detached mill, recently converted to provide comfortable first floor self-contained accommodation. Open plan kitchen/dining room/ spacious sitting room, electric fire, colour TV. Night store heating and fitted carpets throughout. Linen/electricity included. Telephone. Sunny patio, parking, freedom to walk on the farm and enjoy a wealth of nature. Own farm produce. Short breaks. Open all year.

㉒ Moody Farm Cottage, Moody Farm, Longtown, Herefordshire HR2 0LW

Judy Stone
☎ 01873 860685
[SC] From £150–£295
Sleeps 4/5 + cot
Commended

Swans on the lake, woodpeckers in the wood! Wonderful views and setting at foot of Black Mountains. Comfortable, very well equipped cottage, part of barn conversion. River, own lake, fishing and boating. Ideal for children. Walking, birdwatching and exploring castles. One double, one single, one single/twin. Open all year.

㉓ Old Forge Cottage, Lyston Smithy, Wormelow, Nr Hereford HR2 8EL

Shirley Wheeler
☎ 01981 540625
[SC] From £160–£314
Sleeps 4 + cot
Commended

The Forge cottage is all on one level and retains many original features. Large open plan living room, fully equipped kitchenette, one twin en suite, one double bedroom and bathroom. CH, telephone and TV. Linen included. 14 acres of gardens and grounds. 3 day breaks Nov–Mar. Open all year.

㉔ Poolspringe Farm Cottages, Much Birch, Hereford HR2 8JJ

David & Val Beaumont
☎/Fax 01981 540355
[SC] From £80–£285
Sleeps 1–7
Approved

Barn conversion on 17th century, 50-acre farm set in the orchards of south Herefordshire. Midway between Hereford and Ross on Wye. Indoor heated swimming pool, sauna, games room, large garden with games. Coarse fishing on farm. Dogs' walks. Pets very welcome. Reduced fees at Belmont Golf Course 7 miles away. Many excellent pubs for food. Lovely touring area within reach of Forest of Dean, Cotswolds and Wales. Open all year.

⑮ The Vauld House Farm, Marden, Hereford, Herefordshire HR1 3HA

Judith Wells
☎ 01568 797347
Fax 01568 797366
[SC] From £165–£300
EM From £13.50
Sleeps 2/5 + cot
Commended

Set amidst beautiful countryside on family stock farm midway between Hereford and Leominster, this skilfully converted Victorian hop kiln is spacious and well-equipped. Recently renovated 17th century Cider House, retaining character and charm. Ground floor sleeps 2. Lawned and wooded gardens with moat and ponds extend to over an acre.

Please mention *Stay on a Farm* when booking

Worcestershire

Wyre Forest, Severn Valley, Malvern Hills
& Vale of Evesham

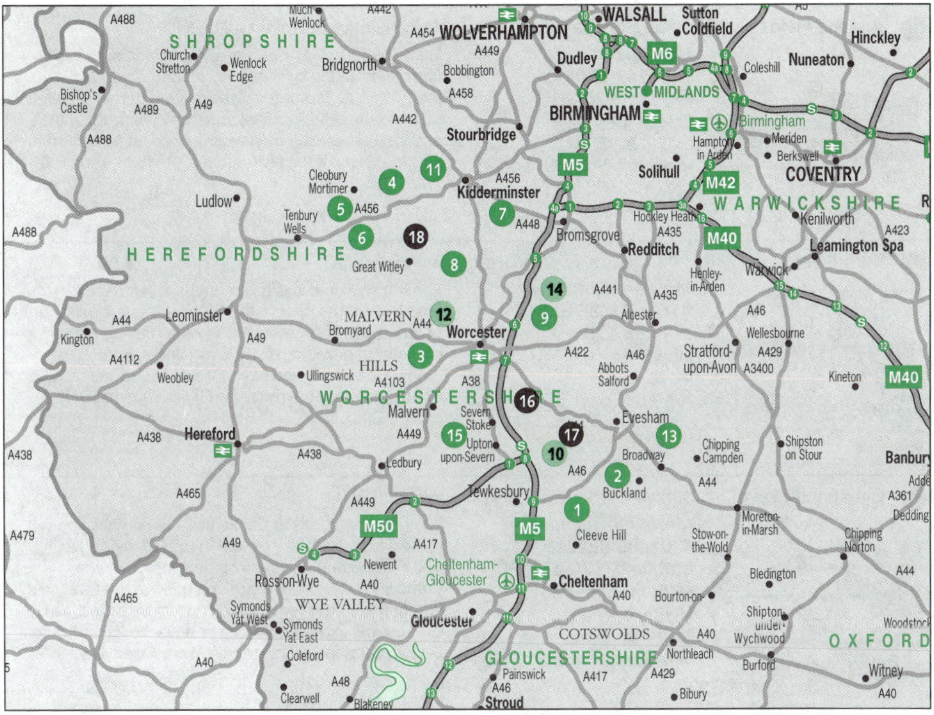

Key

- 1 Bed & Breakfast
- 1 Self-Catering
- 1 B&B and SC
- 1 Camping Barns
- 1 Camping & Caravanning

Worcestershire still has that flavour of Old England with flowering hedges, grazing pastures, rolling hills and bluebelled woodland, winding lanes and sleepy villages. Explore Georgian Bewdley and Bromsgrove; the old spa towns of Tenbury, Droitwich and lovely Malvern; historic Worcester with its beautiful cathedral, porcelain factory and excellent museums; and picturesque Broadway. Follow the gentle flow of the Severn, Teme and Avon as they make their way through the county passing through Evesham, Pershore and Upton-on-Severn. Climb the rolling hills of Malvern, Abberley, Clent and Clee. The county offers great variety and you can be sure of a warm welcome.

If you would like help in finding suitable farm accommodation, turn to the full listing of farm groups on pages 360 to 363 to find appropriate contact details for this area.

 **Heartland**   Worcestershire

Bed and Breakfast
(and evening meal)

---

① Alstone Fields Farm, Teddington Hands, Nr Tewkesbury, Gloucestershire GL20 8NG

Jane Rogers
☎ 01242 620592
BB From £20–£25
Sleeps 12
🐴 ✕ ♿ 🎪
💚💚 *Highly Commended*

Enjoy the friendliest welcome on our traditional family farm, surrounded by sheep, horses and dogs. Wake up in pretty en suite rooms to splendid views of rolling countryside and the delicious smell of bacon! We promise a memorably peaceful holiday and a perfect base from which to explore the picturesque Cotswolds. Open all year.

---

② Burhill Farm, Buckland, Nr Broadway, Worcestershire WR12 7LY

Mrs Pam Hutcheon
☎/Fax 01386 858171
BB From £20
Sleeps 4
✕ ♿ 🎪 ⊛
Applied

A warm welcome awaits our guests at our mainly grass farm lying in the folds of the Cotswolds just 2 miles south of Broadway. The Cotswold Way runs through the middle of the farm providing many lovely walks. Both guest rooms are en suite and have TV and tea/coffee facilities. Come and enjoy the peace and quiet. Open all year except Christmas.

---

③ Chirkenhill, Leigh Sinton, Malvern, Worcestershire WR13 5DE

Mrs Sarah Wenden
☎ 01886 832205
Mobile 07970 430590
BB From £18–£20
Sleeps 6
🐴 🐕 ♿
💚💚 *Commended*

We welcome guests to Chirkenhill – or perhaps you will recognise us as 'Arkley House' in the ITV series 'Noah's Ark'. The second series will be showing this summer. Come and relax in the peace and quiet of our lovely old farmhouse amidst some of Worcestershire's most beautiful countryside. Excellent walking or drive the 'Elgar Route'. Dogs/horses housed by arrangement. Open all year.

---

④ Clay Farm, Clows Top, Nr Bewdley, Worcestershire DY14 9NN

Mike & Ella Grinnall
☎ 01299 832421
BB From £18.50
Sleeps 6
🐴(3) 🎣 🐕 ♿
💚💚 *Highly Commended*

Fully centrally heated farmhouse with outstanding views. Friendly atmosphere, homemade cakes and tea on arrival. En suite bedrooms with tea making facilities. Full English breakfast. Spacious TV lounge, log fires, sun lounge overlooking trout and coarse fishing pools. Close to Bewdley, Ludlow, Severn Valley Railway and Witley Court. On Worcestershire and Shropshire borders on the B4202 Cleobury Mortimer Road. Closed Christmas.

---

⑤ Clod Hall, Milson, nr Kidderminster, Worcestershire DY14 0BJ

Mrs C Morrison
☎ 01584 781421
BB From £17–£25
Sleeps 3
🐴 🐕 ♿ ✕
Listed Commended

Comfortable house on road between Tenbury Wells and Cleobury Mortimer commanding beautiful views over woods and farmland. Horses are bred here. Near Clee Hills, historic town of Ludlow, market towns of Tenbury, Wells and Leominster. CH. One double, one single, both with TV, tea/coffee. Generous breakfasts with homemade preserves. Packed lunches available and good local pubs. Children welcome. Open all year.

Worcestershire   Heartland

Court Farm, Hanley Childe, Tenbury Wells, Worcestershire WR15 8QY

Edward & Margaret Yarnold
☎ 01885 410265
BB From £18–£25
Sleeps 4
Listed *Commended*

A warm and friendly welcome awaits you at Court Farm, a 15th century oak-beamed farmhouse, perfectly situated far from the madding crowd. A family-run farm of 200 acres with outstanding views of the Teme Valley, Clee Hills and the Welsh mountains. Near to Tenbury Wells, Ludlow and Elgar's Birthplace. Spacious en suite bedrooms, hospitality trays and guests' sitting room. Excellent meals available locally. Open Apr–Nov.

The Durrance, Berry Lane, Upton Warren, Bromsgrove, Worcestershire B61 9EL

Helen Hirons
☎/Fax 01562 777533
BB From £22–£25
EM From £7
Sleeps 6
Commended

We welcome you to our Victorian farmhouse in picturesque rural setting with large garden – ideal for children. Comfortably furnished and spacious en suite rooms, all with colour TV. Homemade tea and cakes on arrival. Enjoy total privacy as guests' accommodation is separate to family living area. One downstairs room. Convenient for NEC, 5 miles J5 M5, 7 miles J1 M42.

Eden Farm, Ombersley, Nr Droitwich, Worcester WR9 0JX

Bill & Ann Yardley
☎ 01905 620244
BB From £22–£25
Sleeps 5
Commended

Come and enjoy our 17th century home with its lovely garden, fishing on the Severn and 5-acre marsh with over 100 species of flora. It's just off the A449 and the Wychavon Way, a wonderful centre for exploring the heart of England, with Worcester 7 miles, Droitwich 6 miles. Bedrooms are tastefully decorated, with bathrooms en suite, tea/coffee-making facilities and TV. Homemade produce and preserves used. Closed Christmas.

The Green Farm, Crowle Green, nr Worcester, Worcestershire WR7 4AB

Mrs Lucy Harris
☎/Fax 01905 381807
BB From £20–£22
Sleeps 3
Commended

A peaceful oak-beamed Grade II listed farmhouse set in large garden and surrounding farmland. Comfortable rooms with own basin, private bathroom, tea/coffee-making facilities and CH. Guests' also have sole use of lounge with wood-burning stove and colour TV. Excellent meals within easy walking distance at local country pub. Open all year.

Home Farm, Bredons Norton, Tewkesbury, Gloucestershire GL20 7HA

Mick & Anne Meadows
☎/Fax 01684 772322
BB From £20–£25
Sleeps 6
Commended

Find a friendly welcome at our 18th century farmhouse. The family-run farm is situated in an extremely quiet, unspoilt, little village nestling under famous Bredon Hill. Superb position for walking, touring or simply relaxing. All bedrooms have en suite bathrooms, CH, tea-making facilities, TV. Guests' lounge, garden, separate dining room. Choice of breakfast. Excellent food pubs nearby. Open mid Jan–mid Dec.

Lightmarsh Farm, Crundalls Lane, Bewdley, Worcestershire DY12 1NE

Mrs Pauline Grainger
☎ 01299 404027
BB From £20
Sleeps 4
Highly Commended

Small, pasture farm in elevated position with fine views. Ideal for walking, wildlife and exploring Heart of England. The house is approx 200 years old, with full CH and comfortable accommodation; TV lounge with inglenook fireplace. Both rooms have private facilities. Truly rural setting, only 1 mile from Bewdley's shops and restaurants, Severn Valley Railway and West Midland Safari Park. Closed Christmas and New Year.

Heartland — Worcestershire

12 Little Lightwood Farm, Lightwood Lane, Cotheridge, Worcestershire WR6 5LT

Vee & Richard Rogers
☎ 01905 333236
Fax 01905 333468
BB From £18–£24
Sleeps 6
💤 ⅍ ♿
❦❦ Commended

A friendly and warm welcome awaits you to share our family home in the heart of Worcestershire. All rooms en suite with courtesy tray, TV and CH. Also self-catering. Ours is a working dairy and cheese-making farm where you are welcome to participate. 3 miles west of Worcester, A44 to Leominster, 7 miles M5 J7. Closed Christmas.

13 Lowerfield Farm, Willersey, Broadway, Worcestershire WR11 5HF

Jane Hill
☎ 01386 858273
Fax 01386 854608
BB From £22.50–£25
EM From £12.50
Sleeps 6
💤 ⅍ ♿ 🐴
❦❦ Commended

Lowerfield farm is peacefully located 3 miles from Broadway and provides an ideal base for exploring the Cotswolds, Stratford on Avon, Cheltenham and beyond. Bedrooms are en suite with clock radio, TV, hairdryer and tea/coffee-making facilities. Three-course evening meal available by arrangement or good eating houses nearby. Open all year.

14 Phepson Farm, Himbleton, Droitwich, Worcestershire WR9 7JZ

David & Tricia Havard
☎/Fax 01905 391205
BB From £20–£26
Sleeps 8
💤 🐕 ⅍ ♿ 🐴 ⊛
❦❦ Highly Commended

In our 17th century oak beamed farmhouse we offer a warm welcome, good food and a relaxed and informal atmosphere. The recently converted Granary has two ground floor bedrooms whilst the farmhouse has double, and family accommodation. All rooms en suite with colour TV. Peaceful surroundings on family stock farm. Walking on Wychavon Way. Featured on 'Wish You Were Here'. Open all year except Christmas and New Year.

15 Tiltridge Farm & Vineyard, Upper Hook Road, Upton-on-Severn, Worcestershire WR8 0SA

Sandy Barker
☎ 01684 592906
Fax 01684 594142
BB From £21–£28
Sleeps 6
💤(5) 🐕 ⅍ ♿ 🐴
❦❦ Highly Commended

Period family farmhouse lying between the Malvern Hills and the attractive riverside town of Upton-on-Severn. Set in its own vineyard, the house is fully renovated with one double, one twin and one family room. All rooms are en suite with TV. Warm welcome, bumper breakfast and plenty of our own wine available! New vineyard centre and vineyard walk open. Four minutes from the Three Counties Showground. Open all year except Christmas.

Self-Catering

16 Court Close Farm, Manor Road, Eckington, Pershore, Worcestershire WR10 3BH

Eileen Fincher
☎ 01386 750297
SC From £200–£295
Sleeps 5 + cot
💤 ⅍ 🐕 🐴 ♿
🏠🏠🏠🏠 Commended

A self-contained wing of our lovely 18th century farmhouse and garden on village edge, bordering Gloucestershire. Outstanding views of Bredon Hill. Attractive set dairy farm with meadows sloping to the Avon. Fishing by arrangement. Central for Shakespeare, Malvern and Cotswold jaunts. Convenient kitchen/diner and comfortable sitting room with TV, storage heat and electric fire. 3 bedrooms, linen provided. Closed Christmas.

Worcestershire — Heartland

The Granary, c/o Phepson Farm, Himbleton, Droitwich, Worcestershire WR9 7JZ

David & Tricia Havard
☎/Fax 01905 391205
[SC] From £170–£245
Sleeps 2/3
Commended

The recent conversion of the old granary is reached by an outside stone staircase. The light and airy flat is double-glazed and very comfortably furnished. Situated on working stock farm in peaceful surroundings. Entrance through stable door. Fitted kitchen, colour TV, double bedroom with en suite bathroom. Linen, electricity, night storage heating included. Open all year.

The Granary, Tibbitts Farm, Great Comberton, nr Pershore, Worcestershire WR10 3DT

Mrs Jenny Newbury
☎ 01386 710210
[SC] From £160–£260
Sleeps 2/3
Commended

The Granary is attached to 16th century farmhouse and reached by external stone stairs. Wealth of exposed beams with kitchen/dining area, lounge, bedroom and bathroom for 2/3. Peaceful village location, views to open countryside and walking directly to Bredon Hill. Central for Cotswolds, Malvern Hills and Stratford. Linen and electricity included. Open all year.

Little Lightwood Farm, Lightwood Lane, Cotheridge, Worcestershire WR6 5LT

Vee & Richard Rogers
☎ 01905 333236
Fax 01905 333468
[SC] From £80–£330
Sleeps 2/6
Up to Commended

A friendly and warm welcome awaits you to share our family home in the heart of Worcestershire. Self-catering in a log cabin or converted wain house. Also bed and breakfast. Ours is a working dairy and cheese-making farm where you are welcome to participate. 3 miles west of Worcester, A44 to Leominster, 7 miles M5 J7. Closed Christmas.

Old Yates Cottages, Old Yates Farm, Abberley, Nr Worcester, Worcestershire WR6 6AT

Sarah & Richard Goodman
☎ 01299 896500
Fax 01299 896065
[SL] From £130–£310
Sleeps up to 4
Commended

We invite you to enjoy the home comforts of our cottages, to experience their tranquil surroundings and to relax in our beautiful countryside. Games facilities and launderette on site. 1 mile from village; many restaurants, leisure and recreational facilities within easy reach. Please send for brochure. Open all year.
E-mail: rmgoodma@aol.com.uk

Stable Cottage, Home Farm, Bredons Norton, Tewkesbury, Gloucestershire GL20 7HA

Mick & Anne Meadows
☎/Fax 01684 772322
[SC] From £225–£285
Sleeps 5
Commended

Delightful Cotswold stone stable/barn conversion on a mixed working family farm in a quiet and picturesque village under Bredon Hill. Very cosy and tastefully furnished. Full central heating, lots of beams, own paddock. Perfect location for touring the Cotswolds, Severn Valley and Malverns with many wonderful walks. Open all year.

NO ANSWER?

Farmers are mostly out and about during the day.
Try to telephone before 9.30am or after 4pm.

Gloucestershire

Forest of Dean, Cotswolds & Slad Valley

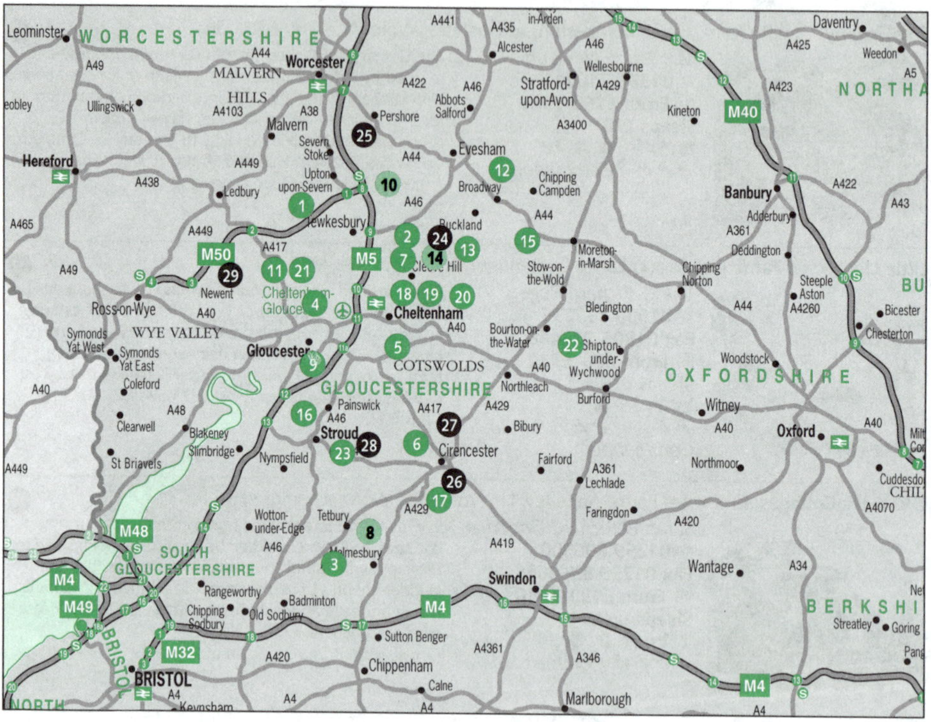

Key

- 1 Bed & Breakfast
- 1 Self-Catering
- 1 B&B and SC
- 1 Camping Barns
- 1 Camping & Caravanning

Gloucestershire is home to the Cotswolds whose villages and scenic beauty are famed throughout the world. The many honey-coloured villages include Bibury, Painswick and Lower Slaughter while some of the finest churches in the country are at Northleach, Fairford and Winchcombe which also has Sudeley Castle. Gloucester with its cathedral and revitalised docks, the elegant Regency town of Cheltenham and picturesque Tewkesbury with its 12th century abbey, are all in the Severn Vale. Bordered by the Severn and the Wye is the beautiful and romantic Forest of Dean and the mining towns of Cinderford, Coleford and Lydney. Any visitor is spoilt for choice in this beautiful county.

If you would like help in finding suitable farm accommodation, turn to the full listing of farm groups on pages 360 to 363 to find appropriate contact details for this area.

Gloucestershire   Heartland

Bed and Breakfast
(and evening meal)

Abbots Court, Church End, Twyning, Tewkesbury, Gloucestershire GL20 6DA

Bernie Williams
☎/Fax 01684 292515
BB From £17–£19
Sleeps 15
⛄🐎✗♨🛍
♨♨ *Commended*

Lovely, quiet farmhouse in 350 acres between Cotswolds and Malverns. All bedrooms have colour TV, most en suite, tea-making facilities. Large lounge, separate dining room, excellent home cooked food. Licensed bar. 3 games rooms with pool table, table tennis, children's TV room, grass tennis court, bowling green, children's play area on lawn. Superb touring area. River and lake fishing on the farm. Open all year (except Christmas and New Year).

Alstone Fields Farm, Teddington Hands, Nr Tewkesbury, Gloucestershire GL20 8NG

Jane Rogers
☎ 01242 620592
BB From £20–£25
Sleeps 12
⛄✗🛍♨
♨♨ *Highly Commended*

Enjoy the friendliest welcome on our traditional family farm, surrounded by sheep, horses and dogs. Wake up in pretty en suite rooms to splendid views of rolling countryside and the delicious smell of bacon! We promise a memorably peaceful holiday and a perfect base from which to explore the picturesque Cotswolds. Open all year.

Avenue Farm, Knockdown, Tetbury, Gloucestershire GL8 8QY

Sonja King
☎ 01454 238207
Fax 01454 238033
BB From £20–£25
Sleeps 6
⛄✗👤🚗🛍♨
Listed Commended

Westonbirt Arboretum adjoins our farm with many miles of walks and a large summer programme of events. We are also near the cities of Bath and Bristol and delightful villages of Lacock and Castle Combe. 'Home from home' is our motto. Open all year.

Brawn Farm, Sandhurst, Gloucester, Gloucestershire GL2 9NR

Sally Williams
☎ 01452 731010
Fax 01452 731102
Mobile 0973 313418
BB From £20
Sleeps 4
⛄🐎✗♨🛍ⓢ
Listed Commended

Working dairy/corn farm with a 15th century listed farmhouse and large garden in an extremely quiet setting. Delightful footpaths through the farm and woods. Two very spacious bedrooms, comfortable sitting room with TV, separate dining room offering excellent breakfasts. Good local pubs. Open all year.

Butlers Hill Farm, Cockleford, Cowley, Cheltenham, Gloucestershire GL53 9NW

Bridget Brickell
☎/Fax 01242 870455
BB From £15
EM From £7
Sleeps 4
⛄(6)✗🛍♨
♨♨ *Approved*

A warm welcome awaits you on this mixed working farm between Cheltenham and Cirencester. Relax in this modern spacious farmhouse, in a quiet part of the Churn Valley with attractive walks and an ideal centre for exploring the Cotswolds. All rooms have H&C and tea/coffee-making facilities, separate guests' sitting room with colour TV and separate dining room. Open Mar–Sept.

Heartland *Gloucestershire*

6 Dix's Barn, Duntisbourne Abbots, Cirencester, Gloucestershire GL7 7JN

Mrs Rosemary Wilcox
☎ 01285 821249
BB From £18–£25
Sleeps 4
♥♥ Commended

Dix's Barn is situated in an Area of Outstanding Natural Beauty. It has breathtaking views of the Cotswolds and one can take lovely walks in any direction. Ideally placed for touring by car. The farm is family run, being a mixture of arable, beef and sheep. Open all year except Christmas.

7 Elms Farm, Gretton, nr Winchcombe, Cheltenham, Gloucestershire GL54 5HQ

Rosemary Quilter
☎ 01242 620150
Fax 01242 620837
Mobile 0374 461107
BB From £17.50–£20
EM From £15
Sleeps 4
♥♥ Commended

Relax and enjoy the Cotswolds in our farmhouse set on the outskirts of Gretton village, with picturesque views north and south. The 120-acre arable, and sheep farm adjoins some of the many footpaths in the area. Ideal for exploring those beautiful Cotswold villages, or just sitting and enjoying the peace and quiet. En suite rooms with TV and tea/coffee. Guests' lounge with log fire. Open all year except Christmas. E-mail: rose@elmfarm.demon.co.uk

8 Folly Farm, Malmesbury Road, Tetbury, Gloucestershire GL8 8XA

Julian Benton
☎ 01666 502475
Fax 01666 502358
BB From £28–£48
Sleeps 7

Listed Commended

Nestled in the Cotswold countryside, a delightful Queen Anne period farmhouse, with Royal Tetbury a five minute walk away. All rooms are en suite, with colour TV and continental breakfast. Easy access to both the M4 and M5. Open all year.

9 Gilbert's, Gilbert's Lane, Brookthorpe, Nr Gloucester, Gloucestershire GL4 0UH

Jenny Beer
☎/Fax 01452 812364
BB From £24–£35
Sleeps 6

♥♥ Highly Commended

Gilbert's, which nestles beneath the Cotswolds close to Gloucester, is listed as an architectural gem. Whilst each room has modern comforts – WC, bath, shower, TV, telephone, etc. – the atmosphere is in keeping with the unpretentious nature of the house and organic smallholding. RAC Highly Acclaimed and *Which? Best Buy*. Open all year. E-mail: jenny@gilbertsbb.demon.co.uk

10 Home Farm, Bredons Norton, Tewkesbury, Gloucestershire GL20 7HA

Mick & Anne Meadows
☎/Fax 01684 772322
BB From £20–£25
Sleeps 6

♥♥ Commended

Find a friendly welcome at our 18th century farmhouse. The family-run farm is situated in an extremely quiet, unspoilt, little village nestling under famous Bredon Hill. Superb position for walking, touring or simply relaxing. All bedrooms have en suite bathrooms, CH, tea-making facilities, TV. Guests' lounge, garden, separate dining room. Choice of breakfast. Excellent food pubs nearby. Open mid Jan–mid Dec.

11 Kilmorie Guest House, Gloucester Road, Snigs End, Corse, Staunton, Gloucestershire GL19 3RQ

Sheila Barnfield
☎ 01452 840224
BB From £15
EM From £7.50
Sleeps 11

♥♥ Commended

Built in 1848 by the Chartists, Kilmorie is a Grade 2 listed smallholding keeping sheep, ponies, goats, ducks and hens. Children may help with animals. All accommodation is on ground floor, warm and cosy with CH, tea/coffee trays, colour TVs, H&C (some en suite available). Relax in large garden or walk waymarked footpaths to discover the countryside. Good home cooking, full English breakfast, 3 course dinner. Ideal for Cotswolds, Malverns, Forest of Dean. Fishing nearby. Closed Christmas & New Year.

Gloucestershire — Heartland

Lowerfield Farm, Willersey, Broadway, Worcestershire WR11 5HF

Jane Hill
☎ 01386 858273
Fax 01386 854608
BB From £22.50–£25
EM From £12.50
Sleeps 6
♥ Commended

Lowerfield farm is peacefully located 3 miles from Broadway and provides an ideal base for exploring the Cotswolds, Stratford on Avon, Cheltenham and beyond. Bedrooms are en suite with clock radio, TV, hairdryer and tea/coffee-making facilities. Three-course evening meal available by arrangement or good eating houses nearby. Open all year.

Lydes Farm, Toddington, Cheltenham, Gloucestershire GL54 5DP

Mrs R Sharpley
☎/Fax 01242 621229
BB From £17.50–£20
Sleeps 5
♥ Commended

Comfortable farmhouse between Broadway and Winchcombe with panoramic views from every room. TV in bedrooms, separate dining room, garden. Dogs taken by arrangement. A grass farm grazed by cattle and horses; visitors are welcome to walk round. Ideal centre for exploring the North Cotswolds. Golf and riding nearby. Open Jan–Nov.

Manor Farm, Greet, Winchcombe, Cheltenham, Gloucestershire GL54 5BJ

Richard & Janet Day
☎/Fax 01242 602423
BB From £22.50–£25
Sleeps 6
♥♥ Highly Commended

Luxuriously restored 16th century cotswold manor on mixed family farm, excellent views, near Sudeley Castle and steam railway. Convenient to Broadway, Cheltenham, Evesham, Tewkesbury and M5. 1½ miles from Cotswold Way and Wychavon Way. Large garden, croquet lawn, children welcome, horses can be accommodated. Self-catering cottages also available and camping space. Open Jan–Nov.

Manor Farm, Weston Sub-Edge, Chipping Campden, Gloucestershire GL55 6QH

Lucy Robbins
☎ 01386 840390
Fax 08701 640638
Mobile 0589 108812
BB From £20
Sleeps 6
♥♥ Commended

Traditional 17th century farmhouse on a 600-acre mixed farm with sheep, cattle and horses. An excellent base for touring the Cotswolds, Shakespeare Country and Hidcote Manor Gardens. Warm, friendly atmosphere with big hearty breakfasts. Beautiful walled garden. All rooms are en suite with tea/coffee making facilities, TV/radio. 1½ miles from Chipping Campden. Lots of excellent walks around beautiful countryside. AA QQQQ selected. Open all year. E-mail: lucy@manorfarmbnb.demon.co.uk

Oaktree Farm, Little Haresfield, Standish, Gloucestershire GL10 3DS

Jackie Guilding
☎ 01453 822300
BB From £18–£20
EM From £12
Sleeps 6
Applied

Enjoy that well-earned break in the friendly atmosphere of our mixed dairy farm, situated in an Area of Outstanding Natural Beauty with open views to the Malvern Hills, Forest of Dean and Cotswolds. Guests are welcome to watch the daily running of this family farm, enjoy the outdoor swimming pool or just relax in the large garden. All rooms are en suite and equipped with the little extras to make your stay enjoyable. Open Feb–Nov.

Oakwood Farm, Upper Minety, Malmesbury, Wiltshire SN16 9PY

Mrs Katie Gallop
☎/Fax 01666 860286
Mobile 0385 916039
BB From £15–£18
Sleeps 6
Listed Commended

A friendly farming couple welcome you to their working dairy farm overlooking Upper Minety church. Meander through the landscaped gardens or just relax on the croquet lawn under the old oak tree. Guests enjoy their own spacious wing with extra touches that make Oakwood Farm a special place to stay. Well situated for touring the Cotswolds, Heart of England and West Country. Open all year.

Heartland Gloucestershire

18 Pardon Hill Farm, Prescott, Gotherington, Cheltenham, Gloucestershire GL52 4RD

Mrs J Newman
☎/Fax 01242 672468
BB From £20
Sleeps 5
♥♥ Commended

A quiet, family-run 300-acre livestock farm, set in the beautiful Cotswold hills just 6 miles from Cheltenham and 3 miles from Winchcombe. Double, twin and single rooms, all en suite with outstanding views. A marvellous base for walking, riding and touring holidays. Open all year except Christmas.

19 Postlip Hall Farm, Postlip, Winchcombe, Cheltenham, Gloucestershire GL54 5AQ

Mrs Valerie Albutt
☎ 01242 603351
BB From £19–£30
Sleeps 6
♥♥ Highly Commended

Spectacular situation, superb scenery in every direction. Set in tiny hamlet of Postlip off B4632, Winchcombe 1¾ miles. This working farm is a fantastic base for exploring Cotswolds, Warwick Castle, Blenheim Palace, Bath, Malverns. Great walking. Golf and horse riding nearby. Cosy, spacious en suite rooms, armchairs, colour TV. Beverages. Lovely welcoming atmosphere. Open all year except Christmas.

20 Sudeley Hill Farm, Winchcombe, Gloucestershire GL54 5JB

Barbara Scudamore
☎/Fax 01242 602344
BB From £22–£28
Sleeps 6
♥♥ Highly Commended

Delightfully situated above Sudeley Castle with panoramic views across the surrounding valley, this is a 15th century listed farmhouse with a large garden on a working mixed farm of 800 acres. Ideal centre for touring the Cotswolds. Family/twin, 1 double, 1 twin, all en suite. Comfortable lounge with TV and log fires. Separate dining room. Open all year except Christmas.

21 Town Street Farm, Tirley, Gloucestershire GL19 4HG

Sue Warner
☎ 01452 780442
Fax 01452 780890
BB From £18–£25
Sleeps 4
♥♥ Commended

Town Street Farm is a typical working family farm close to the River Severn, within easy reach of M5 and M50. The farmhouse offers a high standard of accommodation with en suite facilities in bedrooms and a warm and friendly welcome. Breakfast is served overlooking the lawns, flowerbeds and tennis court which is available for use by guests. Open all year except Christmas.

22 Upper Farm, Clapton-on-the-Hill, Bourton-on-the-Water, Gloucestershire GL54 2LG

Mrs Helen Adams
☎ 01451 820453
Fax 01451 810185
BB From £17.50–£22
Sleeps 8
♥♥ Highly Commended

A mixed family farm of 140-acres in a peaceful, undiscovered village two miles from Bourton-on-the-Water. Our centrally heated period stone farmhouse has been tastefully restored and offers a warm, friendly welcome. Quality accommodation and hearty farmhouse fayre. We are centrally located for touring or walking and our hill position offers panoramic views over the surrounding Cotswold countryside. Open Mar–Nov.

23 Wickridge Court Farm, Folly Lane, Stroud, Gloucestershire GL6 7JT

Gloria & Peter Watkins
☎ 01453 764357
BB From £20–£25
Sleeps 6
♥♥ Commended

Wickridge Court Farm is situated 1 mile from the B4070 holiday route. A farm of 250 acres with cattle and horses. The historic farmhouse is a sympathetically converted Cotswold stone barn offering all en suite rooms. It is a peaceful suntrap set in a fold of the beautiful Slad Valley offering excellent walks through National Trust woods; Stroud Leisure Centre with its heated pool is 1 mile, many places of interest within easy reach. Open all year.

Gloucestershire   Heartland

Self-Catering

Bangrove Farm, Teddington, Tewkesbury, Gloucestershire GL20 8JB
Pat Hitchman
☎/Fax 01242 620223
SC From £280–£330
Sleeps 2/8
❦❦❦❦ Commended

An attractive self-contained property part of 17th century oak-beamed farmhouse on arable/livestock farm in quiet rural setting near Cheltenham. Ideal for walking and touring Cotswolds. Comfortably furnished, fitted carpets throughout. 3 double bedrooms (1 with washbasin), large bathroom. Downstairs cloakroom, kitchen/diner, microwave, large lounge, TV. Linen/electricity/use of washing machine included. Children welcome. Garden, hard tennis court, barbecue. Golf/riding available. Open Mar–Oct.

Court Close Farm, Manor Road, Eckington, Pershore, Worcestershire WR10 3BH
Eileen Fincher
☎ 01386 750297
SC From £200–£295
Sleeps 5 + cot
❦❦❦❦ Commended

A self-contained wing of our lovely 18th century farmhouse and garden on village edge, bordering Gloucestershire. Outstanding views of Bredon Hill. Attractive set dairy farm with meadows sloping to the Avon. Fishing by arrangement. Central for Shakespeare, Malvern and Cotswold jaunts. Convenient kitchen/diner and comfortable sitting room with TV, storage heat and electric fire. 3 bedrooms, linen provided. Closed Christmas.

Folly Farm Cottages, Malmesbury Road, Tetbury, Gloucestershire GL8 8XA
Julian Benton
☎ 01666 502475
Fax 01666 502358
SC From £90–£615
Sleeps 2–8
❦❦❦ – ❦❦❦❦ Commended

Close to Royal Tetbury, 10 superior 18th century cottages. Well furnished, fully equipped throughout. CH, CTV, microwave, linen provided. Some log fires. Laundry, large gardens, barbecue and play area. Fishing, golf, riding, windsurfing nearby. Pubs 4 minutes' walk. Resident host. Ideal for disabled and family reunions. Civilised pets and children welcome! Close to M4/M5. Open all year.

Manor Farm Cottages, Greet, Winchcombe, Cheltenham, Gloucestershire GL54 5BJ
Richard & Janet Day
☎/Fax 01242 602423
SC From £150–£550
Sleeps 3/6
❦❦❦❦ Highly Commended

Beautifully restored 15th century tithe house (pictured) also 'Shuck's Cottage' and 'Bread Oven Cottage', on family farm. Central for Tewkesbury, Broadway, Evesham, Cheltenham. Sleep 3–6, cot and high-chair available. Horses accommodated. Close to Cotswold Way and Wychavon Way, in sight of steam railway. Full central heating, every modern convenience. Camping space also available. Open all year.

Old Mill Farm, nr Cirencester, c/o Ermin House Farm, Syde, Cheltenham, Gloucestershire GL53 9PN
Mrs Catherine Hazell
☎ 01285 821255
Fax 01285 821531
SC From £145–£550
Sleeps 2–7
❦❦❦❦ Commended

Four superior barn conversions featuring Cotswold stone pillars and beams. Situated 4 miles from Cirencester on mixed farm beside River Thames and Cotswold Water Park for walking, birdwatching, fishing, sailing and jet skiing. Trains to London 1¼ hrs. Prices include full central heating, electricity, bed-linen, colour TV. Separate laundry room with pay-phone. Convenient for Stratford-upon-Avon, Oxford, Stonehenge, Bath and Tetbury. Open all year.

Heartland *Gloucestershire*

(10) Stable Cottage, Home Farm, Bredons Norton, Tewkesbury, Gloucestershire GL20 7HA

Mick & Anne Meadows
☎/Fax 01684 772322
SC From £225–£285
Sleeps 5
Commended

Delightful Cotswold stone stable/barn conversion on a mixed working family farm in a quiet and picturesque village under Bredon Hill. Very cosy and tastefully furnished. Full central heating, lots of beams, own paddock. Perfect location for touring the Cotswolds, Severn Valley and Malverns with many wonderful walks. Open all year.

(27) Warrens Gorse Cottages, Home Farm, Warrens Gorse, Cirencester, Gloucestershire GL7 7JD

John & Nanette Randall
☎ 01285 831261
SC From £140–£200
Sleeps 3–5
Approved

2½ miles from Cirencester between Daglingworth and Perrotts Brook, these attractive whitewashed cottages are ideally situated for touring the Cotswolds. The cottages are personally attended by the owners and are comfortably furnished and well equipped. 100-acre sheep and cattle farm. Golf club nearby. Water sports 5 miles. Open Apr–Oct.

(28) Westley Farm, Chalford, Stroud, Gloucestershire GL6 8HP

Julian Usborne
☎/Fax 01285 760262
SC From £130–£300
Sleeps 2/6
Approved

Steep meadows of wild flowers and beech woods are the setting for this old fashioned 80-acre hill farm with breathtaking panoramic views over the Golden Valley. Children especially enjoy the donkey, calves, lambs and foals. Adults may prefer the complete tranquillity and abundant wildlife. Nearby horseriding, golf, gliding, watersports. Midway Cirencester – Stroud. Four cottages, two flats. Brochure available. Open Apr–Nov.

(29) Windmill Annexe, Castle Fruit Farm, Castle Tump, Newent, Gloucestershire GL18 1LS

Mrs Gilli Nicolson
☎/Fax 01531 890428
SC From £265–£350
Sleeps 4
Highly Commended

Windmill Annexe is an extension to a beautiful Georgian country house. Designed on one level, it is spacious and opens on to large lawns and gardens. You are invited to seek secluded corners to relax in or wander through orchards. A unique windmill adds a majestic aspect to the tranquil setting. Open all year.
E-mail:wndmlanx@aol.com.uk

Please mention **Stay on a Farm** when booking

FINDING YOUR ACCOMMODATION

The local FHB Group contacts listed on page 360 can always help you find a vacancy in your chosen area.

Warwickshire

Shakespeare Country & Fosse Way

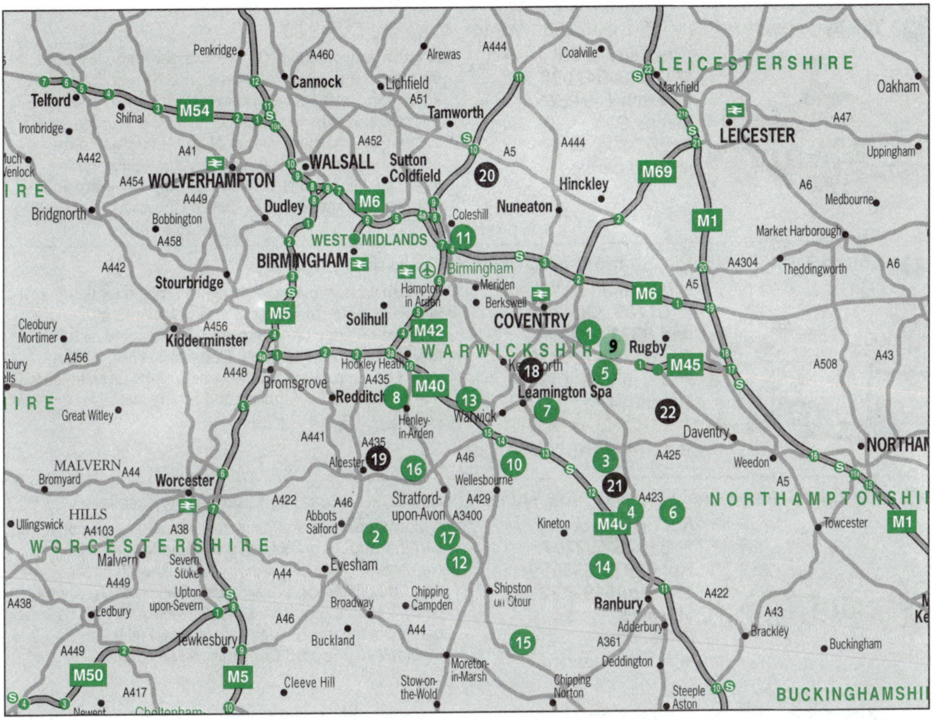

Key

- 1 Bed & Breakfast
- 1 Self-Catering
- 1 B&B and SC
- 1 Camping Barns
- 1 Camping & Caravanning

The native county of William Shakespeare has a lot to offer with its medieval castles, the historic towns of Warwick, Stratford-upon-Avon, Leamington Spa, Rugby and Kenilworth, and its delightful countryside. Stratford-upon-Avon is the provincial home of the Royal Shakespeare Company which performs in the three theatres near the River Avon. At Stoneleigh, near Kenilworth, is the Royal Showground which hosts the Royal Show every July and is a year-round agricultural centre. Warwickshire also has many pretty villages and stately homes such as Packwood House, Ragley Hall, Charlecote Park, Baddesley Clinton and Coughton Court.

If you would like help in finding suitable farm accommodation, turn to the full listing of farm groups on pages 360 to 363 to find appropriate contact details for this area.

Heartland　　　Warwickshire

Bed and Breakfast
(and evening meal)

---

① The Byre, Lords Hill Farm, Coalpit Lane, Wolston, Coventry CV8 3GB

Mrs Betty Gibbs
☎ 01203 542098
BB From £19–£26
Sleeps 6
♿(5) 🐎 ✂ ♣
♛ *Commended*

A warm welcome awaits guests to our home, a converted barn set in a quiet country lane on a 200-acre sheep/arable farm. Attractive, spacious double/twin bedrooms, 1 en suite, 2 with washbasins. Full CH, colour TV, tea/coffee tray and many extras. Numerous village pubs nearby for evening meals. Ideally situated for visiting Stratford, NEC and NAC, 15 mins from Coventry and Rugby. Non smokers only. Closed Christmas.

---

② Church Farm, Dorsington, Stratford-upon-Avon, Warwickshire CV37 8AX

Mrs Marian J Walters
☎ 01789 720471
and 0831 504194
Fax 01789 720830
BB From £18–£19.50
Sleeps 14
🐴 ♿ 🐕 ♣ 🟢
♛♛ *Commended*

A warm welcome awaits you at our mixed working farm with lake, equestrian course and woodlands to explore. Situated on edge of quiet pretty village yet ideal for touring Stratford, Warwick, Cotswolds, NAC, NEC, Worcester and Evesham. Most bedrooms en suite, all with tea/coffee and TV. Stabling and fishing available. Open all year.

---

③ The Coach House, Snowford Hall Farm, Hunningham, Royal Leamington Spa, Warwickshire CV33 9ES

Rudi Hancock
☎ 01926 632297
Fax 01926 633599
BB From £19–£22
Sleeps 6
♿ ♣ 🐾
♛♛ *Commended*

A warm welcome and peaceful surroundings in converted barn farmhouse on 200-acre working farm in rolling countryside. Near the Roman Fosse Way, ideal for visiting Stratford, Warwick, Leamington, Cotswolds, NAC and NEC. 2 double rooms en suite, 1 twin room with basin and bathroom adjacent. Singles extra. CH. Full breakfast. Open all year (closed Christmas & New Year).

---

④ Crandon House, Avon Dassett, Leamington Spa, Warwickshire CV33 0AA

Deborah Lea
☎/Fax 01295 770652
BB From £19.50–£28
Sleeps 10
♿(10) 🐎 🏠 ♣ ♣
♛♛ *Highly Commended*

We offer an an exceptionally high standard of accommodation and a friendly welcome on our small farm with rare breeds. Set in peaceful countryside with beautiful views. Large garden. Full CH. 5 attractive bedrooms with en suite/private facilities, colour TV, tea/coffee tray and many extras. Extensive breakfast menu. Easy access to Stratford, Warwick, Cotswolds. Located between J11 and 12 on M40 (4 miles). Closed Christmas.

---

⑤ Frankton Grounds Farm, Frankton, Nr Rugby, Warwickshire CV23 9PD

Mrs Mary Pritchard
☎ 01926 632391
BB From £15–£20
EM From £10
Sleeps 4
♿ 🐎 ♣
Listed Approved

Beautifully situated in a mixed farm of horses, sheep, pedigree and commercial cattle. A warm welcome for the visitor who enjoys peace and quiet yet, with the benefit of easy access to Warwick, Leamington and Stratford. 2½ miles M45. Full CH, log fires, excellent food. 1 double with bathroom, 1 twin. Open all year.

Warwickshire — Heartland

Hill Farm, Priors Hardwick, Rugby, Warwickshire CV23 8SP

Simon & Angela Darbishire
☎ 01327 260338
BB From £18–£25
Sleeps 4
Applied

We offer a warm, relaxed welcome to our new stone farmhouse on our 400-acre mixed farm situated in beautiful, peaceful countryside with outstanding views. Rooms have TV and tea/coffee with guests' bathroom. Many varied walks/pubs/amenities nearby. Well situated for Stratford, Warwick, Oxford and the NAC. Open all year except Christmas and New Year.

Hill Farm, Lewis Road, Radford Semele, Leamington Spa, Warwickshire CV31 1UX

Mrs Rebecca Gibbs
☎ 01926 337571
BB From £18–£25
Sleeps 10
Commended

Hill Farm is a comfortable, friendly farmhouse situated in 350 acres of mixed farmland. Excellent breakfasts, large garden, attractive double/twin/single bedrooms, some en suite, with CH and tea/coffee-making facilities. Comfortable TV lounge, quiet room, guests' bathroom. Children welcome. AA and Farm Holiday Guide award winner. Caravanning/Camping Club certificated site. Ideal for Shakespeare Country. Open all year (closed Christmas).

Holland Park Farm, Buckley Green, Henley in Arden, Nr Solihull, Warwickshire B95 5QF

Mrs Kathleen Connolly
☎/Fax 01564 792625
BB From £19–£25
Sleeps 6
Commended

A Georgian style farmhouse, set in 300 acres of peaceful farmland, including the historic grounds of 'The Mount' and other interesting walks. Large garden with pond. Livestock includes cattle, sheep and Irish Draught horses. Ideally situated in Shakespeare's country, within easy reach of Birmingham International Airport, NEC, NAC, Stratford-upon-Avon, Warwick and the Cotswolds. Open all year.

Lawford Hill Farm, Lawford Heath Lane, Nr Rugby, Warwickshire CV23 9HG

Mrs Susan Moses
☎ 01788 542001
Fax 01788 537880
BB From £22–£27
Sleeps 12
Commended

You will find a warm welcome at our Grade II listed Georgian farmhouse and converted stables set in an attractive garden, on a mixed family farm. Full CH, log fire, attractive double and twin bedrooms, some en suite. Fishing available. Situated two miles from Rugby. Easy access to Stratford, NAC and NEC. Open all year except Christmas and New Year.

Lower Watchbury Farm, Wasperton Lane, Barford, Warwickshire CV35 8DH

Valerie Eykyn
☎/Fax 01926 624772
BB From £20–£25
Sleeps 5
Highly Commended

In the heart of Shakespeare Country, we offer you a warm welcome in our luxurious accommodation with outstanding views over Warwickshire. 1 large twin/family en suite room with lounge area, 1 double en suite, 1 small double with own bathroom. All have colour TV, tea/coffee facilities. Excellent farmhouse breakfast. Village pubs for dinners. Large garden. Warwick, Stratford, NAC, NEC and Cotswolds nearby. Open all year except Christmas.

Packington Lane Farm, Coleshill, Warwickshire B46 3JJ

Constance Harcourt
☎/Fax 01675 462228
BB From £20–£25
Sleeps 6
Commended

A warm welcome awaits you in a rural oasis when you stay in this charming 17th century farmhouse. Tastefully furnished, comfortable rooms. Full English breakfast served on fine china. Large gardens and parking on a working farm, with pleasant views over surrounding countryside. Within 4 miles of the National Exhibition Centre and Birmingham Airport. Easy access from M6 J4 and M42 J6 & 9.

Heartland   Warwickshire

⑫ The Poplars, Mansell Farm, Newbold on Stour, Stratford on Avon, Warwickshire CV37 8BZ

Judith Spencer
☎/Fax 01789 450540
BB From £17.50–£18
EM From £10.50
Sleeps 5
🐎🐕✗ 🏛
♦♦ Commended

A warm welcome awaits you on our working dairy farm. Enjoy the views of the Cotswolds from our modern farmhouse which is in easy reach of Stratford, Warwick, Oxford and NEC. 1 family and 1 twin, both en suite. All have TV, tea tray and CH. Good food or walk to local hostelry. Open all year except Christmas and New Year.

⑬ Shrewley Pools Farm, Haseley, Warwickshire CV35 7HB

Mrs Cathy Dodd
☎ 01926 484315
BB From £25–£35
EM From £10
Sleeps 6
🐎🐕✗ 🏹 ⛺ 🏛
♦♦ Highly Commended

Why not sample the delights of staying in a beautiful 17th century traditional farmhouse on a working stock/arable farm? Set in an acre of landscaped garden with many interesting features, including timbered barn, huge fireplaces, and beamed ceilings. 2 bedrooms, both en suite, with tea/coffee tray. Close to Warwick, Stratford-upon-Avon, the NEC and NAC. Open all year except Christmas and New Year.

⑭ Sor Brook House Farm, Horley, Banbury, Oxfordshire OX15 6BL

Yvonne Prickett
☎ 01295 738121
BB From £20–£25
EM From £15
Sleeps 4
⌕(10) 🐎 🏹 🚴 🏛 ⚙
Applied

Tea and homemade cake await you in this charming stone farmhouse with oak beams and log fires. 1 twin with en suite, 1 twin with private bathroom. Full CH, colour TV, tea/coffee-making facilities. Guests' own sitting and dining rooms. Large, attractive gardens, peaceful walks. Stabling available. Closed Christmas.

⑮ Tallet Barn, Yerdley Farm, Long Compton, Shipston on Stour, Warwickshire CV36 5LH

Diana Richardson
☎ 01608 684248
BB From £18.50–£20
Sleeps 5
⌕(6) ✗ 🏛 ⛺
Listed Commended

A warm welcome and comfortable rooms await you at Yerdley Farm in the recently converted Tallet Barn annex. Both rooms have en suite shower, TV, tea/coffee. On A3400, Stratford 16 miles, Oxford 22 miles. Central for PO/stores, hotel and pub. Many Cotswold attractions nearby, wonderful walking and interesting gardens to visit. Open all year.

⑯ Walcote Farm, Walcote, Haselor, Alcester, Warwickshire B49 6LY

Prim & John Finnemore
☎/Fax 01789 488264
BB From £18–£19
Sleeps 4
🐎🐕✗ ⛺ 🏛
♦♦ Commended

Come and enjoy the relaxing atmosphere at our attractive 16th century oak-beamed farmhouse with inglenook fireplaces, set in a tranquil, picturesque hamlet near Stratford-upon-Avon. En suite double and twin rooms with TV/Fastext, tea/coffee-making facilities and lovely views. Full central heating with log fires in winter. Ideal for Shakespeare's properties, Warwick Castle, NEC and the Cotswolds. Closed Christmas and New Year.
E-mail: john_finnemore@csi.com.uk

⑰ Whitchurch Farm, Wimpstone, Stratford-upon-Avon, Warwickshire CV37 8NS

Mrs Joan James
☎/Fax 01789 450275
BB From £18–£19
EM From £10.50
Sleeps 6
🐎🏹 ⚙ 🏛
♦♦ Commended

Lovely Georgian farmhouse set in park-like surroundings in peaceful Stour Valley 4½ miles from Stratford. Very convenient for Warwick Castle and Shakespeare properties. Ideal for touring the Cotswolds by car or rambling. The bedrooms are large and well furnished, all with en suite bathrooms, CH and tea/coffee-making facilities. Separate dining room and sitting room for guests. Open all year (closed Christmas Day).

Warwickshire Heartland

Self-Catering

Furzen Hill Farm Cottages, c/o Furzen Hill Farm, Cubbington Heath, Leamington Spa, Warks CV32 6QZ

Mrs Christine Whitfield
☎/Fax 01926 424791
SC From £110–£310
Sleeps 4/7
🐕 🐎 💼
🔑🔑 *Commended*

Furzen Hill is a mixed farm. The cottage is part of 17th century farmhouse with a large shared garden. Sleeping 7. The Barn and Dairy Cottages, both recently converted, each sleep 4. Dairy Cottage has its own small garden. The Barn shares the Cottage garden. All have the use of tennis court. Situated within easy reach of NAC, NEC, Warwick and Stratford. Open all year.

The Granary, c/o Glebe Farm, Kinwarton, Alcester, Warwickshire B49 6HB

Susan Kinnersley
☎/Fax 01789 762554
SC From £90–£145
Sleeps 2
🔑🔑 *Commended*

Off the beaten track, yet near the small market town of Alcester, this cottage retains many interesting features of the original granary combined with modern standards of warmth and comfort. The farm is bounded by the River Alne and there are a variety of attractive country walks in the area. Linen provided, colour TV. Car space. Short breaks by arrangement. Open all year.

Hipsley Farm Cottages, Hipsley Lane, Hurley, Atherstone, Warwickshire CV9 2LR

Mrs Ann Prosser
☎/Fax 01827 872437
SC From £220–£340
Sleeps 2/4 + cots
🔑🔑🔑 – 🔑🔑🔑🔑 *Highly Commended*

Hipsley Farm is situated in beautiful rolling countryside. Very peaceful and quiet yet only 3 miles from jct10, M42/A5, so easy access to all the Midlands. The barns and cowshed have been carefully converted into 6 very comfortable, individually furnished cottages. Fully equipped including gas CH, colour TV, all bed linen and towels. Laundry facilities and putting green. Ample parking on site. Open all year.

Knightcote Farm Cottages, The Bake House, Knightcote, nr Leamington Spa CV33 0SF

Fiona Walker
☎ 01295 770637
Fax 01295 770135
SC From £295–£525
Sleeps 4/6
🔑🔑🔑🔑 *Highly Commended*

Escape to the quiet and historic village of Knightcote and then relax. Three idyllic barn conversions have been lavishly equipped and furnished to ensure you are cosy and comfortable. Explore the many beautiful lanes and footpaths. One cottage wheelchair friendly. Adjacent car parking. No smoking. Open all year.
E-mail: fionawalker@mcmail.com

Lawford Hill Farm, Lawford Heath Lane, Nr Rugby, Warwickshire CV23 9HG

Susan Moses
☎ 01788 542001
Fax 01788 537880
SC From £250–£350
Sleeps 4
Applied

Attractive, newly converted barns adjacent to Georgian farmhouse and garden. Many mature trees, attractive flower/shrub borders and traditional walled vegetable garden. Farm walks, fishing, golfing and sailing facilities nearby, as are the delights of Warwick, Leamington, Stratford-upon-Avon and many wonderful National Trust properties. Open all year.

Heartland   Warwickshire

22 Little Biggin, c/o Broadwell House Farm, Broadwell, Rugby, Warwickshire CV23 8HF

Mrs Linda Denham
☎/Fax 01926 812347
SC From £225–£350
Sleeps 4
⌂(12) ⚔ ♟ ♞ ♣ ✂
♪♪♪♪ Commended

Attractive stone cottage with exposed beams, well equipped and furnished, with full central heating. Radio and colour TV. Cosy double and twin bedrooms have sloping ceilings. Bathroom has shower. Gas hob, electric oven, microwave in modern kitchen. Ample parking. Outstanding views and tranquil walks. Peacefully situated. Linen, electricity and gas included. Open all year.

USE THE INDEX

The comprehensive Index shows which farms offer access to disabled visitors; caravanning/camping facilities; the chance to participate on a working farm; stabling/grazing for visiting horses; en suite rooms; a welcome to business people; acceptance of *Stay on a Farm* gift tokens.

THE 1000+ BUREAU MEMBERS OFFER A UNIQUE LINK TO CUSTOMERS ACROSS THE UK

All Bureau members belong to a local Group. Each member can refer you to an equally high quality member within the Group... or across the UK: England, Northern Ireland, Scotland, Wales.

FOLLOW THE COUNTRY CODE
Leave nothing but footprints,
Take nothing but photographs,
Kill nothing but time!

Northamptonshire

Rockingham Forest, Nene Valley & Grand Union Canal

Key

- 1 Bed & Breakfast
- 1 Self-Catering
- 1 B&B and SC
- 1 Camping Barns
- 1 Camping & Caravanning

Northamptonshire, the county of 'squires and spires', has houses, monuments and fine churches too numerous to mention. There's Sulgrave Manor, home of George Washington's ancestors, Rockingham Castle, Boughton House, the fine Saxon church at Brixworth and, most famous of all, Althorp. The Battle and Farm Museum at Naseby will give you a taste of that decisive Civil War battle in 1645, while the Waterways Museum at Stoke Bruerne provides a fascinating insight into life on the canals, or take a nostalgic trip on the Nene Valley Steam Railway. The world-famous motor racing circuit at Silverstone is situated in the south of the county and will bring you right up-to-date.

If you would like help in finding suitable farm accommodation, turn to the full listing of farm groups on pages 360 to 363 to find appropriate contact details for this area.

 *Heartland* Northamptonshire

Bed and Breakfast
(and evening meal)

① Dairy Farm, Cranford St Andrew, Kettering, Northamptonshire NN14 4AQ

Audrey Clarke
☎ 01536 330273
[BB] From £20–£30
EM From £14
Sleeps 3
👶 🐴 ✂ 🕯 ♿
🏵 🏵 *Commended*

Enjoy a holiday in a comfortable 17th century farmhouse with oak beams and inglenook fireplaces. Four poster bed now available. Peaceful surroundings, large garden containing ancient circular dovecote. Dairy Farm is a working farm situated in a beautiful Northamptonshire village just off the A14 within easy reach of many places of interest or ideal for a restful holiday. Good farmhouse food and friendly atmosphere. Open all year except Christmas.

② Drayton Lodge, Daventry, Northamptonshire NN11 4NL

Ann Spicer
☎ 01327 702449
Fax 01327 872110
[BB] From £25–£30
EM From £15
Sleeps 8
👶 🐴 ✂ 🌿 ♿
🏵 🏵 🏵 *Highly Commended*

Drayton Lodge is a secluded 18th century farmhouse set on the edge of Daventry to one side and rolling Northamptonshire countryside to the other. A warm, friendly welcome awaits you. Beautiful centrally heated bedrooms with en suite bathrooms and TVs. Championship golf course within ½ mile. Historical places of interest to visit. Full traditional English breakfast served. Open all year. E-mail: ann.andmark.spicer@farmline.com.uk

③ The Elms, Kislingbury, Northampton NN7 4AH

Mrs Primrose Sanders
☎ 01604 830326
[BB] From £18.50
Sleeps 5
👶 🐴 ✂ 🕯 ♿ 🌿
Listed *Commended*

A warm welcome awaits you in our Victorian farmhouse with views over the farm. Situated 2 miles from M1 junction 16 and 4 miles from Northampton. Convenient for business stopovers and touring Cotswolds, Stratford, Oxford and Cambridge. Nene Way Walk passes through the farm. Open all year.

④ Green Farm, Weedon Lois, Towcester, Northamptonshire NN12 8PL

Mrs Paddy Elkington
☎/Fax 01327 860249
[BB] From £18.50–£21
Sleeps 6
👶 ⛵ 🕯 ♿
Listed *Commended*

Green Farm is a comfortable 18th century farmhouse set in rolling countryside on a 550-acre mixed farm. You can enjoy private coarse fishing or visit the many local attractions, including Sulgrave Manor, Canons Ashby, and Silverstone Grand Prix circuit to name but a few! The M1 and M40 are both within 15 minutes. Open all year except Christmas.

⑤ Pear Tree Farm, Main Street, Aldwincle, Nr Kettering, Northamptonshire NN14 3EL

Mavis Hankins
☎ 01832 720614
Fax 01832 720559
[BB] From £20
EM From £8.50
Sleeps 8
✂ 🚗 ♿ 🕯
🏵 🏵 *Commended*

Pear Tree Farm is a mixed 400-acre farm consisting of cattle, sheep, poultry and arable. Comfortably furnished with relaxed family atmosphere and excellent breakfasts. Four bedrooms. Excellent for walking, birdwatching, fishing. Large garden for relaxing. Open all year except Christmas and New Year (camping Feb–Sept).

Northamptonshire   Heartland

Spinney Lodge Farm, Forest Road, Hanslope, Milton Keynes, Buckinghamshire MK19 7DE

Mrs Christina Payne
☎ 01908 510267
BB From £20–£22.50
EM From £10
Sleeps 4
⛔(12) ✗ ⚘ ▪
❀❀ Commended

Spinney Lodge is a arable, beef and sheep farm. The lovely Victorian farmhouse with its large garden and rose pergola has en suite bedrooms with colour TV and tea-making facilities. Evening meal by arrangement. M1 J15, 8 minutes, 12 minutes Northampton, 15 minutes Milton Keynes. Silverstone Circuit, Stowe Gardens and Woburn to visit in the area. Ideal base for touring. Open all year except Christmas.

Walltree House Farm, Steane, Brackley, Northamptonshire NN13 5NS

Richard & Pauline Harrison
☎ 01295 811235
Fax 01295 811147
Mobile 0860 913399
BB From £20–£25
EM From £15
Sleeps 18
⛔ ⚐ ⛅ ⛵ ▪ ⚘ ✿
❀❀❀ Commended

Our home is in the middle of nowhere but at the centre of everything. Badger woods to explore, lovely walks. Historic places to visit. Individual ground floor rooms in the courtyard now with four new additional luxury rooms, others in the adjacent licensed Victorian farmhouse. Most rooms en suite. Nearby shopping, fishing, golf, gliding, Silverstone Circuit and leisure centres. Open Feb–Nov.

Wold Farm, Old, Northampton, Northamptonshire NN6 9RJ

Anne Engler
☎ 01604 781258
BB From £22–£25
Sleeps 8
⛔ ⛅ ✗ ▪ ⚘ ✿
❀❀❀ Highly Commended

A friendly, informal atmosphere is offered at this 18th century farmhouse on 250-acre beef/arable farm. Main farmhouse offers attractive bedrooms. Hearty breakfast is served in oak-beamed dining room with inglenook fireplace. Relax by log fire or at snooker table. Recently converted barn provides en suite rooms overlooking pretty garden with colourful Pergola. Open all year.

Self-Catering

Granary Cottage, Brook Farm, Lower Benefield, Peterborough PE8 5AE ⑨

Mrs J Singlehurst
☎ 01832 205215
SC From £150–£250
Sleeps 4
⛔(4) ⚘
♣ ♣ ♣ Commended

At the beginning of a gated road we offer peace and tranquillity with picturesque walks. Granary Cottage is warm, cosy and well equipped with linen provided. Close by are the historic market towns of Oundle and Stamford and the pretty village of Rockingham. Sorry no pets. Open all year.

Rye Hill Country Cottages, Rye Hill Farm, Holdenby Road, East Haddon, Northants NN6 8DH ⑩

Michael & Margaret Widdowson
☎ 01604 770990
Fax 01604 770237
SC From £150–£435
Sleeps 2/6
⛅ ⛵ ⚐ ⚘ ▪ ✿
♣ ♣ ♣ ♣ Highly Commended

Children are most welcome on our delightful, peaceful smallholding. They can help feed our farm animals, collect eggs and have fun in the play area and games room. Our 5 cottages have every modern convenience combined with beams, open fires and log burning stoves. Small licensed restaurant providing good country food and cream teas. Many places of interest for all the family. Open all year.

Heartland — Northamptonshire

⑪ Villiers Suite, Cranford Hall, Cranford, Kettering, Northamptonshire NN14 4AL

Gayle Robinson
☎ 01536 330248
Fax 01536 330203
SC From £255–£295
Sleeps 5

Commended

Lovely Georgian mansion in the heart of a traditional estate village which is set in parkland amidst fine gardens. Many attractive walks and drives to be taken, together with historic spots to visit and a great range of cultural activities. The Villiers Suite is a stylish, self-contained apartment within the Hall.

Our farms offer a range of facilities that are illustrated by symbols in each entry. Turn to page 16 for an explanation of the symbols.

CONFIRM BOOKINGS

Disappointments can arise from misunderstandings over the telephone. Please write to confirm your booking.

Our Internet address is
http://www.webscape.co.uk/farmaccom/

Bedfordshire
Ivel & Ouse Valleys

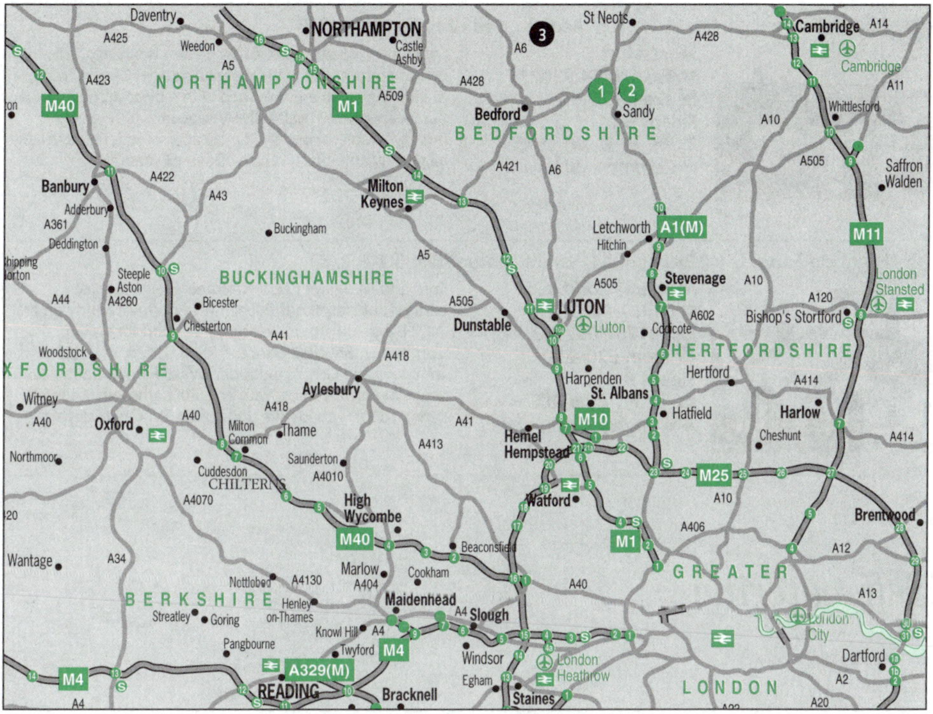

Key
- 🟢 Bed & Breakfast
- 🟢 Self-Catering
- 🟢 B&B and SC
- 🟢 Camping Barns
- 🟢 Camping & Caravanning

Bedfordshire is ideally situated between Oxford and Cambridge and makes perfect cycling, fishing and golfing country, while walkers will enjoy the Greensand Ridge Walk. The stately home is Woburn Abbey and there are many pretty villages with thatched cottages and beamed Tudor buildings such as Old Warden, near Bedford, which houses nearby the Shuttleworth Collection of historic aeroplanes and road vehicles. The River Ouse flows through Bedford which boasts many excellent museums and galleries. For animal lovers there is the RSPB nature reserve at Sandy, Whipsnade Zoo and Woburn's Wild Animal Kingdom.

If you would like help in finding suitable farm accommodation, turn to the full listing of farm groups on pages 360 to 363 to find appropriate contact details for this area.

 *Heartland* *Bedfordshire*

Bed and Breakfast
(and evening meal)

---

① Church Farm, High Street, Roxton, Bedford, Bedfordshire MK44 3EB

Janet Must
☎/Fax 01234 870234
[BB] From £22.50
Sleeps 6
♥ Commended

Set in a secluded village, Church Farm is a lovely 17th century farmhouse with Georgian facade. Guests' lounge and dining room are furnished with a pleasant mixture of family antiques. Local walks. Village inns for evening meals. Double, single and family accommodation available all year. Many guests return. Open all year.

---

② Highfield Farm, Great North Road, Sandy, Bedfordshire SG19 2AQ

Margaret Codd
☎ 01767 682332
Fax 01767 692503
[BB] From £20–£30
Sleeps 8
♥♥ Highly Commended

Tom and Margaret Codd welcome guests to their comfortable farmhouse. Just 1 mile north of Sandy on the A1, Highfield Farm is excellently situated for visiting Cambridge, Shuttleworth, the RSPB, Grafham Water and for taking the Greensand Ridge Walk. Family, double and single bedrooms, most with en suite bathroom. Guests' sitting room with log fire and colour TV. Open all year.

Self-Catering

---

③ Scald End Farm, Scald End, Mill Road, Thurleigh, Bedford MK44 2DP

Jim Towler
☎ 01234 771996
[SC] From £100–£200
Sleep 2–8
⚑ Approved

The Towler family provides self-catering accommodation in 16th century thatched cottages and modern barn conversions. The farm has cattle, horses, sheep, chickens, ducks and geese – so there is always something to see or do on the farm. The market town of Bedford is only about 15 minutes' drive away. Open all year.

NO ANSWER?
Farmers are mostly out and about during the day.
Try to telephone before 9.30am or after 4pm.

Hertfordshire

The Chilterns

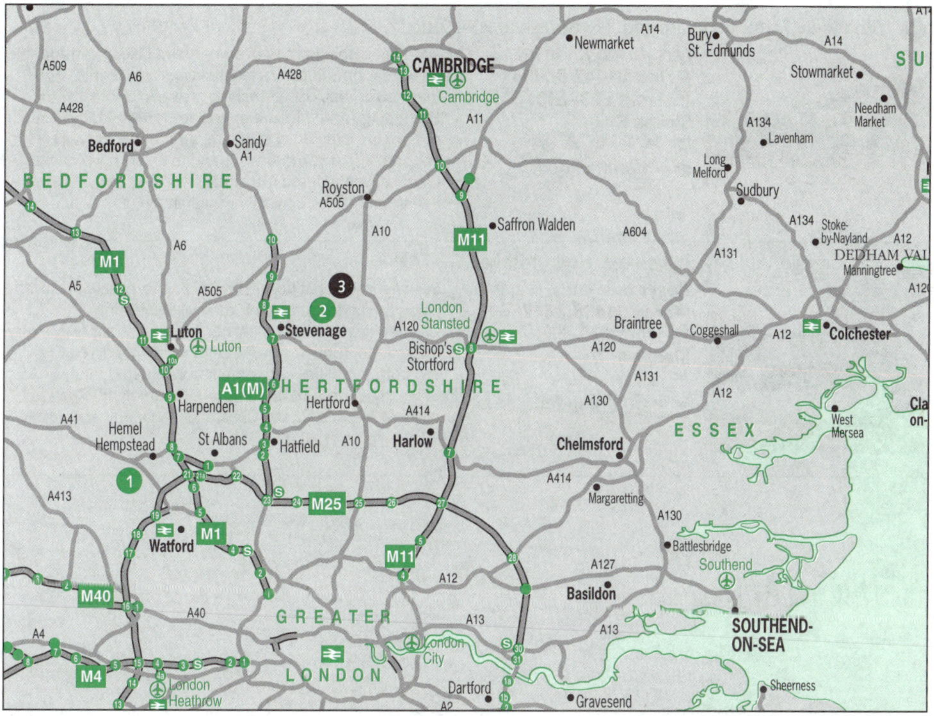

Key

1. Bed & Breakfast
1. Self-Catering
1. B&B and SC
1. Camping Barns
1. Camping & Caravanning

Hertfordshire, a county of contrasts, is in the unique situation of being at the hub of the country's transport network whilst offering some truly unspoilt and varied rural landscapes. It has a great historical heritage with St Albans, once the Roman town Verulamium, the Old Palace and House in Hatfield Park, and Knebworth House. Come and enjoy the Chiltern landscape including many picturesque villages such as Aldbury and Frithsden and the 4,000 acres of ancient woodland of the National Trust's Ashridge Estate. We offer the business guest the chance to unwind in a homely atmosphere as little as half an hour by train from central London.

If you would like help in finding suitable farm accommodation, turn to the full listing of farm groups on pages 360 to 363 to find appropriate contact details for this area.

 **Heartland**   *Hertfordshire*

Bed and Breakfast
(and evening meal)

① Broadway Farm, Berkhamsted, Hertfordshire HP4 2RR

Mrs Alison Knowles
☎/Fax 01442 866541
BB From £20–£30
Sleeps 6
♞ ✈ ✂ ⌒ ▪ ⊚
♛ ♛ *Commended*

Working arable farm with own fishing lake. 3 comfortable en suite rooms in converted buildings adjacent to farmhouse. Tea/coffee-making facilities, colour TV, CH. Everything for the leisure or business guest – the relaxation of farm life in an attractive rural setting, yet easy access to London, airports, motorways and mainline rail services. Open all year (closed Christmas and New Year).
E mail: a.knowles@broadway.nildram.co.uk

② The Grange, Ardeley, Stevenage, Hertfordshire SG2 7AH

Roger & Wendy Waygood
☎/Fax 01438 861260
BB From £25–£30
Sleeps 4
✂ ⚘ ▪
♛ ♛ *Commended*

Seeking traditional hospitality? Come to Ardeley, relax and enjoy the peace of a quiet, rural village setting. Overlooking our tranquil water garden are our two luxury en suite bedrooms with TV, clock radio, hairdryer, CH, tea/coffee facilities and refrigerator. Situated midway A1 Stevenage and A10 Buntingford. No smoking. Regret no children or pets. Closed Christmas, New Year and Easter.

Self-Catering

③ Bluntswood Hall Cottages, Middle Farm, Throcking, Buntingford, Hertfordshire SG9 9RN

Sally Smyth
☎/Fax 01763 281204
SC From £150–£250
Sleeps 4
♞ ▪
🔑🔑🔑🔑 *Commended*

Stables recently converted into 2 cottages with lovely views over the countryside. Ideally situated for Cambridge, Duxford, Wimpole Hall or Knebworth Park. Each beamed cottage has double bedroom, bunk bedroom or single bed, bathroom, fitted kitchen and sitting room. R/C colour TV, CH. Linen and towels included in price. Children welcome. No pets. Open all year.

 Please mention ***Stay on a Farm*** when booking

Cambridgeshire
The Fens & Grafham Water

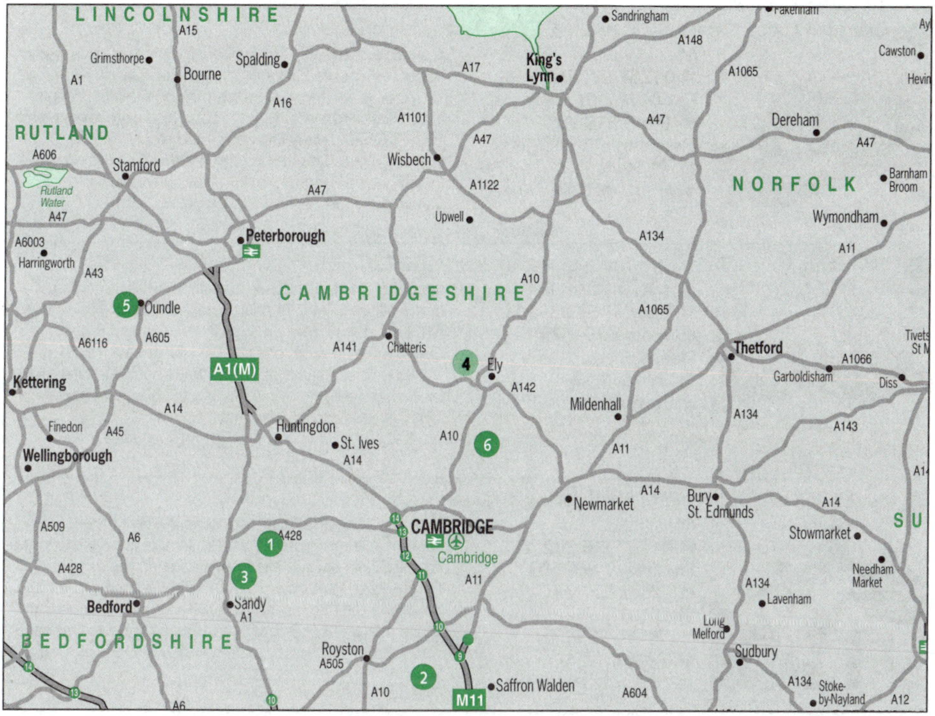

Key
1 Bed & Breakfast
1 Self-Catering
1 B&B and SC
1 Camping Barns
1 Camping & Caravanning

Cambridgeshire, inspiration of Rupert Brooke, is a quintessentially English county of quiet waterways, gentle hills, lanes, pretty villages and busy towns. Best known is Cambridge itself, one of England's oldest university cities where the colleges in their architectural splendour rest near tranquil rivers overhung with willows. North of Cambridge lies the strikingly flat landscape of the Fens. For contrast there is the hustle and bustle of the modern city of Peterborough with its excellent shopping or the stately grandeur of Ely Cathedral, so-called 'Ship of the Fens'. "And is there honey still for tea?" – you never know, at our welcoming farms!

If you would like help in finding suitable farm accommodation, turn to the full listing of farm groups on pages 360 to 363 to find appropriate contact details for this area.

 *Heartland* *Cambridgeshire*

Bed and Breakfast
(and evening meal)

① Gransden Lodge Farm, Little Gransden, Sandy, Bedfordshire SG19 3EB

Mrs Mary Cox
☎ 01767 677365
Fax 01767 677647
[BB] From £18–£20
Sleeps 6
😊 🐎 ⅍ ■
♣♣ *Highly Commended*

A warm and friendly atmosphere awaits you at Gransden Lodge, where we have double, twin and single rooms with TV, clock-radio and tea/coffee-making facilities. Ample bathrooms and WCs. Dining room, also large lounge with TV. AA QQQ. Many local pubs and restaurants for evening meals. Situated on the B1046, 10 miles west of Cambridge. London 50 miles. Also convenient for Stansted Airport (M11, J12). Open all year.

② Hall Farm, Great Chishill, Nr Royston, Hertfordshire SG8 8SH

Mrs Jean Wiseman
☎/Fax 01763 838263
[BB] From £20–£25
Sleeps 6
😊 🐎 ⅍ 🎪 ■
♣ *Commended*

Beautiful, quiet farmhouse in secluded walled garden in a pretty hilltop village 11 miles south of Cambridge on the B1039 midway between Saffron Walden and Royston. One double en suite, one double and one twin with washbasins and share of guests' bathroom. All rooms have tea/coffee facilities, colour TV, electric blankets, hairdryers. Open all year except Christmas.

③ Highfield Farm, Great North Road, Sandy, Bedfordshire SG19 2AQ

Margaret Codd
☎ 01767 682332
Fax 01767 692503
[BB] From £20–£30
Sleeps 8
😊 🐎 ⅍ 🆎 ■ ⊚
♣♣ *Highly Commended*

Tom and Margaret Codd welcome guests to their comfortable farmhouse. Just 1 mile north of Sandy on the A1, Highfield Farm is excellently situated for visiting Cambridge, Shuttleworth, the RSPB, Grafham Water and for taking the Greensand Ridge Walk. Family, double and single bedrooms, most with en suite bathroom. Guests' sitting room with log fire and colour TV. Open all year.

④ Hill House Farm, 9 Main Street, Coveney, Ely, Cambridgeshire CB6 2DJ

Hilary Nix
☎ 01353 778369
[BB] From £20–£22
Sleeps 6
😊(12) ⅍ 🐎 ■ ⊚
♣♣ *Highly Commended*

Spacious Victorian farmhouse in quiet fenland village, 3 miles west of the historic cathedral city of Ely. Open views of the surrounding countryside. Easy access to Cambridge, Newmarket & Huntingdon. Wicken Fen and Welney Wildfowl Trust are nearby. 3 tastefully furnished and decorated bedrooms, all en suite (1 on ground floor). All have own entrance, colour TV, etc full CH. Warm welcome. Open all year except Christmas.

⑤ Lilford Lodge Farm, Barnwell, Oundle, Peterborough, Northamptonshire PE8 5SA

Trudy Dijksterhuis
☎/Fax 01832 272230
[BB] From £20
Sleeps 5
😊 🐕 ⅍ ■
♣♣ *Commended*

Mixed farm set in the attractive Nene Valley situated on the A605, 3 miles south of Oundle and 5 miles north of the A14. Peterborough and Stamford are within easy reach. Guests stay in the recently converted original 19th century farmhouse. All bedrooms have en suite bathrooms, CH, TV, radio and tea/coffee-making facilities. Comfortable lounge with satellite TV and separate dining room. Coarse fishing available. Open all year.

Cambridgeshire   *Heartland*

Spinney Abbey, Wicken, Ely, Cambridgeshire CB7 5XQ

Mrs Valerie Fuller
☎ 01353 720971
[BB] From £20–£21
Sleeps 6
⌂(5) ✕ ♿ ⊛
♚♚ Commended

❻

Enjoy the views across open pasture fields from our attractive Grade II listed Georgian farmhouse. Large garden with tennis court adjacent to our dairy farm which borders the National Trust nature reserve Wicken Fen. 1 double and 1 family room, both en suite and twin with private bathroom. All with TV and hospitality tray. Full CH. Guests' sitting room. Open all year except Christmas.

Self-Catering

Hill House Farm Cottage, 9 Main Street, Coveney, Ely, Cambs CB6 2DJ

Hilary Nix
☎ 01353 778369
[SC] From £230–£350
Sleeps 6
⌂(8) ✕ ♿ ⊛
🗝🗝🗝🗝 Highly
Commended

❹

A tasteful barn conversion on our farm is now a comfortable cottage. Furnished and decorated to a high standard. Set in a quiet village location 3 miles west of Ely with open views of Ely Cathedral and the surrounding countryside. Ideally situated for touring Norfolk, Suffolk and Cambridgeshire. Easy access to Cambridge, Newmarket and Huntingdon. Access form A142 or A10. Regret no smoking, no pets. Open all year.

STAY ON A FARM GIFT TOKENS

If you have enjoyed your Stay on a Farm, why not treat your friends and relatives to *Stay on a Farm* gift tokens? Available from the Bureau office (tel: 01203 696909), they can be redeemed against accommodation and are accepted by the majority of farms (see Index). Please check when booking to avoid disappointment.

FOLLOW THE COUNTRY CODE

Leave nothing but footprints,
Take nothing but photographs,
Kill nothing but time!

Norfolk

The Broads, Norfolk Coast, the Wash, Wensum Valley & Thetford Forest

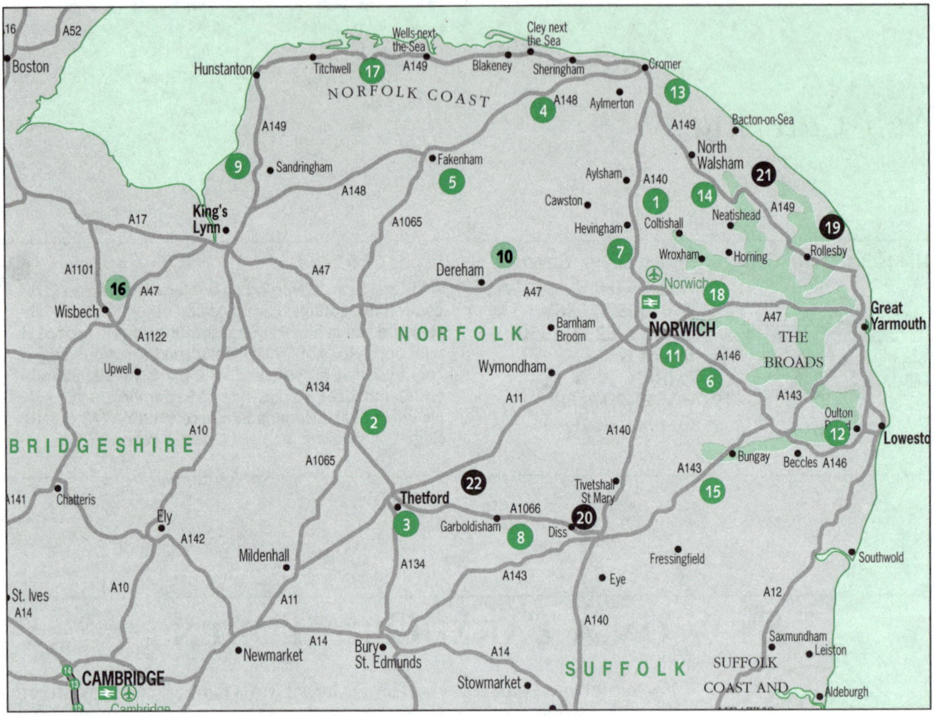

Key

1 Bed & Breakfast
1 Self-Catering
1 B&B and SC
1 Camping Barns
1 Camping & Caravanning

Wherever you go in Norfolk, you are never far from water. There's the glorious North Norfolk coast with its nature reserves and timeless resorts such as Cromer and Wells-next-the-Sea, the picturesque flint houses of Holt and the National Trust's exquisite Blickling Hall. Further down the coast lies the traditional seaside resort of Great Yarmouth. Even inland water tends to be the theme. The famous Broads are a boating paradise of meres and rivers whose reeds are put to good use in the pretty thatched cottages of the surrounding villages. Historic Norwich lies at the confluence of the Rivers Wensum and Yare. Further west you will find royal Sandringham, Thetford, capital of forested Breckland and fascinating attractions such as the Thursford Collection and Bressingham Steam Museum.

If you would like help in finding suitable farm accommodation, turn to the full listing of farm groups on pages 360 to 363 to find appropriate contact details for this area.

Norfolk   Heartland

Bed and Breakfast
(and evening meal)

Birds Place Farm, Back Lane, Coltishall Road, Buxton, Norwich NR10 5HD

Bill and Jenny Catchpole
☎ 01603 279585
BB From £18–£25
EM From £14
Sleeps 6
🐎(8) ⚜ 🏇 ♿
🌹🌹 *Commended*

Small family farm in the Bure Valley in beautiful Broadland countryside. Our 17th century farmhouse is licensed and we offer excellent cuisine, much of the produce home grown. Bedrooms comprise of 1 family and 1 double room en suite, 1 single with private bathroom, all with TV and tea/coffee-making facilities. We have riding stables plus public footpaths and fishing nearby. Open all year.

Colveston Manor, Mundford, Thetford, Norfolk IP26 5HU

Mrs Wendy Allingham
☎ 01842 878218
Fax 01842 879218
BB From £22.50–£27.50
EM From £15
Sleeps 6
🐎(12) ⚜ 🏇 🐕 ♿ 🍴 ⊙
🌹🌹 *Highly Commended*

Peaceful 18th century farmhouse in delightful setting in heart of Breckland. Attractive bedrooms, some en suite. We specialise in delicious cooking from the Aga, using home-grown vegetables. NT properties, cathedrals, gardens and coast within easy reach. Brochure showing location available on request. Open all year.

East Farm, Euston Road, Barnham, Thetford, Norfolk IP24 2PB

Margaret Heading
☎ 01842 890231
Fax 01842 890457
BB From £21–£24
Sleeps 4
🐎 ⚜ ♿ ⊙
🌹 *Commended*

Relax and enjoy the comfort and warm welcome at East Farm in the village of Barnham. We're a 1,000-acre arable farm with beef and sheep and plenty of widlife on the edge of Breckland on Norfolk/Suffolk border between Thetford and Bury St Edmunds. A grey flint-faced house in peaceful surroundings with superb views. Spacious heated rooms with en suite bathrooms. Full English breakfast from local produce. Open all year except Christmas.

Hempstead Hall, Holt, Norfolk NR25 6TN

Lynda-Lee Mack
☎ 01263 712224
BB From £19–£25
Sleeps 6
🐎(3) 🏇 ⚜ 🚗 🍴
🌹🌹 *Commended*

Attractive 19th century flint farmhouse peacefully set in beautiful surroundings. 300 acre arable farm with ducks, donkeys, large gardens, and country walks. Close to the Georgian town of Holt and the North Norfolk coast and its many attractions including steam train rides and boat trips to Blakeney Point Seal Sanctuary. En suite family room, double with private bathroom. Colour TV. Tea/coffee-making facilities in rooms. Open all year.

Highfield Farm, Great Ryburgh, Fakenham, Norfolk NR21 7AL

Mrs E Savory
☎ 01328 829249
Fax 01328 829422
BB From £18–£22
EM from £12.50
Sleeps 6
🐎(12) ⚜ 🍴 ♿ 🍴 ⊙
🌹🌹 *Highly Commended*

Spacious, elegant and comfortable Georgian-style house 10 miles from the coast, set deep in countryside amidst 500 acres of rolling farmland. Central for historic houses and Pensthorpe. Ideal for birdwatchers. Twin room with en suite. Double and twin rooms with washbasin. Guests' sitting room and dining room, log fires, CH. Evening meals by arrangement. Grass tennis court and croquet lawn, horse riding locally. Closed Christmas & New Year.

Heartland — Norfolk

6 Hillside Farm, Welbeck Road, Brooke, near Norwich, Norfolk NR15 1AU

Mrs Carolyn Holl
☎/Fax 01508 550260
BB From £18–£25
EM From £12.50
Sleeps 4
⌚ Commended

This is a 350-acre arable and stock farm. A beautiful 16th century thatched and timber-framed house situated in a pretty village, 7 miles south of Norwich, within easy reach of coast and Broads. One twin/family room, 1 double/family room, both with private facilities. Large games barn with snooker, pool and table tennis. Five acre private lake for coarse fishing. Relaxed family atmosphere. Open all year except Christmas.

7 Lower Farm, Horsford, Norwich, Norfolk NR10 3AW

Mrs Marion Jones
☎ 01603 891291
BB From £19–£25
Sleeps 6
⌚⌚ Highly Commended

Enjoy the comfort and warm welcome at Lower Farm, a mixed farm with sheep and cattle. Beautiful old farmhouse ideal for Norwich, the coast and Broads. Attractive, spacious accommodation in two en suite rooms (1 family, 1 double) with TV and beverage trays. Superb views traditional farmhouse fayre. Cot, babysitting service. Open all year.

8 Malting Farm, Blo Norton Road, South Lopham, Diss, Norfolk IP22 2HT

Cynthia Huggins
☎ 01379 687201
BB From £19–£22
Sleeps 6
⌚⌚ Commended

Situated on Norfolk/Suffolk border amid open countryside. A working dairy farm with some farmyard pets. Farmhouse is Elizabethan timber-framed (inside) with inglenook fireplaces. Central heating. Some four poster beds, some en suite. Easy reach Norfolk Broads, Norwich, Cambridge, Bressingham Steam Museum & Gardens. Cynthia is a keen craftswoman in patchwork, quilting, embroidery and spinning. Closed Christmas & New Year.

9 Marsh Farm, Wolferton, King's Lynn, Norfolk PE31 6HB

Keith Larrington
☎ 01485 540265
Fax 01485 543143
BB From £20
Sleeps 6
⌚⌚ Commended

You can be assured of a warm welcome at our comfortable and relaxing farmhouse, with large garden, in the quiet village of Wolferton. This working arable farm is ideally situated for walking and exploring the countryside and North Norfolk coast. RSPB reserves nearby. Open all year except Christmas.
E-mail: keith.larrington@farmline.com.uk

10 Park Farm, Bylaugh, East Dereham, Norfolk NR20 4QE

Mrs Jenny Lake
☎ 01362 688584
BB From £15–£20
EM From £9
Sleeps 6
⌚⌚ Commended

Charming old family farmhouse with picturesque setting in Wensum Valley, ideally situated for exploring the Norfolk countryside and visits to Norwich, the Norfolk Broads and North Norfolk coast. One large family room, one double and one twin, all en suite. Lounge with colour TV, dining room with inglenook. Children welcome, sorry no pets. Open all year.

11 Salamanca Farm Guest House, 116–118 Norwich Road, Stoke Holy Cross, Norwich, Norfolk NR14 8QJ

Roy & Barbara Harrold
☎ 01508 492322
BB From £18–£22
Sleeps 8
(6)
⌚⌚ Commended

"Real experience of English hospitality" – "All we could have asked for" – just two comments from our visitors' book. The Harrold family have welcomed guests to their farm for 20 years. 4 miles from the cathedral city of Norwich, the valley of the River Tas, with the mill where Colmans began producing mustard, provides an attractive holiday base. All rooms have private facilities. Open 15 Jan–15 Dec.

Norfolk   Heartland

Shrublands Farm, Burgh St Peter, nr Beccles, Suffolk NR34 0BB

Mrs Rachel Clarke
☎/Fax 01502 677241
BB From £18–£21
Sleeps 6
ᗑ(10) ⚹ ♿
❀ ❀ *Commended*

Tranquillity, peaceful surroundings and a warm welcome at this attractive, homely farmhouse. Set in 550 acres of mixed working farmland in the Waveney Valley. Ideal base for touring Norfolk/Suffolk. 2 double en suite, 1 twin with private facilities, all with colour satellite TV and tea/coffee-making facilities. Excellent choice of home-cooked breakfast. Tennis court available. Swimming pool and food at River Centre nearby. Open all year except Christmas.

Shrublands Farm, Northrepps, Cromer, Norfolk NR27 0AA

Mrs Ann Youngman
☎/Fax 01263 579297
BB From £20–£26
EM From £10.50
Sleeps 6
ᗑ(12) ✕ ⚘ ⚹ ♈ ♿ Ⓟ
❀ ❀ *Highly Commended*

A warm welcome awaits you at Shrublands Farm, an arable farm set in the village of Northrepps, 2½ miles SE of Cromer and 20 miles north of Norwich. The Victorian/Edwardian house has 1 twin and 1 double with private bathrooms and 1 twin en suite. Separate sitting room and dining room for guests. Full central heating, log fires in chilly weather. Sorry, no pets. Evening meal by arrangement. Open all year (closed Christmas & New Year). E- mail: www.broadland.com/shrublands

Sloley Farm, Sloley, Norwich, Norfolk NR12 8HJ

Mrs Ann Jones
☎ 01692 536281
Fax 01692 535162
BB From £18–£20
Sleeps 5
ᗑ(10) ⚹ ☗ ⚘ ♿ Ⓟ
❀ ❀ *Commended*

A warm welcome awaits you in our comfortable farmhouse, ideally situated to explore the nearby Norfolk Broads and the coast with its many attractions. One double/twin en suite, 1 double with private bathroom and 1 single. All rooms have colour TV, tea/coffee facilities. Full central heating. Open all year except Christmas and New Year. E-mail: sloley@farmhotel.u-net.com

South Elmham Hall, St Cross, Harleston, Norfolk IP20 0PZ

Mrs Jo Sanderson
☎ 01986 782526
Fax 01986 782203
BB From £18–£35
EM From £12.50
Sleeps 6
ᗑ ⚹ ☗ ♈ ♿ ✿ Ⓟ
❀ ❀ *Highly Commended*

Moated former bishop's palace with large gardens. Mixed farm, peaceful location with rare cattle and farm trails in historic landscape. Tastefully furnished comfortable rooms with tea/coffee tray. Kingsize bed, double antique brass bed and twin bedded rooms all with en suite facilities, colour TV and views of the farm and garden. Guests' lounge and dining room, full CH. Evening meals, cot and baby sitting by arrangement. Open all year.

Stratton Farm, West Drove North, Walton Highway, Norfolk PE14 7DP

Derek & Sue King
☎ 01945 880162
BB From £20.50–£25
Sleeps 6
♿ᗑ(7) ⚹ ⚘ ☗ ♈ ✿ Ⓟ
❀ ❀ *Highly Commended*

We invite you to stay on our peaceful farm which supports a prize winning herd of Shorthorn cattle. Meet our cows and calves, collect fresh eggs for your breakfast, or fish in our lake. All bedrooms have en suite facilities. Home produced sausages, bacon, eggs, bread and marmalades. Heated, covered swimming pool. Open all year (including Christmas).

Whitehall Farm, Burnham Thorpe, King's Lynn, Norfolk PE31 8HN

Valerie Southerland
☎/Fax 01328 738416
BB From £18
Sleeps 6
ᗑ ☗ ♈ ⚘ ♿ ♿
Listed *Commended*

Situated about 2 miles from the North Norfolk coast, Whitehall Farm is a working arable farm with a friendly family atmosphere. Comfortable rooms offering TV, tea/coffee and private bathrooms. Ample parking available and use of the garden and meadow. Valerie and Barry Southerland look forward to ensuring your stay is an enjoyable experience that you will want to repeat. Open all year.

 **Heartland** *Norfolk*

⑱ Witton Hall Farm, Witton, Norwich, Norfolk NR13 5DN

Jane Mack
☎ 01603 714580
BB From £20–£40
Sleeps 6
Commended

This elegant Georgian farmhouse on a dairy and arable farm is set in the heart of Norfolk, 5 miles east of Norwich and 12 miles from the coast, and 3 miles from the Broads. There are two acres of mature garden. Spacious bedrooms, all with TV and en suite bathrooms. Open all year.

Self-Catering

⑲ Burnley Hall, East Somerton, Great Yarmouth NR29 4DU

Penny Beard
☎ 01493 393206
Fax 01493 393745
SC From £250–£550
Sleeps 4–8 + cot
Up to Highly Commended

Arable/livestock farm between Norfolk Broads and sea. We welcome families with children and well behaved dogs to our 4 holiday homes (own gardens). Equipped to a high standard with comfortable beds (linen, towels, heat, electricity included). Three-mile private beach, nature reserve, footpaths, bicycles, access to Broads (boat available). Weekend breaks. Brochure on request. Open all year. E-mail: penny@burnleyhall.co.uk

⑯ Carysfort and Carysfort Too, Stratton Farm, West Drove North, Walton Highway, Norfolk PE14 7DP

Derek & Sue King
☎ 01945 880162
SC From £165–£370
Sleeps 2/4
Highly Commended

We welcome you to our beautiful farm cottages where all 4 bedrooms have en suite bathrooms. Relax in total comfort, peace and seclusion. You may meet the calves or walk for miles with only bird song for company. Come and catch a carp from the lake or plunge into our heated swimming pool. We can guarantee you a perfect holiday. Free secure parking for your car. Open all year including Christmas.

⑳ The Cottage, Walcot Green Farm, Diss, Norfolk IP22 3SU

Nannette Catchpole
☎/Fax 01379 652806
SC From £220–£350
Sleeps 5/6
Commended

Set in peaceful, idyllic countryside, central for exploring Norfolk and Suffolk's many attractions, this tastefully converted and well-equipped cottage is close to the pleasant market town of Diss. Spacious, safe garden and use of indoor swimming pool make for a relaxing holiday. Family room, one bunk, one single. Bed linen, towels, electricity and CH all included. Sorry no pets and no smoking. Colour brochure. Open Mar–Nov.

㉑ Dairy Farm Cottages, Dilham, North Walsham, Norfolk NR28 9PZ

Annabel Paterson
☎ 01692 535178
Fax 01692 536723
SC From £200–£950
Sleeps 4–11 + cot
Highly Commended

Relax at Dairy Farm in Broadland, mixed arable and stock farm. Superb walks, acres of woodland, Victorian folly – Dilham Islands. 15 minutes to coast. Top quality accommodation, each cottage sleeps 4 to 11, all bedrooms en suite. Full kitchen facilities, laundry facilities, games room, secure play area, wheelchair access. Pets welcome. Colour brochure available. Open all year.

Norfolk *Heartland*

Dolphin Lodge, Roudham Farm, Roudham, East Harling, Norfolk NR16 2RJ

Mr & Mrs T Jolly
☎ 01953 717126
Fax 01953 718593
SC From £220–£355
Sleeps 5 + cot

Highly Commended

Let us offer you a country retreat! Conveniently situated in central East Anglia, our cottages are home-from-home. Beautifully restored with beams and woodburning stoves, set in large garden by Thetford Forest. Carefully prepared for you and fully equipped, CH, Aga, washing machine, tumble drier, fridge, microwave, colour TV. Each cottage sleeps 5 in two bedrooms. Many local attractions. You choose, a quiet secluded holiday or a busy sightseeing one? Open all year.

Meadow View, Park Farm, Bylaugh, East Dereham, Norfolk NR20 4QE

Mrs Jenny Lake
☎ 01362 688584
SC From £100–£175
EM From £9
Sleeps 2/3

Commended

Attached to charming old family farmhouse with picturesque setting in Wensum Valley, Meadow View is a comfortable, well equipped one bedroom bungalow with lovely countryside views. Sleeps 2 adults plus cot/child's bed and includes living room, kitchen, bathroom, colour TV and heating. Evening meals available next door served in dining room with inglenook. Children welcome, sorry no pets. Linen provided and laundry service. Open all year.

Please mention *Stay on a Farm* when booking

STAY ON A FARM GIFT TOKENS

If you have enjoyed your Stay on a Farm, why not treat your friends and relatives to *Stay on a Farm* gift tokens? Available from the Bureau office (tel: 01203 696909), they can be redeemed against accommodation and are accepted by the majority of farms (see Index). Please check when booking to avoid disappointment.

USE THE INDEX

The comprehensive Index shows which farms offer access to disabled visitors; caravanning/camping facilities; the chance to participate on a working farm; stabling/grazing for visiting horses; en suite rooms; a welcome to business people; acceptance of *Stay on a Farm* gift tokens.

Suffolk

Constable Country, Waveney Valley, Suffolk Coast & Heaths

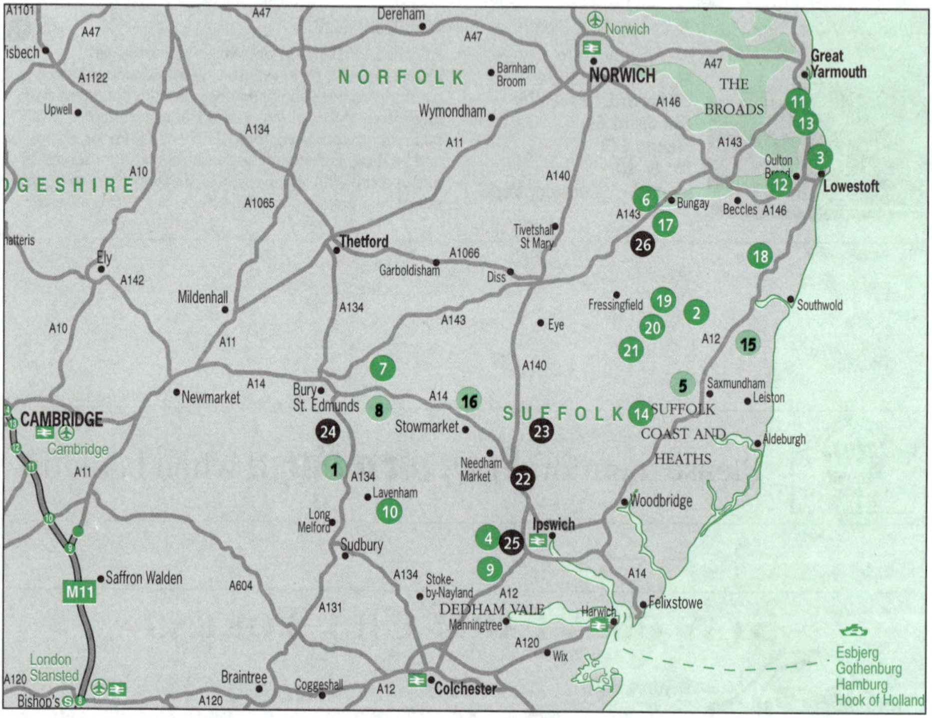

Key

- 1 Bed & Breakfast
- 1 Self-Catering
- 1 B&B and SC
- 1 Camping Barns
- ▲ Camping & Caravanning

This beautiful, unspoilt county was the inspiration of the artists Thomas Gainsborough and John Constable who so brilliantly captured its churches, lanes, mills and farms. Suffolk is famed for its half-timbered market towns and villages – Bury St Edmunds, Sudbury, Long Melford and Lavenham, to name a few. The heritage coast and heathland are a birdwatcher's paradise and the whole county offers easy cycling and excellent walking. Oulton Broad and the Rivers Deben and Orwell are ideal for boating. For a spot of culture, take in the Aldeburgh Festival or visit stately Ickworth House and Somerleyton Hall. Suffolk has something for everyone.

If you would like help in finding suitable farm accommodation, turn to the full listing of farm groups on pages 360 to 363 to find appropriate contact details for this area.

Suffolk   Heartland

Bed and Breakfast
(and evening meal)

Brighthouse Farm, Melford Road, Lawshall, near Bury St Edmunds, Suffolk IP29 4PX

Mr & Mrs Truin
☎/Fax 01284 830385
BB From £18–£25
Sleeps 6
Commended

Timbered Georgian farmhouse, set in beautiful surroundings of the Suffolk countryside, 3 acres of picturesque gardens. We offer homely accommodation. Centrally heated throughout, log fires in TV room in winter. Two double rooms, one twin, all with en suite facilities. Historic Bury St. Edmunds/Lavenham close by. Good restaurants locally. Open all year.

Broad Oak Farm, Bramfield, Halesworth, Suffolk IP19 9AB

Mrs Patricia Kemsley
☎ 01986 784232
BB From £16–£22
Sleeps 6
Commended

Enjoy the peace and quiet of a dairy farm, where the countryside meets the North-East Heritage Coast, only 8 miles from Southwold. Relax in our carefully modernised and spacious 16th century farmhouse, surrounded by attractive gardens and meadowland. Tennis court. One double and 2 twin rooms (2 en suite and 1 private bathroom). Separate guests' sitting room and beautiful beamed dining room. Good home cooking (EM by arrangement). Friendly, informal atmosphere. Bramfield village is on A144. Open all year.

Church Farm, Corton, Nr Lowestoft, Suffolk NR32 5HX

Elisabeth Edwards
☎ 01502 730359
Fax 01502 733426
BB From £18–£19
Sleeps 6
Listed *Highly Commended*

A warm welcome awaits you to relax in our comfortable Victorian farmhouse on the most easterly farm in Britain. Within easy reach of the rural beach and clifftop walks, convenient driving distance for the Norfolk Broads, the Suffolk Heritage Coast and the fine city of Norwich. Double bedded en suite rooms. Quiet garden, ample parking. Non-smoking. Selected for *'Which' Good Bed & Breakfast Guide* and mentioned in London's *Time Out* magazine. Tourist Board International Host. Open Mar–Nov.

College Farm, Hintlesham, Ipswich, Suffolk IP8 3NT

Mrs Rosemary Bryce
☎/Fax 01473 652253
BB From £18–£24
Sleeps 6
(10)
Highly Commended

Relax and unwind at our peaceful 15th century farmhouse on 600-acre farm. Comfortable accommodation, hearty breakfasts and a warm welcome are assured. Three bedrooms (1 single, 1 double en suite, 1 family) tastefully furnished to high standards. Guests' lounge with inglenook fireplace. Explore nearby 'Constable Country', Suffolk's coast. Country walks with golf and riding close by. Open Jan–mid Dec. E-mail: bryce1@agripro.co.uk

---

Colston Hall, Badingham, nr Framlingham, Woodbridge, Suffolk IP13 8LB

John & Liz Bellefontaine
☎/Fax 01728 638375
BB From £20–£30
Sleeps 6
Commended

Colston Hall, easily found just ½ mile from the A1120, is surrounded by beautiful, quiet countryside. Guests' can enjoy country walks, cycling, fishing, indoor bowling and Easter lambs. Our centrally heated Elizabethan farmhouse boasts a wealth of beams and brick flooring. We look forward to meeting you. Open all year.

Heartland   Suffolk

6 Earsham Park Farm, Harleston Road, Earsham, Bungay, Suffolk NR35 2AQ

Mrs Bobbie Watchorn
☎/Fax 01986 892180
BB From £20–£30
EM £15
Sleeps 6
♥ ♥ Highly Commended

Delightful, quiet and friendly farmhouse with panoramic views over the Waveney Valley. Spacious and elegantly furnished en suite rooms (one four-poster bed) with extensive facilities. CH. Guests are welcome to use the large gardens and lovely farm walks. Indulge in the delicious, locally produced, huge Norfolk breakfasts. Evening meal available. Easy access coast/Norwich. Open all year.

7 Elmswell Hall, Elmswell, Bury St Edmunds, Suffolk IP30 9EN

Kate Over
☎/Fax 01359 240215
BB From £20
Sleeps 5
Listed Commended

A fine Georgian house set in open countryside. Large heated rooms with tea/coffee-making facilities and colour TV. Separate lounge with open log fire, hearty breakfasts, relaxed family atmosphere. Easy access A14 (Cambridge, Lavenham, Felixstowe) for touring. One family/double and 1 twin. Private bathroom for guests. Open all year.

8 Grange Farm, Woolpit, Bury St Edmunds, Suffolk IP30 9RG

Kathy Parker
☎ 01359 241143
Fax 01359 244296
BB From £20–£25
Sleeps 6
♥ Commended

Grange Farm is a Grade II listed Victorian house set in the heart of Suffolk, but only 1 mile from the A14 giving easy access. Ideal centre for exploring tranquil Suffolk villages or larger historic towns of Bury St Edmunds, Sudbury, Ely and Cambridge. Two en suite rooms and one with private bath/WC, all with TV and tea/coffee facilities. Guests' lounge and dining room with period furniture. Open all year except Christmas. E-mail: grange@cocoon.co.uk

9 Grove Farm House, Little Wenham, via Colchester, Essex CO7 6QB

Mrs Monica Collins
☎ 01473 310341
BB From £17.50
EM From £7.50–£12
Sleeps 5
♥ Commended

Leave stress behind and enjoy warm hospitality in our 15th century farmhouse. Comfortable, centrally heated accommodation in 1 double, 1 twin and 1 single room all attractively furnished and overlooking open countryside. Cosy lounge with TV and charming dining room in which to enjoy excellent home-cooked meals. 1 mile off A12 giving easy access Constable Country, Ipswich, Harwich. Open all year except Christmas.

10 The Hall, Milden, Sudbury, Suffolk CO10 9NY

Juliet & Christopher Hawkins
☎/Fax 01787 247235
BB From £15–£30
EM From £12
Sleeps 6
Listed Commended

Spacious 16th century hall farmhouse, peacefully surrounded by walled garden, flower meadows, ancient barns and hedged countryside. Explore farm nature trails around award winning woodland, castle earthworks, ponds and museum. Visit nearby historic Lavenham and 'Constable Country'. Evening meals of wild game, homegrown meat, fruit and vegetables. Relaxed family atmosphere. Open all year.

11 Hall Farm, Jay Lane/Church Lane, Lound, Lowestoft, Suffolk NR32 5LJ

Judith Ashley
☎ 01502 730415
BB From £16–£20
Sleeps 6
Listed Commended

Share our peaceful, traditional Suffolk farmhouse 1½ miles from sea on 101-acre arable farm. Very clean, comfortable accommodation in one double and one family room all with en suite facilities and one pretty single, all with tea/coffee. Excellent breakfast with our own farm eggs. Beamed lounge, colour TV and log fire. Convenient for Broads. Open Easter–Oct.

Suffolk — *Heartland*

Laurel Farm, Hall Lane, Oulton, Lowestoft, Suffolk NR32 5DL

Janet Hodgkin
☎/Fax 01502 568724
BB From £20–£22.50
Sleeps 6
Listed *Highly Commended*

A fine Georgian farmhouse set in peaceful landscaped gardens. Spacious bedrooms include 1 twin and 1 double with private bathrooms and 1 double en suite. Drawing room and conservatory are for guests' use. Close to sandy beaches, Broads and historic fishing port of Lowestoft. A no smoking house. Open all year.

Oak Farm, Market Lane, Blundeston, Lowestoft, Suffolk NR32 5AP

Julie and Keith Cooper
☎ 01502 731622
BB From £16–£20
Sleeps 4
Listed *Commended*

140-acre mixed farm set in peaceful countryside crossed by the Waveney Way footpath and 1½ miles from the sea. This Victorian house was originally farm cottages. We take a pride in our breakfast and local pubs offer other meals. Guests' stairs lead to a double and a twin room and a guests' bathroom. Tea/coffee facilities and colour TV in rooms. Children very welcome – reductions under 14. Closed Christmas & New Year.

Park Farm, Sibton, Saxmundham, Suffolk IP17 2LZ

Margaret Gray
☎ 01728 668324
Fax 01728 668564
BB From £17–£20
EM From £12
Sleeps 6
Commended

Do you want comfort, peaceful surroundings and delicious food? If so, enjoy friendly farmhouse hospitality at its best in our spacious 18th century house close to Heritage Coast. English breakfast and 3-course dinners imaginatively cooked from local produce. All tastes and special diets catered for. Two twins en suite, one double with private bathroom, all with tea/coffee. Ideal for birdwatching, sightseeing or relaxing. Closed Christmas.

Priory Farm, Priory Lane, Darsham, Saxmundham, Suffolk IP17 3QD

Suzanne Bloomfield
☎ 01728 668459
Fax 01728 668744
BB From £19–£25
Sleeps 4
Commended

Comfortable 17th century farmhouse situated in peaceful countryside. An ideal base for exploring the Suffolk coast and heathlands and other numerous local attractions. Excellent pubs and restaurants nearby. 1 double, 1 twin, each with private facilities, tea/coffee making in all bedrooms. Separate guests' dining room. Cycle hire available at the farm. Open Mar–Oct.

Red House Farm, Station Road, Haughley, Nr Stowmarket, Suffolk IP14 3QP

Mrs Mary Noy
☎/Fax 01449 673323
BB From £20–£22
Sleeps 6
Commended

A warm welcome and homely atmosphere awaits you at our attractive farmhouse set in the beautiful surroundings of mid Suffolk. Comfortably furnished bedrooms with en suite shower rooms, tea/coffee-making facilities. One double, one twin and two single rooms. CH. Guests' own lounge with TV and dining room. Ideal location for exploring, walking, cycling and birdwatching. No smoking or pets. Open Jan–Nov.

South Elmham Hall, St Cross, Harleston, Norfolk IP20 0PZ

Mrs Jo Sanderson
☎ 01986 782526
Fax 01986 782203
BB From £18–£35
EM From £12.50
Sleeps 6
Highly Commended

Moated former bishop's palace with large gardens. Mixed farm, peaceful location with rare cattle and farm trails in historic landscape. Tastefully furnished comfortable rooms with tea/coffee tray. Kingsize bed, double antique brass bed and twin bedded rooms all with en suite facilities, colour TV and views of the farm and garden. Guests' lounge and dining room, full CH. Evening meals, cot and baby sitting by arrangement. Open all year.

Heartland   *Suffolk*

⑱ Uggeshall Manor Farm, Uggeshall, Nr Southwold, Suffolk NR34 8BD

Annie Davies
☎ 01502 578546
Fax 01502 578560
BB From £23–£30
Sleeps 6
⌂(10) 🐎 ✂ ♿ ⓦ
✿✿ *Highly Commended*

Luxuriously appointed historic farmhouse in 220 acres of its own beautiful heritage countryside just 5 minutes' drive from Southwold and the coast. Explore the 6 miles of private conservation tracks offering a profusion of wildlife, birds and flowers. Two doubles and one twin room, all en suite. Guests' sitting and dining rooms. Open all year except Christmas.

⑲ Walpole Old Hall, Walpole, Halesworth, Suffolk IP19 9AU

Pauline & Rodney Winter
☎ 01986 784234
Fax 01986 784538
BB From £18–£20
EM From £10
Sleeps 6
✂ ⛱ ♿ ⓒ
✿ *Commended*

Walpole Old Hall is a dairy farm surrounded by meadowland. Double and twin en suite rooms with tea/coffee facilities. The 16th century farmhouse has exposed beams and listed chimneys and large lounge with colour satellite TV. Guests' own private dining room. Covered swimming pool (heated in season). Minsmere and coast 9 miles. Open Mar–Oct.

⑳ Watersmeet, Framlingham Road, Laxfield, nr Woodbridge, Suffolk IP13 8DH

Mrs Margaret Jefferies
☎/Fax 01986 798880
BB From £19–£22
EM From £11
Sleeps 4
⌂(10) ✂ ♿ ⛱ 🎄 ⓦ
✿✿ *Highly Commended*

Experience the warm welcome and relax at this comfortable, traditional farmhouse with log fires and wonderful food – English breakfasts, suppers and vegetarian too. One double and one twin, both with private bathroom. Small working farm on edge of pretty village with interesting church, museum and old inns. Cycle or ramble through this part of rural Suffolk. Treat yourself to a weekend or longer stay. Open Jan–mid Dec.

㉑ Woodlands Farm, Brundish, Framlingham, Suffolk IP13 8BP

Jill Graham
☎ 01379 384444
BB From £18–£20
EM From £12.50
Sleeps 6
⌂(10) ✂ ♿ ⓦ
✿✿ *Highly Commended*

A friendly welcome and good home cooking assured in our comfortable, timber-framed farmhouse set in peaceful countryside near Framlingham. Within easy reach of the coast and numerous local attractions. One twin and 2 double bedrooms with en suite bathrooms, and tea/coffee facilities. Separate dining and sitting rooms with inglenooks. Centrally heated with log fires in cold weather. AA Selected QQQQ. Closed Christmas & New Year.

Self-Catering

㉒ Baylham House Farm Annexe and Flat, Mill Lane, Baylham, Suffolk IP6 8LG

Ann Storer
☎/Fax 01473 830264
SC From £120–£295
Sleeps 4 + cot and 2 + cot
🏇 🐎 ♿ 🎄 ⓦ
🏠🏠🏠🏠 *Commended*

Two self-contained units in old farmhouse. Small rare breeds farm on River Gipping with sheep, cattle, poultry, pigs and goats. Peaceful setting, good walks, good touring base. Fishing, garden, barbecue. Both fully equipped to high standard. Children welcome, sorry no pets. Please phone or write for further details. Open all year.

Suffolk — Heartland

The Bothy, Grange Farm, Woolpit, Bury St Edmunds, Suffolk IP30 9RG

Mrs Kathy Parker
☎ 01359 241143
Fax 01359 244296
[SC] From £170–£200
Sleeps 2
Highly Commended

The Bothy is adjacent to farmhouse in the heart of Suffolk, only one mile from A14 corridor giving easy access to East Anglia. Ideal for touring tranquil villages or visiting major towns and cities. The cottage, recently converted, consists of kitchen/diner, lounge, double bedroom, en suite shower room and balcony area. Patio with barbecue. Linen and towels provided. Open all year.
E-mail: grange@cocoon.co.uk

The Coach House, Kenton Hall, Debenham, Stowmarket, Suffolk IP14 6JU

Sharon McVeigh
☎ 01728 860279
Fax 01728 861246
[SC] From £125–£410
Sleeps 8
Highly Commended

Part of beautiful moated Tudor hall set in the centre of our 460-acre arable farm. One double en suite, one bunk bedded room with bathroom and a large additional bedroom en suite to sleep up to 4. Bed linen, towels, electricity and CH all included. Well equipped kitchen/diner, comfortable sitting room, cloakroom. Centrally situated for touring Suffolk coast (½ hour drive). Sorry no pets and no smoking. Open all year.

Colston Cottage, Colston Hall, Badingham, Woodbridge, Suffolk IP13 8LB

John & Liz Bellefontaine
☎/Fax 01728 638375
[SC] From £200–£400
Sleeps 6
Commended

Charming centrally heated cottage enjoying lovely views over the Alde Valley. Idyllically set in the tranquillity of the countryside, yet only minutes from the coast. Downstairs bedroom. Cot and high chair available. Dishwasher, washing machine, tumble drier, freezer, colour TV, telephone. Coarse fishing and indoor bowls available. Open all year.

The Cottage, Red House Farm, Station Road, Haughley, Nr Stowmarket, Suffolk IP14 3QP

Mrs Mary Noy
☎/Fax 01449 673323
[SC] From £150–£190
Sleeps 2/4
Commended

Enjoy the peace and tranquillity of Suffolk staying in our charming cottage which adjoins the farmhouse. Very well furnished and equipped. Ideal location for exploring, cycling, birdwatching and walking. All linen and towels provided. Electricity and heating included. No smoking or pets. Open all year.

The Court, Brighthouse Farm, Melford Road, Lawshall, near Bury St Edmunds, Suffolk IP29 4PX

Roberta Truin
☎/Fax 01284 830385
[SC] From £350–£400
Sleeps 7
Highly Commended

Queen Anne cottage situated in a rural position in the glorious Suffolk countryside. Furnished and equipped to a very high standard. Set in its own garden with access to larger grounds. Local shops, pubs and restaurants, historic Bury St Edmunds, Lavenham and Constable Country nearby. Also small studio flats each sleeping two. Open all year.

The Granary, Priory Fram, Darsham, Nr Saxmundham, Suffolk IP17 3QD

Suzanne Bloomfield
☎ 01728 668459
Fax 01728 668744
[SC] From £135–£340
Sleeps 4
Commended

17th century granary tastefully converted to provide comfortable accommodation. Situated in peaceful Suffolk countryside, an ideal base for touring Suffolk coast and heathlands and other local attractions. 1 double, 2 singles. Shower room, kitchen, dining room, sitting room. Storage heaters, colour TV, washing machine. Cycle hire. Sat–Sat. Weekend lets out of season. Open all year.

Heartland Suffolk

(24) Rowney Cottage, Rowney Farm, Whepstead, Bury St Edmunds, Suffolk IP29 4TQ

Mrs Kati Turner
☎/Fax 01284 735842
SC From £180–£275
Sleeps 5

Commended

Situated atop the rolling countryside of West Suffolk the 500-acre farm is ideally placed for exploring this picturesque and historically fascinating part of East Anglia. The cottage is spacious and fully equipped, with 2 bedrooms, fully fitted kitchen and bathroom and a generous lounge. The farm is safely tucked away at the end of a private drive. Bury St Edmunds 6 miles, Cambridge 32. Linen and electricity included. Children and pets welcome. Open Apr–Oct.

(25) Stable Cottages and The Granary, Chattisham Place, Nr Ipswich, Suffolk IP8 3QD

Mrs Margaret Langton
☎/Fax 01473 652210
SC From £140–£365
Sleeps 2/8

Highly Commended

Come and enjoy the peaceful Suffolk countryside where we have something for everyone. Making our 3 beautifully converted cottages (en suites, dishwashers) your base with all home comforts, you can relax or explore Constable Country, Lavenham and the Heritage Coast. Borrow maps for waymarked walks or bring the family to share our heated outdoor pool, tennis court, games and studio/craft room. Wheelchair users welcome. Open all year.

(26) Tom, Dick and Harry, Church Farm, Withersdale, Mendham, Harleston, Norfolk IP20 0JR

Audrey & Kate Carless
☎/Fax 01379 588090
SC From £100–£240
Sleeps 2 + cot

Commended

Tom, Dick and Harry are three timber-framed converted farm buildings nestling by dewy pastures in the 'Valley of the Rams'. Walk the footpaths, watch birds, go fishing, cycle Norfolk and Suffolk's tranquil lanes, enjoy a coastal drive. Each cottage includes garden, linen/towels, electricity, open fire. Cot/high chair available, ample parking. Open all year.

THE 1000+ BUREAU MEMBERS OFFER A UNIQUE LINK TO CUSTOMERS ACROSS THE UK

All Bureau members belong to a local Group. Each member can refer you to an equally high quality member within the Group... or across the UK: England, Northern Ireland, Scotland, Wales.

CONFIRM BOOKINGS

Disappointments can arise from misunderstandings over the telephone. Please write to confirm your booking.

South & South East England

Farm entries in this regional section are listed under those counties shown in green on the key map. Look at the index below to find on which page the entries start. You will see that we have listed the counties geographically so that you can turn more easily to find farms in neighbouring areas.

At the start of each county section is a detailed map with numbered symbols indicating the location of each farm. Different symbols denote different types of accommodation; see the key below each county map. Farm entries are listed alphabetically under type of accommodation. Some farms offer more than one type of accommodation and therefore have more than one entry.

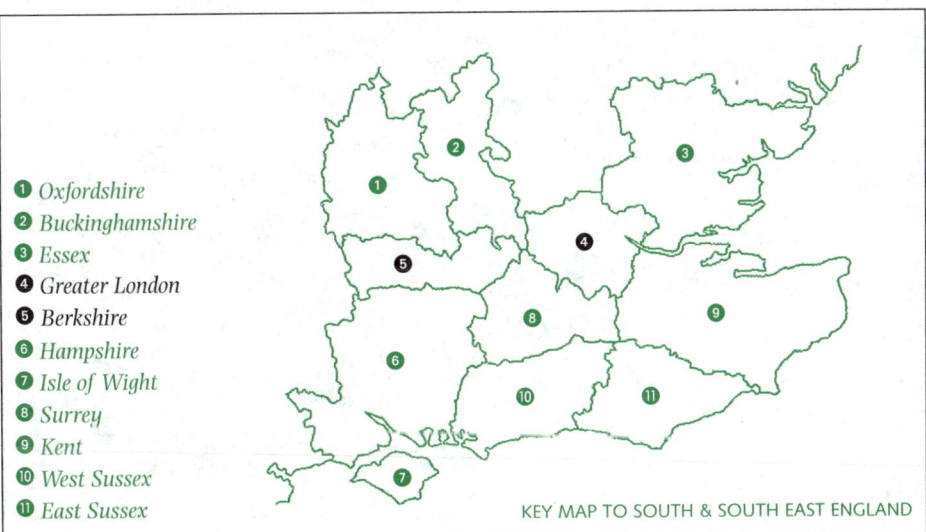

1. Oxfordshire
2. Buckinghamshire
3. Essex
4. Greater London
5. Berkshire
6. Hampshire
7. Isle of Wight
8. Surrey
9. Kent
10. West Sussex
11. East Sussex

KEY MAP TO SOUTH & SOUTH EAST ENGLAND

Oxfordshire — page 206
Cotswolds, Thames Valley, Vale of the White Horse & the Chilterns

Buckinghamshire — page 211
Vale of Aylesbury & the Chilterns

Essex — page 214
Dedham Vale, Essex Way & Epping Forest

Hampshire — page 217
New Forest, South Hampshire Coast, the Solent & Test Valley

Isle of Wight — page 221
The Needles, Medina Valley, the Downs & Sandown Bay

Surrey — page 224
North Downs, Pilgrims' Way & Surrey Hills

Kent — page 226
Kent Downs, High Weald, Weald of Kent & Romney Marsh

West Sussex — page 230
Sussex Weald, Rother & Arun Valleys & Sussex Downs

East Sussex — page 233
Ashdown Forest, High Weald & Sussex Downs

Oxfordshire

Cotswolds, Thames Valley, Vale of the White Horse & the Chilterns

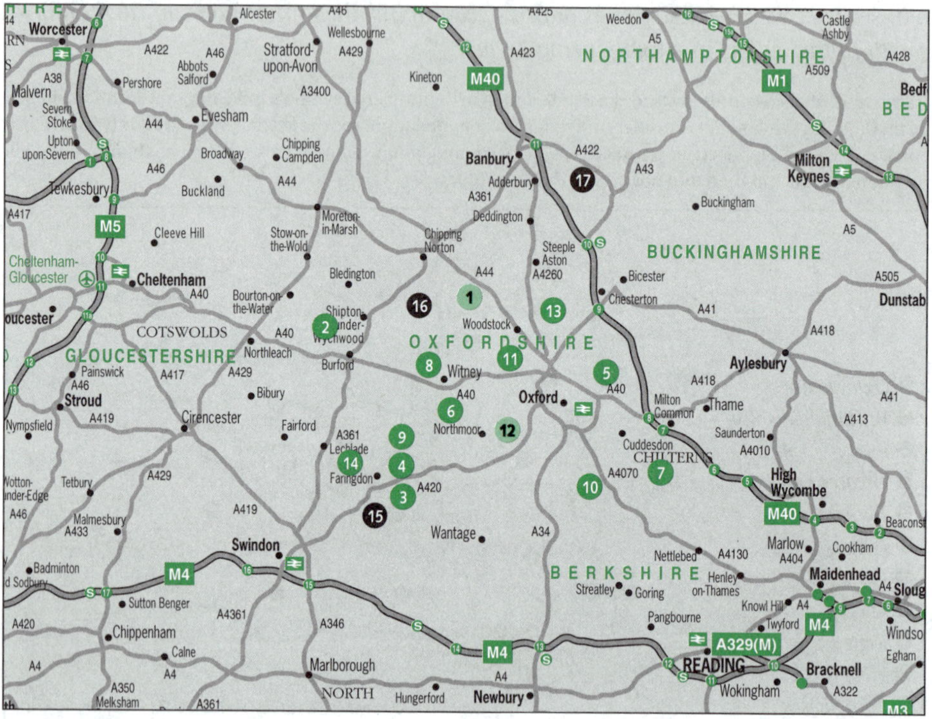

Key

- **1** Bed & Breakfast
- **1** Self-Catering
- **1** B&B and SC
- **1** Camping Barns
- **1** Camping & Caravanning

At the heart of historic Oxfordshire is the Thames Valley, stretching from the Chiltern Hills above Henley to the west of Oxford and the Cotswolds. Oxford itself is of great historic interest with its dreaming spires and great buildings including medieval colleges and Renaissance masterpieces such as the Sheldonian Theatre. Woodstock has many historic associations and is the site of Blenheim Palace, birthplace of Sir Winston Churchill. The county boasts many other beautiful country houses and picturesque villages with welcoming inns. There are numerous places of interest including Burford's Cotswold Wildlife Park and the Cogges Farm Museum near Witney.

If you would like help in finding suitable farm accommodation, turn to the full listing of farm groups on pages 360 to 363 to find appropriate contact details for this area.

Oxfordshire   South & South East

Bed and Breakfast
(and evening meal)

Banbury Hill Farm, Enstone Road, Charlbury, Oxford OX7 3JH

Mrs Angela Widdows
☎ 01608 810314
Fax 01608 811891
[BB] From £16–£25
Sleeps 9
Commended

Natural Cotswold stone farmhouse commanding spectacular view in AONB overlooking the small township of Charlbury with the ancient Wychwood Forest nestling against the River Evenlode. Large variety of animals around the farm. Ideally centred – midway Oxford, Stratford-on-Avon, near Blenheim, Burford and Chipping Norton. Family, double (3 en suite), twin or single rooms. Ideal for families. Also self-catering cottages available.

Bould Farm, Bould, Nr Idbury, Chipping Norton, Oxfordshire OX7 6RT

Mrs Lynne Meyrick
☎/Fax 01608 658850
[BB] From £22.50–£30
Sleeps 6
Highly Commended

Bould Farm is a 17th century Cotswold farmhouse on a 300-acre family farm set in beautiful countryside, 10 minutes' drive from Stow-on-the-Wold and Bourton-on-the-Water and Burford. Within easy reach of Blenheim Palace and the Cotswold Wildlife Park. Children welcome. Spacious rooms with TV, tea/coffee-making facilities. Large garden. Good local pubs. Open Feb–Nov.

Bowling Green Farm, Stanford Road, Faringdon, Oxfordshire SN7 8EZ

Della Barnard
☎ 01367 240229
Fax 01367 242568
[BB] From £22–£24
Sleeps 6
Commended

Attractive 18th century period farmhouse offering 20th century comfort situated in the Vale of the White Horse, just 1 mile south of Faringdon on the A417. Easy access to M4 for Heathrow Airport. A working farm breeding cattle and horses. Large twin/family room on ground floor en suite. All bedrooms have colour TV, electric blankets in winter, tea/coffee-making facilities and CH throughout. Open all year.

Chimney House, Chimney on Thames, Aston, Bampton, Oxfordshire OX18 2EH

Mrs Jean Kinch
☎/Fax 01367 870279
[BB] From £21–£25
Sleeps 4
(12)
Highly Commended

Enjoy the peace and quiet of Chimney Farm, on the Thames path. Our recently renovated 100-year-old centrally heated farmhouse offers comfortable en suite bedrooms with TV, tea/coffee facilities and guests' lounge. Enjoy local walks and golf courses. In easy reach of Oxford, Blenheim and Cotswolds. A warm welcome awaits you. Open Mar–Nov.

Common Leys Farm, Waterperry Common, Waterperry, Oxfordshire OX33 1LQ

Allie Jones
☎/Fax 01865 351266
[BB] From £20–£25
EM From £11
Sleeps 4
(10)
Applied

Allie and Guy take pride in offering delightful accommodation in their picturesque Grade II listed Tudor farmhouse set in 38 acres of beautiful Oxfordshire countryside. Full English breakfasts prepared in the farmhouse kitchen and sumptuous evening meals available by arrangement. TV, tea/coffee-making facilities in all rooms. Oxford 9 miles, Thame 7 miles, M40 6 miles. Open all year.

South & South East   Oxfordshire

6 Ducklington Farm, Coursehill Lane, Ducklington, Witney, Oxon OX8 7YG

Mrs Stacey Strainge
☎ 01993 772175
BB From £19–£21
Sleeps 6
🐴 ⚔ ♿ 🏠 ⚙
👑 Commended

Looking forward to welcoming you to Ducklington Farmhouse. Our family-run mixed farm is situated 1½ miles from Witney on the edge of the Cotswolds. In this recently built house all rooms are en suite, have tea/coffee-making facilities and a TV. Pub meals available in village. Open all year except Christmas.

7 Fords Farm, Ewelme, Wallingford, Oxon OX10 6HU

Marlene Edwards
☎ 01491 839272
BB From £22
Sleeps 4
⚔ 🏠 🌳
👑 Highly Commended

500-acre mixed farm, arable beef and sheep. Attractive farmhouse set in historic part of village with famous church almshouses and school. Peaceful surroundings with good walks and good selection of pubs nearby. Easy access to Henley, Oxford, Reading, Windsor, Heathrow and London. Friendly and comfortable atmosphere. 2 twin rooms. Open all year.

8 Hill Grove Farm, Crawley Dry Lane, Minster Lovell, Witney, Oxfordshire OX8 5NA

Mrs Katharine Brown
☎ 01993 703120
Fax 01993 700528
BB From £20–£22
Sleeps 4
🐴 ⚔ 🌳 🏠 🎣
👑 Highly Commended

Hill Grove is a mixed, family-run 300-acre working farm situated in an attractive rural setting overlooking the Windrush Valley. Ideally positioned for driving to Oxford, Blenheim Palace, Witney (Farm Museum) and Burford (renowned as the Gateway to the Cotswolds and for its splendid Wildlife Park). Riverside walks. Hearty breakfasts. Golf course 1 mile. 1 double/private shower, 1 twin/double en suite. Open all year (closed Christmas).

9 'Morar', Weald Street, Bampton, Oxfordshire OX18 2HL

Janet Rouse
☎ 01993 850162
Fax 01993 851738
BB From £21–£22
EM From £14
Sleeps 6
🐴(6) ⚔ ⚔ 🏠 ⚙
👑 Highly Commended

Wake up to the smell of homemade bread, look out over rolling fields and listen to the birds welcome the new day. Relax over breakfast, make it a feast. Let us help you get the most from your stay in this most beautiful corner of England. Pet cats, sheep, goat. Doubles en suite. Open Mar–mid Dec. E-mail: morar@cwcom.net

10 North Farm, Shillingford Hill, Wallingford, Oxfordshire OX10 8NB

Hilary Warburton
☎ 01865 858406
Fax 01865 858519
BB From £24–£25
Sleeps 4
🐴(10) ⚔ 🐾 🌳 🏠 🎣
👑 Highly Commended

Attractive and quiet farmhouse in the middle of our 500-acre sheep and arable farm bordering the River Thames with a well-tended garden and hard tennis court. Pygmy goats and chickens. Lovely walks and private fishing available. Ideal for Oxford and Henley. One twin with private bathroom, one double en suite. Closed Christmas and New Year.

11 The Old Farmhouse, Station Hill, Long Hanborough, Oxfordshire OX8 8JZ

Vanessa Maundrell
☎ 01993 882097
BB From £19.50–£22.50
Sleeps 4
🐴(12) ⚔ 🚭 🌳 🎣 🏠
👑 Highly Commended

We welcome you to our former farmhouse dating from 1670 with many original features and charming bedrooms. Delicious breakfasts with freshly baked bread, homemade marmalade/jams and fresh orange juice (served in delightful cottage garden on summer mornings). Lovely country walks and good pubs within walking distance. Woodstock and Blenheim Palace nearby and Oxford a 10-minute train ride. Two doubles (one en suite). Closed Christmas.

Oxfordshire
South & South East

Rectory Farm, Northmoor, Witney, Oxfordshire OX8 1SX ⑫

Mary Anne Florey
☎ 01865 300207
Fax 01865 300559
BB From £20–£22
Sleeps 4
Highly Commended

A 16th century farmhouse retaining old charm alongside modern comforts. Both rooms have en suite facilities, CH, tea/coffee-making facilities. Guests' own sitting room with woodburning stove. We are conveniently situated for Oxford (10m), the Cotswolds, Blenheim and the Thames path. A pot of tea, homemade shortbread, along with a warm welcome and a peaceful, comfortable stay await you at Rectory Farm. Open Feb–mid Dec.

Vicarage Farm, Kirtlington, Oxfordshire OX5 3JY ⑬

Mrs Judith Hunter
☎/Fax 01869 350254
BB From £20–£25
Sleeps 4
Commended

Leave behind the bustle of everyday life and sink into the peace of the countryside. Golf on the surrounding 18-hole course, or go on a shopping trip to the Bicester Village, or browse round the shops of nearby Woodstock and on into Blenheim Palace. Spend a day in Stratford or at Warwick Castle. Oxford only 8 miles. One twin, one double, both with their own private bathroom or shower and colour TV, CH and tea/coffee-making facilities. Open Mar–Nov.

Weston Farm, Buscot Wick, Faringdon, Oxfordshire SN7 8DJ ⑭

Mrs Jean Woof
☎/Fax 01367 252222
BB From £20–£25
Sleeps 6
(10)
Highly Commended

Come and share our idyllic 17th century Cotswold farmhouse in peaceful surroundings. Period furniture and well maintained gardens. 500-acre mixed farm. CH, tea/coffee-making facilities and own TV, one four-poster, one double and one twin room, all with private bathroom. Guests' own dining and sitting rooms, with log fires. Ideally situated to explore this beautiful area. Open all year except Christmas.

Self-Catering

Banbury Hill Farm, Enstone Road, Charlbury, Oxford OX7 3JH ①

Mrs Angela Widdows
☎ 01608 810314
Fax 01608 811891
SC From £185–£295
Sleeps 4/6
– Highly Commended

Comfortable Cotswold farm cottages, well appointed with outstanding views in AONB between Oxford and Stratford-on-Avon. Variety of farm animals. Forest trail, play area, tennis and bike hire available. Ample parking. Open Mar–Nov.

Coxwell House, Little Coxwell, Faringdon, Oxfordshire SN7 7LP ⑮

Elspeth Crossley Cooke
☎ 01367 241240
Fax 01367 240911
SC From £375–£725
Sleeps 6
Highly Commended

Coxwell House is the superb main 1760 part (self-contained) of a Georgian farmhouse set in an attractive, secluded walled garden. Every modern convenience. Tennis court, indoor swimming pool. Unspoilt stone walled farming village with thatched cottages and pub. Ideal for the Cotswolds, Oxford. 1½ miles Faringdon south of A420. Open all year. E mail: elspeth@coxwell.u-net.com

South & South East *Oxfordshire*

16 Lower Court Cottage, Lower Court Farm, Chadlington, Oxfordshire OX7 3NQ

Juliet Pauling
☎/Fax 01608 676422
SC From £195–£450
Sleeps 4/6
Commended up to Highly Commended

Alfie's Cottage is a typical, pretty Cotswold stone cottage set on this beautiful farm. Ideally situated for touring the Cotswolds and local Area of Outstanding Natural Beauty. Oxford and Sratford 18 miles, Stow-on-the-Wold, Bourton-on-the-Water, Burford 10 mile radius. Fully fitted kitchen with dishwasher, microwave, etc. Open log fire, CH. Garden with superb views, barbecue. Other cottages available. Open all year.

12 Rectory Farm Cottages, Northmoor, Nr Witney, Oxon OX8 1SX

Mary Anne Florey
☎ 01865 300207
Fax 01865 300559
SC From £220–£360
Sleeps 4
Highly Commended

Two delightful, warm, welcoming cottages tucked away on our farm in quiet village 10mw Oxford with south-facing enclosed gardens, field views and excellent walks. Each cottage is furnished in pine and has 1 double and 1 twin bedroom, bathroom, shower room, lounge with woodburner, TV, dining area and kitchen (washer/drier, dishwasher, electric cooker, fridge, microwave). CH, ample parking, linen/towels provided. Fully inclusive price. Open all year.

17 Walltree House Farm, Steane, Brackley, Northamptonshire NN13 5NS

Richard & Pauline Harrison
☎/Fax 01295 811235
Mobile 0860 913399
SC From £185–£460
Sleeps 2/6
Highly Commended

We have converted the granary and stables into warm, comfortable, well-equipped, quiet cottages in a courtyard adjacent to the farmhouse, overlooking lawns and garden where you are welcome to relax. Near Cotswolds, Stratford, Warwick, Blenheim, Stowe, Waddesdon and other National Trust properties. Shopping, golf and leisure centres. Every activity you can think of. A peaceful haven to return to. Open all year except Christmas and New Year.

STAY ON A FARM GIFT TOKENS

If you have enjoyed your Stay on a Farm, why not treat your friends and relatives to *Stay on a Farm* gift tokens? Available from the Bureau office (tel: 01203 696909), they can be redeemed against accommodation and are accepted by the majority of farms (see Index). Please check when booking to avoid disappointment.

FOLLOW THE COUNTRY CODE

Leave nothing but footprints,
Take nothing but photographs,
Kill nothing but time!

Buckinghamshire
Vale of Aylesbury & the Chilterns

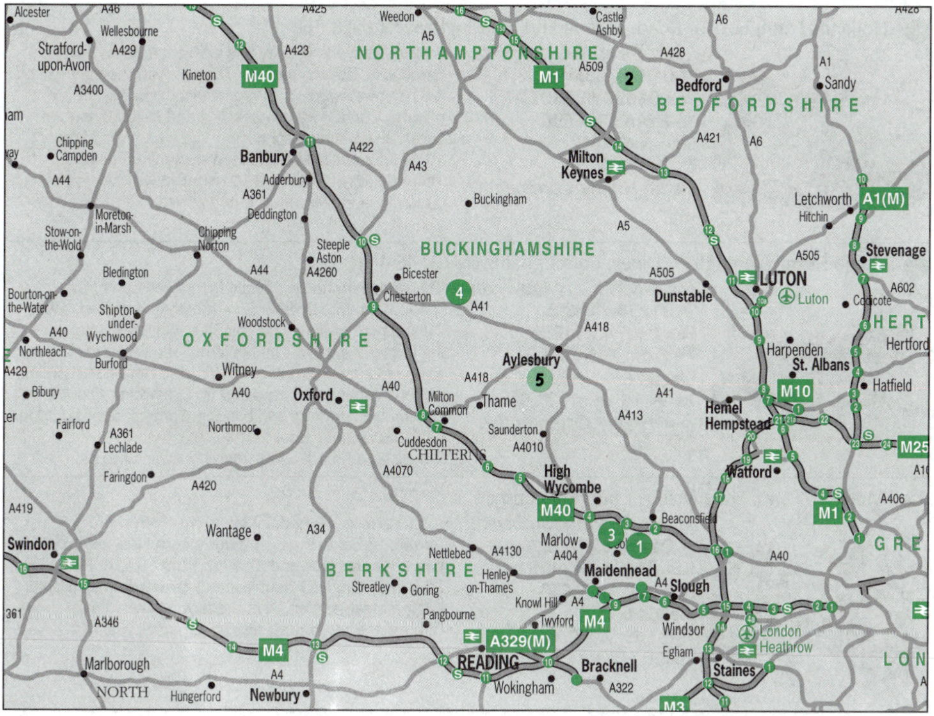

Key

1 Bed & Breakfast
1 Self-Catering
1 B&B and SC
1 Camping Barns
▲ Camping & Caravanning

This is a richly agricultural county yet within easy reach of London, Oxford and Heathrow. The fertile Vale of Aylesbury takes its name from the historic county town of 'Aylesbury Duck' fame. Situated at the foot of the Chiltern Hills, this is a bustling market town offering plenty of entertainment for the visitor. Milton Keynes, Buckingham and High Wycombe are excellent for shopping or you can mess about on the River Thames at picturesque Marlow – or just while away an afternoon watching others doing the messing as they negotiate the locks! You won't be short of places to visit: Waddesdon Manor, Claydon House, Stowe Gardens and Quainton Railway Centre, to name a few.

If you would like help in finding suitable farm accommodation, turn to the full listing of farm groups on pages 360 to 363 to find appropriate contact details for this area.

South & South East Buckinghamshire

Bed and Breakfast
(and evening meal)

① Hollands Farm, Hedsor Road, Bourne End, Buckinghamshire SL8 5EE

Marion Lunnon
☎ 01628 520423
Fax 01628 531602
BB From £20–£30
Sleeps 6
Listed *Highly Commended*

A 550-acre working dairy and arable farm with Victorian farmhouse, close to the river Thames with superb views of the hanging woods of Cliveden. Heathrow Airport 25 minutes, London 30 minutes, M4 and M40 10 minutes. Local railway station connecting to London (Paddington) 10 minutes' walk. Local bus service 5 minutes' walk. Thames Path at Cookham 10 minutes' walk. All rooms have colour TV and tea/coffee. Open all year.

② Home Farm, Warrington, Olney, Buckinghamshire MK46 4HN

Mr & Mrs Garry Pibworth
☎ 01234 711655
Fax 01234 711855
BB From £25
Sleeps 6
Highly Commended

Our stone farmhouse offers a friendly welcome, two spacious en suite bedrooms with bath and shower, colour TV and tea/coffee-making facilities. Guests' lounge with a log burner. A peaceful arable farm 1½ miles from market town of Olney, 10 miles from Bedford, Northhampton and Milton Keynes. Ideally situated for Cotswolds, Oxford, Cambridge, Stratford and London. Summer use of outdoor heated swimming pool.
E-mail: accommodation@ homefarm.force9.co.uk

③ Monkton Farm, Little Marlow, Buckinghamshire SL7 3RF

Jane & Warren Kimber
☎ 01494 521082
Fax 01494 443905
BB From £25–£30
Sleeps 6
Listed *Highly Commended*

A 150-acre working dairy farm with 14th century 'Cruck' farmhouse set in the beautiful Chiltern Hills, yet only 30 miles from London and 27 miles from Oxford. Heathrow 20 mins, 1 single, 1 double and 1 family room available. English breakfast served in the farm kitchen. Large choice of pubs and restaurants nearby. Open all year.

④ Poletrees Farm, Ludgershall Road, Brill, Aylesbury, Buckinghamshire HP18 9TZ

Anita & John Cooper
☎/Fax 01844 238276
BB From £22–£30
EM From £12
Sleeps 6
Listed *Commended*

A 16th century working beef and sheep farm with house of architectural interest. 2 quiet bedrooms, 1 double, 1 twin, both with H&C and tea/coffee-making facilities. Guests have own lounge. En suite barn conversion in garden for couples – suppers can be ordered. Many pubs and restaurants nearby. Places of interest include Waddesdon Manor, Claydon House, Stowe Gardens and Oxford. Bicester Retail Village 6 miles. Elizabeth Gundrey recommended. Open Mar–Dec.

⑤ Wallace Farm, Dinton, Nr Aylesbury, Buckinghamshire HP17 8UF

Jackie Cook
☎ 01296 748660
Fax 01296 748851
BB From £21–£30
Sleeps 6
Commended

This 16th century listed farmhouse is situated in a quiet, rural setting in the Vale of Aylesbury, yet within easy reach of London, Oxford and Heathrow. A small family farm, rearing beef cattle and sheep, plus chickens, ducks and geese. Plenty of opportunitites for country walks, coarse fishing or browsing through our extensive library. Open all year.

Buckinghamshire South & South East

Self-Catering

'The Old Stone Barn', c/o Home Farm, Warrington, Olney, Buckinghamshire MK46 4HN ❷

Mr & Mrs G Pibworth
☎ 01234 711655
Fax 01234 711855
🆂🅲 From £160–£350
Sleep 1/6
👤 🐕 ♿ 🏊 ♀ 🎀 🌀
🍃🍃🍃🍃 *Highly Commended*

A charming combination of old character and modern facilities, the Old Stone Barn is 3 ground floor and 3 first floor spacious self-contained apartments peacefully positioned on an arable farm 1½ miles north of Olney. Relax in the gardens, make use of the outdoor heated swimming pool or take day trips to Oxford, Cambridge, London or the Cotswolds. Open all year.
E-mail: accommodation@homefarm.force9.co.uk

Wallace Farm Cottages, Dinton, Nr Aylesbury, Buckinghamshire HP17 8UF ❺

Jackie Cook
☎ 01296 748660
Fax 01296 748851
🆂🅲 From £170–£300
Sleep 2–5
🌀 🐕 ♿ 💼 ♀ 🎀 🌀 🌀
🍃🍃🍃 *Commended*

The Old Foaling Box and Keepers Cottage are two very charming cottages set across the courtyard of a 16th century farmhouse. These adjoining cottages are on one level and comfortably giving a feeling of cosiness and welcome. This conversion of a former stable block has been kept in complete harmony with the surrounding farm. Open all year.

FINDING YOUR ACCOMMODATION

The local FHB Group contacts listed on page 360 can always help you find a vacancy in your chosen area.

USE THE INDEX

The comprehensive Index shows which farms offer access to disabled visitors; caravanning/camping facilities; the chance to participate on a working farm; stabling/grazing for visiting horses; en suite rooms; a welcome to business people; acceptance of *Stay on a Farm* gift tokens.

Essex

Dedham Vale, Essex Way & Epping Forest

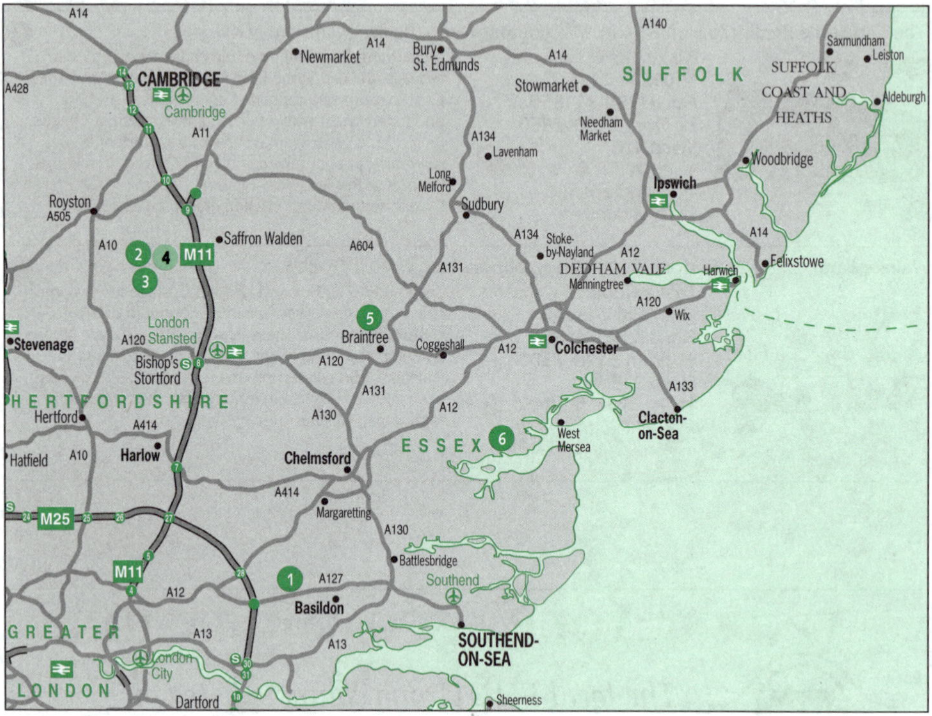

Key

- 1 Bed & Breakfast
- 1 Self-Catering
- 1 B&B and SC
- 1 Camping Barns
- ▲ Camping & Caravanning

Come and discover the real Essex. Once off the beaten track you will be surprised by our pargetted cottages, unspoilt villages set in undulating countryside, stately homes, working museums and gardens like Beth Chatto's. Go back to the time of the Romans at Colchester Castle, the Saxons at unique Greenstead Church and the Second World War at Duxford Air Museum. Or walk the Essex Way from Epping, via Constable Country to the coast where you can sail and birdwatch around the creeks and estuaries. Essex can cater for all tastes and interests and we are ideally placed for travellers with the port of Harwich, Stansted Airport and easy access to London.

If you would like help in finding suitable farm accommodation, turn to the full listing of farm groups on pages 360 to 363 to find appropriate contact details for this area.

Essex South & South East

Bed and Breakfast
(and evening meal)

Bonnydowns Farmhouse, Doesgate Lane, Bulphan, Nr Upminster, Essex RM14 3TB

Rose Newman
☎ 01268 542129
BB From £20
EM From £8
Sleeps 6
Listed *Approved*

Large, comfortably furnished, pleasantly situated in large garden with lovely views. Close to Langdon Hills Country Park and Basildon New Town (modern shopping centre). Convenient for London, Southend, South East England via M25, A13, A127. Sheep/cattle kept on the farm. 2 twin, 1 family bedrooms, 1 bath with toilet/shower, 1 shower room with toilet. Tea/coffee trays. Good cooking. Open all year (closed Christmas).

Duddenhoe End Farm, Duddenhoe End, Nr Saffron Walden, Essex CB11 4UU

Peggy Foster
☎ 01763 838258
BB From £20–£25
Sleeps 6
(12)
Commended

A warm welcome awaits you at this comfortable 17th century farmhouse situated in quiet rural area. All bedrooms have private or en suite bathrooms, tea/coffee-making facilities, TV and radio. Visitors' sitting room. Ideally located for Cambridge, Audley End mansion, Duxford Air Museum and Stansted Airport. Central heating throughout. Non-smokers only. Open all year except Christmas.

Parsonage Farm, Arkesden, nr Saffron Walden, Essex CB11 4 JB

Daniele Forster
☎ 01799 550306
BB From £15–£23
Sleeps 6
Commended

After a hard day's touring come and relax in our beautifully kept Victorian farmhouse, situated in the centre of an attractive small village. En suite facilities available, TV and hot drinks in bedrooms. The farm is arable but a few pets are kept. Hard tennis court and picnic table in large garden. Excellent meals in local pub just 5 minutes' walk. Open all year except Christmas.

Rockells Farm, Duddenhoe End, Saffron Walden, Essex CB11 4UY

Mrs Tineke Westerhuis
☎ 01763 838053
Fax 01763 837001
BB From £18–£20
Sleeps 6
Commended

Rockells is an arable farm in a beautiful corner of Essex. The Georgian house has a large garden with a 3-acre lake for coarse fishing. All rooms have private facilities, one room is downstairs. On the farm are several footpaths, and beautiful villages in the area. Audley End, Duxford and Cambridge nearby. London is about 1 hour by car or train. Stansted Airport 30 mins. Open all year except Christmas.

Spicers Farm, Rotten End, Wethersfield, Braintree, Essex CM7 4AL

Mrs Delia Douse
☎ 01371 851021
BB From £17
Sleeps 6
Highly Commended

Set in a delightful, peaceful position overlooking beautiful countryside. Comfortable and welcoming atmosphere. All rooms en suite with CH, tea/coffee-making facilities, colour TV, clock radio and lovely views. Convenient for Stansted, Harwich, Cambridge and Constable Country. Ideal for touring or walking. Open all year except Christmas and New Year.

South & South East *Essex*

⑥ Wicks Manor Farm, Witham Road, Tolleshunt Major, Maldon, Essex CM9 8JU

Mary Howie
☎/Fax 01621 860629
BB From £18
Sleeps 4
⌂ ⚞ ⚘ ♿
Listed *Commended*

Comfortable 17th century moated farmhouse set in large established garden. You are assured of a warm welcome on our mixed arable farm close to the River Blackwater estuary. Delicious traditional breakfasts or your own requirements. Guests' own bathroom and sitting room. Two attractive bedrooms with TV and tea/coffee-making facilities. Open all year except Christmas.

Self-Catering

④ The Byre, c/o Rockells Farm, Duddenhoe End, Saffron Walden, Essex CB11 4UY

Mrs Tineke Westerhuis
☎ 01763 838053
Fax 01763 837001
SC From £140–£200
Sleeps 3/5
⌂ ⚞ ⚘ ♿ ♞
🔑🔑🔑 *Commended*

The Byre is part of Rockells farmyard, an arable farm in a beautiful corner of Essex. Lounge with kitchen area has original wood panelling. The cottage is fully equipped to high standard. Garden with 3-acre lake for excellent fishing. In the area are several footpaths and beautiful villages with excellent pubs. Audley End, Duxford and Cambridge nearby. London is 1 hour by car or train, Stansted Airport 30 mins by car. Open all year.

NO ANSWER?
Farmers are mostly out and about during the day.
Try to telephone before 9.30am or after 4pm.

 Please mention **Stay on a Farm** when booking

---

CONFIRM BOOKINGS
Disappointments can arise from misunderstandings over the telephone.
Please write to confirm your booking.

Hampshire

New Forest, South Hampshire Coast, the Solent & Test Valley

Key

- 1 Bed & Breakfast
- 1 Self-Catering
- 1 B&B and SC
- 1 Camping Barns
- 1 Camping & Caravanning

Hampshire is a beautiful county of contrasts – of creeks, harbours and beaches, grand rivers and sparkling streams, forests and lush farmland with picturesque villages and hamlets. The county has numerous links with the past. Winchester was the Saxon capital; Southampton bore witness to the Norman invasion; Portsmouth is famous for its naval heritage and as the birthplace of Charles Dickens; and Chawton was the home of Jane Austen. There are excellent walks in the lovely New Forest, along the Solent coastline and inland along the famous Test Valley, or visit a country mansion such as Broadlands, Breamore, Stratfield Saye or Highclere Castle.

If you would like help in finding suitable farm accommodation, turn to the full listing of farm groups on pages 360 to 363 to find appropriate contact details for this area.

South & South East Hampshire

Bed and Breakfast
(and evening meal)

① Brocklands Farm, West Meon, Petersfield, Hampshire GU32 1JN

Sue Wilson
☎/Fax 01730 829228
BB From £18.50–£20
Sleeps 6
Listed *Commended*

Sue's home-baked bread and delicious preserves complement her warm hospitality in the unique, traditionally furnished, modern farmhouse. Lovely views of the countryside and a sheltered sunny terrace. Mown grass walks around the farm and into West Meon, a charming village with shops and 2 friendly pubs. TV in some rooms. There are badgers on the farm. Open all year except Christmas.

② Compton Farmhouse, Church Lane, Compton, Nr Chichester, West Sussex PO18 9HB

Mrs Melanie Bray
☎ 01705 631597
BB From £18–£20
Sleeps 6
Listed *Commended*

Children are especially welcome (half-price) at our old, flint farmhouse. We are 200 yards up a track from the village square, next door to the church and are bordered by fields and woods. Lovely walks and plenty to do in our enclosed, child-orientated garden. Large family bedroom, own bathroom and sitting/dining room with drink-making facilities, fridge, TV. Open Jan–Nov.

③ Moortown Farm, Soberton, Southampton, Hampshire SO32 3QU

Rosemary Taylor
☎ 01489 877256
BB From £17.50–£25
Sleeps 6
Listed *Commended*

A friendly atmosphere is found at Moortown in the heart of the Meon Valley, an Area of Outstanding Natural Beauty. Crossed by the Warfarer's Walk and South Downs Way. 1 twin en suite, 1 4-bedded with private bathroom, both with TV and tea facilities. Set in a peaceful village within easy reach of Winchester, home of King Arthur's Round Table, Portsmouth, with the Mary Rose and Nelson's flagship, Chichester and the New Forest. Open all year.

④ Oakdown Farm Bungalow, c/o Oakdown Farm, Dummer, Basingstoke, Hampshire RG23 7LR

Mrs Elizabeth Hutton
☎ 01256 397218
BB From £15–£18
Sleeps 6
(12)
Commended

Oakdown Farm Bungalow is on a secluded, private road, next to junction 7 on the M3, 1 mile south of Basingstoke and close to the village of Dummer. Excellent road communications to London, Winchester, South coast, the South-West, Oxford and the Midlands. Local historians welcome. B&B for horses. Wayfarer's Walk within 200 metres. Open all year.

⑤ Peak House Farm, Cole Henley, Whitchurch, Hampshire RG28 7QJ

Mrs Jenny Stevens
☎ 01256 892052
BB From £16–£20
Sleeps 6
Listed *Commended*

Come and stay in our attractively furnished and decorated turn of the century farmhouse set in peaceful surroundings on working dairy farm close to Watership Down. Beautiful walks and horseriding nearby. Centrally based for New Forest, Winchester, Stonehenge, Legoland and Oxford. 1 twin en suite (ground floor, self-contained), 1 double and 1 twin with handbasin, all with colour TV, tea/coffee facilities. Lounge with log fire. Large garden, parking. Children welcome. Open all year.

Hampshire — South & South East

Pyesmead Farm, Plaitford, Romsey, Hampshire SO51 6EE

Mrs Christina Pybus
☎/Fax 01794 323386
BB From £16
Sleeps 6
♥ Commended

A warm welcome awaits you, on the northern edge of the New Forest, at our family-run stock farm with its own coarse fishing lakes and indoor heated swimming pool. Many activities locally including horse riding, trout fishing, golf and forest walks. Within easy reach of Salisbury, Winchester, Southampton and the coast. Excellent pubs providing good food within ½ mile. Children welcome. Open all year except Christmas.

Roughwood House, Highwood, Ringwood, Hampshire BH24 3LE

Mrs Carelle Sherwood
☎ 01425 474977
Fax 01425 471005
BB From £20–£25
Sleeps 8
♥♥ Commended

Roughwood is a small elegant country house in 20 acres set in a secluded valley in the heart of the New Forest. The farm has direct access to 45,000 acres of the New Forest and has the ancient rights of 'commoning' to graze cattle, ponies and pigs there. Stabling for guests' own horses. All rooms are self-contained and en suite. Stunning views and abundant wildlife. Easy access to Dorset and the coast.
E-mail: tallyho@bigfoot.com.uk

Vine Farmhouse, Isington, Bentley, Alton, Hampshire GU34 4PW

Mrs G Sinclair
☎/Fax 01420 23262
mobile 0467 767599
BB From £17.50–£22.50
Sleeps 5
Listed Commended

Vine Farmhouse is situated halfway between Alton and Farnham in its own farmland overlooking the River Wey. Gatwick and Heathrow are 1 hour by car as is London. Local attractions are Jane Austen's house, Birdworld, steam museum and railway and numerous gardens. Pubs and restaurants nearby. Open all year except Christmas.
Email: vinefarm@aol.com

Self-Catering

Beacon Hill Farm Cottages, Beacon Hill Lane, Exton, Southampton, Hampshire SO32 3NW

Mrs C Dunford
☎ 01730 829724
Fax 01730 829833
SC From £300–£400
Sleeps 4/5
Applied

Barn conversion comprising 4 self-catering cottages. Stunning location in the Meon Valley with magnificent farmland views. Tastefully furnished with beamed ceilings and galleried landings. One suitable for disabled with carer. Close to Winchester and Portsmouth. Ideal for walkers (South Downs Way). Excellent facilities including dishwasher, microwave, barbecue, garden furniture. Open all year.

Meadow Cottage, c/o Farley Farm, Braishfield, Romsey, Hampshire SO51 0QP

Mrs Wendy Graham
☎ 01794 368265
Fax 01794 367847
SC From £180–£290
Sleeps 5 + cot
Commended

Well equipped, semi-detached cottage on a 400-acre beef and arable farm. Outstanding views of beautiful surrounding countryside. Ideal for walking or riding, or touring historic centres of Romsey, Winchester, Salisbury, Portsmouth, New Forest and coast. Cottage has CH, log fire, colour TV, downstairs WC, washer/dryer, cot. Garden. Phone for brochure. Open Apr–Oct.

South & South East *Hampshire*

(11) Owl Cottage, Lye Farm, West Tytherley, Romsey, Hampshire SP5 1LA

Maxine Vine
☎ 01794 341667
SC From £195–£295
Sleeps 5
Applied

Owl cottage has been skillfully converted from an old barn situated in one of the most beautiful parts of Hampshire. Outstanding views, close New Forest, Salisbury, Winchester. Location perfect for touring, walking, riding in southern England. Excellently equipped cottage, central heating, electric included, washer dryer, TV, cot. Peaceful and relaxing environment. Open all year.

LET THE TELEPHONE RING!
Some farmhouses are big places. Let the telephone ring long enough to give the owner time to answer it.

USE THE INDEX

The comprehensive Index shows which farms offer access to disabled visitors; caravanning/camping facilities; the chance to participate on a working farm; stabling/grazing for visiting horses; en suite rooms; a welcome to business people; acceptance of *Stay on a Farm* gift tokens.

STAY ON A FARM GIFT TOKENS

If you have enjoyed your Stay on a Farm, why not treat your friends and relatives to *Stay on a Farm* gift tokens? Available from the Bureau office (tel: 01203 696909), they can be redeemed against accommodation and are accepted by the majority of farms (see Index). Please check when booking to avoid disappointment.

Isle of Wight

The Needles, Medina Valley, the Downs & Sandown Bay

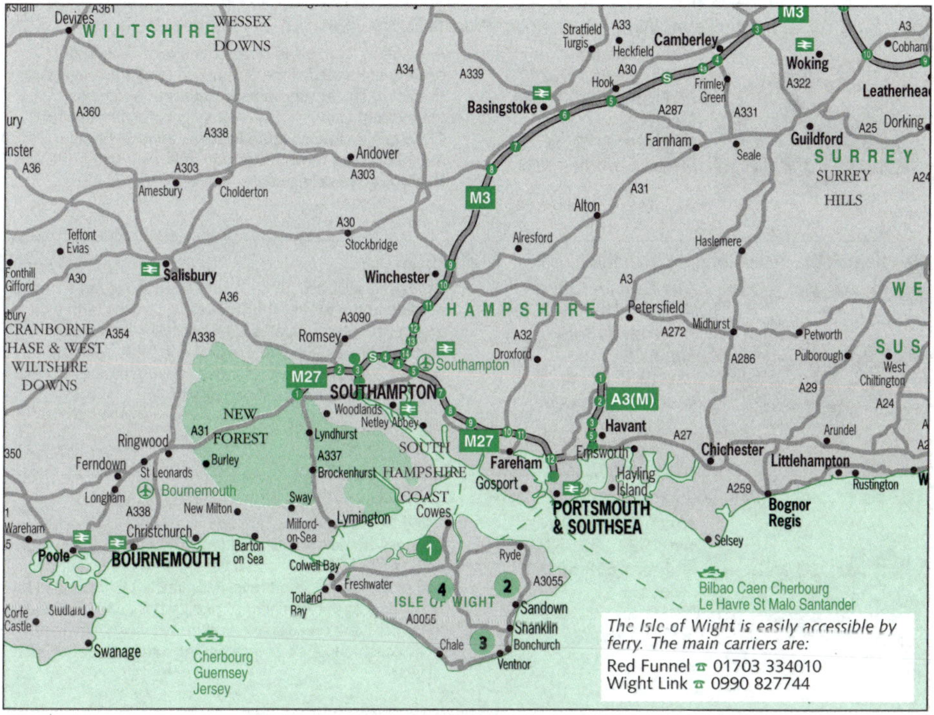

The Isle of Wight is easily accessible by ferry. The main carriers are:
Red Funnel ☎ 01703 334010
Wight Link ☎ 0990 827744

Key

 Bed & Breakfast
 Self-Catering
 B&B and SC
 Camping Barns
▲ Camping & Caravanning

The Isle of Wight, with its sandy beaches and small, secluded coves, and the sea never more than 15 minutes from wherever you may be, has a wide variety of holiday activities and attractions. With Cowes and the Royal Yacht Squadron, an international symbol of all that is finest in yachting, the Island is famous for its seafaring activities. This is the perfect holiday retreat for ramblers on the Downs, birdwatchers, anglers, adventure sports enthusiasts and for those who merely wish to relax and drink in the glorious scenery. A climate that tops the British Isles' Sunshine League makes the Island particularly attractive in Spring or Autumn for short break holidays.

If you would like help in finding suitable farm accommodation, turn to the full listing of farm groups on pages 360 to 363 to find appropriate contact details for this area.

South & South East Isle of Wight

Bed and Breakfast
(and evening meal)

① **Auld Youngwoods Farm,** Whitehouse Road, Porchfield, Newport, Isle of Wight PO30 4LJ

Judith Shanks
☎/Fax 01983 522170
BB From £15.50–£20
Sleeps 5
☼(8) ⚥ ☘ ♨ ♣ ✸
Listed *Commended*

A grassland farm set in open countryside. The 18th century renovated stone farmhouse retains its original character. The guest rooms are spacious and enjoy magnificent views of the West Wight (CH throughout). Close to Newtown Nature Reserve, an ideal base for the naturalist. Wild flowers. Red squirrels, owls and butterflies locally. Cowes sailing centre 4 miles. Open all year.

② **Kern Farm,** Alverstone, Nr Sandown, Isle of Wight PO36 0EY

Mrs Gaynor Oliver
☎/Fax 01983 403721
BB From £18–£20
Sleeps 5
☼(10) ⚥ ♨ ♣ ✸
☻ ☻ *Commended*

Quiet and secluded 16th century listed stone farmhouse nestling at the foot of the Downs on a mixed farm with wonderful views. Situated on Bembridge Trail. Sandy beaches 3 miles. One double and one triple bedroom – both en suite with tea and coffee-making facilities. Colour TV. Minimum 2 nights. Open all year.

③ **Lisle Combe,** Bank End Farm, Undercliff Drive, St Lawrence, Ventnor, Isle of Wight PO38 1UW

Hugh & Judy Noyes
☎ 01983 852582
BB From £18.50–£19
Sleeps 6
☼ ⚥ ♣
☻ *Commended*

Listed Elizabethan style farmhouse overlooking English Channel, home of the late Alfred Noyes (poet and author) and his family. 5 acre coastal garden with rare waterfowl and pheasant collection (over 100 species). Surrounded by farmlands for owner's herd of pedigree Friesians, free entry to owner's rare breeds park. Superb sea views, coves and small beaches in area of outstanding natural beauty. Open all year.

④ **Newbarn Farm,** Newbarn Lane, Gatcombe, Newport, Isle of Wight PO30 3EQ

Mrs Diane Harvey
☎ 01983 721202
BB From £18–£20
Sleeps 3
☼(5) ⚥ ♨
☻ ☻ *Commended*

17th century farmhouse on a 240-acre arable farm in the small hamlet of Gatcombe in the centre of the island. Wonderful walking area enjoying some spectacular views over the island and south coast. One bedroom with en suite shower and tea-making facilities. Dining room and TV lounge with inglenook fireplace. Open Mar–Nov.

 Please mention **Stay on a Farm** when booking

Isle of Wight South & South East

Self-Catering

Combe Lodge, Bank End Farm, Undercliff Drive, St Lawrence, Ventnor, IOW PO38 1UW ❸

Hugh & Judy Noyes
☎ 01983 852582
SC From £220–£360
Sleeps 6 + cot
Approved

Victorian-style cottage in wooded surroundings overlooking owners' rare breeds and waterfowl park to which there is free entry. Own garden within grounds of Bank End Farm. Many small coves for swimming and sunbathing. Colour TV. Everything provided except linen. Fine coastal walks within Area of Outstanding Natural Beauty. Open all year.

The Stable, Newbarn Farm, Newbarn Lane, Gatcombe, Newport, Isle of Wight PO30 3EQ

Mrs Diane Harvey
☎ 01983 721202
SC From £150–£450
Sleeps 6
Highly Commended

Beautiful converted stable offering high standard of accommodation for up to six people. Both bedrooms have double beds, one with 3 ft bunks, other with cot. Secluded valley setting, excellent walking. Centrally situated for island attractions. Enclosed patio and parking. Linen and electricity included. Beds made up on arrival. Open all year.

West Wing, Kern Farm, Alverstone, nr Sandown, Isle of Wight PO36 0EY ❷

Mrs Gaynor Oliver
☎/Fax 01983 403721
SC From £275–£450
Sleeps 6
☾(10)
Highly Commended

Self-contained west wing of 16th century listed stone farmhouse on 250-acre mixed farm. Off beaten track, ideal for walking, painting or just relaxing. Two triple bedrooms. All linen provided. Log fire and CH. Regret no dogs or children under 10. Friday bookings. Open all year.

NO ANSWER?
Farmers are mostly out and about during the day.
Try to telephone before 9.30am or after 4pm.

FARM HOLIDAY BUREAU

Our Internet address is
http://www.webscape.co.uk/farmaccom/

Surrey

North Downs, Pilgrims' Way & Surrey Hills

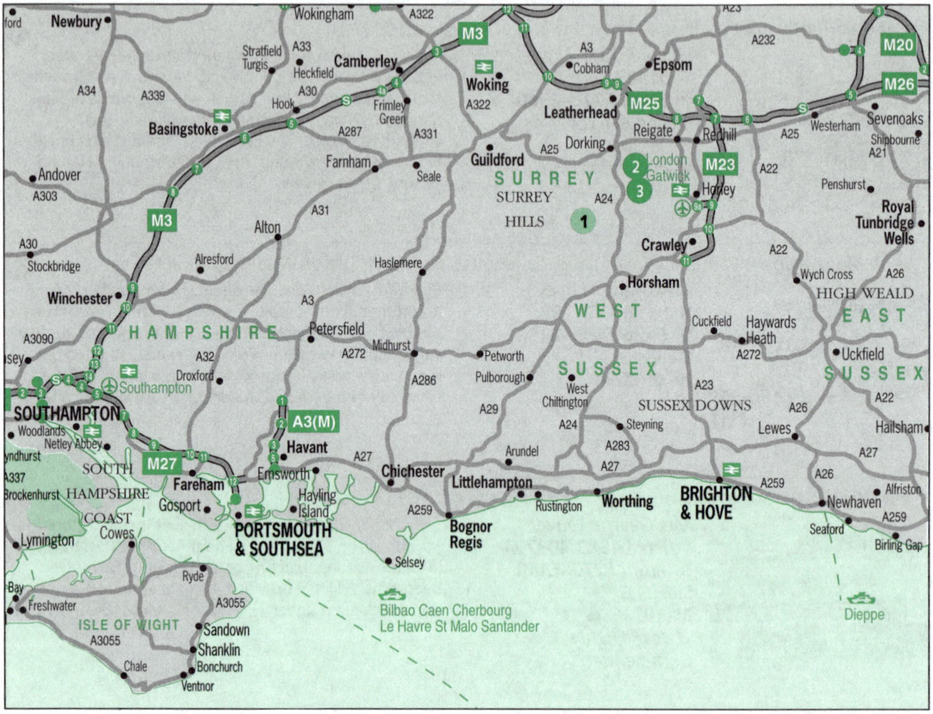

Key

- Bed & Breakfast
- Self-Catering
- B&B and SC
- Camping Barns
- Camping & Caravanning

In Surrey, the North Downs provide dramatic wooded hillsides with small, attractive towns and villages nestling in the valleys. Here you can walk along the track claiming to be the Pilgrims' Way which connects Winchester to Canterbury, or clamber up famous heights like Leith Hill – just short of 1,000ft – or its neighbour Box Hill, coming down via the intriguingly named Zig Zag Hill. The charming towns of Farnham, Guildford and Dorking are excellent for shopping and there are numerous pretty villages for the lover of tea shops and antiques. The National Trust's Polesden Lacey is a jewel in a beautiful setting, yet none of this is more than an hour from London.

If you would like help in finding suitable farm accommodation, turn to the full listing of farm groups on pages 360 to 363 to find appropriate contact details for this area.

Surrey   South & South East

Bed and Breakfast
(and evening meal)

Bulmer Farm, Holmbury St Mary, Dorking, Surrey RH5 6LG ①

Gill Hill
☎ 01306 730210
BB From £20–£32
Sleeps 16
Caravans £3.50
♿ ♘(12) ♞ ♨ ♣ ♃
♣♣ Commended

Warm welcome guaranteed at our 30-acre farm in peaceful, picturesque Victorian village amid Surrey hills. 3 charming rooms in 17th century farmhouse; 5 en suite barn conversion, non-smoking rooms with TV around courtyard adjoining house. Homemade preserves. Large walled garden, woodland walk to award-winning lake. Good pubs nearby. Convenient for London, airports, Wisley, NT properties, sporting venues. Elizabeth Gundrey recommended. Open all year.

Herons Head Farm, Mynthurst, Leigh, Surrey RH2 8QD ②

Ann Dale
☎ 01293 862475
Fax 01293 863350
BB From £20–£40
Sleeps 6
♘ ♞ ♨ ♣ ♃
Applied

Charming, quintessentially British Grade II listed beamed farmhouse set in 5 acres of gardens, paddocks, small lake, tennis court and heated swimming pool. Antique furnishings, farmhouse kitchen, inglenook and log fires. Conservatory for guests' use overlooking the lake and ducks. Near Dorking and Reigate, picturesque Leigh has many inns and restaurants. Gatwick 10 mins, London and Brighton 33 mins. Parking and transfers. Open all year.
E-mail: heronshead@clara.net.co.uk

Sturtwood Farm, Partridge Lane, Newdigate, Dorking, Surrey RH5 5EE ③

Bridget MacKinnon
☎ 01306 631308
Fax 01306 631908
BB From £20–£30
EM From £8.50
Sleeps 5
♘ ♞ ♨ ♣ ♃
♣♣ Commended

An attractive 18th century farmhouse in lovely countryside yet within 12 mins of Gatwick Airport. Many National Trust properties and gardens nearby. Also London, Brighton and several country towns. Open all year except Christmas.

Self-Catering

'Badgersholt' and 'Foxholme', c/o Bulmer Farm, Holmbury St Mary, Dorking, Surrey RH5 6LG ①

Gill Hill
☎ 01306 730210
SC From £160–£310
Sleeps 2/4
♘ ♞ ♨ ♣ ♃
♣♣ – ♣♣♣♣
Commended

Two delightfully cosy, single-storey cottages, sympathetically converted from a Surrey barn, forming a courtyard with the farmhouse. Fully carpeted, electric CH, colour TV and linen (beds made up). Communal laundry room, use of 2-acre farmhouse garden. Situated in picturesque, quiet valley. Ideal walking country. 'Badgersholt' sleeps 2 (also suitable disabled). 'Foxholme' sleeps 4 in 2 bedrooms. Open all year.

Kent

Kent Downs, High Weald, Weald of Kent & Romney Marsh

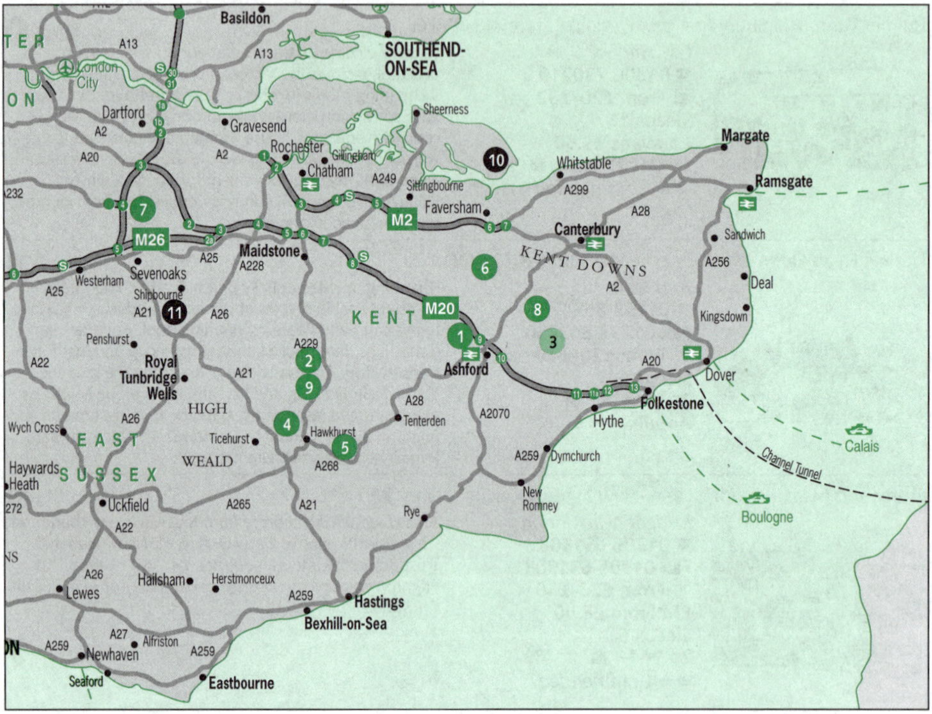

Key

- 🔵 Bed & Breakfast
- 🔵 Self-Catering
- 🔵 B&B and SC
- 🔵 Camping Barns
- 🔺 Camping & Caravanning

Kent is very much farming country, and the distinctive features are the many orchards, hop gardens and oast houses to be found in the aptly named 'Garden of England'. The lovely and varied Kent countryside is dotted with many historic towns and villages, such as the medieval port of Sandwich, Tenterden, West Malling, Cranbrook, Rochester and the hilltop village of Chilham. Kent has a wealth of attractions for the visitor, including world-famous Canterbury Cathedral, fairytale castles such as Leeds, Hever, Dover, Deal and Walmer, numerous historic houses including Churchill's Chartwell, Knole and Penshurst Place, fortifications, museums, vineyards, wildlife parks and glorious gardens.

If you would like help in finding suitable farm accommodation, turn to the full listing of farm groups on pages 360 to 363 to find appropriate contact details for this area.

Kent South & South East

Bed and Breakfast
(and evening meal)

Barnfield, Charing, Ashford, Kent TN27 0BN

Mrs Phillada Pym
☎/Fax 01233 712421
BB From £20–£27
Sleeps 6
Listed *Commended*

Charming and romantic Kent hall farmhouse built in 1420 with a wealth of character. A family home by a wildfowl lake amidst peaceful farmland. England at its very best. Excellent for Leeds Castle, Canterbury, Sissinghurst, Channel Tunnel and coastal ports. 1 family, 1 double, 1 twin and 2 singles. AA QQQ. Open all year except Christmas.

Great Cheveney Farm, Marden, Tonbridge, Kent TN12 9LX

Mrs Diana Day
☎ 01622 831207
Fax 01622 831786
BB From £20–£25
Sleeps 3
(10)
Listed *Highly Commended*

We offer comfort and a friendly welcome in our 16th century farmhouse peacefully situated between Marden and Goudhurst villages on B2079. A perfect base for discovering Kent's attractive countryside, NT properties, gardens and coast. London and Le Shuttle 1 hour. Bedrooms with private facilities, guests' lounge, TV, spacious garden and parking. Open all year except Christmas & New Year.

Great Field Farm, Misling Lane, Stelling Minnis, Canterbury, Kent CT4 6DE

Lewana Castle
☎/Fax 01227 709223
BB From £18–£22.50
Sleeps 6
Listed *Highly Commended*

This comfortable, spacious farmhouse, with a wealth of old pine, sits amidst pleasant gardens and paddocks with friendly ponies. Three en suite rooms with colour TV, 1 double/family room with jacuzzi-style air bath, 2 have own lounges, 1 with kitchen. A warm welcome assured, very child friendly, all day access. Ideal location for exploring Kent, convenient for Canterbury, Chunnel and ferries. Open all year.

Hallwood Farm, Hartley, Hawkhurst Road, Cranbrook, Kent TN17 2SP

David Wickham
☎/Fax 01580 713204
BB From £20–£22
EM From £15
Sleeps 6
Listed *Commended*

A lovely 15th century farmhouse with enchanting garden, surrounded by peaceful countryside. 2 miles from Cranbrook, medieval town associated with Wealden weaving and iron trades. Ideally situated for Sissinghurst Castle, other classic gardens, historic castles, NT properties. Easy access to London, Channel Tunnel. Comfortable, well furnished bedrooms, guests' lounge. Open Apr–Nov.

Hoads Farm, Crouch Lane, Sandhurst, Cranbrook, Kent TN18 5PA

Anne Nicholas
☎/Fax 01580 850296
BB From £19
EM From £11
Sleeps 6
Listed *Approved*

Bed and breakfast available in 17th century farmhouse on hop vine and sheep farm. Comfortable furnishings, sitting room with colour TV. Good centre for the coast, Bodiam Castle, Sissinghurst Castle, Scotney Castle and other National Trust properties. Excellent train service to London from Etchingham or Staplehurst. Dinner by arrangement. Dropside cot available on request. Open all year.

South & South East   Kent

6 Leaveland Court, Leaveland, Faversham, Kent ME13 0NP

Mrs Corrine Scutt
☎ 01233 740596
BB From £20–£25
Sleeps 6
🐴 ⚔ 🎒 🎿 💼 ✈ ⊚
♛ ♛ Highly Commended

Captivating 15th century timbered farmhouse on 300-acre downland farm. Easy access, 3 miles south of M2 junction 6, Faversham 5 minutes, Canterbury 20 minutes. Situated in a quiet setting with attractive garden and outdoor heated swimming pool. All rooms have en suite facilities, colour TV and tea/coffee trays. Traditional farmhouse food and warm welcome assured. Brochure available. Open Feb–Nov.

7 Preston Farm, Shoreham, Sevenoaks, Kent TN14 7UD

Mrs Shirley Montgomerie
☎ 01959 522029
Fax 01959 524375
BB From £20–£22
Sleeps 5
🐴(10) 🎿 💼
♛ Commended

We look forward to welcoming you to our 18th century farmhouse in the beautiful Darenth Valley. We are an ideal base for visiting London, 35 minutes by train, and there are many NT properties in the area. Guests' sitting room, TV and conservatory. Open all year except Christmas.

8 South Wootton House, Capel Road, Petham, Canterbury, Kent CT4 5RG

Frances Mount
☎ 01227 700643
Fax 01227 700613
BB From £18–£25
Sleeps 4
🐴 🐎 ⚔ 👤 🛎 🐕 🎿 💼
♛ Commended

A beautiful farmhouse with a conservatory set in extensive garden, surrounded by fields and woodland. Fully coordinated bedroom with private bathroom. Tea/coffee facilities, colour TV. Children and dogs welcome. Canterbury 4 miles. Open all year.

9 Tanner House, Tanner Farm, Goudhurst Road, Marden, Tonbridge, Kent TN12 9ND

Lesley Mannington
☎ 01622 831214
Fax 01622 832472
BB From £19–£22.50
EM From £12.50
Sleeps 6
🐴(12) ⚔ 🎒 👤 🛎 🐕 🎿 💼
♛ ♛ Commended

For a restful break, holiday or stop over, we are ideally placed in the beautiful Weald countryside. Our Tudor farmhouse in the centre of our working farm offers high standards of accommodation and cuisine. All our rooms, 1 double and 2 twins, are en suite, one with a genuine four-poster bed, and have colour TV, radio, tea/coffee-making facilities. We specialise in a countryside welcome. Visa/Access/Switch. Open all year except Christmas.

Self-Catering

10 'Birdwatcher's Cottage', c/o Newhouse Farm, Leysdown-on-Sea, Sheerness, Kent, ME12 4BA

Sally-Anne Marsh
☎ 01795 510201
Fax 01795 510830
SC From £175–£395
Sleeps 2–8 + cot
🐴 ⚔
🐾 🐾 🐾 Highly Commended

Come and relax in this peaceful, tucked away, quality country cottage on a sheep and arable farm. Panoramic views. Beamed ceilings, four bedrooms, CH. Large garden to sit in and daydream. Visit the nature reserves or wander along to the beach. Ideal touring base and a quiet hideaway. SAE for detailed leaflet. Open all year.

Kent — South & South East

Golding Hop Farm Cottage, c/o Golding Hop Farm, Bewley Lane, Plaxtol, Nr Sevenoaks, Kent TN15 0PS ⑪

Jacqueline Vincent
☎ 01732 885432
SC From £160
Sleeps 5 + cot

Highly Commended

13-acre farm producing Kent cobnuts for London markets. Surrounded by orchards and close to attractive village of Plaxtol. Secluded cottage, but not isolated. Sleeps 5, 2 double and 1 single, CH, colour TV, washer dryer and fridge/freezer, payphone. Horse riding, golf nearby. Car essential. Covered parking. Local station 2 miles with frequent trains to London. Motorway 4 miles. Dogs by arrangement only. Agency mid March to October. Open all year.

Great Field Farm, Misling Lane, Stelling Minnis, Canterbury, Kent CT4 6DE ③

Lewana Castle
☎ /Fax 01227 709223
SC From £150–£275
Sleeps 2 + cot

Commended

Cosy first floor flat in owners' farmhouse with beautiful views over lovely countryside. Double bedroom, lounge/dining room with colour TV, well equipped kitchen, bathroom. Freedom of the garden and grounds. Full CH, double glazing. Heating, power and linen inclusive. Open all year.

NO ANSWER?
Farmers are mostly out and about during the day.
Try to telephone before 9.30am or after 4pm.

FINDING YOUR ACCOMMODATION

The local FHB Group contacts listed on page 360 can always help you find a vacancy in your chosen area.

Our Internet address is
http://www.webscape.co.uk/farmaccom/

West Sussex

Sussex Weald, Rother & Arun Valleys & Sussex Downs

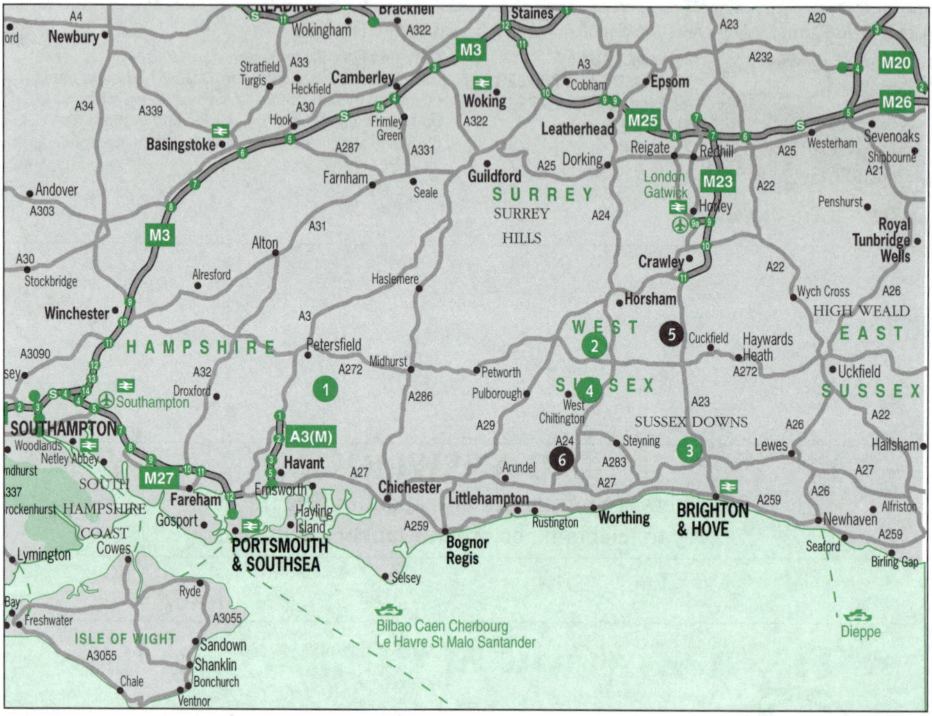

Key
- ① Bed & Breakfast
- ① Self-Catering
- ① B&B and SC
- ① Camping Barns
- ▲ Camping & Caravanning

The West Sussex coast stretches from historic Chichester and its harbour to Shoreham, taking in Bognor Regis, Littlehampton and Worthing and many picturesque smaller resorts on the way. Just inland there is the vast area of lovely downland with the South Downs Way and picturesque villages such as Storrington and Poynings waiting to be explored. West Sussex has a wealth of attractive towns: Midhurst, Horsham and East Grinstead, to name a few, and all surrounded by lush green countryside. There is history here, in Arundel's castle, Petworth House, glorious Goodwood and Fishbourne, site of the remains of a palace once ruled by a King Cogidubnus – really.

If you would like help in finding suitable farm accommodation, turn to the full listing of farm groups on pages 360 to 363 to find appropriate contact details for this area.

West Sussex   South & South East

Bed and Breakfast
(and evening meal)

Compton Farmhouse, Church Lane, Compton, Nr Chichester, West Sussex PO18 9HB

Mrs Melanie Bray
☎ 01705 631597
[BB] From £18–£20
Sleeps 6
Listed *Commended*

Children are especially welcome (half-price) at our old, flint farmhouse. We are 200 yards up a track from the village square, next door to the church and are bordered by fields and woods. Lovely walks and plenty to do in our enclosed, child-orientated garden. Large family bedroom, own bathroom and sitting/dining room with drink-making facilities, fridge, TV. Open Jan–Nov.

Goffsland Farm, Shipley, Horsham, West Sussex RH13 7BQ

Mrs Carol Liverton
☎/Fax 01403 730434
[BB] From £18–£20
EM From £8.50
Sleeps 5
Commended

A friendly welcome awaits you at our 17th century farmhouse on a working farm with sheep and dairy herd. Situated in the Sussex Weald central to Gatwick and the South coast. Family room has double bed and bunk beds with washbasin and tea/coffee-making facilities. Own bathroom with WC and own sitting/dining room with TV. Evening meals by arrangement. Open all year.

Manor Farm, Poynings, Nr Brighton, West Sussex BN45 7AG

Mrs Carol Revell
☎/Fax 01273 857371
[BB] From £22.50–£25
Sleeps 6
(8)
Commended

260-acre family run sheep/arable farm with charming old manor house resting quietly in a green valley under the South Downs. An area of outstanding natural beauty, ideal for riders, walkers, golfers, hang gliders and country lovers. Plenty of country pubs and eating houses nearby. A23 5 mins, Hickstead 10 mins, Gatwick 30 mins, Brighton and Hove 15 mins. Open Mar–Dec.

New House Farm, Broadford Bridge Road, West Chiltington, Nr Pulborough, West Sussex RH20 2LA

Alma Steele
☎ 01798 812215
Fax 01798 813209
[BB] From £20–£35
Sleeps 6
(12)
Commended

Listed 15th century farmhouse with oak beams and inglenook fireplace, in the centre of the village, close to local inns which provide good food. A new 18 hole golf course, open to non-members, is only ¼ mile away. Many places of historical interest in the area including Goodwood House, Petworth House, Parham House, Arundel Castle. Gatwick 35 minutes. En suite facilities and colour TV in bedrooms. Open all year.

Please mention **Stay on a Farm** when booking

South & South East *West Sussex*

Self-Catering

⑤ Black Cottage, c/o Newells Farm, Newells Lane, Lower Beeding, Horsham, West Sussex RH13 6LN

Vicky Storey
☎ 01403 891326
Fax 01403 891530
SC From £140–£260
Sleeps 4
🐕 🐎 🐈 ♨ 🎒
🔑🔑🔑 Approved

A delightful secluded cottage in the centre of a sheep and arable farm, with views to the South Downs. Surrounded by woods and lovely walks. Sleeps 4 in comfort. Recently modernised, it is 40 mins from Brighton, 20 mins from Gatwick, with fishing, golf and beautiful Sussex, Surrey and Kent gardens within easy reach. The ideal holiday cottage. Open all year.

⑥ Byre Cottages, c/o Sullington Manor Farm, Storrington, West Sussex RH20 4AE

Mrs G Kittle
☎/Fax 01903 745754
SC From £120–£350
Sleep 2–6
🐕 🐎 🐈 ♨ 🎒 🚲
🔑🔑🔑🔑 Commended

Mixed farm with many footpaths, including the South Downs Way, providing walks and beautiful views. The four cottages sleep 2, 4 or 6 and have been converted from stables and overlook a shared lawn and 17th century tithe barn. Outdoor pool with springboard and children's slide, tennis court and barbecue may be used by guests. Bike hire. Beaches 30 mins. London 1 hour by train. Many historic houses, castles and gardens.

THE 1000+ BUREAU MEMBERS OFFER A UNIQUE LINK TO CUSTOMERS ACROSS THE UK

All Bureau members belong to a local Group. Each member can refer you to an equally high quality member within the Group... or across the UK: England, Northern Ireland, Scotland, Wales.

STAY ON A FARM GIFT TOKENS

If you have enjoyed your Stay on a Farm, why not treat your friends and relatives to *Stay on a Farm* gift tokens? Available from the Bureau office (tel: 01203 696909), they can be redeemed against accommodation and are accepted by the majority of farms (see Index). Please check when booking to avoid disappointment.

East Sussex

Ashdown Forest, High Weald & Sussex Downs

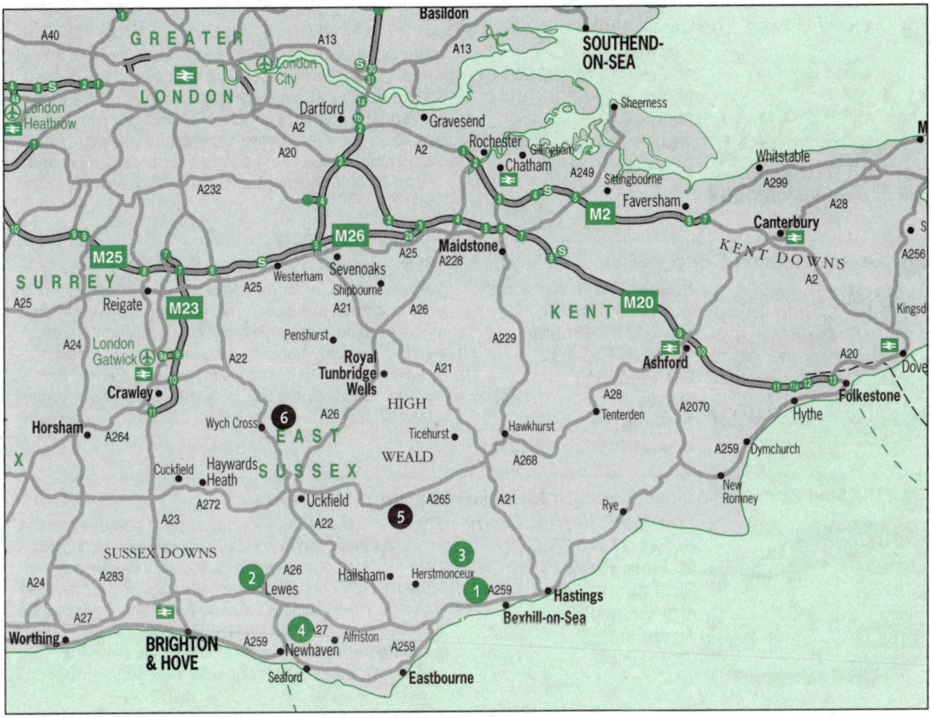

Key

 Bed & Breakfast
 Self-Catering
 B&B and SC
 Camping Barns
Camping & Caravanning

'Sussex by the Sea' conjures up the famous resorts of Brighton and Eastbourne, each of which can easily fill a day out, having so much to offer. But don't forget the lesser-known delights of the East Sussex coast such as Cuckmere Haven in the Seven Sisters Country Park, or picturesque Rye, just inland. For a spot of culture you can't beat Glyndebourne, or visit exquisitely-painted Charleston, once home of the Bloomsbury set. Then there's magnificent Sheffield Park, or Battle for a bit of 1066 and all that. Give the children a turn – they'll love chugging through the glorious countryside on the Bluebell Railway or playing Pooh sticks at A.A. Milne's Hartfield in the Ashdown Forest.

If you would like help in finding suitable farm accommodation, turn to the full listing of farm groups on pages 360 to 363 to find appropriate contact details for this area.

South & South East   East Sussex

Bed and Breakfast
(and evening meal)

① Moonshill Farm, The Green, Ninfield, Battle, East Sussex TN33 9LH

Mrs June Ive
☎/Fax 01424 892645
BB From £17.50–£20
Sleeps 6
⛨(4) ♁ ⚘ ⚭ ♣ ☘ ♨ ⚜ ⓔ
♣♣ *Commended*

In the heart of the '1066 Country' in the centre of Ninfield opposite pub. Farmhouse in 10 acres of garden, orchard, stables. Enjoy beautiful walks, golf and riding arranged. Comfortable rooms, 3 en suite, CH and electric fires, hospitality tray, TV, lounge, parking and garage, babysitting service. Every comfort in our safe, quiet and peaceful home. Reduced rates for weekly bookings. Open Jan–Nov.

② Ousedale House, Offham, Lewes, East Sussex BN7 3QF

Roland & Brenda Gough
☎ 01273 478680
Fax 01273 486510
BB From £24–£32
EM From £13
Sleeps 6
⚘ ⓔ ♣ ⓔ
♣♣ *Highly Commended*

You are warmly welcomed to our spacious Victorian house with its garden and panoramic views of the river valley. We are retired farmers who like music (Glyndebourne nearby/ speciality hampers prepared) and cooking, and are enthusiastic WI members/marketeers. Central for touring 'Sussex by the Sea'. Courtesy car – Lewes station. Open all year.

③ The Stud Farm, Bodle Street Green, Nr Hailsham, East Sussex BN27 4RJ

Philippa & Richard Gentry
☎/Fax 01323 833201
BB From £20–£25
EM From £11 (by arrangement)
Sleeps 6
⚘ ⚘ ♣ ⚜
♣♣ *Commended*

70 acre sheep and cattle farm situated in peaceful surroundings and beautiful countryside, ideal for walking. 8 miles from sea, Eastbourne, Hastings, South Downs in easy reach. Upstairs, family unit of double bedded room/twin bedded room, both with handbasins, and bathroom. Downstairs twin bedded room with shower, toilet, handbasin en suite. All bedrooms with colour TV and tea/coffee-making facilities. Guests' sitting room, colour TV. Sunroom. Open all year.

④ Stud Farm House, Telscombe Village, Lewes, East Sussex BN7 3HZ

Tim & Nina Armour
☎/Fax 01273 302486
BB From £19.50–£24.50
Sleeps 6
⛨(10) ✗ ⚜ ♣ ⚘
♣♣ *Commended*

Family-run working 300-acre sheep farm and 17th century house in quiet hamlet on the South Downs Way in Glyndebourne and Bloomsbury area. Central for touring – Gatwick 30 mins, Brighton 15 mins, London 1 hour by train, Newhaven/Dieppe Sealink Ferries 10 mins. Guests' own 'unique' lounge. Cosy and comfortable, a relaxing break with a family atmosphere. Open Feb–Dec.

LET THE TELEPHONE RING!
Some farmhouses are big places. Let the telephone ring
long enough to give the owner time to answer it.

East Sussex   South & South East

Self-Catering

Boring House Farm, Vines Cross, Heathfield, East Sussex TN21 9AS

Mrs Anne Reed
☎ 01435 812285
SC From £130–£190
Sleeps 6
Commended

Peaceful farm cottage on sheep and beef farm. Marvellous views and walks, fishing available. Traditional local, good atmosphere/food in easy walking distance. Many beautiful places to visit. Beach within 15 miles. Accommodation (portion of farmhouse) comprises utility room, hall, WC, kitchen, dining room, sitting room, 3 bedrooms, 1 with shower, 1 with washbasin, bathroom and WC. Large garden. Open Mar–Nov.

2 High Weald Cottages, Chelwood Farm, Nutley, c/o Sheffield Park Farm, Nr Uckfield, E Sussex TN22 3QR

Mrs Nicky Howe
☎ 01825 790235/790267
Fax 01825 790151
SC From £200–£400
Sleeps 5 + cot
Commended

Picturesque semi-detached farm cottage with garden on dairy farm adjacent Ashdown Forest. Comfortable accommodation comprises 1 double, 1 twin, 1 single room, bathroom, WC, sitting room (log fire, colour TV, phone), kitchen (fridge/freezer, auto washing machine, tumble dryer, electric cooker). Close Sheffield Park Gardens, Bluebell Railway. Easy reach Downs and coast. Cot/high chair available. Beds made up. No cot linen provided; towels on request. Open all year.

STAY ON A FARM GIFT TOKENS

If you have enjoyed your Stay on a Farm, why not treat your friends and relatives to *Stay on a Farm* gift tokens? Available from the Bureau office (tel: 01203 696909), they can be redeemed against accommodation and are accepted by the majority of farms (see Index). Please check when booking to avoid disappointment.

FOLLOW THE COUNTRY CODE

Leave nothing but footprints,
Take nothing but photographs,
Kill nothing but time!

England's West Country

Farm entries in this regional section are listed under those counties shown in green on the key map. Look at the index below to find on which page the entries start. You will see that we have listed the counties geographically so that you can turn more easily to find farms in neighbouring areas.

At the start of each county section is a detailed map with numbered symbols indicating the location of each farm. Different symbols denote different types of accommodation; see the key below each county map. Farm entries are listed alphabetically under type of accommodation. Some farms offer more than one type of accommodation and therefore have more than one entry.

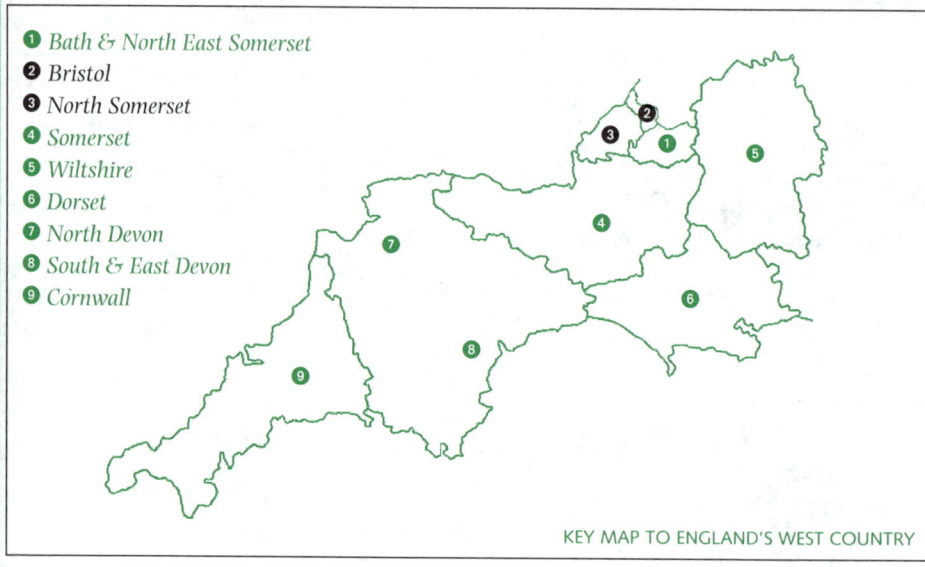

❶ Bath & North East Somerset
❷ Bristol
❸ North Somerset
❹ Somerset
❺ Wiltshire
❻ Dorset
❼ North Devon
❽ South & East Devon
❾ Cornwall

KEY MAP TO ENGLAND'S WEST COUNTRY

Bath & North East Somerset *page 237*
Bristol & Kennet & Avon Canal

Somerset *page 241*
Exmoor National Park, Quantock Hills & Mendip Hills

Wiltshire *page 251*
Stonehenge, Avebury, Wiltshire White Horses & the Ridge Way

Dorset *page 258*
Cranborne Chase, Hardy Country & Dorset Coast

North Devon *page 266*
Exmoor National Park, North Devon Coast & Taw & Torridge Valleys

South & East Devon *page 277*
Dartmoor National Park & South & East Devon Coasts

Cornwall *page 293*
Bodmin Moor, North & South Cornwall Coasts, Land's End & St Michael's Mount

Bath & North East Somerset
Bristol & Kennet & Avon Canal

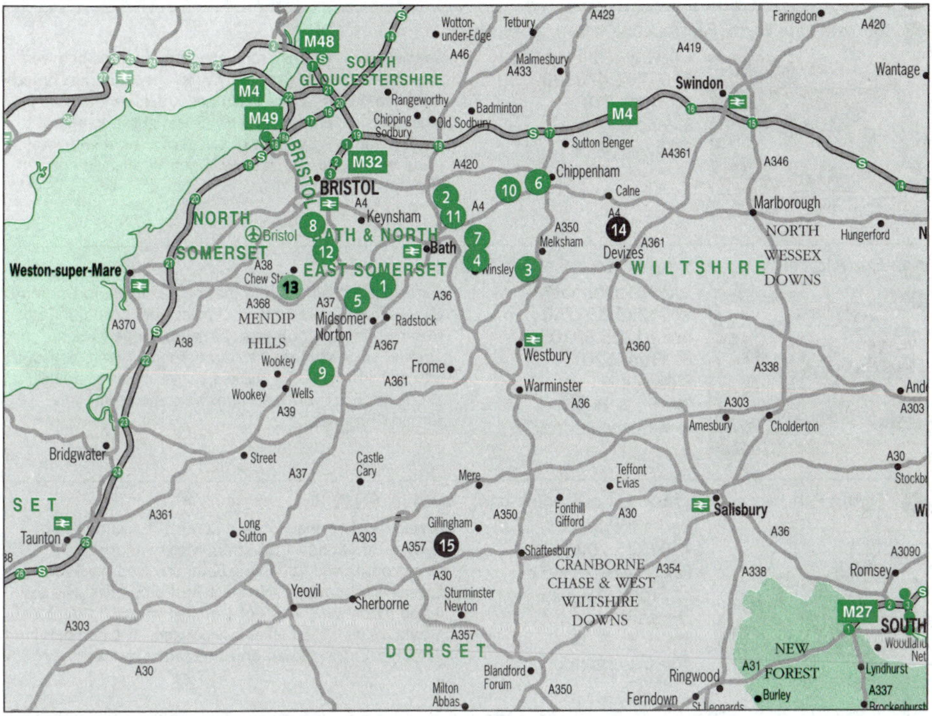

Key
- **1** Bed & Breakfast
- **1** Self-Catering
- **1** B&B and SC
- **1** Camping Barns
- **1** Camping & Caravanning

Though modern in name, this county has a wealth of history. Its namesake, the beautiful city of Bath, is a World Heritage site famed for its Roman remains, in the shape of the fascinating Roman Baths, and elegant Georgian architecture. The whole city is alive with unusual shops, street entertainment and pavement cafes. Around Bath, the lovely countryside rolling away to the Mendip Hills is just as noteworthy as the city attractions. Picturesque villages with charming country pubs are too numerous to mention. You can walk or cycle the newly-restored Kennet and Avon Canal, sail the lakes at Blagdon and Chew Valley or, if that sounds too energetic, try the local cider on one of our farms.

If you would like help in finding suitable farm accommodation, turn to the full listing of farm groups on pages 360 to 363 to find appropriate contact details for this area.

West Country — Bath & North East Somerset

Bed and Breakfast
(and evening meal)

① Barrow Vale Farm, Farmborough, Bath, BA3 1BL

Cherilyn Langley
☎ 01761 470300
BB From £18
Sleeps 6
⌕(5) ✄ ♁ ■
♨ ☙ Commended

Barrow Vale is a family-run dairy farm, situated between the historic cities of Bath and Wells. The farmhouse, which has been comfortably modernised, offers central heating, well furnished en suite bedrooms and guests lounge with TV. It is within easy reach of places of interest with local pubs and restaurants close by. Open all year (except Christmas and New Year).

② Fairfield Farm, Upper Wraxall, Chippenham, Wiltshire SN14 7AG

Julie McDonough
☎ 01225 891750
Fax 01225 891050
BB From £20
Sleeps 4
⌕ ✄ ♁ ■ ☉
♨ ☙ Commended

Fairfield is a friendly family farmhouse in Beaufort country, 8 miles from Georgian Bath, 3 miles from beautiful Castle Combe on route for Bristol (12 miles). Large garden, wonderful views. 1 double/family room, 1 twin, both with private bathrooms, TV and tea/coffee-making facilities. Excellent pubs nearby. A warm welcome awaits you. Closed Christmas.

③ Frying Pan Farm, Broughton Gifford, Melksham, Wiltshire SN12 8LL

Barbara Pullen
☎ 01225 702343
Fax 01225 793652
BB From £19–£25
Sleeps 4
⌕(2) ✄ ♁ ■
♨ ☙ Commended

A warm welcome awaits you at our 17th century farmhouse situated 1 mile from Melksham making it ideally positioned for visiting Bath, Bradford-on-Avon, Lacock and numerous National Trust properties. The cosy accommodation consists of 1 double en suite, 1 double/ 1 twin, all with tea/coffee facilities and TV. Good pub food in village 1 mile. Closed Christmas and New Year.

④ Hatt Farm, Old Jockey, Box, Nr Bath, Wiltshire SN13 8DJ

Mrs Carol Pope
☎ 01225 742989
Fax 01225 742779
BB From £20–£22.50
Sleeps 4
⌕ ✄ ■ ♁ ☉
♨ ☙ Commended

Extremely comfortable Georgian farmhouse in peaceful surroundings. Scrumptious breakfasts served overlooking beautiful countryside views. What could be nicer than sitting by a log fire in winter or enjoying the garden in summer? Lovely walks and good golfing nearby. Ideal for touring Wiltshire and the Cotswolds yet only 15 mins' drive to Bath. One twin with en suite shower, one double/family with private bathroom, both with tea/coffee. CH. Guests' lounge. Closed Christmas and New Year.

⑤ Home Farm, Farrington Gurney, Bristol BS39 6UB

Tish and Andy Jeffery
☎/Fax 01761 452287
BB From £15–£30
Sleeps 6
⌕ ✄ ■ ♁ ✶
♨ ☙ Commended

Our beautifully refurbished 17th century farmhouse and 230-acre mixed farm is set on the northern edge of the Mendips. We offer a friendly welcome and delicious homemade breakfast. One double with four-poster, one four-bedded family room, both en-suite with full facilities. Lounge with woodburner, lovely garden. We are well placed for Bath, Wells, Cheddar, Longleat. Golf course next door. Open Mar–Nov.

Bath & North East Somerset — West Country

Home Farm, Harts Lane, Biddestone, Chippenham, Wilts SN14 7DQ ⑥

Ian & Audrey Smith
☎/Fax 01249 714475
BB From £20–£22.50
Sleeps 6
Commended

A warm welcome awaits you in this 17th century farmhouse on a family-run working mixed farm. Set in beautiful Biddestone just a stroll across village green from the pub. Ideally situated for Bath, Castle Combe and Lacock, Stonehenge, Avebury, Longleat, etc. Both rooms have colour TV, tea and coffee; one en suite, the other has private bathroom. Open all year.

Manor Farm, Wadswick, Box, Corsham, Wiltshire SN13 8JB ⑦

Carolyn Barton
☎ 01225 810700
Fax 01225 810733
BB From £22.50–£25
Sleeps 6
Highly Commended

Visit our arable and horse farm nestling in the quiet hamlet of Wadswick. We are only 7 miles from Bath yet close to Lacock and other beautiful villages. Our 16th century farmhouse has large, spacious rooms, all en suite with tea/coffee making facilities and colour TV. Stabling and riding by arrangement. Open Mar–Nov.

The Model Farm, Norton Malreward, Pensford, Bristol BS39 4HA ⑧

Margaret Hasell
☎ 01275 832144
BB From £16–£20
Sleeps 6
Commended

The farmhouse is situated 2 miles off the A37 in a peaceful hamlet, nestling under the Dundry Hills. A working arable and beef farm in easy reach of Bristol, Bath, and many other interesting places. The accommodation consists of 1 family room and 1 double room, both en suite. Guests' lounge and dining room. Open all year except Christmas and New Year.

Pantiles, Bathway, Chewton Mendip, Nr Bath BA3 4NS ⑨

Pat Hellard
☎ 01761 241519
BB From £18–£22
Sleeps 6
Highly Commended

Delightful house with views over Mendip countryside. Sample the locally baked bread and free range eggs. Ideal base for visits to Bath, Wells, Cheddar, Glastonbury. We offer 3 rooms all with private facilities, colour TV and hospitality trays. Early booking advised. Open all year.

Pickwick Lodge Farm, Guyers Lane, Corsham, Wiltshire SN13 0PS ⑩

Gill Stafford
☎ 01249 712207
Fax 01249 701904
BB From £20
Sleeps 6
Highly Commended

Enjoy a stay at our beautiful home set in wonderful countryside where you can see rabbits, pheasant and occasionally deer. Relax in our garden having started the day with a hearty delicious breakfast. Local produce used when possible. Bath, NT properties, Corsham Court and many interesting villages nearby. Two well appointed and tastefully furnished rooms with en suite/private facilities, hospitality tray, home made biscuits. Closed Christmas and New Year.

Saltbox Farm, Drewetts Mill Lane, Box, Corsham, Wiltshire SN13 8PT ⑪

Mary Gregory
☎ 01225 742608
BB From £17.50–£20
Sleeps 4
Commended

Mary and Tony invite you to relax in their 18th century farmhouse surrounded by the unspoilt Box Valley, offering scenic walks in a wildlife and conservation area. Centrally situated for touring the West Country and Bath. One double room with en suite shower, one twin/family room with guests' bathroom, both with tea/coffee. Visitors lounge/diner with colour TV, CH. Special rates for 3/4 day breaks. Open Feb–Dec.

West Country   Bath & North East Somerset

12 Valley Farm, Sandy Lane, Stanton Drew, Nr. Bristol BS39 4EL

Mrs Doreen Keel
☎ 01275 332723
[BB] From £18–£22
Sleeps 6
🐎 🍴 🚗 🧳 🐎
♥♥ Highly Commended

Modern farmhouse situated on the edge of an ancient village near the river Chew with Druid Stones and many footpaths to walk. Near the Chew Valley Lakes renowned for trout fishing and in easy reach of Bath, Bristol, Wells and Cheddar. Stanton Drew is off A368 Bath to Weston-super-Mare road or the B3130 road. There are 2 rooms with double beds each with wash basins and coffee/tea making facilities. 2 en suite and 1 private bathroom. Open all year (except Christmas).

13 Woodbarn Farm, Denny Lane, Chew Magna, Bristol BS40 8SZ

Mrs Judi Hasell
☎/Fax 01275 332599
[BB] From £19–£23
Sleeps 6
🐎(3) 🍴 🧳
♥♥ Commended

Woodbarn is a working mixed farm. 5 minutes from Chew Valley Lake. Chew Magna is a large village with pretty cottages, Georgian houses and is central for touring. There are two en suite bedrooms, one double and one family, both with tea trays. Guests' lounge and dining room. Open all year except Christmas and New Year.

Self-Catering

14 Home Farm Barn and The Derby, Home Farm, Heddington, Nr Calne, Wiltshire SN11 0PL

Mrs Janet Tyler
☎/Fax 01380 850523
[SC] From £150–£380
Sleeps 2/5
🐎 🎋 🧳 ⊛
🏠🏠🏠🏠 Commended

Home Farm is a large dairy and arable farm in village centre with its own private lake and offering unbeatable downland walks with panoramic views (SSSI). Riding school and golf course adjoin the farm. Also bungalow-style stable conversion set in idyllic courtyard. Sleeps 2. Colour brochure. E mail: W.S.Tyler@farmline.com.uk

15 Lois Barns, Lois Farm, Horsington, Templecombe, Somerset BA8 0EW

Paul & Penny Constant
☎/Fax 01963 370496
[SC] From £189–£399
Sleeps 4/6
🐎 🎋 🧳
🏠🏠🏠🏠 Commended

In the heart of the Blackmore Vale, Lois Barns are situated on a small sheep farm surrounded by meadow fields. Light and spacious, both barns have south-facing patios, beams in the bedrooms and are fully equipped. CH, electricity and linen are all inclusive. Walk, bike, drive or simply enjoy the quiet of our rural landscape. Phone/fax for a brochure. Open all year.

13 Stable & Denny Cottages, Woodbarn Farm, Denny Lane, Chew Magna, Bristol BS40 8SZ

Mrs Judi Hasell
☎/Fax 01275 332599
[SC] From £220–400
Sleeps 2/6
♿ 🐎 🍴 🧳
🏠🏠🏠 – 🏠🏠🏠🏠
Highly Commended

Brand new stone-built barn conversion on farm, close to Chew Valley Lake, 30 minutes from Bath, Wells, Bristol, Cheddar. Stable Cottage, just for two, has its own patio. Denny Cottage, for 6, has 2 bedrooms, 2 bathrooms, lounge, kitchen/diner and is suitable for disabled guests. Beautiful countryside, peaceful location. Short breaks available. Open all year.

Somerset

Exmoor National Park, Quantock Hills & Mendip Hills

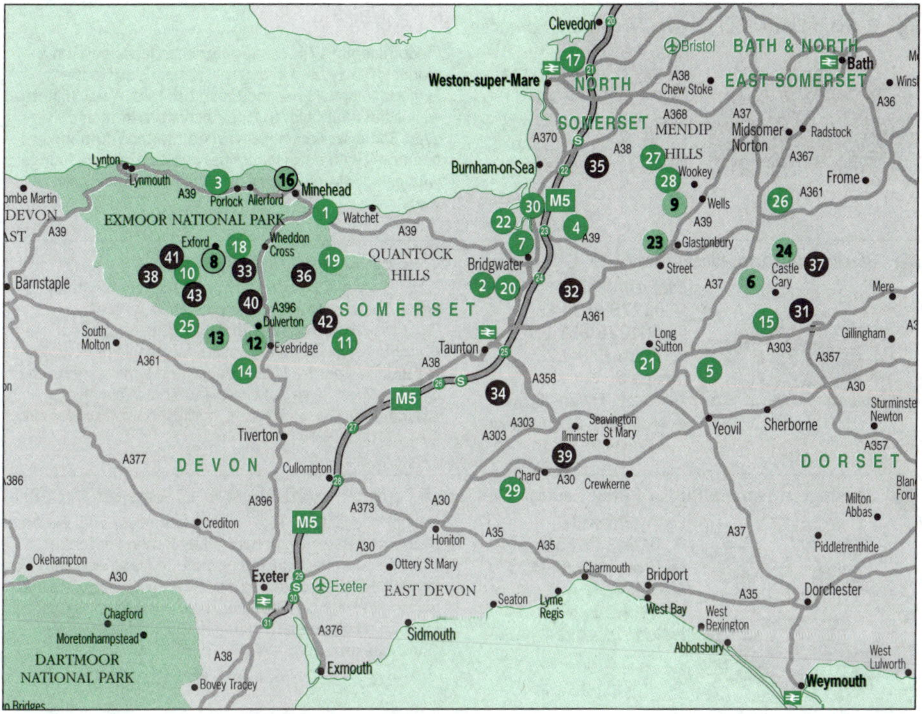

Key

- **1** Bed & Breakfast
- **1** Self-Catering
- **1** B&B and SC
- **1** Camping Barns
- **1** Camping & Caravanning

Originally named by the Saxons as the 'Summer Land', this is a county full of contrasts from ancient gorges to the waterways of the Somerset Levels. We have a wealth of National Trust properties with beautiful buildings and fragrant gardens. The energetic can go caving, cycle or ramble through our wonderful countryside and Exmoor National Park. In our rural museums you can learn about traditional local crafts such as willow basket weaving and paper, cheese and cider making. Children will thrill to the adventure of the legendary Witch of Wookey Hole and the whole family will enjoy a 'bucket and spade' day at one of our coastal resorts, rounded off with a delicious cream tea!

If you would like help in finding suitable farm accommodation, turn to the full listing of farm groups on pages 360 to 363 to find appropriate contact details for this area.

West Country   Somerset

Bed and Breakfast
(and evening meal)

① Binham Farm, Old Cleeve, Minehead, Somerset TA24 6HX

Mrs S Bigwood
☎/Fax 01984 640222
BB From £17–£20
Sleeps 6
🐎 🐕 ⚜ 人 ⚔ ♨ ■
👑👑 Commended

Predominantly 17th-century Jacobean farmhouse on a working family farm in an idyllic setting close to the Exmoor National Park and Quantock Hills. A few minutes walk across our fields to Blue Anchor sea front and the West Somerset Steam Railway. Comfortably furnished bedrooms with en suite facilities available, private lounge with colour TV, mediaeval dining hall. Full CH. Open all year.

② Blackmore Farm, Blackmore Lane, Cannington, Bridgwater, Somerset TA5 2NE

Mrs Ann Dyer
☎ 01278 653442
Fax 01278 653427
BB From £20–£25
Sleeps 8
🐎 🐕 ⚜ 🐕 ■ ♨ ◉
👑👑 Highly Commended

A tastefully restored and furnished 14th century manor house, set in rolling countryside with views to the Quantock Hills. Rooms with oak bedsteads and four poster beds, all en suite. Facilities for disabled guests. As featured in *Country Living* magazine. Within easy reach of Exmoor, West Somerset coast, Taunton, Wells and Glastonbury. Open all year. E-mail:dyerfarm@aol.com.uk

③ Bossington Farm & Birds of Prey Centre, West Lynch Farm, Allerford, Nr Porlock, Somerset TA24 8HJ

Cathy Powell
☎ 01643 862816
BB From £22.50–£25
Sleeps 4
🐎 🐕 ⚜ ■ 🐕 ♨ ◉
Listed Approved

Delightful character 15th century farmhouse with exposed beams and spacious rooms in quiet location at foot of wooded coombes on Exmoor, close to Minehead and Porlock. Ideal for birdwatchers, country lovers, riding and walking in National Trust area. Free entry to animal centre. Exmoor activity breaks arranged. Open all year, except Christmas day.

④ Brookhayes Farm, Bell Lane, Cossington, Bridgwater, Somerset TA7 8LR

Mrs Susan Bell
☎/Fax 01278 722559
BB From £20
Sleeps 6
🐎 🐕 ⚜ ■
Listed Commended

Working dairy farm with outstanding views over moors and hills. Situated between Bridgwater and Glastonbury on the edge of lovely village of Cossington. All rooms en suite plus family room. Large garden. Also good fishing nearby. Good pub within walking distance for evening meal – always a warm welcome. Open all year.

⑤ Cary Fitzpaine, Yeovil, Somerset BA22 8JB

Mrs Susie Crang
☎ 01458 223250
Fax 01458 223372
BB From £18–£20
EM From £9
Sleeps 6
🐎 🐕 ⚜ ⊞ ■ 🐕 ♨
👑👑 Commended

Gracious Georgian manor farmhouse set in two acres of gardens on 600-acre working farm comprising of sheep, cattle, horses and arable. There is a river running through the farm with an abundance of wildlife. The bedrooms are large and attractively decorated, all en suite. Peaceful, relaxed setting. Open all year. E-mail:acrang@aol.com.uk

Somerset — West Country

Clanville Manor, Castle Cary, Somerset BA7 7PJ

Mrs Sally Snook
☎ 01963 350124/350313
Fax 01963 350313
Mobile 0966 512732
BB £17.50–£25
Sleeps 6
Listed *Highly Commended*

Explore Somerset, Bath, Wells and Glastonbury from an elegant Georgian farmhouse on a working dairy farm. Only 2 miles from Castle Cary, with riverbank walks. Outdoor pool in summer. En suite and family room available and all rooms have colour TV and tea/coffee-making facilities. Safe parking. Full CH. Open all year.
E-mail: clanville@aol.com

Cokerhurst Farm, 87 Wembdon Hill, Bridgwater, Somerset TA6 7QA

Derrick and Diana Chappell
☎/Fax 01278 422330
Mobile 0850 692065
BB From £21–£24
Sleeps 6
Highly Commended

We would like to welcome you into our home, a 16th century Somerset longhouse. We have 3 pretty en suite bedrooms, all with comfortable beds, TV, CH, tea/coffee facilities. A good hearty breakfast is served to you in the dining room overlooking the garden and lake beyond. Good central location for exploring the 'Cider' county of Somerset. Open all year except Christmas.

Cutthorne Farm, Luckwell Bridge, Wheddon Cross, Somerset TA24 7EW

Ann Durbin
☎/Fax 01643 831255
BB From £23
EM From £14
Sleeps 6
Highly Commended

Tucked away in the heart of Exmoor, Cutthorne is truly 'off the beaten track'. Share our peaceful home overlooking private trout lakes and valley. The pretty bedrooms all have bathrooms, and one even a four-poster bed. A choice of traditional farmhouse fayre is served in the sunny dining room, using local meat and organic vegetables. Open all year except Christmas.

Double-Gate Farm, Godney, Nr Wells, Somerset BA5 1RX

Mrs H Millard
☎ 01458 832217
Fax 01458 835612
BB From £20
Sleeps 8
Highly Commended

Situated on the banks of the River Sheppey, this lovely old Georgian farmhouse offers – comfortable guests' lounge, games room and en suite bedrooms with tea/coffee facilities, colour TVs and CH. Guest launderette. Lovely flower garden, outdoor breakfast in summer. Ideal base for touring, cycling, birdwatching, etc. Evening meals available in nearby village inn. AA QQQ and RAC acclaimed. Open Feb–Nov. E-mail: hilary@millard.webscape.co.uk

Edgcott House, Exford, Nr Minehead, Somerset TA24 7QG

Gillian Lamble
☎/Fax 01643 831495
BB From £20–£23
EM £13
Sleeps 6
Commended

Country house of great charm and character amidst beautiful countryside in the heart of Exmoor National Park, ¼ mile from village of Exford. Peaceful and quiet. All bedrooms have basins, private bathroom available. Excellent home cooking using fresh local produce is served in the elegant 'longroom' with its unique murals. Large garden. Comfortable, friendly centre for relaxing, walking, riding and fishing. Open all year.

Greenway Farm, Wiveliscombe, Taunton, Somerset TA4 2UA

Mrs M A Woollaston
☎ 01984 623359
Fax 01984 624051
BB From £17
EM From £7
Sleeps 6
Commended

Comfort with peace and quiet. For those who prefer action, help us on the farm or take part in a country pursuit – excellent walks, rides, game or coarse fishing can be arranged and the coast is close. Good food, home-prepared menus, comfortable lounge, excellent views. Facilities for children. Open all year.

West Country   Somerset

12 Highercombe, Dulverton, Exmoor, Somerset TA22 9PT

Sarah Wates
☎ 01398 323451
BB From £20–£35
EM From £10
Sleeps 6/10
♛ Commended

Relax at historic Highercombe, of 14th century origin, and enjoy this beautiful, spacious country home heading the Barle Valley. Peacefully set in 8 acres of formal gardens and paddocks within the Exmoor National Park, adjacent to open moorland, Dulverton 2½ miles. Quality bed & breakfast. En suite bathrooms available. Also self-catering. Stabling if required. Open all year except Christmas.

13 Highercombe Farm, Dulverton, Somerset TA22 9PT

Abigail Humphrey
☎/Fax 01398 323616
BB From £20–£25
EM £15
Sleeps 6
♛ Highly Commended

A 450-acre working farm on the edge of the moor. We have spectacular 60-mile views and red deer can often be seen from the farmhouse. Pretty en suite rooms with tea/coffee facilities and colour TV. Large guest lounge with inglenook and bay window where breakfast is served. A relaxed atmosphere, a friendly welcome, personal service and quality food. Complimentary farm tours. Open Mar–Nov. E-mail: abigail@highercombe.demon.co.uk

14 Higher Langridge Farm, Exebridge, Dulverton, Somerset TA22 9RR

Gill Summers
☎/Fax 01398 323999
BB From £20–£25
EM From £12.50
Sleeps 6
Listed Commended

Come and enjoy comfort, good food and warm hospitality in our 17th century farmhouse. Our working farm is set amidst superbly peaceful countryside on the edge of Exmoor where red deer and other wildlife abound. Most bedrooms have en suite/private bathrooms and all have tea/coffee-making facilities. Central heating throughout. Open all year.

15 Hill Ash Farm, Woolston, North Cadbury, Yeovil, Somerset BA22 7BL

Mrs Jane Pearse
☎/Fax 01963 440332
BB From £20–£24
Sleeps 6
♛ Highly Commended

This lovely thatched house, a listed building constructed in 1766, is set in a beautiful hamlet of south Somerset 1½ miles from A303. It is an ideal centre for visiting the many tourist attractions and NT gardens in Somerset and Dorset. 2 double en suite rooms and 2 singles, all with tea/coffee-making facilities, full central heating. Open Mar–Nov.

16 Hindon Farm, nr Minehead, Somerset TA24 8SH

Penny & Roger Webber
☎/Fax 01643 705244
BB From £20–£22
EM From £15
Sleeps 6
Listed Commended

Escape to our working farm in peaceful Exmoor valley (Minehead 3 miles, Selworthy 1 mile for cream teas!) Wander our acres and adjoining heather moors to coast path. Relax by the stream while ducks dabble and donkeys dawdle. 18th century farmhouse with 20th century hospitality (own produce). Featured on TV *Getaways* and in *Which? Best B&B* and *Country Living*. Brochure.

17 Icelton Farm, Wick-St-Lawrence, Weston-super-Mare, North Somerset BS22 7YJ

Mrs Elizabeth Parsons
☎ 01934 515704
BB From £16–£18
Sleeps 5
♛ Commended

Icelton is a working dairy/sheep farm, just off the M5 (jct21). Ideal for touring Wells, Cheddar, and Mendip Hills. This listed farmhouse offers double room with H/C, family room with H/C and shower. Tea/coffee-making facilities. Oak-beamed dining room and lounge, both with inglenook fireplaces. English breakfast. Good pubs and restaurants close at hand. No dogs. Open Mar–Nov.

Somerset   *West Country*

Larcombe Foot, Winsford, Nr Minehead, Somerset TA24 7HS — 18

Mrs Val Vicary
☎ 01643 851306
BB From £20
EM From £12.50
Sleeps 4
⛔(8) 🐕 ♿
♣ ♣ Highly Commended

Larcombe Foot is an attractive period house set in the beautiful, tranquil Exe Valley. Guests' comfort within a warm, happy atmosphere is paramount. A pretty garden to relax in, superb walks on the doorstep, Larcombe Foot makes an ideal base for exploring Exmoor and the scenic North Devon coast – 12 miles. Open Mar–Nov.

Little Brendon Hill Farm, Wheddon Cross, Nr Minehead, Somerset TA24 7BG — 19

Mrs Shelagh Maxwell
☎/Fax 01643 841556
BB From £19–£21
EM From £14
Sleeps 6
⛔(10) ✗ 🐕 ♿ ♣
♣ ♣ Highly Commended

Enjoy a stay with us in our beautifully appointed farmhouse set in the peace and tranquillity of the Exmoor National Park. Three lovely en suite rooms with colour television. Log fires, cosy candlelit dinners. Central heating. Non-smoking. Short stay or long, a truly relaxing place to pursue country pastimes. You will be most welcome. Open all year except Christmas.

Lower Clavelshay Farm, Clavelshay, North Petherton, Bridgwater, Somerset TA6 6PJ — 20

Sue Milverton
☎/Fax 01278 662347
BB From £16–£20
EM From £8
Sleeps 6
⛔ 🐕 ✗ 👶 ♿ ♣
Listed Approved

Badgers, buzzards and beautiful countryside surround our traditional 17th century farmhouse on 260-acre dairy farm. Spacious, comfortable rooms, beautiful views, peace and quiet. Ideally situated for exploring the Quantock Hills, Exmoor, Somerset Levels and coast. Close to Hestercombe Gardens. Warm welcome and relaxed family atmosphere. Open all year.

Lower Farm, Kingweston, Somerton, Somerset TA11 6BA — 21

David & Jane Sedgman
☎ 01458 223237
Fax 01458 223276
BB From £20–£22
Sleeps 5
⛔(6) ✗ 🐕 ♿ ♣
♣ Commended

This Grade II listed farmhouse, sited in a conservation area and overlooking a wide stretch of open country, was formerly a coaching inn and retains many of its original features. The attractive rooms are excellently equipped to ensure your every comfort. Well placed to visit Wells, Glastonbury and Bath. Good country pubs nearby. AA QQQ and RAC Acclaimed. Open all year except Christmas and New Year.
E-mail: lowerfarm@kingweston.demon.co.uk

Moxhill Farmhouse, Combwich, Bridgwater, Somerset TA5 2PN — 22

Carol Venner
☎ 01278 652285
Fax 01278 653942
mobile 0802 382870
BB From £23–£28
EM From £9.50
Sleeps 12
⛔ 🐕 ✗ 👶 ♣
♣ ♣ Highly Commended

Relax in the peaceful countryside surrounding our 17th century farmhouse. Explore Somerset by day and then indulge yourself at night in our elegant licensed dining room. All our spacious rooms are en suite and have those little extras that will make your stay all the more memorable. Open all year.
E-mail: nigel.verner@ukonline.co.uk

New House Farm, Burtle Road, Westhay, Nr Glastonbury, Somerset BA6 9TT — 23

Mrs M Bell
☎/Fax 01458 860238
BB From £20–£22
EM From £11
Sleeps 5
⛔ 🐕 ✗ ♣
♣ ♣ Highly Commended

Large Victorian farmhouse on dairy farm. Central for touring Wells, Cheddar, etc. Accommodation comprises of double room and 1 family room both en suite with colour TV, tea/coffee facilities, hair drier, etc. Lounge with colour TV, separate dining room, also sun lounge, CH throughout, plenty of local fishing. Open all year except Christmas and New Year.

West Country   Somerset

24 Orchard Farm, Cockhill, Castle Cary, Somerset BA7 7NY

Olive Boyer
☎/Fax 01963 350418
BB From £17–£20
Sleeps 5
🐎 🐕 ♻ ♿ ⊚
🌼 🐚 Commended

Our pleasure is your comfort. We welcome you with tea and homemade cakes in the conservatory or garden. Quiet, beautiful surroundings. Two en suite bedrooms with radio, alarm clock, tea/coffee. Newspapers at breakfast. Bath, Longleat, Stourhead, Yeovilton Air and Haynes Motor Museums close, also many NT properties. Castle Cary with many shops and eating places 1½ miles. Open all year.

25 Springfield Farm, Ashwick Lane, Dulverton, Somerset TA22 9QD

Mrs Patricia Vellacott
☎/Fax 01398 323722
BB From £19–£24
EM From £12.50
Sleeps 6
🐎 🐕 ⚹ ♻
🌼 🐚 Commended

A warm welcome awaits you at our 270-acre working farm. Peacefully situated between Tarr Steps and Dulverton, overlooking the River Barle valley with magnificent moorland and woodland views. Comfortable accommodation and delicious farmhouse meals. All bedrooms have en suite or private facilities and beverage trays. Guests' sitting room with colour TV. Large dining room leading onto patio and garden. Garage on request. Open Easter–Nov.

26 Temple House Farm, Doulting, Shepton Mallet BA4 4RQ

Mrs Veronica Reakes
☎ 01749 880294
Fax 01749 880688
BB From £22
EM From £10
Sleeps 6
🐎(3) ⚹ 🚗 ♻ ♿
🌼 🐚 Commended

Temple House Farm is a family-run dairy farm situated on the eastern end of the Mendip Hills. A 400-year old listed farmhouse with all facilities, set in a rural area within easy reach of the Royal Bath and West Showground, Wells, Bath and many local attractions. All fresh produce used, hearty evening meals also available. Open all year.

27 Tor Farm Guesthouse, Nyland, Cheddar, Somerset BS27 3UD

Mr & Mrs Ladd
☎/Fax 01934 743710
BB From £17.50–£22
EM From £10
Sleeps 16
🐎 ⊞ ♻
🐚 Highly Commended

Our working farm is situated three miles from Cheddar in open countryside. The house has full central heating (log fires on colder evenings) and for those long hot days a heated swimming pool in the garden. Bath, Cheddar, Wells, Glastonbury and the coast close by. Open all year except Christmas. E-mail: bcjbkj@aol.com.uk

28 Townsend Farm, Sand, Wedmore, Somerset BS28 4XH

Sarah Willcox
☎ 01934 712342
BB From £17–£18.50
Sleeps 6
🐎(5) ⚹ ♻
🌼 🐚 Commended

Townsend Farm is a working dairy farm, set in peaceful countryside with views of the Mendip hills, close to Wells, Cheddar and Glastonbury, 6 miles from M5 (jct22). The spacious Victorian farmhouse offers comfortable accommodation and a friendly atmosphere, traditional English breakfast served in dining room, relaxing separate TV lounge. All bedrooms have TV, en suite available. Open Apr–Nov.

29 Wambrook Farm, Wambrook, Nr Chard, Somerset TA20 3DF

Mrs Sue Eames
☎ 01460 62371
BB From £20–£25
Sleeps 6
🐎 ⚹ ♻ 🐾 ♿
🌼 🐚 Commended

Relax in the beautiful countryside of the Blackdown Hills, in our listed farmhouse situated in an unspoilt, peaceful village. Ideal for touring Devon, Dorset and Somerset. One double and one family room, both en suite with tea/coffee-making facilities. Good pub food in village. Open Apr–Nov.

Somerset *West Country*

Wembdon Farm, Hollow Lane, Wembdon, Bridgwater, Somerset TA5 2BD **(30)**

Mrs Mary Rowe
☎ 01278 453097
mobile 0402 272755
Fax 01278 445856
BB From £19–£22
Sleeps 6
☎(10) ✂ ⚘ ♨ ☯
♨ ♨ Highly Commended

Enjoy a refreshing and memorable stay at our homely Georgian farmhouse situated near the Quantocks (AONB). We offer two romantic double en suite bedrooms, one pretty twin with private bathroom, all with tea/coffee, colour TV. Separate lounge and dining room for superb breakfasts. Landscaped gardens, off road parking. Tucked away yet easy to find, a place for all seasons.
E-mail: mary.rowe@btinternet.com

Self-Catering

Cockhill Farm & Orchard Farm, Cockhill, Castle Cary, Somerset BA7 7NY **(24)**

Olive Boyer
☎/Fax 01963 350418
SC From £145–£380
Sleeps 2/7
☎ ⚘ ♨ ⚘ ☯
♔ ♔ – ♔ ♔ ♔
Approved

An attractive listed farmhouse overlooking beautiful countryside, with 3 bedrooms and fully equipped with TV, dishwasher, washing machine and spin dryer. Also 2 attractive cottages converted from a Somerset barn, both fully equipped, electricity and linen inclusive. Bath, Longleat, Stourhead, Yeovilton Air and Haynes Motor Museums and many NT properties nearby. Castle Cary with many shops and eating places 1½ miles. Open all year.

The Courtyard, c/o New House Farm, Burtle Road, Westhay, Nr Glastonbury, Somerset BA6 9TT **(23)**

Mr & Mrs P Bell
☎/Fax 01458 860238
SC From £150–£400
Sleeps 6
☎ ⚘
♔ ♔ ♔ ♔ Highly Commended

The Courtyard is a converted barn which sleeps up to 4 adults and 2 children. Its situation on a dairy farm on the Somerset Levels makes it central for touring Wells, Cheddar, Bath, etc. Superbly equipped, including colour TV, washing machine, microwave, tumble dryer. Bed-linen, electricity and heating included. Good local fishing. Open all year.

Cutthorne Farm, Luckwell Bridge, Wheddon Cross, Somerset TA24 7EW **(8)**

Ann Durbin
☎/Fax 01643 831255
SC From £200–£475
Sleeps 4
☎ ⚘ ♨ ⚘ ☯
♔ ♔ ♔
Highly Commended

'What a wonderful position' – the most frequent comment we hear. Nestling in the heart of Exmoor, we offer two attractive barn conversions on side of farmhouse. These peaceful havens overlook our own trout lakes and valley. Close to Lynton and Lynmouth, Tarr Steps and Dunster, also small unspoilt beaches. Home-cooked meals may be taken in the farmhouse. Open all year.

Hale Farm, Cucklington, Wincanton, Somerset BA9 9PN **(31)**

Mrs Pat David
☎ 01963 33342
SC From £110–£195
Sleeps 4
☎ ⚘
♔ ♔ Approved

Set in a peaceful, but not isolated, position on edge of village, only 2 miles from A303. Ideal touring. Period converted former cowshed, comfortable and well equipped. One twin and one double bedroom, bathroom, kitchen, sitting room. All electric (coin meter). Linen supplied. Open all year.

West Country *Somerset*

12 Highercombe, Dulverton, Exmoor, Somerset TA22 9PT

Sarah Wates
☎ 01398 323451
SC From £130–£410
EM From £10
Sleeps 6
🐕 🐎 💼
🗝🗝🗝🗝 *Up to Highly Commended*

Relax at historic Highercombe, of 14th century origin, and enjoy this beautiful, spacious country home heading the Barle Valley. Peacefully set in 8 acres of formal gardens and paddocks within the Exmoor National Park, adjacent to open moorland, Dulverton 2½ miles. Smart, private self-catering cottages. Also bed and breakfast. Stabling if required. Open Mar–Sept.

13 Highercombe Farm, Dulverton, Somerset TA22 9PT

Abigail Humphrey
☎/Fax 01398 323616
SC From £190–£380
Sleeps 5
🐕 🐎 🐈 ♨
🗝🗝🗝 *Commended*

Self-contained wing of large farmhouse on 450-acre working farm next to the moor. Well furnished in cottage style. Private entrance, large gardens, spectacular views. 2 bedrooms, bathroom, large lounge/dining room with colour TV, CD player/radio, woodburner. Modern pine kitchen. Linen, CH, hot water, logs included. Use of washing machine/dryer. Evening meals arranged, babysitting service. Electricity pound coin meter. Open all year. E-mail: abigail@highercombe.demon.co.uk

16 Hindon Farmhouse Cottage, Hindon Farm, Nr Minehead, Somerset TA24 8SH

Penny & Roger Webber
☎/Fax 01643 705244
SC From £250–£530
Sleeps 6
🐕 🐎 🍴 🐈 ♨ 💼 🐾
🗝🗝🗝🗝 *Commended*

18th century cottage/wing of Exmoor farmhouse between Minehead and Selworthy (short walk for cream teas!) 500-acre NT farm below heather moors and SW coast path – terrific views. Much farm and wild life. Tastefully furnished with original fireplace, log burner. Living/dining/kitchen, CH, TV, video and all mod cons. 1 double en suite, 2 twins with bathroom. Linen and towels provided. Baby listening. Breakfasts available. Featured on TV in *Getaways* and in *Country Living*. Brochure.

32 Holly Farm, Holly Cottage, Stoke St. Gregory, Taunton TA3 6HS

Liz Smith
☎/Fax 01823 490828
SC From £170–£370
Sleeps 4/6
🐕 🐎 💼 ♨
🗝🗝🗝 – 🗝🗝🗝🗝 *Highly Commended*

Come and stay in one of our 5 spacious cottages converted from old stone long barns. Each has its own private, enclosed garden and there is a games barn for the energetic. Plenty of fishing, horse riding or walking and an excellent selection of pub grub and restaurants nearby so give the cook a holiday too. Open all year.

33 Liscombe Farm, Winsford, Dulverton, Somerset TA22 9QA

Sally Wade
☎ 01643 851551
SC From £100–£600
Sleeps 2/9 + cot
🐕 🐎 💼
🗝🗝🗝 – 🗝🗝🗝🗝 *Commended*

Liscombe is a 385-acre beef and sheep farm in Exmoor National Park. Peaceful, spacious farmhouse and two converted barns, each furnished to a high standard with CH, dishwasher, washing machine, drier, hi-fi, video – everything to make a relaxing holiday. Perfect for walking, riding or fishing. Cosy log fires, garden, play area and barbecue. Stabling available. Open all year.

34 Mill Farm, Staple Fitzpaine, Taunton, Somerset TA3 5SP

Stan & Alison Moore
☎ 01823 481214
SC From £160–£260
Sleeps 4
🐕 💼
🗝🗝🗝🗝 *Commended*

A warm and friendly welcome awaits you on our small farm in the tranquil countryside of the Blackdown Hills. Your own character cottage is luxuriously equipped including woodburner and quality linen while outside the children have their own play area adjacent to the patio. Don't forget the chickens, ducks and sheep all need looking after! Open all year.

Somerset   *West Country*

The Old Cart House, Double-Gate Farm, Godney, Nr Wells, Somerset BA5 1RX

Hilary Millard
☎ 01458 832217
Fax 01458 835612
SC From £175–£375
Sleeps 4/5
Highly Commended

First floor barn conversion, with lovely views of the Mendip Hills and Glastonbury Tor, offers excellent, well equipped accommodation including 2 en suite bedrooms. Heating, electricity and bedlinen included. Ground floor games room, open to all residents, with full-size snooker table, table tennis, darts, etc. Guest launderette. Ideal for touring, cycling, birdwatching, fishing. Village inn nearby for those days when you don't want to cook! Open all year. E-mail: hilary@millard.webscape.co.uk

Pear Tree Cottage, Northwick Farm, Mark, Highbridge, Somerset TA9 4PG

Mrs Susan Slocombe
☎ 01278 641228
SC From £200–£350
Sleeps 6
Highly Commended

Situated on the Somerset Levels in an area of outstanding natural beauty. Recent barn conversion. Luxurious and comfortable with beautifully co-ordinated fabrics and furnishings. Perfect for a peaceful relaxing holiday and an ideal base for touring this part of the West Country. Excellent facilities nearby for golf, fishing and riding and only 4 miles from coast. Open all year.

Pembroke Cottage, c/o Brake Cottage, Wheddon Cross, Minehead, Somerset TA24 7EX

Mrs J Escott
☎ 01643 841550
SC From £125–£350
Sleeps 5/6
Commended

A warm welcome to Pembroke. A detached cottage ideally situated on beef and sheep farm, amidst peaceful surroundings with splendid south westerly views of Exmoor countryside. Well equipped, colour TV, video, microwave, washing machine. Linen included. Brochure available. Sorry no pets.

Pigsty, Cowstall & Bullpen Cottages, Barrow Lane Farm, Charlton Musgrove, Wincanton, Somerset BA9 8HJ

Mrs Chilcott
☎/Fax 01963 33217
SC From £150–£315
Sleeps 5–8 + cot
Commended

Pigsty, Cowstall and Bullpen Cottages are conversions from the appropriate farm buildings in rural Somerset. Pleasant garden, barbecue and games room. Pets welcome. Please send for brochure. Open all year.

Riscombe Farm, Exford, Exmoor, Somerset TA24 7NH

Leone & Brian Martin
☎/Fax 01643 831480
SC From £95–£400
Sleeps 2–7
Highly Commended

Four very comfortable cottages converted from stone barns set in attractive courtyard. Ample parking. Quiet, relaxed setting beside River Exe in very heart of Exmoor National Park, 1½ miles from Exford village. Smallholding with ponies, chickens, ducks, etc. Logburning fires. DIY stabling. The perfect place to enjoy Exmoor all year round. Brochure available.

Rull Farm, Otterford, near Chard, Somerset TA20 3QJ

Mrs Pauline Wright
☎ 01460 234398
SC From £100–£170
Sleeps 5/6
Commended

We would like to welcome you to our family farm in the beautiful Blackdown hills with splendid scenic views. This accommodation is part of the farmhouse within easy reach of 5 local towns and coastal resorts. Open all year.

West Country — Somerset

---

(6) The Tallet, Clanville Manor, Castle Cary, Somerset BA7 7PJ

Mrs Sally Snook
☎ 01963 350124/350313
Fax 01963 350313
Mobile 0966 512732
[SC] From £190–£350
Sleeps 4/5 + cot

🐴 ⚒ 🚲 ♿ ⛺
🔑🔑🔑🔑 Highly Commended

In summer, walk or picnic beside the river, swim in the pool or play games in the walled garden. Watch the milking, help collect the eggs. Take a cosy short break in winter and curl up in front of the fire. All-inclusive rent and starter pack. Brochure. Open all year.
E-mail: clanville@aol.com

---

(40) Week Farm, Bridgetown, Dulverton, Somerset TA22 9JP

Hilda England
☎ 01643 851289
Fax 01643 851554
[SC] From £100–£350
Sleeps 6

🐴 🐕 ♿ 👶 ⛺ ⊙
🔑🔑🔑🔑 Commended

Enjoy a break in our comfortable cottage on a sheep and beef farm adjoining moorland. Peaceful setting, magnificent views and excellent walks. TV, video, CD player, microwave, heating. Safe garden and barbecue. Cot, highchair, toys and babysitting. Linen inclusive. Ponies, chickens, geese etc. Pets welcome and stabling available. Brochure. Open all year.

---

(41) Westermill Farm, Exford, Nr Minehead, Somerset TA24 7NJ

The Edwards family
☎ 01643 831238
Fax 01643 831660
[SC] From £139–£399
Sleep 4/8

👣 🐴 🐕 🎣 ⛺ ♿ ✂ ⊙
🔑🔑 – 🔑🔑🔑
Commended

Six delightful log cottages (Gold winners, David Bellamy Conservation Award) in small grassy paddocks on side of valley by a river. Also bright, comfortable cottage adjoining the farmhouse overlooks the river. Patio, garage. Four waymarked walks over 500-acre farm in centre of Exmoor. 2½ miles shallow river, fishing, bathing. Laundry, payphone, information centre, seasonal small shop. Open all year.

---

(42) West Withy Farm, Upton, Taunton, Somerset TA4 2JH

Gareth & Mary Hughes
☎ 01398 371258
Fax 01398 371123
[SC] From £140–£530
Sleep 4–6 + cot

🐕 🐴 ♿ ✂
🔑🔑🔑🔑 Highly Commended

In idyllic rural location on the edge of Exmoor, comfortable and spacious character cottages skillfully converted from stone barns. Exposed beams, central heating, private gardens. Carp lake plus excellent trout fishing at Wimbleball and Clatworthy reservoirs. Dogs welcome. Short breaks available. Open all year.
E-mail: g.hughes@irisi.u-net.com.uk

---

(43) Wintershead Farm, Simonsbath, Exmoor, Somerset TA24 7LF

Jane Styles
☎ 01643 831222
Fax 01643 831628
[SC] From £125–£485
Sleeps 2–6

🐴 🐕 ♿
🔑🔑 – 🔑🔑🔑🔑 Highly Commended

Forget the pressures of everyday life and unwind in one of our warm and cosy cottages. Hidden away in the hills of Exmoor with breathtaking views. You can relax after a wonderful day's exploring, with comfy sofas, log fires, central heating, etc. Short breaks available Nov–Mar. Colour brochure. Open all year.

Please mention *Stay on a Farm* when booking

Wiltshire

Stonehenge, Avebury, Wiltshire White Horses
& the Ridge Way

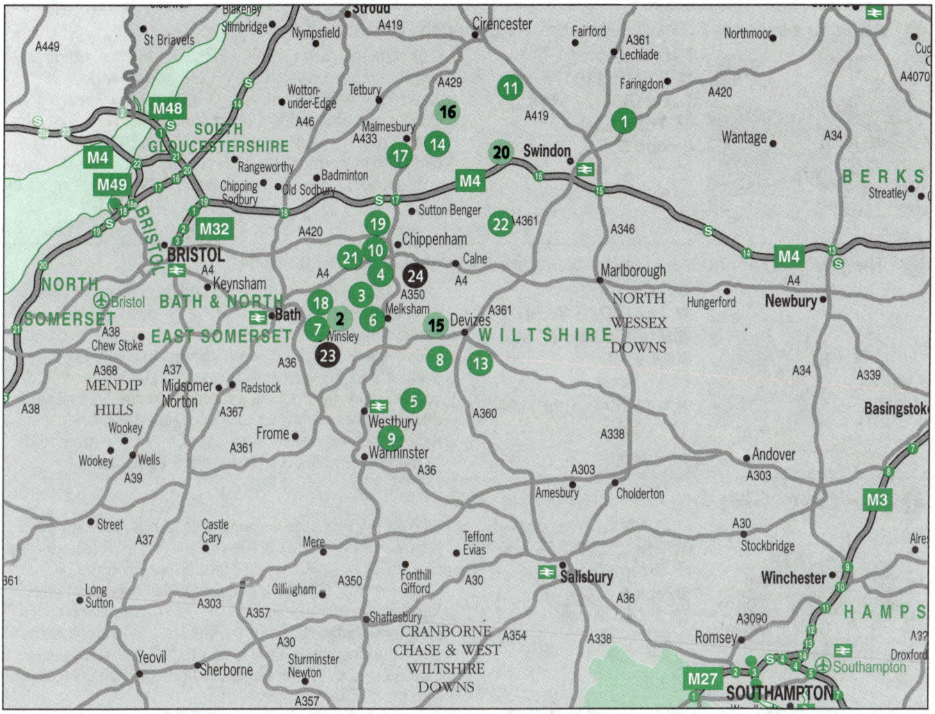

Key

1. Bed & Breakfast
1. Self-Catering
1. B&B and SC
1. Camping Barns
1. Camping & Caravanning

Although easily accessible from London, Wiltshire offers some of the best of rural England. Its wide, peaceful downland is rich in historic interest, with Stonehenge, Avebury and Silbury Hill standing out on the rolling green plain. Picturesque villages such as Castle Combe and Lacock lie tucked away in the valleys and just over the county border lies the Georgian city of Bath. Six hundred years of building are displayed in the magnificent collection of historic homes – Longleat, Bowood House, Corsham Court, Sheldon Manor...Walk the ancient Ridgeway Path or along the Kennet and Avon Canal, now restored along much of its route. Once here, you'll see why almost half the county is designated an Area of Outstanding Natural Beauty.

If you would like help in finding suitable farm accommodation, turn to the full listing of farm groups on pages 360 to 363 to find appropriate contact details for this area.

West Country   Wiltshire

Bed and Breakfast
(and evening meal)

① Ashen Copse Farm, Coleshill, Highworth, Nr Swindon, Wiltshire SN6 7PU

Pat Hoddinott
☎ 01367 240175
Fax 01367 241418
BB From £20–£23
Sleeps 6
😊 ☕ Commended

Our National Trust beef/arable farm is an ideal setting for peace and quiet. Watch the wildlife during wonderful walks in beautiful countryside. Explore pretty Cotswold villages and attractions. Good food, golf and riding nearby. M4 11 miles. 1 family en suite, 1 twin and 1 single bedroom in comfortable 17th century farmhouse. Open all year except Christmas Day. E-mail: pat@hodd.demon.co.uk

② The Beeches Farmhouse, Holt Road, Bradford-on-Avon, Wiltshire BA15 1TS

Mrs Sharon Gover
☎/Fax 01225 863475
BB From £20–£27.50
Sleeps 10
😊 ☕ Highly Commended

Idyllic 18th century farmhouse and recently converted old dairy and old cart house in rural setting east of Bath. Family, double and twin rooms, all en suite and decorated with original country pine furnishings to a very high standard. Exposed beams, breakfast in Victorian-style conservatory overlooking a running stream. Free range ducks and hens – collect your own eggs for breakfast. Riding and golf nearby. Brochure. Closed Christmas and New Year. E-mail: beeches-farmhouse@bath.co.uk

③ Boyds Farm, Gastard, Nr Corsham, Wiltshire SN13 9PT

Dorothy Robinson
☎/Fax 01249 713146
BB From £20–£22
Sleeps 6
😊 ☕ Highly Commended

Enjoy a relaxing stay on our arable farm situated in the peace and tranquillity of the unspoilt Wiltshire countryside. Our delightful 16th century farmhouse, featured by the *Daily Express*, *Observer* and *Daily Mail* accommodates families, couples and individuals. All rooms have en suite/private facilities and TV. Guests' own lounge with woodburning stove. Easy access to M4, Bath, Lacock, Castle Combe, Stonehenge, Bradford-on-Avon. Excellent pub food close by.

④ Church Farm, Hartham Park, Corsham, Wiltshire SN13 0PU

Mrs Kate Jones
☎/Fax 01249 715180
BB From £18–£25
Sleeps 6
😊 ☕ Listed Commended

You will find our Cotswold stone farmhouse enjoys a secluded position with wonderful views across the adjoining valley and fields of our dairy/beef farm. Lovely walks and riding close by, as are pretty villages like Lacock and Castle Combe. Easy access to Bath (8 miles), M4 (4 miles), award-winning local pubs/restaurants. Family room with private bathroom, double room en suite, both with TV, CH and tea/coffee. Hearty breakfasts. Closed Christmas and New Year. E-mail: sbcjones@aol.com.uk

⑤ Church Farm, Steeple Ashton, Trowbridge, Wiltshire BA14 6EL

Susan Cottle
☎ 01380 870518
BB From £17.50–£18.50
Sleeps 4
😊 ☕ Listed Commended

Lovely old farmhouse dating back to 16th century in centre of beautiful village. Ideally situated for Bath, Salisbury, Longleat, Stourhead, Castle Combe. Lacock, Avebury. Spacious rooms, one double with H&C, one family, tea/coffee facilities. Guests' bathroom. Homely atmosphere, use of lounge, TV. Log fire in winter. Tea and homemade cake on arrival. No smoking in bedrooms. Open all year except Christmas and New Year.

Wiltshire   West Country

Great Ashley Farm, Bradford-on-Avon, Wiltshire BA15 2PP ⑥

Helen Rawlings
☎/Fax 01225 864563
BB From £18–£22.50
Sleeps 5
⌂ ⌇ ⚘ ♨
♛ ♛ Commended

A very warm and inviting welcome awaits anyone visiting Great Ashley Farm. Set on the outskirts of Bradford-on-Avon in an Area of Outstanding Natural Beauty with Bath just 15 minutes away. Tastefully decorated farmhouse with delightful en suite bedrooms overlooking a large duck pond. Delicious breakfasts. Family room available. Open all year except Christmas.

Hatt Farm, Old Jockey, Box, Nr Bath, Wiltshire SN13 8DJ ⑦

Mrs Carol Pope
☎ 01225 742989
Fax 01225 742779
BB From £20–£22.50
Sleeps 4
⌂ ⌇ ♨ ⚘ ◉
♛ ♛ Commended

Extremely comfortable Georgian farmhouse in peaceful surroundings. Scrumptious breakfasts served overlooking beautiful countryside views. What could be nicer than sitting by a log fire in winter or enjoying the garden in summer? Lovely walks and good golfing nearby. Ideal for touring Wiltshire and the Cotswolds yet only 15 mins' drive to Bath. One twin with en suite shower, one double/family with private bathroom, both with tea/coffee. CH. Guests' lounge. Closed Christmas and New Year.

Higher Green Farm, Poulshot, Devizes, Wiltshire SN10 1RW ⑧

Marlene & Malcolm Nixon
☎/Fax 01380 828355
BB From £17
Sleeps 6
⌂ ⇄ ⌇ ♨
Listed Commended

Welcome to our peaceful 17th century timbered farmhouse facing village green and cricket pitch. Excellent traditional inn nearby. Our dairy farm is situated between Bath and Salisbury, close to many National Trust properties. Ideal for Stonehenge, Longleat, Avebury and Lacock. 1 double, 1 twin, 2 single rooms. Tea-making facilities. Guests' lounge, colour TV. Take A361 from Devizes, after 2 miles left to Poulshot, farm opposite Raven Inn. Open Mar–Nov.

Hillside Farm, Edington, Westbury, Wilts BA13 4PG ⑨

Carol Mussell
☎/Fax 01380 830437
BB From £17–£18
Sleeps 4
⌂ ♨ ◉
♛ Commended

A warm welcome and wonderful views are yours on our small working farm nestled under the edge of Salisbury Plain. We have one double/family room and one twin room each with wash basins, colour TV and hospitality tray. Lovely conservatory for guests' use. Within easy reach of Bath and NT properties. Closed Christmas & January.

Home Farm, Harts Lane, Biddestone, Chippenham, Wilts SN14 7DQ ⑩

Ian & Audrey Smith
☎/Fax 01249 714475
BB From £20–£22.50
Sleeps 6
⌂ ⌇ ♨ ⚘ ◉
♛ ♛ Commended

A warm welcome awaits you in this 17th century farmhouse on a family-run working mixed farm. Set in beautiful Biddestone just a stroll across village green from the pub. Ideally situated for Bath, Castle Combe and Lacock, Stonehenge, Avebury, Longleat, etc. Both rooms have colour TV, tea and coffee; one en suite, the other has private bathroom. Open all year.

Leighfield Lodge Farm, Cricklade, Swindon, Wiltshire SN6 6RH ⑪

Mrs Claire Read
☎/Fax 01666 860241
BB From £20
Sleeps 6
⌂ ⌇ ♨ ◉
♛ ♛ Commended

Imagine a lovely old farmhouse in a truly rural setting. Step inside and discover comfortable en suite rooms with crisp cotton bedlinen. Relax in the sitting room in front of a warm fire, after explororng the Cotswolds or Wiltshire Downs. Children will enjoy meeting the Jersey cows and may even see the wild deer! Open all year except Christmas and New Year.

West Country — Wiltshire

Please mention *Stay on a Farm* when booking

---

13 Longwater Park Farm, Lower Road, Erlestoke, Nr Devizes, Wiltshire SN10 5UE

Pam Hampton
☎/Fax 01380 830095
From £18–£22
EM From £12
Sleeps 12
Commended

A peaceful retreat overlooking our own lakes and parkland with 2½ acre waterbird area and organic farm with rare sheep. Family suite, double/twin rooms all en suite, TV and tea-making facilities, CH. 2 ground floor bedrooms. Welcoming lounge, large conservatory, separate dining room. Traditional farmhouse fayre using local produce. Special diets. Local wines. Coarse fishing. Erlestoke Sands Golf Course adjacent. Open all year except Christmas and New Year.

---

14 Lovett Farm, Little Somerford, Nr Malmesbury, Wiltshire SN15 5BP

Susan Barnes
☎/Fax 01666 823268
From £20–£25
Sleeps 6
Commended

Enjoy traditional hospitality at our delightful farmhouse on a working farm with beautiful views. Three attractive bedrooms, one double and one twin both en suite and one double with private bathroom, all with tea/coffee and colour TV. Full central heating. Guests' dining room/lounge. Log fires in winter. Convenient M4, Bath, Cotswolds, Lacock and Stonehenge. Excellent food pubs nearby. Open all year except Christmas and New Year.

---

15 Lower Foxhangers Farm, Rowde, Devizes, Wiltshire SN10 1SS

Cynthia & Colin Fletcher
☎/Fax 01380 828254
From £20–£26
Sleeps 6
(touring & static)
Commended

We expectantly await your visit to our 18th century farmhouse alongside the canal with its gaily painted narrow boats. Assist boats through the locks whilst strolling to the pubs. Ideal for walking, cycling, fishing, boating. Easy reach Stonehenge/Bath. Also available for hire our new 40'–60' narrowboats. Twin, double and family rooms, all en suite with TV and hospitality tray. Self-catering units and small campsite with electricity, toilets/shower. Open May–Oct.

---

16 Lower Stonehill Farm, Charlton, Malmesbury, Wiltshire SN16 9DY

Mrs Edna Edwards
☎/Fax 01666 823310
From £17.50–£22
Sleeps 6
Listed *Commended*

Large Cotswold stone 15th century farmhouse on working dairy farm in the lush, rolling countryside on the Wilts/Glos border. Three comfortable rooms, 1 en suite, all with tea/coffee facilities. Children and dogs welcome. Delicious full English breakfast served in guests' sitting/dining room or garden if fine. Central for Oxford, Bath, Stratford, Stonehenge and the Cotswolds. On the B4040 3½ miles from historic Malmesbury. Open all year.

---

17 Manor Farm, Corston, Malmesbury, Wiltshire SN16 0HF

Mrs Ross Eavis
☎ 01666 822148
Fax 01666 826565
From £19–£27
Sleeps 12
Commended

Manor Farm is very easy to find just 3 miles north of M4 J17. Cotswold stone farmhouse full of character and very homely. Six rooms, four en suite all with colour TV and hospitality tray. Large gardens to while away the time or visit local pub just down the road. As featured in the *Daily Express* and *Bella* magazine. Closed Christmas.

Wiltshire   *West Country*

Manor Farm, Wadswick, Box, Corsham, Wiltshire SN13 8JB

Carolyn Barton
☎ 01225 810700
Fax 01225 810733
BB From £22.50–£25
Sleeps 6

Highly Commended

Visit our arable and horse farm nestling in the quiet hamlet of Wadswick. We are only 7 miles from Bath yet close to Lacock and other beautiful villages. Our 16th century farmhouse has large, spacious rooms, all en suite with tea/coffee making facilities and colour TV. Stabling and riding by arrangement. Open Mar–Nov.

Oakfield Farm, Easton Piercy Lane, Yatton Keynell, Chippenham, Wiltshire SN14 6JU

Mrs Margaret Read
☎/Fax 01249 782355
BB From £18–£20
Sleeps 6

Listed Commended

Friendly welcome in Cotswold stone farmhouse with fine views over open countryside. On working livestock farm in a quiet location, excellent for wildlife. One en suite double/family room, 1 double and 1 twin room, all with tea/coffee-making facilities and colour TV. Full central heating. Ideal base for visiting Bath, Castle Combe, Lacock and the Cotswolds. Open Mar–Nov.

Olivemead Farm, Olivemead Lane, Dauntsey, nr Chippenham, Wiltshire SN15 4JQ

Suzanne Candy
☎/Fax 01666 510205
Mobile 0378 667611
BB From £18–£20
Sleeps 6

Commended

Relax and enjoy the warm, informal hospitality at our delightful 18th century farmhouse on a working dairy farm. Thoughtfully decorated twin, double, family rooms with washbasin, colour TV. Tea/coffee facilities. Generous breakfasts. Oak beamed dining room/lounge for guests' exclusive use. Large garden, play area, cot, highchair. Convenient M4, Bath, Cotswolds, Salisbury. Open all year except Christmas and New Year.

Pickwick Lodge Farm, Guyers Lane, Corsham, Wiltshire SN13 0PS

Gill Stafford
☎ 01249 712207
Fax 01249 701904
RR From £20
Sleeps 6

Highly Commended

Enjoy a stay at our beautiful home set in wonderful countryside where you can see rabbits, pheasant and occasionally deer. Relax in our garden having started the day with a hearty delicious breakfast. Local produce used when possible. Bath, NT properties, Corsham Court and many interesting villages nearby. Two well appointed and tastefully furnished rooms with en suite/private facilities, hospitality tray, home made biscuits. Closed Christmas and New Year.

Tockenham Court Farm, Tockenham, Nr Swindon, Wiltshire SN4 7PH

Mrs Elizabeth Bennett
☎/Fax 01793 852315
Mobile 0831 341310
BB From £20–£25
Sleeps 6

Highly Commended

Welcome to our Grade II listed 16th century court house. We have 1 double room with private shower room and toilet, 1 double room with private bathroom and toilet, 1 en suite room. CH, tea/coffee facilities and colour TV. Guests' own sitting room.

LET THE TELEPHONE RING!
Some farmhouses are big places. Let the telephone ring
long enough to give the owner time to answer it.

West Country — Wiltshire

Self-Catering

② The Beeches Farmhouse, Cow Byre and Piggery, Holt Road, Bradford-on-Avon, Wiltshire BA15 1TS

Mrs Sharon Gover
☎/Fax 01225 863475
SC From £200–£390
Sleeps 4/5
Applied

Recently converted south-facing buildings overlooking open countryside. Luxurious, spacious accommodation with olde worlde charm. Exposed beams, wood burning stove and original country pine furnishings. Barbecue and patio furniture. Play area and tree house. Free range ducks and chickens. Golf and pony trekking nearby. Ideal for Bath, Lacock, Castle Combe, Wells, Stonehenge and Longleat. Electricity and linen included. Brochure. Open all year. E-mail: beeches-farmhouse@bath.co.uk

㉓ Church Farm Cottages, Winsley, Bradford-on-Avon, Wiltshire BA15 2JH

Trish Bowles
☎/Fax 01225 722246
Mobile 0468 543027
SC From £165–£315
Sleeps 2–4 + cot
Commended

Five natural stone single-storey cottages with vaulted ceilings and exposed beams. Luxuriously appointed with CH, colour TV, video and microwave. On outskirts of village within 500 metres of pub and shop. Kennet and Avon canal ¾ mile for cycling, walking, boating and fishing. Brochure available. Open all year.
E-mail: churchfarmcottages@compuserve.co.uk

⑮ Lower Foxhangers Farm, Rowde, Devizes, Wiltshire SN10 1SS

Cynthia & Collin Fletcher
☎ 01380 828254/828795
Fax 01380 828254
SC From £170–£230
Sleeps 4/6
(touring and static)
Tourist Board Inspected

Enjoy your holiday with us on our small farm/marina with its diverse attractions. Relax on the patio of your rural retreat. We have four holiday mobile homes. Hear the near musical clatter of the windlass heralding the lock gate opening and the arrival of yet another narrow boat. Hire one of our new narrowboats and cruise to Bath and back. Also B&B and small campsite with electricity and facilities. Open Easter–Nov.

⑯ Stonehill Farm, Charlton, Malmesbury, Wiltshire SN16 9DY

Mrs Edna Edwards
☎/Fax 01666 823310
SC From £170–£210
Sleeps 2/3
Commended

Stonehill is a family-run dairy farm on the Wilts/Glos border, 3 miles from Malmesbury and 8 miles M4. The Cow Byre and Bull Pen are converted cowsheds, comfortably furnished with double bed, bathroom, fitted kitchen/diner and lounge. Full CH, colour TV, microwave, all power and linen included. Facing south-west with gravel patio and garden chairs. Open all year.

⑳ Swallow Cottage, Olivemead Farm, Olivemead Lane, Dauntsey, nr Chippenham, Wilts SN15 4JQ

Suzanne Candy
☎/Fax 01666 510205
Mobile 0378 667611
SC From £160–£350
Sleeps 6
Commended

Imagine a delightful, comfortable, well-equipped cottage on a working dairy farm. Newly converted to offer the luxuries of modern living but retaining its traditional features. Bed settee available for extra guests. Perfectly positioned for days out in Wiltshire, Bath and the Cotswolds. Plenty to do for all the family even on the wettest of days. Brochure available.

Wiltshire   West Country

Wick Farm, Lacock, Chippenham, Wiltshire SN15 2LU

Philip and Sue King
☎ 01249 730244
Fax 01249 730072
SC *From £170–£380*
Sleeps 4/5 + cot
Highly Commended

Philip and Sue invite you to their working dairy farm in The Cheese House or Cyder House, where original cyder press remains, also stepped fireplace with woodburning stove. Some windows in Cheese have original shutters with gallery as extra seating area with portable TV. Both properties have exposed timbers, traditional furnishings. Linen and towels included. Coarse fishing on own lake. Brochure available. Open all year.

(24)

FINDING YOUR ACCOMMODATION

The local FHB Group contacts listed on page 360 can always help you find a vacancy in your chosen area.

CONFIRM BOOKINGS

Disappointments can arise from misunderstandings over the telephone. Please write to confirm your booking.

Our Internet address is
http://www.webscape.co.uk/farmaccom/

Dorset

Cranborne Chase, Hardy Country & Dorset Coast

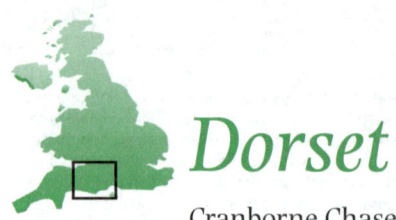

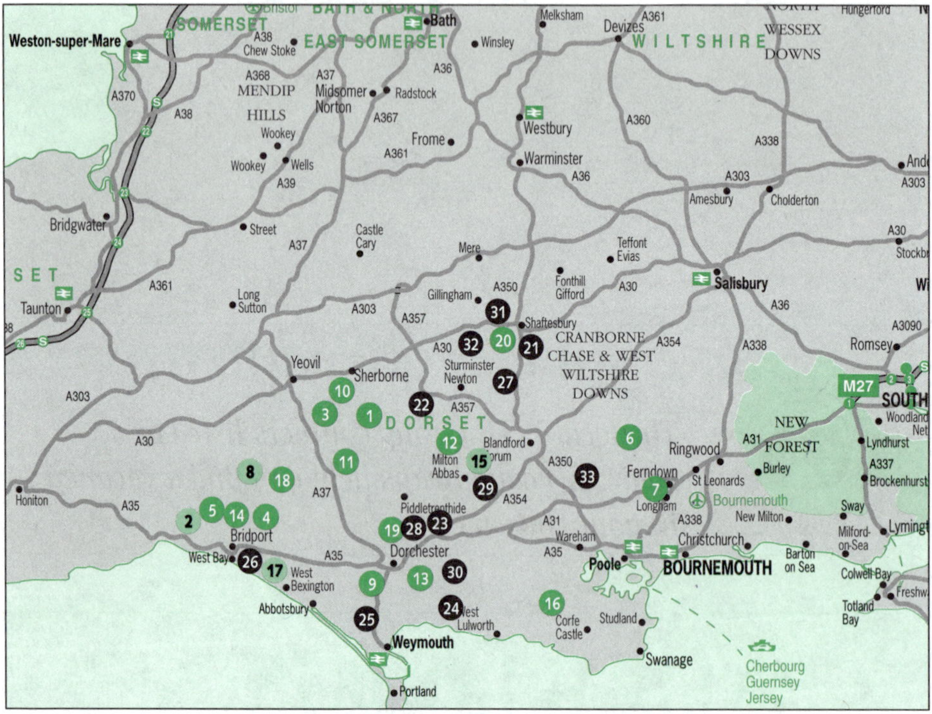

Key
- 1 Bed & Breakfast
- 1 Self-Catering
- 1 B&B and SC
- 1 Camping Barns
- ▲ Camping & Caravanning

Dorset's mild climate makes it an ideal location for a holiday all year round and wherever you stay the coast is but a short distance away with excellent swimming, sailing and fishing. For the country lover, the area has a wide choice of forest trails, nature reserves, coastal and inland walks; there are ancient monuments, historic houses and tropical gardens to explore. You can visit Thomas Hardy's birthplace in Higher Bockhampton, near Dorchester or Lawrence of Arabia's cottage, Clouds Hill. The settings for most of Hardy's novels are based on villages and towns in the area, and many retain the rural atmosphere of his fictional Wessex. Corfe Castle, Brownsea Island, Lulworth Cove, Durdle Door – are just some of the many other places to discover here in Dorset.

If you would like help in finding suitable farm accommodation, turn to the full listing of farm groups on pages 360 to 363 to find appropriate contact details for this area.

Dorset   West Country

Bed and Breakfast
(and evening meal)

Almshouse Farm, Hermitage, Holnest, Sherborne, Dorset DT9 6HA

Mrs Jenny Mayo
☎/Fax 01963 210296
BB From £19–£22
Sleeps 6
♥(10) ♠
♥♥ Highly Commended

Spoil yourself and stay on our traditional working dairy farm situated in a totally unspoiled part of Dorset. Listed farmhouse retains its age and beauty whilst boasting every modern convenience. Wander the charming garden, surrounding fields or lanes and build an appetite for a real farmhouse breakfast. Golf, fishing and riding nearby. AA QQQQ selected. Open Feb–Dec.

Cardsmill Farm, Whitchurch Canonicorum, Bridport, Dorset DT6 6RP

Mrs Sue M Johnson
☎/Fax 01297 489375
BB From £17–£21
Sleeps 6
♥♥ Commended

Freedom to wander around and watch on this working family farm. Nature walks to the village and pub via the woods and fields. Ideal for family and friends to visit the beach, go fossil hunting, touring and walking. One double en suite and one family room with private bathroom. Lounge with CTV and inglenook fireplace. English and varied breakfasts. A warm welcome guaranteed. Open Feb–Nov.

Church Farm, Stockwood, Nr Dorchester, Dorset DT2 0NG

Mrs Ruth House
☎ 01935 83221
Fax 01935 83771
BB From £19–£25
Sleeps 6
♥♥ Highly Commended

Escape for a while to an unspoilt, peaceful landscape. Stroll along the many paths or perhaps visit the coast, just 30 minutes away. Relax in our beautiful Georgian home on working farm and discover in the garden one of England's smallest churches. En suite rooms with TV, CH, tea/coffee-making facilities. Golf, shooting, fishing nearby. Open all year.

Colesmoor Farm, Toller Porcorum, Dorchester, Dorset DT2 0DU

Mrs Rachael Geddes
☎ 01300 320812
Fax 01300 321402
BB From £20
EM From £9.50
Sleeps 4
♥♥ Commended

Colesmoor Farm, reached by its own private track, is surrounded by peaceful countryside with extensive views. We offer a choice of breakfasts with homebaked bread. Our ground floor accommodation consists of a double and a twin/double room. Both rooms have well-equipped en suite bathrooms, CTV and hot drink facilities. Excellent choice of pubs and restaurants nearby. Brochure. Closed Mar, Apr & Dec.

Dunster Farm, Broadoak, Bridport, Dorset DT6 5NR

Mrs Linda Hutchings
☎ 01308 424626
BB From £17–£19
Sleeps 6
♥♥ Commended

Dunster Farm is a family farm situated in the peaceful Vale of Marshwood, surrounded by the rolling hills of West Dorset. Within easy reach of popular sandy beaches including Lyme Regis 8 miles, Charmouth and West Bay 5 miles, our local town Bridport 4 miles. All guests are very welcome to view or participate in some farm activities. Open Mar–Nov.

West Country — Dorset

6. Hemsworth Manor Farm, Witchampton, Nr Wimborne, Dorset BH21 5BN

Mrs A C Tory
☎ 01258 840216
Fax 01258 841278
BB From £25
Sleeps 6
♥♥ Highly Commended

Working family farm of approx 800 acres, mainly arable, but with horses, ponies, cattle, sheep and pigs, and situated in unspoilt countryside with only one other farmhouse in sight! Easy access to Bournemouth, Salisbury, Dorchester and the New Forest. Spacious en suite rooms, 3 double, 1 twin, all with colour TV, tea/coffee-making facilities. Excellent local pubs in the area. Open all year except Christmas.

7. Henbury Farm, Dorchester Road, Sturminster Marshall, Wimborne, Dorset BH21 3RN

Sue & Jonathan Tory
☎ 01258 857306
Fax 01258 857928
BB From £20–£23
Sleeps 6
♥♥ Commended

300-year-old farmhouse facing large front lawn and pond, situated on 200-acre dairy farm. Guests' lounge with colour TV. Near to New Forest and 15 minutes' drive from sandy beaches. Numerous local restaurants to meet your evening requirements. Many local attractions and country walks. Ideally situated for a great holiday. En suite facilities available. Open all year except Christmas.

8. Higher Langdon, Beaminster, Dorset DT8 3NN

Judy Thompson
☎/Fax 01308 862537
BB From £18–£25
EM From £10
Sleeps 4
♥♥ Commended

Tucked away in the green folds of West Dorset, at the end of long quiet lane is our stone built, unstuffy farmhouse with rambling character, big log-fired drawing room and loads of space. 9 miles to coast. Farmyard animals and large playroom make sure everyone can relax! En suite rooms.

9. Higher Park Farm, Bats Lane, Martinstown, Dorchester, Dorset DT2 9TG

Marigold King
☎ 01305 889362
Fax 01305 889541
BB From £20–£22
Sleeps 4
♥♥ Highly Commended

Our farmhouse is at the centre of our 100-acre dairy farm, surrounded by fields. Rooms are en suite, peaceful and comfortably furnished, with TV, etc. Close to Dorchester, in Hardy Country with beautiful coastline and many places of interest. Start the day with a good breakfast, end it at one of the many local restaurants. Open Feb–Nov.

10. Huntsbridge Farm, Batcombe Road, Leigh, Nr Sherborne, Dorset DT9 6JA

Mrs Su Read
☎/Fax 01935 872150
BB From £20
Sleeps 6
♥♥ Highly Commended

Family-run dairy farm situated in open countryside in the beautiful part of Dorset Thomas Hardy chose for his novel 'The Woodlanders'. Tastefully furnished bedrooms, 2 double (one with four-poster) and 1 twin, all en suite with tea/coffee facilities, colour TV, radio/alarm and full CH. Farmhouse breakfast served in conservatory overlooking garden and fields. So why not come and relax 'far from the madding crowd'? Open Feb–mid Dec.

11. Lamperts Farmhouse, 11 Dorchester Road, Sydling St Nicholas, Dorchester, Dorset DT2 9NU

Mrs Rita Bown
☎ 01300 341790
BB From £20–£22
EM From £12
Sleeps 4
♥♥ Commended

Enjoy home comforts in our thatched farmhouse in the unspoilt village of Sydling St Nicholas. Ideal for walking or touring. 1 double family room, 1 twin room, both with en suite bathroom. Guests' own lounge with inglenook fireplace, colour TV, tea/coffee-making facilities. Full CH. Open all year.

Dorset   West Country

Lower Fifehead Farm, Fifehead St Quinton, Sturminster Newton, Dorset DT10 2AP

Mrs Jill Miller
☎/Fax 01258 817335
[BB] From £17.50–£25
Sleeps 4
Commended

Come and stay with us on a working farm in our 17th century listed farmhouse mentioned in Nicolas Pense's and Jo Draper's Dorset books for its architectural interest. En suite or private bathroom, tea/coffee, guests' sitting room. Large peaceful garden, green fields, ideal for relaxing, walking or touring Dorset beauty spots. Riding and golf easily arranged. Open all year.

Maiden Castle Farm, Dorchester, Dorset DT2 9PR

Hilary Hoskin
☎ 01305 262356
Fax 01305 251085
[BB] From £20–£25
Sleeps 6
Highly Commended

Our large working farm, 1 mile from Dorchester and 7 miles from Weymouth in the heart of Hardy country, enjoys magnificent views of Maiden Castle and the surrounding countryside. En-suite bedrooms with CH, TV, tea-making facilities and a telephone for guests' use combine to offer comfort, peace and quiet – ideal for the perfect holiday. Babysitting by arrangement. Open all year.

New House Farm, Mangerton Lane, Bradpole, Bridport, Dorset DT6 3SF

Jane Greening
☎/Fax 01308 422884
[BB] From £18
EM From £10
Sleeps 6
Commended

Modern, comfortable farmhouse set in the rural Dorset hills. Near coast (2½ miles). A warm welcome to guests. Two family rooms, both en suite. Lots to do and see in this historically beautiful area. Evening meals available subject to prior reservation. Open all year except Christmas.

Park Farm, Milton Abbas, Blandford Forum, Dorset DT11 0AX

Mrs A Burch
☎ 01258 880828
[BB] From £20–£25
Sleeps 2
Listed Commended

A Grade II listed thatched building. Our twin bedded room has wonderful views to Poole Harbour and private bathroom overlooks the stables. Some of the best country woodland walking and riding from the farm. Short winter breaks. Open all year.

Priory Farm, East Holme, Wareham, Dorset BH20 6AG

Mrs Jenny Goldsack
☎/Fax 01929 553832
[BB] From £19–£24
EM From £9.50
Sleeps 6
Commended

A 16th century thatched family farmhouse in a quiet backwater of the Isle of Purbeck. It is here that our cows graze the water meadows of the Frome Valley and where we aim to provide you with a warm, friendly, relaxed atmosphere after your days out exploring coast and countryside. Open all year except Christmas and New Year.

Rudge Farm, Chilcombe, Bridport, Dorset DT6 4NF

Sue Diment
☎ 01308 482630
Fax 01308 482635
[BB] From £23
Sleeps 6
(10)
Highly Commended

Peacefully situated in the beautiful Bride Valley, just over 2 miles from the sea. After a day spent exploring the lovely West Dorset countryside, relax in our comfortably furnished farmhouse. Then try one of the many good local pubs and restaurants. All rooms are en suite with TV and tea tray and have far reaching views. Open Mar–Oct.
E-mail: rudge@wdi.co.uk

West Country — Dorset

18. Watermeadow House, Bridge Farm, Hooke, Beaminster, Dorset DT8 3PD

Mrs Pauline Wallbridge
☎/Fax 01308 862619
BB From £20–£25
Sleeps 6
♛ Highly Commended

Watermeadow House stands amidst beautiful countryside on the edge of the small village of Hooke. All bedrooms enjoy splendid rural views and overlook the river Hooke which meanders close by the garden where guests are welcome to sit. Breakfast is served in the sunlounge which attracts the morning sun. Perfect for those seeking peace and quiet in a friendly atmosphere. Open Apr–Nov.

19. Yalbury Park, Frome Whitfield Farm, Dorchester, Dorset DT2 7SE

Tom and Ann Bamlet
☎ 01305 250336
Fax 01305 260070
BB From £22–£24
Sleeps 6
♛ Highly Commended

Stone farmhouse with large garden in parkland to River Frome. Warm and welcoming for all country lovers. All rooms en-suite have TV, tea/coffee-making facilities, fridge, hairdrier. 1 double with french windows to garden, 2 family rooms. Traditional farmhouse breakfasts. Ideal for walking, beaches, fishing, riding and all country pursuits. Open all year.

20. Yew House Farm, Husseys, New Street, Marnhull, Sturminster Newton, Dorset DT10 1PD

Gil Espley
☎ 01258 820412
Fax 01258 821044
BB From £20–£25
Sleeps 6
♛ Highly Commended

Spacious family farmhouse of character in quiet location with superb views over open countryside. No longer a working farm, we welcome guests to enjoy our hospitality. Excellent area for walking, coarse fishing and sightseeing. Two double rooms, 1 twin, all en suite with tea/coffee-making facilities and colour TV. Open all year.

Self-Catering

21. Buddens Farm, Twyford, Shaftesbury, Dorset SP7 0JE

Sarah Gulliford
☎/Fax 01747 811433
SC From £110–£600
Sleeps 2/6 + cot
Commended

HARRASSED? Have a real farm holiday, guests welcome to help feed pigs, sheep, chickens and goats and watch cows being milked. Pony rides over farm. Set in rolling hills and patchwork fields. Relax in superb farmhouse and cottage accommodation. Comfortably furnished, woodburners, dishwasher, colour TV, laundry room, outdoor swimming pool. Fully equipped for babies and children. Open all year.

22. Dairy Farm Cottages, Dairy House Farm, Woolland, Blandford Forum, Dorset DT11 0EY

Mrs Penny Cooper
☎ 01258 817501
SC From £130–£350
Sleeps 4/6 + cot
Applied

Jasmine and Plumtree Cottages at Dairy House Farm are comfortably furnished and well equipped. Set in a peaceful location, a wonderful base from which to explore Dorset's beautiful countryside with its superb views, properties and coastline. Enjoy coarse fishing on the farm and natural woodland for exploring wildlife. Open Mar–Oct.

Dorset **West Country**

2 Deverel Cottages, Deverel Farm, Milborne St Andrew, Blandford, Dorset DT11 0HX

Charlotte Martin
☎ 01258 837195
Fax 01258 837227
SC From £150–£350
Sleeps 6
Commended

In the midst of Hardy Country, 1 mile from Milborne St Andrew and just 2 miles from the picturesque village of Milton Abbas, the cottage is within easy reach of the coast. Situated at the edge of the farmyard, 150 yards from the A354, this modern 3 bedroom semi-detached cottage has a large, well fenced garden and views of rolling countryside. Open all year.

Glebe Cottage, c/o Glebe House, Moreton, Dorchester, Dorset DT2 8RQ

Carol Gibbens
☎ 01929 462468
SC From £140–£280
Sleeps 4
Approved

Glebe Cottage is set in an old rectory garden in the peaceful farming village of Moreton, famous for its church windows engraved by Laurence Whistler and burial place of Lawrence of Arabia. It is a wildlife haven. The cottage is detached, is on one floor with 2 double bedrooms, kitchen, living room, bathroom, night storage heating and has its own garden. Open all year.

Gorwell Farm, Abbotsbury, Weymouth, Dorset DT3 4JX

Mrs Mary Pengelly
☎ 01305 871401
Fax 01305 871441
SC From £160–£500
Sleeps 1–8 + cot
Commended

Relax, unwind and enjoy peaceful and natural surroundings at Gorwell Farm. A family farm in its own scenic valley with lambs in the spring and calves in the summer. Comfortable, well equipped, warm accommodation with log fires. 2 miles from Abbotsbury and the Chesil Beach. Explore the coastal path crossing our farm or enjoy watersports, fishing and birdwatching locally. Wildlife in abundance. Winter short breaks. Open all year. E-mail: gorwell.farm@wdi.co.uk

Graston Farm Cottage, Graston Farm, Burton Bradstock, Bridport, Dorset DT6 4NG

Mrs Sylvia Bailey
☎ 01308 897603
Fax 01308 897016
SC From £160–£480
Sleeps 7–9
Approved

This spacious detached cottage is situated on a dairy farm in the beautiful Bride Valley one mile from Burton Bradstock and the sea. Three bedrooms (1 double, 1 double and single, 1 twin), two bathrooms, sitting room with woodburning stove, large well equipped kitchen/dining room and a further room with bed-settee. Open all year.

Hartgrove Farm, Hartgrove, Shaftesbury, Dorset SP7 0JY

Mrs Susan Smart
☎/Fax 01747 811830
SC From £180–£530
Sleeps 2/5 + cot
Up to Highly Commended

Far from the madding crowd! Discover this glorious, unspoilt corner of Dorset. Our family dairy farm has quite breathtaking views. 4 beautifully equipped, warm, character cottages. Old beams, log fires, laundry room, tennis, games barn, free swimming at leisure centre, fishing. Magnificent walking and wildlife. Children will enjoy cows, calves, sheep, pony, chickens. Pretty villages, good pubs, coast 30 mins. Open all year.

Higher Langdon Flat, Beaminster, Dorset DT8 3NN

Judy Thompson
☎/Fax 01308 862537
SC From £150–£200
Sleeps 2
Approved

Tucked away in the green folds of West Dorset, at the end of long quiet lane is our stone built, unstuffy farmhouse with rambling character. First floor flat has sitting room/kitchen with TV and microwave. Linen, CH, ensuite double bedroom. Ideal for walkers – on the Wessex Way. 9 miles to coast.

West Country   Dorset

㉘ Higher Waterston Farm Cottages, Piddlehinton, Nr Dorchester, Dorset DT2 7SW

Mrs Georgina Pole-Carew
☎/Fax 01305 848208
SC From £185–£495
Sleeps 4/6
Commended

Four extremely comfortable cottages overlooking a lawned courtyard. Fully modernised and exceptionally well-equipped. Safe play area for children, games barn, tennis court. Located in an Area of Outstanding Natural Beauty in the heart of Hardy's Dorset. Sea only 8 miles, historic Dorchester 4 miles. Personally supervised by owner. Open all year.

⑫ Lower Fifehead Farm, Fifehead St Quinton, Sturminster Newton, Dorset DT10 2AP

Mrs Jill Miller
☎/Fax 01258 817335
SC From £100–£300
Sleeps 2/5
Commended

Come and join us on our 400-acre dairy farm in beautiful, peaceful North Dorset staying in the cottage (sleeps 4/5) or flat (2/3). Situated in the heart of Hardy's Blackmore Vale within easy reach of many beauty spots. Large garden, friendly atmosphere.

㉙ Luccombe Farm, Milton Abbas, Blandford, Dorset DT11 0BE

Murray & Amanda Kayll
☎ 01258 880558
Fax 01258 881384
SC From £160–£650
Sleeps 2–7
Highly Commended

Our traditional barn conversions lie in a secluded hidden valley, deep in rolling downland. Beauty, peace and history surround you. Comfortable, well equipped and sleeping 2–7, they stand around a pond in landscaped grounds. Riding, fishing, sailing, clay shooting, good walking, cycling, etc. on farm or locally. Telephone, games room, childcare, maid and laundry service all available. Open all year.

㉚ Old Dairy Cottage and Clyffe Dairy Cottage, c/o Clyffe Farm, Tincleton, Dorchester, Dorset DT2 8QR

Rosemary Coleman
☎ 01305 848252
Fax 01305 848702
SC From £185–£450
Sleeps 3/6 + cot
Commended

Two character cottages, attractively and comfortably furnished, one spacious, both cosy with beams, inglenooks and gardens. CH. Interesting working dairy farm – abundance of wildlife on our ponds and rivers. Fishing, birdwatching, walking, cycling, golf, riding and swimming locally. All year round interest, especially beautiful in spring. Historical houses and gardens and heritage coastline within easy reach. Winter breaks. Open all year.

⑱ Orchard End, Hooke, Beaminster, Dorset DT8 3PD

Mrs Pauline Wallbridge
☎/Fax 01308 862619
SC From £200–£310
Sleeps 6
Approved

Stone-built bungalow on edge of small village of Hooke. Peaceful situation on our dairy farm, large garden, driveway and garage. Three comfortable bedrooms, 2 double, 1 twin. Large sitting room with dining area, well equipped kitchen. Lovely walking area. Price includes bedlinen, towels, electricity, VAT. Open all year.

⑮ Park Farm, Milton Abbas, Blandford Forum, Dorset DT11 0AX

Mrs A Burch
☎ 01258 880828
SC From £180–£600
Sleeps 8
Commended

A perfect setting for a country holiday in the heart of Dorset, either in our Grade II listed thatched barn conversion or chalet adjacent to our small caravan site. Bring your old clothes and even your horse and discover the superb woodland walks and rides. Feed the pigs, ponies and sheep. Coast 30 minutes' drive. Short winter breaks. Open all year.

Dorset   West Country

Rudge Farm Cottages, Chilcombe, Bridport, Dorset DT6 4NF

Sue Diment
☎ 01308 482630
Fax 01308 482635
[SC] From £190–£510
Sleeps 2–6
Highly Commended

Rudge is a peacefully situated livestock farm in the beautiful Bride Valley, just over 2 miles from the sea. The old farm buildings have been converted into superbly comfortable cottages, around a flower-decked cobbled yard, enjoying open views towards our lake and the countryside beyond. Ideal for a family holiday or relaxing short break. Open all year. E-mail: rudge@wdi.co.uk

Shire and Stable Cottages, Middle Farm, Fifehead Magdalen, Nr Gillingham, Dorset SP8 5RR

Mrs Jo Trevor
☎ 01258 820220
Fax 01258 820200
[SC] From £100–£400
Sleeps 4/6
Commended

Stable and Shire Cottages are situated in a courtyard, some distance apart. Explore our 300-acre farm with woodland and riverbank walks. Coarse fishing, riding, cycling and golf nearby. Village shops and good pubs two miles away. One cottage suitable for wheelchair. Children and small pets very welcome. Open all year.

Taphouse and Courthouse Farm, Whitchurch Canonicorum, Bridport, Dorset DT6 6RW

Mrs Sue M Johnson
☎/Fax 01297 489375
[SC] From £160–£880
Sleeps 11/12 + cots
Approved

Taphouse and Courthouse have large, comfortable farmhouses in the quiet Marshwood Vale. Ideal location for walking leafy lanes, footpaths and NT coastal paths. Fossil hunting, golf and beaches at Lyme Regis and Charmouth. Well-equipped kitchen/dining rooms separate lounges, large gardens. Taphouse has Rayburn, part CH, log fire, payphone, games room. Courthouse has full CH. Open all year.

Top Stall, Factory Farm, Fifehead Magdalen, Gillingham, Dorset SP8 5RS

Kathy Jeanes
☎/Fax 01258 820022
[SC] From £200–£380
Sleeps 5 + cot
Highly Commended

Tastefully converted cow stall adjoining listed farmhouse on a dairy farm, formerly a woollen mill. 'Top Stall' has a walled garden with barbecue. It is well equipped throughout. Babysitting can be arranged. Ideal for fishing and walking or just relaxing. Longleat, Stourhead, Bath or the coast all within 30 miles. Open all year.

White Cottage, Tarrant Crawford, Blandford, Dorset DT11 9HY

Mrs Jan Tory
☎ 01258 857417
Fax 01258 857218
[SC] From £220–£420
Sleeps 6
Commended

Enjoy a welcome in a modernised, extremely comfortable cob cottage with enclosed garden. On 550-acre family-run dairy/arable farm. Three bedrooms, CTV, CH, 2 WCs, washing machine, microwave. Ideal for exploring coast, National Trust properties – beach 20 mins. Children welcome, no pets please. Open May–Oct.

 Please mention *Stay on a Farm* when booking

North Devon

Exmoor National Park, North Devon Coast & Taw & Torridge Valleys

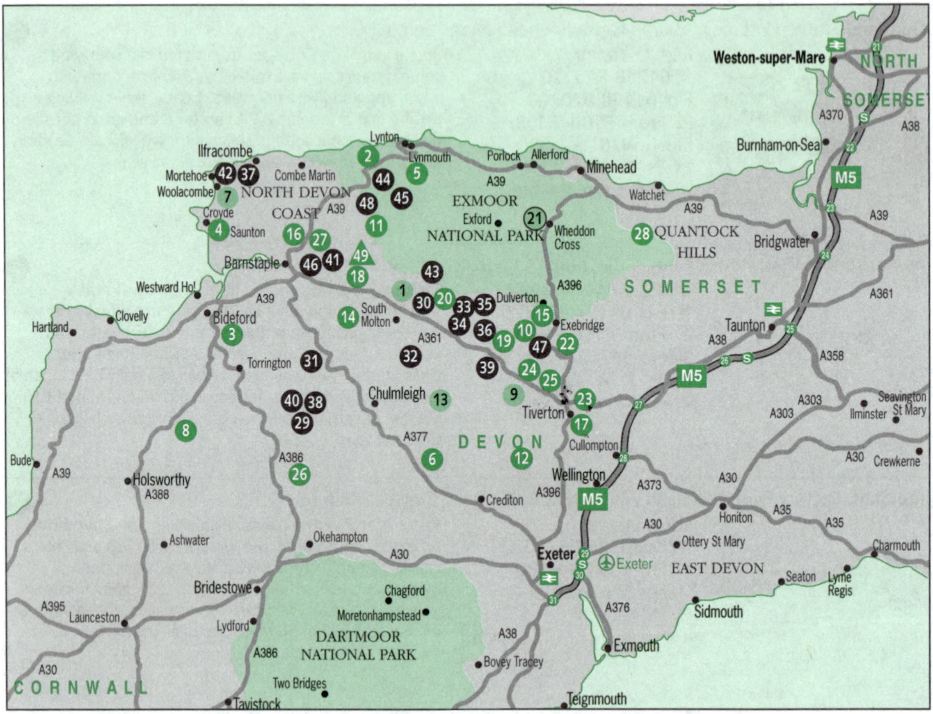

Key
- 1 Bed & Breakfast
- 1 Self-Catering
- 1 B&B and SC
- 1 Camping Barns
- 1 Camping & Caravanning

This is a lovely area, full of contrast. To the west you'll find miles of golden sands, surf-washed beaches, wide rolling hills, winding country lanes, and the valleys of the Taw and Torridge stretching to the Tamar near the Cornish border. In the north there's Exmoor offering wonderfully dramatic and varied scenery – expanses of wild heather-clad moorland, deep wooded coombes and the highest sea cliffs in the country, as well as quiet coves and beaches and 600 miles of waymarked walks. Follow the Tarka Trail, soak up the romance of the Doone Valley, the atmosphere of quaint villages like cobbled Clovelly – there's nowhere quite like it.

If you would like help in finding suitable farm accommodation, turn to the full listing of farm groups on pages 360 to 363 to find appropriate contact details for this area.

North Devon   West Country

Bed and Breakfast
(and evening meal)

Barkham, Sandyway, South Molton, North Devon EX36 3LU ●1

John Adie
☎/Fax 01643 831370
BB From £20–£25
EM From £17
Sleeps 6
Highly Commended

Discover our Georgian farmhouse, tucked away in a hidden moorland valley in the heart of the Exmoor National Park. Eat in the oak panelled dining room, sit on the patio overlooking a croquet lawn or enjoy the comfort of a log fire. Excellent home cooking. Antiques/painting gallery in adjacent barn. Open all year except Christmas.
E-mail: adie.exmoor@btinternet.com.uk

Caffyns Heanton Farm, Lynton, Devon EX35 6JW ●2

Mrs C J Priscott
☎/Fax 01598 753770
BB From £15.50–£18
Sleeps 6
Commended

Caffyns Heanton Farm is a family-run, 260-acre beef and sheep farm. Ideally situated in the heart of Exmoor, with qualified riding nearby. Whether you want beach or bracken, the scenery is stunning and it's all within easy reach – a perfect location. Please phone for brochure. Open Apr–Sept.

Cleave Farmhouse, Weare Giffard, Nr Bideford, North Devon EX39 4QX ●3

Liz Moore
☎ 01805 623671
Fax 01805 623235
BB From £20–£22
Sleeps 5
Listed Commended

Welcome to Cleave Farmhouse on our very busy dairy farm set in the heart of Tarka countryside with lovely walks and panoramic views. Safe, level parking, secluded garden. Golfing and fishing available nearby. Local to RHS garden Rosemoor, Dartington Crystal and Clovelly. Open Jan–Nov.

Combas Farm, Putsborough, Croyde, North Devon EX33 1PH ●4

Mrs Gwen Adams
☎ 01271 890398
BB From £18–£21
EM From £10
Sleeps 12
Commended

140-acre stock farm nestling in its own secluded valley, just 15 mins' walk from miles of golden sands (5 mins from the village pub!). Many repeat bookings confirm claims to a warm welcome and high standard of home cooking using home produce including unusual fruit and veg. Wisteria rambles over this 17th century longhouse overlooking a lovely garden and unspoiled view. In 'Which' Good B&B Guide. Colour brochure. Closed Christmas & Jan.

Coombe Farm, Countisbury, Lynton, Devon EX35 6NF ●5

Rosemary & Susan Pile
☎/Fax 01598 741236
BB From £18.50–£23
Sleeps 14
Commended

Comfortable old farmhouse set on a hillside between picturesque Lynmouth and the legendary Doone Valley. Wholesome breakfast with delicious homemade bread and marmalade, served in large beamed dining room, will set you up for the day exploring Exmoor. After that relax in the lounge with colour TV. 2 bedrooms with shower en suite, 3 with H/C, all with hot drinks facilities. Licensed. Open Mar–Nov.

West Country — North Devon

6. Court Barton, Lapford, Crediton, Devon EX17 6PZ

Sheila Mather
☎/Fax 01363 83441
BB From £19–£21
Sleeps 6
♛ ♛ Commended

Treat yourself. Delightful medieval farmhouse, undulating floorboards, beams and panelling. Quality bedrooms, cosy and warm. En suite or private bathrooms. Nibble or feast – breakfast's a treat. Enjoy our dairy farm and lovely local walks. Deer, foxes, badgers and buzzards abound. It's a different world here. Conservation village with 16th century pub/restaurant. Ideally central. Brochure. Open Jan–Nov.

7. Denham Farm, North Buckland, Braunton, North Devon EX33 1HY

Mrs Jean Barnes
☎/Fax 01271 890297
BB From £25–£28
EM From £12
Sleeps 24
♛ ♛ Commended

A Happy Holiday Recipe
Take a lovely warm farmhouse, pretty en suite bedrooms, a pinch of fun and laughter, mix with nearby attractions and miles of golden sand. Surround with green fields, country walks, keep amused with small pets and games room. Serve up with delicious home cooking and return for a repeat helping. Open Jan–Nov.

8. Forda Farm, Thornbury, Holsworthy, North Devon EX22 7BS

Mrs Valerie Wood
☎ 01409 261369
BB From £16–£20
EM From £10
Sleeps 5
Listed Commended

Roddy and Val invite you to stay on their livestock farm set in a peaceful location four miles from the market town of Holsworthy. Comfortable lounge with exposed beams and inglenook fireplace. Day trips to the North Cornish coast, Rosemoor Gardens, Dartmoor and National Trust properties are highly recommended. Open all year.

9. Great Bradley Farm, Withleigh, Tiverton, Devon EX16 8JL

Mrs Sylvia Hann
☎ 01884 256946
BB From £18–£21
Sleeps 4
♛ ♛ Highly Commended

Lovely, peaceful 16th century farmhouse. Friendly, happy atmosphere. Beautiful countryside. Private bathrooms, comfort and delicious breakfasts. Do come, we will be here to welcome you. Non-smokers only please. Open Easter–Oct.

10. Harton Farm, Oakford, Tiverton, Devon EX16 9HH

Mrs Lindy Head
☎/Fax 01398 351209
BB From £14–£16
EM From £7
Sleeps 6
♛ Commended

Country fare at its best, in peaceful surroundings, with additive-free home-grown meat and vegetables. Meet the sheep, relax in the comfortable old stone farmhouse, explore wonderful countryside and return home revitalised – the perfect get-away-from-it-all break. Vegetarian menu on request. Tea-making facilities, home-spun wool available. Farm walk with nature notes, friendly animals. Reduction for children. Open all year (closed Christmas & New Year).

11. Haxton Down Farm, Bratton Fleming, Barnstaple, Devon EX32 7JL

Mrs Pat Burge
☎ 01598 710275
BB From £16–£19
EM From £9
Sleeps 5
♛ ♛ Commended

Relax among leafy lanes and wonderful scenery on our working stock farm nestling in a peaceful valley. 17th century farmhouse offers warmth and comfort with private or en suite facilities, CTV, tea trays and a warm welcome to all ages. Delicious food with hearty breakfasts and tempting 4-course dinners. Close to beach and moor and attractions galore. Give North Devon a try – you'll be pleased you did. Ring for brochure please. Open Apr–Oct.

North Devon   *West Country*

Hayne Farm, Cheriton Fitzpaine, Devon EX17 4HR

Mrs Margaret Reed
☎/Fax 01363 866392
BB From £15
Sleeps 6
Listed *Commended*

Guests are welcome to our 17th century working farm situated between Cadeleigh and Cheriton Fitzpaine. Exeter 9 miles, Tiverton 8 miles. South and north coasts, Exmoor and Dartmouth are within easy reach. Many great tourist attractions around, three local pubs to visit. Summerhouse overlooking pond with ducks. Open all year except Christmas.

Hele Barton, Black Dog, Thelbridge, Crediton, Devon EX17 4QJ

Mrs Gillian Gillbard
☎/Fax 01884 860278
BB From £16
Sleeps 4
Commended

Relax amid peaceful surroundings with lovely views from our 17th century thatched farmhouse on family-run 273-acre beef and sheep farm. Ideal position just off B3042, 2 miles B3137 pub/restaurant just ½ mile. Double or twin rooms (en suite.available). Guests return year after year. Send for a brochure and the cream tea is waiting to welcome you. Open all year (closed Christmas).

Higher Biddacott Farm, Chittlehampton, Umberleigh, Devon EX37 9PY

Mrs Fiona Waterer
☎ 01769 540222
BB From £15–£20
Sleeps 6
Commended

Wake up to a view of rolling Devon countryside, a scrumptious breakfast and the sound of shire horses going out to work on a traditional working farm. Biddacott's mediaeval farmhouse provides log fires and a plasterwork ceiling. Exmoor and beautiful coastline are close at hand. Open all year except Christmas.

Higher Langridge Farm, Exebridge, Dulverton, Somerset TA22 9RR

Gill Summers
☎/Fax 01398 323999
BB From £20–£25
EM From £12.50
Sleeps 6
Listed *Commended*

Come and enjoy comfort, good food and warm hospitality in our 17th century farmhouse. Our working farm is set amidst superbly peaceful countryside on the edge of Exmoor where red deer and other wildlife abound. Most bedrooms have en suite/private bathrooms and all have tea/coffee-making facilities. Central heating throughout Open all year.

Home Park Farm, Lower Blakewell, Muddiford, Barnstaple, North Devon EX31 4ET

Mrs Mari Lethaby
☎/Fax 01271 342955
BB From £15–£20
EM From £8.50
Sleeps 6
Commended

Paradise for a country and garden lover. Panoramic scenic views combined with warm hospitality, genuine farmhouse cuisine and a relaxing, tranquil atmosphere await you at Home Park. All rooms en suite, TV, hair dryer, hospitality tray. Four-poster beds. CH. Many extras including laundry. Conveniently positioned for Exmoor, N. Devon coast. Many repeat bookings confirm excellent accommodation. 2 miles north of Barnstaple. RAC acclaimed. AA QQQQ. Closed Christmas.

Hornhill Farmhouse, Exeter Hill, Tiverton, Devon EX16 4PL

Barbara Pugsley
☎/Fax 01884 253352
BB From £18–£22
EM From £12
Sleeps 6
Highly Commended

If you appreciate relaxation with comfortable beds (one four-poster and one ground floor), private bathrooms, good breakfasts, on-site parking and no smoking, come and stay with us. Our 17th century farmhouse has superb views and is surrounded by fields. You will be most welcome. AA 5Q Premier Selected. Recommended by *Which? Good B&B Guide*. Open all year.

West Country — North Devon

18 Huxtable Farm, West Buckland, Barnstaple, North Devon EX32 0SR

Jackie & Antony Payne
☎/Fax 01598 760254
BB From £24
EM £15
Sleeps 17
Commended

Enjoy a 4-course candlelit dinner of farm/local produce with a glass of complimentary homemade wine in the medieval dining room of this 16th century Devon longhouse. Secluded sheep farm with abundant wildlife. En suite bedrooms with TV. Log fires, fitness room, sauna, games room and tennis court. Reductions for short/long breaks out of season and for children (£10). Free informative brochure. Open Feb– Nov and New Year.

19 Jubilee House, Highaton Farm, West Anstey, South Molton, North Devon EX36 3PJ

Lesley and Bill Denton
☎/Fax 01398 341312
BB From £18–£21
EM From £12
Sleeps 6
Listed Highly Commended

We are close to the edge of Exmoor, situated on the Two Moors Walk. Peaceful surroundings but easily accessible. Stabling/grazing available. Single/double rooms all with scenic views, large lounge/dining room, gas CH and log fire. Excellent cuisine – home-grown vegetables/preserves. Vegetarians catered for. Non-smokers. Open all year.

20 Kerscott Farm, Ash Mill, South Molton, North Devon EX36 4QG

Mrs Theresa Sampson
☎ 01769 550262
BB From £18
EM From £8.50
Sleeps 6
Highly Commended

Peaceful, 16th century farmhouse and working farm mentioned in Domesday Book, with beef cattle, sheep and shire horses. Beautiful olde world antique interior and furnishings – a rare find. Superb elevated position overlooking Exmoor National Park and surrounding countryside. Pretty en suite bedrooms. Healthy farmhouse food from the Aga. Spring water. Non-smokers only. AA QQQQQ Premier Selected. Open Feb–Nov.

21 Little Quarme Farm, Wheddon Cross, Exmoor National Park, Somerset TA24 7EA

Bob Cody-Boutcher
☎/Fax 01643 841249
BB From £18.50–£22
EM £11
Sleeps 6
Highly Commended

Come and relax in our beautifully furnished and decorated home. Outstanding location in the heart of Exmoor – very peaceful. Two double en suite rooms, one twin with private bathroom, all with panoramic southerly views, colour TV and hospitality tray. Dining room, TV lounge with satellite and racing channels, video and video library, ample car parking, stabling, E-mail and fax facilities. ¼ mile past Wheddon Cross – Exford road B3224.
E-mail:106425.743@compuserve.co.uk

22 Lodfin Farm, Morebath, Bampton, Devon EX16 9DD

Elaine Goodwin
☎/Fax 01398 331400
BB From £17.50–£22.50
EM From £10
Sleeps 6
Listed Highly Commended

The calming ambience of this 17th century farmhouse offers everything to help you relax and unwind. Spacious, comfortable and inviting with log fires and interesting artefacts. Three pretty bedrooms, one en suite, all with tea-making facilities and TV. Hearty, Aga-cooked breakfast. Ideally situated on southern edge of Exmoor National Park. Open Feb–Nov.

23 Lower Collipriest Farm, Tiverton, Devon EX16 4PT

Mrs Linda Olive
☎/Fax 01884 252321
BB From £21–£23
EM From £11
Sleeps 6
Highly Commended

Come and relax and enjoy the beauty of the Exe Valley in our 17th century thatched farmhouse. Comfortable lounge with inglenook fireplace and oak beams. Colour TV. Central heating throughout. Twin/single rooms with bathroom en suite, tea/coffee-making facilities. Delicious, traditional fresh cooking with our/local produce. Lovely walks over 220-acre dairy farm, conservation pond/woodland area. An AA award-winning farm. Open Feb–Oct. Brochure available.

North Devon   *West Country*

Newhouse Farm, Oakford, Tiverton, Devon EX16 9JE — 24

Mrs Anne Boldry
☎ 01398 351347
BB From £18–£21
EM £11
Sleeps 4
⛔(10) ✗ ✿ ■ ⊛
♥♥ *Commended*

A perfect base for discovering Devon, our 17th century farmhouse is close to Exmoor. Tastefully and comfortably furnished featuring oak beams and inglenook. Bedrooms have CH, CTV, tea trays, en suite bathrooms. We aim to provide the best of farmhouse cooking and hospitality – home-baked bread our speciality! AA QQQQ Selected. Recommended by *Which? Good B&B Guide*. Weekly reductions. Open all year (closed Christmas).

Quoit-at-Cross Farm, Stoodleigh, Tiverton, Devon EX16 9PJ — 25

Mrs Linda Hill
☎ 01398 351280
BB From £19
EM From £11
Sleeps 6
⛔ ✗ ■ ✿
♥♥ *Commended*

Beautiful 17th century farmhouse in conservation village. Unwind in the comfort of our home. Make *yourself* at home. Enjoy panoramic views, take a stroll around the lanes and return to a delicious evening meal. Attractive, co-ordinated bedrooms, all en-suite. Full English breakfast. Ideal location for National Trust properties, beaches and Exmoor. Open Apr–Dec.

Seldon Farm, Monkokehampton, Winkleigh, Devon EX19 8RY — 26

Mary Case
☎ 01837 810312
BB From £16
Sleeps 6
⛔ ♞ ■
♥ *Commended*

Relax in our delightful 17th century farmhouse situated in beautiful unspoilt part of the Devonshire countryside. Ideal for touring Dartmoor and Exmoor. Tarka Trail nearby, Rosemoor Gardens a short drive. Two double, one family room, all with H&C and tea/coffee-making facilities. Reductions for weekly bookings and children. Open Easter–Oct.

Waytown Farm, Shirwell, Barnstaple, North Devon EX31 4JN — 27

Hazel Kingdon
☎/Fax 01271 850396
BB From £18–£21
EM From £10.50
Sleeps 10
⛔ ♞ ■ ⊛
♥♥ *Commended*

Enjoy a relaxing, peaceful holiday set in the beautiful rolling countryside of North Devon. We have a family-run beef and sheep farm, easily found just three miles north of Barnstaple. Our 17th century farmhouse offers comfortable, well-appointed bedrooms with superb views. Traditional farmhouse cooking. Send for colour brochure. Reductions for weekly bookings. Open all year except Christmas.

Wood Advent Farm, Roadwater, Watchet, Somerset TA23 0RR — 28

Diana Brewer
☎/Fax 01984 640920
BB From £19.50–£23.50
EM £14
Sleeps 8
⛔(10) ♞ ⊠ ♣ ✿ ■ ⊛
♥♥ *Commended*

Discover peace and tranquillity at our listed farmhouse in the Exmoor countryside. Well-marked footpaths go for miles! Four en suite bedrooms with TV and hospitality trays, glorious views from all windows. Two large reception rooms and dining room where delicious Exmoor dishes are served with good wines. Relax by the heated pool, enjoy afternoon tea in the large gardens. Wonderful base for the West Country. We look forward to welcoming you. Open all year.

NO ANSWER?
Farmers are mostly out and about during the day.
Try to telephone before 9.30am or after 4pm.

West Country   North Devon

Self-Catering

① **Barkham,** Sandyway, South Molton, North Devon EX36 3LU

John Adie
☎/Fax 01643 831370
SC From £190–£415
EM From £17
Sleeps 5
🐴 ♿ 🍽 💼 ✿
♣♣♣♣ Highly
Commended

Hidden in a secluded moorland valley with streams and woodland, you can find peace and quiet throughout the year. Our three well-equipped cottages, once stone barns, are furnished with antiques. Dinner available in main house. Good walking. Tree house and croquet lawn. Also, three lovely B&B rooms available. Open all year.
E-mail: adie.exmoor@btinternet.com.uk

⑦ **Barley Cottage & Old Granary,** c/o Denham Farm, North Buckland, Braunton, North Devon EX33 1HY

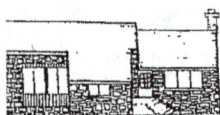

Jean Barnes
☎/Fax 01271 890297
SC £160–£630
EM From £12
Sleeps 4/6/8
🐴 🐕 ♿ £ 💼 ✿
♣♣♣♣ Commended

Welcome to our cottages. Let us surround you with warmth, comfort, peace and green fields. Walk our country lanes or take a short drive to the nearby sandy beaches. Here you can be pampered by having a meal in our farmhouse or a drink in our bar. Come to Denham to see why everyone else does. Open all year.

㉙ **Beech Grove,** East Westacott, Riddlecombe, Chulmleigh, Devon EX18 7PF

Thomas & Joyce Middleton
☎/Fax 01769 520210
SC From £150–£395
Sleeps 4/6
🐴 💼 ✿ ⓘ
♣♣♣♣ Commended

Peace, comfort, charming surroundings and a lovely warm atmosphere make you quickly relax. 2 bedrooms, sleeping 4/6 (cot available). CH, cosy log fires in winter. Superbly equipped, even a dishwasher. Games room for all ages. Delightful views of rolling meadows, pretty gardens with sunny patio. Friendly hosts, 'home from home' comforts, Devon's magnificent scenery and a taste of farming life, all combined ensure many guests often return. Open all year.

㉚ **Churchtown Farm,** West Anstey, South Molton, Devon EX36 3PE

Mrs Nicky Tarr
☎/Fax 01398 341391
SC From £145–£450
Sleeps 8 + cot
🐴 🐕 ♿ 🐎 ✿
♣♣♣♣ Commended

Enjoy a characteristic, spacious and attractively furnished half of Devon longhouse set in 200 acres of working farm adjoining moorland. Farmyard animals and pony rides. Beautiful secluded garden, barbecue, stocked fish ponds. 3 bedrooms, lounge with TV and woodburner, dining hall, well equipped kitchen, bathroom, CH. Linen included. Washing/drying facilities. Babysitting. Ideal family/walking holiday destination. Open all year.

⑨ **Cider Cottage,** c/o Great Bradley Farm, Withleigh, Tiverton, Devon EX16 8JL

Mrs Sylvia Hann
☎ 01884 256946
SC From £150–£375
Sleeps 2–5 + cot
🐴 ♿ 💼 ⓘ
♣♣♣♣ Highly
Commended

This charming cottage, its oak beams hung with cider jars, is cosy, warm, bright and comfortable. It has, we think, the best view in Devon, always changing with the light and seasons. Lean on the gate and watch the cows come home, or laze in the garden with a book. Then at the end of a happy day out, tuck freshly bathed children into bed, enjoy a glass of wine and relax. Lovely! Open all year.

North Devon   West Country

Country Ways, Little Knowle Farm, High Bickington, Umberleigh, Devon EX37 9BJ

Kate Price
☎/Fax 01769 560503
SC From £165–£475
Sleeps 2–6 + cot

♣ ♞ ⚑ ♨ ⚐
🌳🌳🌳 – 🌳🌳🌳🌳 Highly Commended

Beautifully converted stone barns hidden away on a small farm with magnificent views across the Devonshire Dales. Warm and well-equipped, incredibly peaceful with lovely gardens, ideal for barbecues. Walks through ancient woodland. Rare breeds with lots of friendly animals. Children's play area. Within easy reach of Exmoor and the coast. One unit ideal for wheelchairs. Open all year.

Crosse Farm, Bishops Nympton, South Molton, North Devon EX36 4PB

Mrs Dawn Verney
☎/Fax 01769 550288
SC From £140–£340
Sleeps 6 + cot

♞
🌳🌳🌳🌳 Commended

Wing of thatched 12th century Devon longhouse on 230-acre working farm. Magnificent views, unspoilt countryside, peace and tranquillity. Edge of Exmoor, 20 miles Golden Coast. 1 double en suite, 2 twins. Well equipped kitchen, microwave, dishwasher, washing machine. Lounge/diner with colour TV. Shower room. Enclosed garden. Electricity and linen included. Breakfasts and evening meals available. Open all year.

Deer's Leap Country Cottages, Deer's Leap Farm, West Anstey, South Molton, North Devon EX36 3NZ

Michael & Frances Heggadon
☎/Fax 01398 341407
SC From £116–£345
Sleeps 2/4

♞ ⚑ ⚐ ♨
🌳🌳🌳🌳 Up to Highly Commended

Occupying an idyllic, tranquil setting on the edge of Exmoor, this can be described as the perfect antidote to the stress of modern day life! The cottages are equipped to the highest standard. 30 acres of ground and extensive garden. Pets welcome. Stabling. Tennis court, games room and mountain bikes. Farm walk. Brochure available. Open all year. E-mail: dearsleapcottages@lineone.net

---

Drewstone Farm, South Molton, North Devon EX36 3EF

Ruth Ley
☎ 01769 572337
SC From £160–£395
Sleeps 6

♞ ⚑ ✂ ⚐ ♨
🌳🌳🌳🌳 – 🌳🌳🌳🌳🌳 Commended

Escape to farm tranquillity on edge of Exmoor. 16th century luxury cottage and converted barn with beams, woodburner, colour TV, fitted carpets, phone, dishwasher, washing machine. 3/4 bedrooms, bath-shower room. Fully equipped oak kitchen/diner and lounge with panoramic views. Enclosed lawn, children's games room, animals, freedom to explore the farm. Country walks, clay-pigeon shooting, trout lake. Open all year.

Dunsley Farm, West Anstey, South Molton, Devon EX36 3PF

Mrs Mary Robins
☎ 01398 341246
SC From £90–£375
Sleeps 5

♞ ⚑
🌳🌳🌳🌳 Commended

Self-contained cottage forming part of 16th century farmhouse, overlooks meadows and woodland valley. Access off a quiet country road. 2 bedrooms (accommodate 5 people), bathroom, large lounge/diner with colour TV. Large modern equipped kitchen, electric heating (£1 meter). Linen provided, pets welcome. Coarse fishing available on farm. Dulverton 6 miles. Open all year.

Dunsley Mill, West Anstey, South Molton, Devon EX36 3PF

Helen Sparrow
☎/Fax 01398 341374
SC From £200–£450
Sleeps 6

♞ ⚑ ♨ ⚐ ✂ 🎀
🌳🌳🌳🌳 Highly Commended

Beautifully converted detached stone barn set in 30 acres in an idyllic riverside situation. Three bedrooms, 2 doubles, 1 twin. Dishwasher, microwave, electric oven, washing machine. Linen and towels provided. Children, dogs and horses welcome. Bridleways adjoin the property. Fishing, hunting and shooting all in the vicinity. Open all year.

West Country — North Devon

㉑ Little Quarme Cottages, Wheddon Cross, Exmoor National Park TA24 7EA

Tammy Cody-Boutcher & family
☎/Fax 01643 841249
SC From £90–£500
Sleeps 2/6
Highly Commended to De Luxe

Six stone cottages furnished and equipped to the highest standards in the heart of Exmoor. All have microwaves, colour TV, videos, bed linen and towels. Standing amid 18 acres and large informal gardens, direct access to footpaths and bridlepath. Traffic free tranquillity with panoramic southerly views. Ample parking, free laundry room, pay phone, stabling. Many animals, pony rides. Quality, comfort, cleanliness. Brochure available.
E-mail: 106425.743@compuserve.com.uk

㊲ Lower Campscott Farm, Lee, Ilfracombe, Devon EX34 8LS

Mrs Margaret Cowell
☎ 01271 863479
SC From £195–£481
Sleeps 4/8
Up to Commended

Our four cottages have been converted from the farm's original buildings. All have fitted carpets, colour TV, fridge and microwave, the largest ones have freezers. Communal laundry room. Variety of farm animal pets for children to make friends with. Situated at the head of the Fuchsia Valley with a footpath to the village and beach 1½ miles away. Open all year.

㊳ Manor Farm, Riddlecombe, Chulmleigh, North Devon EX18 7NX

Eveline Gay
☎/Fax 01769 520335
SC From £185
Sleeps 7/8 + cot
Commended

Picturesque farmhouse with cosy 3-bedroomed wing in idyllic setting, overlooking cows and sheep grazing in nearby fields. Meet Doris the cow, collect eggs, feed lambs, watch milking on our dairy/sheep farm. Outstanding games room – children call it 'Alladins cave'! Includes play cottage, tractor, trikes, slide, table tennis and much more. Excellent heating for all seasons. Illustrated brochure.

㊴ Nethercott Manor Farm, Rose Ash, South Molton, North Devon EX36 4RE

Carol Woollacott
☎/Fax 01769 550483
SC From £100–£425
Sleeps 4 and 7
Approved

Welcome to Nethercott! Situated in the heart of the Devonshire dales – explore the farm, Exmoor and beautiful coast. Three cottages within traditional thatched farmhouse. Comfortably furnished, cosy and warm atmosphere, woodburners, oak beams, nooks and crannies. Trout pond, games room with skittles, pool table, tennis, darts. Barbecue or relax.

㊵ Northcott Barton Farm, Ashreigney, Chulmleigh, Devon EX18 7PR

Mrs Sandra Gay
☎/Fax 01769 520259
SC From £170
Sleeps 7/8 + cot
Commended

Unwind and relax country-style. Glorious countryside and farm to explore. Beautifully equipped, warm and comfy three bedroomed cottage offers character beams and log fire, plus video, microwave, washer, freezer, etc. Children love helping feed lambs and calves. Collect eggs for breakfast and see the cows come home for milking.

㊶ The Old Granary, Bampfield Farm, Goodleigh, Barnstaple, North Devon EX32 7NR

Lynda Thorne
☎/Fax 01271 346566
SC From £200–£620
Sleeps 8 + cot
Commended

Recently converted from a granary, this delightful detached cottage is situated near the picturesque village of Goodleigh on a 200-acre dairy farm. Spacious accommodation, beamed ceilings, woodburner and 'olde worlde' cottage ambience. Dishwasher, washer/dryer, microwave, CH. En suite master bedroom, family bathroom, separate WC. Play area, barbecue. Ideally placed for north coast/Exmoor and market town of Barnstaple. Open all year.

North Devon   *West Country*

Pickwell Barton Holiday Cottages, Pickwell Barton, Georgeham, Braunton, North Devon EX33 1LA

Mrs Sheila Cook
☎/Fax 01271 890987
⑯ From £160–£410
Sleeps 7/8
🐎 🐕 ✕ ■
✿ ✿ Commended

Visit Pickwell Barton and you have the best of both worlds – gorgeous country walks with a fantastic view of Putsborough, Woolacombe beach. Stroll across our fields in the evening to view the sun setting into the ocean. Each cottage has 3 bedrooms on our sheep and arable farm just 20 minutes' walk to the golden, sandy beach. Warm, cosy open fires in winter. Open all year.

Stable Cottage, Pitt Farm, North Molton, North Devon EX36 3JR

Mrs Gladys Ayre
☎ 01598 740285
⑯ From £150–£380
Sleeps 5/6
🐎 🐕 ✕ ✕
✿ ✿ ✿ ✿ Commended

Enjoy peaceful surroundings at our charming cottage, set in unspoilt Exmoor countryside, 1 mile from village shops, pubs, garage, equipped to high standard with night storage heating throughout. 3 bedrooms. Bath/shower/beamed lounge with woodburner. Colour TV, oak fitted kitchen/diner. Autowasher, fridge, microwave, etc. Own patio. Barbecue. Pond with ducks and geese. Freedom to explore the farm. Open all year.

West Ilkerton Farm, Barbrook, Lynton, North Devon EX35 6QA

Chris & Victoria Eveleigh
☎/Fax 01598 752310
⑯ From £190–£460
Sleeps 6 + cot
🐎 🐕 ✕ ■ 🐎 ✿ ✕ ◉
✿ ✿ ✿ ✿ Commended

Luxurious semi-detached cottage on secluded hill farm bordering open moor. Sheep, cattle, carthorses and Exmoor ponies. Coast 3 miles, riding ½ mile. 3 bedrooms (2 king size, 1 twin) 2 bathrooms, living/dining room, kitchen (Rayburn and full range of appliances). CH. TV, video. Baby equipment and evening babysitting. Children, dogs and horses welcome. Special winter breaks from £95. Ideal for walking, riding, family farm holidays. Open all year.

Whitefield Barton, Challacombe, Barnstaple, Devon EX31 4TU

Rosemarie Kingdon
☎ 01598 763271
⑯ From £100–£360
Sleeps 6 + cot
🐎 🐕 ✕ ✕ ■
✿ ✿ ✿ ✿ Commended

Spacious characteristic accommodation in half of 16th century farmhouse with modern luxuries. Tastefully furnished to high standard. Warm cosy lounge, well equipped kitchen, family & twin rooms, bathroom/shower, babysitting. Ample parking. Private patio, BBQ, streamed garden. Linen & electricity incl. Peaceful surroundings with scenic walks and farm animals on 200-acre farm. Central for beaches, moors. Open May–Dec.

White Witches and Stable Lodge, Hele Barton, Black Dog, Crediton, Devon EX17 4QJ

Mrs Gillian Gillbard
☎/Fax 01884 860278
⑯ From £150–£450
Sleeps 6–8 + cot
🛏 🐕 ■ ◉
✿ ✿ ✿ ✿ Up to Highly Commended

Dream of a pretty, well-equipped thatched cottage in the country with a garden leading to fields with a river meandering by. Listen to the birds singing on a summer evening or enjoy cosy nights by an open fire, or the luxury of en suite bedrooms and a four-poster bed in our listed barn. Sounds like heaven? Well this is reality. Send for a brochure and we shall be here to welcome you. Open all year.

Willesleigh Farm, Goodleigh, Barnstaple, North Devon EX32 7NA

Charles & Anne Esmond-Cole
☎/Fax 01271 343763
⑯ From £157–£642
Sleeps 6
🐎 🐕 ✕ ■ ◉
✿ ✿ ✿ ✿ Highly Commended

86-acre family-run dairy farm in glorious countryside, ½ mile from village, within ½ hour's drive of dramatic coastlines, Exmoor, glorious gardens, superb walks. Lovingly cared for, The Cottage and The Gatehouse welcome all ages and abilities to year-round comfort and peace. Enclosed heated swimming pool May–Oct. Open all year.

West Country — North Devon

47 Wonham Barton, Bampton, Tiverton, Devon EX16 9JZ

Anne McLean Williams
☎/Fax 01398 331312
[SC] From £125–£290
Sleeps 4/6
Commended

Conveniently explore sleepy Devon from our friendly, comfortable farmhouse wing overlooking the Exe Valley. Discover Domesday hamlets, majestic moorland, dramatic coastlines – or enjoy country pursuits and leisurely cream teas. Children are fascinated by soaring buzzards, Exmoor red deer and traditional shepherding on horseback with skilled Border Collies. TV drama and films have been made here; you too can share our secrets. Tell us when you are coming!

48 Yelland Cottage, c/o West Whitefield Farm, Challacombe, Barnstaple, Devon EX31 4TU

Jean Kingdon
☎ 01598 763433
[SC] From £120–£270
Sleeps 6
Approved

Semi-detached cosy farm cottage on working hill farm amidst beautiful countryside within easy reach of village pub and shop. Log fire, Rayburn plus electric conveniences. Relaxing lounge, colour TV. Linen provided. Friendly, relaxed atmosphere with farm animals. Spacious garden with ample parking. Ideal for beaches, walking, fishing, riding and touring North Devon. Open all year.

Camping & Caravanning

49 Welcombe Farm, Charles, Nr Barnstaple, North Devon EX32 7PU

Mrs Margaret Faulkner
☎/Fax 01598 710440
[SC] From £100–£260
Sleeps 4/5
Tourist Board Inspected

Imaginative private setting for a luxury caravan holiday. Comfortable and peaceful, with full facilities, two bedrooms and heating throughout. Small, family run farm with dairy cows and sheep, on the foothills of Exmoor. Panoramic views of hills and valleys from enclosed garden. Close to Tarka Trail and easy reach of sandy beaches, moors and gardens. Wildlife in abundance. Open Easter–Oct.

CONFIRM BOOKINGS

Disappointments can arise from misunderstandings over the telephone. Please write to confirm your booking.

South & East Devon

Dartmoor National Park & South & East Devon Coasts

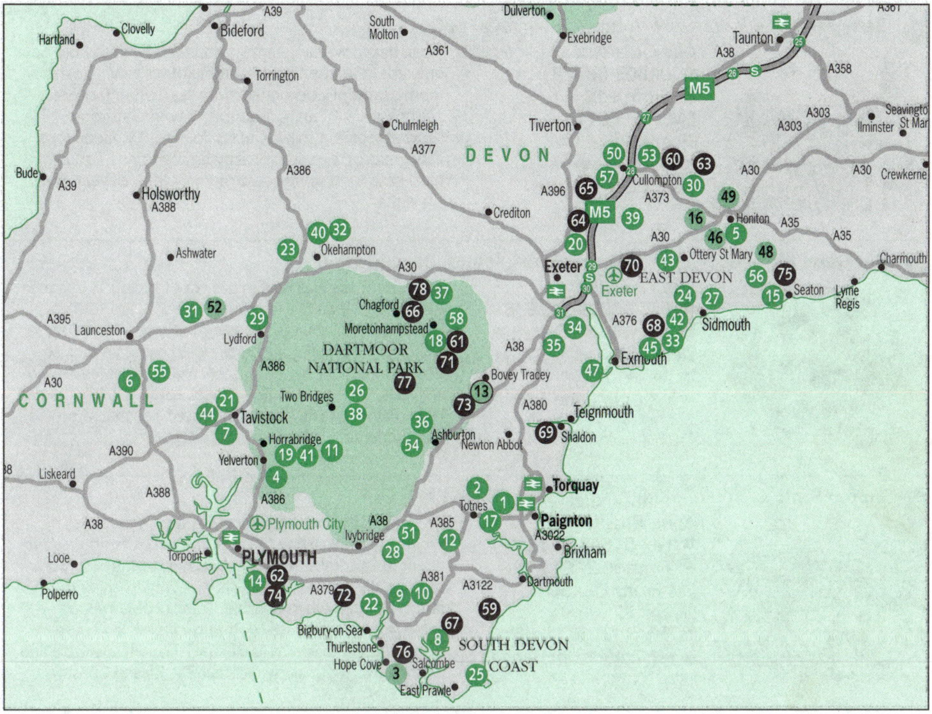

Key

- **1** Bed & Breakfast
- **1** Self-Catering
- **1** B&B and SC
- **1** Camping Barns
- **1** Camping & Caravanning

With its thatched cottages, lush meadows, steeply wooded valleys, rivers and streams, this is a special place. The 365 spectacular square miles of Dartmoor are wild, open and free and stretch down to the coves and hamlets of the south coast. Ancient small country towns abound – Moretonhampstead, Ottery St Mary, Totnes, Dartmouth, Ashburton – all unspoilt and tempting you to stop and browse. This is an area rich in the treasures of the National Trust, historic cities like Exeter and Plymouth, castles, abbeys, local crafts and cultures. Bustling seaside towns like Torquay, Paignton, Kingsbridge, Salcombe, Teignmouth and Exmouth are its hallmark. Come and enjoy 'heaven in Devon'.

If you would like help in finding suitable farm accommodation, turn to the full listing of farm groups on pages 360 to 363 to find appropriate contact details for this area.

West Country — South & East Devon

Bed and Breakfast
(and evening meal)

① Berry Farm, Berry Pomeroy, Totnes, Devon TQ9 6LG

Mrs Geraldine Nicholls
☎ 01803 863231
BB From £16
EM From £11
Sleeps 6
☼(5) ⚞ ⚒ ♞ 🛁 ⚱ ⊚
Listed *Commended*

Large mixed working farm surrounded by lovely old cider orchards in village 1½ miles from Totnes town. Spacious rooms, tastefully decorated, with tea/coffee facilities, washbasins – 1 family, 1 double, 1 twin. Bathroom, shower, separate toilet. Guests' lounge, TV. Good local eating places, evening meal by arrangement. Parking. Ideal base for touring coast/moors. Open all year except Christmas.

② Buckyette Farm, Buckyette, Littlehempston, Totnes, Devon TQ9 6ND

Mrs EP Miller
☎/Fax 01803 762638
BB From £18–£23
Sleeps 12
☼ ⚒ 🛁 ♞
☙☙ *Commended*

The farmhouse was built in the era of Victorian elegance with lovely views over the valley. Nearby are Totnes, Dartington cultural centre, steam railways, River Dart for fishing and several golf courses welcoming visitors, so don't forget your handicap card. Many other leisure activities. Beds have cotton sheets. Large garden, croquet lawn. Breakfast with locally produced bacon and sausages and homemade rolls. Open Mar–Oct.

③ Burton Farm, Galmpton, Kingsbridge, South Devon TQ7 3EY

Anne Rossiter
☎/Fax 01548 561210
BB From £22–£26.50
EM From £13.50
Sleeps 22
☼ ⚒ ⚞ ⊞ 🛁 ⚱ ⊚
☙☙ *Highly Commended*

Working dairy and sheep farm situated in the valley running towards Hope Cove. 3 miles from famous sailing haunt of Salcombe. Walking, beaches, sailing, windsurfing, bathing, diving, fishing. Guests welcome to enjoy the farm's activities when possible. Traditional farmhouse cooking, home produce (clotted cream, etc). 4 course dinner. Access to rooms at all times. En suite available and washbasins. Tea-making facilities, TV. Closed Christmas.

④ Callisham Farm, Meavy, Yelverton, Devon PL2 6PS

Esmé Wills
☎/Fax 01822 853901
BB From £18–£25
Sleeps 6
☼ ⚒ ⚞ ♞ 🛁 ⚱
☙☙ *Commended*

Traditional Dartmoor farmhouse nestling in the pretty Meavy valley. Perfect for walking and fishing – riding and golf nearby. A warm welcome, comfortable beds and huge breakfasts await you. ¼ mile from 12th century inn and picturesque village. Homely atmosphere with all comforts, log fires in winter. Full central heating. Open all year.

⑤ Catshayes Farm, Gittisham, Honiton, Devon EX14 0AE

Mrs Christine Broom
☎ 01404 850302
BB From £15.50
EM From £7.50
Sleeps 6
☼ ⚒ 🛁
Listed *Approved*

Countryside lovers will enjoy the peace and tranquillity of our 15th century thatched Devon longhouse on our working dairy farm. Near charming thatched village, market town, woodland walks. Abundance of wildlife and panoramic views. Shooting and riding by arrangement. Log fires, oak beams, farmhouse cooking. Studio nearby offering creative and personal development workshops. Open all year.

South & East Devon West Country

Claw House, Clawton, Holsworthy, Devon EX22 6QT

Diana Wallis
☎ 01409 253930
BB From £16–£18
Sleeps 6
Listed Commended

Come and relax in our comfortable Georgian farmhouse in a pretty village. Lovely views, plenty of off-road secure parking. Children welcome. Home cooking using fresh produce and brown eggs. Ideal base for touring Devon and Cornwall. Reasonable rates. Brochure available. Open all year.

Colcharton Farm, Gulworthy, Tavistock, Devon PL19 8HU

Mrs Lowenna Edwards
☎/Fax 01822 616435
BB From £18–£22
Sleeps 6
Highly Commended

Enjoy every home comfort in tasteful surroundings – good food and hearty breakfasts a speciality. We are situated in quiet and peaceful surroundings, central for touring, with splendid Dartmoor views. Relax in a charming garden or beside a cosy log fire. Good eating houses and National Trust properties nearby. Only 2 miles from beautiful historic town of Tavistock. Open all year.

Coombe Farm, Kingsbridge, South Devon TQ7 4AB

Beni & Jonathan Robinson
☎ 01548 852038
BB From £20–£22.50
Sleeps 6
Commended

Come and enjoy the peace and beauty of Devon in our lovely 16th century farmhouse. Wonderful breakfast, large elegant rooms, all en suite with colour TV, hot drink facilities. Artists have use of an art studio, and fishermen the well known Coombe Water fishery. Open Mar–Nov.

Court Barton Farmhouse, Aveton Gifford, Kingsbridge, Devon TQ7 4LE

John & Jill Balkwill
☎/Fax 01548 550312
BB From £22–£28
Sleeps 15
Highly Commended

Delightful 16th century listed manor farmhouse set in extensive gardens and situated on 40-acre farm. Seven bedrooms, mostly en suite, all with colour TV. Sunny breakfast room to enjoy delicious country farmhouse breakfasts and log fires in the comfortable lounge in colder weather. Close to moorland, beaches, ideal centre for walking, sailing, fishing, birdwatching. Open all year except Christmas. E-mail: jill@courtbarton.avel.co.uk

Crannacombe Farm, Hazelwood, Loddiswell, Nr Kingsbridge, South Devon TQ7 4DX

Shirley & Stephen Bradley
☎ 01548 550256
BB From £19
Sleeps 6
Commended

In an Area of Outstanding Natural Beauty near Kingsbridge. Working farm, Georgian farmhouse, comfortable, informal, absolutely peaceful. We have family/double bedrooms with private bathrooms and TV, hot drink facilities and a separate children's room sleeping 2. Lovely walks, stunning views and a clean river to paddle, play and picnic by. 15 minutes beach. Excellent food and cider.

Eggworthy Farm, Sampford Spiney, Yelverton, Devon PL20 6LJ

Linda Landick
☎ 01822 852142
BB From £16–£18
Sleeps 6
Commended

Away-from-it-all Dartmoor farm with secluded, informal gardens and beautiful moorland walks. Relax and enjoy our comfortable rooms with colour TV, tea/coffee-making facilities, H&C. Full English breakfast. Pets welcome. We look forward to seeing you. Open all year except Christmas.

West Country — South & East Devon

12 Foales Leigh, Harberton, Totnes, Devon TQ9 7SS

Carol Chudley
☎ 01803 862365
BB From £20–£25
Sleeps 6
⚘(5) ⚘ ⚘ ⚘ ⚘
⚘⚘ Highly Commended

A charming 16th century farmhouse in traditional courtyard setting. This family farm is situated in peaceful, unspoilt countryside within easy reach of beaches, moors and towns. Comfortable accommodation includes large oak-beamed lounge and 3 spacious bedrooms: 1 double, 1 family, 1 twin, all en suite with TV, CH and beverage trays. Delicious Aga-cooked breakfast. Closed Christmas & New Year.

13 Frost Farm, Hennock, Bovey Tracey, South Devon TQ13 9PP

Linda Harvey
☎/Fax 01626 833266
BB From £20–£22
EM From £10
Sleeps 6
⚘ ⚘ ⚘
⚘ Commended

A great place to stay, really homely and informal. Pretty country rooms, excellent en suites (bath and separate showers), bedrooms that are large enough to relax in. Find heritage and history here on our traditional Devonshire farmstead, and the food is great too! Open Mar–Nov.

14 Gabber Farm, Down Thomas, Plymouth, Devon PL9 0AW

Margaret MacBean
☎/Fax 01752 862269
BB From £16.50–£18.50
EM From £10
Sleeps 12
⚘ ⚘ ⚘ ⚘ ⚘
⚘⚘ Commended

A warm welcome is assured on this working dairy farm in an area of outstanding natural beauty. Situated on the coast near Plymouth with lovely walks and within easy reach of the beaches. Good home cooking, hot drinks facilities in all rooms, double and family with en suite showers. Open all year.

15 Gatcombe Farm, Seaton, Devon EX12 3AA

Julie Reed
☎ 01297 21235
Fax 01297 23010
BB From £16–£20
Sleeps 6
⚘ ⚘ ⚘ ⚘ ⚘
⚘ Commended

Only 5 minutes from the coast, Gatcombe is a family-run dairy farm in the beautiful Axe valley. Spacious farmhouse with double, twin and family rooms with washbasins. Guests' dining room and lounge with traditional beams, stonework and woodburner. Tea/coffee-making facilities, TV, video, large enclosed gardens. Hearty breakfasts, many local inns. Open Mar–Oct.

16 Godford Farm, Awliscombe, Honiton, Devon EX14 0PW

Sally Lawrence
☎/Fax 01404 42825
BB From £15–£21
Sleeps 6
⚘ ⚘ ⚘
⚘⚘ Commended

We invite you to stay on this family-run dairy farm, set in a beautiful river valley. Listed farmhouse with large sitting and dining rooms. Colour TV. Central heating. Drinks facilities in bedrooms. Scrumptious Devonshire breakfasts, local meat, homemade preserves. Delightful area for walking and wildlife. Cots and highchairs provided. Family and twin room, en suite/ private bathrooms. Child reductions. Brochure. Open Easter–Sept.

17 Great Court Farm, Weston Lane, Totnes, Devon TQ9 6LB

Janet Hooper
☎ 01803 862326
BB From £16–£18.50
EM From £10
Sleeps 6
⚘ ⚘ ⚘ ⚘ ⚘
⚘⚘ Highly Commended

Relax and enjoy the warm hospitality and country cuisine in our Victorian farmhouse overlooking the historic town of Totnes and surrounding countryside. Dairy farm with lanes and fields running down to River Dart. Ideal for coast and Dartmoor. Spacious double/family rooms have tea/coffee facilities, washbasins, TV, CH. Twin room en suite, WC and basin. Guests' bathroom, shower. Lounge, garden. South Hams Accommodation Award winner 1998. Open all year.

South & East Devon — West Country

Great Sloncombe Farm, Moretonhampstead, Newton Abbot, Devon TQ13 8QF

Mrs Trudie Merchant
☎/Fax 01647 440595
[BB] From £21–£22
EM From £11–£12
Sleeps 6
❦(8) ⚞ ⚘ ⚐ ⚑ ⚒
♣ ♣ ♣ Highly Commended

Share the magic of Dartmoor all year round whilst staying in our lovely 13th century farmhouse. A working dairy farm set amongst meadows and woodland, abundant in wild flowers and animals. A welcoming place to relax and explore Devon. Comfortable double and twin rooms all en suite with central heating, TV. Plenty of delicious home-cooked Devonshire food. Open all year.

Greenwell Farm, Nr Meavy, Yelverton, Plymouth, Devon PL20 6PY

Bridget Cole
☎/Fax 01822 853563
[BB] From £21–£24
EM From £14
Sleeps 6
❦ ⚐ ⚒
♣ ♣ Commended

Fresh country air, breathtaking views and scrumptious farmhouse cuisine. This busy farming family welcomes you to share the countryside and wildlife. Greenwell nestles on the slopes of Dartmoor and is ideal for walking. Touring Devon and Cornwall is easy with many gardens and National Trust properties locally or you may just prefer to relax and enjoy the peace and tranquillity. Liscensed, brochure available. Open all year (closed Christmas).

Hayne House, Silverton, Exeter, Devon EX5 4HE

Mrs L Kelly
☎ 01392 860725
[BB] From £16–£18
EM From £10
Sleeps 6
⚘ ⚐
♣ ♣ Commended

Explore Devon from our spacious and elegant Georgian farmhouse in delightful rural location. Centrally situated for touring coast, moors and NT properties. Killerton House is close by. 1 family, 1 twin room, both with private bath, 1 single with H&C, all with tea/coffee. Separate drawing room with colour TV and dining room. Tea and homemade cake on arrival. Evening meal sometimes available by prior arrangement. Open Easter–Oct.

Hele Farm, Gulworthy, Tavistock, Devon PL19 8PA

Mrs Rosemary Steer
☎ 01822 833084
[BB] From £18–£20
Sleeps 5
❦ ⚞ ⚘ ⚐
♣ ♣ Commended

A welcoming tea awaits you at the architecturally listed farmhouse (1780) on our working dairy farm which is in the process of converting to farming organically. Two fully en suite bedrooms with CH and tea/coffee. Central location for Dartmoor, both coasts and National Trust properties. Abundant good pubs and restaurants nearby. Dogs accepted. Open Apr–Oct.

Helliers Farm, Ashford, Aveton Gifford, Kingsbridge, Devon TQ7 4ND

Christine Lancaster
☎/Fax 01548 550689
[BB] From £20
Sleeps 9
❦ ⚘ ⚑
♣ ♣ Highly Commended

Small working sheep farm on a hillside set in the heart of Devon's unspoilt countryside. An ideal spot for touring the coast, Dartmoor, Plymouth, NT houses and walks. Family room with own private bathroom, double and twin both en suite and a single room, all tastefully appointed with washbasins and tea/coffee facilities. Comfortable lounge with TV. Dining room where excellent breakfasts, using local produce, are served.

Higher Cadham Farm, Jacobstowe, Okehampton, Devon EX20 3RB

John & Jenny King
☎ 01837 851647
Fax 01837 851410
[BB] From £18–£25
EM From £10
Sleeps 17
❦ ⚞ ⚐ ⚑ ⚒
♣ ♣ ♣ Highly Commended

Superb farmhouse accommodation, tasty home cooking, and breathtaking Devon scenery, that's the appetising recipe on offer at Higher Cadham in the heart of Tarka Country. Facilities for the less agile, en suite, flexible meal times, riverside walks and lots more! Ring for a brochure and details of our special offers. Open all year except Christmas and New Year.

West Country   *South & East Devon*

---

(24) Higher Coombe Farm, Tipton St John, Sidmouth, Devon EX10 0AX

Kerstin Farmer
☎/Fax 01404 813385
From £17–£19
Sleeps 10

♣ *Commended*

Find a warm, friendly welcome and comfortable, fully equipped rooms in our Victorian farmhouse, family owned since 1913. We offer total relaxation and a superb breakfast. After exploring East Devon's towns and villages, rolling countryside and beaches, take tea on the patio overlooking mature garden. Ideal for families. Easily reached, 4 miles inland from Sidmouth. Open Mar–Dec.

---

(25) Higher Kellaton Farm, Kellaton, Kingsbridge, Devon TQ7 2ES

Mrs Angela Foale
☎/Fax 01548 511514
From £15–£20
EM From £9
Sleeps 6

Listed *Highly Commended*

Our traditional, family-worked farm welcomes you to an area of peaceful and natural unspoilt beauty. Friendly farm animals. Children welcome. Nearby safe, sandy beaches, coastal walks and family attractions. Georgian farmhouse with attractive gardens. Comfortable, well furnished, spacious rooms. Guests' own lounge. Delicious Aga cooking, flexible meal times. Tea/coffee-making facilities. Open Easter–Sept.

---

(26) Higher Venton Farm, Widecombe-in-the-Moor, Newton Abbot, South Devon TQ13 7TF

Helen Hicks
☎ 01364 621235
From £18–£21
EM From £9
Sleeps 6

Listed *Commended*

A friendly welcome awaits you at Higher Venton Farm, a 16th century thatched farmhouse and working farm. Peaceful and relaxing, ideal for touring Dartmoor. Riding stables nearby. Coast 16 miles, ½ mile from Widecombe village. Good local eating places recommended. 2 double en suite with colour TV and 1 twin with washbasin. CH, tea/coffee-making facilities, lounge with colour TV. Open all year except Christmas.

---

(27) Higher Weston Farm, Weston, Nr Sidmouth, Devon EX10 0PH

Sandy MacFadyen
☎ 01395 513741
From £19–£22
Sleeps 6

♣ *Highly Commended*

Enjoy a relaxed, comfortable holiday in superb Heritage coast location, 3 miles from Sidmouth. Fully equipped en suite rooms, comfortable lounge. Breakfast menu includes vegetarian. Lovely garden, croquet, badminton, stabling available. Conservation award winning, working farm. Fields extend to coastal footpath, superb views of Lyme Bay, and to unspoilt Combe and beach. Closed Jan.

---

(28) Hillhead Farm, Ugborough, Ivybridge, Devon PL21 0HQ

Mrs J Johns
☎ 01752 892674
Fax 01752 690111
From £18–£20
EM From £10
Sleeps 6

♣ *Highly Commended*

Comfortable, welcoming family farmhouse. Guests' sitting room with TV and woodburner. 1 twin room, 2 double rooms both with TV and all with beverage trays and H&C. 2 en suite bathrooms, 1 private, also separate toilet. Full CH, open log fire in dining room. Good, home cooked and largely home produced food. Open all year except Christmas.

---

(29) The Knole Farm, Bridestowe, Okehampton, Devon EX20 4HA

Mrs Mavis Bickle
☎ 01837 861241
From £20–£22
EM From £10
Sleeps 8

♣ *Highly Commended*

Family working farm in area of outstanding beauty overlooking Dartmoor. Farmhouse with spacious rooms, large garden, sunlounge. Enjoy good home cooking. Ideally based to visit numerous places of interest with birdwatching, horseriding, fishing and walking for the energetic. En suite rooms available. Breakfast to your choice, four-course evening meal optional. Open all year except Christmas.

South & East Devon   West Country

Lane End Farm, Broadhembury, Honiton, Devon EX14 0LU

Mrs Molly Bennett
☎/Fax 01404 841563
BB From £17–£20
EM From £10
Sleeps 6
Commended

(30) At Lane End Farm you will enjoy delicious home cooking in glorious surroundings. Panoramic views of the Blackdown Hills, an Area of Outstanding Natural Beauty. With cattle and sheep grazing, floral gardens all within walking distance of the unspoilt thatched village of Broadhembury. Tea/ coffee facilities in bedrooms (2 en suite). CH, colour TV. Colour brochure. Children reduced rates. Evening meals optional. Open all year.

Little Bidlake Farm, Bridestowe, Okehampton, Devon EX20 4NS

Jo Down
☎/Fax 01837 861233
BB From £16–£17
EM From £8
Sleeps 6
Commended

(31) We are a working dairy/beef farm which is family run. Come and unwind in a relaxed atmosphere and enjoy traditional farmhouse fare. Walking, riding, golf and fishing can easily be arranged and Dartmoor is on our doorstep. Kennels and stabling available, as are packed lunches. Phone/fax for details. Open Mar–Nov.
E-mail: bid_boys@aol.com.uk

Lower Nichols Nymet Farm, North Tawton, Devon EX20 2BW

Mrs Jane Pyle
☎/Fax 01363 82510
BB From £18–£19.50
EM From £11
Sleeps 6
Highly Commended

(32) We offer a haven of comfort and rest on a modern working dairy farm and provide the perfect base for exploring the beauties of the West Country. Residents' lounge, colour TV. All rooms en suite, plus tea/coffee-making facilities. An ideal holiday centre – beaches, golf, good walks, riding, fishing, fine houses and gardens nearby to visit. Open Easter–Oct (incl).

Lower Pinn Farm, Peak Hill, Sidmouth, Devon EX10 0NN

Elizabeth Tancock
☎/Fax 01395 513733
BB From £19–£21
Sleeps 6
Commended

(33) A friendly welcome and comfortable, spacious rooms await you at Lower Pinn. 2 miles west of the coastal resort of Sidmouth. Many coastal and country walks. Bedrooms are en suite, fully centrally heated and have colour TV, hot drink making facilities. Own keys for access at all times. Guests' lounge, dining room with separate tables. Good hearty breakfasts. Ample parking. Several local pubs and restaurants. Open most of the year.

Lower Thornton Farm, Kenn, Exeter, Devon EX6 7XH

Mrs Alison Clack
☎/Fax 01392 833434
BB From £18–£20
Sleeps 6
Commended

(34) Come and relax at our secluded family farm with panoramic views. Just 2 miles from A38. Ideal base to visit Exeter, Torquay, Dartmoor, coast and racecourse. Our ground floor bedrooms are spacious and comfortable. One room en suite opening onto patio and garden, other has private bathroom. Both with tea/coffee facilities. Guests' lounge, colour TV, CH throughout. Child reductions. Open all year except Christmas.

Mill Farm, Kenton, Exeter, Devon EX6 8JR

Delia Lambert
☎ 01392 832471
BB From £19
Sleeps 14
Commended

(35) Mill Farm – a charming farmhouse with delightful, sunny en suite bedrooms with colour TV. Lovely rural setting. Ideal base to explore Devon. Good parking. Very easy to find. Don't miss out. Send for a brochure now!

West Country — South & East Devon

36 Mill Leat Farm, Holne, Ashburton, Newton Abbot, Devon TQ13 7RZ

Dawn Cleave
☎/Fax 01364 631283
BB From £16–£18
EM From £9
Sleeps 6
✿ Approved

200-acre hill farm situated on the edge of Dartmoor, an ideal place for touring Devon's beautiful countryside, moorland or beaches. Comfortable accommodation in 18th century farmhouse with large spacious bedrooms, en suite available, with tea/coffee facilities. Very peaceful surroundings, just right for relaxing. Closed Christmas.

37 Moor Farm, Dunsford, Exeter, Devon EX6 7DP

Mrs Joyce Dicker
☎ 01647 24292
BB From £14–£16
Sleeps 5
Listed *Commended*

The farmhouse is quietly situated on the edge of Dartmoor National Park with beautiful views of the surrounding Devon Hills and countryside. The guests have their own wing of the farmhouse, making it ideal for families. One family, one double room, each with tea/coffee-making facilities. Open Mar–Oct.

38 New Cott Farm, Poundsgate, nr Ashburton, Newton Abbot, Devon TQ13 7PD

Margaret Phipps
☎/Fax 01364 631421
BB From £18.50–£19.50
EM From £11
Sleeps 8
✿✿ *Commended*

A friendly welcome, beautiful views, pleasing accommodation at New Cott, a working farm in the Dartmoor National Park. Relax in our conservatory after enjoying the freedom and tranquillity of open moorland, the Dart Valley or one of the many attractions in Devon. Lots of lovely homemade food. Tea/coffee/chocolate in your en suite bedroom. Weekly reductions. Ideal for less able guests. OS: SY 703727. Closed Christmas Day.

39 Newcourt Barton, Langford, Cullompton, Devon EX15 1SE

Mrs Helen Hitt
☎ 01884 277326
BB From £16–£19
Sleeps 6
Applied

A friendly welcome awaits you at Newcourt Barton. Quietly situated just 5 mins from M5/J28, an ideal base for touring Devon's coast and countryside with many attractions nearby. Enjoy our large garden with grass tennis court or coarse fishing on farm. One twin/double en suite, one family room with private bathroom. Tea/coffee facilities, cot, highchair. Guests' own TV lounge, dining room. Child reductions. Local inn and restaurants for evening meal. Closed Christmas.

40 Oaklands Farm, North Tawton, Devon EX20 2BQ

Winifred Headon
☎ 01837 82340
BB From £17.50
EM From £10
Sleeps 5
✿ *Commended*

A warm welcome awaits you at Oaklands, a 130-acre farm in the centre of Devon. Easy to find on a level drive from a good road. Traditional farmhouse cooking with ample of everything. Heating, TV and electric blankets in bedrooms. Lounge with colour TV. Pleasant gardens. Open Mar–Nov.

41 Peek Hill Farm, Dousland, Yelverton, Devon PL20 6PD

Justine Colton
☎/Fax 01822 854808
BB From £17–£20
EM From £10
Sleeps 6
✿✿ *Commended*

Situated on the southern slopes of Dartmoor with sweeping views to Cornwall and adjacent to wooded Burrator Lake. Comfortable, sunny bedrooms, with antique furniture and en suite bathrooms. Log fire in lounge and much more. Mountain cycle hire. We are friendly and informal and are easily located off B3212. Open all year.

South & East Devon — West Country

Pinn Barton Farm, Pinn Lane, Peak Hill, Sidmouth, Devon EX10 0NN

Betty Sage
☎/Fax 01395 514004
BB From £19–£21
Sleeps 6
⌂(2) ⚞ ♿
♥ ♥ Commended

Enjoy a warm welcome on our 330-acre farm by the coast, 2 miles from Sidmouth seafront. Lovely walks in Area of Outstanding Natural Beauty. Comfortable bedrooms (all en suite) with CH, colour TV, hot drink facilities, electric blankets, access at all times. TV lounge and dining room with separate tables. Substantial breakfast, bedtime drinks. Many restaurants, inns and places to visit nearby. Open most of the year.

Pitt Farm, Fairmile, Ottery St Mary, Devon EX11 1NL

Susan Hansford
☎ 01404 812439
BB From £17–£20
Sleeps 14
⌂ ♿
♥ ♥ Commended

A warm family atmosphere awaits you at this 16th century thatched farmhouse which nestles in the picturesque Otter Valley ½ mile from A30 on B3176. Within easy reach of all East Devon resorts and pleasure facilities. A working cattle/arable farm surrounded by lovely countryside and rural walks. Family, double and twin rooms. Lounge with colour TV. Fire certificate. Open Mar–Nov.

Rubbytown Farm, Gulworthy, Tavistock, Devon PL19 8PA

Mary Steer
☎ 01822 832493
BB From £20–£25
EM From £12
Sleeps 6
⌂(12) ⚞ ⚘ ♿
♥ ♥ Highly Commended

Stay in our lovely old farmhouse and sleep in four-poster beds. Enjoy woodland walks. There is abundant wildlife, you may see deer if you are lucky and at dusk the foxes and badgers at play. Help with feeding the calves. Good farmhouse cooking with evening meals served by candlelight. St Mellion Golf and Country Club nearby. 2 double, 4 posters, en suite, 1 twin with private bathroom. Evening meal served by candlelight by prior arrangement. Closed Christmas.

Rydon Farm, Woodbury, Exeter, Devon EX5 1LB

Sally Glanvill
☎/Fax 01395 232341
BB From £22–£26
Sleeps 6
⌂ ⚞ ♿
♥ ♥ Highly Commended

Come and enjoy the peaceful tranquillity of our 16th century Devon longhouse on a working dairy farm. Exposed beams and inglenook fireplace. Bedrooms with tea/coffee facilities, hairdryers, full CH, private or en suite bathrooms. Romantic four-poster. Full English breakfast with free range eggs. Several local pubs and restaurants. AA QQQQ Selected. Open all year.

Skinners Ash Farm, Fenny Bridges, Honiton, Devon EX14 0BH

Mrs Jill Godfrey
☎ 01404 850231
BB £17
EM £9
Sleeps 6
⌂ ⚞ ⚘ ♿
Listed Commended

Enjoy a relaxing holiday on a family-run rare breeds farm. Two large family rooms with tea/coffee facilities, TV, private bathroom. Farmhouse cooking, cream teas. Farm walk, pony rides, egg collections. Lovely views. Near local beaches. Walk to two local inns. Please send for brochure. Open all year.

Smallacombe Farm, Aller Valley, Dawlish, Devon EX7 0PS

Mrs Alison Thomson
☎ 01626 862536
BB From £16–£18
EM From £9.50
Sleeps 6
⌂ ♿
♥ ♥ Commended

Off the beaten track, yet only two miles from Dawlish and the beach. Enjoy the best of both worlds, 'country and coast'. Children play freely with no fear of busy roads. Meet our 3 friendly dogs. Relax in the peaceful surroundings and homely atmosphere. 2 double rooms, 1 twin room, family unit available, en suite. Fridges in bedrooms. Reductions for children, weekly discounts. Ring or write for brochure. Open all year.

West Country — South & East Devon

48 Smallicombe Farm, Northleigh, Colyton, Devon EX13 6BU

Maggie Todd
☎ 01404 831310
Fax 01404 831431
BB From £18.50–£22
EM From £10
Sleeps 6
♕ Commended

Taste real pork, bacon and sausages from our prize-winning rare breed pigs in idyllic setting little changed over the centuries. Meet traditional farm animals and watch for the surrounding wildlife. Explore coast and country in this unspoilt corner of Devon. Featured in *Good Food Guide to the West Country*. Family or ground floor twin/double room, all en suite. Laundry, games room with Devon skittles, snooker and table tennis. Open all year.

49 Stafford Barton, Broadhembury, Honiton, Devon EX14 0LU

Anne Barons
☎/Fax 01404 841403
BB From £18–£22
EM From £10
Sleeps 6
♕♕♕ Highly Commended

Come and share our lovely home for a holiday treat. We are situated beneath the Blackdown Hills, ¼ mile from picturesque thatched village. Glorious walks through woodland and country lanes. Roam our farm and meet cows, sheep, horses and hens. Family, double, twin rooms, all en suite with colour TV, etc. Large lounge/dining room overlooking beautiful garden. Delicious home cooking using own produce. Weekly terms. Brochure. Open all year except Christmas.

50 Upton, Old Hill, Cullompton, Devon EX15 1RA

Fay Down
☎/Fax 01884 33097
BB From £18–£22
Sleeps 6
(12) ♕♕ Highly Commended

A warm welcome is assured in this beautiful, tranquil 17th century farmhouse. Set in its own parkland grounds with picturesque fishing lake, only 1½ miles from M5/J28. Guest rooms are charmingly furnished with a wealth of beams. All rooms en suite with TV and tea/coffee facilities. Golf course 1 mile. A perfect place to explore coast, moors and NT properties. Open all year except Christmas.

51 Venn Farm, Ugborough, Ivybridge, Devon PL21 0PE

Pat Stephens
☎/Fax 01364 73240
BB From £20–£22
EM £11
Sleeps 12
(5) ♕ Commended

We are well placed to offer you a peaceful and relaxing holiday 'off the beaten track'. Secluded gardens, streams, Gypsy caravan, an abundance of fresh local produce. Our guests become friends and keep returning. Carve your own roasts, still popular after 20 years. Also two bedroomed ground floor garden cottage for B&B guests. Open Feb–Nov.

52 Week Farm, Bridestowe, Okehampton, Devon EX20 4HZ

Margaret Hockridge
☎/Fax 01837 861221
BB From £23–£24
EM From £11
Sleeps 12
♕ Commended

Guests return annually to our 17th century farmhouse. Set in rolling countryside ¾ mile from old A30. Good home cooking and every comfort. Central for Dartmoor and coast, 8 miles Cornwall. Lounge with colour TV and log fires. 3 doubles, 2 family rooms all en suite (1 ground floor). Tea/coffee-making facilities, night storage heaters, colour TV. Heated outdoor swimming pool. Come and spoil yourselves. Fire certificate held. Open all year (closed Christmas).

53 Weir Mill Farm, Jaycroft, Willand, Cullompton, Devon EX15 2RE

Rita Parish
☎ 01884 820803
Fax 01884 820973
BB From £18–£20
EM From £10
Sleeps 6
♕♕ Highly Commended

Luxurious rooms, beautiful views and peaceful surroundings make Weir Mill, in the beautiful Culm Valley, something very special. Only 3 miles from M5 J27, giving easy access to coasts, moors and NT properties. There is one double en suite, one family en suite and one double room with private bathroom. All have CH, TV and tea/coffee-making facilities. Large garden, ample parking. Open all year.

South & East Devon — West Country

Wellpritton Farm, Holne, Ashburton, South Devon TQ13 7RX 54

Sue Gifford
☎ 01364 631273
BB From £19
EM From £9
Sleeps 11
♥♥ Highly Commended

Delightful character farmhouse set in Dartmoor National Park with beautiful views. Exposed beams, woodburner, scrumptious farmhouse cuisine. An ideal base, 3 miles from A38, within easy reach of all main attractions and NT properties. Perfect for staying off the beaten track. Elizabeth Gundrey recommended. Riviera Care Award winner. Brochure available. Open all year.

Whitecroft Farm, Clawton, Holsworthy, Devon EX22 6PW 55

Mrs J Morris
☎/Fax 01409 254623
BB From £18–£20
Sleeps 6
♥♥ Commended

Welcome, we offer comfort, superb farmhouse cuisine, log fires and solitude. Off the beaten track but within easy reach of coast and moors. Take a riverside walk around the farm or a dip in the heated pool. Whether you come for a short or long break, you're sure to feel refreshed. Open all year. E-mail: melvyn.j.morris@btinternet.com.uk

Wiscombe Linhaye Farm, Southleigh, Colyton, Devon EX13 6JY 56

Sheila Rabjohns
☎ 01404 871342
BB From £18–£22
EM From £9
Sleeps 6
♥♥ Commended

A spacious farm bungalow on a small working farm in quiet countryside but in easy reach of Sidmouth, the Donkey Sanctuary and Lyme Regis. Ideal for senior citizens and those who cannot use stairs. Private en suite bathrooms. Drink facilities, TV and hair dryers in all bedrooms. Separate dining tables. Home/local produce. Open Mar–Nov.

Wishay Farm, Trinity, Cullompton, Devon EX15 1PE 57

Mrs Sylvia Baker
☎/Fax 01884 33223
BB From £16–£17
Sleeps 6
♥♥ Commended

Comfortable and spacious 17th century farmhouse, set amid the peace and seclusion of the countryside. Ideal base for touring. Comfortable lounge with colour TV. Central heating. 1 family room with en suite bathroom, double with separate guests' bathroom, both with colour TV, fridge and tea/coffee-making facilities. Children welcome. Open Feb–Nov.

Wooston Farm, Moretonhampstead, Newton Abbot, Devon TQ13 8QA 58

Mary Cuming
☎/Fax 01647 440367
BB From £19–£21
Sleeps 6
♥♥ Highly Commended

Wooston Farm is situated above the Teign Valley in the Dartmoor National Park with views over open moorland. The farmhouse is surrounded by a delightful garden. There are plenty of walks on the moor and wooded Teign Valley adjoining farm. Good home cooking and cosy log fires await you at Wooston. 2 double en suite, 1 with four-poster, 1 twin room. Also mountain bikes available. AA listed QQQQ Selected. Open all year except Christmas.

Please mention *Stay on a Farm* when booking

West Country   South & East Devon

Self-Catering

59 Alston Cottage, Alston Farm, Slapton, Kingsbridge, Devon TQ7 2QE

Mrs Suzanne Hutchings
☎ 01548 580337
SC From £130–£350
Sleeps 5 + cot
Commended

Alston is a family-run beef and arable farm tucked away between Dartmouth and Kingsbridge. Sea views. Alston Cottage is completely modernised, self-contained part of farmhouse. Separate driveway, entrance. Large garden. Ideal for a family holiday. Family and twin bedrooms, beds ready made. Well fitted kitchen, elegant lounge/diner, colour TV, NSH. Open all year.

46 Bertie's and Porky's Barns, Skinners Ash Farm, Fenny Bridges, Honiton, Devon EX14 0BH

Mrs J S Godfrey
☎ 01404 850231
SC From £170–£420
EM £9
Sleeps 5/7
Up to Highly Commended

Enjoy a relaxing holiday on a family-run rare breeds farm in a luxury flat and converted barn. Enjoy pony rides, farm walks, egg collections. Meals available. Near local beaches and tourist attractions. On A30 Honiton to Exeter road. Please send for colour brochure. Open all year.

60 Bodmiscombe Farm, Blackborough, Cullompton, Devon EX15 2HR

Mrs Brenda Northam
☎/Fax 01884 266315
SC From £115–£310
Sleeps 4 + cot
Commended

For three generations our family has been farming in this tiny peaceful hamlet set in the Blackdown Hills now designated an Area of Outstanding Natural Beauty. The self-contained part of our 17th century farmhouse with beamed ceilings is furnished to a high standard. Cleanliness and comfort guaranteed. Come and share 200 acres of rolling Devonshire countryside with us. Nature trails, private fishing. Looking forward to meeting you! Open all year.

61 Budleigh Farm, Moretonhampstead, Devon TQ13 8SB

Mrs Judith Harvey
☎ 01647 440835
Fax 01647 440436
SC From £95–£350
Sleeps 2–6
Commended

Seven properties, created with flair from traditional granite barns, on a farm at the end of a stunning valley in the Dartmoor National Park – rural but not remote. Superb gardens, delightful pubs, beaches and castles are not too far away. Come especially in May when the bluebells turn the woods to a smoky haze. Open all year.
E-mail: farmleigh@aol.com.uk

3 Burton Farm Cottages, Burton Farm, Galmpton, Kingsbridge, South Devon TQ7 3SR

Anne Rossiter
☎/Fax 01548 561210
SC From £85–£495
Sleeps 4/5 + cot
Commended

Situated in a pretty hamlet adjoining open farmland, 5 mins walk from farm, these cob and slate cottages are 5 miles from Kingsbridge, 3 miles from sailing haunt of Salcombe and 1 mile from lovely beaches of Hope Cove and Thurlestone. Traditionally decorated and furnished, many original features with stone-built fireplaces and electric heating. Guests welcome to enjoy farm activities. Meals (from £10.50) available on request.

South & East Devon — West Country

Coombe Farm Cottage, Wembury Road, Plymstock, Plymouth, Devon PL9 0DE ⓖ

Suzanne MacBean
☎ 01752 401730
[SC] From £100–£350
Sleeps 5/6
Commended

A warm welcome with tea and cake awaits you to our comfortable and homely cottage, set in a peaceful valley on a working dairy farm. Close to beaches, moor and city centre. Off road parking, linen and towels included, small garden with barbecue. Pets welcome by arrangement. Open all year.

Droughtwell Farm, Sheldon, Honiton, Devon EX14 0QW ⓖ

Mrs Sue Cochrane
☎ 01404 841349
[SC] From £110–£200
Sleeps 2 + cot
Commended

Come to a cosy, comfortable self-contained wing of our farmhouse, with log fire. We are a small working sheep farm in peaceful countryside. Lovely walks in fields and forest where foxes, badgers, roe deer and a great variety of birds can be seen. Open all year.

The Garden Lodge, Stafford Barton, Broadhembury, Honiton, Devon EX14 0LU ⓖ

Mrs Anne Barons
☎/Fax 01404 841403
[SC] From £275–£325
Sleeps 4
Commended

In need of a break? Then come and relax in our spacious Garden Lodge. Enjoy the beautiful scenery and garden. Watch the sun set over the Blackdown Hills. Stroll into nearby idyllic thatched village with pub and shop. Plenty to see and do. Lovely farm walks with lots of animals. Brochure available. Open all year.

The Granary and Little Week Barn, Week Farm, Bridestowe, Okehampton, Devon EX20 4HZ ⓖ

Margaret Hockridge
☎/Fax 01837 861221
[SC] From £240–£635
Sleeps 5/8 + cot
Up to Highly Commended

A cream tea awaits you at these semi-detached barn conversions situated in a pretty part of Devon countryside where scenery, moorland and wildlife are magnificent. Near A30, ideal touring base for both coasts, Cornwall, Dartmoor and numerous attractions. Attractive garden with patio, BBQ, heated outdoor swimming pool. Well fitted kitchen, (washing machine, microwave, dish-washer, fridge freezer), lounge, colour TV. Open end May–end Oct.

Hele Payne Farm, Hele, Exeter, Devon EX5 4PH ⓖ

Irene and Sally Maynard
☎ 01392 881530/ 881356
Fax 01392 881530
[SC] From £170–£430
Sleeps 3/5/6
Up to Highly Commended

Relax in our heated swimming pool and slip into the tranquillity of rural life as recently featured on BBC 1's *Holiday* programme. Explore our dairy farm – children may help to feed the baby calves. All three cottages are surrounded by beautiful gardens, ideal for barbecues, and have colour TV, bed linen, laundry room, cot, highchair and CH. Games barn with pool, table tennis etc provides fun for any age. Open all year.

Highdown Farm, Bradninch, Exeter, Devon EX5 4LT ⓖ

Mrs Sandra Vallis
☎ 01392 881028
Fax 01392 881272
[SC] From £120–£500
Sleeps 2/4/7 + cot
Highly Commended

Situated high above the Culm Valley, our partly organic Duchy of Cornwall mixed/dairy farm boasts spectacular views, an abundance of wildlife and lovely walks. We have three warm and welcoming cottages to choose from, all tastefully decorated and furnished, each with its own garden. An ideal holiday base whatever the season. Open all year.

West Country — South & East Devon

66 Howton Linhey, Great Howton Farm, Moretonhampstead, Newton Abbot, Devon TQ13 8PP

Jane & Alastair Wimberley
☎/Fax 01647 440100
SC From £225–£475
Sleeps 6

Commended

Comfortable, well-designed barn conversion standing in its own garden. Spacious accommodation with well-equipped kitchen. Working livestock family farm with ponds, streams and woodland walks. Easy access to open moorland with its wonderful scenery, walking, cycling, horseriding, other outdoor pursuits and many tourist attractions. Open all year.

67 Ledstone Farm, Ledstone, Kingsbridge, South Devon TQ7 2HQ

Ann Lidstone
☎ 01548 852662
SC From £175–£273
Sleeps 2/3

Highly Commended

In a tiny village near Kingsbridge we offer a choice of two converted haylofts. The Loft has two bedrooms and Swallow Barn one bedroom. Both have living rooms with corner kitchens, lots of extras. Lovely locations and a happy, comfortable atmosphere. Phone, towels, VCR, etc. Convenience and contentment guaranteed. Open all year.

68 Lemprice Farm, Yettington, Budleigh Salterton, Devon EX9 7BW

Mrs Hanneke Coates
☎ 01395 567037
Fax 01395 567585
SC From £228–£496
Sleeps 4–6

Highly Commended

National award winning stone barn cottages suitable for disabled. Exceptional walking area of outstanding natural beauty and scientific interest. Home of the rare barn owl. All cottage gardens overlook small lake and marshes abundant with wildlife, hills and open countryside beyond. All linen and electricity included. Dogs by arrangement only. Three miles to beach. Brochure. Open Easter–Nov.
E-mail: dickcoates@compuserve.com.uk

69 Longmeadow Farm, Coombe Road, Ringmore, Shaldon, Teignmouth, Devon TQ14 0EX

Mrs Anne Mann
☎ 01626 872732
Fax 01626 872323
SC £140–£300
Sleeps 4

Approved

Enjoy the best of both worlds on our South Devon farm set in lovely countryside but less than a mile from the beach and Shaldon village. Comfortable accommodation (in two units each sleeping 4) adjoining traditional style farmhouse overlooking estuary. Garden, patio, barbecue. Ideal location for touring coast, moors. Walks, fishing, riding nearby. Ample parking. Brochure available. Open all year.

70 Middle Cobden Farm, Whimple, Exeter, Devon EX5 2PZ

Mrs Cathie Cottey
☎ 01404 822276
SC £160–£370
Sleeps 6

Commended

A warm and friendly welcome awaits you on our real working dairy farm. Peace and quiet with comfortable surroundings offered in half of our farmhouse. Self-contained, the accommodation offers large lounge, kitchen/diner, family room, twin room and bathroom upstairs. Easy access to M5, Exeter and East Devon resorts. Brochure available. Open all year.

71 Narramore Farm Cottages, Narramore Farm, Moretonhampstead, Devon TQ13 8QT

Sue Horn
☎ 01647 440455
Fax 01647 440031
SC From £100–£480
Sleeps 2/5

Commended to Highly Commended

Stressed out? Let Narramore work its magic on you! Six comfortable cottages situated on 107-acre horse stud/deer farm. A really warm pool, bubbling hot spa, satellite TV, games/laundry room, payphone, play area, fishing lake, boat, barbecue, small animals plus the opportunity to badgerwatch amidst glorious countryside – all these make us special. Colour brochure. Open all year.

South & East Devon — *West Country*

Oldaport Farm Cottages, Modbury, Ivybridge, Devon PL21 0TG

Miss C Evans
☎ 01548 830842
Fax 01548 830998
[SC] From £149–£441
Sleeps 2/6
Highly Commended

Oldaport is a small sheep farm of 70 acres, lying in the Erme Valley, and offering lovely views of the countryside. The four cottages, which sleep 2/6, were redundant stone barns which have been carefully converted into comfortable holiday homes. All fully equipped, heating in all rooms. Sandy beaches nearby, Dartmoor 8 miles. Excellent birdwatching. No dogs in high season. Brochure available. Open all year.
E-mail: cathy.evans@dial.pipex.com.uk

Otter Holt and Owl Hayes, c/o Godford Farm, Awliscombe, Honiton, Devon EX14 0PW

Sally Lawrence
☎/Fax 01404 42825
[SC] From £125–£350
Sleeps 4 + cot
Commended

Come and see where the hayracks are in our beautiful barn cottages, one of the many features that make them unique. Each cottage has beamed lounge with colour TV/video, pine kitchen/diner with washer/dryer, microwave, fridge/freezer. CH. 2 bedrooms (linen incl). Walkers' paradise, wildlife abundant. Floral gardens, games barn, pets and calves to feed. Farm map. Children welcome, large play area. Cot available. Brochure. Open all year.

Shippen and Dairy Cottages, c/o Lookweep Farm, Liverton, Newton Abbot, Devon TQ12 6HT

Averil Corrick
☎ 01626 833277
[SC] From £160–£430
Sleeps 4/5 + cot
Commended

Come and relax in the peace and tranquillity of these two delightful barn converted cottages. Set within the Dartmoor National Park with easy access to the coast, golf, riding, walking and fishing locally. Sleeps 4/5, fully equipped and well furnished throughout. Own gardens with beautiful views. Ample parking. Use of outdoor heated swimming pool. High chairs, cots and linen available. Open all year.

Smallicombe Farm, Northleigh, Colyton, Devon EX13 6BU

Maggie Todd
☎ 01404 831310
Fax 01404 831431
[SC] From £95–£650
Sleeps 2–8
Commended – Highly Commended

Escape the stresses of modern living to converted barns in idyllic rural setting little changed over the centuries. Meet our traditional farm animals and watch for the surrounding wildlife. Try Devon skittles in our games room. Explore coast and country in this unspoilt corner of Devon. ETB 'England for Excellence' Award 1995. Holiday Care Service 'Best Self-Catering Accommodation' 1996. Open all year.

Stick Wick Holiday Homes, c/o Frost Farm, Hennock, Bovey Tracey, South Devon TQ13 9PP

Linda Harvey
☎/Fax 01626 833266
[SC] From £125–£1,250
Sleeps 2–12
Commended

Three good country homes with excellent facilities. Long farmland views, garden, play area, games barn, friendly farm animals. 10 mins Bovey. Craft centre, working pottery/glass blowing, Becky Falls, Trago Mills, Dartmoor, Exeter. Seaside at Teignmouth. Golf, fishing, riding, swimming nearby. Come and join us and have fun in Devon. Open all year.

Traine Farm, Wembury, Plymouth, Devon PL9 0EW

Sheila Rowland
☎/Fax 01752 862264
[SC] From £105–£375
Sleeps 5 (+ 2) + cot
Commended

Come and enjoy a relaxed holiday in lovely surroundings, on farm overlooking village of Wembury and beautiful heritage coastline. Ideal for families, children can enjoy rockpool rambling, pony rides. Good centre for walking with waymarked trails through the farm. Sailing, diving, golf nearby. Short breaks. Open all year.

West Country — South & East Devon

75 Vine & Grooms Cottage, Lovehayne Farm, Southleigh, Colyton, Devon EX13 6JE

Mrs Philippa Bignell
☎/Fax 01404 871216
SC From £175–£595
Sleep 4/8 + cot
Commended

Delightful cottages in secluded private valley. Explore our 200-acre mixed farm with woods and streams, abundant wildlife, horses and sheep. In an Area of Outstanding National Beauty, 3 miles from the sea at Branscombe. Hard tennis court. Bedlinen provided, Central heating. Brochure available. Open Mar–Nov.
E-mail: fairway@globalnet.co.uk

76 Withymore Cottage, Withymore Farm, Malborough, Kingsbridge, South Devon TQ7 3ED

Mrs Jo Hocking
☎/Fax 01548 561275
SC From £135–£440
Sleeps 6 + cot
Commended

Recently modernised cottage nestling in a peaceful valley on a family-run dairy farm within a short distance of Salcombe. Very comfortable and furnished to a high standard throughout. Colour TV, bed linen, CH. Well equipped kitchen. Large enclosed garden. Ideal centre for family holiday with many beaches, sailing, fishing, golf, horse riding and spectacular coastal walks. Open all year.

77 Wooder Manor, Widecombe-in-the-Moor, Newton Abbot, Devon TQ13 7TR

Mrs Angela Bell
☎/Fax 01364 621391
SC From £100–£800
Sleeps 2/16
Commended

Cottages and converted coachhouse on 150-acre family farm, nestled in picturesque valley surrounded by unspoilt woodland, moors and granite tors. Central for touring Devon and exploring Dartmoor by foot or on horseback. Clean and fully equipped. Colour TVs, laundry facilities, microwaves, CH. Gardens, courtyard for easy parking. Good food at local inn (½ mile). Choose a property to suit you from our colour brochure. Open all year.

78 Yarningale, Exeter Road, Moretonhampstead, Devon TQ13 8SW

Sarah Radcliffe
☎/Fax 01647 440560
SC From £150–£350
Sleeps 6
Commended

A secluded, tranquil property offering exceptional panoramic views of Dartmoor. An individual, totally private self-contained flat offering two large double (or triple) bedrooms, each with their own bathroom, lounge, kitchen/diner. Ample level parking. Stables/kennels available. Superb walking country – 500 acres of open moorland within 5 minutes of house.

Please mention **Stay on a Farm** when booking

FOLLOW THE COUNTRY CODE

Leave nothing but footprints,
Take nothing but photographs,
Kill nothing but time!

Cornwall

Bodmin Moor, North & South Cornwall Coasts, Land's End & St Michael's Mount

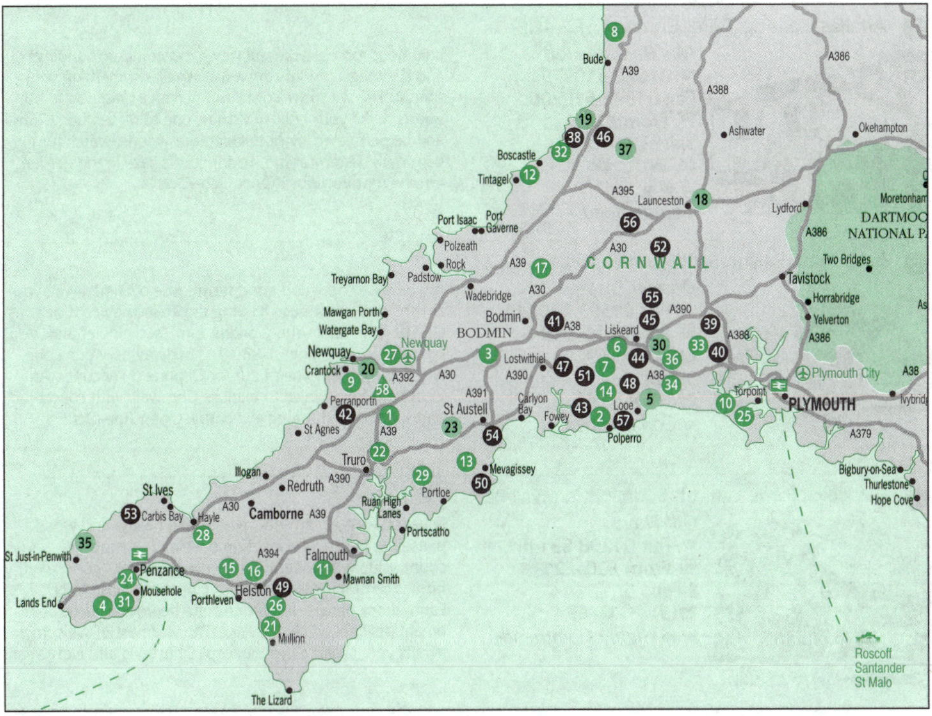

Key

- **1** Bed & Breakfast
- **1** Self-Catering
- **1** B&B and SC
- **1** Camping Barns
- **1** Camping & Caravanning

Cornwall has a coastline of 326 miles, varying from wonderful stretches of firm, golden sands and soaring cliffs on the north coast, to tiny coves, picturesque fishing villages and sheltered, wooded estuaries in the south. Beaches from Bude to St Ives are famous for the exhilarating Atlantic surf, while Looe, Fowey, Mevagissey and Falmouth are ideal for sailing, fishing and windsurfing. Inland lies the atmospheric Bodmin Moor with its mysterious standing stones. Visitors have a wide choice of art galleries, potteries, famous gardens and National Trust properties such as St Michael's Mount, Lanhydrock and Trelissick, while Arthurian Tintagel sums up the mystical quality of Cornwall.

If you would like help in finding suitable farm accommodation, turn to the full listing of farm groups on pages 360 to 363 to find appropriate contact details for this area.

West Country — Cornwall

Bed and Breakfast
(and evening meal)

---

1 Arrallas, Ladock, Truro, Cornwall TR2 4NP

Mrs Barbara Holt
☎ 01872 510379
Fax 01872 510200
BB From £21
Sleeps 6
♥ ♥ ♥ *Highly Commended*

Luxurious rooms, beautiful views, peaceful surroundings and the magic of birdsong make Arrallas something very special. The warm welcome and personal attention to our guests make your holiday with us one to remember. Come and be pampered, walk through our woods, watch for the barn owls. Listen for the woodpeckers, laze in the garden. (Phone for directions.) Open Feb–Oct.

---

2 Bake Farm, Pelynt, Looe, Cornwall PL13 2QQ

Doreen Eastley
☎/Fax 01503 220244
BB From £16–£18
EM From £9
Sleeps 6
(3)
♥ *Commended*

A warm welcome and good farmhouse cooking await you at this listed farmhouse bearing the Trelawney coat of arms (1610). The family-run working farm, set in quiet and peaceful surroundings, is situated midway between Looe and Fowey, the home of author Daphne du Maurier. An ideal base from which to explore Cornwall, with coastal paths, riding and fishing all nearby. Open Apr–Oct.

---

3 Bokiddick Farm, Lanivet, Bodmin, Cornwall PL30 5HP

Gill Hugo
☎/Fax 01208 831481
BB From £20–£21
Sleeps 5
(3)
♥ ♥ *Highly Commended*

Lovely Georgian farmhouse with oak beams and wood panelling, in peaceful location nestling in beautiful countryside with magnificent views. Our 180-acre dairy farm is central for touring all of Cornwall. Close to NT Lanhydrock House. Lovely en suite bedrooms, delicious breakfasts cooked on the Aga. The warmest of welcomes awaits you. Open all year except Christmas and New Year.

---

4 Boskenna Home Farm, St Buryan, Penzance, Cornwall TR19 6DQ

Julia Hosking
☎/Fax 01736 810705
BB From £19–£20.50
Sleeps 6
♥ ♥ *Commended*

Our 17th century listed farmhouse which has been in our family for generations lies in the far west of Cornwall close to Land's End, nestling south of the rugged moorland, near the coastal path. Stay on our working dairy farm, with Guernsey cows, farm pets and Redde-Wood the pony. Open Mar–Oct.

---

5 Bucklawren Farm, St Martin-by-Looe, Cornwall PL13 1NZ

Mrs Jean Henly
☎ 01503 240738
Fax 01503 240481
BB From £20–£22
EM From £10.50
Sleeps 14
(5)
♥ ♥ ♥ *Highly Commended*

Tucked away in the Cornish countryside is Bucklawren, a beautiful Domesday hamlet. The delightful 19th century farmhouse enjoys spectacular sea views over Looe Bay. Come and enjoy good food, comfort and relaxation. An award-winning farm where every effort is made to ensure you have a memorable stay. Open mid Mar–Oct.

Cornwall — West Country

Caduscott, East Taphouse, Liskeard, Cornwall PL14 4NG ⑥

Lindsay Pendray
☎/Fax 01579 320262
[BB] From £16–£21
Sleeps 4
Listed *Commended*

Sweet dreams and peaceful nights broken only by the owl's hooting in the clear night sky; from stargazers to shellseekers, all the ingredients are here to match your mood! A positive approach to all your needs. Log fires to brighten your return after days spent on the rugged cliffs or exploring the sheltered valleys. Open Apr–Sept incl. Easter.

Carglonnon Farm, Duloe, Liskeard, Cornwall PL14 4QA ⑦

Mrs Ann Bray
☎/Fax 01579 320210
[BB] From £16–£18
Sleeps 6
Commended

A lovely 18th century Georgian farmhouse which is part of the Duchy of Cornwall Estate. A working mixed farm of 230 acres, situated 4½ miles from fishing port of Looe. Forestry walks from farm. Golf, horse-riding, Theme Park, coastal walking, moors all nearby. Two doubles en suite. One twin with private bathroom. Tea/coffee-making facilities, central heating. Open Mar–Dec.

Cornakey Farm, Morwenstow, Bude, Cornwall EX23 9SS ⑧

Mrs Monica Heywood
☎ 01288 331260
[BB] From £16–£19
EM From £8
Sleeps 6
Listed *Commended*

This is a 220-acre mixed coastal farm with extensive views of sea and Lundy island from bedrooms and bathroom. Good touring centre with easy reach of quiet beaches. The farmhouse offers one family room en suite and two double rooms. Bathroom, toilet, lounge (colour TV), dining room, games room. Children welcome at reduced rates. Cot, highchair, babysitting. Good home cooking with fresh vegetables. Open Jan–Nov.

Degembris Farmhouse, St Newlyn East, Newquay, Cornwall TR8 5HY ⑨

Kathy Woodley
☎ 01872 510555
Fax 01872 510230
[BB] From £20–£22
EM From £12
Sleeps 12
Highly Commended

Degembris nestles in a south facing hillside overlooking a beautiful wooded valley. Its low beams and log fires make this listed 18th century farmhouse a delight. Come inside (mind your head!) and enjoy the charming Georgian surroundings, complete with creaky floorboards! Take a stroll along our farm trail that wanders through woodland and fields of corn. Open all year except Christmas.

Hendra Farm, Polbathic, Torpoint, Cornwall PL11 3DT ⑩

Mrs A Hoskin
☎/Fax 01503 250225
[BB] From £15–£18
Sleeps 5
Commended

Hendra is a working farm situated in an area of outstanding natural beauty. The fishing port of Looe is 6 miles, and safe bathing beaches of Downderry and Seaton only 2 miles. The main shopping centre of Plymouth is within ½ hours travelling. TV lounge. Family room with en suite shower and WC. Babysitting. Open Mar–Nov.

Higher Kergilliack Farm, Budock, Falmouth, Cornwall TR11 5PB ⑪

Jean Pengelly
☎ 01326 372271
[BB] From £17.50–£19.50
Sleeps 6
Commended

18th century Georgian listed farmhouse on 130-acre dairy farm, former residence of Bishop of Exeter. Overlooks Falmouth Bay and near the seal sanctuary. See the flowers in the hedgerows and daffodil fields. Trebah, Trelissick and Glendurgan Gardens 15 mins. 1 double with en suite WC and shower, 1 twin/family with en suite WC and bath. Take 2nd right on A39 at Hillhead roundabout. Open Mar–Dec.

West Country — Cornwall

⑫ Home Farm, Minster, Boscastle, Cornwall PL35 0BN

Jackie Haddy
☎/Fax 01840 250195
BB From £16–£19
Sleeps 6
⛹ ⛺ 💼
👑 Commended

A warm welcome awaits you at Home Farm, our family working farm situated overlooking picturesque Boscastle and the Atlantic coastline. The farm is surrounded by National Trust countryside and walks. The traditional farmhouse has three tastefully decorated bedrooms. Delicious farmhouse breakfasts, homemade bread and plenty of Cornish hospitality. Open all year except Christmas.

⑬ Kerryanna Country House, Treleaven Farm, Mevagissey, Cornwall PL26 6RZ

Linda Hennah
☎/Fax 01726 843558
BB From £20–£26
EM £12
Sleeps 12
⛹(5) 💼 ⓖ
👑 👑 Highly Commended

Surrounded by farmland, wildlife and flowers, the farm is only 8 minutes' walk from the centre of Mevagissey. Romantic en suite bedrooms with TV and beverage tray. Beautiful gardens with heated outdoor pool and stunning views. Games barn, putting green. Hearty breakfasts and delicious evening meals. A warm welcome assured. Mentioned in the *Daily Telegraph* and Gill Charlton's *A Week in Cornwall*. Open Easter–Oct.

⑭ Little Larnick Farm, Pelynt, Looe, Cornwall PL13 2NB

Angela Eastley
☎/Fax 01503 262837
BB From £18–£21
Sleeps 7
⛹(3) ✕ 💼 ⓖ
👑 Commended

Little Larnick is situated in a sheltered part of the West Looe river valley. Walk to the bustling fishing town of Looe from our working dairy farm and along the coastal path to picturesque Polperro. Popular with our guests is our new annexe bedroom with its separate entrance. Open Feb–Nov.

⑮ Little Pengwedna Farm, Helston, Cornwall TR13 0AY

Iris White
☎/Fax 01736 850649
BB From £18–£22
Sleeps 10
⛹ 💼 ⓖ
👑 👑 Highly Commended

A friendly Cornish welcome and hearty home-cooked breakfast make a stay at this charming farmhouse a real treat. Ideally positioned for touring either coast, you'll find this 19th century granite house prettily and comfortably decorated with original paintings and fresh flowers. It's easily reached, on the B3302 between Helston and Hayle. Open all year including Christmas.

⑯ Longstone Farm, Trenear, Helston, Cornwall TR13 0HG

Gillian Lawrance
☎/Fax 01326 572483
BB From £17–£20
EM From £8.50
Sleeps 14
⛹ ⛺ 💼 ⓖ
👑 Commended

Enjoy the warm and friendly atmosphere of our home which is off the beaten track overlooking rolling fields and peaceful countryside. Central for sandy beaches and many attractions, particularly Flambards. All bedrooms en suite or private facilities. Delicious meals using local produce, attractively presented in our dining room overlooking spacious garden. Relax and unwind in our TV lounge and sunlounge. Open Mar–Oct.

⑰ Loskeyle Farm, St Tudy, Bodmin, Cornwall PL30 3PW

Mrs Sandra Menhinick
☎/Fax 01208 851005
BB From £15–£16
EM From £10
Sleeps 6
⛹ ✕ 💼 ⓖ
👑 Commended

Welcome to Loskeyle, a real 'home from home'. Wake up to a choice of breakfasts and home baked bread. Perfectly situated for touring, cycling and walking, then return to cosy log fires, a delicious supper, and listen out for our resident barn owls – a truly relaxing holiday. Open Mar–Nov.

Cornwall — West Country

Lower Dutson Farm, Launceston, Cornwall PL15 9SP

Mrs Kathryn Broad
☎/Fax 01566 776456
BB From £17.50
Sleeps 3
♥ Commended

Welcome to Lower Dutson, the home of the Broad family since 1897. Guests may use the spacious lounge/dining room with wood burner and colour TV. Tea/coffee facilities in large en suite bedroom. Guests may walk along or fish the River Tamar and coarse fishing lake. Open all year.

Lower Tresmorn Farm, Crackington Haven, Bude, Cornwall EX23 0NU

Rachel Crocker
☎/Fax 01840 230667
BB From £18–£22
EM From £13
Sleeps 10
♥ Highly Commended

Beautiful medieval farmhouse situated on a secluded National Trust clifftop farm, just north of a sandy cove at Crackington Haven. Massive oak beams, granite fireplace, real fires, fine furnishings and superb home cooking. Stunning coastal walks from the front door. A lovely welcoming place to stay, whatever the season. Open all year except Christmas.

Manuels Farm, Quintrell Downs, Newquay, Cornwall TR8 4NY

Mrs Jean Wilson
☎/Fax 01637 873577
BB From £18.50–£20
Sleeps 6
♥ Highly Commended

A delightful 17th century farmhouse situated in a sheltered valley, 2 miles from Newquay's magnificent beaches. Bedrooms have brass beds and window seats overlooking the charming gardens, and are enhanced by antique and pine furniture. There is a lounge and fascinating dining room with huge inglenook fireplace and antique dining table around which guests gather for substantial farmhouse breakfasts. Closed Christmas.

Polhormon Farm, Polhormon Lane, Mullion, Helston, Cornwall TR12 7JE

Alice Harry
☎/Fax 01326 240304
BB From £16–£20
Sleeps 8
♥ Commended

Treat yourselves to a relaxing Cornish break in our comfortable Georgian farmhouse. Spectacular views over the sea and sandy Poldhu beach on the unspoilt Lizard Peninsula. Watch the milking or help feed our newborn calves. Ideal base for beaches, cliffwalking or boat trips around Mullion Island with local fisherman, Barry. Scrumptious breakfasts. Open Mar–Nov.

Polsue Manor Farm, Tresillian, Truro, Cornwall TR2 4BP

Geraldine Holliday
☎ 01872 520234
Fax 01872 520616
BB From £18–£22
EM From £10
Sleeps 14
♥ Commended

The farmhouse on this 190-acre working farm, set in glorious countryside, overlooks the tidal Tresillian River and one of the prettiest parts of Cornwall, 'gateway' to the Roseland Peninsula. Beautiful cathedral city of Truro 2 miles. Centrally situated between north and south coasts, ideal centre for touring Cornwall. Delightful woodland and estuary walks. Traditional home cooking, comfortable, relaxed atmosphere. Open most of year.

Poltarrow Farm, St Mewan, St Austell, Cornwall PL26 7DR

Judith Nancarrow
☎/Fax 01726 67111
BB From £22–£25
EM From £10
Sleeps 12
♥ Highly Commended

Our charming farmhouse is the ideal place for you to take time to relax. Tucked away, yet so central that you can do as much or as little as you want. Gardens in the spring, beaches in summer, the warm days of Autumn, but a log fire in the evenings. Open all year except Christmas.

West Country — Cornwall

24 Rose Farm, Chyanhal, Buryas Bridge, Penzance, Cornwall TR19 6AN

Mrs Penny Lally
☎/Fax 01736 731808
BB From £20–£25
Sleeps 8
♛ Commended

Rose Farm is a small working farm in a little hamlet close to the picturesque fishing villages of Mousehole and Newlyn and 7 miles from Lands End. The 200-year-old granite farmhouse is cosy with pretty, en suite rooms. 1 double, 1 family suite and a romantic 15th century four poster room in barn annexe. We have all manner of animals, from pedigree cattle to pot-bellied pigs! Open all year (closed Christmas).

25 Stone Farm, Whitsand Bay, Millbrook, Torpoint, Cornwall PL10 1JJ

Mrs Sarah Blake
☎/Fax 01752 822267
BB From £17–£20
Sleeps 6
♛♛ Highly Commended

Dairy farm 400 yards from the cliff path leading to miles of sandy beaches in an Area of Outstanding Natural Beauty, with panoramic views from Rame to Looe. Large garden with croquet lawn. Everyone can help feed the animals or watch the milking. Children's pony rides and games room. Open all year except Christmas.

26 Tregaddra Farm, Cury, Cross Lanes, Helston, Cornwall TR12 7BB

June Lugg
☎/Fax 01326 240235
BB From £19.50–£24
EM From £9
Sleeps 14
♛♛♛ Highly Commended

Unwind in this beautifully furnished 18th century farmhouse (1717) on working farm. Situated in an Area of Outstanding Natural Beauty, our views of rolling countryside are unrivalled. All-weather tennis court, heated outdoor pool and large relaxing garden. Pretty en suite bedrooms, two with balconies, one four-poster. Winter breaks with blazing open log fires. A warm family welcome awaits. Closed Christmas.

27 Tregaswith Farmhouse, Tregaswith, near Newquay, Cornwall TR8 4HY

John & Jacqui Elsom
☎/Fax 01637 881181
BB From £22–£25
EM From £13
Sleeps 6
♛♛♛ Highly Commended

Tregaswith is a small hamlet just outside Newquay, 5 minutes' drive to beaches and several National Trust properties near. The elegant farmhouse built over 250 years ago, now a smallholding with many friendly animals. Pony rides and an introduction to carriage driving can be arranged. We have a reputation for delicious food. 3 beautiful bedrooms, all en suite. Antiques and oak beams throughout. Open all year except Christmas.

28 Treglisson, Wheal Alfred Road, Hayle, Cornwall TR27 5JT

Carole Runnalls
☎/Fax 01736 753141
BB From £21–£24
Sleeps 15
♛♛ Highly Commended

Just one mile from the A30 you will find Treglisson, an 18th century former 'mine captains'' home. All the en suite rooms have been delightfully decorated and furnished with antiques. There is even an indoor heated swimming pool. Although dinner is not provided there are many pubs and restaurants in the area offering a wide variety of excellent food. Ideally situated for gardens, galleries, beaches and much, much more. Closed Nov.

29 Tregonan, Tregony, Truro, Cornwall TR2 5SN

Sandra Collins
☎/Fax 01872 530249
BB From £16
Sleeps 6
♛ Commended

Discover Tregonan, a spacious, comfortable farmhouse tucked away down a ½-mile private lane and set in a secluded garden amidst our 300-acre farm. 6 miles west of Mevagissey, we are on the threshold of the Roseland Peninsula, with a good selection of gardens, beaches and eating places locally. Open Apr–Oct. Advanced booking only Nov–Mar (closed Christmas and New Year).

Tregondale Farm, Menheniot, Liskeard, Cornwall PL14 3RG 30

Stephanie Rowe
/Fax 01579 342407
BB From £19–£22.50
EM From £10
Sleeps 6
(3)
Highly Commended

Feeling like a break? Relax in style in the peace of the countryside near the coast. Three charming en suite bedrooms with TV/radio. Home produce a speciality. Play tennis, explore the woodland farm trail. See pedigree cattle, lambs in spring amidst wildlife and flowers. Activities arranged, golf, cycling, walking and fishing. A warm welcome awaits you. Open all year.

Tregurnow Farm, St Buryan, Penzance, Cornwall TR19 6BL 31

Edwina Jeffery
/Fax 01736 810255
BB From £20–£25
Sleeps 6
Commended

Our tastefully furnished farmhouse is situated in a magnificent coastal position above Lamorna Cove. Ideal base for the South West Way, Minack Theatre, Land's End, The Tate and beaches. Romantic four-poster. Spectacular views across Mount's Bay. Superb Aga-cooked breakfasts. We combine comfort and luxury with peace and tranquillity. Open Easter–Nov.
E-mail: tregurno@eurobell.co.uk

Trerosewill Farm, Paradise, Boscastle, Cornwall PL35 0DL 32

Mrs Cheryl Nicholls
/Fax 01840 250545
BB From £19–£35
EM From £18
Sleeps 13
Highly Commended

Luxurious farmhouse offering bed & breakfast on a working farm. Situated a short walk from the picturesque village of Boscastle. All rooms equipped to the highest standards and there are unsurpassed panoramic sea views of Lundy Island and the North Devon coast from most rooms. Traditional farmhouse fare. Special spring/autumn breaks. FHG award winner.
E-mail: nicholls@trerosewill.telme.com

Tresulgan Farm, Nr Menheniot, Liskeard, Cornwall PL14 3PU 33

Mrs E Elford
/Fax 01503 240268
BB From £19–£22
EM From £9
Sleeps 6
(2)
Highly Commended

Relax and unwind at Tresulgan, our 17th century farmhouse on a livestock/arable farm enjoying picturesque views of the wooded Seaton Valley. Beamed dining room and attractive en suite bedrooms with tea/coffee facilities and colour TV. An ideal location for touring this most beautiful area. A friendly welcome is assured. Open all year.

Treveria Farm, Widegates, Looe, Cornwall PL13 1QR 34

Mrs J Kitto
/Fax 01503 240237
BB From £20–£22
Sleeps 6
Applied

Treveria is a delightful manor house set in a large garden overlooking the farm and surrounding countryside. A high standard of accommodation is offered with beautifully decorated en suite rooms, one with four-poster. All rooms have colour TV and beverage facilities. Looe and Polperro with their quaint harbours and excellent restaurants are only a short drive away. Open Easter–Nov.

Trewellard Manor Farm, Pendeen, Penzance, Cornwall TR19 7SU 35

Mrs Marion Bailey
/Fax 01736 788526
BB £20
Sleeps 6
Commended

The farm is situated in a superb coastal position between Lands End and St Ives. We offer a friendly, relaxed atmosphere with seasonal fires and CH. 3 bedrooms (2 en suite, 1 with private bathroom) all with tea/coffee facilities. Use of swimming pool (June–Sept) with good beaches within easy reach. Golf available nearby. This is an outstanding area for walking, either inland or on the coast path. Open all year (closed Christmas).

West Country   Cornwall

36 Trewint Farm, Menheniot, Liskeard, Cornwall PL14 3RE

Elizabeth Rowe
☎/Fax 01579 347155
BB From £18–£21
EM From £8
Sleeps 6
♥ ♥ Commended

Ideally situated only minutes from the A38, yet in peaceful, tranquil surroundings. Wander around our 200-acre working farm known for its prize-winning pedigree cattle. Meet Rusty the pony and Lucy the lamb in pets' corner. En suite rooms with matching decor. Breakfast overlooking the garden watching the birds while you enjoy the farmhouse fare using home/local meats and produce. Open all year except Christmas and New Year.

37 Wheatley Farm, Maxworthy, Launceston, Cornwall PL15 8LY

Valerie Griffin
☎/Fax 01566 781232
BB From £17–£23
EM From £13
Sleeps 12
♥ ♥ ♥ Highly Commended

Raymond and Valerie welcome you to Wheatley, their lovingly restored Victorian farmhouse built by Duke of Bedford in 1871. Close to North Cornish coast, the ideal place to escape and unwind. Warm country bedrooms, one four-poster. Enjoy splendid food, carefully presented. Silver B&B award winners 1997 'England for Excellence'. Judge's comments "Wheatley offers real Cornish hospitality at its best". Open Easter–Nov.
E-mail: wheatleyfrm@compuserve.com.uk

Self-Catering

30 Beechleigh Cottage, Tregondale Farm, Menheniot, Liskeard, Cornwall PL14 3RG

Stephanie Rowe
☎/Fax 01579 342407
SC From £95–£405
Sleeps 4 (+ cot)
♣ ♣ ♣ ♣ ♣ Highly Commended

In the leigh of our farmhouse beech tree, this peaceful, attractive character cottage nestles. Warm and cosy in winter, barbecue on the patio in summer, play tennis. Explore the woodland farm trail. Hear birds singing, enjoy wild flowers and lambs in Spring. See pedigree South Devon cattle, naturally reared. Special activities arranged – golf, cycling, fishing. A warm welcome awaits you – come and discover the beauty of Cornwall. Open all year.

38 Brevean, Smallhill Barton, St Gennys, Bude, Cornwall EX23 0BQ

Mr & Mrs Harry Mead
☎/Fax 01840 230230
SC From £100–£450
Sleeps 6
♣ ♣ ♣ ♣ Highly Commended

By the North Cornwall coast, between Bude and Tintagel and surrounded by rolling farmland, our spacious holiday cottage, standing in its own garden, offers a chance to relax in peace and comfort. Excellent home base from which to explore the mysteries and delights of this renowned and attractive area. Open all year.

5 Bucklawren Farm, St Martin-by-Looe, Cornwall PL13 1NZ

Mrs Jean Henly
☎ 01503 240738
Fax 01503 240481
SC From £120–£490
Sleeps 2/6
♣ ♣ ♣ ♣ Highly Commended

Step back in time and enjoy our character cottages, tastefully converted and furnished to a high standard. Come and enjoy our spectacular scenery with exceptional sea views. Plenty to do with walks, golf, fishing, all close by. An award-winning farm where you can come and discover a true Cornish farm holiday. Open all year.

Cornwall

West Country

Cadson Manor Farm, Callington, Cornwall PL17 7HW ⓛ39

Brenda Crago
☎/Fax 01579 383969
SC From £150–£480
Sleeps 6 + cot
Highly Commended

Wing of manor house with large garden on 200-acre working farm set in the beautiful Lynher Valley with lovely views of two-acre fishing lake for guests' exclusive use. Three pretty bedrooms, bathroom, lounge/diner and separate kitchen, all tastefully decorated and equipped to a very high standard. Cosy and comfortable. Farm and river walks. Open all year except Christmas.

The Coach House, c/o Lantallack Farm, Landrake, Nr Saltash, Cornwall PL12 5AE ⓛ40

Nicky Walker
☎/Fax 01752 851281
SC From £235–£530
Sleeps 6/7 + cot
Highly Commended

Georgian farm coach house, extremely comfortable with outstanding views across undulating countryside and wooded valleys. The perfect retreat for a relaxing holiday. We keep ponies, sheep, ducks, hens and a pig called Polly. Golf at St Mellion, 10 mins. away. Close to sea and moors. 2 bathrooms, log fire, CH, phone, microwave, dishwasher and games room. Linen/electricity inclusive. Open Apr–Oct.

Glynn Barton Farm Cottages, Glynn Barton, Cardinham, Bodmin, Cornwall PL30 4AX ⓛ41

Diana Mindel
☎/Fax 01208 821375
SC From £150–£580
Sleeps 2/6
Commended

Whatever the season, make the most of our comfortable cottages – four poster, wood beams and traditional cast iron stove. From your cottage enjoy beautiful views and take woodland or farmland walks. Play tennis or relax by heated pool in walled 'Mediterranean' atmosphere. Central for golf, beaches, cycling, fishing, horseriding and gardens. Open all year.

Hendra Farm, Rose, Truro, Cornwall TR4 9PS ⓛ42

Josephine Symons
☎/Fax 01872 572273
SC From £250–£700
Sleeps 7 + cot
Commended

Spacious old farmhouse with pretty garden, two bathrooms and private coarse fishing in a secluded lake. Footpaths lead to the coast and glorious beaches. Tariff includes central heating, electricity, log fire, linen, well behaved pet.

Katie's Cottage, Bocaddon, Lanreath, Looe, Cornwall PL13 2PG ⓛ43

Mrs Alison Maiklem
☎/Fax 01503 220245
SC From £140–£400
Sleeps 4
Highly Commended

A warm welcome awaits you all the year round at this tastefully converted barn situated in peaceful countryside, on our 350-acre dairy farm. Central heating, fully equipped kitchen, wheelchair access, close parking. Six miles from fishing villages and beaches. Central for wonderful gardens, walks and children's entertainments. Open all year. E-mail: alimaik@aol.com.uk

Lodge Barton Farm, Liskeard, Cornwall PL14 4JX ⓛ44

Rosanne Hodin
☎/Fax 01579 344432
SC From £120–£500
Sleeps 2/5 + cot
Commended

Lodge Barton is set in a beautiful river valley flanked by woodland. We keep goats and also have ducks, hens and geese. Everyone can help collecting eggs and feeding. Our character cottages are luxuriously equipped including heating, woodburners, video, linen, laundry room, private gardens and playground. We are close to sea, moors, sailing, windsurfing, riding, fishing, golf. Open all year. E-mail: lodgebart@aol.com.uk

West Country   Cornwall

⑱ Lower Dutson Farm, Launceston, Cornwall PL15 9SP

Mrs Kathryn Broad
☎/Fax 01566 776456
SC From £120–£350
Sleeps 6
♞ ♘ ⚒
🐎🐎🐎🐎 Commended

A warm welcome awaits you at our 17th century farmhouse, centrally situated for Devon, Cornwall, Dartmoor and Bodmin Moors. Wander across to the River Tamar or coarse lake (good fishing available). Fully equipped kitchen, microwave, washing machine, tumble dryer, electric cooker, colour TV, storage heaters, two bathrooms. Open all year.

㊺ Lower Trengale Farm, Liskeard, Cornwall PL14 6HF

Louise Kidd
☎ 01579 321019
Fax 01579 321432
SC From £140–£495
Sleeps 4–6
♞ ♘ ⚒ ♞ ⓢ
🐎🐎🐎🐎 Highly Commended

A small farm, set in beautiful countryside, offering three comfortable and well equipped cottages with woodburners, videos and dishwashers. Super for children with pony, playground and games room. Lovely views from the garden. Ideally located for beaches, moors, golfing, fishing and walking. All linen, cots, highchairs supplied. Open all year. E-mail: lkidd@eurobell.co.uk

⑲ Lower Tresmorn Cottage, Lower Tresmorn Farm, Crackington Haven, Bude, Cornwall EX23 0NU

Rachel Crocker
☎/Fax 01840 230667
SC From £160–£450
EM From £13
Sleeps 4
♞ 🐕 ♘ ⚒ ♞ ⓢ
🐎🐎🐎🐎 Highly Commended

Cosy cottage enjoying spectacular views to the cliffs and sea. Situated on working National Trust farm. Superb coastal walks start at the door and beaches are close by. Comfortably and tastefully furnished, the cottage is surrounded by an enclosed lawned garden. Home-cooked dinners are available at the farmhouse. Open all year.

⑳ Manuels Farm, Quintrell Downs, Newquay, Cornwall TR8 4NY

Alan & Jean Wilson
☎/Fax 01637 873577
SC From £100–£510
Sleeps 2/5 + cot
♞ ♘ ⚒ ♞ ♞ ⓢ
🐎🐎🐎 Commended

Imagine a family holiday close to Newquay's magnificent beaches but tucked away in your own quiet valley. Secluded from the crowd but perfectly placed for touring, walking and riding. Your own character cottage in the country, on the farm, with gardens, flowers, pets and farm animals around you. The children will enjoy the calves, tractor and ponies while you relax. Electricity and linen included. Short breaks available. Open all year.

㊻ Old Newham Farm, Otterham, Camelford, Cornwall PL32 9SR

Mrs Mary Purdue
☎ 01840 230470
Fax 01840 230303
SC From £120–£495
Sleeps 2/4/8
♞ 🐕 ♘
🐎🐎🐎🐎 Commended

Three individual stone and slate cottages around an old farmyard dating back to medieval times, at the end of a quiet country lane. Our 30-acre farm is managed in a traditional way with cattle, sheep and other small animals for the children. Here you can find the peace of the Cornish countryside yet be only 3 miles from the most spectacular coastline in the area. Cottages with character, open fire, CH. Open all year.

㉓ Poltarrow Farm, St Mewan, St Austell, Cornwall PL26 7DR

Judith Nancarrow
☎/Fax 01726 67111
SC From £130–£550
Sleeps 2/6
♞ ♞ 🐕 ♘ ♞ ♞ ⚒
🐎🐎🐎🐎 Up to Highly Commended

Tucked away in the countryside between Fowey and Mevagissey, discover your cottage, restored with care, with all the touches that make you feel at home. Wood fires for the coldest weather and summer barbecues. You'll find nature on your doorstep. Children love the animals, particularly Taffy the pony. Short breaks. Open all year.

Cornwall — West Country

Tredethick Farm Cottages, The Guildhouse, Tredethick, Lostwithiel, Cornwall PL22 0LE ㊼

Tim & Nicky Reed
☎/Fax 01208 873618
SC From £135–£650
Sleeps 2/6

Highly Commended

Award-winning cottages set amongst beautiful rolling countryside. Walk from your door through meadows and woods to the River Fowey and on to the quiet creekside village of Lerryn – the inspiration behind *The Wind in the Willows*. Ideal year round base for exploring the delights of coast and countryside or simply relaxing and enjoying the rural idyll. Open all year.

Tredinnick Farm, Duloe, Liskeard, Cornwall PL14 4PJ ㊽

Mrs Angela Barrett
☎ 01503 262997
Fax 01503 265554
SC From £150–£705
Sleeps 2/10 (+ cot)

Highly Commended

Enjoy a relaxing and tranquil holiday on our family-run mixed farm which offers something for everyone, whatever the season. Our spacious Victorian farmhouse with en suite bedrooms, is situated in the rolling countryside. Local pub nearby serving excellent food. Many beautiful and interesting local walks, golf and leisure facilities within easy reach. In Looe you can hire a boat, explore the rivers or go deep-sea fishing. Open all year.

Tregevis Farm, St Martin, Helston, Cornwall TR12 6DN ㊾

Julie Bray
☎/Fax 01326 231265
SC From £170–£450
Sleeps 6

Highly Commended

Come and relax at Tregevis, a working dairy farm in the picturesque Helford River area, just ½ mile from the little village of St. Martin and 5 miles from sandy beaches. The accommodation is a self-contained, spacious part of the farmhouse, very comfortable, well equipped and with a games room. The large lawn area with swings will prove popular with children, as will our farm animals. Open Mar–Oct.

Treleaven Farm Cottages, Treleaven Farm, Mevagissey, Cornwall PL26 6RZ ㊿

Mrs Linda Hennah
☎/Fax 01726 843558
SC From £180–£600
Sleeps 4–6

Highly Commended

Surrounded by rambling countryside, wildlife and flowers, the farm is only 8 minutes' walk from the centre of Mevagissey. Each cottage has luxury pine fitted kitchen with dishwasher, microwave, fridge/freezer and cooker. Lovely bathroom with shower, cosy lounge with TV, some en suite bedrooms. CH included. Linen and electricity inclusive. Laundry room. Ample parking. Games barn. Next to Heligan Gardens and central for touring. Open all year.

Tremadart Farm, Duloe, Liskeard, Cornwall PL14 4PE 51

Evelyn Julian
☎/Fax 01503 262855
SC From £200–£695
Sleeps 2–12

Commended

The wing of our Victorian farmhouse is situated in a secluded garden on a 330-acre working farm. Ideally located three miles from Looe for beaches and walking, cycling and fishing. Short breaks and smaller numbers welcomed in low season. Open all year.

Trevadlock Farm Cottages, Trevadlock Farm, Trevadlock, Congdon's Shop, Launceston, Cornwall PL15 52

Mrs Barbara Sleep
☎/Fax 01566 782239
SC From £90–£550
Sleeps 3/6

Highly Commended

A truly Cornish welcome awaits you at Trevadlock Farm, offering a wonderful retreat, in one of our beautifully restored cottages. Log fires, dishwasher, TV/video and much more. Ideally situated for both coasts, walk the moors, visit Jamaica Inn, explore the many gardens, or golf at St Mellion – Trevadlock is perfectly placed. Open all year.

West Country   Cornwall

---

53 Trevalgan Farm, St Ives, Cornwall TR26 3BJ

Jean Osborne
☎/Fax 01736 796433
[SC] From £150–£450
Sleeps 2/6

🐴 🐕 ♿ 🎾 🚲 🍴 ⊚
🔑🔑🔑🔑 *Commended*

Trevalgan is a coastal stock-rearing farm surrounded by magnificent scenery, just 2 miles from St Ives. Enjoy walking our farm trail to the cliffs overlooking the sea, a paradise for nature lovers. Traditional granite barns have been carefully converted into 7 lovely holiday homes around an attractive courtyard. Land's End, St Michael's Mount, Mousehole and Lamorna within easy reach by car. Open Mar–Jan.

---

54 Trevissick Manor, Trevissick Farm, Trenarren, St Austell, Cornwall PL26 6BQ

Anita Treleaven
☎/Fax 01726 72954
[SC] From £140–£390
Sleeps 2–4 + cot

🐴 🍴
🔑🔑🔑🔑 *Commended*

The east wing of the manor farmhouse on our coastal mixed farm is situated between St Austell and Mevagissey Bays. Spectacular views across the gardens down the valley to the sea. Ideal for a couple or family. Meet the animals, view the milking, play tennis or take the farm trail to Hallane Cove. Near sandy beaches, sailing, watersports, cycling, 18-hole golf. Heligan Gardens 5–10 mins. Open all year except Christmas.

---

55 Trewalla Farm Cottages, Trewalla Farm, Minions, Liskeard, Cornwall PL14 6ED

Fiona Cotter
☎/Fax 01579 342385
[SC] From £210–£420
Sleeps 3/4 (+ cot)

🐴 🐕 🎾
🔑🔑🔑 *Commended*

Our small, traditionally-run farm on Bodmin Moor has rare breed pigs, sheep, hens and geese, all free-range and very friendly. Our three cottages are beautifully furnished and very well equipped. Their moorland setting offers perfect peace, wonderful views, ideal walking country and a good base for exploring – if you can tear yourself away! Linen and electricity included. Open Mar–Dec and New Year.

---

35 Trewellard Manor Farm, Pendeen, Penzance, Cornwall TR19 7SU

Mrs Marion Bailey
☎/Fax 01736 788526
[SC] From £150–£435
Sleeps 4

🐴 🍴 ⊚
🔑🔑🔑🔑 – 🔑🔑🔑🔑🔑
Commended

In the heart of Poldark Country, between Land's End and St Ives, attractive stone cottages converted from old stables. Situated across courtyard from owner's farmhouse and swimming pool (June–Sept). On edge of village within easy reach of beaches and coast path. Special winter short breaks. Open all year.

---

56 Trewithen Country Lodges, Trewithen Farm, Laneast, Launceston, Cornwall PL15 8PW

Mrs Margaret Colwill
☎/Fax 01566 86343
[SC] From £200–£405
Sleeps 4

🐴 🐕 🎾 ⊚
🔑🔑🔑🔑 *Commended*

Come on down to our Cornish farm to stay,
Where the hedgerows are wonderful, changing each day,
Just two pine lodges, beautifully designed,
Away from the noise, relax and unwind,
Tastefully furnished and cosy as pie,
Fun for the family and jacuzzi to try,
Panoramic views of the surrounding moors,
Enjoy animals and walks in the great outdoors.
Open Mar–Jan.

---

57 West Kellow Farmhouse & Meadow Bank, West Kellow, Lansallos, Looe, Cornwall PL13 2QL

Mrs E Julian
☎/Fax 01503 262855
[SC] From £200–£620
Sleeps 9/4

🐴 🍴 ⊚
🔑🔑🔑🔑 *Up to Highly Commended*

In a secluded position with panoramic views, our Victorian farmhouse and converted stone cottage are reached down a country lane. Visitors are welcome to walk around our 160-acre working beef and sheep farm. Close to the secluded bays of Lansallos and Lantivet with quiet, sandy beaches, we are just a mile from picturesque Polperro. Open all year.

Cornwall *West Country*

Wheatley Farm Cottages, Maxworthy, Launceston, Cornwall PL15 8LY (37)

Valerie Griffin
☎/Fax 01566 781232
SC From £100–£550
Sleeps 4/7
⊗ ■ ⚶ ◉
♙ ♙ ♙ ♙ *Highly Commended*

Something special – two quality character cottages, each with private garden, providing you with all you need for the perfect holiday. Crackling log fire for cooler evenings, TV, video, luxury kitchen, dishwasher, washing machine. Situated on family dairy sheep farm close to spectacular North Cornish Coast. Children's play area, pony rides, farm animals to visit. Open all year.
E-mail: wheatleyfrm@compuserve.com.uk

Camping & Caravanning

Nancolleth Farm Caravan Gardens, Newquay, Cornwall TR8 4PN

Joan Luckraft
☎ 01872 510236
SC From £115–£350
Sleeps 4/6
⊗ ⚶ ⚶ ◉
✓ ✓ ✓ ✓

A little gem, in the countryside near the sea, that's Nancolleth Caravan gardens. We offer a comfortable, relaxing holiday in our six spacious 2- and 3-bedroomed Rose Award holiday homes, in a garden setting with parking beside. Laundry, phone, country trail. Perfectly placed for exploring Cornwall's delights and where a warm welcome and cleanliness are guaranteed. Open May–Oct.

CONFIRM BOOKINGS

Disappointments can arise from misunderstandings over the telephone. Please write to confirm your booking.

Our Internet address is
http://www.webscape.co.uk/farmaccom/

Our Internet address is
http://www.webscape.co.uk/farmaccom/

USE THE INDEX

The comprehensive Index shows which farms offer access to disabled visitors; caravanning/camping facilities; the chance to participate on a working farm; stabling/grazing for visiting horses; en suite rooms; a welcome to business people; acceptance of *Stay on a Farm* gift tokens.

THE 1000+ BUREAU MEMBERS OFFER A UNIQUE LINK TO CUSTOMERS ACROSS THE UK

All Bureau members belong to a local Group. Each member can refer you to an equally high quality member within the Group... or across the UK: England, Northern Ireland, Scotland, Wales.

STAY ON A FARM GIFT TOKENS

If you have enjoyed your Stay on a Farm, why not treat your friends and relatives to *Stay on a Farm* gift tokens? Available from the Bureau office (tel: 01203 696909), they can be redeemed against accommodation and are accepted by the majority of farms (see Index). Please check when booking to avoid disappointment.

FINDING YOUR ACCOMMODATION

The local FHB Group contacts listed on page 360 can always help you find a vacancy in your chosen area.

North Wales

Farm entries in this regional section are listed under those areas shown in green on the key map. Look at the index below to find on which page the entries start. You will see that we have listed the areas geographically so that you can turn more easily to find farms in neighbouring areas.

At the start of each area section is a detailed map with numbered symbols indicating the location of each farm. Different symbols denote different types of accommodation; see the key below each area map. Farm entries are listed alphabetically under type of accommodation. Some farms offer more than one type of accommodation and therefore have more than one entry.

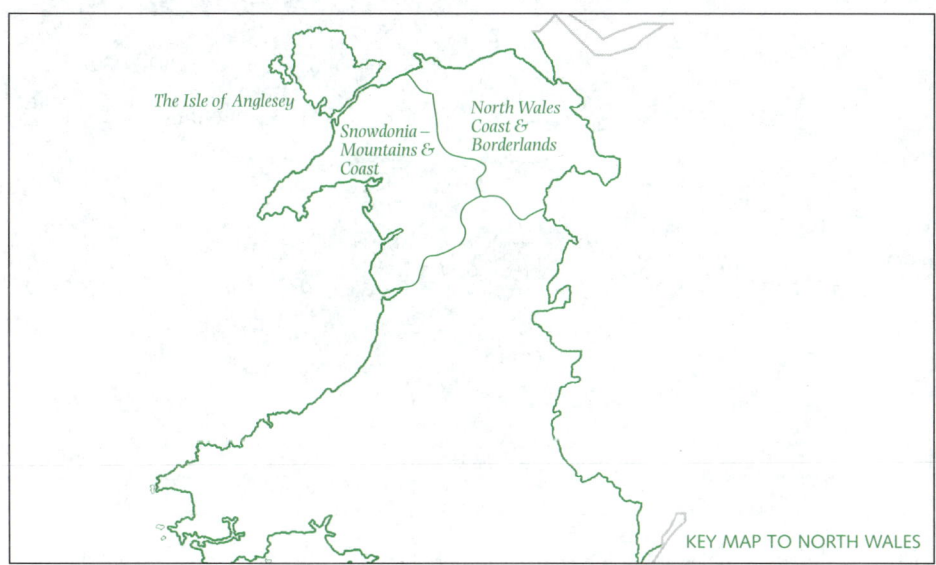

KEY MAP TO NORTH WALES

The Isle of Anglesey *page 308*

Snowdonia – Mountains & Coast *page 311*
Snowdonia National Park, Lleyn Peninsula, Southern Gwynedd & Cambrian Coast

North Wales Coast & Borderlands *page 319*
Llandudno, Colwyn Bay, Rhyl, Prestatyn & Clwydian Range

The Isle of Anglesey

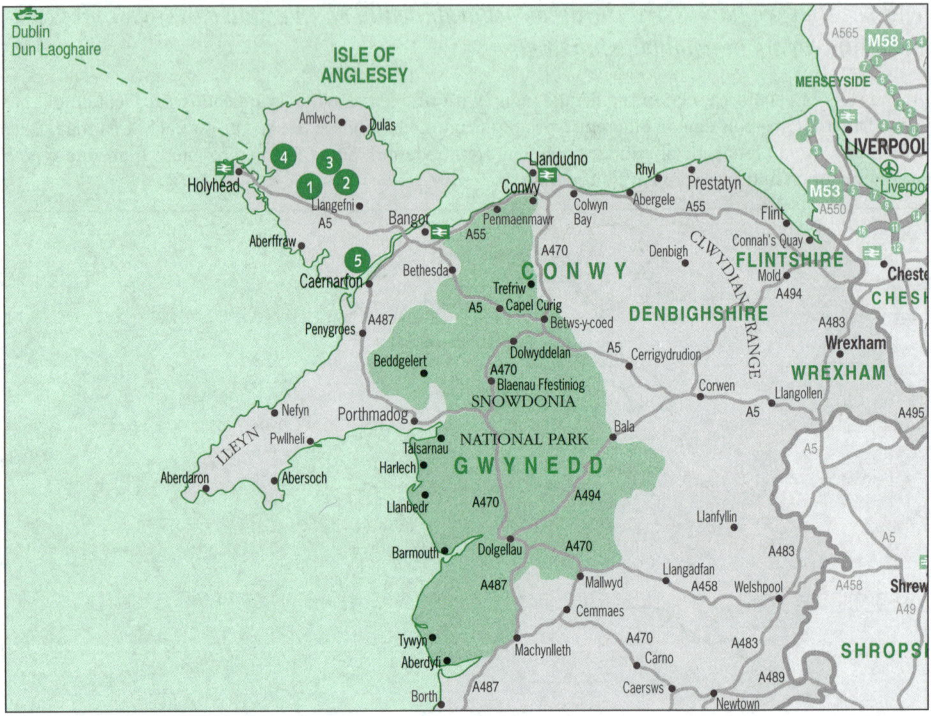

Key

- ① Bed & Breakfast
- ① Self-Catering
- ① B&B and SC
- ① Camping Barns
- ▲ Camping & Caravanning

Anglesey, known as the 'mother of Wales', is a largely agricultural island. The signs are everywhere, from the inland cornfields to the coastal pastures, and from the whitewashed cottages of the smallholdings to the 'home farms' of the great country estates. Anglesey's history is written in the stone of its prehistoric burial chambers and tall standing stones, Roman walls, the little churches and chapels, and the ramparts of Beaumaris Castle which serve as a reminder of the invaders from across the border. Holiday makers will find that the island's lovely coast – much of it an Area of Outstanding Natural Beauty – includes some of Europe's most thrilling beaches.

If you would like help in finding suitable farm accommodation, turn to the full listing of farm groups on pages 360 to 363 to find appropriate contact details for this area.

The Isle of Anglesey 　　　　　　　　　　　　　　　　　　　　　　　　　　　　　　　　North Wales

Bed and Breakfast
(and evening meal)

Bwlch-y-Fen, Tyn Lon, Holyhead, Isle of Anglesey LL65 3LX ①

Sian Stephen
☎ 01407 720273
[BB] From £16–£18
Sleeps 6
Applied

A friendly Welsh welcome awaits you at Bwlch-y-Fen, a fully renovated farmhouse with all bedrooms en suite and offering tea/coffee-making facilities and colour TV. Delicious, traditional home cooking using local produce. Centrally situated for touring coast and many local attractions. Open all year except Christmas.

Drws-y-Coed, Llannerch-y-medd, Isle of Anglesey LL71 8AD ②

Mrs Jane Bown
☎/Fax 01248 470473
[BB] From £21.50–£23.50
EM From £13
Sleeps 6
★★★★
FARM

Enjoy excellent hospitality, food and tranquil surroundings with panoramic views of Snowdonia. Centrally situated to explore Anglesey's coastline and attractions. Comfortable en suite bedrooms with all facilities. Inviting spacious lounge with log-fire. Interesting historical farmstead and private walks on a 550-acre mixed farm. Games room. WTB Farmhouse Award, Farm Holiday Guide Diploma Award. Closed Christmas.

Llwydiarth Fawr, Llanerchymedd, Isle of Anglesey LL71 8DF ③

Mrs Margaret Hughes
☎ 01248 470321/470540
[BB] From £25
EM From £12.50
Sleeps 6
Applied

Secluded Georgian mansion set in 850 acres of woodland and farmland. Ideal touring base for island's coastline, Snowdonia and North Wales coast. Nearby is Llyn Alaw for trout fishing. Reputation for excellent food using farm and local produce. En suite bedrooms. TV, CH, log fires. Walks and private fishing. Winner of the BBC 'Welsh Farm housewife of the Year' competition. Member of Taste of Wales. Warmest Welcome Award 1993. Closed Christmas.

Penyrorsedd Farm, Llanfachraeth, Holyhead, Isle of Anglesey LL65 4YB ④

Mrs Joyce Roberts
☎/Fax 01407 730630
[BB] From £19–£20
Sleeps 6
★★★
FARM

Charming 18th century farmhouse, tastefully decorated and furnished throughout. 15 minutes' drive from Holyhead on the A5025. Close to sandy beach, conveniently located for many nearby tourist attractions. One double en suite, one double and one twin with private bathroom. Separate lounge with TV and dining room. A warm welcome awaits you. Open Mar–Nov.

Plas Trefarthen, Brynsiencyn, Isle of Anglesey LL61 6SZ ⑤

Marian Roberts
☎ 01248 430379
[BB] From £19–£22
Sleeps 14
★★★
COUNTRY HOUSE

Secluded Georgian house in glorious location in 200 acres on the shore of the Menai Strait. Outstanding views of Snowdonia and Caernarfon Castle, 6 miles Menai Bridge. Ideal base for touring Anglesey and Snowdonia, walking, birdwatching and visiting NT properties. Most bedrooms en suite with beverage tray, colour TV. Full size snooker table. Owned and run by Marian, a well-known soprano. Winner of Warmest Welcome Award for 1995. Closed Christmas.

Snowdonia – Mountains & Coast

Snowdonia National Park, Lleyn Peninsula, Southern Gwynedd & Cambrian Coast

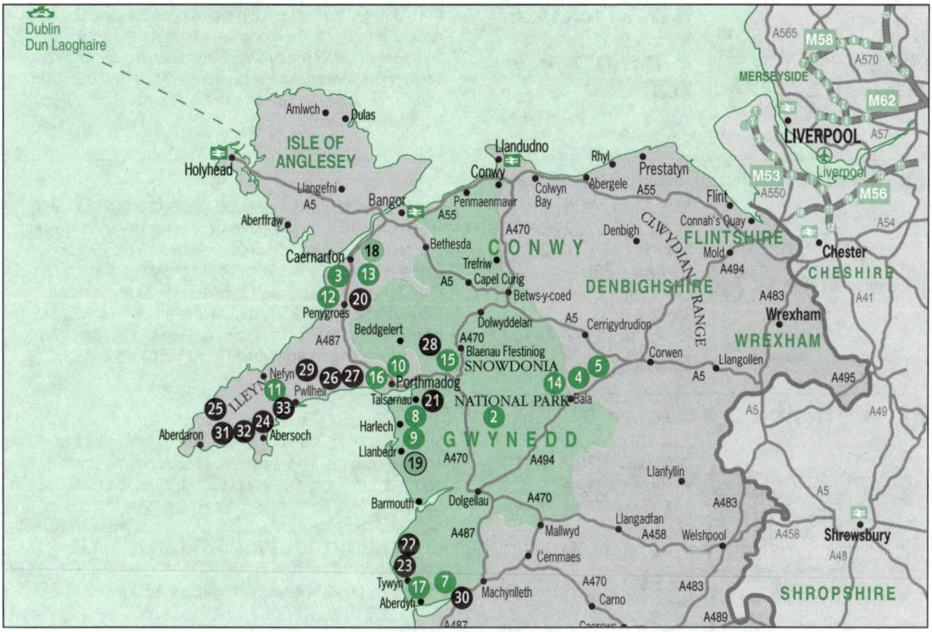

Key
- 1 Bed & Breakfast
- 1 Self-Catering
- 1 B&B and SC
- 1 Camping Barns
- 1 Camping & Caravanning

There's so much to do here, and in such a dramatic setting. Take a ride on a steam train into the mountains with the Talyllyn or Ffestiniog Railways, alongside Llanberis or Bala Lake or even up Mount Snowdon itself. Visit the heart of a Welsh slate cavern, or a remote bird sanctuary at the foot of the Lleyn Peninsula, go to the theatre in Bangor, see craftsmen at work or explore lovely Bodnant Garden. See historic ruins, magnificent castles at Caernarfon, Harlech, Criccieth and Conwy and many National Trust properties. Add to this the mountains, lakes, waterfalls and fine beaches awaiting you here in the heartland of the Welsh language.

If you would like help in finding suitable farm accommodation, turn to the full listing of farm groups on pages 360 to 363 to find appropriate contact details for this area.

 **North Wales** — Snowdonia Mountains & Coast

Bed and Breakfast
(and evening meal)

② Bryn Celynog Farm, Cwm Prysor, Trawsfynydd, Gwynedd LL41 4TR

Mrs G E Hughes
☎/Fax 01766 540378
BB From £18–£19.50
Sleeps 6
★★★ FARM

Relax in peaceful setting with splendid views of Cwmprysor Valley, on 700-acre working beef and sheep farm 3 miles from Trawsfynydd village. Spacious twin, double and family bedrooms, one en suite, all with washbasins, beverage trays. Guests' lounge with colour TV, log fire. Reputation for excellent food and friendliness. Welsh speaking. WTB Farmhouse Award. Open all year except Christmas.

③ Cae'r Efail, Llanfaglan, Caernarfon, Gwynedd LL54 5RE

Mrs Mari Williams
☎ 01286 676226/672824
Fax 01286 676226
BB From £20
EM From £12
Sleeps 4
★★★★ FARM

Modernised farmhouse enjoying perfect tranquillity and seclusion with splendid views of Snowdonia and the Menai Straits. Central for Snowdonia, Isle of Anglesey, Llŷn Peninsula and all attractions of North Wales. Caernarfon only 2 miles. Homely atmosphere and warm welcome. Good home cooking. En suite bedrooms with colour TV, hairdryer and tea/coffee facilities. TV/video lounge and separate dining room. Open Easter–Oct.

④ Cwm Hwylfod, Cefn-Ddwysarn, Bala, Gwynedd LL23 7LN

Joan Best
☎/Fax 01678 530310
BB From £16–£18
EM From £11
Sleeps 6
★★★ FARM

Set in hills near Bala, our 400-year-old farmhouse is warm and welcoming. The views are spectacular. Animals abound and everyone, especially children, can take part in farm activities. Bedrooms have washbasins and tea making facilities. The guest lounge has TV, books and games. Full central heating. For our home-cooked evening meals we use the best of local produce. All diets catered for. Taste of Wales. Open all year except Christmas Day.

⑤ Erw Feurig Farm, Cefn-Ddwysarn, Bala, Gwynedd LL23 7LL

Glenys Jones
☎/Fax 01678 530262
BB From £16.50–£19
Sleeps 6
★★★ FARM

Facing the Berwyn Mountains, Erw Feurig is a guesthouse set on the 200-acre family farm, 3½ miles from Bala. The old farm cottage has been extended to provide modern, comfortable accommodation in family, double and twin rooms, some en suite. All bedrooms have heating and tea/coffee. Separate guests' dining room and lounge. Good home cooking using local produce. Coarse fishing on the farm. Open all year except Christmas.

 Please mention **Stay on a Farm** when booking

Snowdonia Mountains & Coast   *North Wales*

Gogarth Hall Farm, Gogarth, Pennal, Machynlleth, Powys SY20 9LB ⑦

Deilwen Breese
☎/Fax 01654 791235
BB From £18–£20
EM From £8
Sleeps 6

★★★
FARM

It's a pleasure to welcome guests for a quiet, relaxing stay. Feel the warmth and quality of a Welsh welcome in traditional style on our farm in magnificent setting overlooking the Dovey estuary opening to Cardigan Bay. Aberdovey beach 4 miles. En suite facilities, guests' sitting and dining rooms. See the farm animals and wildlife (kites, barn owls, etc). Farmhouse Award. Brochure. Open all year except Christmas Day.

Gwrach Ynys, Talsarnau, Nr Harlech, Gwynedd LL47 6TS ⑧

Mrs Deborah Williams
☎ 01766 780742
Fax 01766 781199
BB From £20–£23
EM From £14
Sleeps 15

★★★★
COUNTRY HOUSE

Relax in the peace and comfort of our secluded Edwardian House. Conveniently located, close to sea and mountains with many tourist attractions nearby. Ideal golfing, rambling, birdwatching area. En suite bedrooms with TV, telephone, beverage facilities. Renowned for superb home cooking using fresh local produce. WTB Farmhouse Award. AA Selected. Open Apr–Oct.

Hendy Farm, Llanbedr, Gwynedd LL45 2LT ⑨

Eirian Williams
☎/Fax 01341 241263
Mobile 0402 446949
BB From £19
EM From £12
Sleeps 6

★★★
FARM

Hendy Farm is a 200-acre mixed working farm run by Welsh speaking family, located overlooking Cardigan Bay in Snowdonia. Convenient for walking, fishing, swimming, riding, golfing, etc. Good country food provided using fresh produce whenever possible. Three en suite bedrooms, all with tea/coffee facilities. A warm welcome awaits you. Open all year.

Llwyn Mafon Isaf, Criccieth, Gwynedd LL52 0RE ⑩

Mrs Buddug Anwyl Jones
☎ 01766 530618
BB From £16–£20
Sleeps 6

★★
FARM

Traditional 17th century farmhouse, sympathetically modernised and offering superb views of Cardigan Bay and the Snowdonia mountain range. Two double en suite bedrooms, a spacious single bedroom and 1 twin bedroom, both with private bathroom. Relax in the comfortable beamed lounge with colour TV and enjoy a hearty breakfast on separate tables in the dining room. Please ring for directions. Open all year.

Mathan Uchaf Farm, Boduan, Pwllheli, Gwynedd LL53 8TU ⑪

Mrs Jean Coker
☎ 01758 720487
Fax 01758 720020
BB From £18–£20
Sleeps 6

★★
FARM

A 190-acre dairy farm, situated off the main Pwllheli to Nefyn road. Centrally positioned for northern and southern beaches of peninsula. Guests can participate in farm activities. Large garden provides safe play area. We have a dog who plays ball. 1 double room, 1 family room with washbasins, 1 twin bedded room. Dining room, sitting room with colour TV. Good food and friendly atmosphere are our aim. Farmhouse Award. Open Feb–Nov.

LET THE TELEPHONE RING!
Some farmhouses are big places. Let the telephone ring long enough to give the owner time to answer it.

North Wales — Snowdonia Mountains & Coast

12 Pengwern, Saron, Llanwnda, Caernarfon, Gwynedd LL54 5UH

G & J Lloyd Rowlands
☎/Fax 01286 831500
Mobile 0378 411780
BB From £20–£35
EM From £12.50
Sleeps 6
★★★★
FARM

Charming, spacious farmhouse of character, situated between mountains and sea. Unobstructed views of Snowdonia. Well appointed bedrooms, all with en suite bathrooms. Set in 130 acres of land which runs down to Foryd Bay. Jane has a cookery diploma and provides the excellent meals with farmhouse fresh food, including home-produced beef and lamb. Excellent access. Open Feb–Nov.

13 Plas Tirion Farm, Llanrug, Caernarfon, Gwynedd LL55 4PY

C H Mackinnon
☎/Fax 01286 673190
BB From £18–£25
Sleeps 6
★★★★
FARM

Peacefully located in 300 acres of lowland pastures, commanding panoramic views of Snowdonia and historic Caernarfon. Ideally situated for touring North Wales. Traditional stone farmhouse, offering guests warm and comfortable accommodation. All en suite bedrooms with beverage facilities and TV. Recommended for wide range of breakfast dishes and packed lunches. Open Apr–Oct.

14 Rhydydefaid Farm, Frongoch, Bala, Gwynedd LL23 7NT

Olwen Davies
☎/Fax 01678 520456
BB From £16.50–£18
Sleeps 6
★★★
FARM

A true Welsh welcome awaits you at our traditional Welsh stone farmhouse. 3 miles from Bala in secluded position. 100-acre working farm. Oak beamed lounge with inglenook fireplace. Three comfortable bedrooms with CH, 1 with exposed beams and trusses, 2 en suite. All with tea/coffee-making facilities. Ideal for touring Snowdonia. Open all year except Christmas.

15 Tyddyn Du Farm, (b), Gellilydan, Ffestiniog, nr Porthmadog, Gwynedd LL41 4RB

Paula Williams
☎/Fax 01766 590281
BB From £19–£27
EM From £12
Sleeps 8
★★★★
FARM

Enchanting 400 year-old farmhouse on our working sheep farm, set amidst spectacular scenery in superb central Snowdonia location. Choice of cosy farmhouse bedrooms or beautifully converted luxury ground floor stable suites – some with whirlpool baths and patio window gardens. (Non-smoking inside.) Delicious farmhouse cuisine. Luxury self catering suite also available. Weekly dinner B&B from £180–£240. Open all year except Christmas Day.

16 Tyddyn Iolyn, Pentrefelin, Nr Criccieth, Gwynedd LL52 0RB

Maurice & Charlotte Lowe
☎/Fax 01766 522509
BB From £17–£23
EM From £11
Sleeps 12
★★★
FARM

Lovingly restored, secluded 16th century oak-beamed farmhouse, set in idyllic farmland. Breathtaking views of Snowdonia and coastline. Perfect base for exploring Portmeirion, Snowdonia, Llŷn Peninsula. Four en suites (including 4-poster), twin with basin, all with beverage trays. Traditional cooking/vegetarian, candlelit dinners, homemade jams. Abundance of books/local information. Cats, chickens, ponies. Farm Tourism Award. Closed Christmas.
E-mail: tyddyniolyn@compuserve.co.uk

17 Tyddyn Rhys Farm, Aberdovey, Gwynedd LL35 0PG

Mrs Mair Jones
☎/Fax 01654 767533
BB From £18–£20
Sleeps 5
★★★
FARM

A warm Welsh welcome awaits you at Tyddyn Rhys with its fantastic panoramic view of the Dovey Estuary and Cardigan Bay. Only ½ mile from the centre of Aberdovey with its beautiful sandy beaches. Full central heating with colour TV, tea/coffee-making facilities in bedrooms. One en suite, one double, one single. Also static caravan. Very nice walks in the area. Open Mar–Nov.

Snowdonia Mountains & Coast — North Wales

Ty-Mawr Farm, Llanddeiniolen, Caernarfon, Gwynedd LL55 3AD

Mrs Jane Llewelyn Pierce
☎/Fax 01248 670147
BB From £18–£25
EM From £12.50
Sleeps 6
★★★ provisional
FARM

Charming, warm country farmhouse on 100-acre farm with superb views of Snowdonia mountain range. Ideal for touring North Wales and Anglesey. Caernarfon only 5 miles. All rooms have en suite bathrooms, TV and tea and coffee facilities. Two lounges with wood fires and a separate dining room. Good home cooking. Ample parking area. Open all year.

Ystumgwern, Hall Farm, Dyffryn Ardudwy, Gwynedd LL44 2DD

Jane E Williams
☎ 01341 247249
Fax 01341 247171
BB From £20–£22
Sleeps 16
★★★★
FARM

A warm Welsh welcome awaits you at Ystumgwern where the mountains of Snowdonia slope down to the sea. The traditional 16th century farmhouse has a wealth of antiques and heavy oak timbers creating a luxurious homely atmosphere. Each bedroom is charmingly decorated with many extras including the luxury of a well-equipped kitchen and its own lounge with colour TV and video. Farmhouse Award. Colour brochure sent with pleasure. Open all year.

Please mention **Stay on a Farm** when booking

Self-Catering

Bryn Beddau, Bontnewydd, Caernarfon, Gwynedd LL54 7YE

Eleri Carrog
☎ 01286 830117/673795
Fax 01286 675664
SC From £80–£375
Sleeps 5
★★★★

Cosy stone-built stable cottage with views of mountains and sea. Excellent centre for walks, touring, lovely beaches and Snowdonia. Secluded setting yet only 3 miles from Caernarfon. Lovely gallery bedroom with graceful arch windows, twin room, cot. Ideal for families or that romantic break. Spacious beamed lounge of great character and many books. Patio, barbecue. "Croeso Cymreig". Open all year.

Caerwych Farmhouse, Llandecwyn, Near Harlech, Gwynedd LL47 6YT

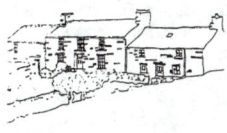

Richard Williams-Ellis
☎ 01766 770913/771270
SC From £200–£450
Sleeps 9/10
Applied

Secluded and set in marvellous scenic countryside with stupendous views to the sea. We are a typically traditional sheep farm but also breed horses and are replanting ancient woodlands. The stone farmhouse is old, large and handsome. Central heating throughout. Five bedrooms. Perfection for walkers. Accompanied trail riding in the mountains. Open all year.

North Wales — Snowdonia Mountains & Coast

㉒ Carn y Gadell Uchaf, c/o Henblas, Llwyngwril, Gwynedd LL37 2QA

Mrs Swancott Pugh
☎/Fax 01341 250350
SC From £144–£485
Sleeps 6

An historic 16th century farmhouse situated 1 mile from A493, a perfect retreat with panoramic views of Cardigan Bay. Stone spiral staircase, inglenook fireplace with log fire, 3 bedrooms, 2 bathrooms, colour TV, video, dishwasher, washing machine, fridge/freezer, microwave, games room, drying room. Excellent accommodation, ideal for exploring Snowdonia National Park. Welsh speaking family. No extra charges. Brochure. Open all year.

㉓ Cartref, Ty Newydd, Llanegryn, Tywynl, Gwynedd LL36 9SR

Ian & Catrin Rutherford
☎/Fax 01654 711726
SC From £120–£400
Sleeps 4
Applied

An attractive cottage in the charming hamlet of Llanegryn nestling in the Dysynni Valley at the foot of Cader Idris the Snowdonia National Park. Convenient for walking, swimming, golfing etc. and 4 miles from the beach. Tastefully decorated, storage heaters, washing machine, private garden. Ideal for summer or winter breaks. Open all year. E-mail: cartref@corris-wales.co.uk

㉔ Castellmarch, Abersoch, Pwllheli, Gwynedd LL53 7UE

Mrs H M Jones
☎ 01758 712242
SC From £100–£500
Sleeps 4/5 (+ cot)

Castellmarch, a family-run beef and sheep farm, 1 mile from the village of Abersoch, and minutes' walk from safe sandy beach. Listed 16th century farmhouse, once the home of fabled March Ap Meirchion – a man with horse's ears. Cegin-Isa (wing of farmhouse) sleeps 4 + cot (gas CH). All rooms have exposed beams, inglenook in living area. The Granary sleeps 5 in 2 bedrooms. A chalet set on elevated position also sleeps 5. Brochure. Open all year.

㉕ Cefnamwlch, Tudweiliog, Pwllheli, Gwynedd LL53 8AX

Mrs R Wynne-Finch
☎ 01758 770209
Fax 01758 770548
SC From £110–£295
Sleeps 4/6 + cot

Houses 1 & 2 sleep 6 in 3 double bedrooms. Cot available. Converted from wing of owner's 17th century manor farmhouse on ancient Welsh estate. Situated in beautiful woodland setting 1 mile from village of Tudweiliog, along rhododendron drive. Easy reach sandy beaches, golf course. Ideal touring centre. Colour TV, tumble dryer and spindryer. Play area. Electric £1 meter. Ty Thimble Cottage sleeps 4 in 2 double bedrooms. Open Easter–end Oct.

㉖ Chwilog Fawr, Chwilog, Pwllheli, Gwynedd LL53 6SW

Catherine Jones
☎/Fax 01766 810506
SC From £125–£450
Sleeps 2/6

Enjoy the comforts of a home from home holiday with panoramic views of the Welsh coastline while sheep and cattle graze peacefully nearby. Walk along the footpath pass the fishing lake to the village or down to the beach (3 miles). Choice of accommodation to suit you. Request our colour brochure today. Open Mar–Nov.

㉗ Dwyfach Cottages, Pen-y-Bryn, Chwilog, Pwllheli, Gwynedd LL53 6SX

Mrs Sulwen Edwards
☎ 01766 810208
Fax 01766 810064
SC From £100–£525
Sleeps 2–8

We offer a choice of luxury accommodation for the discerning. Enjoy a memorable holiday in our tastefully restored farmhouse or bungalow. Both are set in their own garden with permanent barbecue and enjoy panoramic views of Cardigan Bay and Snowdonia. Here you will find peace and tranquillity yet be within easy reach of towns, beaches, tourist attractions, fishing and shooting, children's play area. Open all year.

Snowdonia Mountains & Coast — North Wales

Garth-y-Foel, Croesor, Penrhyndeudraeth, Gwynedd LL48 6SR

Richard Williams-Ellis
☎ 01766 770913
SC From £200–£400
Sleeps 7

Absolute seclusion! And set in its own gentle, park-like, miniature valley with views to the sea in this otherwise wild mountain landscape – an unexpected, special, compelling place. Own wooded 90 acres include river with falls, pools and firewood for free. Oil, Aga and CH. 3/4 bedrooms (plus there's a large bell tent). Be forewarned about the rough, narrow, gated and bridged access track. Open all year.

28

Gwynfryn Farm, Gwynfryn, Pwllheli, Gwynedd LL53 5UF

Sharon B Ellis
☎ 01758 612536
Fax 01758 614324
SC From £135–£495
Sleeps 2/8

Our **organic** dairy farm is a haven for nature lovers, away from the madding crowd, yet only 1½ miles from Pwllheli. Cottages for romantic couples/houses 4–8 persons, all personally supervised, WTB 5 dragons – quality assured. Snowdon 25 miles, sea 2 miles – vary your activity to suit the weather or your mood. Beds made up, storage/central heating. Mini breaks Oct–Mar. Cooked dishes to order. Gold Award Welcome Host. Farmhouse Award. Colour brochure. Open all year.

29

Hafod & Hendre, c/o Ty-Mawr Farm, Llanddeiniolen, Caernarfon, Gwynedd LL55 3AD

Mrs Jane Llewelyn Pierce
☎/Fax 01248 670147
SC From £100–£400
EM From £12.50
Sleeps 2/4

Two luxurious, self-catering converted granaries situated in a private courtyard on our working farm. Hafod sleeps 3 and Hendre 5. Camp beds are available for extra children. Both are centrally heated and have wood burning stoves. CH, electricity, towels and full bedding included in price. Caernarfon 5 miles, Snowdon 4 miles. Brochures available. Open all year.

18

Penmaenbach Farm Cottages, Cwrt, Pennal, Machynlleth, Powys SY20 9LD

Mrs Shana Rees
☎/Fax 01654 791616
SC From £140–£425
Sleep 5/6

Come and stay in our newly converted stable or in our delightful 18th century keeper's cottage. Both provide an interesting blend of 'olde worlde' charm and every modern comfort. Ideally located with Aberdovey beach, Talyllyn Railway, Celtica, Centre for Alternative Technology and lots more all within 8 miles. Children are welcome to see the farm animals and feed the hens. Welsh speaking family. Brochure. Open all year.

30

Rhydolion, Llangian, Abersoch, Pwllheli, Gwynedd LL53 7LR

Catherine Morris
☎/Fax 01758 712342
SC From £110–£400
Sleeps 6 + cot

Unwind and relax in our 'olde worlde' farmhouse and cottage (disabled facilities) offering all modern comfort. Exposed beams and stone walls, inglenook fireplaces, both 3-bedroomed. Four-poster in farmhouse, attractively furnished – all conjure up a cosy homestead. Surrounded by farm interest yet only ¾ mile from beach. Explore the peninsula on foot or bike. Sandy beaches, ideal sailing and surfing area. Colour brochure. Open Feb–Nov.

31

Tai Gwyliau Tyndon Holiday Cottages, c/o Penlan, Rhos Isaf, Caernarfon, Gwynedd LL54 7NG

Mrs Elisabeth Evans
☎ 01286 831184
SC From £99–£420
Sleeps 2/8

120 acre sheep farm on the beautiful Llŷn heritage coast. Peaceful and relaxing self-catering units. 1 mile from Llanengan with its country pub and 6th century church. Boating resort of Abersoch only 2 miles away. Beautiful sandy beach of Porthneigwl within 200 yards (with private access). Most cottages have glorious views of the bay. Ideal family holiday. Personal supervision. Free brochure. Short breaks. Open all year.

32

North Wales — Snowdonia Mountains & Coast

33 Towyn Farm, Tudweiiliog, Pwllheili, Gwynedd LL53 8PD

Iona Wynne Owen
☎ 01758 770230
[SC] From £150–£380
Sleeps 6/7 + cot

Enjoy a relaxing holiday in unspoilt Area of Outstanding Natural Beauty. 200 yds from Towyn beach. Ideal fishing, surfing boating. Nefyn golf course 5 miles. A 300-year-old modernised farmhouse, carpeted throughout, colour TV, 4 bedrooms, duvets and heaters. Open fire in autumn/winter. Bathroom with bath and shower. Fitted kitchen, washing machine, tumble dryer, microwave. Sheltered lawn garden with barbecue. Free babysitting. Cot and high chair. Also ground level cottage sleeping 6. Open all year.

19 Ynys, Ystumgwern, Dyffryn Ardudwy, Gwynedd LL44 2DD

Jane & John Williams
☎ 01341 247249
Fax 01341 247171
[SC] From £140–£650
Sleeps 2/8

A taste of luxury with cosy, relaxed atmosphere. Situated between sea and mountains. 16th century farmhouse and barn conversions furnished and equipped to the highest standards. Oak beams, inglenook fireplace, gas CH. From one to four bedrooms, many en suite. Laundry room, play area. Barbecue, picnic table. Ample parking via private drive. Farmhouse Award. Warm welcome to all. Colour brochure available. Open all year.

LET THE TELEPHONE RING!

Some farmhouses are big places. Let the telephone ring long enough to give the owner time to answer it.

THE 1000+ BUREAU MEMBERS OFFER A UNIQUE LINK TO CUSTOMERS ACROSS THE UK

All Bureau members belong to a local Group. Each member can refer you to an equally high quality member within the Group... or across the UK: England, Northern Ireland, Scotland, Wales.

STAY ON A FARM GIFT TOKENS

If you have enjoyed your Stay on a Farm, why not treat your friends and relatives to *Stay on a Farm* gift tokens? Available from the Bureau office (tel: 01203 696909), they can be redeemed against accommodation and are accepted by the majority of farms (see Index). Please check when booking to avoid disappointment.

North Wales Coast & Borderlands

Llandudno, Colwyn Bay, Rhyl, Prestatyn & Clwydian Range

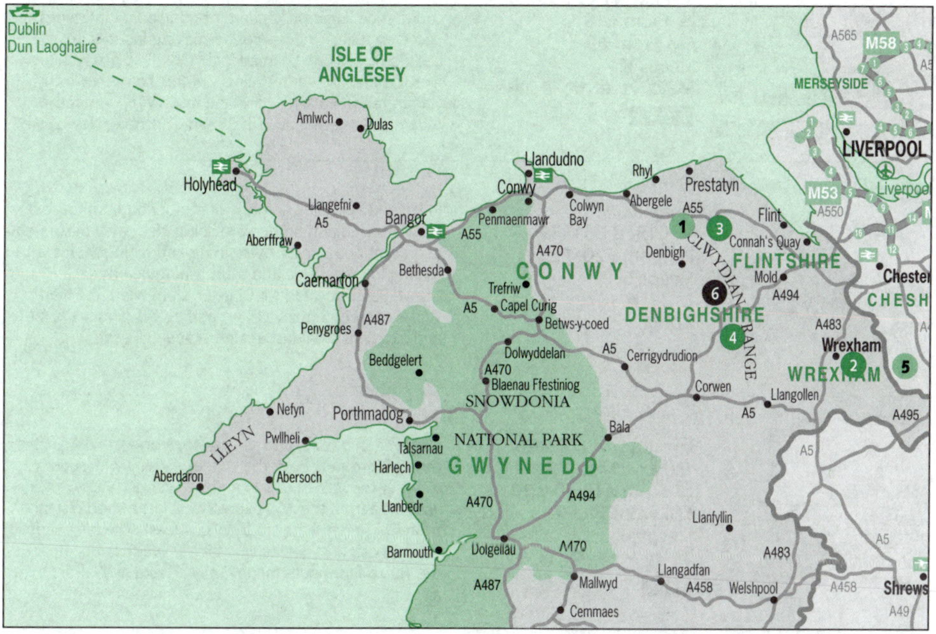

Key

- 1 Bed & Breakfast
- 1 Self-Catering
- 1 B&B and SC
- 1 Camping Barns
- 1 Camping & Caravanning

Pride of this area is the Clwydian Range of rolling hills overlooking the Vale of Clwyd and the Denbigh Moors beyond. St Asaph, at the head of the Vale, might appear to be a large village, but it is also a 'city' with one of the oldest cathedrals in Wales. Further into Clwyd lies Ruthin with its castle and 'Maen Huail' stone where King Arthur is said to have beheaded his rival in love. Visit Ruthin's craft centre and those at Afon-wen and Llanasa. Craft of a different nature are to be found in Llangollen where horse-drawn barges glide along the Shropshire Union Canal. Catch the International Eisteddfod here, try a world-class theatre production in Mold or visit the National Trust's Erddig near Wrexham.

If you would like help in finding suitable farm accommodation, turn to the full listing of farm groups on pages 360 to 363 to find appropriate contact details for this area.

North Wales

North Wales Coast & Borderlands

Bed and Breakfast
(and evening meal)

---

① Bach-y-Graig, Tremeirchion, St Asaph LL17 0UH

Anwen Roberts
☎/Fax 01745 730627
BB From £18
EM From £9
Sleeps 6
★★★★ FARM

A 16th century listed farmhouse nestling at the foot of the Clwydian Range with beautiful views of the surrounding countryside. Highest standard of traditional furnishings and decor, en suite, TVs, tea/coffee-making facilities in bedrooms, full CH, beamed inglenook fireplace with log fires. Central for North Wales, Chester, coast 9 miles. Games room. 40 acre woodland trail. WTB Farmhouse Award. AA selected award. Closed Christmas/New Year.

---

② Erlas Hall, Erlas Lane, Wrexham, LL13 9UD

Anne Done
☎ 01978 661339
BB From £20–£25
Sleeps 5
Applied

Relax and enjoy the comfort of our period farmhouse on the Welsh/English border, providing pleasantly decorated bedrooms and guests' own sitting and dining rooms with roaring log fires. Golf and trout fishing nearby. Conveniently located for Chester, Llangollen, the North Wales coast and many NT properties. A warm welcome and excellent breakfast assured. Open all year.

---

③ Fron-Haul, Bodfari, Denbigh, Denbighshire LL16 4DY

Gwladys M Edwards
☎/Fax 01745 710301
BB From £18.50–£20
EM From £8.50
Sleeps 6
★★★ FARM

Discover an oasis of calm and taste. Fron-Haul dominates the high ground above the Wheeler Valley with superb views of the Vale of Clwyd and Snowdonia. Easily accessible from the A55 expressway, just a short distance from Chester and the North Wales coast. The farm supplies the freshest, best quality vegetables, Welsh lamb, etc for the varied farmhouse menu. Truly a Taste of Wales. Open all year.

---

④ Llainwen Ucha, Pentrecelyn, Ruthin, Denbighshire LL15 2HL

Elizabeth Parry
☎ 01978 790253
BB From £15–£17
EM From £8
Sleeps 5
★★ FARM

Our 130 acre farm overlooks the beautiful Vale of Clwyd. Centrally situated to coast, Snowdonia, Chester and Llangollen. Modern house with 2 pleasant bedrooms to accommodate 5 persons. CH and good home cooking, a warm welcome to visitors throughout the year. Take A525 from Ruthin towards Wrexham; after 4 miles turn left after college, we are a mile up this road. Open all year except Christmas and New Year.

---

⑤ Mill House, Higher Wych, Malpas, Cheshire SY14 7JR

Chris & Angela Smith
☎ 01948 780362
Fax 01948 780566
BB From £18
EM From £8
Sleeps 4
★★★ GUEST HOUSE

Modernised Mill House on the Cheshire/Clwyd border in a quiet valley, convenient for visiting Chester, Shrewsbury and North Wales. The house is centrally heated and has an open log fire in the lounge. Bedrooms have washbasins, radios and tea-making facilities. 1 bedroom has an en suite shower and WC. Reductions for children and senior citizens. Open Jan–Nov.

North Wales Coast & Borderlands — North Wales

Self-Catering

Bach-y-Graig, Tremeirchion, St Asaph LL17 0UH

Anwen Roberts
☎/Fax 01745 730627
SC From £90–£350
Sleeps 6 + cot

Stay on a working dairy farm in this 16th century farmhouse, retaining the charm but offering comforts and convenience of modern living in high standard accommodation. Dark oak, fully equipped kitchen. 3 bedrooms, 1 four-poster bed. Bathroom with shower/bath. Downstairs toilet, CTV heating. Log fires. Linen provided. Games room, large garden with swings/slide. Central for Chester, Snowdonia and coastal resorts. No pets. Open all year.

The Granary, c/o Mill House, Higher Wych, Malpas, Cheshire SY14 7JR

Chris & Angela Smith
☎ 01948 780362
Fax 01948 780566
SC From £75–£175
Sleeps 4/5 + cot

The Granary is a self-contained bungalow adjacent to Mill House. Sleeps 4/5 in 2 double bedrooms, kitchen/living area, shower and WC. TV. CH. Cot and babysitting available. Situated in a quiet valley with a small stream in the garden. Convenient for visiting Chester, Shrewsbury and North Wales. Open May–Nov.

Tyddyn Isaf, Rhewl, Ruthin, Clwyd LL15 1UH

Elsie Jones
☎ 01824 703142/703367
SC From £90–£260
Sleeps 4/6 + cot

Stay in self-contained part of farmhouse or recently converted granary in picturesque Vale of Clwyd. Both fully equipped to high standard. Farmhouse has kitchen lounge/diner, 2 bedrooms sleeping 4/6, bathroom, separate toilet. Granary has 1 bedroom with vanity unit, sofa bed in lounge, sleeps 2/4, shower room. 3 miles from Ruthin and within easy reach of Chester, the coast, Snowdonia. Bedlinen provided. No pets. Open all year.

FOLLOW THE COUNTRY CODE

Leave nothing but footprints,
Take nothing but photographs,
Kill nothing but time!

Mid Wales

Farm entries in this regional section are listed under those areas shown in green on the key map. Look at the index below to find on which page the entries start. You will see that we have listed the areas geographically so that you can turn more easily to find farms in neighbouring areas.

At the start of each area section is a detailed map with numbered symbols indicating the location of each farm. Different symbols denote different types of accommodation; see the key below each area map. Farm entries are listed alphabetically under type of accommodation. Some farms offer more than one type of accommodation and therefore have more than one entry.

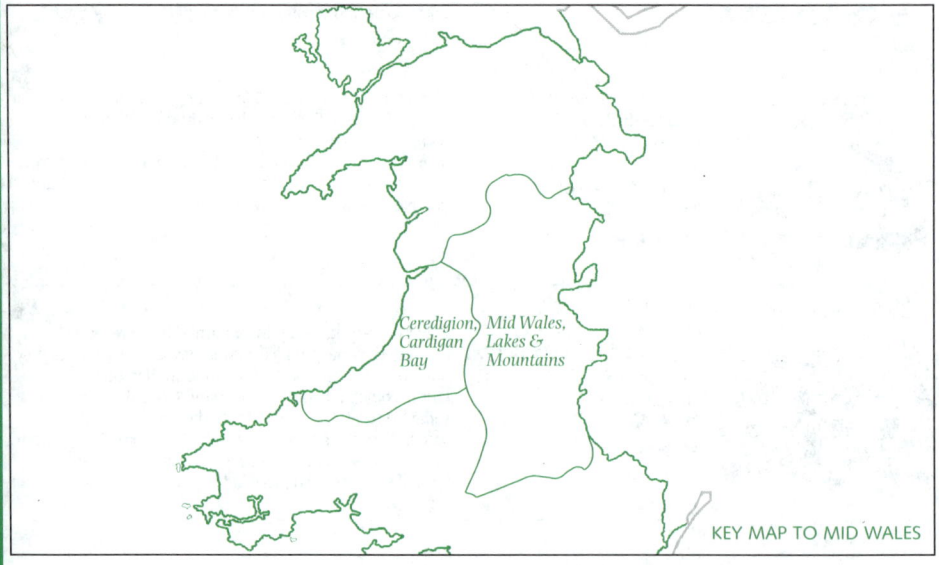

KEY MAP TO MID WALES

Ceredigion, Cardigan Bay page 323

Mid Wales, Lakes & Mountains page 327
Berwyn Mountains through Heart of Wales to Brecon Beacons National Park & Black Mountains

Ceredigion, Cardigan Bay

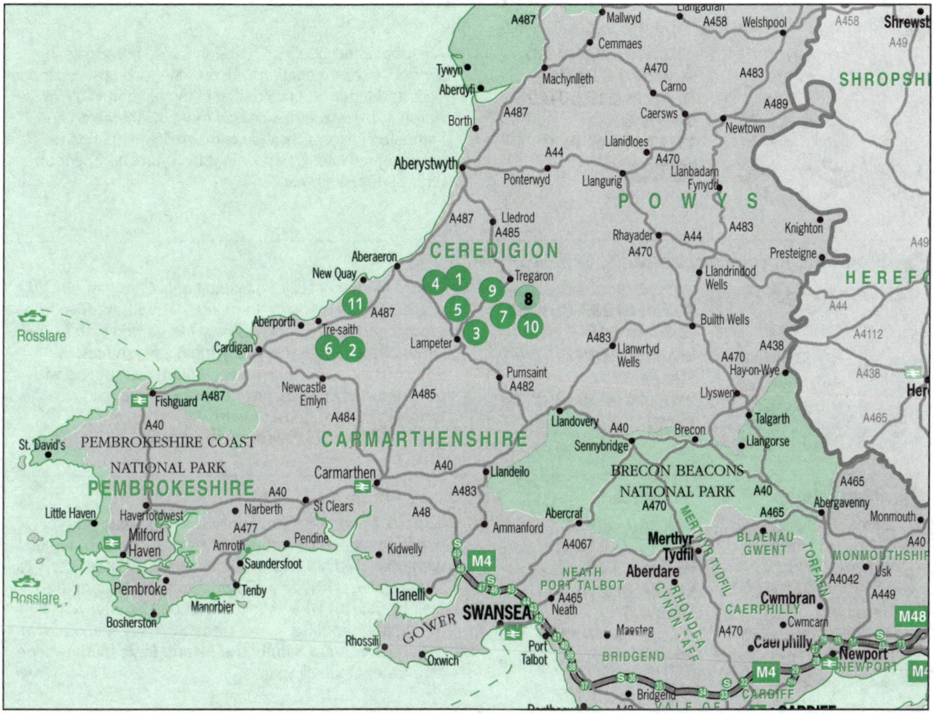

Key

- 1 Bed & Breakfast
- 1 Self-Catering
- 1 B&B and SC
- 1 Camping Barns
- 1 Camping & Caravanning

The magic of Cardiganshire will enchant you with its gentle mountains and 52 miles of unspoilt coastline encircling pastureland threaded with salmon rivers and providing a haven for wildlife. The coastline, with its safe, sandy beaches and spectacular walks, stretches from Cardigan to the university town of Aberystwyth. The county's main river, the Teifi, is shared by fishermen, canoeists and the famous coracle men of Cenarth. Woollen mills, potteries and Celtic crafts abound. Here, in the ancient kingdom of Ceredigion, a rural way of life persists in the small farms and villages where Welsh is still the first language. Come and join us.

If you would like help in finding suitable farm accommodation, turn to the full listing of farm groups on pages 360 to 363 to find appropriate contact details for this area.

Mid Wales

Ceredigion, Cardigan Bay

Bed and Breakfast
(and evening meal)

---

① Abermeurig Mansion, Abermeurig, Lampeter, Ceredigion, SA48 8PP

Mrs M J Rogers-Lewis
☎ 01570 470216
BB From £19.50–£25
Sleeps 6
★★★★
COUNTRY HOUSE

Ancestral listed Georgian mansion family home offering spacious accommodation with en suite four-poster, canopy beds and family room. Situated in the beautiful Vale of Aeron, 7 miles from the coastal town of Aberaeron and Lampeter. Peaceful location with wildlife in abundance including red kite. Free private fishing. Brochure sent on request. Open all year.

---

② Broniwan, Rhydlewis, Llandyssul, Ceredigion SA44 5PF

Carole Jacobs
☎/Fax 01239 851261
BB From £19–£20
EM From £11
Sleeps 4
★★★
FARM

Unwind in the peace of our traditional Cardiganshire home. Explore our small farm just 10 minutes' drive from sandy beaches at Penbryn. Enjoy our garden with its quiet views of the Preseli Hills. Cosy rooms, warm fires, generous meals (including vegetarian) wait for you with our welcome. En suite/private facilities. Reduced weekly terms. WTB Farmhouse Award.
E-mail: 101535.2310@compuserve.com.uk

---

③ Bryncastell Farm, Llanfair Road, Lampeter, Ceredigion SA48 8JY

E A Beti Davies
☎ 01570 422447
BB From £18–£20
EM From £10
Sleeps 6
★★★
FARM

'Croeso' to our 140-acre family farm commanding panoramic views over the Teifi Valley. All modern facilities with unrivalled hospitality and excellent cuisine. Access to farm activities, hillside walks or gentle strolls along the river bank in an area of unspoilt natural beauty. ¾ mile fishing and shooting, 1 mile from university market town of Lampeter. WTB Farmhouse Award. Basic food hygiene certificate. Open all year.

---

④ Brynog Mansion, Felinfach, Lampeter, Ceredigion SA48 8AQ

Eleanor Davies
☎ 01570 470266
BB From £18.50–£19
Sleeps 6
★★★
FARM

Secluded spacious 250 year old country mansion and 170-acre grazing farm, approached by ¾ mile rhododendron-lined drive off the A482 main road. 15 mins by car. Lampeter University town and seaside resort of Aberaeron and coast. Full Welsh breakfast in the grand old dining room. Rough shooting, birdwatching, riverside walks. Brochure available. Open all year except Christmas & New Year.

---

⑤ Dremddu Fawr, Creuddyn Bridge, Lampeter, Ceredigion SA48 8BL

Mrs Ann Jones
☎ 01570 470394
BB From £20
EM From £12.50
Sleeps 4
★★★
FARM

Come to us for a genuine taste of Welsh farming life. Small farmhouse on 163-acre cattle and sheep farm set in rolling countryside between Lampeter and the Cardigan Bay coast. Guest bedrooms have pine furniture, tapestry bedspreads and chocolates – all made in Wales! WTB Farmhouse Award. Member of Wales – Great Little Places and Taste of Wales. 'All Wales Top Cook' award – mouthwatering food. Open all year.

Ceredigion, Cardigan Bay — Mid Wales

Llwyn yr Eos, Rhydlewis, Llandyssul, Ceredigion SA44 5QU ⑥

Judith Rodwell
☎/Fax 01239 851268
BB From £19–£21
EM From £11
Sleeps 6

★★★ FARM

Escape to our sheep farm in the beautiful Teifi valley. Comfortable, south-facing bedrooms with superb views. Watch buzzards and red kites on the farm or dolphins and seals off the coast 10 minutes' drive away. Good food using fresh local produce with fruit and vegetables from the garden. Open all year.

Nantymedd Farm, Llanfair Clydogau, Lampeter, Ceredigion SA48 8JZ ⑦

Eleanor Evans
☎ 01570 493208
BB From £17–£18
EM From £9
Sleeps 2

★★★ provisional
FARM

Situated in quiet countryside overlooking the River Teifi, a 250-acre working farm with free trout and salmon fishing and riding ponies. Ideally situated to explore and enjoy coastal resorts, the rugged Cambrian Mountains and large nature reserves. Golf club, riding centres, craft centre, activity centre all nearby. Evening meals served using fresh farm and local produce. Brochure available. Open all year.

Pant-Teg, Llanfair Clydogau, Lampeter, Ceredigion SA48 8LL ⑧

Mrs Pat Brown
☎ 01570 493416
BB From £19–£20
Sleeps 5

★★★ GUEST HOUSE

Welcome to Pant-Teg! Once an old stone hill farm, now a peaceful country home, it rests on the gentle mountainside with magnificent views. Red kites wheel overhead and wildlife surrounds us. Beautiful lawned gardens, pond, meandering brook. Enticing meals, vegetarian if preferred, served in our charming conservatory. Cosy woodburner and en suite facilities. Come and join us! Open all year except Christmas.

Penlanmedd, Llanfair Road, Lampeter, Ceredigion SA48 8JZ ⑨

Mrs Elaine Coombes
☎ 01570 493438
BB From £18–£20
EM From £10
Sleeps 6

★★★ GUEST HOUSE

Set in farmland above the River Teifi, we extend a very warm welcome at our secluded 18th century Penlanmedd. We offer good fresh food, log fires, cosy en suite bedrooms, pretty gardens and glorious views. Visit the mountains or the deep blue sea – every day the choice is yours! Open all year.

Pentre Farm, Llanfair Clydogau, Lampeter, Ceredigion SA48 8LE ⑩

Eleri Davies
☎/Fax 01570 493313
BB From £19–£20
EM From £10
Sleeps 6

★★★ FARM

Pentre, a family farm overlooks the Teifi Valley. Comfortable en suite accommodation in large stonebuilt farmhouse of traditional charm and character dating back to 1870. Excellent farmhouse fare using fresh local produce reflecting a taste of Wales. Peaceful countryside walks, free fishing for salmon and trout. Brochure supplied. Open Apr–Oct.

Wervil Grange Farm, Pentregat, Nr Llangranog, Llandyssul, Ceredigion SA44 6HW ⑪

Ionwen Lewis
☎ 01239 654252
BB From £20–£25
Sleeps 6

★★★★ FARM

A very warm welcome awaits you in this superb de luxe Welsh Georgian farmhouse, offering a very high standard of accommodation. All bedrooms en suite with colour TV. The house has been beautifully decorated and furnished and has a very relaxed atmosphere. Enjoy the true 'Taste of Wales' with mouth-watering food and wine, mostly grown on the farm or locally supplied. Free coarse and trout fishing for guests. Just off the A487, halfway between the Georgian towns of Aberaeron and Cardigan.

Mid Wales   *Ceredigion, Cardigan Bay*

Self-Catering

⑧ Pant-Teg Studio Cottage, Llanfair Clydogau, Lampeter, Ceredigion SA48 8LL

Mrs Pat Brown
☎ **01570 493416**
SC From £150–£300
Sleeps 4–6

Set on the bank, its patio area next to our tumbling brook, and surrounded by meadows of grazing sheep, Pant-Teg Studio, tastefully converted, fully equipped and with en suite facilities, shares the beautiful views and tranquil gardens of the main farmhouse, whilst offering privacy and independence. Coast and countryside abound with wildlife and our peaceful haven is a perfect base from which to explore – or just relax! Brochure available. Open all year.

Please mention **Stay on a Farm** when booking

CONFIRM BOOKINGS

Disappointments can arise from misunderstandings over the telephone. Please write to confirm your booking.

Our Internet address is
http://www.webscape.co.uk/farmaccom/

Mid Wales, Lakes & Mountains

Berwyn Mountains through Heart of Wales to Brecon Beacons National Park & Black Mountains

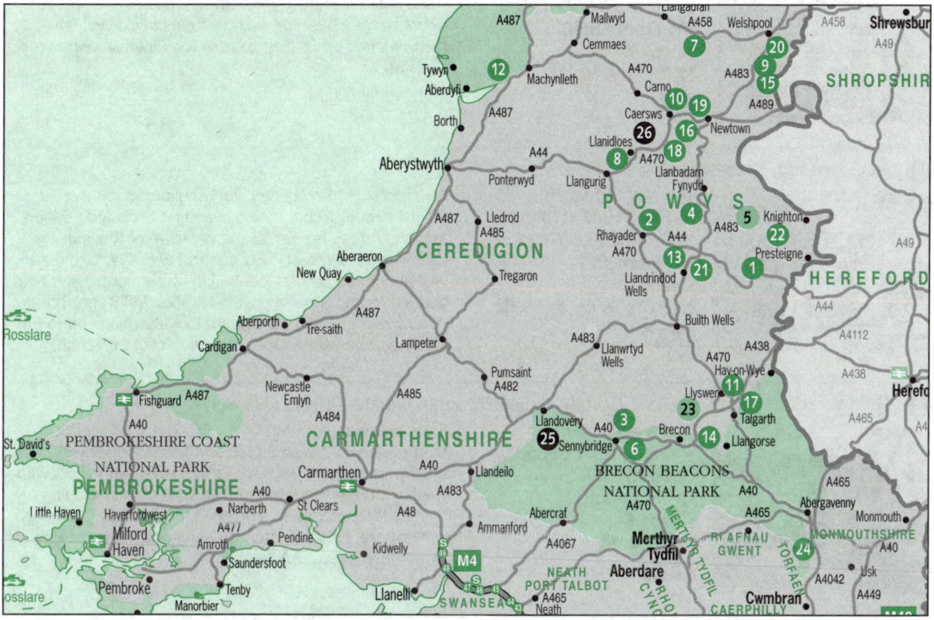

Key

- 1 Bed & Breakfast
- 1 Self-Catering
- 1 B&B and SC
- 1 Camping Barns
- 1 Camping & Caravanning

With its rugged mountain scenery, lakes, gentle hills and beautiful valleys, Mid Wales is the perfect habitat for wild flowers and rare birds such as the red kite. This breathtaking landscape is ideal for walking, from gentle rambles or following the long-distance footpaths of Glyndwr's Way and the Upper Wye Valley, to tackling the remote areas of the vast Elan Valley watershed. In the Brecon Beacons you can scale a peak or follow a guided walk, cycle one of the graded tracks, go pony trekking, fish, or take a trip on the Monmouthshire and Brecon Canal or Brecon Mountain Railway. The whole area is steeped in history, with Roman encampments, castles, caves, old mine workings, churches and monuments.

If you would like help in finding suitable farm accommodation, turn to the full listing of farm groups on pages 360 to 363 to find appropriate contact details for this area.

 **Mid Wales** — Mid Wales, Lakes & Mountains

Bed and Breakfast
(and evening meal)

① Bache Farm, New Radnor, Presteigne, Powys LD8 2TG

May Hardwick
☎ 01544 350680
BB From £17.50–£19
EM From £9.50
Sleeps 6
★★ FARM

Situated near to the village of New Radnor – gateway to the heart of Wales. 'Bache', a family-run mixed farm with stone built farmhouse with exposed beams and log fires, offers an ideal base for walking/touring Mid Wales and the borders. Special diets catered for. Open all year except Christmas.

② Beili Neuadd, Rhayader, Powys LD6 5NS

Mrs Ann Edwards
☎/Fax 01597 810211
BB From £19.50–£21
EM From £11
Sleeps 6 (8)
★★★ FARM

An attractive 16th century stone-built farmhouse set amidst beautiful countryside in a quiet, secluded position approx. 2 miles from small market town of Rhayader. Guests are assured of every comfort with CH, log fires and well appointed accommodation in single, double and twin bedded rooms, all with private facilities. WTB Farmhouse Award winner. We look forward to welcoming you to this lovely part of Wales. Open all year except Christmas.

③ Bryn y Fedwen Farm, Trallong Common, Sennybridge, Brecon, Powys LD3 8HW

Mrs Mary Adams
☎/Fax 01874 636505
BB From £20
EM From £10
Sleeps 6
★★★ FARM

Enjoy peace and quiet at Bryn y Fedwen, a hill livestock farm situated between Brecon and Sennybridge overlooking the Brecon Beacons and Usk Valley. Lovely farm walks with wildlife. Comfortable, spacious en suite rooms including twin bedded apartment (equipped for disabled). TV lounge with log fire. Personal attention and good home cooking. Farmhouse Award. AA Selected.

④ Bwlch Farm, Llananno, Llandrindod Wells, Powys LD1 6TT

Dorothy Taylor
☎/Fax 01597 840366
BB From £18.50–£21
EM From £12.50
Sleeps 6
★★★ FARM

Come to the Bwlch and spend a peaceful holiday in our beautiful 16th century farmhouse. Go walking, birdwatching or touring or just laze and admire the magnificent views. You will be made welcome. We're ½ mile from A483 and 12 miles north of Llandrindod Wells. Open Apr–Oct.

⑤ Cefnsuran Farm, Llangunllo, Knighton, Powys LD7 1SL

Gill & Gordon Morgan
☎ 01547 550219
BB From £21–£25
EM From £10.50
Sleeps 6 (8)
★★★ FARM

Cefnsuran is a 16th century farmhouse set in isolated valley with large gardens and extremely picturesque countryside. 5 mins from A483. Recently refurbished, it retains its farmhouse feel with woodburning inglenook fireplaces and exposed beams. High standard of traditional cooking using fresh local produce whenever possible. Vegetarian and special diets. Open all year.

Mid Wales, Lakes & Mountains — Mid Wales

Cwmcamlais Uchaf Farm, Cwmcamlais, Sennybridge, Brecon, Powys LD3 8TD ⑥

Mrs Jean Phillips
☎/Fax 01874 636376
BB From £19–£20
EM From £12
Sleeps 6
★★★ FARM

Cwmcamlais Uchaf is a working farm situated on the route of a popular walk in the Brecon Beacons National Park. 1 mile off the A40 between Brecon and Sennybridge. Our 16th century farmhouse has exposed beams and stonework, inglenook fireplace and tastefully decorated bedrooms (2 double en suite, one twin with own shower room, all with tea/coffee). The River Camlais with its waterfalls, flows through the farmland. A warm Welsh welcome awaits you. Closed Christmas.

Cwmllwynog, Llanfair Caereinion, Welshpool, Powys SY21 0HF ⑦

Joyce Cornes
☎/Fax 01938 810791
BB From £20
EM From £10
Sleeps 4
★★★ FARM

Built in the early 17th century Cwmllwynog is a traditional long farmhouse of character on a working dairy farm. We have a spacious garden with a stream at the bottom and a lot of unusual plants. All bedrooms have colour TV and drink making facilities. Double room en suite, twin with hot and cold and private bathroom. Delicious home-cooked meals cooked. Just for you! We can help you with routes. WTB Farmhouse Award. Open Jan–Nov.

Dol-Llys Farm, Llanidloes, Powys, SY18 6JA ⑧

Olwen S Evans
☎ 01686 412694
BB From £18–£20
Sleeps 6
★★★ provisional FARM

Dol-Llys is a working farm situated on the banks of the River Severn. This intriguing farmhouse has many levels and small staircases with character throughout. Three en suite bedrooms with all facilities. Ideal for walking, fishing and birdwatching yet within walking distance of the historic town of Llanidloes. Open Easter–Nov.

The Drewin Farm, Churchstoke, Montgomery, Powys SY15 6TW ⑨

Mrs Ceinwen Richards
☎/Fax 01588 620325
BB From £19–£20
EM From £10
Sleeps 5
★★★ FARM

Relax in our 17th century farmhouse which has a wealth of charm and character, with original features such as exposed beams and inglenook fireplace. En suite bedrooms with TV and drinks facilities. Offa's Dyke footpath runs through the farm, from which its elevated position, commands outstanding views of the surrounding countryside. A warm Welsh welcome with kettle always on the boil. AA Selected, WTB Farmhouse Award. Open Mar–Oct.

Dyffryn Farmhouse, Aberhafesp, Newtown, Powys SY16 3JD ⑩

Dave & Sue Jones
☎ 01686 688817
Fax 01686 688324
BB From £22–£25
EM From £12
Sleeps 6
★★★ provisional BED & BREAKFAST

Set on the banks of a stream, Dyffryn has luxurious, en suite accommodation, full central heating and pretty decor. Lovely walks along stream and in woods, lakes and nature reserve nearby. Traditional farmhouse fare including vegetarian specialities. Walkers and cyclists welcome. 'Come and enjoy life on a Welsh hill farm – you might want to stay!' Open all year.
Mobile 0585 206412 E-mail: daveandsue@clara.net.uk

Ffordd-Fawr Farmhouse, Fforddfawr, Hay-on-Wye, Glasbury via Hereford HR3 5PT ⑪

Mrs Barbara Eckley
☎/Fax 01497 847332
BB From £18–£20
Sleeps 6
★★★ FARM

Charming 17th century farmhouse set in idyllic open countryside, nestling between the Black Mountains and Radnor hills, 3 miles from the famous bookshops of Hay-on-Wye. The three en suite bedrooms each have their own individual charm and enjoy views over the countryside. The farm is bordered by the River Wye and is noted for its birdlife and natural beauty. Open Mar–Nov.

Mid Wales

Mid Wales, Lakes & Mountains

12 Gogarth Hall Farm, Gogarth, Pennal, Machynlleth, Powys SY20 9LB

Deilwen Breese
☎/Fax 01654 791235
BB From £18–£20
EM From £8
Sleeps 6

★★★
FARM

It's a pleasure to welcome guests for a quiet, relaxing stay. Feel the warmth and quality of a Welsh welcome in traditional style on our farm in magnificent setting overlooking the Dovey estuary opening to Cardigan Bay. Aberdovey beach 4 miles. En suite facilities, guests' sitting and dining rooms. See the farm animals and wildlife (kites, barn owls, etc). Farmhouse Award. Brochure. Open all year except Christmas Day.

13 Highbury Farm, Llanyre, Llandrindod Wells, Powys LD1 6EA

Shirley Evans
☎/Fax 01597 822716
BB From £17–£21
EM From £9.50
Sleeps 6

★★★
FARM

Come and visit our comfortable Victorian farmhouse at our smallholding one mile from the spa town of Llandrindod Wells. Three tastefully decorated bedrooms with private facilities and hospitality trays. TV lounge, separate dining room. WTB Farmhouse Award. Brochure available. Ideally situated for the Elan Valley dams and for touring the heart of Wales. Open Mar–Nov.

14 Highgrove Farm, Llanhamlach, Brecon, Powys LD3 7SU

Mrs Ruth Williams
☎ 01874 665489
BB From £18–£25
Sleeps 6

★★★★
FARM

Highgrove, situated between Brecon and Llangorse Lake in the National Park, is a 16th century farmhouse in a superb position overlooking the Brecon Beacons. Conservation award for renovation. An ideal base for a relaxing, touring or sporting holiday. Good choice of restaurants and pubs for evening meals nearby. Open Mar–Oct.

15 Little Brompton Farm, Montgomery, Powys SY15 6HY

Gaynor Bright
☎/Fax 01686 668371
BB From £19–£20
EM From £10
Sleeps 6

★★★
FARM

A true oasis of tranquillity in beautiful scenery, this 17th century oak framed farmhouse on working farm offers friendly hospitality. Pretty rooms enhanced by quality furnishings and antiques, all amenities, en suites available. Traditional farmhouse cooking. Offa's Dyke footpath runs through farm. WTB Farmhouse Award. AA selected. Welcome Host. Situated 2 miles east of Montgomery on B4385. Open all year.

16 Llettyderyn, Mochdre, Newtown, Powys SY16 4JY

Mrs Margaret Jandrell
☎ 01686 626131
BB From £19–£25
EM From £12
Sleeps 6

★★★
FARM

Llettyderyn – a restored 18th century farmhouse with exposed beams, inglenook fireplace and traditional parlour. A working farm rearing sheep and beef. 2 miles from Newtown; an ideal base for touring Mid-Wales. Excellent farmhouse cooking, with home-made bread. Vegetarians catered for. Double and twin-bedded rooms en suite, tea-making facilities and TV. Full central heating. Ample parking. Open all year.

17 Lodge Farm, Talgarth, Brecon, Powys LD3 0DP

Mrs Marion Meredith
☎/Fax 01874 711244
BB From £19–£22
EM From £12
Sleeps 6

★★
FARM

Enjoy the tranquillity on this working farm nestling in the Brecon Beacons National Park. Relax in cottage-style garden with spectacular mountain views, wander along country lanes or climb well-known mountains. Return to 18th century house for interesting homemade meals including vegetarian. Dining room has inglenook and flagstone floor. Retire to cosy en suite period furnished bedrooms. Talgarth 1½ miles, Hay-on-Wye 8 miles. Open all year.

Mid Wales, Lakes & Mountains Mid Wales

Lower Gwerneirin Farm, Llandinam, Powys SY17 5DD

Mrs Anne Brown
☎ 01686 688286
[BB] From £20–£25
EM From £12
Sleeps 4

★★★ FARM

 18

Beautifully situated in the Severn Valley, the farmhouse is a spacious Victorian dwelling offering comfortable accommodation. All rooms have CH, drinks facilities and colour TV. One double and 1 twin en suite. Guests lounge with log fire. Fishing in own trout pool. We have a wealth of wildlife. Ideally located for exploring Mid Wales. Large garden with beautiful views. Superb home cooking. Open all year.

Lower Gwestydd, Llanllwchaiarn, Newtown, Powys SY16 3AY

Iris Jarman
☎ 01686 626718
[BB] From £20–£25
EM From £11
Sleeps 4

★★★ FARM

19

Lower Gwestydd is a listed half-timbered farmhouse set on a quiet hillside 2 miles north of Newtown just off the B4568 road. Guests have own lounge and dining room. All rooms centrally heated, 2 bedrooms en suite, all have beverage trays. WTB Farmhouse Award, hygiene certificate, Hostess Award. Finalist in the Best British Breakfast 1991 competition. Large garden with beautiful views, own produce. Open all year.

Moat Farm, Welshpool, Powys SY21 8SE

Gwyneth Jones
☎/Fax 01938 553179
[BB] From £20–£22
EM From £11
Sleeps 6

★★★ FARM

 20

Moat Farm is a 260-acre dairy farm set in the beautiful Severn Valley. The 17th century farmhouse offers warm and comfortable accommodation with good home cooking served in a fine timbered dining room, traditionally furnished with Welsh dresser. All rooms en suite with tea/coffee facilities and colour TV. Quiet lounge, pool table and spacious garden. Good touring centre. Near Powis Castle. Golf, riding and fishing nearby. Open Mar–Nov.

Neuadd Farm, Penybont, Llandrindod Wells, Powys LD1 5SW

Peter & Jackie Longley
☎/Fax 01597 822571
[BB] From £19.50–£22
EM From £11
Sleeps 6

★★★ FARM

21

Enjoy a relaxing break in our comfortably furnished 16th century farmhouse looking over the lovely Ithon Valley. Historic location with no traffic. Separate guests' sitting and dining rooms, both with inglenook fireplaces. Good traditional home cooking. Ideal for exploring Mid Wales or walk direct from our door. Brochure available. Open all year except Christmas.

Pilleth Court, Whitton, Knighton, Powys LD7 1NP

Mrs Heather Hood
☎/Fax 01547 560272
[BB] From £18–£20
EM From £8.50
Sleeps 6

★★★ FARM

 22

A listed Elizabethan house, tastefully furnished to retain its character and atmosphere, on a large working farm set in marvellous, unspoilt countryside. All guest rooms have panoramic views. One room is en suite and all rooms have tea/coffee-making facilities and TV. A wonderful centre for walking and touring. Open all year except Christmas.

Trehenry Farm, Felinfach, Llandefalle, Brecon, Powys LD3 0UN

Mrs Theresa Jones
☎/Fax 01874 754312
[BB] From £20–£21
Sleeps 6

★★★ FARM

23

Trehenry is a 200 acre mixed farm situated east of Brecon, 1 mile off A470. The impressive 18th century farmhouse with breathtaking views, inglenook fireplaces and exposed beams offers comfortable accommodation, good food and cosy rooms. TV lounge, separate dining tables, central heating, tea-making facilities, all rooms en suite. Brochure on request. Farmhouse Award winner. Open all year except Christmas.

Mid Wales

Mid Wales, Lakes & Mountains

24 Ty-Cooke Farm, Mamhilad, Pontypool, Monmouthshire NP4 8QZ

Mrs Marion Price
☎ 01873 880382
BB From £18–£25
Sleeps 6

★★
FARM

A comfortable 18th century farmhouse set in a cobbled courtyard. The family-run mixed farm is set on the edge of the Brecon Beacons National Park. Goytre Wharf on the Monmouthshire–Brecon Canal is ½ mile away. Ty-Cooke is the ideal centre for exploring the mountains and valleys of South Wales. Open all year.

Self-Catering

5 Cefnsuran Farm, Llangunllo, Knighton, Powys LD7 1SL

Gill & Gordon Morgan
☎/Fax 01547 550219
SC From £165–£360
Sleeps 6

The 16th century house is set in an isolated valley on a 300-acre working farm, 7 miles from Knighton. Beautiful location for a peaceful, interesting and private holiday. Accommodation in a wing of the farmhouse has 3 bedrooms, family en suite room, one double, with colour TV, one single and private bathroom. Lounge and dining room with traditional inglenook fireplaces and oak beams, small kitchen with all modern appliances and full CH. Large, well-maintained gardens.

25 Gwydre Cottage, Gwydre, Llanddeusant, Llangadog, Carmarthenshire SA19 9YS

Mrs D J Price
☎ 01550 740242
SC From £200–£386
Sleeps 6 + cot

Gwydre Cottage is situated at the foot of the Brecon Beacons on a working farm where you are welcome to lend a hand. With rolling acres to explore, feel the fresh hill breezes and see the breathtaking scenery. Ideal for birdwatching (red kites, etc). Safe, large lawn with children's play equipment. Open Mar–Nov.

26 Red House, Trefeglwys, Nr Caersws, Powys SY17 5PN

Gwyneth Williams
☎ 01686 688194
SC From £120–£270
Sleeps 5 + cot

A highly furnished, self-contained part of the farmhouse, situated on a mixed working family farm. Panoramic views, unspoilt scenery and the tranquillity of the Trannon Valley. Ideal base for touring Mid Wales. Golf, riding and fishing available within 6 miles. Llanidloes 6 miles. Guests' comfort is the priority. Log fire, oak beams, garden with furniture, ample parking and wildlife. Open all year.

23 Trehenry Farm, Felinfach, Llandefalle, Brecon, Powys LD3 0UN

Mrs Theresa Jones
☎/Fax 01874 754312
SC From £280–£450
Sleeps 8

For a holiday to remember then come to Trehenry 200 acre working farm. Tranquillity surrounded by breathtaking views. 17th century farmhouse modernised to a high standard with oak beams, inglenook fireplace. 3 bedrooms, 2 en suite, 1 private. Bed settee in second lounge. Very well equipped kitchen, lounge with TV, video, CH, wood stove. Price includes linen, electric, heating. Brochure. Open all year.

South & West Wales

Farm entries in this regional section are listed under those areas shown in green on the key map. Look at the index below to find on which page the entries start. You will see that we have listed the areas geographically so that you can turn more easily to find farms in neighbouring areas.

At the start of each area section is a detailed map with numbered symbols indicating the location of each farm. Different symbols denote different types of accommodation; see the key below each area map. Farm entries are listed alphabetically under type of accommodation. Some farms offer more than one type of accommodation and therefore have more than one entry.

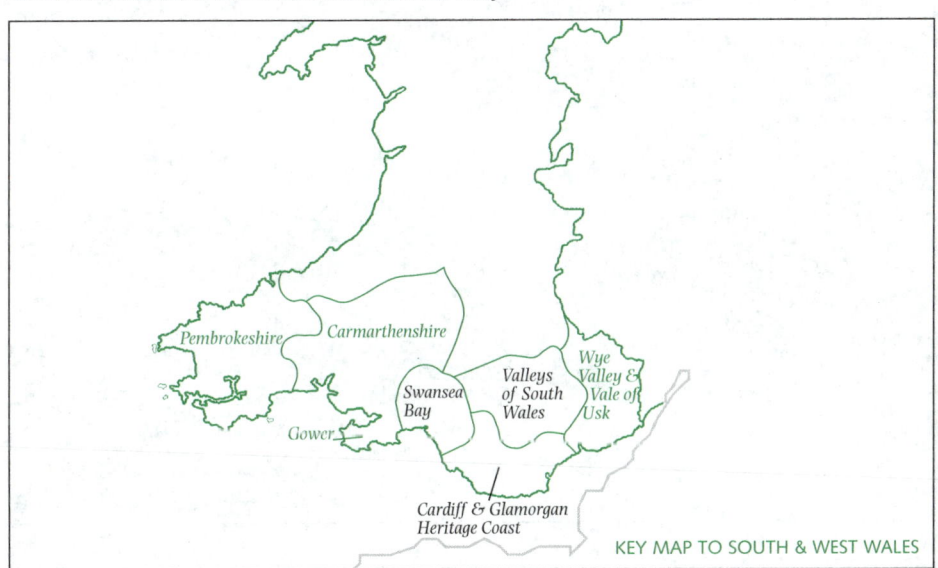

KEY MAP TO SOUTH & WEST WALES

Pembrokeshire   page 334
Pembrokeshire Coast National Park

Carmarthenshire & the Gower   page 340
West Wales, Swansea Bay & Mumbles

Wye Valley & Vale of Usk   page 342

333

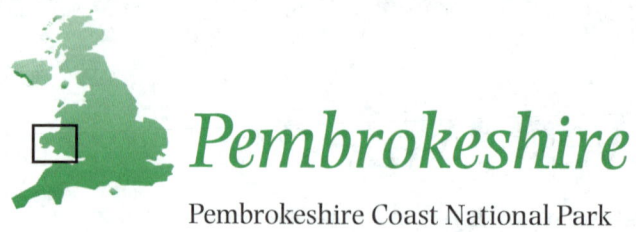

Pembrokeshire

Pembrokeshire Coast National Park

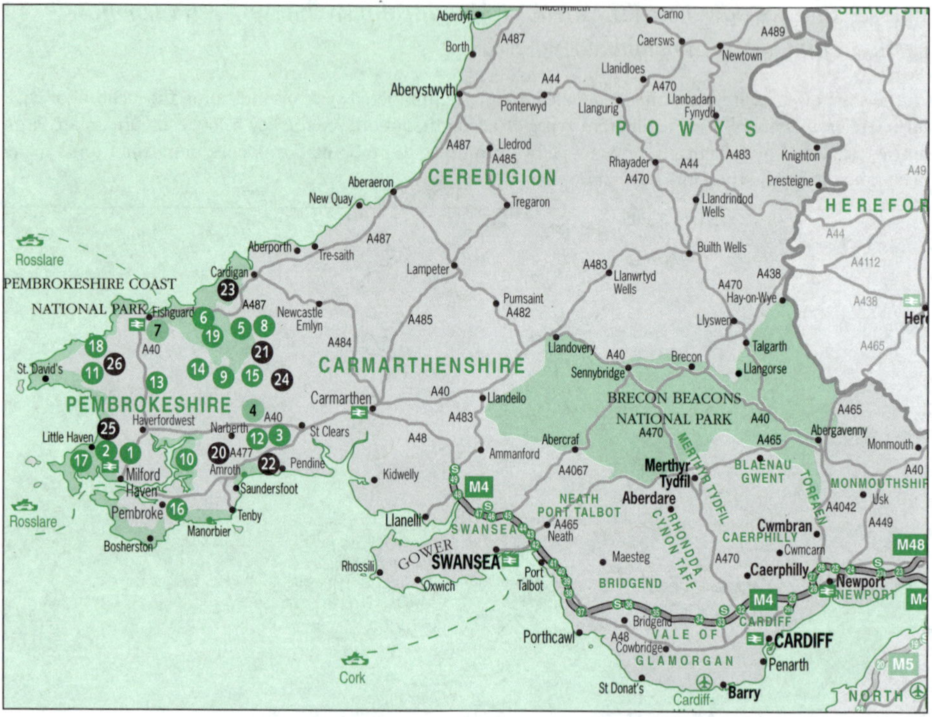

Key

 Bed & Breakfast
 Self-Catering
 B&B and SC
 Camping Barns
Camping & Caravanning

Pembrokeshire's unique standing as Britain's only coastal National Park is reflected in its spectacular coastline with its lovely sandy beaches, bird sanctuary islands and coastal path offering 200 miles of varied walking and breathtaking views across the Irish Sea. In contrast, the heart of the countryside, with the tranquil, wooded creeks of the Cleddau estuary and the peaceful, rolling uplands of the Preseli Hills, provides an idyllic rural setting for a relaxing holiday. Pembrokeshire is rich in history with dramatic castles, stone circles and the beautiful cathedral at St David's. As for activities, there's something for everyone – sailing, windsurfing, riding, fishing, walking, family attractions and theme parks.

If you would like help in finding suitable farm accommodation, turn to the full listing of farm groups on pages 360 to 363 to find appropriate contact details for this area.

Pembrokeshire South & West Wales

Bed and Breakfast
(and evening meal)

Barley Villa, Walwyns Castle, Haverfordwest, Pembrokeshire SA62 3EB ①

Sandra Davies
☎ 01437 781254
BB From £17–£19
EM From £9.50
Sleeps 4
★★★ FARM

Our spacious family homestead and smallholding overlooks a nature reserve and woodland abundant with wildlife. Ideally situated for bird islands, sandy bays, coastal path and walks. Double and twin rooms with tea-making facilities, en suite available. TV lounge, parking, packed lunches, special diets. A non-smoking establishment. Warm welcome. Open Apr–Oct.

The Bower Farm, Little Haven, Haverfordwest, Pembrokeshire SA62 3TY ②

John Birt-Llewellin
☎ 01437 781554
BB From £20–£30
EM £16
Sleeps 8
★★ provisional
FARM

An extensively modernised traditional farmhouse on working sheep farm offering peace, warmth, comfort and friendliness to the casual or longer stay visitor. Run by local historic family. Dogs, horses (livery available) and children welcome. Walking distance of Broad Haven beach and coast path. Impressive sea views over St Brides Bay and islands. All rooms en suite. Licensed. Farmhouse Dragon Award. WTB Farmhouse Award

Brunant Farm, Whitland, Carmarthenshire SA34 0LX ③

Mrs O Ebsworth
☎/Fax 01994 240421
BB From £20–£22
EM £12
Sleeps 6
★★★ FARM

'Never enough time to enjoy this to the full, never enough words to say how splendid it was': John Carter, Thames TV (Wish You Were Here). Welcome to our 200 year old farmhouse centrally situated for touring, beaches, walking, golf or just relaxing. Comfortable, spacious bedrooms, all en suite, tea/coffee, TV, hairdriers. Good home cooking. Comfortable lounge, separate tables in dining room. Open Easter–Oct.

Cilpost Farm, Whitland, Carmarthenshire SA34 0RP ④

Ann Lewis
☎ 01994 240280
BB From £12.75–£23
EM From £15
Sleeps 18
Applied

Our 300-year old farmhouse has been tastefully modernised to provide every modern amenity, including en suite facilities, central heating, colour TV in every bedroom, and is just 7 miles from the coast. The heated indoor swimming pool and snooker room are set amidst extensive lawns providing absolute safety for our younger visitors. You are warmly welcomed. Open Apr–Sept.

Dolau Isaf Farm, Mynachlog-ddu, Clunderwen, Pembrokeshire SA66 7SB ⑤

Mrs V C Lockton
☎/Fax 01994 419427
BB From £18–£20
EM From £10
Sleeps 4
★★★ FARM

Nestling in the Preseli Hills, over which we have superb views, we are centrally situated for exploring Pembrokeshire. Relax in our cosy sitting room with its log fire. See our sheep and mohair-producing goats from your bedroom window (1 en suite). Enjoy a real farmhouse breakfast with our own free-range eggs, honey and homemade marmalade. Walkers catered for. Riding and fishing nearby. WTB Farmhouse Award. Closed Christmas.

South & West Wales Pembrokeshire

6 Fron Isaf, Y Cross, Dinas Cross, Newport, Pembrokeshire SA42 0SW

Mrs Claire Urwin
☎ 01348 811339
BB From £20
EM From £14
Sleeps 5

★★
FARM

Quiet farm in the National Park enjoying panoramic views of coast and Preseli Hills. Two beaches within 1½ miles. Map ref SN 018 384. Bedrooms overlook the sea and have tea/coffee-making facilities. Friendly, relaxed atmosphere. Lounge has books, maps, TV and woodburner. Packed lunches and vegetarian meals available. Pub nearby. Open Apr–Oct.

7 Gilfach Goch Farmhouse, Fishguard, Pembrokeshire SA65 9SR

June Devonald
☎/Fax 01348 873871
BB From £23–£26
EM £13
Sleeps 12

★★★
FARM

Charming farmhouse with attractive grounds in National Park for people who want somewhere relaxing, peaceful and very comfortable. Oak beams, stone walls, ingle-nook, pretty bedrooms (en suite), magnificent views to the sea. Small holding with friendly animals and friendly Welsh people too! Superb meals – own produce giving variety, quality and quantity. Residential licence, fire certificate, pay phone. Farmhouse Award. Open Easter–Nov.
E-mail: devgg@netwales.co.uk

8 Glandy Mawr, Efailwen, Clynderwen, Pembrokeshire SA66 7RS

Annabel Sampson
☎ 01994 419422
BB From £17–£21
EM From £12.50
Sleeps 6

Applied

A grass and arable farm of 140 acres, home to the Bluestone herd of suckler cows. Centrally located for all south-west resorts. Looking towards the Preseli Hills from which the Blue Stones were taken to Stonehenge. Spacious farmhouse, centrally heated, with guests' private lounge/dining room and comfortable en suite bedrooms. Closed Christmas and New Year.

9 Golwg-y-Foel, Maenclochog, Clynderwen, Pembrokeshire SA66 7LA

Gwyneth Williams
☎ 01437 532681
BB From £16.50–£18.50
EM From £10
Sleeps 6

★★★
FARM

Welcome to our smallholding located in a peaceful village at the foot of the Preseli Hills, 2 miles from Llys-y-fran dam and central to places of interest. Comfortable bedrooms and lounge. We offer hearty breakfasts in comfortable dining rom. Ring for directions. Open Apr–Nov.

10 Knowles Farm, Lawrenny, Kilgetty, Pembrokeshire SA68 0PX

Mrs Virginia Lort-Phillips
☎ 01834 891221
Fax 01834 891344
BB From £20–£21
EM From £15
Sleeps 6

★★★
FARM

With land sloping down to the shores of the Upper Cleddau river, we provide the perfect base for boating, birdwatching, walking or fishing. Bedrooms all face south and are cosy and bright. All have tea/coffee-making facilities and are either en suite or with private bathroom. Woodland garden at its best in spring but with calming effect all year. Relax and unwind in total tranquillity. Open Easter–Oct. E-mail: owenlp@globalnet.co.uk

11 Lochmeyler Farm, Llandeloy, Pen-y-Cwm, Nr Solva, Haverfordwest, Pembrokeshire SA62 6LL

Mrs Morfydd Jones
☎ 01348 837724
Fax 01348 837622
BB From £20–£30
EM From £12.50
Sleeps 24

★★★★
FARM

Lochmeyler is a 220-acre dairy farm in the centre of St David's Peninsula, 4 miles from Solva Harbour. Twelve en suite bedrooms (no smoking in bedrooms), TV. 4-poster beds available. Two lounges, 1 non-smokers. Choice of menus, traditional and vegetarian. RAC highly acclaimed. Member of Taste of Wales, WTB Farmhouse Award. RAC Guesthouse of the Year '93. Licensed, credit cards accepted. Open all year including Christmas.

Pembrokeshire — South & West Wales

Lower End Town House, Lampeter Velfrey, Narberth, Pembrokeshire SA67 8UJ

Judy Smith
☎ 01834 831738
BB From £20
EM From £12
Sleeps 4 + cot
★★★ FARM

Beef and sheep farm owned and run by a young couple. Recent total refurbishment of the farmhouse has been aimed at recalling the peace and tranquillity of a bygone age whilst incorporating the comforts of a modern one. Easily accessible from the A40. Ideal for touring, walking or just unwinding. Evening meals by arrangement. Babies, dogs, and horses welcome. Open all year except Christmas & New Year.

Lower Haythog, Spittal, Haverfordwest, Pembrokeshire SA62 5QL

Nesta Thomas
☎/Fax 01437 731279
BB From £20–£25
EM From £15
Sleeps 12–15
★★★ FARM

For a taste of country life, join us in our charming 13th century farmhouse, oozing with character, on a working farm 5 miles north of Haverfordwest. Award winning cuisine, friendly hosts; relaxing, peaceful and entertaining. Haven for garden lovers. Come to be spoilt and enjoy the fun in an easy-going, informal atmosphere. WTB Farmhouse Award. Fire certificate. Pay Phone. Open all year except Christmas.

Penygraig Farm, Puncheston, Haverfordwest, Pembrokeshire SA62 5RJ

Betty Devonald
☎/Fax 01348 881277
BB From £17–£19
Sleeps 6
★★ FARM

A warm welcome awaits you at Penygraig, a working farm, situated near the picturesque Preseli Hills, with plenty of walks, natural trails and places of unspoilt beauty to be enjoyed. The rugged coastline of North Pembrokeshire being not far away. In the spacious dining room good wholesome cooking is served. There is 1 double room en suite, 1 family room. All rooms have tea trays, reductions for children sharing. Open Easter–Nov.
E-mail: p.devonald@compuserve.com.uk

Plas-y-Brodyr, Rhydwilym, Llandissilio, Clynderwen SA66 7QH

Mrs Janet Pogson
☎ 01437 563771
Fax 01437 563294
BB From £18
EM £15
Sleeps 6
★★★★ FARM

Our restful farmhouse will appeal to people seeking comfort and total relaxation. An ideal base for walking and only a short, quiet drive to many sandy beaches and spectacular Coastal Path. At the end of the day, after delicious home cooking, unwind in the sitting room beside log fires in the inglenook. WTB Farmhouse Award. Open all year except Christmas.

Poyerston Farm, Cosheston, Pembroke, Pembrokeshire SA72 4SJ

Mrs Sheila Lewis
☎/Fax 01646 651347
Mobile 0973 907665
BB From £20
EM From £12.50
Sleeps 10–12
★★★ FARM

Welcome to Poyerston, a 300-acre dairy farm in unspoilt countryside, 2 miles east of Pembroke on A477. Tasteful, comfortable accommodation in 5 en suite bedrooms (2 ground floor), CH. Relax in guests' lounge or Victorian conservatory and dine in our attractive dining room. Good farm-house cooking in friendly atmosphere. Spacious and attractive gardens. Ample parking. Ideal for beaches, castles, lily-ponds and inns nearby. Food hygiene certificate. AA QQQQ Selected. Brochure. Closed Christmas and New Year.

Skerryback, Sandy Haven, St. Ishmaels, Haverfordwest, Pembrokeshire SA62 3DN

Mrs Margaret Williams
☎ 01646 636598
Fax 01646 636595
BB From £18
EM From £15
Sleeps 4
★★★ FARM

Warm Pembrokeshire welcome in 18th century farmhouse set in an attractive garden surrounded by farmland and the coastal footpath on the doorstep. A haven for walkers and bird lovers. All home comforts, home cooking, en suite available, tea-making facilities and central heating backed up by log fires on chilly evenings. Farmhouse Award.

South & West Wales — Pembrokeshire

18 Torbant Farmhouse, Croesgoch, Haverfordwest, Pembrokeshire SA62 5JN

Mrs Barbara Charles
☎/Fax 01348 831276
BB From £20–£22
Sleeps 6

A warm welcome awaits you at Torbant, peacefully situated near St Davids, 1½ miles from sea. The Pembrokeshire Coast National Park is all around us. Two comfortable bedrooms, both en suite with tea/coffee tray and TV. Useful utility room and cosy lounge with log fire if needed. Open Easter–Oct.

FARM

19 Trepant Farm, Morvil, Rosebush, Nr Maenclochog, Pembrokeshire SA66 7RE

Marilyn Salmon
☎/Fax 01437 532491
BB From £16.50–£19.50
EM From £10.50
Sleeps 4

★★★ provisional
FARM

Nestling at the foot of the Preseli hills, our family farm offers a warm Welsh welcome. Ideal base for walking, cycling, pony trekking or just a leisurely drive through the quiet countryside, enjoying the unspoilt views and historical monuments. One double and one twin, both with en suite facilities. Imaginative meals, including vegetarian, using the finest local produce. Food hygiene certificate.

Self-Catering

20 Blackmoor Farm, Ludchurch, Amroth, Nr Saundersfoot, Pembrokeshire SA67 8PG

Len & Eve Cornthwaite
☎/Fax 01834 831242
SC From £156–£396
Sleeps 6

Relax in the peaceful and friendly environment of our 36-acre farm. Ideal location for Coastal National Park and beautiful beaches; walking, birdwatching, riding and fishing. Our attractively furnished holiday cottages are light and airy, south facing in a sheltered courtyard setting. Children enjoy rides on Dusty, our friendly donkey. Open Mar–Oct.

21 Castell Pigyn Cottage, Llanboidy, Whitland, Carmarthenshire SA34 0LJ

Mrs Marian Davies
☎ 01994 448391
Fax 01994 448755
SC From £150–£350
Sleeps 4

Situated 4 miles north of Whitland in a peaceful area with views of undulating farmland, semi-detached to our farmhouse, the cottage is completely self-contained with 1 double and 1 twin bedded room, each with washbasins and shaver points, bedlinen and towels. Bathroom with bath and shower. Pine kitchen units and dining room furniture. Three piece suite, colour TV, fitted carpets. Own secluded garden with furniture, ample parking. Open all year.

22 Craig-y-Dyfor Cottage, Tavernspite, Pembrokeshire SA34 0NP

Yvette Kilbey
☎ 01994 240422
Fax 01994 241069
SC From £135–£300
Sleeps 4

Craig-y-Dyfor Cottage is a cosy detached cottage tucked away on our lovely, secluded 112-acre farm. It is the only cottage on the farm, approximately 50 metres from our own farmhouse. We are well away from roads and peaceful all year round yet well placed for exploring the region. Open all year.
E-mail: yvette.kilbey@dial.pipex.com.uk

Pembrokeshire — **South & West Wales**

Croft Farm and Celtic Cottages, Croft, Nr Cardigan, Pembrokeshire SA43 3NT

Andrew & Sylvie Gow
☎/Fax 01239 615179
SC From £160–£645
Sleeps 2/7

Luxury indoor heated pool, sauna, spa pool and fitness room complement these lovingly furnished, fully equipped stone cottages. Croft Farm, situated amidst beautiful North Pembrokeshire countryside is near unspoilt, sandy beaches, stunning coastal path and National Park. Help feed Tabitha (pig), Pearl and Hazel (goats) and other friendly farm animals. Open all year.

Gilfach Goch Cottages, Gilfach Goch, Fishguard, Pembrokeshire SA65 9SR

June Devonald
☎/Fax 01348 873871
SC From £200–£482
Sleeps 5/6

Choose from the 200 year old stone walls, beamed ceiling and inglenook of Garn Madog, or Edwardian elegance, vivid colours and style of Brynawelon, two outstanding renovations in quiet, sheltered location. Panoramic landscape of sea/hills. National Park. Each house has secluded private patio, lawns, parking, woodburner, elec heating, microwave, dishwasher, washing machine. Open all year. E-mail: devgg@netwales.co.uk

Gwarmacwydd, Llanfallteg, Whitland, Carmarthenshire SA34 0XH

Mrs A Colledge
☎ 01437 563260
Fax 01437 563839
SC From £149–£410
Sleeps 22

Gwarmacwydd is a country estate of over 450 acres, set in the idyllic Taf river valley, with two miles of trout fishing, woodland and farm walks. Watch the farming and feed new born calves or lambs. Interesting and sandy local beaches at Saundersfoot and Pendine. The spacious character heated stone cottages are nicely furnished and equipped. Electricity and linen included. Open all year.
E mail: farm.holidays@btinternet.com.uk

Rogeston Cottages, Portfield Gate, Haverfordwest, Pembrokeshire SA62 3LH

John & Paula Rees
☎/Fax 01437 781373
SC From £138–£552
Sleep 2–6

Enchanting smallholding tucked away in peaceful countryside yet only 1½ miles to glorious St Brides Bay and National Park coastal footpath. Our scrupulously clean 200-year old natural stone cottages are surrounded by delightful gardens, adjoining croquet and badminton lawns, boules pitch and barbecue area. Farm trail. Pet Jersey cows, hens, ducks. Mouthwatering food available. Open all year.

The Stable & Coach House, Cilpost Farm, Whitland, Carmarthenshire SA34 0RP

Ann Lewis
☎ 01994 240280
SC From £180–£580
Sleeps 4–8

Just 7 miles from the Pembrokeshire coast, The Stable and Coach House are delightful stone-built cottages providing the most luxurious accommodation for eight and four people respectively. Guests are welcomed to use the indoor heated swimming pool and snooker room and, by arrangement, have breakfast or dinner in the main farmhouse. Early booking is recommended. Open Apr–Sept.

Ty Geifr, Pant-y-Crwyn, Letterston, Pembrokeshire SA62 5TU

Jim & Ann Sibley
☎ 01348 840897
SC From £190–£475
Sleeps 6

Cottage in peaceful valley on 80-acre farm with cattle, sheep, ponies, goats, dogs and cats. Ground floor open plan accommodation, fully equipped with kitchen/dining/lounge, bathroom, shower and bunk bedroom. First floor has twin bedded gallery bedroom and double bedroom. Also cot and high chair. Full CH, electricity and linen (excluding towels) included. Enclosed garden, barbecue. Pets welcome, kennelling available. Open Mar–Dec.

Carmarthenshire & the Gower

West Wales, Swansea Bay & Mumbles

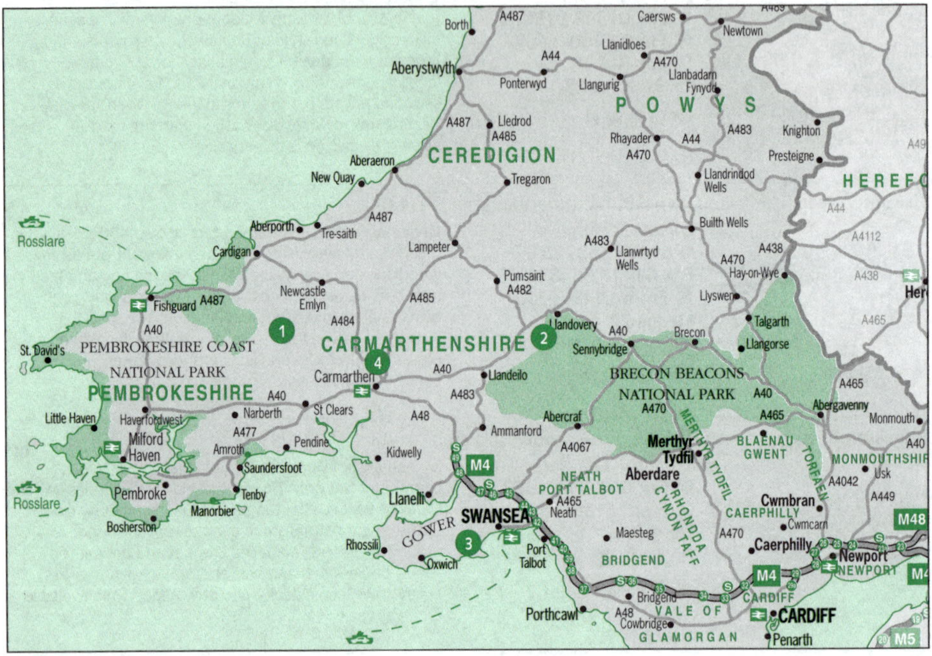

Key
- 1 Bed & Breakfast
- 1 Self-Catering
- 1 B&B and SC
- 1 Camping Barns
- 1 Camping & Caravanning

Carmarthenshire, at the heart of West Wales, is a county of contrasts from the Black Mountain through the tranquil Towy, Teifi and Taf valleys and the Brechfa Forest to the picturesque coastal villages and golden sands of Dylan Thomas's beloved Carmarthen Bay. Welsh is spoken throughout the county and all the main towns are steeped in history, many with their own castles such as Kidwelly and Llansteffan near the coast and Carreg Cennen in the hills. Further south lies the beautiful Gower Peninsula, a holiday paradise of glorious beaches, dramatic cliffs, deep valleys and wild moorland. Here you will find charming villages and the popular resort of Mumbles jutting into Swansea Bay.

If you would like help in finding suitable farm accommodation, turn to the full listing of farm groups on pages 360 to 363 to find appropriate contact details for this area.

Carmarthenshire & the Gower   South & West Wales

Bed and Breakfast
(and evening meal)

Castell Pigyn Farm, Llanboidy, Whitland, Carmarthenshire SA34 0LJ

Marian Davies
☎ 01994 448391
Fax 01994 448755
BB From £19–£21
EM From £12
Sleeps 6
★★★ FARM

Castell Pigyn is situated 4 miles north of Whitland in a peaceful area with fabulous views of undulating farmland. Accommodation with en suite bedrooms. Lounge with TV, dining room with family tables, good home cooking. CH throughout, ample parking. WTB Farmhouse Award, food hygiene certificate, residential licence. (Also self-catering cottage sleeping 4.) Brochure available. Closed Christmas and New Year.

Cwmgwyn Farm, Llangadog Road, Llandovery, Carmarthenshire SA20 0EQ

Marian Lewis
☎ 01550 720410
Fax 01550 720262
BB £20
Sleeps 6
★★★★ FARM

Welcome to the country on our livestock farm with superb views overlooking the River Towy, 2 miles from Llandovery on A4069. The 17th century farmhouse is full of charm and character with inglenook fireplace, exposed stonework and beams. 3 spacious luxury en suite bedrooms with bath/shower, hairdryer, TV, tea/coffee. Enjoy tranquil riverside setting from garden or picnic area. Ideal for touring mid/South Wales. Open Easter–Oct.

Parc Le Breos House, Parkmill, Gower, Swansea SA3 2HA

Olive Edwards
☎/Fax 01792 371636
BB From £18–£19.50
Sleeps 30
★★ FARM

Spacious 19th century farmhouse, formally a shooting lodge in the heart of the beautiful Gower Peninsula. A quiet, scenic sitting within easy reach of magnificent cliffs and beaches. Ideal base for walking and holiday activities. Riding holidays and day rides available, paddock rides for children. TV lounge, games room. We offer homegrown food and warm welcome. Open all year.

Trebersed Farm, St Peters, Travellers Rest, Carmarthen, Carmarthenshire SA31 3RR

Mrs Rosemary Jones
☎ 01267 238182
Fax 01267 223633
BB From £19–£23.50
Sleeps 6
★★★ FARM

A warm welcome awaits you at our working dairy farm. Wellingtons available! Excellent touring base overlooking thriving market town of Carmarthen, just off main A40. Three comfortable rooms, one family, all en suite, with tea/coffee tray, central heating, radio alarm and colour TV. WTB Farmhouse Award. Open all year except Christmas.

Please mention **Stay on a Farm** when booking

# Wye Valley & Vale of Usk

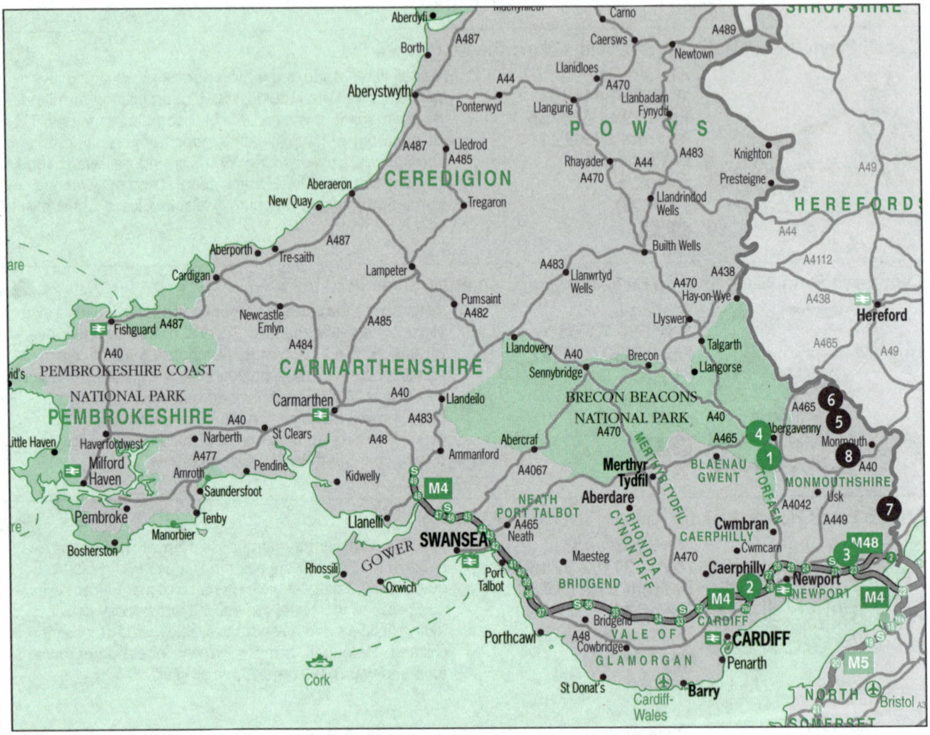

Key

- 1 Bed & Breakfast
- 1 Self-Catering
- 1 B&B and SC
- 1 Camping Barns
- ▲ Camping & Caravanning

This is a pastoral landscape of undulating, wooded hills and tranquil river valleys dotted with ancient market towns and picturesque villages. Part of the Welsh Marches falls within this region and there are a number of strategically-placed castles, including Raglan and Chepstow, serving as reminders of less peaceful times, while Tintern Abbey, immortalised by Wordsworth, shows a gentler aspect. This is excellent walking and fishing country or you can take a trip on the Monmouthshire and Brecon Canal or Brecon Mountain Railway. There are craft centres to visit and museums and secondhand bookshops to browse. To the west is an area of rich industrial heritage for those fascinated by the way we used to live.

If you would like help in finding suitable farm accommodation, turn to the full listing of farm groups on pages 360 to 363 to find appropriate contact details for this area.

Wye Valley & Vale of Usk — South & West Wales

Bed and Breakfast
(and evening meal)

Hardwick Farm, Hardwick, Abergavenny, Monmouthshire NP7 9BT

Mrs Carol Jones
☎ 01837 853513
BB From £18–£20
Sleeps 7

★★ FARM

Situated on the outskirts of Abergavenny (A4042) in peaceful surroundings with scenic views of Holy Mountain, Sugar Loaf and Blorenge. Family run farm with riverside walks. Close to Brecon and Monmouthshire Canal and easy access to golf courses. Open all year.

Pentre-Tai Farm, Rhiwderin, Newport, Monmouthshire NP1 9RQ

Susan Proctor
☎/Fax 01633 893284
BB From £19–£25
Sleeps 6

★★ FARM

Gateway to Wales. A warm welcome awaits you at our peaceful sheep farm located in the countryside yet only 3 miles from M4. Most rooms en suite, all with TV and beverage facilities. Children welcome at reduced rates. Ideal base for Cardiff and Wye Valley. Perfect stopover en route for Irish ferries. Approved camping and caravan site. Open Feb–Nov.

Penylan Farm, St Brides, nr Magor, Newport, Monmouthshire NP6 3AS

Anne Arthur
☎ 01633 400267
Fax 01633 400997
BB £20
Sleeps 4

★★★ FARM

Splendid Elizabethan farmhouse with oak beams and inglenook fireplaces. Set on hilltop overlooking beautiful St Brides Valley in rural setting, 2 miles from M4 and Wentwood Forest. Heated indoor swimming pool. Many golf courses (St Pierre, Celtic Manor), castles, excellent eating places. Good overnight stop for Irish ferries. Welsh hospitality assured. Open Mar–Nov.

The Wenallt Farm, Gilwern, near Abergavenny, Monmouthshire NP7 0HP

The Harris Family
☎ 01873 830694
BB From £18.50–£22
EM From £12
Sleeps 10

★ FARM

A 16th century Welsh longhouse set in 50 acres of farmland in the Brecon Beacons National Park commanding magnificent views over the Usk Valley. Retaining all its old charm with oak beams, inglenook fireplace, yet offering a high standard with en suite bedrooms, good food and a warm welcome. An ideal base from which to see Wales and the surrounding areas. Licensed. AA listed. Brochure available. Open all year.

Our farms offer a range of facilities that are illustrated by symbols in each entry. Turn to page 16 for an explanation of the symbols.

South & West Wales *Wye Valley & Vale of Usk*

Self-Catering

5 **Granary & Coach House,** Upper Cwm Farm, Brynderi, Llantilio Crossenny, Abergavenny, Mon. NP7 8TG

Ann Ball
☎ 01873 821236
SC From £195–£360
Sleeps 6

Holidays and short breaks in beautifully converted old barn on working sheep farm. Family accommodation with CH, TV, electricity, bed linen, towels included. Peaceful superb views, ideal for walking, birdwatching, exploring Welsh castles, Brecon Beacons, Wye and Usk Valleys. The Granary (upper) and Coach House (ground) each have 1 double and 2 twin bedrooms, lounge/dining/kitchen, bathroom with shower. Brochure. Open all year.

6 **Lower Green Farm,** Llanfair Green, Cross Ash, Abergavenny, Monmouthshire NP7 8PA

Mrs Sheila Pritchard
☎ 01873 821219
SC From £100–£260
Sleeps 4/6

High-quality, comfortable, well-equipped barn conversions near farmhouse on 170-acre farm situated between Brecon Beacons and Wye Valley. Peaceful, friendly atmosphere, beautiful scenery and abundant wildlife. Ideal for walking, cycling, visiting the many local attractions or just relaxing. Near to Offa's Dyke, Three Castles walk and cycle route. Brochure available. Open all year.

7 **Parsons Grove,** Earlswood, nr Shirenewton, Chepstow, Monmouthshire NP6 6RD

Frances Marchant
☎/Fax 01291 641382
SC From £135–£360
Sleeps 4/6

On the edge of beautiful Wye Valley, set in 15 acres of peaceful countryside, with heated swimming pool. Three cottages, furnished to very high standard. Fully carpeted with colour TV, fitted kitchen, refrigerator, cooker, microwave, CH. All linen (duvets) and towels included. Panoramic views of beautiful valley and Wentwood Forest. Riding, golf and fishing nearby. Free use of barbecue, boules, croquet. Brochure. Open Mar–Nov.

8 **Worcester House,** Castle Farm, Raglan, Monmouthshire NP5 2BT

Mrs Vivien Jones
☎ 01291 690492
SC From £150–£250
Sleeps 6/7

Part of a 17th century manor house. The oldest brick building in Monmouthshire. Easy access to Wye Valley, Brecon Beacons and Forest of Dean. Many castles and golf courses nearby. Raglan Castle 20 yards, overlooking picturesque village of Raglan. A 200-acre working dairy/arable farm with 3 bedrooms bathroom and separate shower room with WC. Living/dining room with french windows leading to large lawn, separate kitchen. Open Easter–Nov.

NO ANSWER?
Farmers are mostly out and about during the day.
Try to telephone before 9.30am or after 4pm.

Northern Ireland

Farm entries in this regional section are listed under those counties shown in green on the key map. Look at the index below to find on which page the entries start. You will see that we have listed the counties geographically so that you can turn more easily to find farms in neighbouring areas.

At the start of each county section is a detailed map with numbered symbols indicating the location of each farm. Different symbols denote different types of accommodation; see the key below each county map. Farm entries are listed alphabetically under type of accommodation. Some farms offer more than one type of accommodation and therefore have more than one entry.

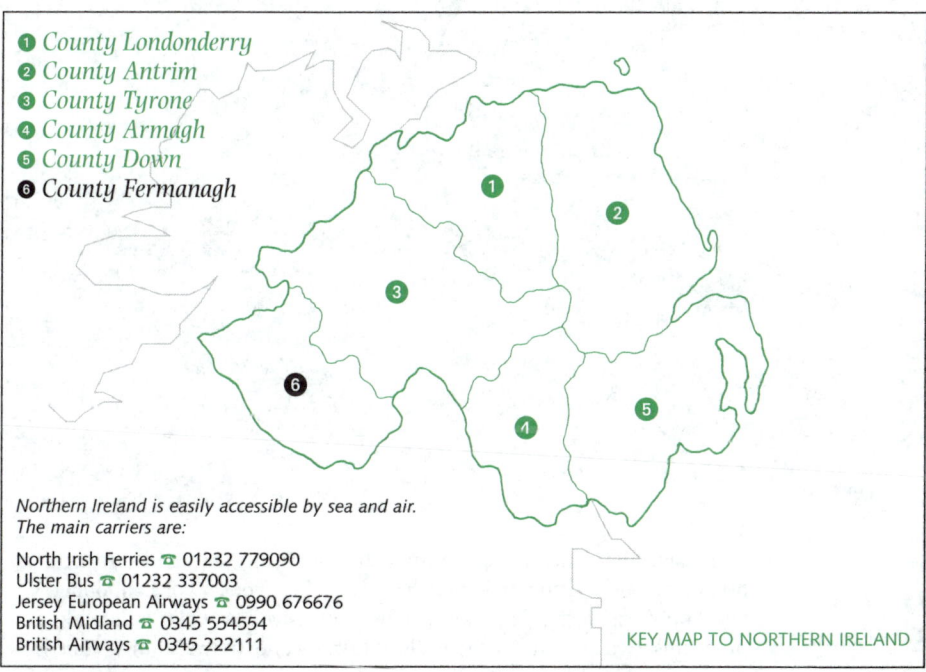

❶ *County Londonderry*
❷ *County Antrim*
❸ *County Tyrone*
❹ *County Armagh*
❺ *County Down*
❻ *County Fermanagh*

Northern Ireland is easily accessible by sea and air. The main carriers are:

North Irish Ferries ☎ 01232 779090
Ulster Bus ☎ 01232 337003
Jersey European Airways ☎ 0990 676676
British Midland ☎ 0345 554554
British Airways ☎ 0345 222111

KEY MAP TO NORTHERN IRELAND

County Londonderry	page 346	*County Armagh*	page 354
Sperrin Mountains		The Orchard County	
County Antrim	page 349	*County Down*	page 356
Causeway Coast & Glens of Antrim		Ards Peninsula & Mourne Mountains	
County Tyrone	page 352		
Sperrin Mountains			

County Londonderry

Sperrin Mountains

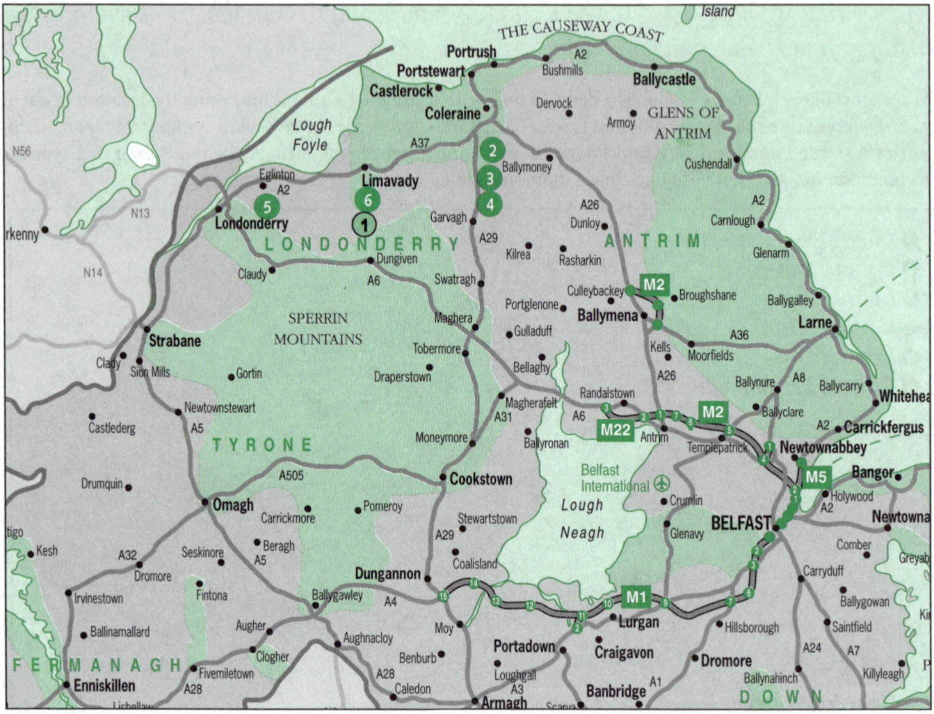

Key
- 1 Bed & Breakfast
- 1 Self-Catering
- 1 B&B and SC
- 1 Camping Barns
- Camping & Caravanning

This is a fertile agricultural county with small farms scattered across the broad, sweeping land and long Atlantic beaches. The city of Londonderry, also known as Derry, is best known for its massive city walls, outstanding museums, two cathedrals and lively cultural scene. In the county's north-east corner is Coleraine which is conveniently close to the seaside resorts of Portstewart and Castlerock for sea angling, golf and children's amusements. For rewarding scenic drives, the Sperrin Mountains are best approached from Limavady and the beautiful Roe Valley Country Park. The Bann river is noted for trout and salmon.

If you would like help in finding suitable farm accommodation, turn to the full listing of farm groups on pages 360 to 363 to find appropriate contact details for this area.

County Londonderry   Northern Ireland

Bed and Breakfast
(and evening meal)

Drumcovitt House, 704 Feeny Road, Feeny, Co Londonderry BT47 4SU ①

Florence Sloan
☎/Fax 01504 781224
[BB] From £16–£22
EM From £5–£20
Sleeps 6
Grade A

Listed Georgian farmhouse with established gardens, 2 miles from Banagher Glen. Ideal centre for exploring Sperrins, Derry City, Donegal and the Causeway Coast. Fishing Roe, Faughan. Golf at Derry, Limavady. Archaelogical sites from pre-history onwards. Half mile east of Feeny on B74 off A6 Derry to Belfast. 1 family room, 1 twin, 1 single. Visa/Mastercard/Eurocard/Delta cards accepted. Open all year.
E mail: drumcovitt.feeny@btinternet.com

Greenhill House, 24 Greenhill Road, Aghadowey, Coleraine, Co Londonderry BT51 4EU ②

Mrs Elizabeth Hegarty
☎ 01265 868241
Fax 01265 868365
[BB] From £24.50
EM From £16 (booked in advance) Sleeps 14
Grade A

Georgian country guest house (with central heating). Good views across wooded countryside in the Bann Valley and the Antrim hills. Convenient to Giant's Causeway and north coast for golf, touring, fishing. Six rooms are en suite with direct-dialling telephones, colour TV, tea/coffee. From Coleraine take A29 south for 7 miles, then turn left on Greenhill Road – B66 and Greenhill House is on right. Recommended in international guides. Egon Ronay, Taste of Ulster, AA Premier Selected QQQQQ. Open Mar–Oct.

Heathfield Farm, 31 Drumcroone Road, Killykergan, Coleraine, Co Londonderry BT51 4EB ③

Mrs Heather Torrens
☎ 012665 58245
[BB] From £20
EM From £12
Sleeps 6
Certified

Winner of AIB Agr-Tourism Farm Guest House. Comfortable, spacious 17th century farmhouse on working beef and sheep farm, set in large garden in lovely countryside. Ideal base for touring Causeway coast. Golf, fishing and horse riding nearby. Walk country lanes. Central heating, guests' lounge with piano, log fire. En suite rooms, colour TV, tea/coffee facilities, hairdrier, etc. On A29 Garvagh-Coleraine road. Open all year.

Killeague Farm, 157 Drumcroone Road, Blackhill, Coleraine, Co Londonderry BT51 3SG ④

Margaret Moore
☎ 01265 868229
[BB] From £20
EM From £12
Sleeps 6
Certified

Relax and enjoy the comfort and warm welcome at our 130-acre dairy farm which is on A29, convenient to North Antrim coast, sandy beaches and Giant's Causeway. Stabling on the farm and horse riding can be arranged. Air and sea ports 1 hour's drive. Three en suite luxury bedrooms with tea/coffee. Open fires. TV lounge. Special off-season terms. Open all year.

Killenan House, 40 Killenan Road, Drumahoe, Co Londonderry BT47 3NG ⑤

Mrs Averil Campbell
☎ 01504 301710
[BB] From £17
Sleeps 6
(5)
Certified

A 19th century farmhouse on working farm with spacious gardens close to historic city. Ideal base for touring to Giant's Causeway and Donegal. Airport, fishing, golf, flying and riding nearby. 1 twin, 1 double, 1 family room, all en suite, with CH, colour TV, tea/coffee facilities. A6 Claudy direction from Londonderry, 5m B118 (Eglinton) 1½m left Killenan Road, first right. Open all year.

Northern Ireland   *County Londonderry*

6 Whitehill Farm, 70 Ballyquin Road, Limavady, Co Londonderry BT49 9EY

Mrs Maud McCormick
☎ 01504 722306
BB From £16–£18
Sleeps 6
Certified

Centrally heated farmhouse, situated on B68, one mile from town centre. Convenient to Roe Valley Country Park, sandy beaches and golf courses. An ideal base for touring Giant's Causeway and Donegal. Open all year.

Self-Catering

1 Drumcovitt Cottages, 704 Feeny Road, Feeny, Co Londonderry BT47 4SU

Florence Sloan
☎/Fax 01504 781224
SC From £240–£350
Sleeps 4/5
4 star

Three 4-star cottages, each fully equipped (dishwasher, washer/dryer, microwave, telephone, etc). One wheelchair accessible, all oil centrally heated, two with log fires. Experience Sperrins, Donegal, Giant's Causeway, Derry and much more within an hour's drive from Drumcovitt. Return to quiet 240-acre farm in beautiful Sperrin foothills. Open all year. E-mail: drumcovitt.feeny@btinternet.com.

FINDING YOUR ACCOMMODATION

The local FHB Group contacts listed on page 360 can always help you find a vacancy in your chosen area.

Our Internet address is
http://www.webscape.co.uk/farmaccom/

County Antrim

Causeway Coast & Glens of Antrim

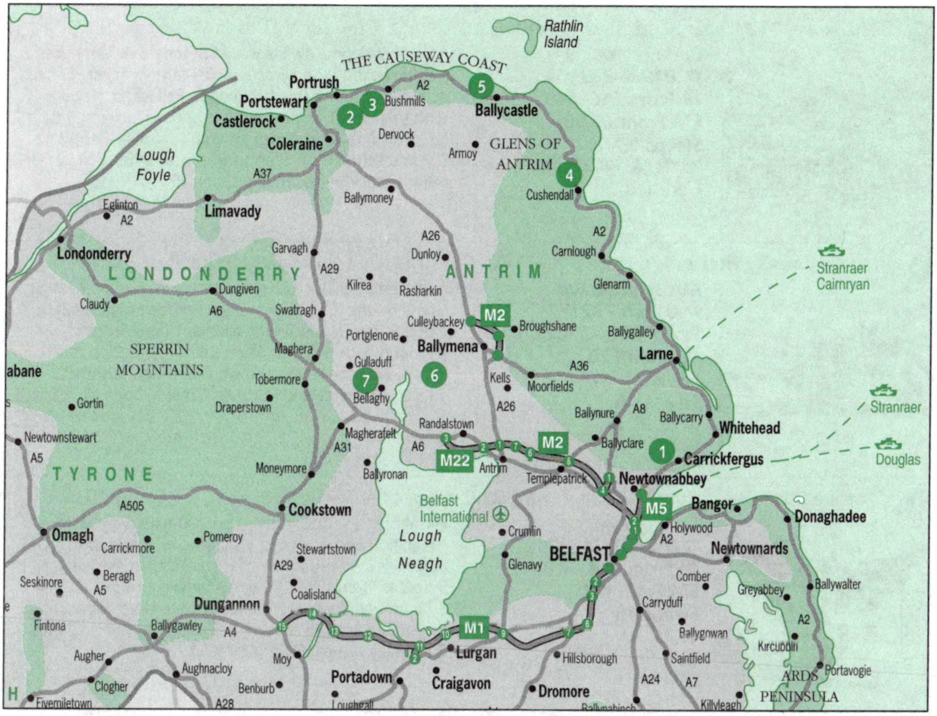

To the south east of the county Belfast provides excellent shopping and city entertainment, while in the north west lies the Causeway Coast and famous Giant's Causeway. Between lie the nine Glens of Antrim and their quaint waterfoot villages, the spectacular coast road, Carrickfergus Castle and Antrim with its ancient round tower and splendid park. There's pony trekking near Ballycastle, a spectacular swinging rope bridge at Carrick-a-rede, golf at Royal Portrush, and bathing, boating and fishing along the hundred miles of shore. The Irish Linen Centre at Lisburn recreates Ulster's greatest industry and is a great place for souvenir shopping.

Key
- 1 Bed & Breakfast
- 1 Self-Catering
- 1 B&B and SC
- 1 Camping Barns
- 1 Camping & Caravanning

If you would like help in finding suitable farm accommodation, turn to the full listing of farm groups on pages 360 to 363 to find appropriate contact details for this area.

Northern Ireland   County Antrim

Bed and Breakfast
(and evening meal)

① **Beechgrove,** 412 Upper Road, Trooperslane, Carrickfergus, Co Antrim BT38 8PW

Betta Barron
☎ 01960 363304
BB From £16–£18
EM From £9.50
Sleeps 13
Certified

A warm welcome awaits you at Beechgrove farmhouse (central heating) on 16 acre mixed farm near sea. Fishing, golf, riding. Knochagh monument, Belfast zoo, leisure centre nearby. 3 single, 1 double, 2 family rooms, 1 twin (all H/C). Babysitter. Dogs allowed (outside). Off A2, 1 mile south of Carrickfergus. Larne 10 miles. Belfast 10 miles. Carrickfergus 3 miles. Open all year.

② **Brown's Country House,** 174 Ballybogey Road, Coleraine, Co Londonderry BT52 2LP

Mrs Jean Brown
☎ 01265 732777
Fax 01265 731627
BB From £20
EM From £11
Sleeps 16
Grade A

A chalet bungalow with spacious lawns. Central heating. Home baking. On Ballymoney – Portrush road (B62). 2 double bedrooms, 4 twin rooms, 1 family room, 3 ground floor, 1 single, all en suite. Tea/ coffee in all rooms. Babysitter. Dogs allowed (outside). Bushmills 4 miles, Coleraine and Portrush 5 miles. Open all year.

③ **Carnside Farm Guest House,** 23 Causeway Road, Giant's Causeway, Bushmills, Co Antrim BT57 8SU

Frances Lynch
☎ 012657 31337
BB From £14–£18
EM From £10
Sleeps 15
Certified

Farmhouse (central heating) on 200-acre dairy farm. Magnificent coastal view. Fishing, golf, water sports. Old Bushmills Distillery 2 miles has weekday tours. 1 single, 3 double (1 en suite), 1 twin, 3 family rooms (1 en suite), 2 on ground floor, all H&C. Babysitter. Dogs allowed (outside). Bushmills 2 miles, Ballycastle 12 miles, Giant's Causeway ¼ mile. Open Mar–Oct.

④ **Cullentra House,** 16 Cloghs Road (off Gaults Road), Cushendall, Co Antrim BT44 0SP

Olive McAuley
☎/Fax 012667 71762
BB From £14–£16
Sleeps 6/8
Certified

Award-winning country house nestling amid breathtaking scenery of Glenballyeamon and Glenaan, overlooking Sea of Moyle. Golf course, Ballycastle and Giant's Causeway nearby. 1 family room, 1 double and 1 twin, all en suite. TV, tea/coffee-making facilities. Homely atmosphere and warm welcome extended to all guests. Last B&B on Cloghs Road. Open all year except Christmas.

⑤ **Glenmore House,** Whitepark Road, Ballycastle, Co Antrim BT54 6LR

Valerie Brown
☎/Fax 01265 763584
BB From £14–£19.50
EM From £9.50
Sleeps 25
Applied

New building, set in 20 acres, with panoramic sea view and restaurant. Central for visiting Giant's Causeway and Glens, 2 miles from Ballycastle. Walks and 2-acre fishing lake. TV and coffee-making facilities in rooms. Choice of appetising breakfasts. Open all year.

County Antrim *Northern Ireland*

Neelsgrove Farm, 51 Carnearney Road, Ahoghill, Ballymena, Co Antrim BT42 2PL

Mrs Margaret Neely
☎ 01266 871225
BB From £16–£18.50
EM From £10
Sleeps 6
☼(3) ⚭ 🐕 🧳
Certified

Country house (central heating) in 1 acre of grounds on mixed farm. Home baking. Water skiing 2 miles, golf nearby. 6 miles from Ballymena, 15 miles from International Airport. Convenient to Glens of Antrim and River Bann. Fishermen welcome, tackle space available. 1 double en suite, 1 double, 1 twin room with H/C. Dogs allowed outside. Car parking. Food hygiene certificate. Open Jan–Nov. E-mail: msneely@btinternet.com

Sprucebank, 41 Ballymacombs Road, Portglenone, Co Antrim BT44 8NR

Mrs Thomasena Sibbett
☎ 01266 822150
Fax 01266 821422
BB From £16–£18
Sleeps 8
☼ 🐕 🧳 ⚭ 🏛
Certified

Relax in the tranquil surroundings of our 18th century farmhouse conveniently situated for touring the province and on route to Ireland's north and west coast. Golf, fishing, forest and river walks nearby. One hour from ports of entry on A54, 1½ miles from Portglenone. Open Mar–Oct or by arrangement.

LET THE TELEPHONE RING!
Some farmhouses are big places. Let the telephone ring long enough to give the owner time to answer it.

USE THE INDEX

The comprehensive Index shows which farms offer access to disabled visitors; caravanning/camping facilities; the chance to participate on a working farm; stabling/grazing for visiting horses; en suite rooms; a welcome to business people; acceptance of *Stay on a Farm* gift tokens.

FOLLOW THE COUNTRY CODE

Leave nothing but footprints,
Take nothing but photographs,
Kill nothing but time!

County Tyrone

Sperrin Mountains

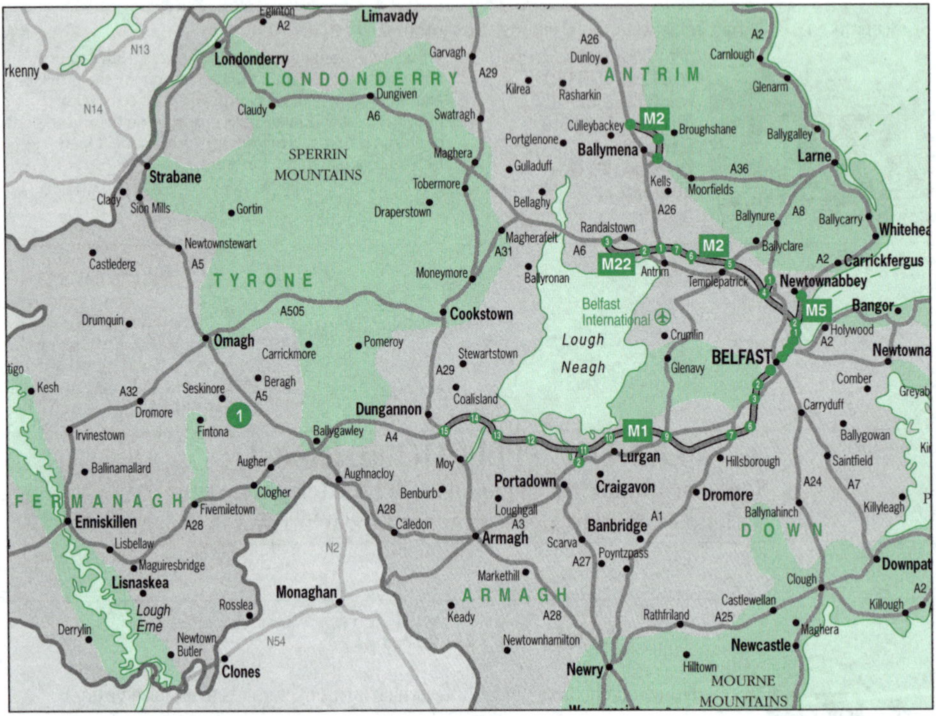

Key

- **1** Bed & Breakfast
- **1** Self-Catering
- **1** B&B and SC
- **1** Camping Barns
- **▲** Camping & Caravanning

Between the Sperrins in the north and the green Clogher Valley with its village cathedral in the south lies this county of great historic interest. You can discover its past at the Ulster-American Folk Park and Ulster History Park, both near Omagh, while the story of the Lough Neagh fishing and eel industry is told at Kinturk Cultural Centre, east of Cookstown. A mysterious ceremonial site of stone circles and cairns has recently been discovered at Beaghmore and there are numerous Stone Age and Bronze Age remains in the area. There are forest parks, Gortin Glen and Drum Manor for rambling, excellent fishing near Newtownstewart and market towns such as Dungannon for souvenir Tyrone Crystal.

If you would like help in finding suitable farm accommodation, turn to the full listing of farm groups on pages 360 to 363 to find appropriate contact details for this area.

County Tyrone   Northern Ireland

Bed and Breakfast
(and evening meal)

Greenmount Lodge, 58 Greenmount Road, Gortaclare, Omagh, Co Tyrone BT79 0YE

Mrs F Louie Reid
☎ 01662 841325
Fax 01662 840019
[BB] From £18–£21
EM From £12
Sleeps 20
♿ 🐎 🐴 ✄ 🏕 🧳
Grade A

Farm guest house on 150-acre farm. Superb accommodation, excellent cuisine. Central for sightseeing Fermanagh, Lakeland, the Sperrin Mountains. A5 from Ballygawley to Omagh, left before Carrick Keel pub at Fintona sign 1 mile. Open all year.

 Please mention *Stay on a Farm* when booking

---

USE THE INDEX

The comprehensive Index shows which farms offer access to disabled visitors; caravanning/camping facilities; the chance to participate on a working farm; stabling/grazing for visiting horses; en suite rooms; a welcome to business people; acceptance of *Stay on a Farm* gift tokens.

THE 1000+ BUREAU MEMBERS OFFER A UNIQUE LINK TO CUSTOMERS ACROSS THE UK

All Bureau members belong to a local Group. Each member can refer you to an equally high quality member within the Group... or across the UK: England, Northern Ireland, Scotland, Wales.

County Armagh
The Orchard County

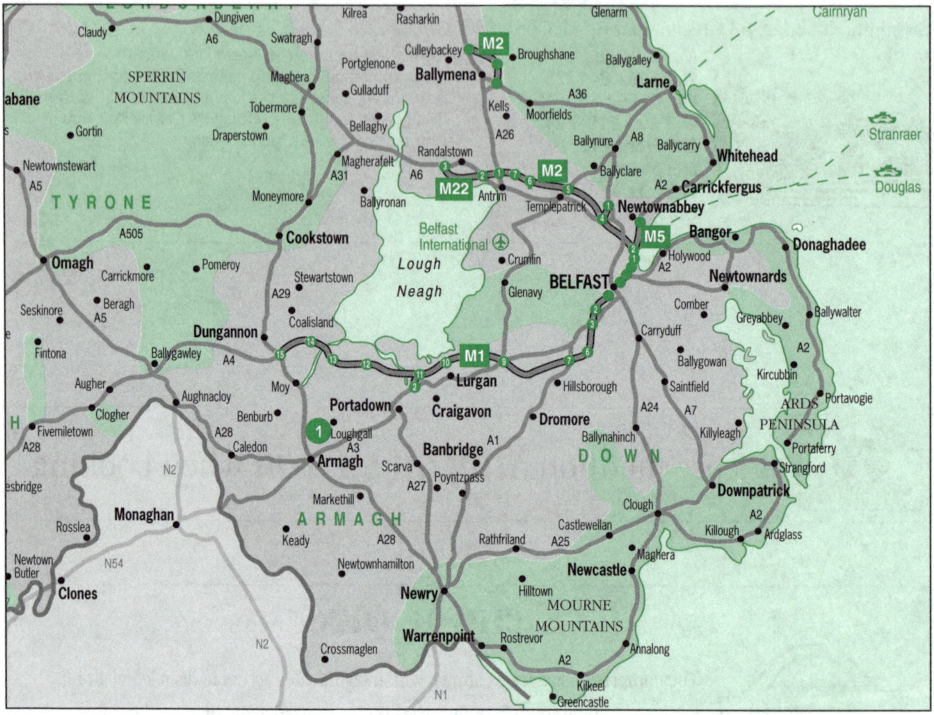

Key

- 🟢 Bed & Breakfast
- 🟢 Self-Catering
- 🟢 B&B and SC
- 🟢 Camping Barns
- 🔺 Camping & Caravanning

Northern Ireland's smallest county rises gently from Lough Neagh's banks, southward through apple orchards, farmland and hill forest to the rocky summit of Slieve Gullion, mountain of Cuchulain. The city of Armagh is a religious capital older than Canterbury, with two cathedrals, the Georgian Mall and a Planetarium and Observatory. Visit the famous hill fort, 'Emain Macha', capital of the kings of Ulster from 600BC and interpreted at the Navan Centre just outside the city. Craigavon has a leisure centre, ski slope and lakes for water sports, and there is sailing on Lough Neagh and angling and canoeing on the Blackwater river.

If you would like help in finding suitable farm accommodation, turn to the full listing of farm groups on pages 360 to 363 to find appropriate contact details for this area.

County Armagh   Northern Ireland

Bed and Breakfast
(and evening meal)

Ballinahinch House, 47 Ballygroobany Road, Richhill, Co Armagh BT61 9NA

Elizabeth Kee
☎/Fax 01762 870081
BB **From £15**
Sleeps 6

Grade B

Early Victorian farmhouse with traditional furnishings, landscaped lawns and rose garden. Tea/coffee-making facilities, home cooking. Shooting over farm. Pony riding, golf, fishing and NT properties nearby. From A3 turn off at junction B131 to Richhill. 2nd road left – Ballyleny Road – go to end, cross roads, straight across – Ballygroobany Road. House 1 mile on left. 1 single, 1 twin, 1 double, 1 family, 1 en suite.

Our farms offer a range of facilities that are illustrated by symbols in each entry. Turn to page 16 for an explanation of the symbols.

USE THE INDEX

The comprehensive Index shows which farms offer access to disabled visitors; caravanning/camping facilities; the chance to participate on a working farm; stabling/grazing for visiting horses; en suite rooms; a welcome to business people; acceptance of *Stay on a Farm* gift tokens.

Our Internet address is
http://www.webscape.co.uk/farmaccom/

County Down

Ards Peninsula & Mourne Mountains

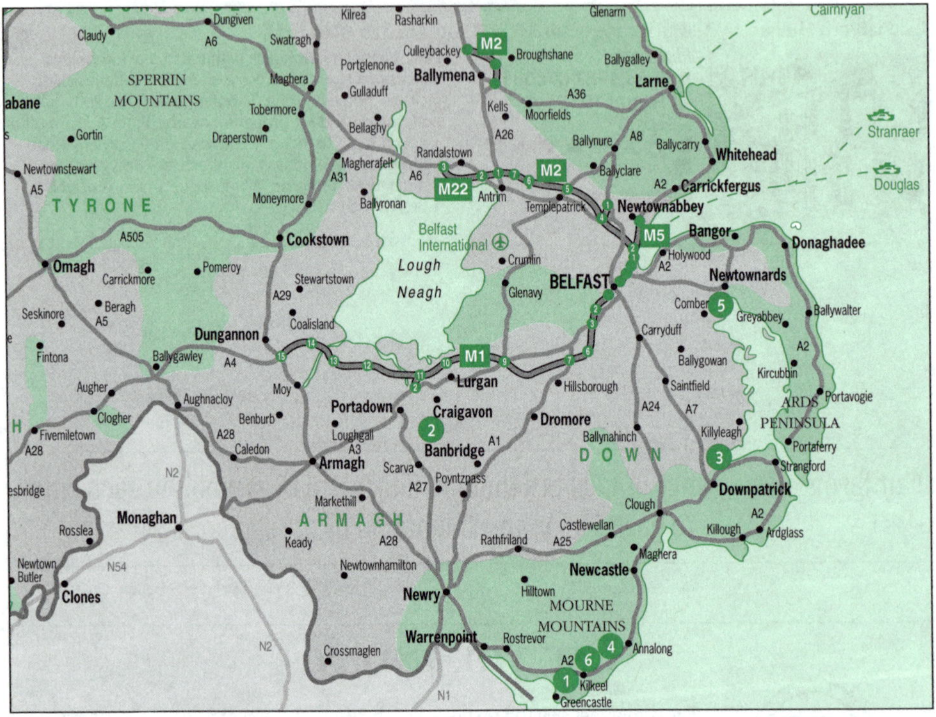

This area includes the Ulster Folk and Transport Museum at Cultra by Belfast Lough, the ancient shrines of St Patrick's Country round the cathedral hill at Downpatrick, the golden beaches of the Ards Peninsula and the mountainous kingdom of Mourne, an ancient town with some of the richest heritage in Ireland including St Patrick's grave. Lively Newcastle is famous for its seaside festival and there are beautiful historic houses to visit such as Mount Stewart and Castle Ward. Horseriding, sailing, angling and golf are everywhere within reach, there is motor racing at Kirkistown, sea angling in Strangford Lough and an intriguing aquarium at Portaferry.

Key
- 1 Bed & Breakfast
- 1 Self-Catering
- 1 B&B and SC
- 1 Camping Barns
- 1 Camping & Caravanning

If you would like help in finding suitable farm accommodation, turn to the full listing of farm groups on pages 360 to 363 to find appropriate contact details for this area.

County Down   Northern Ireland

Bed and Breakfast
(and evening meal)

Morne Abbey Guest House, 16 Greencastle Road, Kilkeel, Co Down BT34 4DE

Mrs Annabel Shannon
☎ 016937 62426
BB From £16–£17.50
EM From £10.40
Sleeps 11
Grade B

Country house on mixed farm in magnificent setting. A warm welcome assured, home cooking a speciality. Fishing, riding, tennis, bowls, golf nearby. 1 single, 2 twin, 1 double, 1 family room. All with H&C, 3 en suite. Sea 1 mile, Silent Valley 4 miles. Kilkeel ½ mile. Open Apr–Sept.

Mourneview, 32 Drumnascamph Road, Laurencetown, Gilford, Co Down BT63 6DU

Esther & Nettie Kerr
☎ 01820 626270/624251
Fax 01820 624251
BB From £17–£20
Sleeps 8
Certified

Superbly appointed bungalow beautifully designed on 200 acre farm providing a welcoming homely atmosphere. Guests TV lounge, dining room, tea/coffee-making facilities, payphone. Health/hygiene and fire certificates. Good base for touring. Linen. Homelands and participating in the full range of leisure activities nearby. 4 en suite rooms which are also suitable for disabled guests. Open all year except Christmas.

Pheasants' Hill Country House, 37 Killyleagh Road, Downpatrick, Co Down BT30 9BL

Janis Bailey
☎/Fax 01396 617246
BB From £20–£24.50
EM From £17.50
Sleeps 4
Certified

Luxury Irish country house accommodation in St Patrick's Country, beside National Nature Reserve and Strangford Lough (AONB/ASSI). Turf fire, pretty en suite bedrooms, fresh flowers, comfy beds. Delicious Irish cooking, vegetarian available. Market garden, orchard, cottage garden, wildflowers, herbs, rare breeds, pond, stream, woodland. On Ulster Way. Airport 30 minutes. Open all year. E-mail: pheasants.hill@dnet.co.uk

---

Sharon Farmhouse, 6 Ballykeel Road, Ballymartin, Kilkeel, Co Down BT34 4PL

M. Bingham
☎ 016937 62521
BB From £15–£17
Sleeps 6
Certified

Farm bungalow – 1 family, 1 twin, 1 single, all with H/C and central heating. Guest bathroom/shower. With excellent sea and mountain views. Situated ideally for mountaineering and 10 minutes from beach. 2 miles from Kilkeel town and fishing port. The area is rich in varied birdlife. Good wholesome home cooked food served in abundance. A warm and welcoming atmosphere. Your comfort is our pleasure. Open all year.

Trench Farm, 35 Ringcreevy Road, Comber, Newtownards, Co Down BT23 5JR

Maureen Hamilton
☎/Fax 01247 872558
BB From £17.50
Sleeps 6
Certified

Farmhouse on working horticultural farm overlooking Strangford Lough excellent for birdlife. H&C and tea/coffee facilities in all bedrooms. Close to Scrabo Tower and golf course. Public health and hygiene certificate. Take A 21 Newtownards Road from Comber, first road on right. Vouchers accepted. Open all year.

Northern Ireland   *County Down*

6 **Wyncrest,** 30 Main Road, Ballymartin, Kilkeel, Co Down BT34 4NU

Robert & Irene Adair
☎ 01693 763012
Fax 01693 765988
BB £21
EM £14
Sleeps 11

Grade A

A warm welcome awaits you at our farm guesthouse where we are renowned for our food and hospitality. Enjoy a holiday in the beautiful 'Mourne' country, a rambler's paradise. Relax in our conservatory and sample our home baking. Most rooms en suite with tea/coffee facilities and colour TV. Visa/Mastercard accepted. Open Apr–Oct.

LET THE TELEPHONE RING!
Some farmhouses are big places. Let the telephone ring long enough to give the owner time to answer it.

THE 1000+ BUREAU MEMBERS OFFER A UNIQUE LINK TO CUSTOMERS ACROSS THE UK

All Bureau members belong to a local Group. Each member can refer you to an equally high quality member within the Group... or across the UK: England, Northern Ireland, Scotland, Wales.

FOLLOW THE COUNTRY CODE

Leave nothing but footprints,
Take nothing but photographs,
Kill nothing but time!

Reference section

FHB Group contacts	**360**
European contacts	**365**
Further information	**366**
Index to farms	**367**

FHB Group Contacts

Every member of the Farm Holiday Bureau belongs to one of 92 local Groups, each of which has its own nominated contact person. (Occasionally, different contacts are given for bed and breakfast (**B&B**) and self-catering (**SC**) accommodation.) If you need help finding accommodation, try the local Group contacts in your chosen area. They may be able to tell you which members have vacancies.

Listed in the order in which their appropriate counties/tourism areas appear in the guide, FHB Group contacts are as follows:

Scotland

Scottish Highlands & Islands

Highlands
Highlands Group
B&B Mrs M Pottie   Tel/Fax 01667 462213
SC Mrs J Masheter   Tel/Fax 01463 782423

Aberdeen & Grampian
Grampian Group
Mrs Patricia Duncan   Tel 01261 851261
Highlands Group (as for *Highlands*)

Perthshire
Perthshire Group
Mrs Jo Andrew   Tel/Fax 01350 724254

Argyll, the Isles & Stirling
Heart of Scotland Group
Mrs Anne Lennox   Tel/Fax 01389 850231
Oban, Mull, Kintyre & Fort William Group
Mrs Kathie Lambie   Tel 01866 833339

Scottish Lowlands

Angus & Dundee
Angus & Dundee Group
B&B Mrs Deanna Lindsay   Tel/Fax 01307 462887
SC Mrs Moira Clarke   Tel/Fax 01575 560213

Fife
Kingdom of Fife Group
Mrs Kathleen Baird   Tel 01337 840218
                     Fax 01337 842226

Glasgow & Clyde Valley
Around Glasgow Group
Mrs Elsie Hunter   Tel/Fax 01236 830243
Biggar & Clyde Valley Group
Mrs Margaret Kirby   Tel/Fax 01899 810338
Heart of Scotland Group
(as for *Argyll, the Isles & Stirling*)

Edinburgh & the Lothians
East Lothian – Edinburgh's Coast & Countryside
Mrs M Whiteford   Tel 01620 810327
Heart of Scotland Group
(as for *Argyll, the Isles & Stirling*)

Ayrshire & Arran
Ayrshire & Arran Group
Mrs Jessie Bone   Tel/Fax 01563 820567

Scottish Borders
Scottish Borders Group
Mrs Ann Prentice   Tel 01361 882811

Dumfries & Galloway
Dumfriesshire (Annandale) Group
B&B Mrs Kate Miller   Tel/Fax 01683 221900
South West Scotland Group
Mrs Vera Dunlop   Tel/Fax 01465 861220

England

England's North Country

Isle of Man
Manx Farm Stay Group
Mrs Jean Jackson   Tel 01624 801871
                   Fax 01624 801543

Cumbria
Carlisle's Border Country Group
Mrs Jane Lawson   Tel 01228 577214
                  Fax 01228 577014
Central Lakeland Group
Mrs Margaret Harryman   Tel 017687 78544
Eden Valley & North Pennines Group
Mrs Ann Ivinson   Tel 016974 76230
                  Fax 016974 76523

FHB Group contacts

Hadrian's Wall, North Cumbria & the Borders Group
Mrs Elizabeth Woodmass   Tel 016977 47285
North Pennines Group
Mrs Susan Huntley   Tel/Fax 01434 381372
South Lakeland Group
Mrs Linda Nicholson   Tel 01434 673240
West Lakeland Group
Mrs Carolyn Heslop   Tel/Fax 01900 824222

Northumberland
North Northumberland Group
Mrs Sally Lee   Tel/Fax 01665 574277
Northumberland South Group
Mrs Susan Dart   Tel/Fax 01434 673240

Durham
Durham & its Dales Group
Mrs Judith Stephenson   Tel/Fax 01388 527285
North Pennines Group (as for Cumbria)

Lancashire
Lancashire Coast & Country Group
Mrs Maureen Smith   Tel 01253 882537
Lancashire Pennines Group
Mrs Carole Mitson   Tel 01282 865301
South Pennines Group
Mrs Charlotte Walsh   Tel 0161 368 4610
                       Fax 0161 367 9106

Yorkshire – Dales, Brontë Country, South, West & Harrogate
Harrogate & Nidderdale Group
Mrs Christine Ryder   Tel 01943 880354
                       Fax 01943 880374
Mrs Sheila Smith   Tel 01423 771040
                    Fax 01423 771515
South & West Yorkshire Group
Mrs Marie Gill   Tel 01924 848339
Yorkshire Dales & Bronte Country Group
Mrs Anne Pearson   Tel 01756 791579

Yorkshire – Coast, Moors & Dales
Cleveland & North Yorkshire Borders Group
Mrs Patricia Weighell   Tel/Fax 01642 712312
Herriot's Yorkshire, Moors & Dales Group
B&B Mrs Diana Greenwood   Tel 01748 822152
SC   Lady Mary Furness   Tel 01609 748614
Ryedale Group
B&B Mrs Sarah Wood   Tel 01439 798277
SC   Mrs Sally Robinson   Tel 01439 798221

Stay on a farm

Yorkshire Moors, National Park & Coast Group
Mrs Jean & Miss Lorraine Allanson
                         Tel/Fax 01723 859333

Yorkshire – Vale of York & the Wolds
Vale of York & the Wolds Group
Mrs Helen Middleton   Tel 01757 228775
                       Fax 01757 228004

Greater Manchester
South Pennines Group (as for Lancashire)

Cheshire
Cheshire Group
Mrs Hilary Bennion   Tel/Fax 01270 811324

England's Heartland

Derbyshire
Derbyshire Dales & Dovedale Group
B&B Mrs Janet Hinds   Tel 01335 360346
SC   Mrs Linda Adams   Tel 01335 360352
Peak District Group
Mrs Joy Lomas   Tel/Fax 01629 540250
             E-mail: joy.lomas@btinternet.com

Nottinghamshire
Sherwood Forest/Nottinghamshire Group
B&B Mr Fernie Palmer   Tel 01623 842666
SC   Mrs Janet Carr   Tel 01623 861088

Lincolnshire
Lincolnshire Group
Mrs Gill Grant   Tel 01673 842283

Shropshire
Shrewsbury, Ironbridge & Shropshire Group
Mrs Janet Jones   Tel/Fax 01939 220223
South Shropshire Group
Mrs Christine Price   Tel/Fax 01547 530249

Staffordshire
Peak District Group (as for Derbyshire)
Staffordshire Group
Mrs Christine Shaw   Tel/Fax 01538 702830

Leicestershire
Leicestershire Group
Mrs Janet Clarke   Tel 0116 260 0472

Herefordshire
Herefordshire Group
B&B Mrs Elizabeth Godsall   Tel 01531 670408

Stay on a farm — FHB Group contacts

Herefordshire Group (cont)
SC Mrs Judy Wells Tel 01568 797347
  Fax 01568 797366

Worcestershire
Worcestershire Group
Mrs Helen Hirons Tel/Fax 01562 777533

Gloucestershire
Cotswolds & Royal Forest of Dean Group
Mrs Barbara Scudamore Tel/Fax 01242 602344

Warwickshire
Warwickshire Group
Mrs Deborah Lea Tel/Fax 01295 770652
  Mobile 07775 626458

Northamptonshire
Northamptonshire Group
Mrs A Singlehurst Tel 01832 205222

Bedfordshire
Bedfordshire Group
B&B Mrs Alison Knowles Tel/Fax 01442 866541
SC Mrs Ruth Pibworth Tel 01234 711655
  Fax 01234 711855

Hertfordshire
Hertfordshire Group
Mrs Alison Knowles Tel/Fax 01442 866541

Cambridgeshire
Cambridgeshire Group
Mrs Jean Wiseman Tel/Fax 01763 838263

Norfolk
Norfolk & Suffolk Group
B&B Mrs Carrie Holl Tel/Fax 01508 550260
SC Mrs Margaret Langton Tel/Fax 01473 652210
  E-mail: keith.larrington@farmline.com

Suffolk
Norfolk & Suffolk Group (as for *Norfolk*)

South & South East England

Oxfordshire
Thames Valley Group
Mrs Mary Anne Florey Tel 01865 300207
  Fax 01865 300559

Buckinghamshire
Thames Valley Group (as for *Oxfordshire*)

Essex
Essex Group
Mrs Tineke Westerhuis Tel 01763 838053

Hampshire
Hampshire Group
Mrs Melanie Bray Tel 01705 631597

Isle of Wight
Isle of Wight Group
Mrs Judy Noyes Tel 01983 852582

Surrey
Sussex & Surrey Group
Mrs Gill Hill Tel 01306 730210

Kent
Kent Group
Mrs Corrine Scutt Tel 01233 740596

England's West Country

Bath & North East Somerset
Bath & Wells Group
Mrs Elizabeth Parsons Tel 01934 515704
Bath & Wiltshire Group
Mrs Julie McDonough Tel 01225 891750

Somerset
Exmoor Coast & Country Group
Mrs Penny Webber Tel/Fax 01643 705244
Exmoor National Park Group
B&B Mrs Elaine Goodwin Tel/Fax 01398 331400
SC Mrs Abigail Humphrey Tel/Fax 01398 323616
Somerset Group
B&B Mrs Jane Sedgman Tel 01458 223237
  Fax 01458 223276
SC Mrs Liz Smith Tel/Fax 01823 490828

Wiltshire
Bath & Wiltshire Group
(as for *Bath & North East Somerset*)

Dorset
Dorset Group
B&B Mrs Jane Greening Tel/Fax 01308 422884
SC Mrs Kathy Jeanes Tel/Fax 01258 820022

Heart of Dorset Group
Mrs Rosemary Coleman Tel 01305 848252
  Fax 01305 848702

North Devon
Exmoor National Park Group (as for *Somerset*)
Friendly Farms of West Devon Group
Mrs Jenny King Tel 01837 851647
  Fax 01837 851410

FHB Group contacts

Stay on a farm

Heart of Devon Group
Mrs Anne McLean Williams Tel/Fax 01398 331312
North Devon Coast & Country Group
B&B Mrs Pat Burge Tel 01598 710275
SC Mrs Ruth Ley Tel 01769 572337

South & East Devon
Dartmoor & South Devon Group
Mrs Anne Barons Tel/Fax 01404 841403
Friendly Farms of West Devon Group
(as for *North Devon*)
Heart of Devon Group
(as for *North Devon*)
Moor to Shore in Devon Group
Mrs Anne Barons Tel/Fax 01404 841403

Cornwall
Cornish Farm Holidays Group
Mrs Diana Mindel Tel 01208 821375
  Fax 01208 821378

Wales

North Wales

Isle of Anglesey
Isle of Anglesey Group
Mrs Joyce Roberts Tel 01407 730630

Snowdonia – Mountains & Coast
Heart of Snowdonia Group
Mrs Paula Williams Tel/Fax 01766 590281
Llyn Peninsula Group
Mrs Jean Coker Tel 01758 720487
  Fax 01758 720020
Snowdonia Group
Mrs Jane Llewelyn Pierce Tel/Fax 01248 670147

North Wales Coast & Borderlands
Vale of Clwyd Group
Mrs Elsie Jones Tel 01824 703142

Mid Wales

Ceredigion, Cardigan Bay
Ceredigion Group
Mrs E A Beti Davies Tel 01570 422447
Mid Wales, Lakes & Mountains
Brecon Group
Mrs Mary Adams Tel/Fax 01874 636505

Carmarthenshire Group
Mrs Marian Lewis Tel 01550 720410
  Fax 01550 720262
Croeso Cader Idris Group
Mrs Deilwen Breese Tel/Fax 01654 791235
Monmouthshire Group
Mrs Ann Ball Tel 01873 821236
Montgomeryshire – Heart of Wales Group
Mrs Joyce Cornes Tel 01938 810791
Radnor Group
Mrs Gill Morgan Tel/Fax 01547 550219

South & West Wales

Pembrokeshire
Carmarthenshire Group
(as for *Mid Wales, Lakes & Mountains*)
Pembrokeshire Group
Mrs Vivienne Lockton Tel/Fax 01994 419123

Carmarthenshire & the Gower
Carmarthenshire Group
(as for *Mid Wales, Lakes & Mountains*)
Pembrokeshire Group (as for *Pembrokeshire*)

Wye Valley & Vale of Usk
Monmouthshire Group
(as for *Mid Wales, Lakes & Mountains*)

Northern Ireland

County Londonderry
County Londonderry Group
Mrs Heather Torrens Tel 012665 58245
County Tyrone
County Tyrone Group
Mrs Louie Reed Tel 01662 841325
County Armagh
County Armagh Group
Mrs Elizabeth Kee Tel/Fax 01762 870081
County Down
County Down Group
Miss Esther Kerr Tel 01820 626270/624251
  Fax 01820 624251

Host & Guest Service

Central reservation service for

The Farm Holiday Bureau
For overseas visitors

Easy and convenient method to book your farm holiday accommodation

Directions and maps supplied with your booking
Itineraries arranged if you require more than one location

103 Dawes Road London SW6 7DU
Tel: 0171 385 9922 Fax 0171 386 7575
E-mail: farm@host-guest.co.uk
Web: http:www.host-guest.co.uk

The British Incoming Tour Operators Association

European contacts

For information on farm holidays in various countries in Europe please contact the following:

GERMANY
Arbeitsgemeinschaft für Urlaub auf dem Bauernhof in der Bundesrepublik Deutschland e.V.
Godesberger Allee 142-148
53175 BONN
☎ [49] 228 81 98 220
Fax [49] 228 81 98 231

Deutsche Landwirtschafts gesellschaft
Eschborner Landstraße 122
60489 FRANKFURT
☎ [49] 69 247 880
Fax [49] 69 247 88 110

BELGIUM
Gîtes de Wallonie
Rue de Millénaire, 53
6941 VILLERS SAINTE GERTRUDE
☎ [32] 86 49 95 31
Fax [32] 86 49 94 07

FINLAND
Lomarengas
Malminkaari 23
00700 HELSINKI
☎ [358] 0 351 61 321
Fax [358] 0 351 61 370

FRANCE
Fédération Nationale des Gîtes de France
56, rue Saint Lazare
75009 PARIS
☎ [1] 49 70 75 75
Fax [1] 49 70 75 76

Agriculture et Tourisme
Assemblée Permanente des Chambres d'Agriculture
9, avenue George V
75008 PARIS
☎ [1] 47 23 55 40
Fax [1] 47 23 84 97

HUNGARY
Association of Village Farm Houses
Szoboszlai u. 2-4
1126 BUDAPEST
☎ [36] 1 155 533 312
Fax [36] 1 155 18 57

Hungarian Federation of Rural Tourism
Klauzal Ter 5
1072 BUDAPEST
☎/Fax [36] 1 268 05 92

ICELAND
Icelandic Farm Holidays
Hafnarstraeti 1
101 REYKJAVIK
☎ [354] 562 36 40
Fax [354] 562 36 44

IRELAND
Irish Farm Holidays
2 Michael Street
LIMERICK
☎ [353] 61 400 700
☎ [353] 61 400 707
Fax [353] 61 400 771

Irish Country Holidays
Rural Development Centre
ATHENRY CO GALWAY
☎ [353] 91 44 473
Fax [353] 91 44 296

ITALY
Agriturist
C. SO Vittorio Emmanuelle, 101
00186 ROMA
☎ [39] 66 85 23 42
Fax [39] 66 85 24 24

LUXEMBOURG
Association pour la Promotion du Tourisme
Rural au Grand-Duché du Luxembourg
c/o Centrale Paysanne
2980 LUXEMBOURG
☎ [352] 48 81 61
Fax [352] 40 03 75

PORTUGAL
Privetur
Nucleo Regional Do Minho E Litoral Norte
Largo das Pereiras
4990 PONTE DE LIMA
☎/Fax [351] 58 741 493

ROMANIA
Antrec
National Association of Rural, Ecological, Cultural, Tourism
B. P. 22-559
BUCAREST
☎/Fax [40] 1 222 83 22

Bran Imex
Bran Jud. Brasov
Str. dr. A. Stoian 395
☎ [40] 68 23 66 42
☎ [40] 1 666 59 48
Fax [40] 68 15 25 98

SLOVAKIA
Slovensky Zväz Vidieckej Turistiky A Agroturistiky
Trencianska 55
82101 BRATISLAVA
☎ [42] 7 215 800/209
Fax [42] 7 214 903

SPAIN
Red Andaluza de Alojamientos Rurales
Apartado Correos 2035
04080 ALMERIA
☎ [34] 50 26 50 18
Fax [34] 50 27 04 31

SWEDEN
The Sweddish University of Agricultural Sciences
Ala Box 7013
75007 UPPSALA
☎ [46] 18 67 19 12
Fax [46] 18 67 19 80

SWITZERLAND
Verein "Ferien auf dem Bauernhof"
Feierlenhof
8595 ALTNAU
☎/Fax [41] 71 695 2372

Further information

These official Tourist Boards will be happy to supply you with further general information on their areas.

National Tourist Boards

English Tourist Board
Thames Tower, Black's Road, Hammersmith, London W6 9EL
☎ (0181) 846 9000

Northern Ireland Tourist Board
59 North Street
Belfast BT1 1NB
☎ (01232) 246609 Fax (01232) 312424

Scottish Tourist Board
23 Ravelston Terrace, Edinburgh EH4 3EU
☎ (0131) 332 2433

Wales Tourist Board
Brunel House, 2 Fitzalan Road, Cardiff CF2 1UY
☎ (01222) 499909

Regional Tourist Boards

Isle of Man Tourism
Department of Tourism and Leisure, Sea Terminal, Douglas, Isle of Man IM1 2RG
☎ (01624) 686801

Cumbria Tourist Board
(covering the county of Cumbria)
Ashleigh, Holly Road, Windermere, Cumbria LA23 2AQ
☎ (015394) 44444

Northumbria Tourist Board
(covering Durham, Northumberland, Tees Valley and Tyne & Wear)
Aykley Heads, Durham DH1 5UX
☎ (0191) 384 6905

North West Tourist Board
(covering Cheshire, Greater Manchester, High Peak District of Derbyshire, Lancashire and Merseyside)
Swan House, Swan Meadow Road, Wigan Pier, Wigan WN3 5BB
☎ (01942) 821222

Yorkshire Tourist Board
(covering East Riding of Yorkshire, North Lincolnshire, North East Lincolnshire, North Yorkshire, South Yorkshire and West Yorkshire)
312 Tadcaster Road, York, North Yorkshire YO24 1GS
☎ (01904) 707961

Heart of England Tourist Board
(covering Derbyshire, Gloucestershire, Herefordshire, Leicestershire, Northamptonshire, Nottinghamshire, Rutland, Shropshire, Staffordshire, Warwickshire, West Midlands and Worcestershire)
Woodside, Larkhill, Worcester WR5 2EF
☎ (01905) 761100

East of England Tourist Board
(covering Bedfordshire, Cambridgeshire, Essex, Hertfordshire, Lincolnshire, Norfolk and Suffolk)
Toppesfield Hall, Hadleigh, Suffolk IP7 5DN
☎ (01473) 822922

London Tourist Board
(covering the Greater London area)
6th Floor, Glen House, Stag Place, London SW1E 5LT
Written enquiries only.

West Country Tourist Board
(covering Bath & North East Somerset, Bristol, Cornwall, Devon, North Somerset, Somerset, South Gloucestershire, Isles of Scilly, Western Dorset and Wiltshire)
60 St David's Hill, Exeter EX4 4SY
☎ (01392) 76351

Southern Tourist Board
(covering Berkshire, Buckinghamshire, Eastern Dorset, Hampshire, Isle of Wight and Oxfordshire)
40 Chamberlayne Road, Eastleigh, Hampshire SO5 5JH
☎ (01703) 620006

South East England Tourist Board
(covering Kent, East Sussex, Surrey and West Sussex)
The Old Brew House, Warwick Park, Tunbridge Wells, Kent TN2 5TU
☎ (01892) 540766

Britain On-Line
Information about all aspects of holidaying in Britain can be found on the British Tourist Authority Website: www.visitbritain.com

Tourist Information Centres

There are over 800 Tourist Information Centres (TICs) throughout the UK and they are there for you to use both before your holiday and during your holiday.
Look in your local telephone directory under 'Tourist Information' to find your nearest TIC, or for details of any TIC in England call Scoot™ on 0800 192 192. TICs can provide details about local attractions, events and accommodation and many will even be able to book it for you. Look out for the information sign.

Index to farms

Key
B&B — Bed & Breakfast
SC — Self-Catering
C&C — Camping & Caravanning
B/CB — Bunkhouse/Camping Barn

INDEX

SCOTLAND

Area/Farm		Page no.	Accessibility category	Caravans and/or camping	Working farm (p=participation)	Stabling/grazing for visiting horses	En suite available	Business people welcome	Meeting room (capacity)	Gift tokens accepted
Aberdeen & Grampian										
B&B	Bandora	39			✔		✔	✔		✔
	The Palace Farm	39			✔p	✔	✔	✔		
Angus & Dundee										
B&B	Blibberhill Farm	49			✔p		✔	✔	✔(10)	✔
	Purgavie Farm	49		✔	✔	✔	✔	✔	✔(10)	✔
	Wemyss Farm	49		✔	✔p	✔			✔(20)	✔
SC	Purgavie Farm	49	⚡	✔	✔	✔		✔	✔(10)	✔
Argyll, Isles, Loch Lomond, Stirling & Trossachs										
B&B	Belsyde Farm	44			✔		✔	✔	✔(12)	✔
	Inchie Farm	44			✔			✔		✔
	Lochend Farm (Carronbridge)	44			✔	✔		✔		✔
	Lochend Farm (Port of Menteith)	44			✔p		✔			✔
	Lower Tarr Farm	44			✔		✔	✔	✔(10)	✔
	Mains Farm	45					✔	✔		✔
	Shantron Farm	45			✔		✔	✔		✔
	Thistle-Doo	45		✔			✔			
	The Topps Farm	45			✔		✔	✔	✔(20)	✔
	Trean Farm	45			✔		✔	✔	✔	
	Wester Carmuirs Farm	45			✔			✔		✔
	West Plean	46			✔p	✔	✔	✔	✔(12)	✔
SC	Shemore Farm Cottage	46			✔			✔		✔
Ayrshire & Arran										
B&B	Auchencloigh Farm	59			✔			✔		✔
	Dunduff Farm	59			✔p		✔	✔		✔
	East Lochhead	53					✔	✔		✔
	Fisherton Farm	59			✔		✔	✔		
	Glen Cloy Farmhouse	59			✔		✔	✔		
	Muirhouse Farm	59			✔p		✔	✔		✔
SC	Bothy Cottage	60			✔p		✔	✔		✔
	East Lochhead	54						✔		✔
Dumfries & Galloway										
B&B	Airds Farm	66				✔	✔	✔		✔
	Blair Farm	66			✔		✔	✔		✔
	Broomlands Farm	66			✔		✔	✔		✔
	Coxhill Farm	66			✔		✔	✔		✔
	Ericstane	66			✔		✔	✔		
	Glengennet Farm	67			✔			✔		✔
	Mains of Collin	67			✔p	✔	✔	✔		✔
	Rascarrel Cottage	67			✔		✔	✔		✔
SC	Upper Barr Farm	67			✔		✔	✔		✔
Edinburgh & the Lothians										
B&B	Ashcroft Farmhouse	56			✔		✔	✔		
	Bankhead Farm	56			✔p	✔	✔	✔		
	Belsyde Farm	56			✔		✔	✔	✔(12)	✔
	Carfrae Farmhouse	56			✔		✔	✔		✔
	Coates Farm	56			✔		✔	✔		✔
	Eaglescairnie Mains	57			✔	✔	✔	✔	✔(12)	✔
	Rowan Park	57			✔		✔	✔	✔(8)	✔
	Whitekirk Mains	57			✔		✔	✔		

INDEX

SCOTLAND

Area/Farm		Page no.	Accessibility category	Caravans and/or camping	Working farm (p=participation)	Stabling/grazing for visiting horses	En suite available	Business people welcome	Meeting room (capacity)	Gift tokens accepted
Edinburgh & Lothians (cont)										
SC	Crosswoodhill Farm	57	♿		✔			✔	✔(8)	✔
	Eastside Farm	57			✔P					✔
Fife										
B&B	Cambo House	51			✔	✔	✔	✔	✔(50)	✔
	Easter Clunie Farmhouse	51			✔		✔	✔		✔
SC	Cambo House	51			✔	✔		✔	✔(50)	✔
	Parkend Cottage	51			✔P		✔	✔		✔
Glasgow & Clyde Valley										
B&B	Allanfauld Farm	53			✔			✔		✔
	Bandominie Farm	53			✔			✔		✔
	East Lochhead	53				✔		✔		✔
	Easter Glentore Farm	53			✔		✔	✔		✔
	Walston Mansion Farmhouse	53			✔P		✔	✔	✔(10)	✔
SC	Carmichael Country Cottages	54			✔P	✔		✔	✔(50)	✔
	East Lochhead	54						✔		✔
Highlands										
B&B	Balaggan Farm	35			✔			✔		✔
	Cherry Trees	35			✔			✔		✔
	Daviot Mains Farm	35			✔	✔		✔		✔
	Drumbuie Farm	35			✔	✔		✔		✔
	Easter Dalziel Farm	35			✔			✔		✔
	Strone Farm	36			✔	✔		✔		✔
	Upper Latheron Farm	36			✔P	✔		✔		✔
SC	Achmony Holidays	36			✔			✔		✔
	Culligran Cottages	36			✔			✔		✔
	Easter Dalziel Farm	36			✔			✔		✔
	Laikenbuie Holidays	37	♿	✔	✔P	✔		✔		✔
	Mains of Aigas	37			✔			✔		✔
	Milton Bank	37		✔	✔	✔		✔		✔
	Strone Cottage	37			✔P		✔	✔		✔
	Tomich Holidays	37			✔			✔		✔
Perthshire										
B&B	'Avonlea' at Pitmurthly	41			✔	✔	✔	✔	✔(10)	✔
	Bankhead	41			✔P		✔	✔		✔
	Blackcraigs Farm	41			✔		✔	✔	✔(10)	✔
	Letter Farm	41			✔P		✔	✔		✔
SC	Milton of Duchally Cottage	42			✔			✔		✔
	Wester Riechip	42			✔			✔		✔
Scottish Borders										
B&B	Cockburn Mill	62			✔P		✔	✔		✔
	Lyne Farm	62			✔	✔		✔	✔(12)	✔
	Morebattle Tofts	62			✔	✔	✔	✔	✔(6)	✔
	Over Langshaw Farm	62			✔P		✔	✔		✔
	Wiltonburn Farm	62			✔P	✔	✔	✔	✔(8)	✔
SC	Broadmeadows Holiday Cottages	63			✔P			✔	✔(12)	✔
	The Cottage	63			✔P			✔		✔
	Craggs Cottage	63						✔		✔
	Kerchesters Cottages	63			✔			✔		✔
	Rowan Tree Cottage	63			✔P			✔		✔

INDEX

SCOTLAND
Area/Farm

Area/Farm	Page no.	Accessibility category	Caravans and/or camping	Working farm (p=participation)	Stabling/grazing for visiting horses	En suite available	Business people welcome	Meeting room (capacity)	Gift tokens accepted
Scottish Borders (cont)									
Roxburgh Newtown Farm	64			✔	✔		✔		✔
Thirlestane Farm Cottages	64			✔					✔

INDEX

ENGLAND County/Farm		Page no.	Accessibility category	Caravans and/or camping	Working farm (p=participation)	Stabling/grazing for visiting horses	En suite available	Business people welcome	Meeting room (capacity)	Gift tokens accepted
Bath & North East Somerset										
B&B	Barrow Vale Farm	238			✔P		✔	✔	✔	
	Fairfield Farm	238			✔		✔	✔		✔
	Frying Pan Farm	238			✔		✔	✔		
	Hatt Farm	238			✔		✔	✔		✔
	Home Farm (Biddestone)	239			✔P		✔	✔		✔
	Home Farm (Farrington Gurney)	238			✔P		✔	✔	✔	
	Manor Farm	239			✔	✔	✔			✔
	The Model Farm	239			✔		✔			
	Pantiles	239			✔			✔	✔(12)	✔
	Pickwick Lodge Farm	239			✔	✔	✔	✔		✔
	Saltbox Farm	239			✔		✔	✔		✔
	Valley Farm	240		✔	✔		✔	✔	✔(12)	✔
	Woodbarn Farm	240			✔		✔	✔		✔
SC	Home Farm Barn & The Derby	240			✔		✔	✔		✔
	Lois Barns	240			✔P	✔		✔		✔
	Stable & Denny Cottages	240	♿		✔		✔	✔		✔
Bedfordshire										
B&B	Church Farm	186			✔			✔	✔(6)	✔
	Gransden Lodge Farm	190			✔		✔	✔		
	Highfield Farm	186			✔		✔	✔		✔
SC	Scald End Farm	186			✔P			✔	✔(40)	
Bristol										
B&B	Home Farm	238			✔P		✔	✔	✔	
	The Model Farm	239			✔		✔			
	Valley Farm	240		✔	✔		✔	✔	✔(12)	
	Woodbarn Farm	240			✔		✔	✔		✔
SC	Stable & Denny Cottages	240	♿		✔		✔	✔		✔
Buckinghamshire										
B&B	Hollands Farm	212			✔		✔	✔	✔	✔
	Home Farm	212		✔			✔			
	Monkton Farm	212		✔	✔P			✔	✔(36)	
	Poletrees Farm	212			✔		✔	✔		
	Spinney Lodge Farm	183			✔		✔			
	Wallace Farm	212			✔	✔		✔	✔(6)	✔
SC	The Old Stone Barn	213	🚶		✔			✔		
	Wallace Farm Cottages	213			✔	✔		✔	✔(6)	✔
Cambridgeshire										
B&B	Gransden Lodge Farm	190			✔		✔	✔		
	Hall Farm	190			✔		✔	✔		✔
	Highfield Farm	190			✔		✔	✔		✔
	Hill House Farm	190			✔		✔	✔		✔
	Lilford Lodge Farm	190			✔		✔	✔		✔
	Spinney Abbey	191			✔		✔	✔		✔
SC	Hill House Farm Cottage	191			✔			✔		✔
Cheshire										
B&B	Adderley Green Farm	123			✔P	✔	✔	✔		✔
	Ash House Farm	123			✔		✔	✔	✔(10)	✔
	Beechwood House	123			✔		✔	✔		✔
	Bridge Farm	123			✔P	✔	✔	✔		✔

INDEX

ENGLAND County/Farm	Page no.	Accessibility category	Caravans and/or camping	Working farm (p=participation)	Stabling/grazing for visiting horses	En suite available	Business people welcome	Meeting room (capacity)	Gift tokens accepted
Cheshire (cont)									
Carr House Farm	123			✓p			✓		✓
Ford Farm	124			✓p	✓		✓		
Golden Cross Farm	124			✓	✓		✓		
Goose Green Farm	124			✓	✓	✓	✓		✓
Henhull Hall	124			✓p		✓	✓	✓(10)	✓
Lea Farm	124			✓p	✓	✓	✓	✓(10)	✓
Little Heath Farm	124		✓	✓		✓	✓	✓(12)	✓
Manor Farm	125		✓	✓	✓	✓	✓	✓(10)	✓
Mill House	320					✓	✓		✓
Millmoor Farm	125			✓p		✓	✓		✓
Newton Hall	125			✓			✓	✓(7)	
Oldhams Hollow Farm	125			✓			✓		✓
Sandhole Farm	125	⚐		✓	✓	✓	✓	✓(15)	✓
Sandpit Farm	125			✓		✓	✓		✓
Shire Cottage Farmhouse	126			✓		✓	✓		✓
Snape Farm	126			✓		✓	✓	✓(50)	✓
Stoke Grange Farm	126					✓	✓	✓(12)	
Yew Tree Farm	126			✓p		✓	✓		✓
SC The Granary	321						✓		✓
Lake View	126			✓	✓		✓		✓
The Old Byre	127	⚐		✓p			✓		✓
Plattwood Farm Cottage	135			✓		✓	✓	✓(6)	✓
Stoke Grange Mews	127						✓		
Cornwall									
B&B Arrallas	294			✓		✓	✓		✓
Bake Farm	294			✓					
Bokiddick Farm	294			✓		✓	✓		✓
Boskenna Home Farm	294			✓p		✓	✓		✓
Bucklawren Farm	294			✓		✓	✓		✓
Caduscott	295			✓		✓	✓		
Carglonnon Farm	295			✓		✓	✓		
Cornakey Farm	295			✓p		✓	✓		✓
Degembris Farmhouse	295			✓		✓	✓	✓(10)	✓
Hendra Farm	295			✓		✓	✓		✓
Higher Kergilliack Farm	295			✓		✓	✓		✓
Home Farm	296			✓p	✓	✓	✓	✓(6)	✓
Kerryanna Country House	296			✓		✓	✓		✓
Little Larnick Farm	296			✓		✓	✓	✓(8)	✓
Little Pengwedna Farm	296			✓		✓	✓		✓
Longstone Farm	296			✓p			✓		✓
Loskeyle Farm	296			✓			✓		✓
Lower Dutson Farm	297			✓p		✓	✓		✓
Lower Tresmorn Farm	297			✓p		✓	✓		✓
Manuels Farm	297			✓p					✓
Polhormon Farm	297			✓p					✓
Polsue Manor Farm	297			✓		✓	✓	✓(10)	✓
Poltarrow Farm	297			✓			✓		
Rose Farm	298			✓		✓	✓		
Stone Farm	298			✓p		✓	✓	✓(6)	

INDEX

ENGLAND County/Farm		Page no.	Accessibility category	Caravans and/or camping	Working farm (p=participation)	Stabling/grazing for visiting horses	En suite available	Business people welcome	Meeting room (capacity)	Gift tokens accepted
Cornwall (cont)										
	Tregaddra Farm	298			✔P		✔	✔		✔
	Tregaswith Farmhouse	298			✔P	✔	✔	✔		✔
	Treglisson	298		✔	✔		✔	✔	✔(30)	
	Tregonan	298			✔			✔	✔(12)	
	Tregondale Farm	299			✔P		✔	✔	✔(6)	✔
	Tregurnow Farm	299			✔		✔	✔		
	Trerosewill Farm	299		✔	✔P		✔	✔		
	Tresulgan Farm	299			✔P		✔	✔		
	Treveria Farm	299			✔P		✔	✔		✔
	Trewellard Manor Farm	299			✔		✔	✔		
	Trewint Farm	300			✔P	✔	✔	✔		
	Wheatley Farm	300			✔P		✔	✔		✔
SC	Beechleigh Cottage	300			✔P				✔(10)	✔
	Brevean	300			✔					
	Bucklawren Farm	300			✔			✔		✔
	Cadson Manor Farm	301			✔P			✔		✔
	The Coach House	301			✔P	✔		✔		
	Glynn Barton Farm Cottages	301			✔P			✔		
	Hendra Farm	301			✔P					
	Katie's Cottage	301	✝		✔P			✔		
	Lodge Barton Farm	301			✔P					
	Lower Dutson Farm	302			✔P			✔		
	Lower Trengale Farm	302			✔P	✔		✔		
	Lower Tresmorn Cottage	302			✔P			✔		
	Manuels Farm	302			✔P			✔		✔
	Old Newham Farm	302			✔P	✔		✔		
	Poltarrow Farm	302	✝		✔			✔		
	Tredethick Farm Cottages	303			✔	✔	✔	✔		✔
	Tredinnick Farm	303			✔		✔	✔		✔
	Tregevis Farm	303			✔	✔				
	Treleaven Farm Cottages	303			✔		✔	✔		
	Tremadart Farm	303			✔P		✔	✔	✔(12)	
	Trevadlock Farm Cottages	303			✔P		✔	✔		
	Trevalgan Farm	304			✔			✔		
	Trevissick Manor	304			✔			✔		
	Trewalla Farm Cottages	304			✔P					
	Trewellard Manor Farm	304			✔			✔		
	Trewithen Country Lodges	304			✔P					
	West Kellow Farmhouse & Meadow Bank	304			✔P		✔	✔		
	Wheatley Farm Cottages	305			✔P			✔		✔
C&C	Nancolleth Farm Caravan Gardens	305			✔					✔
Cumbria										
B&B	Augill House Farm	73			✔	✔	✔	✔		
	Bessiestown Farm Country Guest House	73			✔		✔	✔	✔(10)	✔
	Birkrigg Farm	73			✔					✔
	Bridge End Farm	73			✔	✔	✔	✔		✔

INDEX

ENGLAND County/Farm	Page no.	Accessibility category	Caravans and/or camping	Working farm (p=participation)	Stabling/grazing for visiting horses	En suite available	Business people welcome	Meeting room (capacity)	Gift tokens accepted
Cumbria (cont)									
Cracrop Farm	73			✔p	✔	✔	✔	✔(8)	✔
Craigburn Farm	74			✔		✔	✔	✔(50)	✔
Crossgill Farm	74			✔	✔	✔	✔		✔
Dufton Hall Farm	74			✔		✔			
Fell Foot Farm	74			✔p		✔	✔		
Garnett House Farm	74			✔		✔	✔		✔
Gateside Farm	74			✔		✔	✔		✔
High Gregg Hall	75			✔		✔			
Howard House Farm	75			✔p	✔	✔	✔		✔
Howe Farm	75			✔			✔	✔(6)	✔
Keskadale Farm	75		✔	✔			✔		✔
Low Rigg Farm	75			✔p			✔		
New Pallyards	75			✔p		✔	✔	✔(30)	✔
Park House Farm	76			✔		✔	✔		✔
Slakes Farm	76			✔			✔		✔
Stanger Farm	76			✔p	✔		✔	✔(6)	✔
Town Head Farm	76		✔	✔p	✔		✔		✔
Tranthwaite Hall	76				✔	✔	✔		✔
Tymparon Hall	76		✔	✔		✔	✔		✔
Walton High Rigg	77			✔p					
Wickerslack Farm	77		✔	✔		✔			✔
SC Arch View & Riggfoot Cottages	77	♿	✔	✔p	✔		✔		✔
Bessiestown Farm	77			✔			✔	✔(10)	✔
Birchbank Cottage	77		✔	✔p			✔		✔
Burn and Meadow View	78			✔p			✔	✔(30)	✔
Chestnuts	78			✔			✔	✔(10)	✔
Collin Bank	78			✔p	✔		✔		
Ghyll Burn Cottage	78						✔		✔
Green View Lodges & Well Cottage	78	🚶					✔		✔
High Swinklebank Farm	78			✔p			✔		✔
Jenkin Cottage	79			✔p			✔		
Long Byres	79			✔p			✔		
Lyvennet Cottages	79			✔p			✔		
Preston Patrick Hall Cottage	79			✔					✔
Skirwith Hall Cottage	79			✔			✔		✔
Smithy Cottage	79			✔			✔		✔
Stanger Farm	80			✔p	✔		✔		
Stonefold	80		✔	✔			✔		
Swarthbeck Farm	80			✔	✔		✔		
Tarnside Cottages	80			✔p	✔		✔		
West View Cottages	80			✔			✔		✔
Derbyshire									
B&B Beechenhill Farm	130			✔p	✔	✔	✔	✔(10)	✔
Beeches Farmhouse	130			✔p		✔	✔	✔(12)	✔
Chevin Green Farm	130		✔			✔	✔		✔
Cote Bank Farm	130			✔p		✔	✔		✔
Dannah Farm	130			✔		✔	✔	✔(40)	✔
Lane End Farm	131		✔	✔p	✔	✔	✔		✔
Lydgate Farm	131			✔p		✔	✔		✔

INDEX

ENGLAND County/Farm	Page no.	Accessibility category	Caravans and/or camping	Working farm (p=participation)	Stabling/grazing for visiting horses	En suite available	Business people welcome	Meeting room (capacity)	Gift tokens accepted
Derbyshire (cont)									
Mercaston Hall	131		✔	✔	✔	✔	✔	✔(12)	✔
Middlehills Farm	131		✔	✔P		✔	✔	✔(20)	✔
The Old Bake & Brewhouse	131		✔	✔		✔	✔		✔
Park View Farm	131			✔		✔	✔		✔
Shallow Grange	132		✔	✔P	✔	✔	✔	✔(12)	✔
Shirley Hall	132			✔		✔	✔		✔
Throwley Hall Farm	132				✔	✔	✔		✔
Wolfscote Grange Farm	132		✔	✔P	✔	✔	✔		✔
Yeldersley Old Hall Farm	132			✔			✔		✔
SC									
Archway Cottage	133		✔	✔P	✔		✔		✔
Beechenhill Cottage & The Cottage by the Pond	133	♿		✔P	✔		✔	✔(10)	✔
Briar, Bluebell & Primrose Cottages	133			✔			✔		✔
Chapelgate Cottage	133			✔P			✔		✔
Chevin Green Farm	133		✔				✔		✔
The Chop House	134			✔P	✔		✔		✔
Cote Bank Farm Cottages	134			✔P			✔		✔
Cruck & Wolfscote Cottages	134		✔	✔P	✔		✔		✔
Culland Mount Farm	134			✔P			✔		
Hall Farm Bungalow, New House Farm & The Saddlery	134			✔			✔		
The Hayloft	134		✔	✔P	✔		✔		✔
Honeysuckle & Brook Cottages	135			✔			✔		✔
Honeysuckle, Jasmine & Clematis Cottages	135		✔	✔P			✔	✔(20)	
The Old House	135			✔P			✔		
Old House Farm Cottage	135			✔			✔		
Plattwood Farm Cottage	135			✔		✔	✔	✔(6)	✔
Shatton Hall Farm Cottages	135			✔	✔		✔		
Shaw Farm	136			✔P	✔	✔	✔		✔
Throwley Moor Farm & Throwley Cottage	136				✔		✔		
Devon									
B&B									
Barkham	267					✔	✔	✔(50)	
Berry Farm	278			✔			✔		✔
Buckyette Farm	278			✔			✔		
Burton Farm	278			✔P		✔	✔	✔(40)	✔
Caffyns Heanton Farm	267			✔		✔	✔	✔(10)	
Callisham Farm	278			✔	✔	✔	✔		
Catshayes Farm	278			✔P			✔		
Claw House	279		✔			✔	✔	✔(6)	
Cleave Farmhouse	267			✔			✔		✔
Colcharton Farm	279			✔P			✔		
Combas Farm	267		✔	✔			✔		✔
Coombe Farm (Countisbury)	267			✔	✔	✔	✔		✔
Coombe Farm (Kingsbridge)	279		✔	✔			✔		✔
Court Barton	268			✔			✔		✔
Court Barton Farmhouse	279			✔		✔	✔	✔(25)	✔
Crannacombe Farm	279			✔P	✔		✔		

375

INDEX

ENGLAND County/Farm	Page no.	Accessibility category	Caravans and/or camping	Working farm (p=participation)	Stabling/grazing for visiting horses	En suite available	Business people welcome	Meeting room (capacity)	Gift tokens accepted
Devon (cont)									
Denham Farm	268			✔		✔	✔	✔(30)	✔
Eggworthy Farm	279			✔P	✔		✔		
Foales Leigh	280			✔		✔	✔		
Forda Farm	268			✔P		✔	✔		✔
Frost Farm	280			✔		✔	✔		✔
Gabber Farm	280			✔P		✔			✔
Gatcombe Farm	280			✔P	✔		✔		✔
Godford Farm	280			✔P		✔	✔		✔
Great Bradley Farm	268			✔			✔		✔
Great Court Farm	280			✔		✔	✔		✔
Great Sloncombe Farm	281			✔	✔	✔	✔		✔
Greenwell Farm	281			✔P	✔	✔	✔	✔(16)	✔
Harton Farm	268			✔			✔		✔
Haxton Down Farm	268			✔P	✔	✔	✔	✔(8)	✔
Hayne Farm	269			✔			✔		
Hayne House	281			✔			✔		✔
Hele Barton	269			✔		✔	✔	✔(8)	
Hele Farm	281			✔		✔	✔		
Helliers Farm	281			✔		✔			✔
Higher Biddacott Farm	269	✔		✔P	✔		✔	✔(12)	✔
Higher Cadham Farm	281			✔		✔	✔		
Higher Coombe Farm	282			✔P			✔		✔
Higher Kellaton Farm	282			✔P	✔	✔	✔		
Higher Langridge Farm	269			✔		✔	✔	✔(20)	✔
Higher Venton Farm	282			✔			✔		
Higher Weston Farm	282		✔	✔		✔	✔	✔(6)	
Hillhead Farm	282		✔	✔P		✔	✔		
Home Park Farm	269			✔			✔		
Hornhill Farmhouse	269			✔		✔	✔	✔(12)	✔
Huxtable Farm	270	✔		✔P		✔	✔	✔(10)	✔
Jubilee House	270				✔		✔		
Kerscott Farm	270			✔		✔	✔		✔
The Knole Farm	282		✔	✔	✔	✔	✔	✔(15)	
Lane End Farm	283			✔P		✔			
Little Bidlake Farm	283			✔P	✔		✔		
Little Quarme Farm	270			✔	✔	✔	✔	✔(25)	
Lodfin Farm	270			✔P	✔	✔	✔		
Lower Collipriest Farm	270			✔P		✔	✔		✔
Lower Nichols Nymet Farm	283			✔P		✔	✔		
Lower Pinn Farm	283			✔		✔	✔		✔
Lower Thornton Farm	283			✔P		✔	✔		✔
Mill Farm	283			✔		✔	✔	✔(10)	✔
Mill Leat Farm	284			✔P	✔	✔	✔	✔	✔
Moor Farm	284			✔			✔		
New Cott Farm	284	♿		✔	✔	✔	✔	✔(12)	✔
Newcourt Barton	284		✔	✔P		✔	✔		
Newhouse Farm	271			✔P			✔		✔
Oaklands Farm	284					✔	✔		
Peek Hill Farm	284			✔	✔	✔	✔		✔

376

INDEX

ENGLAND County/Farm	Page no.	Accessibility category	Caravans and/or camping	Working farm (p=participation)	Stabling/grazing for visiting horses	En suite available	Business people welcome	Meeting room (capacity)	Gift tokens accepted
Devon (cont)									
Pinn Barton Farm	285			✔	✔	✔	✔		✔
Pitt Farm	285			✔		✔	✔		
Quoit-at-Cross Farm	271			✔		✔	✔	✔(15)	✔
Rubbytown Farm	285			✔p		✔	✔	✔(20)	
Rydon Farm	285			✔		✔	✔	✔(6)	✔
Seldon Farm	271			✔p			✔		
Skinners Ash Farm	285			✔p			✔	✔(25)	
Smallacombe Farm	285			✔p	✔	✔	✔		✔
Smallicombe Farm	286			✔p		✔	✔		✔
Stafford Barton	286			✔p	✔	✔	✔		✔
Upton	286					✔	✔		
Venn Farm	286			✔p		✔	✔		✔
Waytown Farm	271			✔p	✔	✔	✔		
Week Farm	286	♿		✔p		✔	✔	✔(12)	✔
Weir Mill Farm	286			✔		✔	✔		
Wellpritton Farm	287			✔			✔		
Whitecroft Farm	287			✔p	✔	✔	✔		✔
Wiscombe Linhaye Farm	287	♿		✔p		✔	✔		✔
Wishay Farm	287			✔		✔	✔		
Wood Advent Farm	271		✔	✔	✔	✔	✔	✔(20)	✔
Wooston Farm	287			✔			✔	✔(8)	
SC Alston Cottage	288			✔p			✔		
Barkham	272				✔		✔	✔(50)	
Barley Cottage & Old Granary	272			✔			✔	✔(35)	✔
Beech Grove	272			✔p			✔		✔
Bertie's & Porky's Barns	288			✔p			✔	✔(25)	
Bodmiscombe Farm	288			✔p	✔		✔		
Budleigh Farm	288		✔	✔			✔	✔(25)	✔
Burton Farm Cottages	288			✔p			✔	✔(40)	✔
Churchtown Farm	272			✔p	✔		✔		
Cider Cottage	272			✔p			✔		
Coombe Farm Cottage	289			✔			✔		✔
Country Ways	273	♿		✔p			✔		
Crosse Farm	273			✔	✔	✔	✔		✔
Deer's Leap Country Cottages	273			✔p	✔		✔	✔(12)	
Drewstone Farm	273			✔p	✔		✔		
Droughtwell Farm	289			✔p					
Dunsley Farm	273			✔	✔		✔		
Dunsley Mill	273			✔	✔	✔	✔		
The Garden Lodge	289			✔p			✔		✔
The Granary & Little Week Barn	289			✔p			✔	✔(12)	✔
Hele Payne Farm	289			✔p		✔	✔		✔
Highdown Farm	289			✔	✔	✔	✔		✔
Howton Linhay	290			✔p	✔	✔	✔		✔
Ledstone Farm	290			✔		✔	✔		✔
Lemprice Farm	290	♿♿		✔p			✔		
Little Quarme Cottages	274			✔	✔		✔		
Longmeadow Farm	290		✔	✔			✔		
Lower Campscott Farm	274			✔p			✔		

ENGLAND County/Farm		Page no.	Accessibility category	Caravans and/or camping	Working farm (p=participation)	Stabling/grazing for visiting horses	En suite available	Business people welcome	Meeting room (capacity)	Gift tokens accepted
Devon (cont)										
	Manor Farm	274			✔p			✔		✔
	Middle Cobden Farm	290			✔					
	Narramore Farm Cottages	290			✔	✔		✔		
	Nethercott Manor Farm	274			✔p		✔	✔		
	Northcott Barton Farm	274			✔p					✔
	Oldaport Farm Cottages	291			✔p			✔		
	The Old Granary	274			✔p	✔	✔	✔		✔
	Otter Holt & Owl Hayes	291			✔p			✔		✔
	Pickwell Barton Holiday Cottages	275			✔			✔		✔
	Shippen & Dairy Cottages	291				✔		✔		
	Smallicombe Farm	291	♿		✔p	✔		✔		✔
	Stable Cottage	275			✔p					
	Stick Wick Holiday Homes	291			✔					✔
	Traine Farm	291			✔p			✔		
	Vine Cottage & Grooms Cottage	292			✔p	✔		✔		
	West Ilkerton Farm	275			✔p	✔		✔		✔
	Whitefield Barton	275			✔p			✔	✔(8)	
	White Witches & Stable Lodge	275	♿		✔		✔	✔		✔
	Willesleigh Farm	275			✔		✔	✔		✔
	Withymore Cottage	292			✔p					✔
	Wonham Barton	276			✔p	✔		✔	✔(12)	✔
	Wooder Manor	292			✔p	✔	✔	✔		✔
	Yarningale	292			✔p	✔				✔
	Yelland Cottage	276			✔					
C&C	Welcombe Farm	276		✔	✔			✔		✔
Dorset										
B&B	Almshouse Farm	259			✔p		✔	✔		✔
	Cardsmill Farm	259			✔p		✔	✔	✔(12)	✔
	Church Farm	259			✔p		✔	✔	✔(8)	✔
	Colesmoor Farm	259			✔p	✔	✔	✔		✔
	Dunster Farm	259			✔p	✔				
	Hemsworth Manor Farm	260			✔p	✔	✔	✔	✔(10)	✔
	Henbury Farm	260			✔		✔	✔		
	Higher Langdon	260			✔		✔	✔	✔(12)	
	Higher Park Farm	260			✔		✔	✔		
	Huntsbridge Farm	260			✔	✔	✔	✔		✔
	Lamperts Farmhouse	260			✔p	✔	✔	✔		✔
	Lower Fifehead Farm	261			✔p	✔	✔	✔		
	Maiden Castle Farm	261			✔p	✔	✔	✔	✔(12)	✔
	New House Farm	261			✔p		✔	✔		
	Park Farm	261		✔	✔p	✔		✔	✔(6)	
	Priory Farm	261			✔p	✔	✔	✔	✔(15)	✔
	Rudge Farm	261			✔p		✔	✔		✔
	Watermeadow House	262			✔		✔	✔		✔
	Yalbury Park	262			✔	✔	✔	✔	✔(10)	✔
	Yew House Farm	262					✔	✔		✔
SC	Buddens Farm	262			✔p	✔		✔		✔
	Dairy Farm Cottages	262			✔			✔		
	2 Deverel Cottages	263			✔p			✔		✔

INDEX

ENGLAND County/Farm		Page no.	Accessibility category	Caravans and/or camping	Working farm (p=participation)	Stabling/grazing for visiting horses	En suite available	Business people welcome	Meeting room (capacity)	Gift tokens accepted
Dorset (cont)										
	Glebe Cottage	263								
	Gorwell Farm	263		✓	✓p	✓		✓	✓(6)	✓
	Graston Farm Cottage	263		✓	✓			✓		✓
	Hartgrove Farm	263	♿		✓p			✓		✓
	Higher Langdon Flat	263			✓		✓	✓	✓(20)	✓
	Higher Waterston Farm Cottages	264			✓	✓		✓		
	Lower Fifehead Farm	264			✓p	✓		✓		
	Luccombe Farm	264	🚶	✓	✓	✓	✓	✓	✓(12)	
	Old Dairy Cottage & Clyffe Dairy Cottage	264			✓	✓		✓		✓
	Orchard End	264			✓					
	Park Farm	264		✓	✓p	✓		✓	✓(6)	
	Rudge Farm Cottages	265	♿		✓p			✓		✓
	Shire & Stable Cottages	265			✓p	✓	✓	✓		
	Taphouse & Courthouse Farm	265			✓p			✓	✓(12)	
	Top Stall	265	♿		✓p					✓
	White Cottage	265			✓			✓		
Durham										
B&B	Bee Cottage Farm	90			✓	✓	✓	✓	✓(12)	✓
	East Mellwaters Farm	90		✓	✓p	✓	✓	✓	✓(15)	✓
	Greenwell Farm	90			✓p	✓	✓	✓	✓(16)	✓
	Lands Farm	90			✓	✓	✓	✓		✓
	Lonton South Farm	90			✓p	✓		✓		
	Low Cornriggs Farm	91			✓p	✓	✓	✓	✓(10)	✓
	Low Urpeth Farm	91			✓		✓	✓		✓
	Wilson House	91			✓		✓	✓		✓
	Wythes Hill Farm	91			✓p		✓	✓		✓
SC	Bail Hill	91			✓p			✓		✓
	Brackenbury Leases Farm	92			✓p			✓		
	Bradley Burn Holiday Cottages	92	🚶	✓	✓	✓		✓		✓
	Browney Cottage	92			✓p			✓		
	Buckshott Farm Cottage	92			✓p			✓		
	Greenwell Hill Stables & Byre	92			✓p	✓		✓	✓(16)	✓
	High House Farm Cottages	92			✓p	✓		✓		✓
	Katie's Cottage	93			✓		✓	✓		✓
	Stonecroft	93			✓p	✓		✓		✓
East Riding of Yorkshire										
B&B	Clematis House	115			✓		✓	✓		
	High Belthorpe	116			✓	✓		✓		
	High Catton Grange	116			✓		✓	✓	✓(6)	✓
	Kelleythorpe Farm	116			✓	✓	✓	✓		✓
	West Carlton	117		✓	✓		✓	✓	✓(8)	✓
	The Wold Cottage	117		✓	✓p	✓	✓	✓	✓(14)	✓
SC	The Cottage	118			✓			✓		✓
	Field House	118			✓p	✓		✓		
East Sussex										
B&B	Moonshill Farm	234		✓	✓		✓	✓		✓
	Ousedale House	234			✓	✓	✓	✓	✓(25)	✓
	The Stud Farm	234			✓	✓	✓	✓		✓

INDEX

ENGLAND

County/Farm		Page no.	Accessibility category	Caravans and/or camping	Working farm (p=participation)	Stabling/grazing for visiting horses	En suite available	Business people welcome	Meeting room (capacity)	Gift tokens accepted
East Sussex (cont)										
	Stud Farm House	234			✔p	✔	✔	✔	✔(20)	✔
SC	Boring House Farm	235			✔					
	2 High Weald Cottages	235		✔	✔			✔		✔
Essex										
B&B	Bonnydowns Farmhouse	215				✔				
	Duddenhoe End Farm	215					✔			✔
	Grove Farm House	200			✔			✔		✔
	Parsonage Farm	215			✔	✔	✔	✔		✔
	Rockells Farm	215			✔		✔	✔		✔
	Spicers Farm	215			✔			✔	✔	✔(6)	✔
	Wicks Manor Farm	216			✔			✔		✔
SC	The Byre	216			✔			✔		✔
Gloucestershire										
B&B	Abbots Court	169			✔		✔	✔		✔
	Alstone Fields Farm	169			✔		✔	✔		
	Avenue Farm	169		✔	✔	✔	✔	✔		✔
	Brawn Farm	169			✔			✔		
	Butlers Hill Farm	169			✔	✔		✔		
	Dix's Barn	170			✔			✔		
	Elms Farm	170			✔p	✔		✔		✔
	Folly Farm	170		✔	✔			✔	✔(300)	
	Gilbert's	170			✔		✔	✔	✔(8)	✔
	Home Farm	170			✔	✔	✔	✔		✔
	Kilmorie Guest House	170		✔	✔p		✔	✔		✔
	Lowerfield Farm	171			✔	✔		✔		
	Lydes Farm	171			✔			✔		
	Manor Farm (Greet, Winchcombe)	171		✔	✔p	✔	✔	✔	✔(10)	✔
	Manor Farm (Weston Sub-Edge)	171			✔p		✔	✔		✔
	Oaktree Farm	171			✔p	✔	✔			✔
	Oakwood Farm	171			✔			✔		✔
	Pardon Hill Farm	172			✔p	✔	✔	✔	✔(10)	✔
	Postlip Hall Farm	172			✔p	✔	✔	✔		✔
	Sudeley Hill Farm	172			✔	✔	✔	✔		✔
	Town Street Farm	172			✔	✔	✔	✔	✔(10)	✔
	Upper Farm	172			✔		✔	✔		✔
	Wickridge Court Farm	172			✔		✔	✔		
SC	Bangrove Farm	173			✔			✔		
	Court Close Farm	173			✔			✔		
	Folly Farm Cottages	173		✔				✔	✔(300)	
	Manor Farm Cottages	173		✔	✔p	✔	✔	✔	✔(10)	✔
	Old Mill Farm	173			✔	✔		✔		✔
	Stable Cottage	174			✔	✔		✔		✔
	Warrens Gorse Cottages	174			✔p	✔		✔		✔
	Westley Farm	174		✔	✔p	✔		✔		✔
	Windmill Annexe	174	↟		✔p		✔	✔	✔(8)	✔
Greater Manchester										
B&B	Boothstead Farm	121				✔		✔		✔
	Globe Farm	121		✔	✔	✔	✔	✔		✔

ENGLAND County/Farm		Page no.	Accessibility category	Caravans and/or camping	Working farm (p=participation)	Stabling/grazing for visiting horses	En suite available	Business people welcome	Meeting room (capacity)	Gift tokens accepted
Greater Manchester (cont)										
	Needhams Farm	121			✓	✓	✓	✓		
Hampshire										
B&B	Brocklands Farm	218		✓	✓	✓		✓	✓(12)	✓
	Compton Farmhouse	218			✓			✓		✓
	Moortown Farm	218					✓	✓		
	Oakdown Farm Bungalow	218			✓	✓		✓		
	Peak House Farm	218			✓	✓	✓	✓	✓(6)	✓
	Pyesmead Farm	219			✓p	✓	✓	✓		✓
	Roughwood House	219			✓	✓	✓	✓		
	Vine Farmhouse	219			✓		✓	✓		✓
SC	Beacon Hill Farm Cottages	219	↑		✓			✓		✓
	Meadow Cottage	219		✓	✓	✓		✓		✓
	Owl Cottage	220		✓	✓p	✓		✓		✓
Herefordshire										
B&B	Amberley	158			✓			✓	✓(4)	
	The Barn Farm	158			✓			✓		✓
	Grafton Villa Farm	158		✓	✓p	✓		✓		✓
	Hill Top Farm	158		✓	✓			✓		
	The Hills Farm	158			✓			✓	✓(10)	✓
	Home Farm	159		✓	✓			✓		
	Linton Brook Farm	159			✓			✓	✓(12)	
	Moor Court Farm	159			✓p	✓	✓	✓	✓(20)	✓
	New House Farm	159			✓p	✓		✓		✓
	Old Court Farm	159			✓p			✓	✓(120)	✓
	Penrhos Farm	159			✓	✓		✓		
	Red Ley Farmhouse	160			✓			✓	✓(20)	
	Sink Green Farm	160			✓			✓	✓(10)	
	Upper Gilvach Farm	160		✓	✓p			✓		
	The Vauld House Farm	160			✓p		✓	✓	✓(8)	✓
	Warren Farm	160			✓	✓	✓	✓		
SC	Anvil Cottage	161	↑	✓	✓p	✓	✓	✓		✓
	Brick House Farm	161			✓p	✓		✓		
	Brooklyn	161			✓			✓		
	Carey Dene & Rock House	161			✓p					
	Grafton Cottage	161			✓p	✓		✓		
	Mill House Flat	162		✓	✓			✓		✓
	Moody Farm Cottage	162			✓p			✓		✓
	Old Forge Cottage	162			✓p		✓	✓		✓
	Poolspringe Farm Cottages	162			✓			✓		
	The Vauld House Farm	162			✓p			✓	✓(8)	
Hertfordshire										
B&B	Broadway Farm	188			✓		✓	✓	✓(10)	✓
	The Grange	188			✓		✓	✓	✓(6)	
	Hall Farm	190			✓		✓	✓		✓
SC	Bluntswood Hall Cottages	188						✓	✓(100)	✓
Isle of Man										
B&B	Ballavell Farm	70			✓p			✓		✓
	Kerrowgarrow Farm	70		✓	✓p			✓		
SC	Ballachrink Bungalow	70			✓			✓		

INDEX

ENGLAND

County/Farm	Page no.	Accessibility category	Caravans and/or camping	Working farm (p=participation)	Stabling/grazing for visiting horses	En suite available	Business people welcome	Meeting room (capacity)	Gift tokens accepted
Isle of Man (cont)									
Cronk-Dhoo Farm Cottages	70			✔P		✔			
Kionslieu Farm Cottages	71	↑		✔P			✔		✔
Little Cresta	71			✔					✔
Smeale Cottage	71			✔			✔		✔
Soalt Veg	71		✔	✔P		✔	✔		✔
Isle of Wight									
B&B Auld Youngwoods Farm	222		✔	✔P	✔		✔	✔(10)	✔
Kern Farm	222			✔P	✔	✔	✔	✔	✔
Lisle Combe	222			✔	✔		✔		✔
Newbarn Farm	222			✔		✔	✔		✔
SC Combe Lodge	223				✔		✔		✔
The Stable	223			✔					✔
West Wing	223			✔P			✔		✔
Kent									
B&B Barnfield	227		✔	✔	✔		✔		✔
Great Cheveney Farm	227			✔		✔	✔		✔
Great Field Farm	227			✔		✔	✔		✔
Hallwood Farm	227			✔	✔		✔		✔
Hoads Farm	227			✔			✔		✔
Leaveland Court	228			✔		✔	✔	✔(12)	✔
Preston Farm	228			✔			✔	✔(6)	✔
South Wootton House	228		✔	✔P	✔	✔	✔	✔	✔
Tanner House	228		✔	✔		✔	✔	✔(25)	✔
SC Birdwatcher's Cottage	228			✔	✔				✔
Golding Hop Farm Cottage	229			✔			✔		✔
Great Field Farm	229			✔			✔		✔
Lancashire									
B&B Blakey Hall Farm	95			✔		✔	✔		✔
Galley Hall Farm	95		✔	✔			✔		
Higher Wanless Farm	95			✔	✔	✔	✔		✔
Middle Flass Lodge	95			✔		✔	✔		✔
Parson Lee Farm	95			✔P	✔	✔	✔		✔
Pasture Bottom Farm	96			✔			✔		✔
Rakefoot Farm	96			✔P	✔	✔	✔		✔
Sandy Brook Farm	96	♿		✔		✔	✔		✔
Todderstaffe Hall Farm	96			✔			✔		✔
SC Brackenthwaite Cottages	96		✔	✔P	✔		✔		✔
Garden Cottage	97			✔			✔		✔
Higher Gills Farm	97	♿		✔P			✔		✔
Rakefoot Barn	97			✔P	✔	✔	✔		✔
Sandy Brook Farm	97	♿		✔			✔		✔
Leicestershire									
B&B Knaptoft House Farm	155			✔		✔	✔	✔	✔
Three Ways Farm	155						✔	✔(10)	✔
White Lodge Farm	155			✔	✔	✔	✔		✔
SC Brook Meadow Holiday Chalets	155		✔	✔	✔		✔	✔(10)	✔
Stonehurst	156		✔	✔P			✔	✔(50)	✔
Lincolnshire									
B&B Cackle Hill House	141			✔		✔	✔		✔

ENGLAND County/Farm		Page no.	Accessibility category	Caravans and/or camping	Working farm (p=participation)	Stabling/grazing for visiting horses	En suite available	Business people welcome	Meeting room (capacity)	Gift tokens accepted
Lincolnshire (cont)										
	Church Farm	141			✔		✔	✔		
	East Farm House	141			✔	✔	✔	✔		✔
	Gelston Grange Farm	141			✔		✔	✔		
	The Grange	141		✔	✔	✔	✔	✔	✔(12)	
	Greenfield Farm	142			✔		✔	✔		✔
	Greenoaks	142			✔	✔	✔	✔		
	Guy Wells Farm	142			✔		✔	✔		
	The Manor House (Manor Farm)	142			✔		✔	✔		✔
	The Manor House (West Barkwith)	142			✔		✔	✔		
	Midstone Farmhouse	142			✔p	✔	✔	✔		✔
	Sycamore Farm	143			✔			✔	✔(6)	✔
SC	Bridle Cottage	143			✔p	✔		✔		✔
	Mill Lodge	143			✔			✔		
	Red House Farm Cottage	143			✔			✔		
Norfolk										
B&B	Birds Place Farm	193			✔p	✔	✔	✔		✔
	Colveston Manor	193			✔p	✔	✔	✔	✔(20)	
	East Farm	193			✔	✔	✔	✔	✔(10)	✔
	Hempstead Hall	193		✔	✔		✔			
	Highfield Farm	193			✔	✔	✔	✔	✔(8)	✔
	Hillside Farm	194			✔	✔	✔	✔	✔(12)	✔
	Lower Farm	194			✔	✔	✔	✔	✔(5)	✔
	Malting Farm	194			✔p		✔	✔		✔
	Marsh Farm	194			✔p		✔	✔		✔
	Park Farm	194			✔		✔	✔		✔
	Salamanca Farm Guest House	194			✔			✔	✔(14)	
	Shrublands Farm (Burgh St Peter)	195			✔		✔	✔		✔
	Shrublands Farm (Northrepps)	195		✔	✔		✔	✔		✔
	Sloley Farm	195		✔	✔	✔	✔	✔	✔(8)	✔
	South Elmham Hall	195			✔		✔	✔		✔
	Stratton Farm	195	♿		✔p		✔	✔	✔(10)	✔
	Whitehall Farm	195		✔	✔		✔	✔		✔
	Witton Hall Farm	196			✔		✔	✔	✔(10)	
SC	Burnley Hall	196			✔	✔	✔			
	Carysfort & Carysfort Too	196	♿		✔p		✔	✔		✔
	The Cottage	196			✔			✔		
	Dairy Farm Cottages	196	♿		✔		✔	✔	✔(15)	
	Dolphin Lodge	197			✔	✔		✔		
	Meadow View	197			✔			✔		✔
	Tom, Dick and Harry	204			✔		✔	✔		
North Somerset										
B&B	Icelton Farm	244			✔			✔		✔
North Yorkshire										
B&B	Ainderby Myers Farm	106			✔p			✔		✔
	Barn Close Farm	106			✔p	✔	✔	✔		✔
	Bay Tree Farm	99			✔		✔	✔		✔
	Beech Tree House Farm	115			✔p			✔		✔
	Bushey Lodge Farm	99					✔	✔		✔
	Carr House Farm	106			✔	✔	✔	✔		✔

INDEX

ENGLAND County/Farm	Page no.	Accessibility category	Caravans and/or camping	Working farm (p=participation)	Stabling/grazing for visiting horses	En suite available	Business people welcome	Meeting room (capacity)	Gift tokens accepted
North Yorkshire (cont)									
Church Farm	115			✔p		✔	✔		
Clough House Farm	99			✔	✔	✔	✔		✔
Croft Farm	106			✔	✔	✔	✔		✔
Cuckoo Nest Farm	115		✔	✔		✔	✔		
Dimple Wells	115					✔	✔		
Dromonby Hall Farm	106		✔	✔	✔	✔	✔		
Easterside Farm	107			✔	✔	✔	✔		
Elmfield Country House	107				✔	✔	✔	✔(40)	
Fowgill Park Farm	100			✔	✔		✔		✔
Gatehouse Farm	100			✔		✔	✔		✔
Goose Farm	116		✔	✔	✔	✔	✔	✔(6)	
The Grainary	107	♿		✔p		✔	✔		
Graystone View Farm	100			✔p		✔	✔		
Haregill Lodge	107			✔p	✔	✔	✔	✔(12)	✔
Harker Hill Farm	107			✔	✔		✔		
High Force Farm	107			✔p			✔		✔
Island Farm	108			✔	✔	✔	✔	✔(10)	
Killerby Cottage Farm	116			✔		✔	✔		
Knabbs Ash	100			✔p		✔	✔		
Lane House Farm	101		✔	✔		✔	✔		
Laskill Farm Country House	108		✔	✔p	✔	✔	✔	✔(15)	✔
Lovesome Hill Farm	108	⚤	✔	✔p		✔	✔		
Lund Farm	116		✔	✔p		✔	✔		
Manor Farm	117		✔	✔		✔	✔	✔(6)	
Mill Close Farm	108			✔	✔	✔	✔	✔(8)	
Mount Grace Farm	108			✔		✔	✔		✔
Mount Pleasant Farm	108	⚤		✔p		✔	✔	✔(6)	
Newgate Foot Farm	109		✔	✔p		✔	✔	✔(16)	
North Pasture Farm	101		✔	✔p		✔	✔		
Oldstead Grange	117			✔p	✔	✔	✔	✔(10)	
Oxnop Hall	109			✔	✔	✔	✔		
Plane Tree Cottage Farm	109			✔			✔		
Rains Farm	117					✔	✔		✔
Redmire Farm	101			✔		✔	✔		✔
St George's Court	101			✔	✔	✔	✔		
Seavy Slack	109			✔p			✔		✔
Stonebeck Gate Farm	109			✔	✔	✔	✔	✔(6)	✔
Studley House	109		✔	✔		✔	✔		✔
Summer Lodge	110			✔	✔	✔	✔		✔
Sunley Court	117			✔p	✔	✔	✔		✔
Valley View Farm	110		✔	✔	✔	✔	✔		✔
Walburn Hall	110			✔			✔		✔
Wenningber Farm	101		✔	✔			✔		✔
Whashton Springs Farm	110			✔p		✔	✔	✔(15)	✔
Wilson House	91			✔		✔	✔		✔
SC Blackmires Farm	110			✔			✔		✔
Cawder Hall Cottages	102	⚤			✔		✔	✔(12)	✔
Clematis, Well & Shepherd's Cottages	111		✔	✔p			✔		

INDEX

ENGLAND County/Farm		Page no.	Accessibility category	Caravans and/or camping	Working farm (p=participation)	Stabling/grazing for visiting horses	En suite available	Business people welcome	Meeting room (capacity)	Gift tokens accepted
North Yorkshire (cont)										
	Clough House Farm	102						✔		✔
	The Coach House	111			✔p			✔		✔
	Croft Farm Cottage	111			✔	✔		✔		✔
	Dove Cottage	118			✔			✔		✔
	Dufton's House	111			✔	✔	✔			
	Dukes Place	102			✔	✔		✔		✔
	The Farm Cottage	111			✔	✔		✔		✔
	Farsyde Farm Cottages	111		✔	✔	✔		✔		✔
	Layhead Farm Cottages	103			✔p			✔		
	Lund Farm Cottage	118		✔	✔p	✔	✔	✔		✔
	Manor Cottage	118			✔	✔		✔		✔
	Maypole Cottage	103			✔p			✔		✔
	Mount Pleasant Farm	112	✝		✔p	✔		✔		✔
	Old Spring Wood Lodges	103	✝		✔			✔		✔
	Rains Farm	119						✔		✔
	Rhuss Cottage	112			✔p			✔		
	Stanhow Farm Bungalow	112			✔	✔		✔		✔
	Studley House	112		✔	✔			✔		✔
	Sunset Cottages	119			✔p			✔		
	Valley View Farm	112		✔	✔	✔	✔	✔		✔
	Wren Cottage	112			✔			✔		✔
C&C	Pond Farm	113		✔	✔					✔
	Woodhouse Farm Caravan Park	104		✔	✔p	✔		✔		
B/CB	Lovesome Hill Barn	113		✔	✔p	✔		✔		✔
	West End Outdoor Centre	104			✔		✔	✔		
Northamptonshire										
B&B	Dairy Farm	182			✔	✔	✔	✔	✔(10)	✔
	Drayton Lodge	182			✔	✔	✔	✔	✔(10)	✔
	The Elms	182			✔			✔		✔
	Green Farm	182			✔			✔		✔
	Lilford Lodge Farm	190			✔		✔	✔		✔
	Pear Tree Farm	182		✔	✔		✔	✔		
	Spinney Lodge Farm	183			✔		✔	✔		
	Walltree House Farm	183			✔		✔	✔	✔(14)	✔
	Wold Farm	183			✔		✔	✔	✔(8)	
SC	Granary Cottage	183			✔		✔			✔
	Rye Hill Country Cottages	183	✝					✔	✔(20)	
	Villiers Suite	184			✔	✔		✔	✔(80)	✔
	Walltree House Farm	210			✔			✔	✔(14)	✔
Northumberland										
B&B	Ald White Craig Farm	82			✔	✔	✔	✔		
	Burton Hall	82			✔		✔	✔		✔
	Cornhills	82			✔		✔	✔		✔
	Elford Farmhouse	82		✔	✔		✔	✔		✔
	Fenham-le-Moor Farmhouse	82			✔		✔	✔		✔
	Flothers Farm	83			✔		✔	✔		✔
	Gairshield Farm	83			✔p	✔		✔		
	Gibbs Hill Farm	83			✔p		✔	✔		✔
	Hawkhill Farmhouse	83			✔		✔	✔		

INDEX

ENGLAND

County/Farm	Page no.	Accessibility category	Caravans and/or camping	Working farm (p=participation)	Stabling/grazing for visiting horses	En suite available	Business people welcome	Meeting room (capacity)	Gift tokens accepted
Northumberland (cont)									
Hipsburn Farm	83			✔		✔			✔
Howick Scar Farm	83			✔			✔		✔
The Lee Farm	84			✔P	✔	✔	✔		✔
Lumbylaw Farm	84			✔			✔	✔(10)	✔
Middle Ord Manor House	84			✔P		✔	✔		✔
Ridge End Farm	84			✔P	✔	✔	✔		✔
Rock Farmhouse	84		✔			✔	✔	✔	✔
Rye Hill Farm	84		✔	✔P	✔	✔	✔		✔
Struthers Farm	85			✔		✔	✔		✔
Thistleyhaugh Farm	85			✔	✔	✔	✔	✔(10)	✔
Tosson Tower Farm	85			✔		✔	✔		✔
SC Ald White Craig Farm Cottages	85			✔	✔		✔		
Broome Hill Farm Cottages	85			✔					
Doxford Newhouses	86			✔P	✔				
East Burton Farm Holiday Cottages	86			✔					✔
The Farmhouse	86			✔P			✔		✔
Firwood Bungalow & Humphreys House	86			✔			✔		
Gardeners Cottage & Dunes Cottage	86			✔					
Gibbs Hill Farm Cottages	86			✔P			✔		
The Herdsman Cottage	87			✔					✔
Honeysuckle Cottage	87			✔P			✔		
Keepers Cottages	87			✔			✔		✔
Lumbylaw & Garden Cottages	87			✔			✔		
Nos. 1, 2 & 3 Cottages	87			✔	✔		✔		
Rowan Cottage	87			✔P		✔			
Shepherd's Cottage	88			✔P	✔		✔		✔
West Ord Holiday Cottages	88			✔					
Nottinghamshire									
B&B Blue Barn Farm	138			✔		✔	✔		✔
Far Baulker Farm	138		✔	✔P	✔	✔	✔		
Forest Farm	138			✔		✔	✔		✔
Jerico Farm	138			✔		✔	✔	✔(6)	
Manor Farm	138			✔			✔		
Norton Grange Farm	139			✔P			✔	✔(12)	
SC Blue Barn Cottage	139			✔			✔		✔
Foliat Cottages	139			✔			✔	✔(8)	✔
The Granary	139			✔			✔		
The Mews	139			✔			✔		✔
Oxfordshire									
B&B Banbury Hill Farm	207		✔	✔		✔	✔		
Bould Farm	207			✔	✔	✔	✔		✔
Bowling Green Farm	207			✔	✔	✔	✔		✔
Chimney House	207			✔		✔	✔		
Common Leys Farm	207			✔			✔	✔(12)	
Ducklington Farm	208		✔	✔		✔	✔		✔
Fords Farm	208			✔			✔		
Hill Grove Farm	208			✔	✔	✔	✔		✔

INDEX

ENGLAND County/Farm		Page no.	Accessibility category	Caravans and/or camping	Working farm (p=participation)	Stabling/grazing for visiting horses	En suite available	Business people welcome	Meeting room (capacity)	Gift tokens accepted
Oxfordshire (cont)										
	Morar	208			✔		✔	✔		✔
	North Farm	208			✔	✔	✔	✔		✔
	The Old Farmhouse	208					✔	✔	✔(8)	✔
	Rectory Farm	209			✔		✔	✔		✔
	Sor Brook House Farm	178		✔	✔	✔	✔	✔		
	Vicarage Farm	209			✔	✔				
	Weston Farm	209			✔p		✔	✔		✔
SC	Banbury Hill Farm	209			✔					
	Coxwell House	209			✔	✔		✔		
	Lower Court Cottage	210			✔	✔				
	Rectory Farm Cottages	210			✔			✔		✔
	Walltree House Farm	210			✔			✔	✔(14)	✔
Shropshire										
B&B	Acton Scott Farm	145			✔		✔	✔		✔
	Avenue Farm	145			✔	✔		✔		
	Brereton House	145			✔		✔			✔
	Broughton Farm	145			✔p	✔	✔	✔		✔
	Church Farm	145			✔		✔	✔	✔(12)	✔
	Dearnford Hall	146			✔		✔	✔	✔(10)	
	Grove Farm	146			✔			✔		
	The Hall	146			✔		✔	✔		
	Haynall Villa	146					✔	✔		✔
	Horseman's Green Farm	146			✔			✔	✔(12)	
	Hurst Mill Farm	146		✔	✔p	✔	✔	✔		✔
	Lane End Farm	147			✔p			✔		✔
	Llanhedric	147			✔			✔		✔
	Mickley House	147	⚐		✔	✔	✔	✔	✔(10)	✔
	New House Farm	147		✔	✔	✔	✔	✔		
	North Farm	147			✔	✔		✔		
	Parkside Farm	147			✔					
	Petton Hall Farm	148			✔		✔	✔		✔
	Pool House Farm	148			✔	✔		✔		
	Soulton Hall	148			✔		✔	✔	✔(25)	✔
	Strefford Hall Farm	148			✔		✔	✔	✔(12)	✔
	Willow House	148			✔	✔		✔		✔
	Wood Farm	148			✔p			✔	✔(12)	✔
SC	Brooklyn	161			✔			✔		
	Garden Cottage	149			✔	✔		✔		
	The Granary	149			✔p	✔		✔		
	Hesterworth	149						✔	✔(50)	✔
	Keepers Cottage	149			✔			✔	✔(10)	✔
	The Sett	149			✔			✔		✔
	Strefford Hall Farm	150			✔		✔	✔	✔(12)	✔
B/CB	Broughton Bunkhouse	150			✔p	✔		✔		✔
Somerset										
B&B	Binham Farm	242		✔	✔p		✔	✔		✔
	Blackmore Farm	242	♿		✔		✔	✔	✔(25)	✔
	Bossington Farm & Birds of Prey Centre	242			✔p	✔		✔		

INDEX

ENGLAND County/Farm

County/Farm	Page no.	Accessibility category	Caravans and/or camping	Working farm (p=participation)	Stabling/grazing for visiting horses	En suite available	Business people welcome	Meeting room (capacity)	Gift tokens accepted
Somerset (cont)									
Brookhayes Farm	242			✔p		✔	✔	✔(8)	
Cary Fitzpaine	242			✔p	✔	✔	✔		✔
Clanville Manor	243			✔p		✔	✔		✔
Cokerhurst Farm	243			✔		✔	✔		✔
Cutthorne Farm	243			✔		✔	✔		✔
Double-Gate Farm	243			✔		✔	✔		✔
Edgcott House	243						✔		
Greenway Farm	243			✔p	✔		✔	✔(8)	✔
Highercombe	244			✔p	✔	✔	✔	✔(6)	
Highercombe Farm	244			✔p	✔	✔			✔
Higher Langridge Farm	244			✔	✔	✔	✔	✔(20)	✔
Hill Ash Farm	244		✔	✔		✔	✔		✔
Hindon Farm	244			✔p	✔	✔	✔	✔(12)	✔
Icelton Farm	244			✔			✔		
Larcombe Foot	245				✔				
Little Brendon Hill Farm	245			✔		✔	✔		
Little Quarme Farm	270			✔	✔	✔	✔	✔(25)	
Lower Clavelshay Farm	245		✔	✔p	✔	✔	✔		✔
Lower Farm	245			✔		✔	✔		✔
Moxhill Farmhouse	245			✔p		✔	✔		✔
New House Farm	245			✔		✔	✔	✔(5)	✔
Orchard Farm	246			✔		✔	✔		✔
Springfield Farm	246			✔	✔	✔			
Temple House Farm	246		✔	✔		✔	✔		✔
Tor Farm Guesthouse	246			✔			✔	✔(20)	
Townsend Farm	246			✔p	✔	✔	✔		✔
Wambrook Farm	246			✔p	✔	✔	✔		✔
Wembdon Farm	247			✔		✔	✔		✔
Wood Advent Farm	271		✔	✔	✔	✔	✔	✔(20)	✔
SC Cockhill Farm & Orchard Farm	247			✔			✔		✔
The Courtyard	247			✔			✔		✔
Cutthorne Farm	247			✔		✔			✔
Hale Farm	247								
Highercombe	248			✔p	✔		✔	✔(6)	
Highercombe Farm	248			✔p	✔				✔
Hindon Farmhouse Cottage	248			✔p	✔	✔	✔	✔(12)	✔
Holly Farm	248			✔			✔		
Liscombe Farm	248			✔	✔		✔		
Little Quarme Cottages	274			✔	✔		✔		
Lois Barns	240			✔p		✔	✔		
Mill Farm	248			✔p					
The Old Cart House	249			✔		✔	✔		✔
Pear Tree Cottage	249		✔	✔					
Pembroke Cottage	249								
Pigsty, Cowstall & Bullpen Cottages	249			✔					✔
Riscombe Farm	249				✔		✔		✔
Rull Farm	249			✔					
The Tallet	250			✔p			✔		✔
Week Farm	250			✔p	✔		✔		✔

ENGLAND County/Farm	Page no.	Accessibility category	Caravans and/or camping	Working farm (p=participation)	Stabling/grazing for visiting horses	En suite available	Business people welcome	Meeting room (capacity)	Gift tokens accepted
Somerset (cont)									
Westermill Farm	250	↟	✔	✔P	✔	✔	✔		✔
West Withy Farm	250			✔			✔		
Wintershead Farm	250			✔	✔	✔	✔		
Staffordshire									
B&B									
Brook House Farm	152			✔P		✔	✔		
The Church Farm	152			✔P					✔
Ley Fields Farm	152			✔P		✔	✔		✔
Oulton House Farm	152			✔		✔	✔		✔
Parkside Farm	152			✔					
Ribden Farm	153			✔		✔	✔		
SC									
Rosewood Holiday Flats	153			✔	✔		✔		
Swallows Nest	153			✔					✔
Suffolk									
B&B									
Brighthouse Farm	199		✔	✔			✔	✔	
Broad Oak Farm	199			✔P			✔	✔	✔
Church Farm	199		✔	✔			✔	✔	
College Farm	199			✔			✔	✔	✔(8)	✔
Colston Hall	199		✔	✔			✔	✔	✔(6)	✔
Earsham Park Farm	200			✔P	✔		✔	✔	✔(14)	✔
Elmswell Hall	200									
Grange Farm	200		✔	✔			✔	✔		✔
Grove Farm House	200			✔				✔		✔
The Hall	200			✔				✔		✔
Hall Farm	200			✔						
Laurel Farm	201			✔	✔			✔		
Oak Farm	201			✔	✔			✔		✔
Park Farm	201			✔			✔	✔		✔
Priory Farm	201		✔	✔	✔		✔			✔
Red House Farm	201		✔	✔			✔	✔		✔
Shrublands Farm	195			✔			✔	✔		
South Elmham Hall	201			✔			✔	✔		✔
Uggeshall Manor Farm	202			✔	✔		✔	✔		
Walpole Old Hall	202		✔	✔			✔			✔
Watersmeet	202			✔				✔	✔(6)	✔
Woodlands Farm	202			✔				✔		✔
SC									
Baylham House Farm Annexe & Flat	202			✔P				✔		✔
The Bothy	203		✔				✔	✔		✔
The Coach House	203			✔			✔	✔		
Colston Cottage	203		✔	✔				✔	✔(6)	✔
The Cottage	203		✔	✔				✔		
The Court	203		✔	✔			✔	✔		
The Granary	203		✔	✔	✔			✔		
Rowney Cottage	204			✔				✔		
Stable Cottages & The Granary	204	♿		✔			✔	✔		✔
Tom, Dick & Harry	204			✔			✔	✔		✔
Surrey									
B&B									
Bulmer Farm	225	♿		✔	✔	✔	✔	✔	✔(12)	✔
Heron's Head Farm	225		✔	✔	✔	✔	✔	✔	✔(6)	

INDEX

ENGLAND County/Farm		Page no.	Accessibility category	Caravans and/or camping	Working farm (p=participation)	Stabling/grazing for visiting horses	En suite available	Business people welcome	Meeting room (capacity)	Gift tokens accepted
Surrey (cont)										
	Sturtwood Farm	225					✔	✔		✔
SC	Badgersholt & Foxholme	225	♿	✔	✔	✔	✔	✔	✔(12)	✔
Warwickshire										
B&B	The Byre	176			✔	✔	✔	✔		✔
	Church Farm	176	♿		✔	✔	✔	✔		
	The Coach House	176			✔		✔	✔		
	Crandon House	176			✔		✔	✔	✔(12)	✔
	Frankton Grounds Farm	176			✔	✔	✔	✔		✔
	Hill Farm (Priors Hardwick)	177		✔	✔p			✔		✔
	Hill Farm (Radford Semele)	177		✔	✔		✔	✔		✔
	Holland Park Farm	177			✔	✔	✔	✔	✔	
	Lawford Hill Farm	177			✔		✔	✔		
	Lower Watchbury Farm	177			✔		✔	✔	✔(8)	
	Packington Lane Farm	177		✔	✔p		✔	✔		
	The Poplars	178			✔		✔	✔		✔
	Shrewley Pools Farm	178			✔p	✔	✔	✔		✔
	Sor Brook House Farm	178		✔	✔	✔	✔	✔		✔
	Tallet Barn	178			✔		✔	✔	✔(4)	✔
	Walcote Farm	178			✔		✔	✔		✔
	Whitchurch Farm	178		✔	✔		✔	✔		✔
SC	Furzen Hill Farm Cottages	179			✔			✔		✔
	The Granary	179			✔			✔		✔
	Hipsley Farm Cottages	179	♿		✔			✔		✔
	Knightcote Farm Cottages	179	♿		✔p		✔	✔	✔(30)	✔
	Lawford Hill Farm	179			✔			✔		✔
	Little Biggin	180			✔	✔		✔		✔
West Sussex										
B&B	Compton Farmhouse	231			✔			✔		✔
	Goffsland Farm	231		✔	✔p	✔		✔	✔(6)	✔
	Manor Farm	231			✔	✔	✔	✔		
	New House Farm	231			✔		✔	✔		✔
SC	Black Cottage	232			✔			✔	✔(8)	
	Byre Cottages	232			✔			✔		
West Yorkshire										
B&B	Birch Laithes Farm	99			✔p	✔		✔	✔(10)	✔
	Brow Top Farm	99			✔p		✔	✔		✔
	Far Laithe Farm	100			✔		✔	✔		✔
	Hole Farm	100			✔p		✔	✔		✔
	Scaife Hall Farm	101			✔p		✔	✔		✔
	White Cross Farm	102			✔		✔	✔		✔
SC	Bottoms Farm Cottages	102			✔p	✔		✔		
	Heather & Bilberry Cottages	103			✔p			✔		✔
	Meadow & Field Cottages	103						✔		✔
	Well Head Cottage	103			✔p	✔		✔		✔
	Westfield Farm Cottages	104	♿		✔p	✔	✔	✔		✔
Wiltshire										
B&B	Ashen Copse Farm	252			✔		✔	✔	✔(6)	✔
	The Beeches Farmhouse	252					✔	✔	✔(10)	
	Boyds Farm	252			✔		✔	✔	✔(10)	

INDEX

ENGLAND County/Farm		Page no.	Accessibility category	Caravans and/or camping	Working farm (p=participation)	Stabling/grazing for visiting horses	En suite available	Business people welcome	Meeting room (capacity)	Gift tokens accepted
Wiltshire (cont)										
	Church Farm (Hartham Park)	252		✓	✓	✓	✓	✓		
	Church Farm (Steeple Ashton)	252			✓			✓		✓
	Fairfield Farm	238			✓		✓	✓		✓
	Frying Pan Farm	238			✓		✓	✓		
	Great Ashley Farm	253				✓	✓	✓		
	Hatt Farm	253			✓		✓	✓		✓
	Higher Green Farm	253			✓			✓		
	Hillside Farm	253			✓			✓		
	Home Farm	253			✓P		✓	✓		✓
	Leighfield Lodge Farm	253			✓			✓		✓
	Longwater Park Farm	254	♿		✓			✓	✓(10)	
	Lovett Farm	254			✓P	✓		✓		
	Lower Foxhangers Farm	254		✓	✓	✓	✓	✓	✓(12)	✓
	Lower Stonehill Farm	254			✓		✓	✓		✓
	Manor Farm (Corston)	254			✓		✓	✓		✓
	Manor Farm (Wadswick)	255			✓	✓	✓	✓		✓
	Oakfield Farm	255			✓			✓		✓
	Oakwood Farm	171			✓			✓		✓
	Olivemead Farm	255			✓			✓		✓
	Pickwick Lodge Farm	255			✓	✓	✓	✓		✓
	Saltbox Farm	239			✓		✓	✓		✓
	Tockenham Court Farm	255			✓P		✓	✓		
SC	The Beeches Farmhouse	256						✓	✓(10)	
	Church Farm Cottages	256		✓	✓	✓		✓	✓(15)	✓
	Home Farm Barn & The Derby	240						✓		
	Lower Foxhangers Farm	256		✓	✓	✓		✓	✓(12)	✓
	Stonehill Farm	256			✓			✓		✓
	Swallow Cottage	256			✓	✓		✓		✓
	Wick Farm	257		✓	✓			✓		
Worcestershire										
B&B	Alstone Fields Farm	164			✓		✓	✓		
	Burhill Farm	164			✓			✓		✓
	Chirkenhill	164			✓	✓	✓	✓	✓(12)	
	Clay Farm	164		✓	✓P		✓	✓	✓(25)	
	Clod Hall	164			✓	✓				
	Court Farm	165			✓P	✓	✓	✓	✓	
	The Durrance	165			✓		✓	✓	✓	✓
	Eden Farm	165			✓	✓		✓		
	The Green Farm	165			✓P	✓		✓		
	Home Farm	165			✓	✓	✓	✓		✓
	Lightmarsh Farm	165			✓			✓		✓
	Little Lightwood Farm	166			✓P			✓		
	Lowerfield Farm	166			✓	✓	✓	✓		✓
	Phepson Farm	166			✓	✓	✓	✓	✓	✓
	Tiltridge Farm & Vineyard	166			✓		✓	✓		✓
SC	Court Close Farm	166			✓			✓		
	Grafton Cottage	161			✓P	✓		✓		
	The Granary (Phepson Farm)	167			✓	✓		✓		
	The Granary (Tibbitts Farm)	167			✓			✓		✓

ENGLAND County/Farm	Page no.	Accessibility category	Caravans and/or camping	Working farm (p=participation)	Stabling/grazing for visiting horses	En suite available	Business people welcome	Meeting room (capacity)	Gift tokens accepted
Worcestershire (cont)									
Little Lightwood Farm	167			✔p			✔		
Old Yates Cottages	167	↑		✔			✔	✔(20)	✔
Stable Cottage	167			✔	✔		✔		✔

INDEX

WALES

Region/Farm	Page no.	Accessibility category	Caravans and/or camping	Working farm (p=participation)	Stabling/grazing for visiting horses	En suite available	Business people welcome	Meeting room (capacity)	Gift tokens accepted
North Wales									
B&B									
Bach-y-Graig	320			✔P		✔	✔	✔(10)	✔
Bryn Celynog Farm	312			✔		✔	✔		✔
Bwlch-y-Fen	309			✔P		✔	✔	✔(6)	
Cae'r Efail	312		✔		✔	✔	✔		
Cwm Hwylfod	312			✔P	✔				✔
Drws y Coed	309			✔P					✔
Erlas Hall	320			✔			✔	✔(10)	
Erw Feurig Farm	312			✔					
Fron-Haul	320		✔	✔P	✔		✔	✔(30)	✔
Gogarth Hall Farm	313		✔	✔P	✔	✔	✔		✔
Gwrach Ynys	313					✔	✔		
Hendy Farm	313		✔	✔		✔	✔		
Llainwen Ucha	320								
Llwydiarth Fawr	309			✔P	✔	✔	✔	✔(12)	
Llwyn Mafon Isaf	313			✔P	✔	✔	✔		✔
Mathan Uchaf Farm	313			✔P	✔		✔		✔
Mill House	320					✔	✔		✔
Pengwern	314			✔		✔	✔	✔(6)	
Penyrorsedd Farm	309			✔	✔	✔	✔		✔
Plas Tirion Farm	314			✔P		✔	✔		✔
Plas Trefarthen	309			✔		✔	✔	✔(12)	✔
Rhydydefaid Farm	314			✔		✔	✔		✔
Tyddyn Du Farm	314			✔P	✔	✔	✔		✔
Tyddyn Iolyn	314				✔	✔	✔		✔
Tyddyn Rhys Farm	314		✔	✔P					
Ty-Mawr Farm	315			✔P	✔	✔	✔	✔(8)	✔
Ystumgwern	315	↟	✔	✔P		✔	✔		✔
SC									
Bach-y-Graig	321			✔P		✔	✔		✔
Bryn Beddau	315			✔	✔		✔		
Caerwych Farmhouse	315			✔P	✔		✔		
Carn y Gadell Uchaf	316			✔P		✔	✔		✔
Cartref	316						✔		
Castellmarch	316			✔P			✔		
Cefnamwlch	316			✔					
Chwilog Fawr	316			✔P	✔				✔
Dwyfach Cottages	316			✔		✔	✔		✔
Garth-y-Foel	317		✔	✔	✔		✔		
The Granary	321						✔		✔
Gwynfryn Farm	317	↟	✔	✔P			✔		✔
Hafod & Hendre	317			✔P	✔		✔		✔
Penmaenbach Farm Cottages	317			✔P		✔	✔		✔
Rhydolion	317		✔	✔P	✔		✔		✔
Tai Gwyliau Tyndon Holiday Cottages	317		✔	✔			✔		✔
Towyn Farm	318		✔	✔P			✔		
Tyddyn Isaf	321			✔			✔		✔
Ynys	318		✔	✔P	✔	✔	✔		✔

INDEX

WALES

Region/Farm		Page no.	Accessibility category	Caravans and/or camping	Working farm (p=participation)	Stabling/grazing for visiting horses	En suite available	Business people welcome	Meeting room (capacity)	Gift tokens accepted
Mid Wales										
B&B	Abermeurig Mansion	324			✔	✔	✔	✔		✔
	Bache Farm	328		✔	✔p	✔	✔	✔		✔
	Beili Neuadd	328			✔	✔	✔	✔		✔
	Broniwan	324			✔p	✔	✔	✔	✔(6)	
	Bryncastell Farm	324	♿	✔	✔p	✔	✔	✔		✔
	Brynog Mansion	324			✔		✔	✔		
	Bryn y Fedwen Farm	328			✔	✔	✔	✔		✔
	Bwlch Farm	328				✔	✔	✔		
	Cefnsuran Farm	328			✔	✔	✔	✔	✔(8)	✔
	Cwmcamlais Uchaf Farm	329			✔p	✔	✔	✔		✔
	Cwmllwynog	329			✔p		✔	✔		
	Dol-Llys Farm	329		✔	✔p		✔	✔		
	Dremddu Fawr	324			✔p	✔	✔	✔	✔(5)	
	The Drewin Farm	329		✔	✔	✔	✔	✔		
	Dyffryn Farmhouse	329			✔p		✔	✔		
	Ffordd-Fawr Farmhouse	329		✔	✔		✔	✔	✔(10)	
	Gogarth Hall Farm	330		✔	✔p	✔	✔	✔		
	Highbury Farm	330			✔p		✔	✔		✔
	Highgrove Farm	330			✔	✔	✔	✔	✔(10)	✔
	Little Brompton Farm	330		✔	✔		✔	✔		
	Llettyderyn	330			✔p		✔	✔		
	Llwyn yr Eos	325			✔p	✔	✔	✔		✔
	Lodge Farm	330			✔	✔	✔	✔		✔
	Lower Gwerneirin Farm	331			✔		✔	✔		✔
	Lower Gwestydd	331			✔		✔	✔		
	Moat Farm	331			✔		✔	✔		✔
	Nantymedd Farm	325								
	Neuadd Farm	331			✔	✔	✔	✔		
	Pant-Teg	325			✔		✔	✔		
	Penlanmedd	325					✔	✔		
	Pentre Farm	325			✔p		✔	✔		✔
	Pilleth Court	331			✔	✔	✔	✔		
	Trehenry Farm	331			✔p		✔	✔		
	Ty-Cooke Farm	332		✔	✔			✔	✔(12)	
	Wervil Grange Farm	325			✔p	✔	✔	✔	✔(6)	✔
SC	Cefnsuran Farm	332			✔	✔	✔	✔	✔(8)	✔
	Gwydre Cottage	332			✔p		✔	✔	✔	✔
	Red House	332			✔p		✔	✔		✔
	Pant-Teg Studio Cottage	326			✔		✔	✔		
	Trehenry Farm	332			✔p		✔	✔		
South & West Wales										
B&B	Barley Villa	335					✔	✔		
	The Bower Farm	335		✔	✔	✔	✔	✔	✔(10)	
	Brunant Farm	335			✔					✔
	Castell Pigyn Farm	341			✔		✔	✔		✔
	Cilpost Farm	335			✔		✔	✔	✔(18)	
	Cwmgwyn Farm	341			✔			✔		✔
	Dolau Isaf Farm	335		✔	✔p	✔	✔	✔		✔
	Fron Isaf	336			✔p			✔		

WALES

Region/Farm	Page no.	Accessibility category	Caravans and/or camping	Working farm (p=participation)	Stabling/grazing for visiting horses	En suite available	Business people welcome	Meeting room (capacity)	Gift tokens accepted
South & West Wales (cont)									
Gilfach Goch Farmhouse	336			✔		✔	✔		
Glandy Mawr	336			✔P		✔	✔		
Golwg-y-Foel	336			✔		✔	✔		✔
Hardwick Farm	343			✔		✔	✔		✔
Knowles Farm	336		✔	✔	✔	✔	✔	✔(10)	✔
Lochmeyler Farm	336			✔P	✔	✔	✔	✔(24)	✔
Lower End Town House	337			✔P		✔	✔	✔(8)	✔
Lower Haythog	337			✔P		✔	✔		✔
Parc le Breos House	341			✔		✔	✔	✔(30)	✔
Pentre-Tai Farm	343		✔	✔P	✔	✔	✔		✔
Penygraig Farm	337			✔	✔	✔	✔		
Penylan Farm	343			✔		✔	✔		
Plas-y-Brodyr	337			✔P		✔	✔		✔
Poyerston Farm	337			✔P		✔	✔		✔
Skerryback	337			✔	✔	✔	✔		✔
Torbant Farmhouse	338			✔		✔	✔		✔
Trebersed Farm	341			✔P		✔	✔		✔
Trepant Farm	338			✔		✔	✔		✔
Ty-Cooke Farm	332		✔	✔			✔	✔(12)	
The Wenallt Farm	343		✔	✔P	✔	✔	✔	✔(32)	✔
SC Blackmoor Farm	338			✔	✔		✔		
Castell Pigyn Cottage	338			✔			✔		✔
Craig-y-Dyfor Cottage	338			✔	✔		✔		✔
Croft Farm & Celtic Cottages	339		✔	✔P			✔	✔(15)	✔
Gilfach Goch Cottages	339			✔			✔		
Granary & Coach House	344			✔P			✔		✔
Gwarmacwydd	339			✔P			✔		✔
Lower Green Farm	344	♿		✔P	✔		✔		✔
Parsons Grove	344						✔		
Rogeston Cottages	339			✔P			✔		✔
The Stable & Coach House	339			✔			✔	✔(12)	
Ty Geifr	339			✔P	✔		✔		✔
Worcester House	344			✔			✔		

395

INDEX

NORTHERN IRELAND

County/Farm		Page no.	Accessibility category	Caravans and/or camping	Working farm (p=participation)	Stabling/grazing for visiting horses	En suite available	Business people welcome	Meeting room (capacity)	Gift tokens accepted
Antrim										
B&B	Beechgrove	350		✔	✔p	✔	✔	✔	✔(26)	✔
	Brown's Country House	350	✝				✔	✔		✔
	Carnside Farm Guest House	350		✔	✔		✔			✔
	Cullentra House	350	✝		✔		✔	✔		
	Glenmore House	350	✝	✔	✔p		✔			✔
	Neelsgrove Farm	351			✔		✔	✔		
	Sprucebank	351			✔		✔	✔		✔
Armagh										
B&B	Ballinahinch House	355		✔	✔p	✔	✔	✔	✔(30)	✔
Down										
B&B	Morne Abbey Guest House	357			✔		✔	✔		✔
	Mourneview	357	✝		✔		✔	✔	✔(8)	
	Pheasants' Hill Country House	357			✔p	✔	✔	✔	✔(10)	✔
	Sharon Farmhouse	357	✝		✔p		✔			✔
	Trench Farm	357				✔	✔	✔		✔
	Wyncrest	358			✔		✔	✔	✔(12)	✔
Londonderry										
B&B	Brown's Country House	350	✝				✔	✔		✔
	Drumcovitt House	347			✔p		✔	✔	✔(32)	✔
	Greenhill House	347			✔p	✔	✔	✔	✔(14)	✔
	Heathfield Farm	347			✔p		✔	✔	✔(15)	✔
	Killeague Farm	347			✔p	✔	✔			✔
	Killennan House	347			✔		✔	✔	✔(6)	
	Whitehill Farm	348					✔	✔		✔
SC	Drumcovitt Cottages	348			✔p		✔	✔	✔(32)	✔
Tyrone										
B&B	Greenmount Lodge	353	♿		✔p	✔	✔	✔	✔(70)	✔

You don't have to be a farmer to insure with us.

NFU Mutual

The best in the country.

For details of your nearest local agent call 0345 045031.